PROCEEDINGS OF THE COLLOQUIUM ON GLOBAL ASPECTS OF CORAL REEFS: HEALTH, HAZARDS AND HISTORY

Compiled by Robert N. Ginsburg

Commemorating the Fiftieth Anniversary of

University of Miami's

ROSENSTIEL SCHOOL OF MARINE AND ATMOSPHERIC SCIENCE

and its Founder and Long-Time Dean

F.G. WALTON SMITH

With the cooperation of

THE INTERNATIONAL SOCIETY FOR REEF STUDIES

JUNE 10, 11, 1993

SPONSORED BY

The John D. and Catherine T. MacArthur Foundation

The National Science Foundation

The National Oceanic and Atmospheric Administration

The Minerals Management Service

ORGANIZING COMMITTEE

ROBERT N. GINSBURG, CHAIRMAN

JAMES BOHNSACK   ARTHUR MYRBERG JR.

PETER W. GLYNN   ALINA SZMANT   PETER K. SWART

ACKNOWLEDGEMENTS

The Colloquium would not have been possible without the generous financial support of the Sponsors listed on the Title Page and the F.G. Walton Smith Fund. The Organizing Committee is grateful for the willing and skilled help from a number of persons: Karen Fleites and Jeanne Masters for handling all the correspondence and registration; Robert Warzeski for advice on planning; William Kirsch for help in editing and assembling the case histories and maps; Alan Buck for the preparations; Eberhard Gischler, Julie Firman and Maria A. Bitner for editorial assistance; Victoria Meyers and Siobhan MacCready for guidance in developing support; and Don Heuer, Robert Suarez and Joe Lucena for printing the collection of case histories.

Robert N. Ginsburg, Chairperson
Organizing Committee

This volume should be cited as
Ginsburg, Robert N. Compiler, 1994, Proceedings of the Colloquium on Global Aspects of Coral Reefs: Health, Hazards and History, 1993.
Rosenstiel School of Marine and Atmospheric Science, University of Miami.

To purchase additional copies write University of Miami, RSMAS, Global Reefs, 4600 Rickenbacker Causeway, Miami, Florida 33149-1098

COVER: Charles Darwin's map of the world's reefs appeared in his landmark work, THE STRUCTURE AND DISTRIBUTION OF CORAL REEFS, 1842. In the original, colored version he distinguished between atolls, barrier reefs and fringing reefs.

The Global Reef Logo was designed by Harold Hudson; the layout of the cover by Robert Warzeski.

ISBN-0-932981-79-8

© Rosenstiel School of Marine and Atmospheric Science, University of Miami

Table of Contents

Section Title	Pages
Summary of the Colloquium and Forum on Global Aspects of Coral Reefs: Health, Hazards and History	i - ix
History of Reefs	1 - 26
Methods of Assessing Coral Reefs	27 - 86
Hazards and Human Intervention	87 - 145
Reefs of Florida, Bahamas, Bermuda, and Gulf of Mexico	147 - 187
Reefs of the Caribbean	189 - 232
Reefs of South and Central America	233 - 278
Reefs of Java and South China Seas	279 - 317
Reefs of the Pacific Ocean	319 - 370
Reefs of the Indian Ocean	371 - 416
Index by Author	417 - 420

SUMMARY OF THE COLLOQUIUM AND FORUM ON

GLOBAL ASPECTS OF CORAL REEFS: HEALTH, HAZARDS AND HISTORY

Prepared by Robert N. Ginsburg and Peter W. Glynn

BACKGROUND

For two reasons, the topic of the two meetings was chosen as appropriate to the commemoration of the Fiftieth Anniversary of the Rosenstiel School of Marine and Atmospheric Science and the lasting contributions of its Founder and long-time Dean, F. G. Walton Smith. First, Walton Smith had a keen interest in coral reefs and authored a much-used guide to the identification of Atlantic corals. Second, the numerous press reports of dead and declining reefs in various areas have produced widespread concern about the condition of living reefs and the stresses to which they are subjected, but the basic information on impacted reefs is inadequate.

As a first step in assembling basic information on reefs, the Organizing Committee solicited seven-page case histories of the health, hazards and history of reefs worldwide as the basis for a critical evaluation. Sixty-two case histories about reefs in 28 locations were received and preprinted as the basis of the three-day Colloquium that was held June 7-10, 1993 at the University of Miami's Main Campus. Nearly 120 scientists, managers of reef parks, students and representatives of conservation organizations participated in the Colloquium. Unlike most scientific meetings with formal presentations, the Colloquium consisted instead of extended discussion of key topics: 1) the influence of geological history and sea level rise on reefs; 2) methods of assessment of the condition of reefs; 3) regional evaluations of the condition of reefs; and 4) natural and anthropogenic hazards of reefs. All the participants were aware that the results of their deliberations were to be presented to the general public in the two-day Forum that followed the Colloquium.

The two-day Forum that was held at the Rosenstiel School on May 10 and 11 attracted some 200 participants; it featured a report of the results of the Colloquium and nine keynote talks with ample time for questions and discussion from the audience. The keynote speakers and the titles of their talks are given at the end of this Summary.

MAJOR CONCLUSIONS OF THE COLLOQUIUM AND FORUM

1. **There are significant declines in the condition of many of the world's reefs, but vast areas of remote reefs have not been studied, thus an accurate global evaluation is not possible.** Nearshore reefs adjacent to large populations are among those most impacted. In some, it is evident that combinations of anthropogenic impacts play the principal role: degraded water quality from runoff of untreated sewage and/or sediment; over-fishing; mining of coral; and shoreline development. For other reefs, natural impacts are responsible for their declines: unusually high temperatures associated with the El Nino-Southern Oscillation in the eastern Pacific; various coral diseases in the Western Atlantic;

and predators (crown of thorns) in the Pacific and Indian Oceans; demise of a key animal in the reef ecosystem such as grazing urchins; and hurricanes. Often, the natural and anthropogenic impacts coincide to reduce what were thriving reefs to wastelands of coral rubble.

    2. **The data base for evaluating the condition of the world's reefs is quite inadequate on all counts.** For those that show decline, neither the extent of the area affected is known, nor is the relative importance of natural vs. anthropogenic impacts clearly understood. Similarly, far too little is known about reef areas without obvious impacts that provide the baselines for gauging the extent of impacts. For example, far too little is known about the two largest areas of reefs in the Western Atlantic, the Bahamas and Belize. Vast areas of reefs in the Pacific and Indian Oceans have never been visited by reef scientists.

    3. **There is an urgent need for reef researchers to appreciate how fundamental research can provide the necessary tools for management of these major resources.** Establishing the critical levels of nutrients and sediment impact on the reef community is both a fundamental scientific question as well as a needed ingredient in designing and managing reef preserves. Determining the pattern of coral recruitment is just as essential to understanding the maintenance and renewal of reefs as it is to evaluating the long-term effects and remediation of the damage by ship groundings. Knowledge of the pattern of water movements can help to explain the distribution of reefs as well as the fate of an oil spill.

    4. **Most of the world's reefs are in or near developing countries with large populations of impoverished inhabitants who exploit the nearby reefs for food or saleable items.** Starving people are understandably immune to suggestions that they practice resource management. Yet there are some small signs that incentives can be developed to encourage conservation. The greatest success in encouraging resource management has come from examples in which the local population was convinced that their management practices could make a difference in the yield of food or saleable goods.

RECOMMENDATIONS

Declines in the world's tropical rain forests are well established. It is possible that observed declines in coral reef condition are harbingers of a similar situation that is less obvious. **There is, therefore, an urgent need to provide a comprehensive assessment of reefs, both those impacted by natural and anthropogenic disturbances as well as those that are unaffected.**

An ongoing dialogue needs to be established between reef scientists, environmentalists and those charged with the management of reefs.

A major program of education needs to be established that can promote resource management in developing countries and make user groups and the general public aware of this remarkable and integrated ecosystem, its resources and biodiversity.

To initiate the programs that can accomplish these goals, it was proposed that 1996 be designated the Year of the Reef. The organization and planning required for the various initiatives demands the international collaboration of scientists, administrators of reef parks and reserves and environmental groups. A first step in the development of the Year should be to establish a Steering Committee to prepare formal statement of goals and outline the principal initiatives.

SUMMARY OF THE DISCUSSIONS DURING THE COLLOQUIUM

Geological history of reefs:

Five of the case histories in this collection, Section H, addressed two aspects of history that influence the present-day condition of reefs.

1. The changing rate of sea level rise during the past 10,000 years and its interaction with the pre-existing limestone landscapes have had a profound effect on the present state of development. Early during this period the rise was so rapid that some reefs were literally drowned. During the last several thousand years, as the rising sea flooded larger and more areas of suitable foundation and the rate of rise decelerated, reef communities were established widely and many have been able to grow up to sea level. In several areas around the world, the patterns and ages of modern reef development were dictated by the configuration of the foundations either by providing local elevations for initiation or by controlling water movements to provide more favorable habitats. Information of history may help to identify reefs killed naturally.

2. The present-day coral fauna is geologically young with a third of the modern genera in the Western Atlantic only a few million years old. During this period, corals have been subjected to numerous periods of sea level rise and fall that have forced migrations up and down the margins of shelves and platforms worldwide. This entirely natural stress may have acted to select hardier species both for the shallower communities near sea level as well as those that are vigorous at depths near the lower limits of coral growth.

Methods of assessing the condition of coral reefs:

Assessing the condition of coral reefs is as difficult as evaluating the condition of a city or town using remote sensing. It is, therefore, not surprising that a wide variety of field observations are in current use. Some form of census of reef builders and/or inhabitants is probably the most widely used method. Estimates of the percentages of corals, fishes, algae or other reef organisms, and in some instances their condition, can provide useful snapshots of populations. Evaluating these estimates of abundance and condition demands similar data from either a standard "pristine" reef or, more realistically, data from a large number of reefs close enough together to have similar physical conditions. Just as repeated censuses of human populations are needed to evaluate demographic changes, so for reef building communities is there a need for long-term monitoring both on the small scale in unit areas (quadrats) as well as over larger areas with transects. One model program of monitoring reefs, their physical environments and related sea grass and mangrove ecosystems is underway in the Caribbean with the participation of some 25 laboratories and marine stations in the CARICOMP Program organized by the Florida Institute of Oceanography. Similar programs are in operation in Australia and Southeast Asia and a UNEP Task Force has developed plans for a global network of monitoring sites.

It is evident that the census approach is only a starting point for evaluating the condition of coral reefs. Just as in the analysis of plant communities or human populations, there is a need to know the demographics of the various elements of the reef community and their interactions, metabolism and history of disturbances. Thus, similar information is needed to understand changes in the coral reef builders and residents. Assembling this kind of essential information on marine communities is just beginning, and to develop it will require major commitments in effort and funding.

Three of the case histories in this Collection described the use of indicator species as canaries of reef condition. Among the candidates proposed are a single species of fish, benthic invertebrates like certain sponges, and relatively rare coral species whose reported distributions suggest sensitivity.

Missing from the discussions of methods was consideration of methods and measurement of the physical environment of reefs. Yet it is well established, for example, that changes in temperature and circulation can result in declines or even the demise of reef builders. The recent serious decline in coral reef development in the eastern Pacific as a result of the warming associated with the El Nino-Southern Oscillation event is a case in point. Clearly, there is an urgent need for expanded collection of continuous records of the physical environment of reefs like those of the monitoring programs mentioned above.

A major conclusion of the discussion of methods is that there is no single method for assessing the condition of coral reefs, but instead, the selection of methods should be question driven. For example, some reefs are in such a state of decline that their condition is obvious from a cursory, non-quantitative survey. For other reefs, such as those under attack by predators (crown of thorns) or disease (black band), quantitative data are needed on the amount of decline, selectivity by species, and rates of expansion of the epidemic. The identification of the causes of reef decline is often most challenging because impacts are often multiple and synergistic. Among the case histories in this volume are numerous examples of the combined effects of natural and anthropogenic impacts.

Regional Assessment of Coral Reefs:

Background.
A major goal of the Colloquium was to critically evaluate the condition of reefs in the major areas of reefs worldwide and to rank the principal hazards. It was expected that the case histories within each of the major regions of reef building could provide the starting point for these evaluations and that those participants with experience in the various regions could expand the data base. Accordingly, the entire assembly was divided into six regional groups: 1) Florida, Bahamas, Bermuda and Gulf of Mexico; 2) Caribbean; 3) South and Central America; 4) Java and South China Seas; 5) Pacific; and 6) Indian Ocean. Participants familiar with the reefs of each region met together to consider the evidence from the case histories and the wider base of information. Then, in a plenary session, each region reported to the entire Colloquium.

Caveats.
This attempt to evaluate the condition of reefs worldwide produced only some

tentative first-order conclusions for several reasons. First, although the case histories are an unprecedented collection of reports on reef conditions and histories, the number is so small compared to the total world reefs that they can not be considered to be representative of the overall regions from which they come. Second, from the discussions of all the regions, it was evident that an adequate inventory of large-scale assessment needs to draw not only on published scientific literature and the data from reef scientists, but also on the considerable body of "gray literature" of government reports, popular articles and the observations of knowledgeable divers, resort and tour leaders, and tourists. Some participants were aware of the existence and implications of this type of information, but the lack of access and documentation is a major barrier to incorporating it into assessments. Third, for regions like the Caribbean where marine stations are numerous and the density of local observations is high, the data base appears adequate for first order conclusions, but suffers from a lack of coordinated, areally-extensive surveys. Fourth, there are few organizations in the world comparable to Australia's coordinated, technically-oriented Great Barrier Reef Marine Park Authority and its world class Australian Institute of Marine Sciences that can provide large-scale assessments; in most regions of the world, vast areas of reefs have never been visited by reef scientists.

Bermuda, Florida, Bahamas and the Gulf of Mexico.

There are no obvious signs of decline in the reefs of atoll-like Bermuda and the few reef-capped prominences of the northwestern Gulf of Mexico. In southeast Florida, where the reefs are heavily used for fishing, diving and tourism, there are well-substantiated reports of local declines in coral populations based on long-term monitoring of quadrats, but there remains uncertainty about the areal extent of these changes. The newly-established Florida Keys National Marine Sanctuary plans the first-ever extensive surveys of the reefs and an ongoing program of measurements of water quality. On the other hand, the extensive reefs rimming the vast archipelago of Bahama Banks are poorly known.

Caribbean.

The reefs of the Caribbean are relatively small and almost all are near islands with large populations and extensive tourism. The presence of marine stations and national parks has provided more localized data on the nearby reefs than probably in any other part of the world. In four of the well-studied sites, there are significant declines in coral cover and fish populations. Destruction of reefs by hurricanes and the loss of grazing sea urchins that feed on macroalgae are believed to be principal causes of the declines at several sites; over-fishing is probably a major factor in Jamaica and elsewhere. For some local areas, runoff from the islands or from dredging are considered to be contributory causes of reef decline.

Two aspects of the Caribbean deserve expanded attention by reef specialists: 1) reefs near marine stations are generally well-studied, but those beyond easy access are often poorly known; and 2) the presence of well-established impacts, both natural (e.g., hurricanes, bleaching from elevated temperatures, loss of grazing urchins) and anthropogenic (e.g., over-fishing, runoff, tourism), makes the Caribbean a natural laboratory for assessing the short and long-term effects of these impacts.

Central and South America Mainland Areas.

In this region, as in the Caribbean, a combination of natural and anthropogenic effects have produced significant local declines in reef populations. Examples include Barbados, where hurricane damage and the loss of urchins that graze on macroalgae are the culprits; Colombia off Santa Marta City, where reefs suffer from pollution and runoff, are less diverse, have lower coral cover and show more dead coral than those at a distance; Costa Rica, where a small fringing reef is being smothered by terrestrial runoff from areas cleared for agriculture; and San Blas Islands, where the combination of bleaching and the loss of grazing urchins along with the suspected effects of coral mining and runoff of sediment and excess nutrients, has led to declines in abundance and in variety of coral species.

Included in this region is the Belize Barrier Reef Complex with the largest, most varied and most luxuriant array of reefs in the entire Western Atlantic. The Smithsonian Institution has long maintained a Laboratory there for research on one area and there has been considerable mapping of bottom communities by volunteers of Coral Cay.

Java and South China Seas.

This region is remarkable for the abundance and variety of reefs and for the high diversity of corals. It is also notable for its large population (over 440 million for peninsular and insular SE Asia alone) and its examples of locally-severe reef degradation. For example, the reefs in the vicinity of Jakarta, a city of 9.5 million, are dead or destroyed as a result of the combined effects of eutrophication from untreated sewage, sedimentation, reduced light intensity, coral mining and physical destruction of reefs. Similar problems occur locally throughout the Philippines. There are reasons to believe that reefs in more remote areas are in better condition, although the presence of wide-ranging fishing fleets may have more impact than is now known.

Information on the condition of reefs in this vast region is highly variable. For areas such as Taiwan, the Philippines and Thailand, at least reconnaissance surveys by reefs workers have been carried out for up to half the total reefs, with greater emphasis on nearshore than on offshore reefs. For other areas, including the reef-rich country of Indonesia, fewer than 10% of the reefs have been examined by scientists. There is a large amount of less specialized information on reef conditions available in the form of observations and reports of divers, tour operators, fishermen and government officials, but it has not been assembled or reviewed.

Pacific.

In this, by far the largest region of coral reefs in the world's oceans, there are extremes in the condition of reefs and in the extent of information on them. On the one hand, there are reef areas that have undergone major degradation. Some examples are: severe decline in coral populations in the Eastern Pacific as a result of warming by ENSO events; burial and destruction of reefs in the Ryukus from construction activities; and severe, but local and temporary reef destruction from cyclones on some atolls of French Polynesia. At the other extreme, most of the Great Barrier Reef in Australia and other areas remote from centers of human population are evidently quite healthy, such as most reefs of the atolls in the Marshalls, Caroline and Cook Islands. Overall, the condition of the reefs in the Pacific was rated to be about 70% excellent to good and about 30% fair to poor. Regarding causal factors of reef stress, approximately 50% of the impacts were judged to be natural, such as El Nino events and large storms, and the other half related to anthropogenic factors. The most serious sources of induced stress were judged to be sedimentation, eutrophication (nutrient enrichment) and over-fishing. Another serious problem in the Pacific is lack of information; overall, it was estimated that only about 10% of the reefs in the Pacific have been visited by reef scientists.

Indian Ocean.

Reefs of coastal Kenya provide a model of how reduction in fishing pressure effects the community. In protected marine parks, reef fishes are more abundant and diverse than in nearby unprotected areas. Conversely, large populations of rock-boring sea urchins characterize unprotected areas, while predation by trigger fish reduces their numbers significantly in protected areas.

In Sri Lanka, reefs that are accessible to large human populations along the coast are severely affected by mining of coral for building, and by a variety of destructive and intense methods of fishing (e.g., use of dynamite, special nets, and uncontrolled collection of ornamental reef organisms). Reefs in the remote offshore areas of the northwest and southeast are relatively immune from these impacts.

The reef flats of reefs fringing the islands of Reunion and Mauritius that have been well-studied all show significant declines from various combinations of runoff from agricultural areas, sewage discharge, over-fishing and hurricane damage.

Red Sea.

Red Sea reefs generally are in good shape. As most of the bordering countries neither have large cities nor large populations along the coast, the human stress to reefs is low. Only the drastically increasing tourist boom along the Egyptian coast is having a locally-severe impact and some reefs are already partly dead. Apart from human impacts, there is a slight increase in <u>Drupella</u> grazing in the northern Red Sea reefs, especially in the Gulf of Aqaba.

Ranking of Hazards to reefs:

As a part of the review of reefs in each of the six regions, participants were asked to prepare lists of all the potential hazards and then rank their impacts as high, medium or low. This attempt to produce a single evaluation for any of the regions ignores spatial and temporal variability. For example, ship grounding and coral disease are locally serious in the Florida reefs, but possibly much less so in the nearby Bahamas. Hurricanes may have locally destroyed reefs in Jamaica, St. Croix and on some atolls in French Polynesia, yet reefs nearby are unaffected.

An equally serious limitation to this ranking are the biases of those who participated in the exercise. A listing of hazards developed by resource managers would likely differ from that prepared by reef scientists or conservationists. Scientists tend to focus on the proximate causes, manager's interests are on those hazards that might be controlled, and conservationists often emphasize anthropogenic effects.

Accepting the limitations of the ranking, the consensus view that degradation of water quality from runoff (nutrient enrichment and excess turbidity and/or sedimentation) and over-fishing are major hazards provides a point of departure for future efforts to evaluate hazards.

PROGRAM OF THE FORUM

June 10, 1993

Review of the conclusions and recommendations of the Colloquium.
Robert Ginsburg and a Panel composed of Robert Buddemeir (Kansas Geological Survey), Wendy Craik (Great Barrier Reef Marine Part Authority), Richard Grigg (University of Hawaii), Jeremy Jackson (Smithsonian Institution), Vance Vicente (Southeast Fisheries Science Center), and Susan Wells (ICLARM).

Reefs and you.
Frank Talbot, Smithsonian Natural History Museum

Oil pollution effects on coral community structure at Eilat, Red Sea.
Yossi Loya, Tel Aviv University.

Do deep-ocean sewage outfalls impact coral reefs? An example from Hawaii.
Richard Grigg and Steven Dollar (University of Hawaii).

June 11, 1993

Development of the comprehensive management and zoning plans for the Florida Keys National Marine Sanctuary.
Billy Causey (Florida Keys National Marine Sanctuary.

Can the Great Barrier Reef model of marine protected areas save reefs worldwide?
Wendy Craik (Great Barrier Reef Marine Park Authority).

Why conservation by legal fiat does not work.
Howard Latin (Rutgers University)

Is there a loss of diversity in corals?
J.E.N. Veron (Australian Institute of Marine Science).

El Nino-induced coral mortality: a model of global warming.
Peter Glynn (University of Miami)

Coral reefs, climate and global change.
Robert Buddemeier (Kansas Geological Survey)

HISTORY OF REEFS

	PAGES
The Coral Record of Late Glacial Sea Level Rise	**1 - 6**
Arthur L. Bloom	
Plio-Pleistocene Extinctions and the Origin of the Modern Caribbean Reef-Coral Fauna	**7 - 13**
Ann F. Budd, Kenneth G. Johnson, and Thomas A. Stemann	
How Have Holocene Sea Level Rise and Antecedent Topography Influenced Belize Barrier Reef Development?	**14 - 20**
Randolph B. Bruke	
Preferential Distribution of Reefs in the Florida Reef Tract: The Past is the Key to the Present	**21 - 26**
Robert N. Ginsburg, and Eugene A. Shinn	

THE CORAL RECORD OF LATE GLACIAL SEA LEVEL RISE

Arthur L. Bloom
Dept. Geol. Sci., 2122 Snee Hall, Cornell Univ.
Ithaca, NY 14853

ABSTRACT

Each new improvement in radiometric dating has provided new insights into the growth history of coral reefs during the latest deglaciation. High precision U-series dates on corals now serve to calibrate the ^{14}C time scale beyond the range of dendrochrology. Corrected ages incidentally show distinct fluctuations in the late glacial rate of sea level rise, which have useful implications for reef growth.

INTRODUCTION

This is an exciting decade for the field of Quaternary research. As a recent manuscript reviewer noted, "One has the distinct feeling that with the necessary time control now nearly in hand, a crucial breakthrough in our paleoclimatic understanding is just on the horizon". Corals are more than ever before providing radiometric dates and isotopic ratios that integrate sea level change, atmospheric and ocean circulation, and late Quaternary climate history into a single subject. This "case study" is a review of recent research by others, much of which will be familiar to participants in this colloquium and forum. My purpose is to record my personal admiration for, and amazement at, the quality of research now in progress on the history of the late glacial rise in sea level, with emphasis on its record in coral reefs, and to ask some questions that may already be in the process of being answered.

IMPROVED DATING METHODS

During the nearly 50 years that radiocarbon dating has been revolutionizing Quaternary studies there have been repeated examples of great promises suddenly tempered by new problems, only to have those problems resolved in unexpected ways that lead to more great promises. Within two decades after the discovery of radiocarbon dating in 1947 by Willard Libby, the impact of the industrial revolution on recent radiocarbon dates was recognized by Hans Suess. Soon thereafter, atmospheric nuclear testing introduced new problems of ^{14}C productivity and mixing rates, but almost immediately, one person's contaminant became another's tracer. In rapid succession, sunspots and the fluctuating secular magnetic field of the earth were shown to perturb the classic concept of ^{14}C dating with its assumptions of constant generation and decay. In each case, the "problem" became an exciting and fruitful research topic, touching on broader issues such as the sun as a variable star, the origin and history of the earth's magnetic field, and mixing rates in the atmosphere and ocean.

New and improved equipment and techniques continued to revolutionized radiometric dating. By 1966, Veeh had dated emerged coral reefs of last interglacial age at many locations in the Pacific and Indian Ocean by U-series alpha spectrometry, with ages ranging from "90,000 ± 20,000 to 160,000 ± 40,000 years" and from "80,000 ± 50,000 to 180,000 ± 60,000 years". By 1970, the Milankovitch theory was finding support in U-series dates from Barbados (Broecker et al., 1968), Papua New Guinea (Veeh and Chappell, 1970), and elsewhere, with Emiliani's isotope stage 5 subdivided into intervals centered at about 80,000, 105,000, and 125,000 years, all with 2σ counting errors reduced to the range of ±10%.

Reef corals, by virtue of their close correlation with sea level, clean mineralogy, readily observed diagenesis, generally good preservation, and wide geographic distribution, have been a favored dating material for many investigators using both ^{14}C and U-series techniques. It is worth noting that the entire chronologic support for reading the deep sea and ice core oxygen isotope records in terms of Milankovitch cycles rests on :(1) interpolation from the age of the Brunhes-Matuyama paleomagnetic boundary, which has recently been revised from ca. 730,000 to 780,000 BP (Baksi et al., 1992), (2) ^{14}C dates on deep-sea carbonates back to only ca. 20,000 BP, and (3) U-series dates from last interglacial and Wisconsin interstadial coral reefs. While we have no reason to doubt the established chronology, neither can we assume that it is proven.

The coral reef record of the late Wisconsin-Holocene sea level rise is primarily submerged and accessible only by diving or drilling. Lighty et al. (1982) assembled 42 radiocarbon dates on in situ *Acropora palmata* specimens from 16 reefs in 6 regions of the western Atlantic into a minimum sea-level curve for the past 10,000 years (Fig. 1). For the first time, sea level researchers had a comprehensive coral reef record to compare with previously produced sea level curves based on salt marsh stratigraphy and molluscan shell banks. The radiocarbon ages by this time had counting errors of ±1 or 2 per cent, but were uncorrected for the several ills to which such dates are liable. No seawater age correction was made, based on analyses of living specimens. This sea level curve shows many general features of the final 10,000 years of sea level rise. As ice sheet volume diminished, the rate at which water returned to the sea also diminished. Of the total of about 120 m of sea level rise since about 18,000 BP, only some 30 m remained 10,000 years ago.

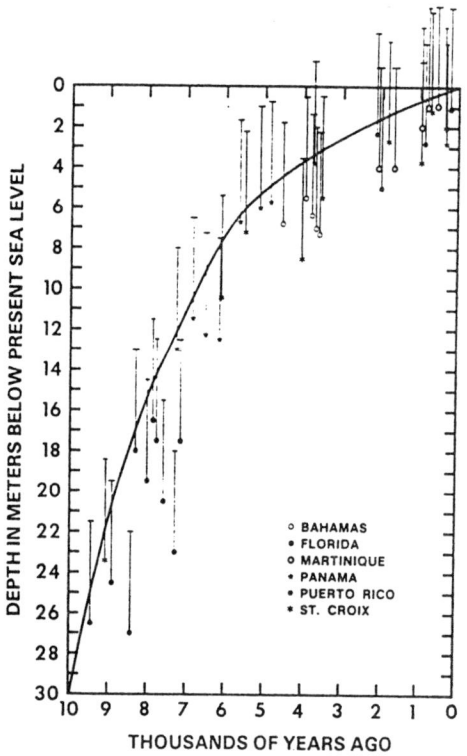 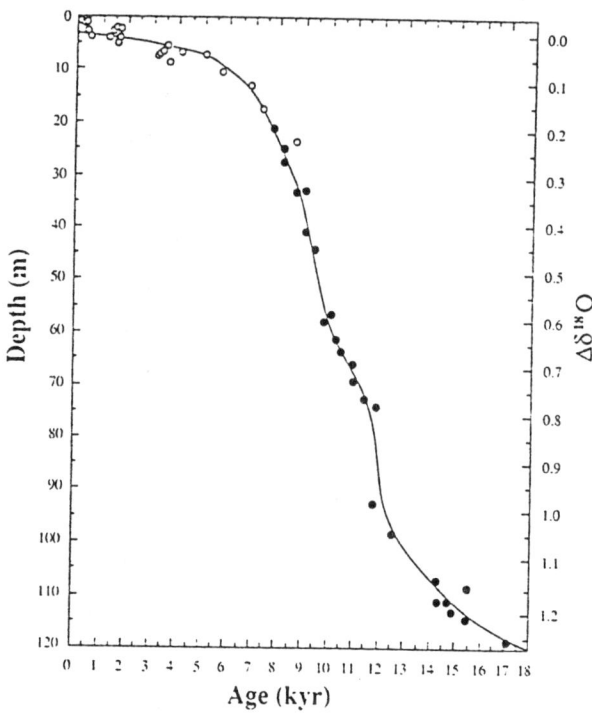

Figure 1. Minimum Holocene sea level curve based on ^{14}C ages and depths of 42 in situ Acropora palmata framework samples from tropical western Atlantic. (Lighty et al., 1982). Vertical bars represent paleo water depths of 0 to 5 m.

Figure 2 (right). Barbados sea level curve based on ^{14}C-dated A. palmata. All ages corrected for seawater age by subtracting 400 years from measured ^{14}C ages. Open circles from Lighty et al. (1982) (Fairbanks, 1989).

Adding to the effect of meltwater returning to the sea was the isostatic response of the ocean floor, which produced a variety of flexural responses on islands and contintental margins. No two regions have exactly the same sea level history for the last 10,000 years; some regions were uplifted, some subsided. The isostatic response added or subtracted only a few meters of vertical displacement relative to changing sea level, however. In most regions of coral reef growth, the decelerating rise of sea level permitted reefs to establish and expand only during middle to late Holocene time. Most modern reefs are a veneer less than 10 m in thickness, built in the Holocene on a much older substrate. A similar record of Holocene fringing-reef growth in North Queensland was compiled from borehole samples by Hopley et al. (1978, 1983). Holocene reef growth was established by 9,500 years ago at a depth of about 20 m, although most of the fringing reefs in North Queensland are veneers less than 7 m in thickness and younger than 7,000 years.

Suddenly, within the last 5 years, the subject of late Wisconsin-Holocene sea level history from coral reefs has exploded. Fairbanks (1989) published the first radiocarbon-dated sea level curve that covered the entire deglacial hemicycle, based on offshore drilling in several drowned reefs off the west coast of Barbados (Fig. 2). The last 9000 years and 20 m of his submergence history merge into the data of Lighty et. al. (1982), when the latter are corrected for a seawater age of 400 years. The sigmoid curve covers 121 ± 5 m of submergence during the past 18,000 radiocarbon years, with two intervals of more rapid rise. The only bothersome feature of this scientific triumph is its lack of continuity among the several reefs that were drilled and dated.

A 52 m borehole in the emerged Holocene reef near Sialum, on the Huon Peninsula in Papua New Guinea, has also provided a sea level chronology for the late glacial interval from 11,000 to 7,000 years BP (Chappell and Polach, 1991). When corrected for tectonic uplift, the Sialum borehole ^{14}C dates from shallow water coral species impressively complement the discontinuous Barbados record (Fig. 3). Whereas the Barbados reefs could not keep up with the rapidly rising sea level, the Sialum reef kept pace from 11,000 years ago until tectonic uplift caused its emergence about 7,000 years ago. The average uplift rate of 1.9 m per 1000 years near Sialum is slow compared to the vertical reef growth rate of 12.7 m per 1000 years. The Barbados and Huon Peninsula radiometrically dated records of the deglacial sea level rise are the focus of the remainder of this case study.

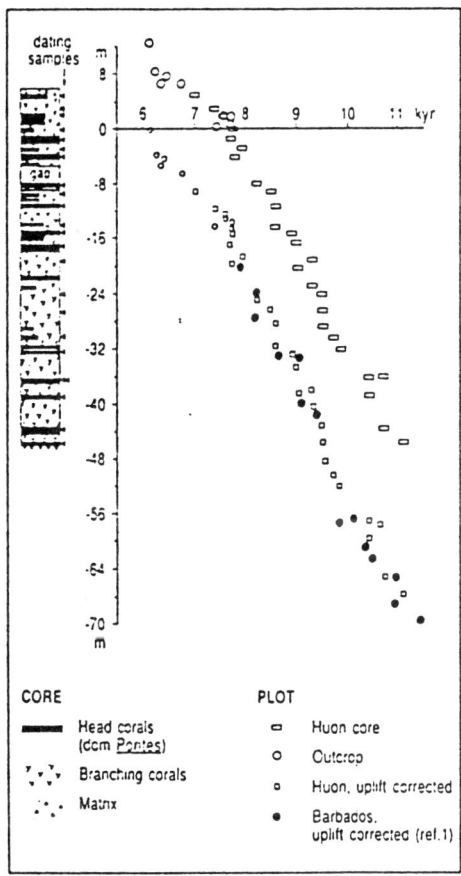

Figure 3. Core log and age-depth plot of Sialum borehole, Papua New Guinea. ^{14}C ages corrected by subtracting 400 years for seawater age. Upper rectangles are uncorrected for tectonic uplift of ca 2 mm/yr. Lower rectangles are corrected for uplift and compared with Barbados curve (Fairbanks, 1989) (Chappell and Polach, 1991).

IMPACT OF HIGH PRECISION CORAL DATING

Both ^{14}C and Uranium-series dating methods have been radically improved by mass spectrometry, better calibration, and better instruments and techniques. Counting errors are now routinely smaller than 1 per cent of the age of the sample. Radiocarbon dates are now precisely calibrated by dendrochronology to at least 9,200 BP (Stuiver et al., 1986). U-series dates by thermal emission mass spectrometry now routinely carry counting errors (2σ) of approximately 0.5 per cent, good enough to extend the calibration of the ^{14}C time scale to at least 30,000 BP (Bard et al., 1990 a and b). The U-series dates from corals in Barbados and Papua New Guinea not only consistently record a "French two step" model of late glacial sea level rise, but they promise to link a whole series of events: reef growth, sea level, the late-glacial Younger Dryas climate oscillation, ^{14}C in the atmosphere, and the δ^{18}O record in pelagic foraminifera and Greenland ice cores.

Consider late glacial sea level history from the viewpoint of a coral reef in Barbados (Fig. 4). Acropora palmata and other species of the impoverished Atlantic coral province were building a fringing reef 120 m below present sea level on the exposed island shelf of Barbados, 18,000-20,000 BP. As sea level rise accelerated to a maximum of 45-50 mm/yr during Fairbank's meltwater pulse 1A, about 14,100 BP (U-series; equivalent to 12,000 ^{14}C BP) the fringing reef was drowned. A second, shallower fringing reef was established during the Younger Dryas time, when sea level rise markedly slowed to between 6-10 mm/yr (Fig. 4), but it too was subsequently drowned by rapid sea level rise during meltwater pulse 1B, when sea level rose at a maximum rate of 35 to 40 mm/yr at about 11,300 BP (U-series; equivalent to 9500 BP 14C years). Near the end of meltwater pulse 1B, a third, even shallower, fringing reef began, from which Fairbanks established the Holocene part of his curve with additional dates from other western Atlantic reefs by Lighty et al. (1968).

The testable hypotheses offered to students of Atlantic coral reefs by Fairbanks (1989, 1990) and Bard et al. (1990a, 1990b) is clear: were other fringing reefs of the region overtopped during the late-glacial meltwater pulses? With the varied rates of sea level rise and the history of surface water temperature reasonably inferred for the region, the late-glacial paleoecology of reef-building corals has been largely circumscribed, although additional variables such as substrate composition, shelf gradient, and turbidity need to be considered. How did the reefs of the region respond? How many other islands have triple drowned reefs at depths of less than 120 m? Someone should take a submersible ride down to look at them.

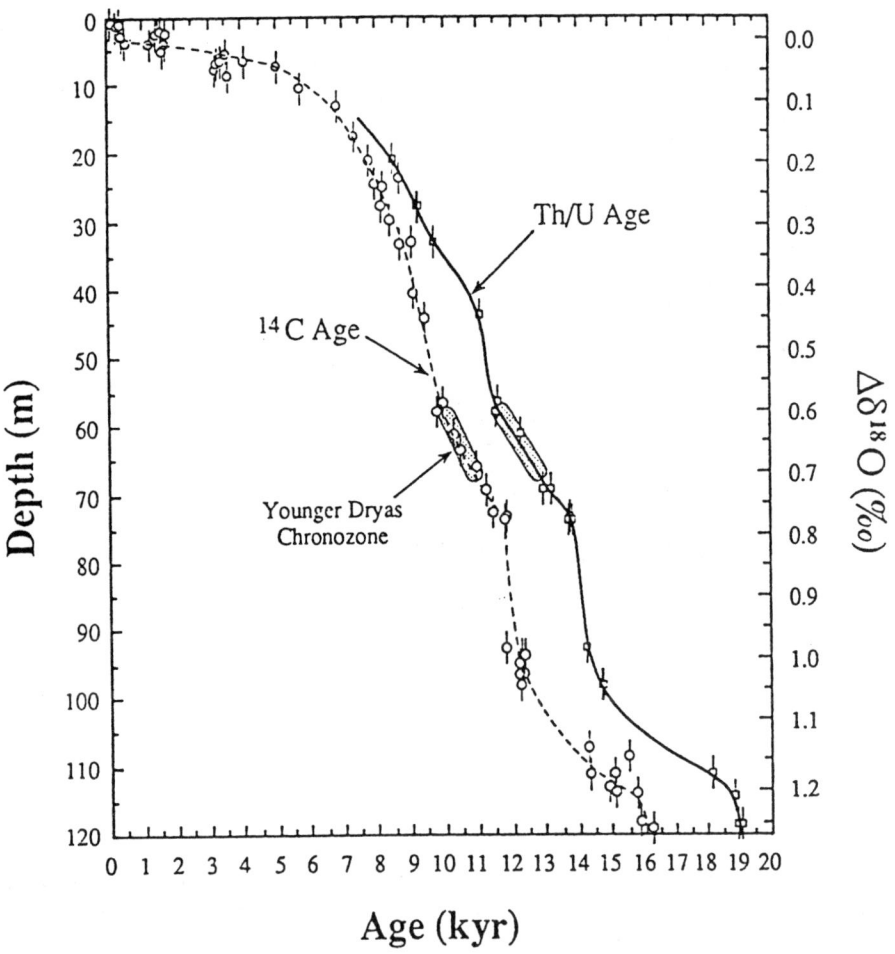

Figure 4. Barbados ^{14}C- and U-series ages compared. The difference between the two curves is a measure of the ^{14}C calibration correction (Fairbanks, 1990).

The Holocene reef crest near Sialum in Papua New Guinea is now about 6 m above sea level. The depth-corrected radiocarbon sea level curve from Fig. 3 is supported by a new series of high precision ^{14}C and U-series ages (Fig. 5). The tectonic uplift rate of nearly 2 m/1000 yr at this part of the Huon Peninsula at least partially negated the rapid pulses of late glacial sea level rise recorded in the Sialum borehole, but even without tectonic uplift, the more abundant and prolific corals of the Indo-Pacific reef province would have been more likely to keep up with the rapid rises than the less vigorous Caribbean reefs. Back to at least 13,100 BP (U-series; equivalent to 10,970 ^{14}C BP), the Sialum reef did so; 48.3 m of vertical accretion occurred in the interval from 13,129 to 8363 BP (U-series) at an average rate of slightly more than 10 mm/yr. Incremental rates of sea level rise varied from 16 mm/yr prior to 12,325 BP to only 2 mm/yr in the Younger Dryas period of reduced melting from 12,325 to 11,045 BP, then increased rapidly to a maximum of 28 mm/yr thereafter (all U-series) (Edwards et al., in press).

Because of the spacing of dated samples, the maximum rates of sea level rise inferred for Barbados and the Huon Peninsula cannot be directly compared. Nevertheless, there are no indications of interupted growth in the Sialum borehole, and coral growth seems to have kept up. The Sialum borehole passed though many thick Porites sections, probably large single heads. We have no idea how much deeper we might have been able to drill in the Holocene reef at Sialum; one could hope for another, deeper borehole at the site. It would be exciting to find a reef anywhere that "kept up" with sea level for the entire deglacial hemicycle.

For coral reefs struggling to avoid drowning in Barbados, Papua New Guineas, and elsewhere, the 1000 year cold interval of reduced glacier melting and slower sea level rise known as the Younger Dryas may have provided a "breathing spell". Polyps could settle on newly submerged suitable substrates and perhaps build small fringing reefs, before the renewed rapid sea level rise defeated them. This may be what is recorded by Fairbank's middle drowned reef. On many coasts, this brief event may not be recorded, or if it is, it will be found only under the reef talus of the younger and much larger Holocene reef that succeeded it.

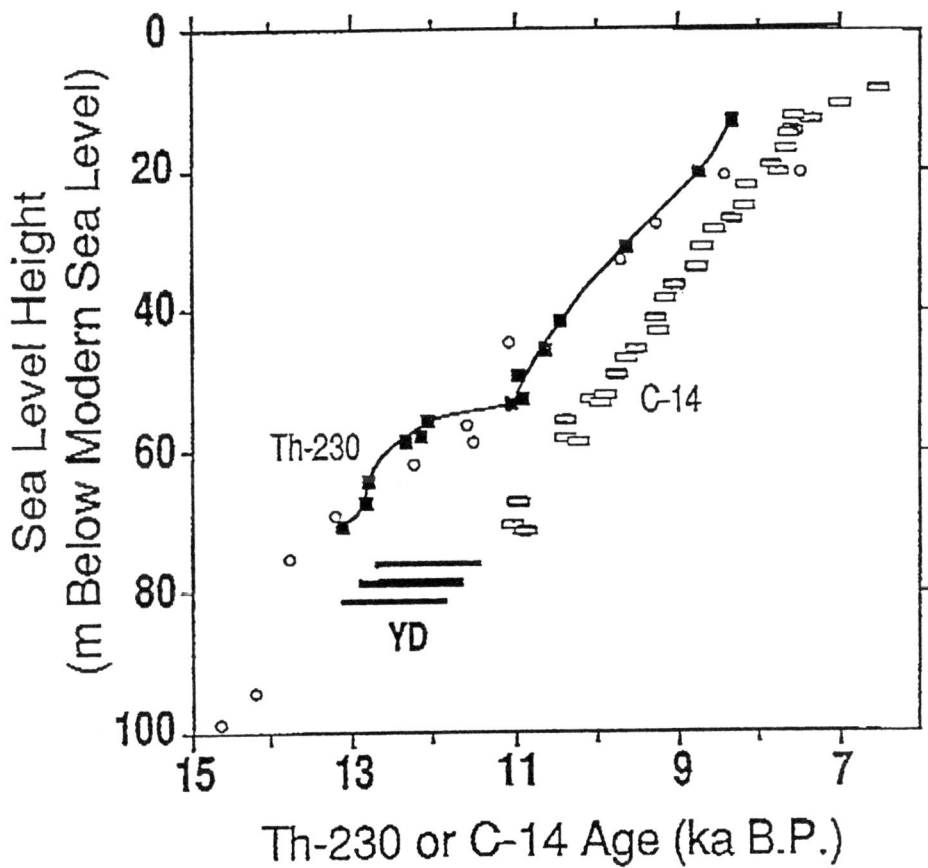

Figure 5. Sialum borehole, Papua New Guinea ^{14}C and U-series ages compared. During part of the Younger Dryas interval, the ^{14}C ages changed by only 210 years while the U-series ages record 1280 years. The Younger Dryas rate of sea level rise is much less than the rate inferred from the Barbados U-series ages (Edwards, et al., in press).

CONCLUSIONS

The real significance of the new high precision paired ^{14}C and U-series dates on corals lies in their ability to calibrate the ^{14}C content of the atmosphere, oceans, and ice sheets, and identify abrupt, step-like climate changes in the late Pleistocene. Coral samples are commonly large enough for a variety of analyses to be done on the same material--even on single, probably annual, layers. With the new analytical tools now available, and coralline aragonite as a proven and in many ways ideal analytical material, we can look forward to additional exciting developments.

REFERENCES

Baksi, A.K., V. Hsu, M.O. McWilliams, and E.Farrar. 1992. ^{40}Ar/^{39}Ar dating of the Brunhes - Matuyama geomagnetic field reversal. Science 25: 356-357.

Bard, E., B. Hamelin, R.G. Fairbanks, and A. Zindler. 1990. Calibration of the ^{14}C timescale over the past 30,000 years using mass spectrometric U-Th ages from Barbados corals. Nature 345: 405-410.

Bard, E., B. Hamelin, R.G. Fairbanks, A. Zindler, G. Mathieu, and M. Arnold. 1990. U/Th and ^{14}C ages of corals from Barbados and their use for calibrating the ^{14}C time scale beyond 9000 years B.P. Nuclear Inst. and Methods in Phy. Res. B52: 461-468.

Broecker, W., D. Thurber, and J. Goddard. 1968. Milankovitch hypothesis supported by precise dating of coral reefs and deep-sea sediments. Science 159: 297-300.

Chappell, J., H. Polach. 1991. Post-glacial sea-level rise from a coral record at Huon Peninsula, Papua New Guinea. Nature 349: 147-149.

Edwards, R.L., J.W. Beck, G. Burr, D. Donahue, J.M.A. Chappell, A.L. Bloom, E.R.M. Druffel, and F.W. Taylor (1993). A large drop in atmospheric ^{14}C/^{12}C and reduced melting in the Younger Dryas, documented with ^{230}Th ages of corals. Science (in press).

Fairbanks, R.G. 1989. A 17,000-year glacio-eustatic sea level record: Influence of glacial melting rates on the Younger Dryas event and deep-ocean circulation. Nature 342: 637-642.

Fairbanks, R.G. 1990. The age and origin of the "Younger Dryas climate event" in Greenland ice cores. Paleoceanography 5 (6): 937-948.

Hopley, D., R.F. Mclean, J. Marshall, and A.S. Smith. 1978. Holocene-Pleistocene boundary in a fringing reef: Hayman Island, North Queensland. Search 9:323-325.

Hopley, D., A.M. Slocombe, F. Muir, and C. Grant. 1983. Nearshore fringing reefs in north Queensland. Coral Reefs 1:151-160.

Lighty, R.G., I.G. Macintyre, and R. Stuckenrath. 1982. Acropora palmata reef framework: A reliable indicator of sea level in the western Atlantic for the past 10,000 years. Coral Reefs 1:125-130.

Stuiver, M., B. Kromer, B. Becker, and C.W. Ferguson. 1986. Radiocarbon age calibraton back to 13,300 Years BP and the ^{14}C age matching of the German oak and U.S. bristlecone pine chronologies. Radiocarbon 28 (2B): 969-979.

Veeh, H.H. 1966. Th^{230}/U^{238} and U^{234}/U^{238} ages of Pleistocene high sea level stand. Jour. Geophys. Res. 71 (14): 3379-3386.

Veeh, H.H., and J. Chappell. 1970. Astronomical theory of climatic change: Support from New Guinea. Science 167: 862-865.

PLIO-PLEISTOCENE EXTINCTIONS AND THE ORIGIN OF THE MODERN CARIBBEAN REEF-CORAL FAUNA

Ann F. Budd[1], Kenneth G. Johnson[2], and Thomas A. Stemann[3]

[1]Department of Geology, University of Iowa, Iowa City, IA 52242, U.S.A. [2]Department of Palaeontology, The Natural History Museum, Cromwell Road, London SW7 5BD, United Kingdom. [3]Geologisches Institut, Universität Bern, Baltzerstrasse 1, CH-3012 Bern, Switzerland.

ABSTRACT

Quantitative analyses of change in the Caribbean reef-coral fauna over the past 22 million years show that a major episode of accelerated faunal turnover occurred during the middle Pliocene to early Pleistocene (4-3 Ma). During turnover, origination and extinction rates of species were found to be equally and simultaneously high, and a relatively constant, "equilibrium" number of species was supported in the fauna. A second smaller episode of accelerated extinction occurred at 2-1 Ma, but was not accompanied by increased origination. Equilibrium was maintained during long periods of faunal stability before turnover (8-4 Ma), and a slightly lower equilibrium was maintained after the second extinction episode (1-0 Ma). As in species, high extinction rates are also detected in genera during the Plio-Pleistocene; however, unlike species, no new genera originated. More than 50% of the genera that became extinct in the Caribbean still live today in the Indo-Pacific. Comparison of extinction rates between grass flat, shallow reef, and deep reef assemblages shows that grass flat corals were most susceptible to extinction. The observed patterns cannot be easily explained by any one environmental agent. However, close correspondence in timing with closure of the isthmus of Panama suggests that associated changes in oceanic circulation may have been at least partially responsible. Understanding long-term patterns of equilibrium and ecological balance will be important to modern reef conservation.

INTRODUCTION

Study of large-scale patterns in the fossil record suggests that tropical reef biotas are among the most vulnerable to extinction during times of extreme global environmental stress (Jablonski, 1991). Yet, little is known about long-term patterns of species extinctions and originations. For example, it remains unclear if and when episodes of accelerated species extinctions occurred in the Caribbean region over the past 50 million years. As a consequence, many questions of significance to modern reef conservation have yet to be addressed, including: (1) which external environmental agents have triggered regional extinction episodes in the geologic past, (2) how have reef communities recovered from such episodes, and (3) which members of reef communities have been most susceptible to extinction. Much of the reason for this lack of knowledge can be attributed to three factors which have hampered investigations of long-term evolutionary patterns in reef-corals: (1) inadequate systematics, (2) the poor resolution of age dates assigned to many fossil reef deposits, and (3) the lack of continuous fossil sequences and patchy distribution of reef deposits in time and space.

In the present paper, we report on preliminary research documenting patterns of extinction and origination in Neogene to Recent Caribbean reef-corals. To study these patterns, we have had to assemble a new compilation of stratigraphic ranges of Neogene to Recent Caribbean reef-coral species (Budd et al., in press). The new compilation differs from previous compilations (e.g., Frost, 1977) by using more up-to-date and consistent taxonomic methods, by including more Pliocene sites (15 Pliocene sites as opposed to six in Frost, 1977), and by using more refined age dates for many fossil deposits. Here we quantitatively analyze occurrences of species and genera in the compilation to identify periods of accelerated extinction and origination. We also evaluate changes in species richness over the past 22 million years. Because the localities in our data set are not evenly scattered through geologic time, we give special consideration to the problem of sampling bias. To determine if certain components of reef communities were more susceptible to extinction than others, we subdivide the data set into three habitat subgroups (grass flat, shallow reef, deep reef) and rerun the analyses. Finally, to assess possible causal agents for the observed patterns, we consider our results in light of reported patterns of regional environmental change.

MATERIAL AND METHODS

Our compilation consists of occurrences of 175 species and 49 genera (Budd et al., in press) (Fig. 1). It includes all recorded hermatypic taxa, except the families Oculinidae and Rhizangiidae which only variably contain zooxanthellae. The data consist of new occurrences from exposed Neogene siliciclastic sequences in the northern Dominican Republic (Saunders et al., 1986) and Costa Rica (Coates et al., 1992), as well as occurrences in the Bahamas Drilling Project cores. Also included are revised occurrences in faunal lists for 21 fossil sites scattered across the Caribbean region (Table 1). The sites comprise all known Caribbean reef assemblages, and consist of both carbonate and siliciclastic sections deposited in a range of near-shore to deeper forereef environments. Age dates for the localities have been estimated using published occurrences of microfossils within the same stratigraphic unit, interpreted relative to the Neogene time-scale of Berggren et al. (1985). Occurrences in the Recent were derived from a faunal list for the north coast of Jamaica (Wells and Lang, 1973), which we modified to include subsequent findings (e.g., Knowlton et al., 1992).

We identified species in newly collected material and revised faunal lists following a rigorous morphometric protocol designed to detect distinct morphologic entities through geologic time (Budd and Coates, 1992). In the protocol, cluster and canonical discriminant analyses are performed on 5-10 replicates per colony in well-preserved, large sample populations (n>10).

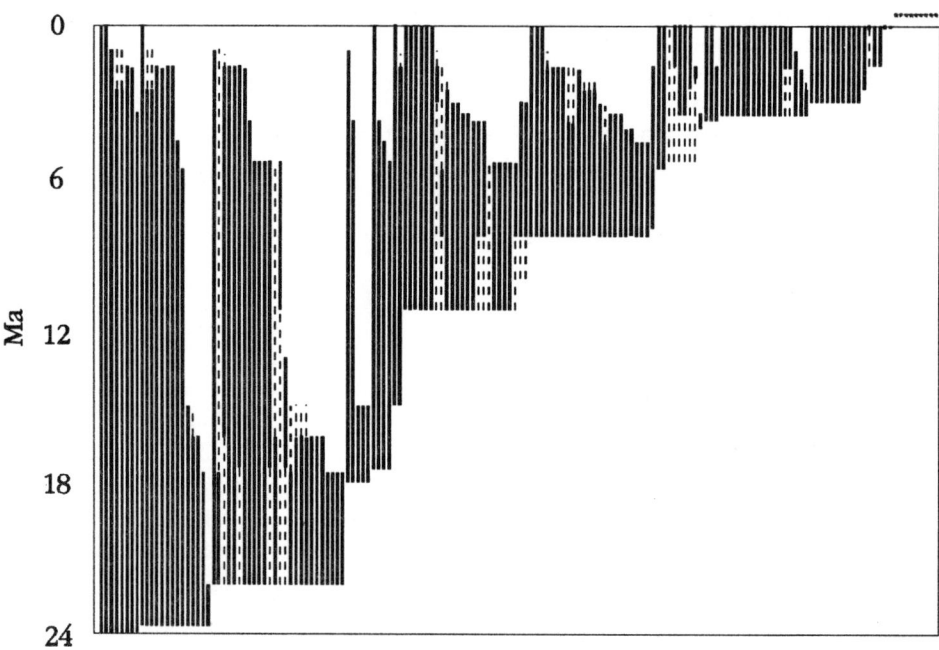

Figure 1. Stratigraphic ranges of all Caribbean reef-coral species over the past 24 million years. Dashed lines indicate occurrences in sites with uncertain age dates.

Preliminary tests on living material comparing these procedures with molecular methods have found >90% agreement between approaches. The results of analyses on well-preserved material were used to define a set of morphologic features which served as a guide in the identification of less well-preserved material. Comparisons with similar taxa in the Mediterranean and Indo-Pacific regions indicate that almost all species in our compilation are restricted in geographic distribution to the Western Atlantic and Caribbean regions. Thus first and last occurrences recorded in the compilation represent true first and last occurrences for species.

We divided the total time period in the compilation into four sets of intervals of equal duration and made three calculations for each time interval: (1) extinction rate, the relative proportion of last occurrences in the interval; (2) origination rate, the relative proportion of first occurrences in the interval; (3) species richness, a count of the total number of species whose ranges extended through or terminated within the interval. Extinction and origination rates for each interval were calculated by dividing by species richness for the interval and by time. The intervals were respectively 1, 2, 3, and 4 million years in duration. In making the calculations, we attempted to account for two major sources of sampling bias: (1) unnecessarily long time intervals assigned to localities with poor stratigraphic resolution, and (2) uneven sampling resulting from some time intervals containing many more localities than others. To correct for poor resolution, we have weighted first and last occurrences relative to the duration assigned to the locality in which they took place. To correct for uneven sampling, nine species which occurred in only one locality were not used in the calculations. In addition, three localities with highly speculative age dates were also dropped. To evaluate the effects of sampling further, correlations were examined between each of the three calculated parameters (extinction rate, origination rate, and species richness) and number of localities for each time interval ("sampling intensity").

Changes in extinction and origination rates and species richness were then examined through geologic time (Figs. 2, 3). Observed periods of accelerated extinction and origination were confirmed using bootstrap resampling methods to establish statistical significance. Changes in faunal composition were evaluated quantitatively by performing cluster analysis on presence-absence data for each locality. They were also examined qualitatively by studying patterns of survivorship (Fig. 4).

Finally, we compared susceptibility among three different habitat subgroups recognized using assemblages associated with different paleoenvironments in the Dominican Republic sequence. To identify these subgroups, cluster analysis was performed on occurrence data for all species collected in 18 different lithostratigraphic units showing little evidence of transport. The subgroups included: (1) a low diversity assemblage of free-living and branching colonies characteristic of reef-marginal grass flats; (2) a low diversity assemblage of mound-shaped and branching colonies characteristic of shallow (<10m) reef environments; and (3) a high diversity assemblage of mound-shaped, plate-shaped, branching, and free-living colonies

Table 1. -- Twenty-one fossil sites whose faunal lists were used in the compilation. S = siliciclastic; C = carbonate; SB = soft bottom; SR = shallow reef; DF = deep forereef; MIX = transported; + = localities excluded in stratigraphic range charts and in calculations of origination and extinction rates.

Site	Absolute age	Environment
early to middle Miocene:		
1. Tampa Formation, Florida	22-23.7 Ma	S/SB,SR
2. Emperador Limestone, Panama	17.6-22 Ma	S/SR
3. Anguilla Formation, Anguilla	16.2-22 Ma	C/SB,SR
4. Chipola Formation, Florida	15-18 Ma	S/SB,SR
+5. Providencia	15-22 Ma	C/SB,SR
6. Brasso and Tamana Formations, Trinidad	11.2-15 Ma	S/SB,SR
late Miocene to early Pliocene:		
7. Manzanilla Formation, Trinidad	5.3-11.2 Ma	S/SB,SR
+8. Lirio Limestone, Mona	5.3-11.2 Ma	C/SB,SR,DF
9. Buff Bay Formation, Jamaica	5.3-11.2 Ma	S/MIX
10. Imperial Formation, California	4.5-8 Ma	S/SB,SR
middle to late Pliocene:		
11. Bowden Formation, Jamaica	2-3.8 Ma	S/MIX
12. Pinecrest Sandstone, Florida	3-3.5 Ma	C/SB,SR
13. La Cruz Marl, Cuba	1.6-3.5 Ma	?C/SB,SR
14. Matanzas, Cuba	1-3.5 Ma	?C/SB,SR
15. Old Pera Beds, Jamaica	1.6-2.5 Ma	C/SB,SR
16. Caloosahatchee Formation, Florida	1.6-1.8 Ma	C/SB
early Pleistocene:		
17. Manchioneal Formation, Jamaica	1-1.6 Ma	C/SB,SR
18. Glades Formation, Florida	1-1.6 Ma	C/SB
late Pleistocene:		
19. Santo Domingo, Dominican Republic	100,000-500,000 yr	C/SB,SR
20. San Andrés	100,000-500,000 yr	C/SB,SR
21. Key Largo Limestone, Florida	100,000-500,000 yr	C/SB,SR

characteristic of deeper (>10m) or more turbid reef environments. Extinction rates were calculated for each subgroup, and the resulting patterns compared (Fig. 5).

RESULTS AND INTERPRETATIONS

In general, our results indicate that an episode of accelerated turnover followed by accelerated extinction occurred in the Caribbean reef-coral fauna between 4 Ma and 1 Ma. These events resulted in the replacement of a late Miocene to early Pliocene reef-coral fauna by a Pleistocene to Recent fauna. The Mio-Pliocene fauna was dominated by taxa such as Stylophora, Goniopora, and a suite of agariciid and poritid species which more closely resemble modern Pacific species than those of the modern Caribbean. Numerous free-living meandroid corals (Teleiophyllia, Thysanus, Trachyphyllia, Placocyathus) dominated Mio-Pliocene reef-associated grass flats. The modern Caribbean fauna (including Acropora palmata, Diploria strigosa, Porites astreoides, and the Montastraea annularis complex) originated during middle Pliocene to early Pleistocene time, as components of the Mio-Pliocene fauna became extinct. Five findings with regard to these patterns are particularly significant.

(1) Accelerated Plio-Pleistocene extinction and origination rates.-- Examination of extinction and origination rate plots over time (Fig. 2) and results of bootstrap resampling tests indicate that extinction and origination rates were both

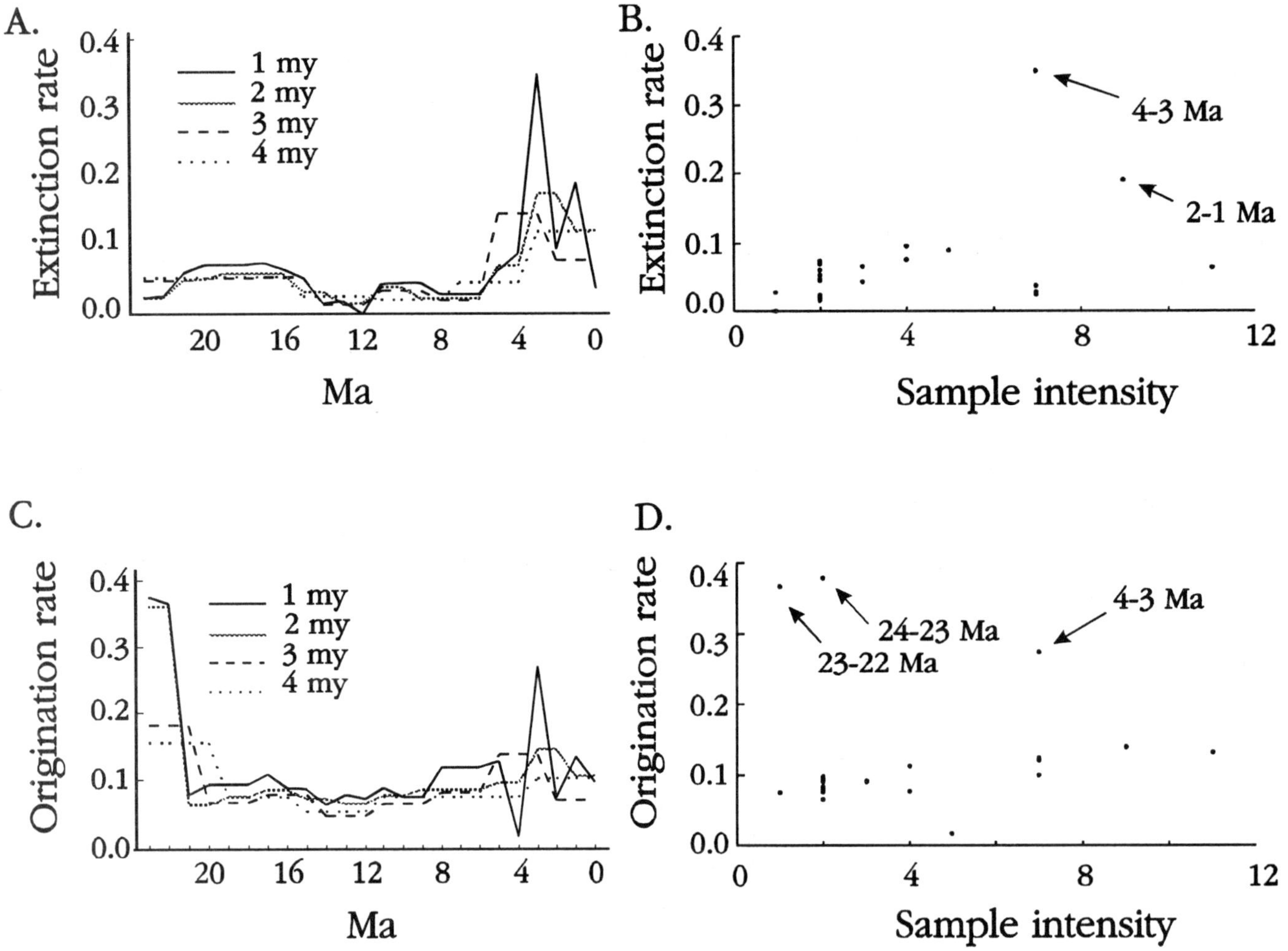

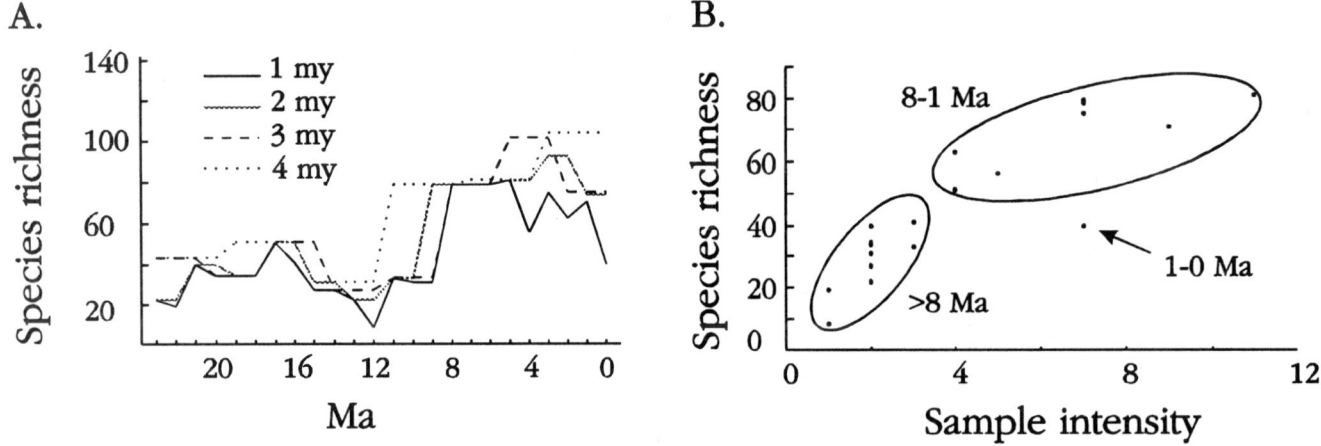

Figure 2. Evolutionary rates in Caribbean reef-coral species over the past 22 million years. Plots A and C show patterns calculated with interval durations of 1, 2, 3, and 4 million years. Plots B and D show the relationship between evolutionary rates and sampling intensity using 1 million year intervals. Each point represents one time interval.

Figure 3. Species richness over the past 22 million years. Plot A shows pattern calculated using interval durations of 1, 2, 3, and 4 million years. Plot B shows the relationship between species richness and sampling intensity using 1 million year intervals. Each point represents one time interval.

accelerated between 4 Ma and 3 Ma, and that extinction rates alone were accelerated between 2 Ma and 1 Ma. Miocene background rates of extinction range between 0-8% per million years. Beginning approximately 4 Ma, extinction rates doubled, with extinction rates of 10 to possibly >35% per million years. Also at 4 Ma, origination rates rose. A smaller second wave of accelerated extinction with rates of up to 20% per million years followed later. Neither extinction nor origination rates are correlated with sampling intensity.

Extinction rates and origination rates were therefore accelerated, at least initially, over the same period of time. Consequently, whatever caused increased extinction did not inhibit simultaneous origination. This result argues against widespread, long-term environmental degradation as a possible initial extinction agent.

(2) Equilibrium number of species.-- Species richness appears to have been relatively high (~80-100) throughout most of the late Miocene to Pleistocene (8-1 Ma), and slight lower (40-60) in the late Pleistocene to Recent (1-0 Ma) (Fig. 3). In time intervals older than 8 Ma, species richness is strongly correlated with sampling intensity; therefore, the low values shown for these intervals in Fig. 3a may be a result of reduced sampling. However, little correlation with sampling intensity or with time exists for samples younger than 8 Ma indicating that the observed temporal patterns (Fig. 3a) are less affected by sampling. Of these intervals, only the 1-0 Ma interval appears less rich than would be predicted by sample density alone.

The observed constancy in species richness between 8-1 Ma indicates that an equilibrium number of species may have been maintained in the Caribbean reef coral fauna at least for much of the past 8 million years. This equilibrium persisted during times of relative faunal stability as well as during times of accelerated faunal turnover. Thus, on a large scale, reef communities appear to have retained ecological structure during Plio-Pleistocene reorganization. This result contrasts observations on smaller scales that reef communities are unstable, disturbed systems which never reach equilibrium over periods of tens of years (Connell, 1978). Fossil reefs provide important tools for monitoring long-term biotic change.

(3) Stable taxonomic composition before and after turnover.-- Low extinction and origination rates (Fig. 2), as well as results of cluster analysis and survivorship data, indicate that the taxonomic composition of the Caribbean reef coral fauna was stable

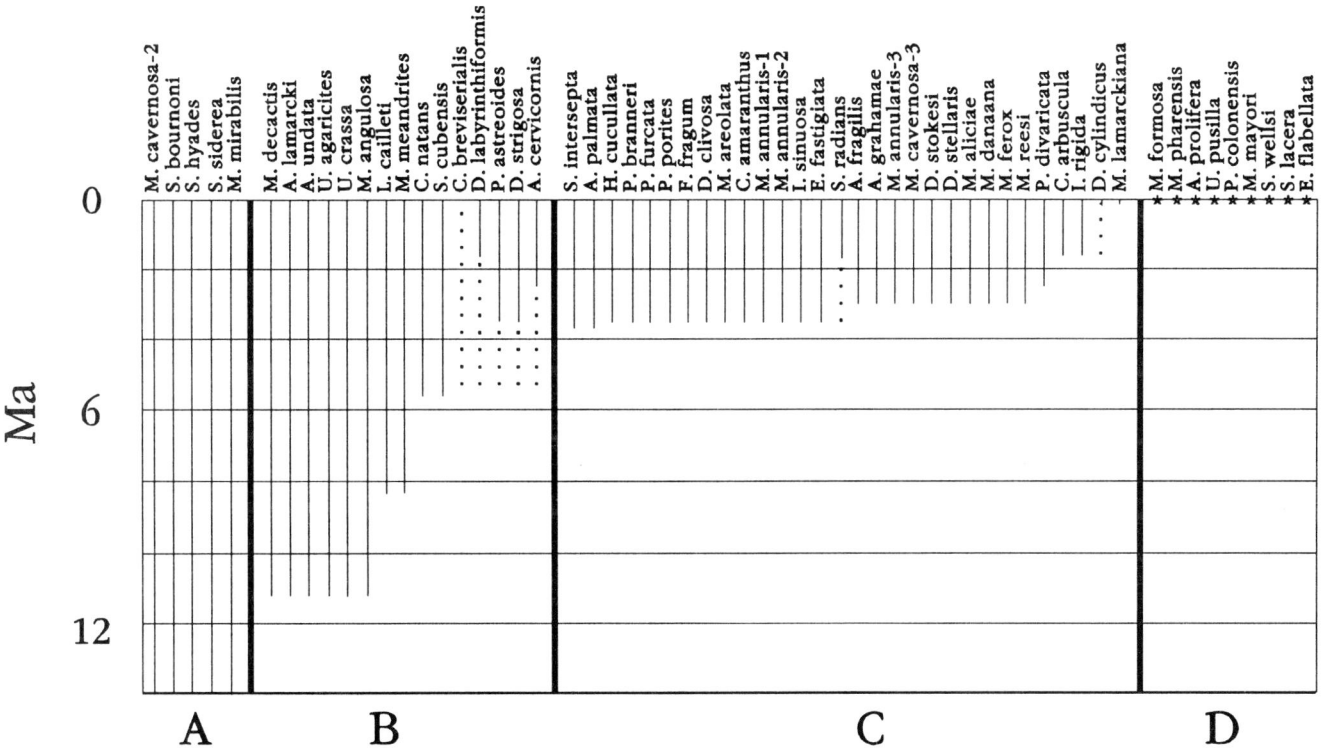

Figure 4. Stratigraphic ranges of species of modern Caribbean reef-corals. Dashed lines indicate occurrences in sites with uncertain age dates. Group "A", species with originations before late Miocene time; group "B", species with late Miocene to early Pliocene originations; group "C", species with mid Pliocene to Pleistocene originations; group "D", species with no reported fossil record.

for long periods of time before (8-4 Ma) and after (1-0 Ma) after turnover. Of the 96 species that lived in the Caribbean during the late Miocene to early Pliocene, 78% became extinct during Plio-Pleistocene time. Of the 59 species currently living in the Caribbean, 51% originated during middle to late Pliocene time, and only 15% have no fossil record (Fig. 4).

Thus, faunal stability represents the norm in the long-term evolution of Caribbean reef communities, and continued throughout the glacial episodes and associated high frequency oscillations in temperature and sea level of the late Pleistocene (see also Jackson, 1992).

(4) Decrease in genera.-- Preliminary counts of genera in the compilation indicate that, during the period of accelerated turnover, 32% of the 38 genera that lived in the Caribbean during the Pliocene became extinct. Four subgenera and genera became globally extinct, and eight genera became extinct in the Caribbean region. The four taxa that became globally extinct (Teleiophyllia, Thysanus, Placocyathus, Antillia) were all free-living corals, common in reef-marginal grass flats. The eight genera that became regionally extinct include seven genera which occur today in the Indo-Pacific (Pocillopora, Gardineroseris, Pavona, Stylophora, Goniopora, Caulastrea, Trachyphyllia), and one genus which is currently restricted to Brazil (Mussismilia). Only two genera in the compilation (Dendrogyra, Mussismilia) have first occurrences after early Pliocene time; however, both of these genera are known in older Mediterranean deposits.

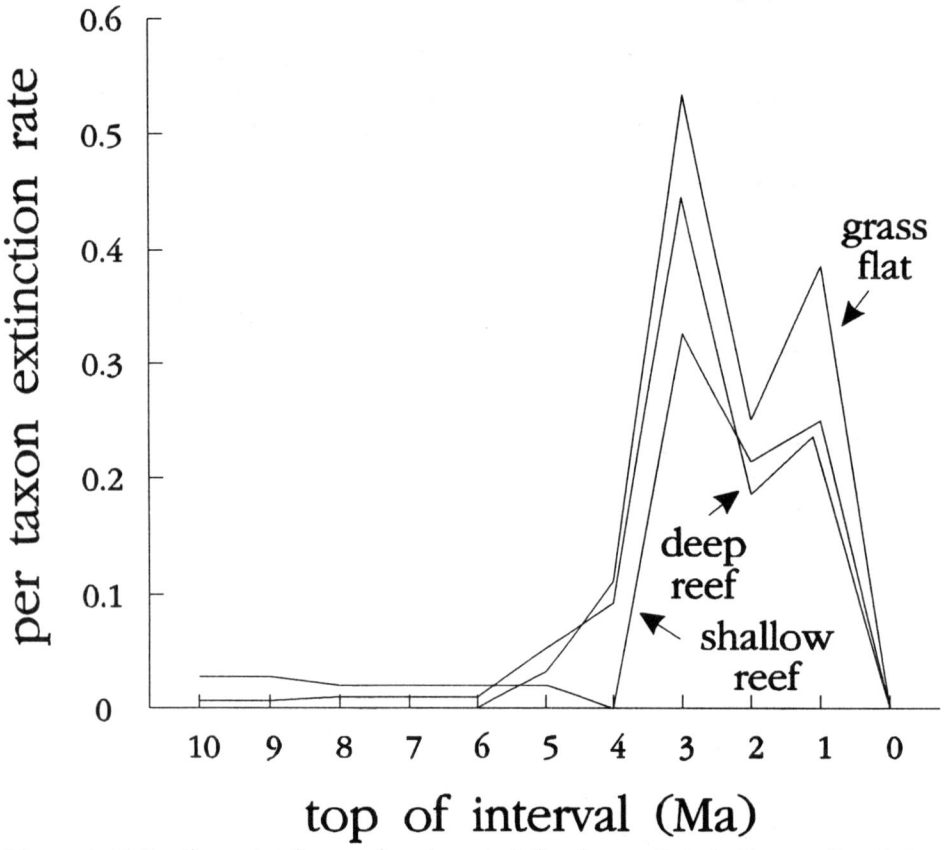

Figure 5. Extinction rates for species characteristic of grass flat, shallow reef, and deep reef communities.

Thus, it appears that although many genera became at least regionally extinct during Plio-Pleistocene time, no new genera arose. Even though species richness remained the same throughout turnover, the number of genera in the reef-coral fauna of the modern Caribbean is considerably less than during early Pliocene time.

(5) High susceptibility to extinction in grass flat corals.-- Examination of plots of extinction rates (Fig. 5) for the three habitat subgroups (grass flat, shallow reef, deep reef) shows that all three groups experienced accelerated rates at 4-3 Ma and 2-1 Ma. The grass flat subgroup was most heavily impacted, with extinction rates of 30-50% per million years. The other subgroups were slightly less affected, especially during the second extinction wave.

Therefore, whatever caused increased rates of turnover and subsequent extinction, its most potent effects were felt in soft bottom environments with communities characterized by small, short-lived, free-living species. Taxa with large colony sizes were less likely to become extinct.

DISCUSSION AND CONCLUSIONS

The fact that Plio-Pleistocene turnover and extinctions have also been reported in Caribbean molluscs (Stanley, 1986) and bryozoans (A.H. Cheetham, pers. comm. 1993), but not in Indo-Pacific reef-corals (Veron and Kelley, 1988), suggests that regional abiotic factors may have been ultimately responsible for the observed turnover and subsequent extinction in corals. However, to date, our attempts to relate the findings to possible external causal agents have not yielded clear answers. Since Indo-Pacific corals did not experience turnover or extinction, the observed Caribbean turnover does not appear to have been caused by global changes in sea level. Also, the fact that faunal stability prevailed throughout the high frequency temperature and sea level oscillations of late Pleistocene time argues against sea level or temperature being primary causal agents.

Furthermore, no evidence supports the existence of decreased temperatures in tropical areas of the Caribbean region during Pliocene to Recent time (T.M. Cronin, pers. comm. 1993). Although soft bottom corals appear to have been more susceptible to extinction, the fact that coastal areas and offshore carbonate platforms were equally affected argues against increased runoff or associated siltation being important agents. Nevertheless, the close correspondence in timing with closure of the isthmus of Panama at 3.5 Ma (Coates et al., 1992) suggests that factors associated with regional changes in oceanic circulation may have been at least partially responsible.

Regardless of its actual cause, the episode of accelerated turnover played a major role in shaping the modern reef biota of the Caribbean region. It is remarkable that throughout the period of turnover species richness remained roughly the same and reef communities were common across the Caribbean region. This long-term integrity contrasts strikingly with the breakdown of reef communities reported in association with the late Devonian and late Cretaceous mass extinctions, after which 4-10 million years elapsed before reefs were again common. Understanding the factors responsible for long-term taxonomic equilibrium and ecological balance will be critical for designing measures to protect species endangered by the rapid and widespread degradation reported on tropical reefs today.

ACKNOWLEDGEMENTS

We thank J. Geister, P. Jung, and J.B. Saunders for assistance with Dominican Republic material; R.N. Ginsburg and C. Kievman with Bahamanian material; and J.B.C. Jackson, A.G. Coates, and J.A. Obando with Costa Rican material. We are especially grateful to L.S. Collins, S.M. Stanley, and members of the Panama Paleontological Project for discussions.

LITERATURE CITED

Berggren, W.A., D.V. Kent, and J.A. VanCouvering. 1985. Neogene geochronology and chronostratigraphy. Pages 211-260 *in* N.J. Snelling, ed. The chronology of the geological record. Geological Society of London, Memoir 10.

Budd, A.F. and A.G. Coates. 1992. Non-progressive evolution in a clade of Cretaceous Montastraea-like corals. Paleobiology 15: 425-446.

Budd, A.F., T.A. Stemann, and K.G. Johnson, in press. Stratigraphic distributions of genera and species of Neogene to Recent Caribbean reef corals. Journal of Paleontology.

Coates, A.G., and 7 others. 1992. Closure of the isthmus of Panama: the marine near-shore record of Costa Rica and western Panama. Geological Society of America Bulletin 104: 208-218.

Connell, J.H. 1978. Diversity in tropical rain forests and coral reefs. Science 199: 1302-1310.

Frost, S.H. 1977. Miocene to Holocene evolution of Caribbean province reef-building corals. Proceedings of the Third International Coral Reef Symposium 2: 353-360.

Jablonski, D. 1991. Extinctions: a paleontological perspective. Science 253: 754-757.

Jackson, J.B.C. 1992. Pleistocene perspectives on coral reef community structure. American Zoologist 32: 719-731.

Knowlton, N., E. Weil, L.A. Weigt, and H.M. Guzman. 1992. Sibling species in Montastraea annularis, coral bleaching, and the coral climate record. Science 255: 330-333.

Saunders, J.B., P. Jung, and B. Biju-Duval. 1986. Neogene paleontology in the northern Dominican Republic. 1. Field surveys, lithology, environment, and age. Bulletins of American Paleontology 89: 1-79.

Stanley, S.M. 1986. Anatomy of a regional mass extinction: Plio-Pleistocene decimation of the western Atlantic bivalve fauna. Palaios 1: 17-36.

Veron, J.E.N. and R. Kelley. 1988. Species stability in reef corals of Papua New Guinea and the Indo-Pacific. Association of Australasian Palaeontologists Memoir 6: 1-69.

Wells, J.W. and J.C. Lang. 1973. Systematic list of Jamaican shallow-water Scleractinia. Bulletin of Marine Science 23: 55-58.

How Have Holocene Sea Level Rise and Antecedent Topography Influenced Belize Barrier Reef Development?

Randolph B. Burke

North Dakota Geological Survey, 600 East Blvd., Bismarck
North Dakota 58505

ABSTRACT

Based on reef vitality, the Belize barrier reef platform can be divided into three provinces: northern, central, and southern. The central province is by far the best developed and most continuous; the northern and southern provinces are characterized by much smaller and discontinuous reefs. A model developed for eastern Caribbean reefs using shelf depth, water quality, and wave energy as the primary factors controlling reef development can be used to explain current Belize reef distribution and vitality. Application of this model requires understanding the regional geologic history relative to Holocene sea level rise. Reef development in each province corresponds to segments of three regional ridge systems. Each ridge is comprised of landward-tilting horst blocks and graubens that constitute a generally southerly dipping platform on which the reef is built. With the rise of sea level during the Holocene, the blocks were inundated at different rates and at different times related to their different elevations. The central province has the most vital reef due to its elevation during a relatively slow period of Holocene sea level rise and because of good water quality and a modified wave regime. Reef development in the southern province was not as extensive due to its deeper starting elevation and faster sea level rise and more open exposure. The northern province would be expected to have extensive reef development based on its elevation and rate of sea level rise, but poor water quality and exposure to damaging high-energy waves prevented such development. This type of assessment is useful for distinguishing between anthropogenic impact on reefs and the natural succession of reef communities and structures.

INTRODUCTION

The Belize barrier reef along the coast of Central American is the longest continuous, and most diverse, barrier reef in the Atlantic ocean (fig. 1 and Rutzler and Macintyre, 1982). The barrier reef platform (< 5.5 m depth) seaward of Belize is 257 km long, of which 147 km consists of shallow-water reefs (< 0.2 m depth). The remainder of the shelf-edge platform is cut by channels or is composed of carbonate shoals, fleshy-algae covered hard bottom, or deeper reef development.

A general model has been developed (Adey and Burke, 1977; Adey 1978) to explain windward reef structural development and gross community composition and distribution for eastern Caribbean reefs. The model was based on three factors: shelf depth, wave energy, and water quality. In an unpublished thesis, Burke (1979) applied this model to the Holocene development of the Belize barrier reef. Two-dimensional computer models (Graus and Macintyre, 1989; Bosscher and Schlager, 1990) using factors of the Adey and Burke model have been able to simulate reef community zonation patterns and structural development similar to those of existing reefs.

Geologic control on reef development is fundamental to these models (Adey and Burke, 1977). Reefs tend to achieve maximal growth and accretion rates at depths less than 15 meters. Sea level has risen over 118 m since the last deglaciation which includes the Holocene (Bard, et al., 1990). Shelf depth (i.e., elevation), therefore differs at any two points in time during the Holocene. Graus and Macintyre's (1989) computer model demonstrated the importance of bathymetric variations in causing differences in zonation patterns of reef communities. They also concluded that submerging the reef produced the greatest modification of the zonation pattern.

One can predict, therefore, with some degree of confidence the general vitality of a reef if one knows the configuration of the surface on which the reef is built, knows the local sea level history, and understands the effects of water quality and wave energy on reef community development. If the vitality of a reef seems extremely different then predicted, one might consider the possibility of anthropogenic impact on the reef. The importance of geologic history and the dynamic nature of reef development, however, are frequently overlooked in current management and conservation efforts. The purpose of this case study is to update and compile available data to show the correlation between current reef vitality and antecedent topography within the context of Holocene sea level rise.

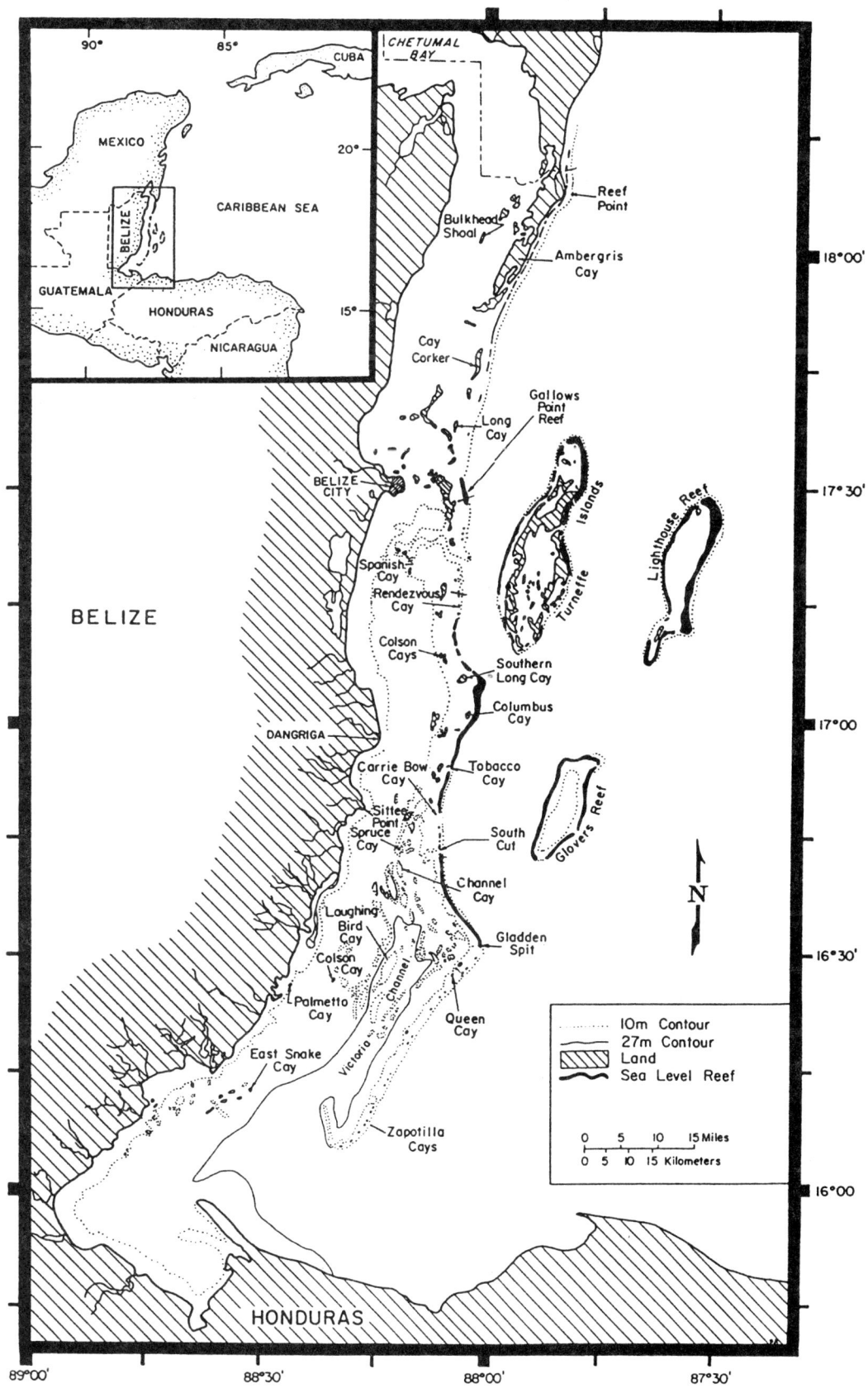

Figure 1. Map of the coastal areas of Belize showing distribution of sea level reefs.

BELIZE REEF VITALITY AND PROVINCES

Vitality in this case is determined by the robustness of reef structural development, species diversity, and species abundance of major reef building organisms on the barrier reef's seaward side. Using these criteria, the Belize barrier reef can be divided into three biogeomorphic provinces: 1) the northern province with 46 km of shallow-water reefs; 2) the central province, with 91 km of shallow-water reefs; and 3) the southern province with only 10 km of shallow-water

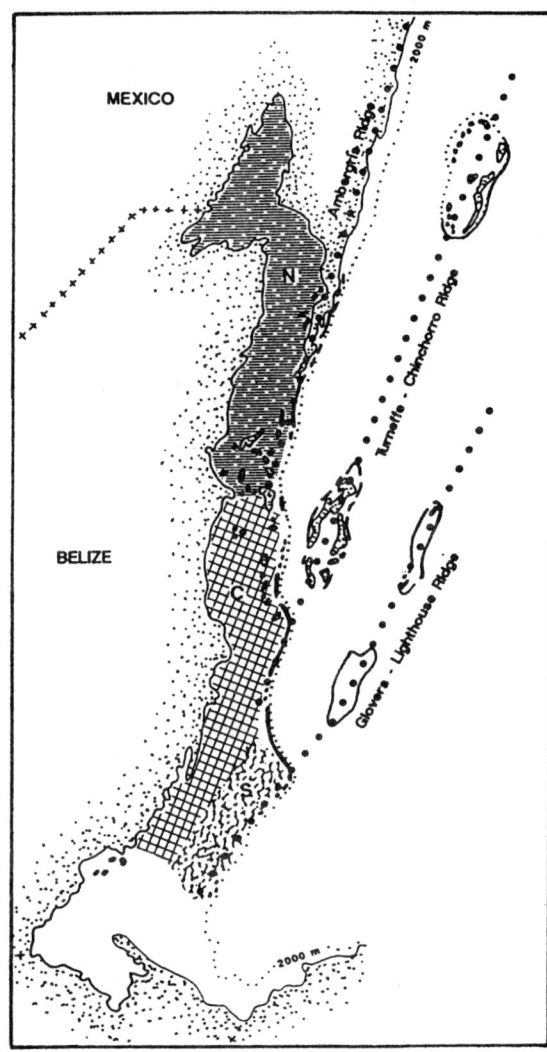

Figure 2. Illustration showing reef community provinces and the location of fault block ridges that control barrier reef development. N = northern, C = central, S = southern.

reefs (fig. 2). Central province reefs exhibit the greatest vitality. They are wide and continuous with flourishing, diverse reef communities. The fore reef is characterized by high-relief spurs and grooves and a ridge along the shelf edge commonly capped by *Acropora cervicornis*. The reef in the northern and southern provinces is discontinuous except along Ambergris Cay. In general, passages through the reef in the northern province are wide and of uniform depth, whereas passes in the southern province are narrow with deep channels. In both the north and south, the reef occurs adjacent to islands and generally is further from the shelf edge than the reef along the central province. In the south, however, some reefs at reentrants are closer to the shelf edge. The major reef-building communities have the same composition along the length of the reef, but relative species abundance and density vary significantly. The greatest abundance occurs in the central province where it accounts for the robust structural development.

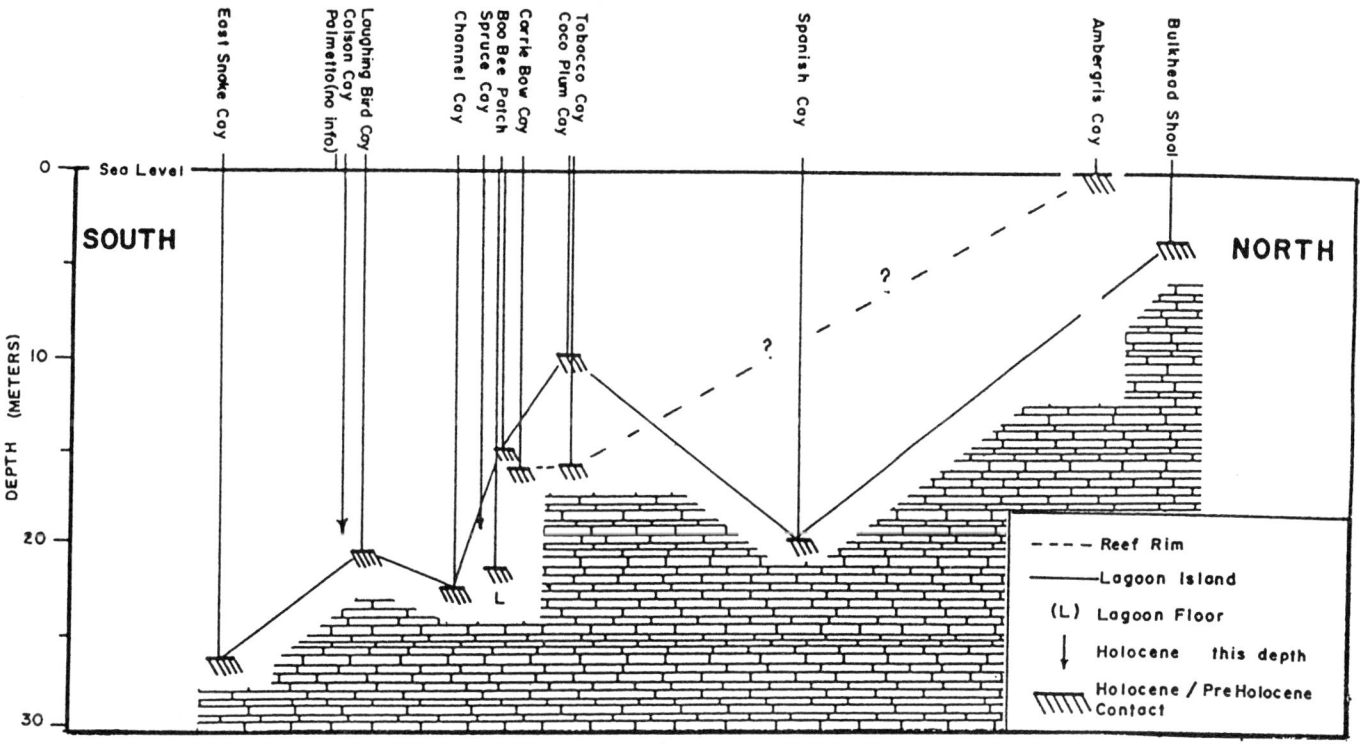

Figure 3. Known Holocene/Pleistocene contacts along the Belize barrier reef. Note the southerly dip indicated in the lagoon and on the reef rim.

GEOLOGIC SETTING - ANTECEDENT TOPOGRAPHY

The regional geologic history indicates that the Belize continental margin has been tectonically active to varying degrees since the Mesozoic (Dillion and Vedder, 1973). It is characterized by a basin and range system of five landward-tilting, block-faulted ridges that dip to the south (figs. 2 & 3 and Purdy, 1974a). Three of these ridges serve as the foundation for the Belize barrier platform (fig. 2). The ridges are segmented into individual horst blocks separated by graubens (Purdy, 1974b). The tops of some of the blocks are capped with Holocene reef complexes. The most landward ridge is the Ambergris Cay ridge which serves as the foundation for the northern province. The next ridge seaward is the Chinchorro Bank - Turneffe Islands ridge which serves as a foundation for the central province. The southern province is founded on the Glovers Reef-Lighthouse Reef structure. Tertiary and Pleistocene deposition and erosion have modified these structures (Purdy, 1974a; James and Ginsburg, 1979; Halley et al., 1977; Choi and Ginsburg, 1982) and undoubtedly have contributed to local variations in reef development, but the ridges clearly serve as the template for the Belize barrier reef.

HOLOCENE SEA LEVEL AND REEF DEVELOPMENT

No regional Holocene sea level curve exists for the Belize barrier reef. A sea level curve extending back 6,000 YBP has recently been proposed for the northern reef province (Mazzullo et al., 1992), but the data are sparse and some of the materials dated have inherent analytical and interpretive difficulties. A compilation of radiocarbon dates taken from cores from the Belize barrier reef shows a distribution pattern that is explainable by Neumann's (personal communications) sea level curve for Bermuda (fig. 4). Peat dates are on or above the sea level curve, and dates from marine samples are below or near the curve. An exception, however, is a cluster of samples above the curve collected from the northern province. These, in conjunction with those added by Mazzullo et al. (1992), can be interpreted to indicate uplift during the Holocene of the northern reef province along the Ambergris ridge.

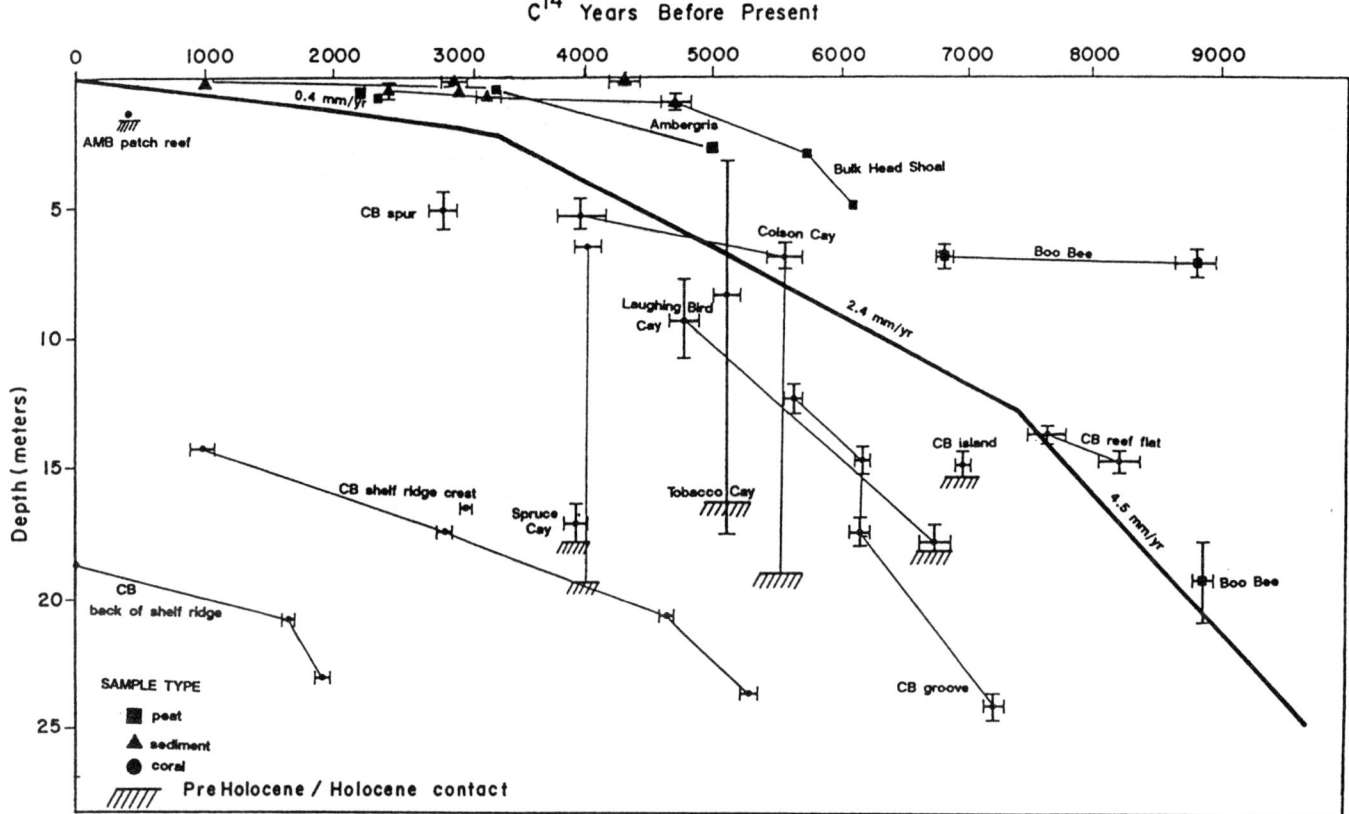

Figure 4. Compilation of radiocarbon dates for the Belize barrier reef plotted relative to Neumann's sea level curve for Bermuda. C = Carrie Bow Cay; AMB = Ambergris Cay = northern province proximal to Ambergris Cay.

The rate of sea level rise slowed from 4.5 m/1000 years to 2.4 m/1000 years between 7,000 to 8,000 years ago (James and Ginsburg, 1979). Thus, sea level would have been rising rapidly when the southern province was submerged approximately 10,000 years ago. The rate of rise was reduced to 2.4 m/1000 years by the time sea level crested the central and northern provinces, approximately 7,000 to 6,000 years ago, respectively.

The weak reef development in the southern province is consistent with the greater shelf depth and rapid sea level rise; the reef could not catch up or keep up with the rising water. The open exposure to high energy waves and poor water quality also contributed to limited reef development in the south. Starting at a higher elevation and facing a slower rate of sea level rise, the northern reef had ample opportunity to develop vigorously from a geologic perspective, but a multitude of water quality factors prevented such development. High terrestrial run-off, high turbidity, variable salinity, and a prevalence of winds and hurricanes that lower water levels have all been documented in the northern province (Wantland and Pusey, 1975). The most substantial reef accumulations in the northern province occur adjacent to cay coastlines protected from the inner shelf effluent.

A schematic interpretation of Holocene reef development in the central province is shown in figure 5 (Burke, 1979). Sea level rose rapidly (approximately 9 m/1000 yrs) up the reef wall allowing only about 10 m of Holocene deposition between 8,000 - 10,000 YBP (James and Ginsburg, 1979). Soil accumulation was probably very limited along the steep and narrow escarpment margin so that turbidity quickly cleared, allowing *Acropora palmata* to establish. Contemporaneously, extensive marshes and mangroves flourished shoreward of the shelf edge Pleistocene rim (Halley et al, 1977).

Between 6,000 to 7,000 YBP, the outer rim was flooded, presumably subjecting the reef tract to poor quality

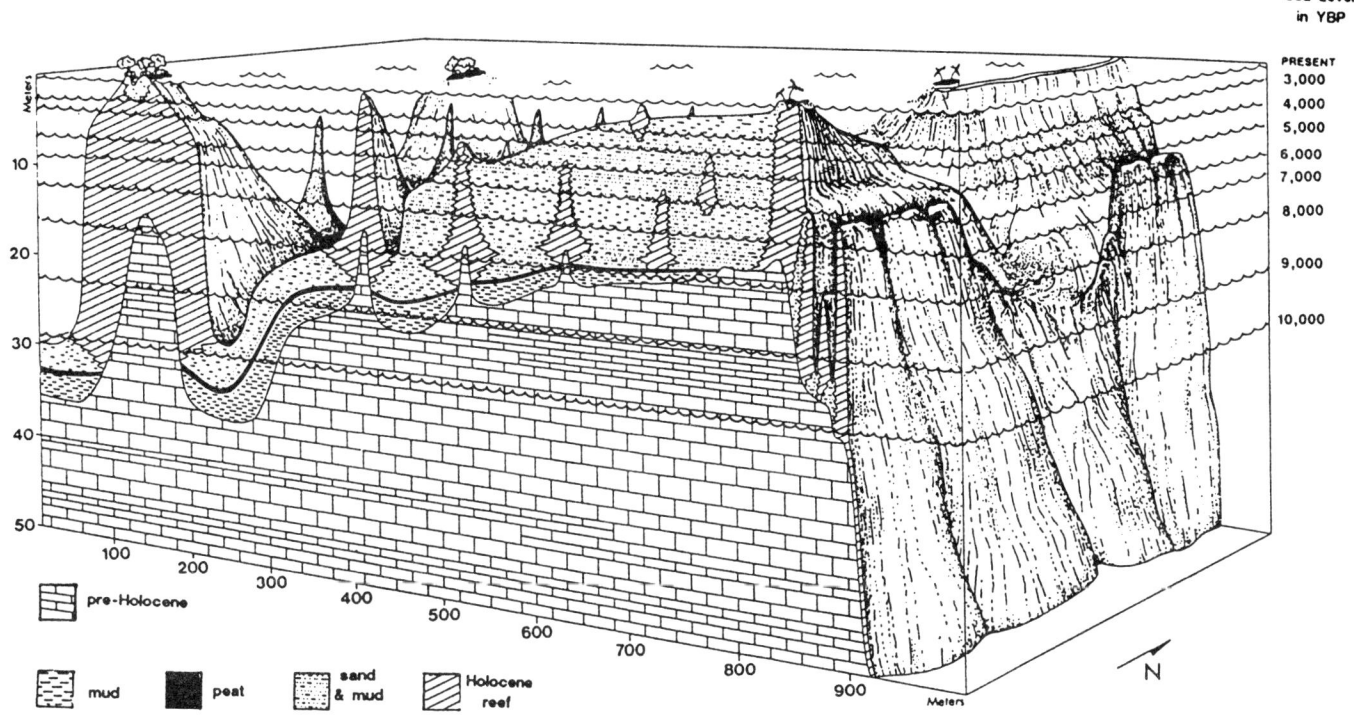

Figure 5. Diagramatic interpretation of Holocene barrier reef development for the central Belize reef province. A cross section from the shelf edge to the inner lagoon. Stratigraphy based on borings at Carrie Bow Cay, Boo Bee patch reef and Spruce Cay. Holocene sea levels are indicated by wavy lines at 1,000 year intervals between 3,000-9,000 YBP.

water as the transgressing sea engulfed the mangroves and marshes. Approximately 7,000 YBP, corals were able to establish on the rim (Shinn et al., 1982), and with the rapid growth rates of *A. cervicornis*, the reefs were able to quickly build to the surface by around 5,000 YBP (Adey, 1978a). A series of *A. cervicornis* and *Montastrea annularis* ridges (Macintyre et al., 1981) have probably contributed to the present fore-reef terrace development by subsequent rubble infilling between troughs as vertical accumulation rates decreased with increasing wave energy. Wave energy is differentially reduced along the central section of the barrier reef by the offshore reef platforms (Glovers, Turneffe, and Lighthouse; Burke, 1982).

Contemporaneous with fore-reef platform development carbonate production along the reef crest was shifted from vertical accumulation to leeward deposition, and many patch reefs have probably been incorporated into the back reef platform. Seaward progradation is proceeding at slower rates. The rates appear to be inversely related to wave energy exposure. Fleshy algae-dominated relief spur and groove areas have the slowest accretion rates, and the high spur and groove and *A. cervicornis* reef areas have the fastest rates.

CONCLUSIONS

Holocene sea level rose over the differentially elevated blocks comprising the foundation of the barrier reef platform. The elevation of the blocks relative to the rate of sea level rise, in conjunction with water quality and wave energy, strongly influenced the pattern of reef development. The most elevated block (north) has sparse reef development because of open exposure to high wave energy and natural effluents from the very shallow lagoon and Chetumal Bay complex. The central block, with intermediate elevation, has the best developed reefs because of the reduced rate of sea level rise after the sea crested the block, and because of good water quality and moderate wave energy. The southern block has the lowest elevation and exhibits the least reef development because of the high rate of rise at the time sea level crested the block in conjunction with reduced water quality and exposure to high energy waves. This analysis shows the importance of considering geologic controls as well as current ecological factors affecting reef development and health when assessing the status and future prognosis of a reef.

ACKNOWLEDGEMENTS

I would like to thank Walter Adey, Ian Macintyre, Klaus Rutzler for their advice and encouragement with this project. I would like to acknowledge the financial support provided by the Smithsonian Institution. I extend special thanks to Margaret Burke for incisive editing, and to LaRae Fey for the "beyond the call of duty" expert word processing. I appreciate the time and support provided by the NDGS necessary to prepare this report.

LITERATURE CITED

Adey, W. H. 1978. Coral Reef Morphogenesis: Multidimensional model - new data from coring and C^{14} dating provide data for unravelling some classical enigmas. Science 202(4370): 831-847.

Adey, W. H. and R. B. Burke. 1977. Holocene bioherms of Lesser Antilles - geological control of development. Pages 67-81. *in* S. H. Frost, M. P. Weiss, J. B. Saunders, eds. Reefs and Related Carbonates - Ecology and Sedimentology. Studies in Geology No. 4, American Association of Petroleum Geologists, Tulsa, OK.

Bard, E., B. Hamlin and R. G. Fairbank. 1990. U-Th ages obtained by mass spectrometry in corals from Barbados: sea level during the past 130,000 years. Nature 346:456-458.

Bosscher, H. and Schlager, W. 1992. Computer simulation of reef growth. Sedimentology 39(3):503-512.

Burke, R. B. 1979. Morphology, benthic communities, and structure of the Belize Barrier Reef, Unpublished Masters Thesis, University of South Florida, 78 pp.

Burke, R. B. 1982. Reconnaissance study of the geomorphology and benthic communities of the outer barrier reef platform, Belize. Pages 509-526. *in* K. Rutzler and I. G. Macintyre, eds. The Atlantic Barrier Reef Ecosystem at Carrie Bow Cay, Belize. 1. Structure and communities. Smithsonian Contributions to Marine Science 12.

Choi, D. R. and R. N. Ginsburg. 1982. Siliciclastic foundations of Quaternary reefs in southernmost Belize lagoon, British Honduras. Geological Society of American Bulletin, 93(2):116-126.

Dillon, W. P., J. G. Vedder, and D. L. Taylor, ed. 1973. Structure and development of the continental margin of British Honduras. Geological Society of America Bulletin 84(8):2713-2732.

Graus, R. R. and I. G. Macintyre. 1989. The zonation patterns of Caribbean coral reefs as controlled by wave and light energy input, bathymetric setting and reef morphology: Computer simulation experiments. Coral Reefs, 8(1):9-18.

Halley, R. B., Shinn, E. A., Hudson, J. H. and Lidz, B. 1977. Recent and relict topography of BooBee patch reef, Belize. *in* D. L. Taylor, ed. Geology - Proceedings Third International Coral Reef Symposium, Miami, 2:29-35.

James, N. P. and R. N. Ginsburg. 1979. The Seaward Margins of Belize Barrier and Atoll Reefs: Morphology, sedimentology, organism distribution and late Quaternary history. Special Publication No. 3, International Association of Sedimentologists, Oxford, U.K. 191 pp.

Mazzullo, S. J., K. E. Anderson-Underwood, C. D. Burke, W. D. Bischoff. 1992. Holocene coral patch reef ecology and sedimentary architecture, northern Belize, Central America. Palaios, 7(6):591-601.

Purdy, E. G. 1974a. A karst-determined facies patterns in British Honduras: Holocene sedimentation model. American Association of Petroleum Geologists Bulletin, 58(5):825-855.

Purdy, E. G. 1974b. Reef configurations: cause and effect. Pages 9-76. *in* L. F. Laporte, ed. Reefs in Time and Space. Society of Economic Paleontologists and Mineralogists Spec. Pub. 18.

Purdy, E. G., Pusey, W. C., and K. F. Wantland. 1975. Continental shelf of Belize - regional shelf attributes. Pages 1-52. *in* K. F. Wantland and W. C. Pusey, eds. Belize shelf - Carbonate Sediments, Clastic Sediments, and Ecology. Studies in Geology No. 2. American Association of Petroleum Geologists, Tulsa, OK.

Rutzler, K. and I. G. Macintyre. 1982. The habitat distribution and community structure of the barrier reef complex at Carrie Bow Cay, Belize. Pages 9-45. *in* K. Rutzler, I. G. Macintyre, eds. The Atlantic Barrier Reef ecosystem at Carrie Bow Cay, Belize. 1. Structure and communities. Smithsonian Contributions to Marine Science 12.

Shinn, E. A., J. H. Hudson, R. B. Halley, B. Lidz, D. M. Robbin, and I. G. Macintyre. 1982. Geology and sediment accumulation rates at Carrie Bow Cay, Belize. Pages 63-75. *in* K. Rutzler, I. G. Macintyre, eds. The Atlantic Barrier Reef ecosystem at Carrie Bow Cay, Belize. 1. Structure and communities. Smithsonian Contributions to Marine Science 12.

Wantland, K. F. and W. C. Pusey III, eds. 1975. Belize Shelf - Carbonate Sediments, Clastic Sediments, and Ecology. Studies in Geology No. 2. American Association of Petroleum Geologists, Tulsa, OK. 599 pp.

PREFERENTIAL DISTRIBUTION OF REEFS IN THE FLORIDA REEF TRACT: THE PAST IS THE KEY TO THE PRESENT

Robert N. Ginsburg[1] and Eugene A. Shinn[2]

[1] University of Miami, Rosenstiel School of Marine and Atmospheric Science, 4600 Rickenbacker, Miami, Florida 33149. [2] U.S. Geological Survey, Center for Coastal Studies, 600 4th St. South, St. Petersburg, Florida, 33701.

ABSTRACT

In the Florida reef tract, shelf-margin and patch reefs occur preferentially seaward of islands of Pleistocene limestone. Where these islands are absent or separated by wide passes, the shelf is open and reefs are absent or poorly developed. The principal reason for the lack of reefs where there are no islands is the inimical effect of water from restricted Florida Bay that moves out across the open shelf areas. These waters can at various times be hot ($32°+C$) or cool ($13-16°$ C); have salinities less than or greater than normal sea water depending on runoff from the mainland; be turbid from suspended sediment; or possibly have increased nutrients, all of which are unfavorable for corals and associated reef builders. A secondary reason is that the open shelf areas have extensive areas of mobile calcareous sands. Where islands are present as in the Upper and Lower Keys, the seaward areas are shielded from waters issuing out of Florida and Biscayne Bays, and sand movement is reduced. A similar pattern of topographic control of living reefs is seen off Andros Island in the nearby Bahamas.

INTRODUCTION

Distribution of Living Reefs

It has long been evident that the distribution and vigor of living reefs in Florida are related to the distribution of the Florida Keys, islands of Pleistocene limestone (Ginsburg and Shinn, 1964). In Figure 1, it can be seen that the areas of most abundant shelf-margin or outer reefs are seaward of islands that are continuous, as off Key Largo, or where a complex of islands is effectively a continuous barrier, as off the Lower Keys. Where the islands are separated by wide passes and channels leading into Florida Bay, as in the Middle Keys, only three isolated reefs are present: Tennessee, Sombrero Key and Looe Key reefs. Tennessee reef has only scattered massive corals (*Siderastrea sp.; Montastrea cavernosa; Porites astreoides*). Sombrero and Looe Key reefs that are both directly seaward of an island (Vaca Key-Grassy Key and Big Pine Key) have some of the same massive corals and there are scattered colonies of the principal reef-building coral *Acropora palmata* at Sombrero and a well-developed spur and groove margin at Looe Key (H. Hudson, personal communication, 1993 and Shinn et al. 1989). The near-absence of living reefs seaward of areas where islands are absent is also seen at the northern end of the reef tract that is open to Biscayne Bay. Further descriptions of the individual shelf-margin reefs can be found in Shinn et al.1989.

The distribution of inner-shelf patch reefs shows the same preferential development related to the distribution of islands as do the shelf-margin reefs. These patch reefs are most numerous off the northernmost Upper Keys (Key Largo to Elliot Key) where Shinn et al.1989, report at least 3000 individual reefs. Inner-shelf patch reefs extend southward, albeit in lesser abundance, to Hen and Chickens reef off Upper Matecumbe Key (Fig.1). No flourishing patch reefs occur off the Middle Keys southwest of Hen and Chickens reef. Patch reefs do occur off the Lower Keys, although the inner shelf is significantly deeper (10 to 12 m) than the inner shelf off the Upper Keys (2 to 8 m). These reefs are locally abundant but relatively unstudied (Shinn et al. 1989).

The inner-shelf areas where all reefs are absent or poorly developed, i.e., the Middle Keys and the area seaward of Biscayne Bay, have unfavorable substrates for reef development, namely mobile skeletal sands as evidenced by the large-scale sand waves and mega-ripples (Fig. 1) that are seen both on the hydrographic charts and from the air.

HOW THE PRESENCE OR ABSENCE OF ISLANDS DETERMINES REEF DISTRIBUTION

Earlier, Ginsburg and Shinn (1964) proposed that a principal reason for the preferential distribution of reefs is the presence or absence of waters inimical to reef-building corals and associated organisms that emanate from Florida or Biscayne Bays. Where the islands are continuous or act as a barrier, no water from either bay can reach the shelf, but where the islands are absent, as off Biscayne Bay, or are separated by wide passes, as off the Middle Keys, bay waters can move across the shelf.

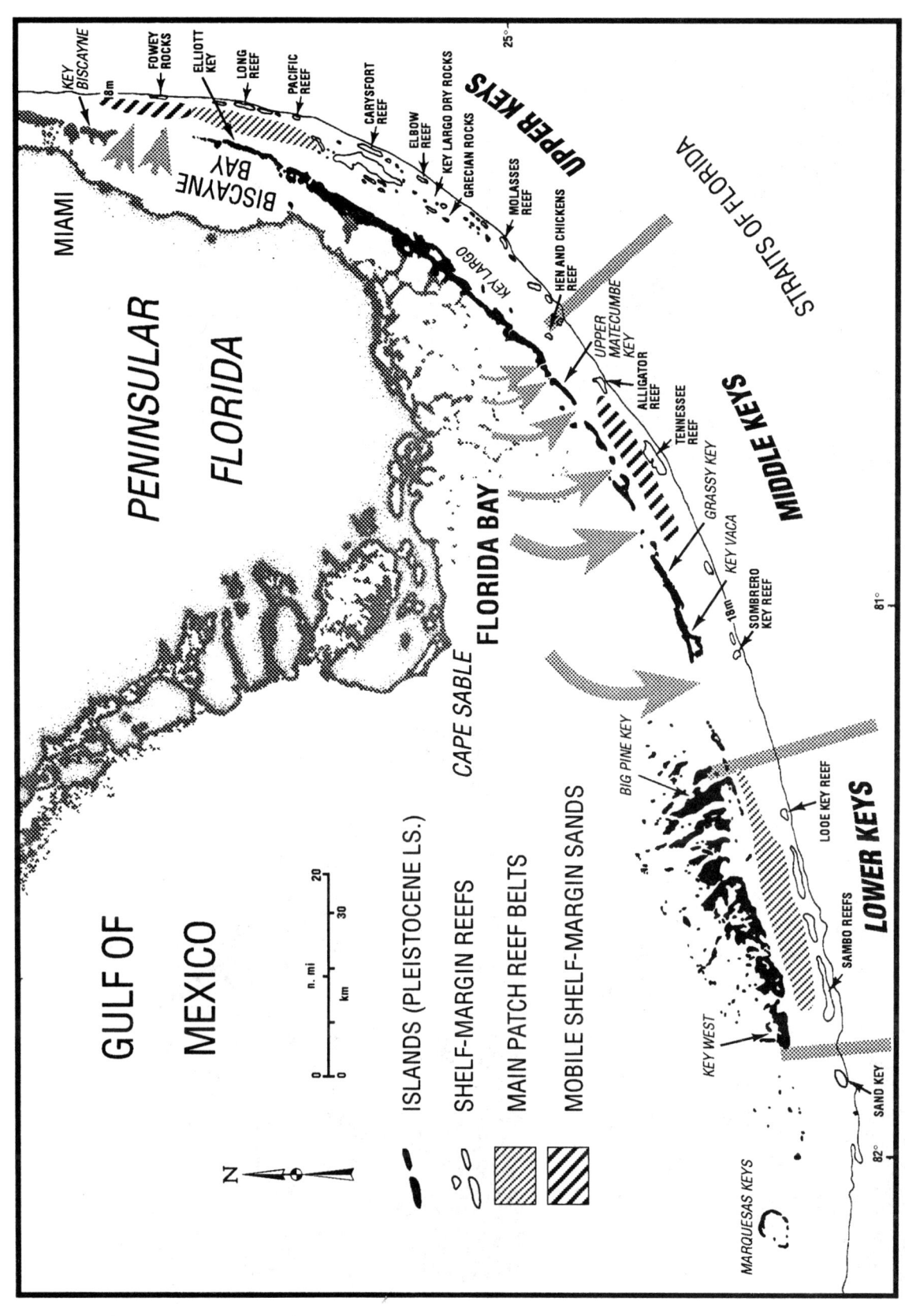

Figure 1. Southeast Florida and the Florida Keys showing the preferential distribution of reefs seaward of islands. Modified from Shinn et al, 1989.

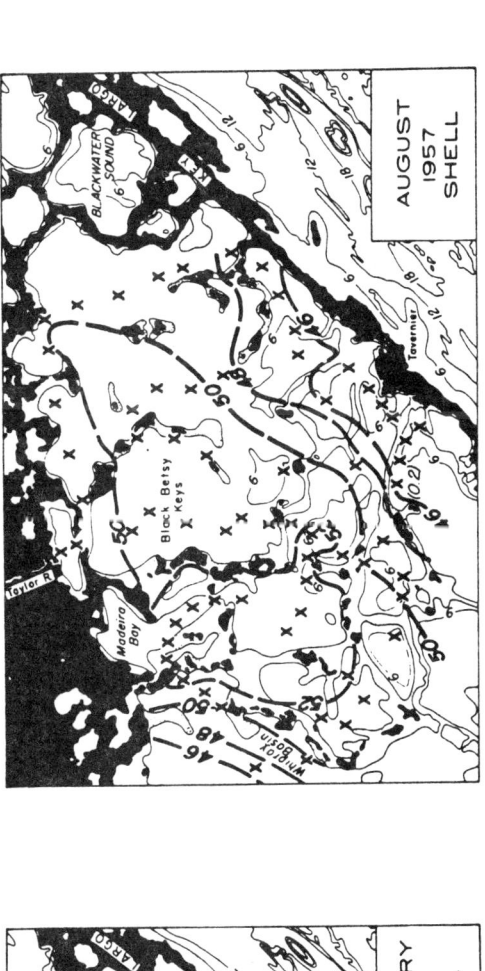

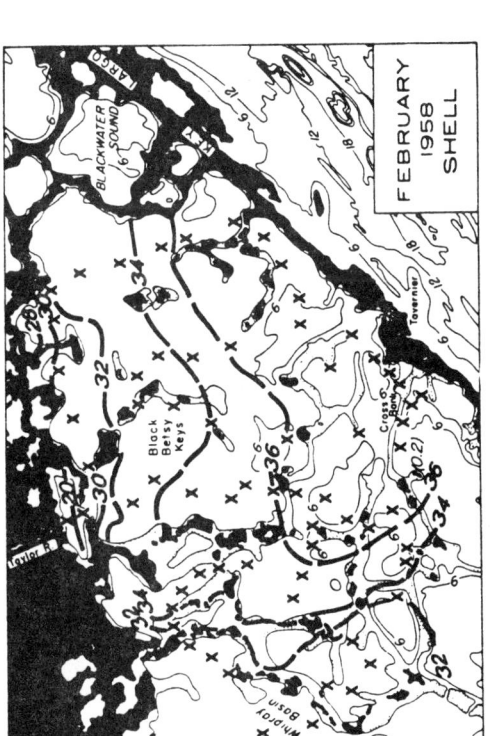
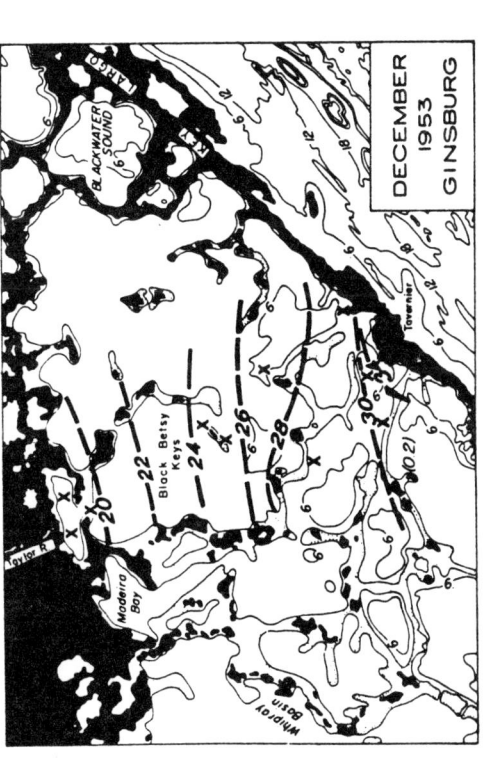

Figure 2. Examples of variation in salinity, northeastern Florida Bay; McCallum and Stockman, 1964.

Florida Bay is so shallow and so restricted by networks of near-surface mud banks that its waters vary widely in temperature, salinity and possibly in nutrients. During years with high rainfall and resulting runoff of fresh water from the Florida mainland into the Bay, the salinity is reduced to below that of normal sea water, and conversely, during years of reduced rainfall, the salinity becomes elevated up to 50 o/o (Fig. 2). Temperatures also vary widely from up to 32^0 C in summer to a few degrees below 15^0 C during a winter cold front (Hudson, 1981), both of which are beyond the accepted limits for corals (Roberts et al. 1982). Roberts et al.(1982) used satellite imagery to document the occurrence of an eight-day period of temperatures of below 16^0 C for Florida Bay and the reef tract during January of 1977. There are no systematic measurements of nutrients, but reports of "low-visibility, green waters" off the Middle Keys (B. Lapointe, personal communication, 1993) suggest that at times water with excess nutrients from Florida Bay may move out across the inner shelf area. Biscayne Bay is somewhat deeper and less restricted than Florida Bay, but its waters can also have significant variations in salinity and temperature.

Three lines of evidence indicate that waters from Florida Bay and the Gulf of Mexico that may prevent or deter reef development can move across the reef tract in the Middle Keys. First, Ball et al. (1967) found that, following Hurricane Donna in 1960, sediment-laden water from Florida Bay issued from inter-island passes onto the inner shelf; moreover, divers reported seeing flocculent mud on the shelf-margin reefs off Key Largo some days after passage of the storm. Secondly, Roberts et al. (1982) used satellite imagery to map plumes of unusually cold and sediment-laden water that moved from Florida Bay through tidal passes between islands of the Middle Keys to the inner shelf, where they remained for up to eight days. Third, long-term records of currents in one of the passes through the Middle Keys found a persistent outflow of water from Florida Bay (Smith, 1993). A further deterrent to the development of reefs off the Middle Keys and off Biscayne Bay is the presence of mobile sand substrates in both areas, as indicated in Figure 1.

PRE-HOLOCENE LIMESTONE TOPOGRAPHY

The key feature of the pre-Holocene topography that controls the distribution of reefs is the arc of limestone islands that now form the Florida Keys on the southeast side of the submerged extension of peninsular Florida (Fig. 1). Radiometric dating of the limestones (Key Largo Limestone and Miami Formation) yielded ages of from 120-130,000 years B.P. (Osmond et al. 1965; Broecker and Thurber, 1965). Three subdivisions of the Keys can be recognized based on their elevation, continuity, orientation and the composition of their limestone. **Upper Keys, from Elliot Key to Upper Matecumbe Key,** are mostly less than 3 km wide, continuous, and oriented parallel the shelf-break; they are generally 3 m or more above present sea level and are composed of limestone rich in reef-building corals, the Key Largo Limestone. **Middle Keys, from Upper Matecumbe to Big Pine Key,** are less than 2 m above sea level, often only two km or less wide and notably discontinuous with breaks and passes between them that are in aggregate more extensive than the islands themselves; limited core borings and reconnaissance observations of dredging from these islands indicate that they contain more skeletal sand and less coral than occur in the Key Largo Limestone of the Upper Keys. **Lower Keys, from Big Pine Key to Key West and the Marquesas,** are a tapering wedge-shaped array of islands oriented east-west that are mostly less than 3 m above sea level and are separated by channels and bays less than a few meters deep; they are composed of oolitic limestone presumed to be the same age as the Key Largo Limestone and the oolitic member of the Miami Limestone that forms the coastal elevation on which the city of Miami is developed (Shinn et al.1989).

DISCUSSION

If the presence or absence of islands on the Florida Shelf determines the preferential distribution of reefs, as proposed here, this same relationship should exist on other shelves and carbonate platforms. One confirming example of the island effect is seen in the distribution of reefs on western Great Bahama Bank. There, the discontinuous barrier reef is preferentially developed seaward of Andros and is absent seaward of channels (bights) through the island, as well as to the north and south (Fig. 3).

One can only speculate on the explanations for the topography of the Pleistocene limestone surface that is here proposed to control the distribution of living reefs. Increased subsidence in the Middle Keys could explain why the islands are lower, less numerous, and contain less coral than the Upper Keys. For the area north of Elliot Key, where the surface of the Pleistocene reef limestone lies several meters below sea level, it is possible that periodic low temperatures may have reduced reef growth, just as they do at the present time (Ginsburg, 1956).

The preferential development of reefs in Florida that is determined by the presence or absence of pre-existing islands has significant implications for concerns about the state of health of the only shallow reefs of North America and their management in the newly-established Florida Keys Marine Sanctuary. The near-absence of reefs off the Middle Keys and seaward of Biscayne Bay as a result of unfavorable water quality and mobile sand substrate means that deterioration and demise of corals and reefs should be expected in these areas. The near-death of Hen and Chickens reef and the reports of loss of corals at Looe Key are evidence of this effect. Coral growth in these areas must therefore not be used as indications of the state of health of the entire Florida reef tract. In effect, the reef-building biota in the paths of effluents from Florida and Biscayne Bays is probably impoverished and chronically ill from entirely natural causes.

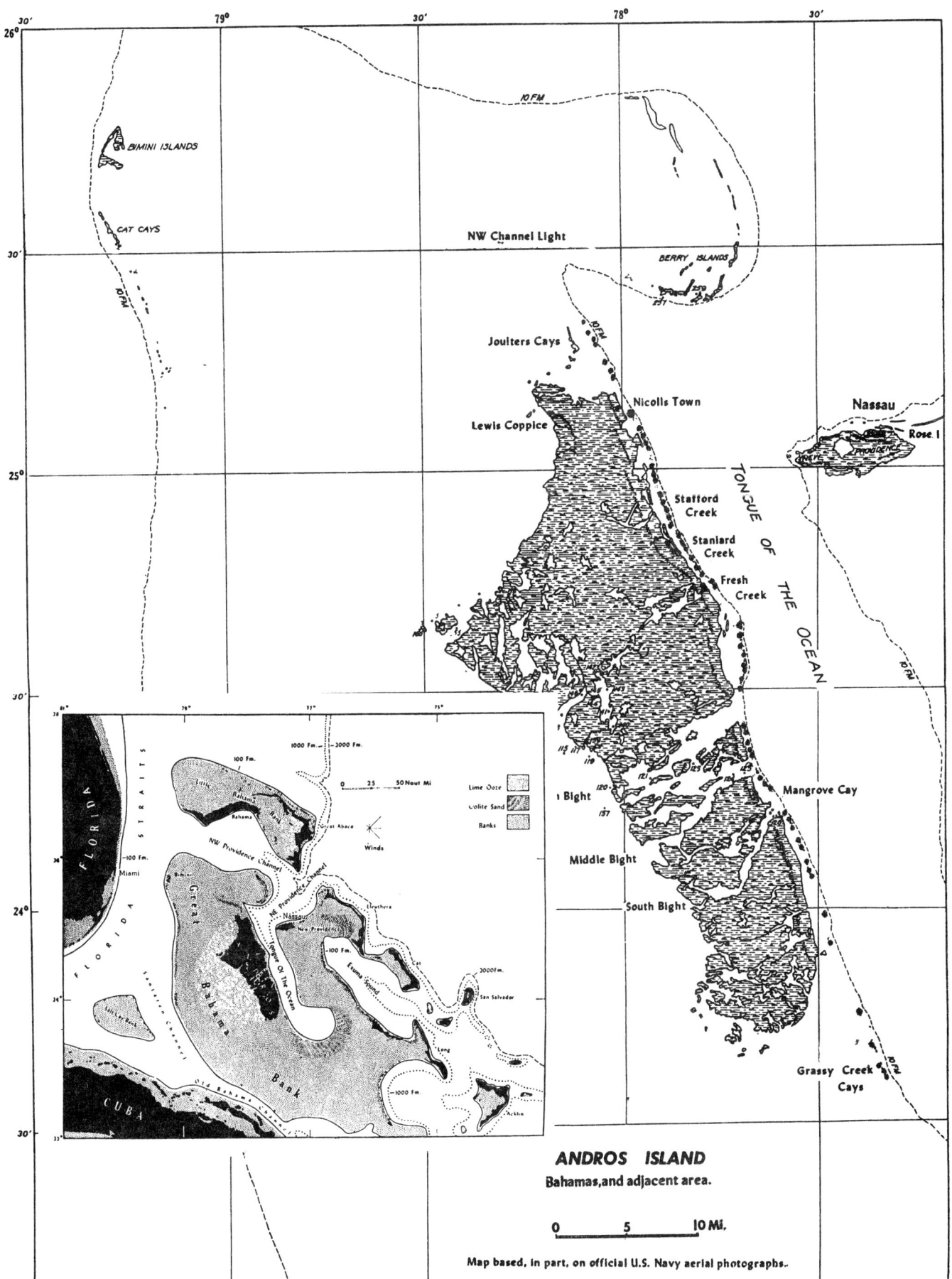

Figure 3. Andros Island, Bahamas showing the barrier reef; modified from Newell and Rigby, 1954. Note the absence of a barrier reef seaward of the bights as well as south of the Island and north of the sand shoals of Joulter Cays. Insert for location.

CONCLUSIONS

The preferential distribution of living reefs in the Florida reef tract is determined by the presence or absence of pre-existing islands of Pleistocene limestone. Where the islands block the movement of reef-deterring waters from Florida and Biscayne Bays, there are well-developed shelf-margin and patch reefs; where these islands are absent and inimical effluent from these bays moves across the shelf, reefs are absent or at best poorly developed. Furthermore, the shelf areas undefended by islands have mobile sand substrates that are not conducive to reef establishment or growth.

The relationship between antecedent topography and reef growth seen in Florida is not unique and a similar relationship is seen in the distribution of reefs on Western Great Bahama Bank.

The conditions of corals and isolated reefs that exist in the areas of unfavorable environment (water quality and substrate) should not be used as indications of the health of the entire Florida reef tract.

ACKNOWLEDGMENT

We thank Robert Warzeski for preparing Figure 1 and Barbara Lidz for thorough and perceptive editing.

LITERATURE CITED

Ball, M.M., E.A. Shinn, and K. W. Stockman, 1967, The geologic effects of Hurricane Donna in south Florida. Journal of Geology, 75:583-597.

Broecker, W.S. and D.L. Thurber, 1965, Uranium-series dating of corals land oolites from Bahamian and Florida Keys limestones. Science 149: 58-60.

Ginsburg, R.N., 1956, Environmental relationships of grain size and constituent composition in some south Florida carbonate sediments. Amer. Association of Petroleum Geologists Bull. 40:2384-2427.

Ginsburg, R.N. and E.A. Shinn, 1964, Distribution of reef-building community in South Florida and the Bahamas. (abstract) American Association of Petroleum Geologists Bull. 48:527.

Hudson, J. H., 1981, Response of *Montastrea annularis* to environmental change in the Florida Keys. Proceedings of the Fourth International Coral Reef Symposium, Manila, 1981, vol. 2:233-240.

Lidz, B. H. and E. A. Shinn, 1991, Paleoshorelines, reefs, and a rising sea: South Florida, U.S.A. Jour. of Coastal Research, 7(1):203-229.

McCallum, J. W. and K. W. Stockman, 1964, Florida Bay Water Circulation. in Ginsburg, R. N., ed. South Florida Carbonate Sediments, Guidebook, Field Trip #1, Annual Meeting, Geological Society of America, 11-13. Reprinted, 1972 as Sedimenta II, Comparative Sedimentology Laboratory, University of Miami, 11-13.

Newell, N. D. and J. K. Rigby, 1957, Geological Studies on Great Bahama Bank. In Le Blanc, Rufus J. and Julia G. Breeding eds., Regional Aspects of Carbonate Deposition, Society of Economic Paleontologists and Mineralogists, Special Publication 5: 15-73.

Osmond, J.K., J.R. Carpenter, and H.L. Windom, 1965, ^{230}Th/^{234}U age of the Pleistocene corals and oolites of Florida. Jour. Geophys. Research, 70:1843-1847.

Roberts, H.H., L.J. Rouse, N.D. Walker and J.H. Hudson, 1982, Cold-water stress in Florida Bay and Northern Bahamas: a product of winter cold-air outbreaks. Journal of Sedimentary Petrology, 52(1): 145-155.

Shinn, E. A., B. H. Lidz, R. B. Halley, J. H. Hudson, and J. L. Kindinger, Reefs of Florida and the Dry Tortugas. Field Trip Guidebook T 176, 28th International Geological Congress, American Geophysical Union, ISBN: 0-87590-648-6, 53p.

Smith, N. P., 1992, Long-term net transport through tidal channels in the Florida Keys. Abstract, 1992 Symposium on Florida Keys Regional Ecosystem, Miami, Florida (unpaginated).

METHODS OF ASSESSING CORAL REEFS

	PAGES
Sessile Communities as Environmental Bio-Monitors in Cuban Coral Reefs	27 - 33

Pedro M. Alcolado, Alejandro Herrera-Moreno, and Nereida Martinez-Estalella

Comparison of Linear Growth Rates in *Porites* Between Undisturbed and Stressed Environments, Gulf of Aqaba, Red Sea — 34 - 37

Wolf-Christian Dullo, Georg A. Heiss, and Elja de Vries

Developing Methods for Assessing Coral Reef Vitality: A Tale of Two Scales — 38 - 44

Phillip Dustan

Non-Invasive Research and Monitoring in Coral Reefs — 45 - 51

Judith C. Lang, Bassett Maguire, Jr., Allison J. King, and Phillip Dustan

Quantification of Loss and Change in Floridian Reef Coral Populations — 52 - 58

James W. Porter and Ouida W. Meier

Reef Fishes as Indicators of Conditions of Coral Reefs — 59 - 65

Ernst S. Reese

Reef Monitoring in Maldives and Zanzibar: Low-Tech and High-Tech Science — 66 - 72

Michael J. Risk, Jennifer J. Dunn, William R. Allison, and Chris Horril

Status and Recent History of Coral Reefs at the CARICOMP Network of Caribbean Marine Laboratories — 73 - 79

Struan R. Smith and John C. Ogden(Editors)
Pedro M. Alcolado, David Bone, Phillippe Bush, Jorge Cortes,

Jaime Garzon-Ferreira, Richard Laydoo, Hazel A. Oxenford, Joe Ryan,
Joth Singh, John Tschirky, Francisco Ruiz, Susan White, and Jeremy Woodley

Global Status of Scleractinia, Alcyonaria, Antipatharia, Stylasterina and Milleporina in the Tropical Western Atlantic: Guidelines and Assessment

K.M. Sullivan, R. Roca, E.C. Peters, and M. Chiappone

SESSILE COMMUNITIES AS ENVIRONMENTAL BIO-MONITORS IN CUBAN CORAL REEFS

Pedro M. Alcolado, Alejandro Herrera-Moreno, Nereida Martinez-Estalella

Instituto de Oceanologia, Academia de Ciencias de Cuba, Ave. 1a No. 18406, Playa, Ciudad de La Habana, Cuba.

ABSTRACT

We present the Cuban experience on employing descriptive ecological features of sessile marine communities as bio-monitors of environmental favorability and constancy. Using indices of heterogeneity (H') and equitability (J'), we interpret the environment at several reefs, taking into account the general requirements of each investigated taxon (sponges, gorgonians, and scleractinians). Dominant species indicate the primary physical factors influencing sessile communities. The range and the comparative intensity of the influence of pollution of Havana Bay on the neighboring reefs were inferred by the species-heterogeneity index. The classification of sampled stations with regard to their level of pollution was obtained by means of cluster analysis. The size-frequency distribution of *Siderastrea radians* also proved to be influenced by the degree of pollution. Variability with regard to depth has been obtained for several indices from numerous stations. These graphs can be used to assess the environmental status of any sampled reef station. All of these methods, if used with caution and in combination, give deductive or predictive outputs that reflect the average conditions of the environment in some cases, while in others indicate the most recent strong events that have affected reef communities.

INTRODUCTION

The inference of environmental quality by means of species or community composition and structure, or by observing the phenotypical adaptations of some species, is a comparatively simple and economical way to monitor and interpret environmental issues. Coral reefs are probably the most sensitive and vulnerable ecosystems in the sea, due to their past evolution under comparatively narrow ranges of environmental variability. For this reason, they are a promising reference choice for monitoring the changes in tropical marine biota. Being aware of this, The Institute of Oceanography of the Cuban Academy of Sciences has been dealing with the composition and structure of coral reef faunal and algal associations since the middle of the 1970's. The purpose of this paper is to offer a brief panorama of our experience in the research of coral reef sessile communities and their potential as bio-monitors.

RESULTS AND DISCUSSION

Species as Indicators of Environmental Stresses

Every ecosystem can be characterized by its species composition which, when compared with other systems, can reveal its particular ecological characteristics, including its biological processes (Grassle, *et al.*, 1991). Sessile taxa, such as sponges, gorgonians, and scleractinians, are more suitable than their motile counterparts to assess the favorability and predictability of the physical environment (Alcolado, 1984).

Dominant species are good indicators of the prevailing environment, provided species-specific habitat requirements are already known. Co- or sub-dominant species may also be good indicators. Species that are well adapted but are not dominant or even rare because they have low reproductive potential or success are unlikely to be good indicators. We have selected a series of species of sponges, gorgonians, and scleractinians that are good indicators of different environmental disturbances. As examples we can mention the dominance of the sponges *Clathria venosa* and *Iotrochota birotulata* f. *musciformis* (Figure 1); the scleractinian *Siderastrea radians*, and the gorgonians *Plexura f. kuekenthali,* and *Pseudoplexaura flagellosa,* so far observed only on reefs affected by organic pollution (Herrera-Moreno and Alcolado, 1983; Alcolado and Herrera-Moreno, 1987; Herrera-Moreno and Martinez-Estalella, 1987). A conditions of stress is inferred when the dominance of some species is coupled to low values of species richness or heterogeneity (Figure 2).

Functional groups can also be used as indicators by summing up the relative abundances (percentages) of species with similar tolerance features. Another way of utilizing species as indicators is by means of a cluster analysis using either species composition alone (Sorenson's or Jacard's indices) or in combination with species relative abundances (Canberra's or Sander' or Bray-Curtis'). Cluster analysis has successfully segregated polluted reef stations using sponge, scleractinian and gorgonian communities as indicators (Figure 3).

Bio-indication of Environmental Favorability and Predictability

Preston and Preston (1975) deserve the merit for integrating and applying the theoretical criteria of some eminent ecologists in a simple and practical scheme to infer the intensity and predictability (constancy) of environmental stresses. By means of the values of H' (Shannon Weaver's heterogeneity index) and J' (Pielou's equitability index), Three different ecological situations can be inferred: high values of both indices suggest a favorable and predictable environment; a low value of H' coupled with a high value of J' indicates a constantly severe environment; and low values of both indices reflect an unpredictably severe environment. That scheme was utilized by us in several investigations.

Due to the fact that this scheme seemed to over-simplify the real situations and led to a misinterpretation of the specific case of extremely low values of both indices, it was recently modified by Alcolado (in press a). This modification consists of a diagram (designed for sponge communities) obtained from a scatter graph of pairs of values of H' and J' from 104 sampled stations. The resulting scatter area was divided into 11 "environmental inference zones" reflecting corresponding ecological situations (Figure 4). These zones conform to the following scale: 1 = extremely stressed by both, a constant basal level of disturbance and intermittent unpredictable strong events (H' = 0-1.3 nats; J' = 0-0.5); 2 = very severe and unpredictable environment (0-1.3 nats; 0.5-0.69); 3 = severe and unpredictable environment (1.3-2.0 nats; 0.5-0.69); 4 = almost constantly severe (1.3-2.0 nats; 0.7-0.8); 5 = constantly severe (1.3-2.0 nats; 0.8-1); 6 = moderately and unpredictably severe (2.0-2.5 nats; 0.5-0.69); 7 = moderately and almost constantly severe (2.0-2.5 nats; 0.7-0.8); 8 = moderately and constantly severe (2.0-2.5 nats; 0.8-1); 9 = favorable and almost constant (2.5-2.9 nats; 0.7-0.8); 10 = favorable and constant (2.5-2.9 nats; 0.8-1); and 11 = very favorable and constant (>2.9 nats; 0.8-1).

Rank 1 show a situation that is not considered by Preston and Preston. It is the case of the surf zone of some Cuban reefs where there are usual average (basal) conditions of fairly strong surf beating and also occasional strong meteorological events, such as severe storms and hurricanes. Under such circumstances, there is only one highly predominant species within each sessile taxa: *Cliona aprica*, among sponges; *Gorgonia flabellum* among gorgonians; and *Acropora palmata*, among scleractinians. for that reason, J' shows very low values. The same happens to H'. This combination within Preston and Preston's method, would suggest an unpredictable environment.

Alcolado's (in press a) inference diagram also differentiates the very favorable and constant environments of the deep reefs (e.g. at 20-30 m) within the rank 11, from those that are simply favorable and quasi-constant (rank10). Nevertheless, it is advisable to be aware of specific situations of very long-term environmental stability in which some species can escape from a certain demographic control and become dominant, consequently diminishing H' and J'. This case seems to be common at reef sites deeper than 25 m. This phenomenon of community senescence is not contemplated in either of the two mentioned inference methods and has to be elucidated by the investigator's acuteness.

Similar inference diagrams have been obtained by us for gorgonians and scleractinians, but remain unpublished. Of course, the frontier values of the boundaries of the inference zones of both indices are not the same among different sessile taxa. We do not consider the "environmental inference diagram" a perfect tool, but a practical way to get a first approach to the coral reef local average environmental situations.

Size-frequency Distributions

Size-frequency distributions (diameter) of populations of the stony coral *siderastrea radians* at 10 m depth were tested by Herrera-Monero and Martinez-Estallel (1987) to detect the responses to organic pollution exported from Havana Bay. The nearer the sampled stations were to the bay, the smaller the dominating diameter classes and the maximum attained diameter were (Figure 5). There was a "paradoxical" exception at the station located just at the entrance of the bay, where the frequencies were more even and the maximum diameter was greater than expected. We explain this by the estuarine circulation pattern of the bay which results in the deeper entering water flow "overwashing" the underlying reef.

Scatter of Variability of Ecological and Population Indices

The scatter of variability with regard to depth for diversity indices, population density and substrate coverage is being obtained for sponge, gorgonian, and scleractinian communities from numerous Cuban reef stations. The graphs that display the area of variation of those indices can be used as a reference pattern to infer the status of a community within a stress gradient. the upper border of this area (an ascending convex line with a slight diminution at depths greater than 25 m) reflects the best conditions registered at different depths for species richness and heterogeneity in sponge communities, while the lower border (an asymptotically ascending curve) shows the worst environmental conditions (Alcolado, in press b).

General Status of Cuban Coral Reefs

Cuban coral reefs stretch along virtually the entire border of the Cuban shelf. About 54% of that border is separated from the mainland by broad shallow water bodies and by groups of keys that prevent anthropogenic influences from reaching the reefs. Great stretches of mainland coasts are poorly urbanized or industrialized. However, they are extensively deforested. For this reason, pollution affects coral reefs only at a few localized stretches, and sedimentation seems to be the most generalized problem.

Organic and /or chemical pollution has been observed to affect the coral reefs of Havana City coast due to the heavily polluted Havana Bay, the Almendares River, and the Quibu River. Nutrient enrichment produces a dense algal growth at a shallow reef located west of the entrance of Mariel Bay. Thermal pollution caused by the cooling system of a power plant located east of Mariel Bay has killed a shallow reef area. Mechanical pollution produced by fiber wastes from a heneguen fiber factory was observed at a shallow reef near the Mosquito River (east of Mariel Bay). Some degree of pollution may be affecting the reefs near the mouths of the bays of Cienfuegos and Santiago de Cuba (south of Cuba), Mantanzas Bay (northwest), Baracoa City (northeast), and some other sites, but this has not been assessed yet. Disregarding storm events, natural stress produced by sedimentation has been detected along long stretches of the east sides of the gulfs of Batabano and Ana Maria, due to the outflowing currents that are often heavily loaded with fine sediments. The same was observed at the reef or Key Cantiles (south of the Gulf of Batabano).

ACKNOWLEDGMENTS

We are deeply grateful to Dr. Rodolfo Claro and Dr. Georgina Bustamente for the critical reading of our manuscript and to the Institute of Oceanology for their great support and for undertaking research on reef ecology

LITERATURE CITED

Alcolado, P.M. 1984. Utilidad de algunos indices ecologios estructurales en el estudio de comunidades marinas de Cuba. Ciencias Biologicas, 11: 61-77.

____. In press a. Sobre la interpretation del ambiente marino mediante el empleo de los indices de diversidad y equalitatividad. Editora Academia de Ciencias de Cuba.

____. In press b. General trends in coral reef sponge communities of Cuba. Univ. of Amsterdam.

Alcolado, P.M. and A. Herrera-Moreno. 1987. Efectos de la contaminacion sobre las comunidades de esponjas al Oeste de la Bahia de la Habana. Reporte de Investigacion del Instituto de Oceanologia, 68: 1-17.

Grassle, J.F., P. Lasserre, A.D. McIntyre and C.G. Ray. 1991. Marine biodiversity and ecosystem function. A proposal for an international programme of research. Biology International (IUBS/SCOPE/UNESCO), special issue 23: 1-19.

Herrera-Moreno, A. and P. Alcolado. 1983. Efectos de la contaminacion sobre las comunidades de gorgonaceos al Oeste de la Bahia de la Habana. Ciencias Biologicas, 10: 69-86.

Herrera-Moreno, A. and N. Martinez-Estalella. 1987. Efectos de la contaminacion sobre las comunidades de corales escleractinios al Oeste de la Bahia de la Habana. Reporte de Investigation del Instituto de Oceanologia, 62: 1-29.

Preston, E.M. and J.L. Preston. 1975. Ecological structure in a West Indian gorgonian fauna. Bulletin of Marine Science, 25: (2); 248-258.

Titles of figures.

Fig. 1. Dominance of two indicator species of sponges at several reef stations (10 m depth) with varying degrees of organic pollution (Stations as in Figure 2).

Fig. 2. Heterogeneity index (H'), equitability index (J') and Sanders' rarefaction curves at different reef stations (10 m depth) affected in varying degrees by organic pollution from Havana Bay and Almendares River.

Fig. 3. Cluster analysis with stations affected by varying degree of influence of organic pollution from Havana Bay and Almendares River (Stations as in Figure 2).

Fig. 4. Diagram for the inference of favorability and predictability of reef environments by means of heterogeneity and equitability indices of sponge communities (Alcolado, in press a).

Fig. 5. Size-frequency distributions of Siderastrea radians at several reef stations affected by varying degrees of organic pollution from Havana Bay and Almendares River (Stations as in Figure 2).

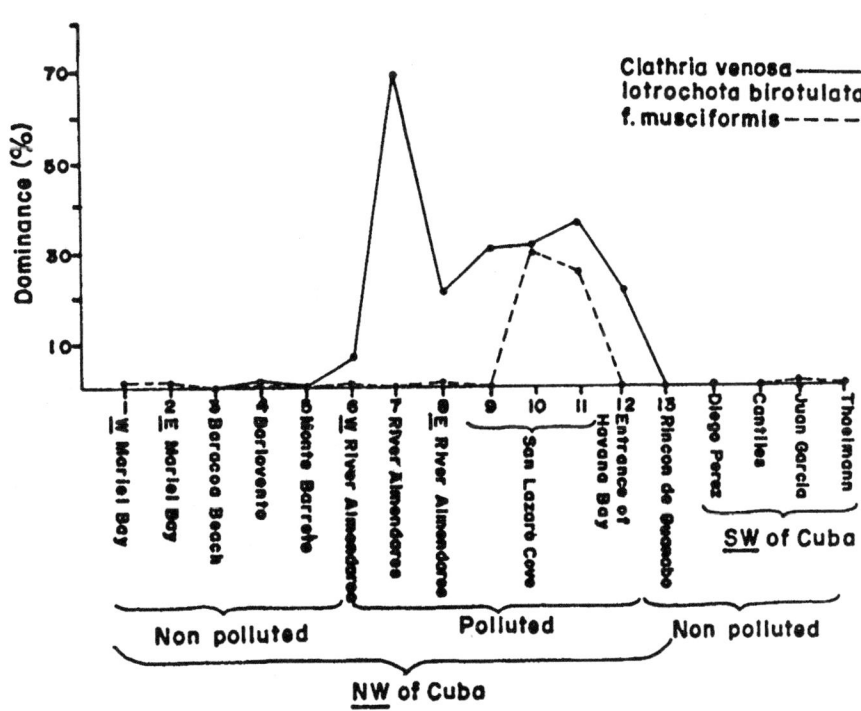

Fig. 1. Dominance of two indicator species of sponges at several reef stations (10 m depth) with varying degrees of organic pollution (Stations as in Figure 2).

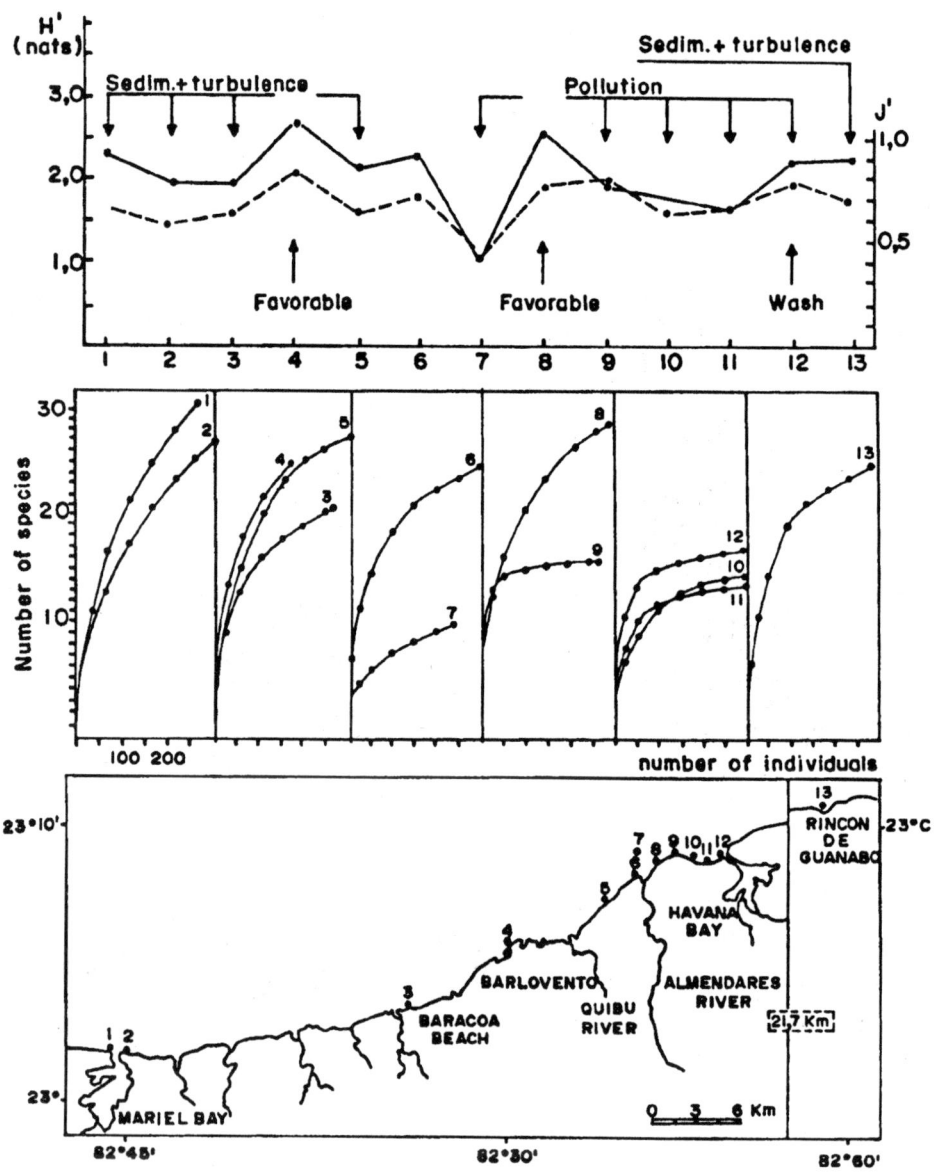

Fig. 2. Heterogeneity index (H'), equitability index (J') and Sanders' rarefaction curves at different reef stations (10 m depth) affected in varying degrees by organic pollution from Havana Bay and Almendares River.

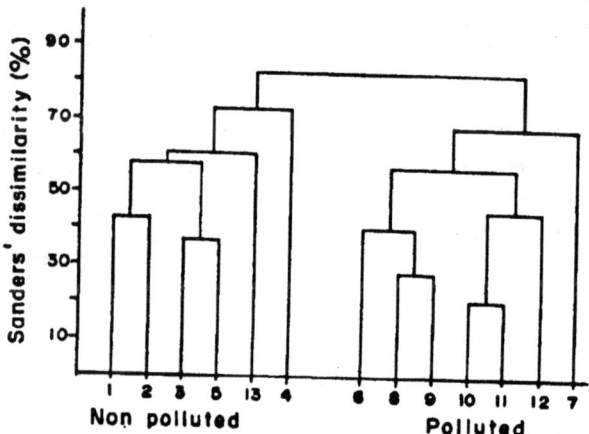

Fig. 3. Cluster analysis with stations affected by varying degree of influence of organic pollution from Havana Bay and Almendares River (Stations as in Figure 2).

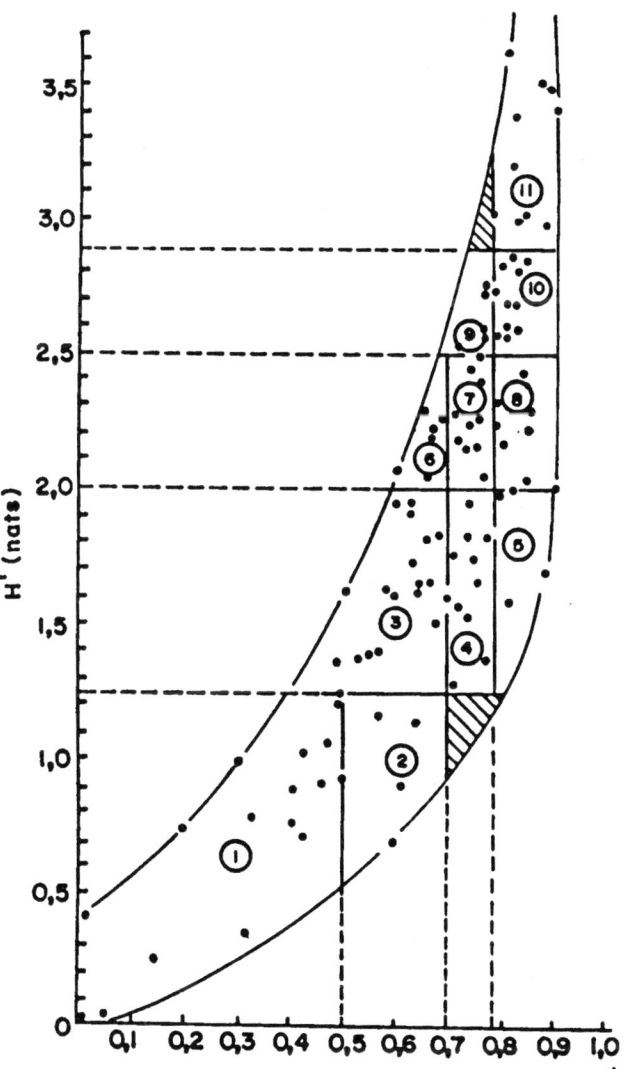

Fig. 4. Diagram for the inference of favorability and predictability of reef environments by means of heterogeneity and equitability indices of sponge communities (Alcolado, in press a).

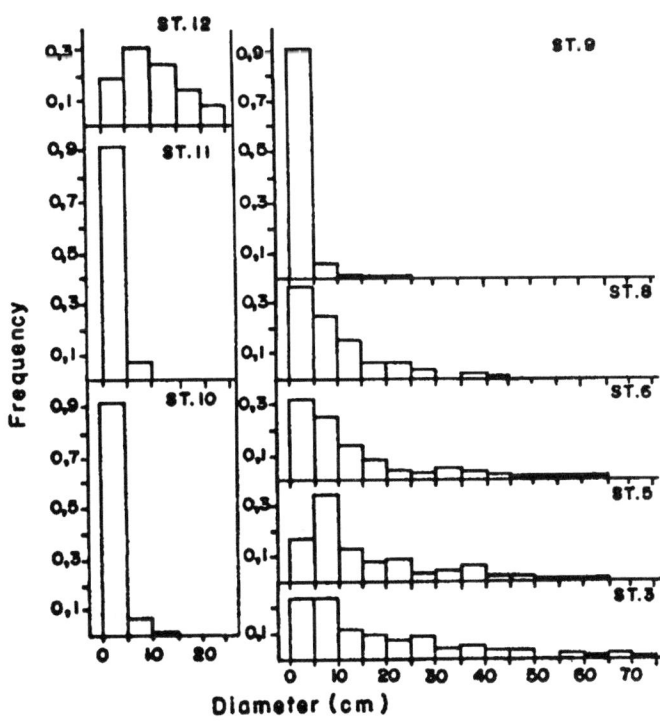

Fig. 5. Size-frequency distributions of Siderastrea radians at several reef stations affected by varying degrees of organic pollution from Havana Bay and Almendares River (Stations as in Figure 2).

33

COMPARISON OF LINEAR GROWTH RATES IN PORITES BETWEEN UNDISTURBED AND STRESSED ENVIRONMENTS, GULF OF AQABA, RED SEA

Wolf-Christian Dullo[1], Georg A. Heiss[1], and Elja de Vries[1]

[1]GEOMAR Forschungszentrum für marine Geowissenschaften, Wischhofstr. 1-3, D-24148 Kiel FRG

ABSTRACT

Investigations were carried out on reef building corals in the Northern Gulf of Aqaba. Using a pneumatic drill we obtained cores of over 1.3 m length. The sclerochronological record shows changes in average linear growth rates of *Porites* sp. over the last 100 years, with a continuos increase since the 1970s. Growth rate and biomineralization were compared between an undisturbed and a stressed environment. At the first site average linear growth rates for *Porites* sp. lie between 8 and 12.26 (max. 16 mm/yr). At the second site corals are smaller and growth rates lie between 5 and 6.5 mm/yr (max. 12 mm/yr). The ultrastructural pattern of *Gyrosmilia interrupta* shows differences in size and density of aragonite accretion between the two sites.

The relationship between the increase of coral growth rate over the last 100 years and global warming, as recorded in the $\partial^{18}O$ record, is discussed. The increase in growth rate in the undisturbed area as opposed to the reduced growth rate in the stressed area is possibly related with decreased sediment input at the former and a significant increase at the latter site.

INTRODUCTION

The coral reefs in the Northern Gulf of Aqaba are amongst the northernmost reefs in the world, lying at 29°27´N. In 1990, we began to study the growth rates of some major reef building scleractinia at the reefs of the Marine Science Station and at the phosphate loading berths in Aqaba, Jordan. Our studies have focused on two major objectives. The first was to obtain a long-term record of linear growth of scleractinians and the second to compare the growth rates between undisturbed and stressed environments as well as their differences in biomineralisation.

The data published on coral growth in the Red Sea and the Gulf of Aqaba are very scarce and cover either the very recent history (Klein & Loya 1991; Klein et al. 1992) or the growth of Pleistocene corals (Klein et al.1990).

The phenomenon of annual density banding patterns in scleractinian corals has been confirmed since it´s first description (Knutson et al. 1972) by several authors (see Barnes & Lough 1989 for a review). For the Gulf of Aqaba (Eilat), the deposition of high-density (HD) in winter and low-density bands (LD) in summer could be correlated to seasonal changes in seawater temperatures (Klein & Loya 1991; Klein et al. 1992).

MATERIALS AND METHODS

Compressed air was chosen as power source for the drill, since Scuba tanks could be conveniently transported and handled on small boats as well as under water. A commercially available RODCRAFT 4200- pneumatic drill was selected working at a speed of 2000 rpm with an air consumption of 220 l/min. Although the operating pressure is 0.6 MPa (6 bar, manufacturer´s information), we operated the drill at a pressure of 8-9 bar which is the pressure supplied by most regulator first stages used for Scuba-diving. The air was supplied by 15 l dive tanks, connected to the drill with a standard industrial pressure hose of 2 m length. The core-cutter is a professionaly manufactured, diamond-tipped steel tube of 300 mm length and an outside diameter of 41 mm (36 mm inside). With this set up we could easily obtain cores of 30 cm length and by using varying extensions we got complete records of more than 1.3 m.

A large colony of *Porites* sp. situated south of the Marine Science Station in Aqaba provided the material for the analysis of the undisturbed environment. The colony grows in front of the reef crest from a depth of approx. 5 m to a height of 3.5 m with a maximum diameter of approx. 5.5 m. The living scleractinians in the stressed environment of the phosphate loading berth are much smaller in size and the *Porites* colonies in the equivalent water depth could be drilled without extension. Core holes were filled with cement plugs after drilling to prevent bioerosion (see Hudson 1981; Winter et al. 1991). In addition to this core material we sampled *Gyrosmilia interrupta* in both environments at water depths of 10 m, 15 m and 25 m to study the differences in biomineralisation.

All cores were sectioned to a thickness of approx. 3 mm using a diamond rock saw. Coral slabs were cleaned in an ultrasonic bath (demineralized water) to remove saw mud. The slabs were x-rayed using a SEIFERT-Industry-X-ray-unit (Type ERESCO 120kV/5ma) at 35kV and 5mA to reveal annual density banding (Knutson et al. 1972; Hudson et al. 1976). Agfa Gevaert Structurix D4 film was used and positive prints developed. From these the growth rates were measured along the major (vertical) growth axis (Buddemeier et al. 1974; Logan & Tomascik 1991) as the distance between the top edges of low-density bands (LD) which are the most distinct boundaries in our samples. Those parts of the cores not drilled parallel to the growth axis were rejected.

SEM samples were cleaned with a fine water jet to remove the tissue and then dried. We have studied the surface of the penultimate accretion pattern as well as fresh fractures of the skeleton.

RESULTS

At present we have a sclerochronological record of coral growth which reaches back to the year 1880. This means we actually see skeletal carbonate that was deposited at the time when Johannes Walther visited the coral reefs in the Gulf of Aqaba. He was one of the first geologists to describe modern reefs and their uplifted pleistocene counterparts (Walther 1888)

In the undisturbed environment mean linear growth rates for *Porites* colonies growing in shallow water (1-3 m) at or close to the reef edge lie between 8.64 and 12.26 mm/yr with maximum values of 16 mm/yr. These growth rates are relatively high for reefs growing at this latitude (compare among others Grigg 1982). The average linear growth rates for the five cores taken from the "big" *Porites*-colony show some interesting changes over time. From 1880 to the first decade of this century we see an increase of mean annual band widths followed by a decrease to the 1940s, strong oscillations until the end of the 1960s and a remarkably steep increase since 1970.

The cores from *Porites* colonies growing in the stressed environment show slightly reduced growth rates compared to those from the undisturbed environment. Maximum values are 12 mm/yr. Minimum values, however, show only 2 mm/yr, while the mean values lie between 5 and 6.5 mm/yr. The production of stress bands is a well known phenomenon (Brown et al. 1986), that may camouflage annual growth patterns.

The ultrastructural pattern in *Gyrosmilia interrupta* from both environments is mostly the same, however the size and the density of both fusiform aragonite crystals of the penultimate accretion (Gladfelter 1982, 1983) and the bundles of parallel aragonite needles vary. They are slightly smaller in samples from the stressed environment. The bundles of aragonite fibres are more compact and more densely packed in specimens from the undisturbed environment.

Skeletal oxygen isotope values indicate a continuous warming of surface waters since about 1900. Carbon isotope values tend to lighter values since the 1950's. Since 1975 a strong $\partial^{13}C$ decrease is measured which coincides with the accelerating extension rate, although the correlation between growth rate and $\partial^{13}C$ for the earlier record is weak

DISCUSSION

Light and temperature have been shown to be the most important variables controlling skeletal growth of scleractinian corals (Knutson et al. 1972; Bosscher 1992 for a review). Other factors influencing coral growth are hydraulic energy (Scoffin et al. 1992), light intensity, sediment resuspension/turbidity (Dodge et al. 1974; Hudson 1981), and nutrients (Dodge & Vaisnys 1975). Endogenic factors (e.g. reproduction) are of varying importance (Klein & Loya 1991).

Sea-surface temperature and light intensity in the Gulf of Aqaba show strong seasonal patterns with highest temperatures occuring in July and August (26-27°C) and minimum in March (ca. 20°C, Paldor & Anati 1979; Klein & Loya 1991). Klein & Loya (1991) suggested that seawater temperature and light intensity are the major factors influencing density patterns in *Porites* corals in the Red Sea. We believe that the same is valid for coral growth rates. The question arises whether the fluctuation (and/or the overall increase) in coral growth rate in the Gulf of Aqaba is related to the well-documented warming of the atmosphere in the Northern Hemisphere (air-land) by about 0.5°C (Grigg 1992) and the increase in global sea surface temperature (SST) by about 0.5°C. These data are well-correlated with solar irradiance (Reid 1991) and discussed for the 100 year skeletal record in the paper of Heiss et al. (1993). The general tendency to lighter oxygen isotope values in our samples in the past 100 years reflects this global warming trend.

The strong increase in growth rate in the undisturbed environment since the early 1970s falls together with major building activities along the coastline south of Aqaba. A road and ferry harbour were built and the Marine Science Station was founded. The road to the southern harbour passes quite close by the reef. Large gullys are built as outlets for the wadis, that drain the hinterland and channel the rain that falls in rare episodic events during winter (Hulings 1989). Even though weather conditions are extremely dry in this region the road may function as a sediment barrier reducing continuos sediment input to the reef. Sedimentation is known to decrease coral growth (Dodge & Vaisnys 1977; Cortés & Risk 1985), therefore reduced sediment load should enhance coral growth. On the other hand man made input of sediment has increased dramatically in vicinity of the phospahte loading berth, where large amounts of apatite dust (Freemantle et al. 1978; Walker & Osmond 1982) are discharged into the water. This dust does not dissolve and increases the particle load in the water, thus causing reduced skeletal accretion as linear growth and the production of biomineralisates.

ACKNOWLEDGEMENTS

We thank the Universities of Jordan and Yarmouk and the staff at their Marine Science Station at Aqaba. We appreciate the help of Caroline Slegtenhorst during fieldwork. Samples were cut by Mr. Reimers. We thank Wilma Rehder for preparation of X-radiographs. Financial support was provided by the Deutsche Forschungsgemeinschaft (Du 129/4, part of the DFG-Schwerpunktprogramm "Globale und regionale Steuerungsprozesse biogener Sedimentation"), which is gratefully acknowledged.

LITERATURE CITED

Barnes, D. J. & Lough, J. M. (1989): The nature of skeletal density banding in scleractinian corals: fine banding and seasonal patterns.- J. exp. mar. Biol. Ecol., 126: 119-134.

Bosscher, H. (1992): Growth potential of coral reefs and carbonate platforms.- PhD thesis, Vrije Universiteit Amsterdam, 160 pp.

Brown, B., Le Tissier, M., Howard, L.S., Charuchinda, M. & Jackson, J.A. (1986): Asynchronous deposition of dense skeletal bands in *Porites lutea*.- Marine Biology, 93: 83-89.

Buddemeier, R. W. & Maragos, J. E. & Knutson, D. W. (1974): Radiographic studies of reef coral exoskeletons: rates and patterns of coral growth.- J. exp. mar. Biol. Ecol., 14: 179-200.

Cortés, J. & Risk, M. J. (1985): A reef under siltation stress: Cahuita, Costa Rica.- Bull.Mar.Sci., 36: 339-356.

Dodge, R. E. & Vaisnys, J. R. (1975): Hermatypic coral growth banding as environmental recorder.- Nature, 258: 706-708.

Dodge, R. E. & Vaisnys, J. R. (1977): Coral populations and growth patterns response to sedimentation and turbidity associated with dredging.- J. Mar. Res., 35: 715-730.

Dodge, R. E. & Aller, R. C. & Thomson, J. (1974): Coral growth related to resuspension of bottom sediments.- Nature, 247: 574-576.

Freemantle, M. H. & Hulings, N. & Mulqi, M. & Watton, E. C. (1978): Calcium and phosphate in the Jordan Gulf of Aqaba.- Mar. Poll. Bull., 9: 79-80.

Gladfelter, E. H. (1982): Skeletal development in *Acropora cervicornis*: I. patterns of calcium carbonate accretion.- Coral Reefs, 1: 45-52.

Gladfelter, E. H. (1982): Skeletal development in *Acropora cervicornis*: II. patterns of calcium carbonate accretion.- Coral Reefs, 2: 91-100.

Grigg, R. W. (1982): Darwin point: A threshold for atoll formation.- Coral Reefs, 1: 29-34.

Grigg, R. W. (1992): Environmental impacts of point-source pollution on coral reef ecosystems in Hawaii.- Pacif. Sci., 46(3): 379.

Heiss, G. A., Dullo, W.-Chr. & Reijmer, J. J. G. (1993): Short- and long-term growth history of massive *Porites* sp. from Aqaba (Red Sea).- Senckenbergiana marit.,23 (4/6) (in press).

Hudson, J. H. (1981): Growth rates in *Montastrea annularis*: a record of environmental change in Key Largo Reef Marine sanctuary, Florida.- Bull. Mar. Sci., 31(2): 444-459.

Hulings, N. C. (1989): A review of marine science research in the Gulf of Aqaba.- Publications of the Marine Science Station Aqaba, Jordan, 6: 267; The University of Jordan Press.

Klein, R. & Loya, Y. (1991): Skeletal growth and density patterns of two *Porites* corals from the Gulf of Eilat, Red Sea.- Mar. Ecol. Progr. Ser., 77: 253-259.

Klein, R. & Loya, Y. & Gvirtzman, G. & Isdale, P. J. & Susic, M. (1990): Seasonal rainfall in the Sinai Desert during the late Quaternary inferred from flourescent bands in fossil corals.- Nature, 345(6271): 145-147.

Klein, R. & Pätzold, J. & Wefer, G. & Loya, Y. (1992): Seasonal variations in the stable isotopic composition and the skeletal density pattern of the coral *Porites lobata* (Gulf of Eilat, Red Sea).- Mar. Biol., 112: 259-263.

Knutson, D. W. & Buddemeier, R. W. & Smith, S. V. (1972): Coral Chronometers: Seasonal Growth Bands in Reef Corals.- Science, 177: 270-272.

Logan, A. & Tomascik, T. (1991): Extension growth rates in two coral species from high-latitude reefs of Bermuda.- Coral Reefs, 10: 155-160.

Paldor, N. & Anati, D. A. (1979): Seasonal variations of temperature and salinity in the Gulf of Elat (Aqaba).- Deep-Sea Res., 26(6a): 661-672.

Reid, G. C. (1991): Solar total irradiance variations and the global sea surface temperature record.- J. Geophys. Res., 96(D2): 2835-2844.

Scoffin, T. P. & Tudhope, A. W. & Brown, B. E. & Chansang, H. & Cheeney, R. F. (1992): Patterns and possible environmental controls of skeletogenesis of *Porites lutea*, South Thailand.- Coral Reefs, 11: 1-11.

Walther, J. (1888): Die Korallenriffe der Sinai Halbinsel. Geologische und biologische Betrachtungen.- Abh. Math.-Naturwiss. Kl. Königl. Sächs. Gesellsch. Wissensch., 14: 439-506.

Winter, A. & Goenaga, C. & Maul, G. A. (1991): Carbon and oxygen isotope time series from an 18-year Caribbean reef coral.- J. Geophys. Res., 96(C9): 16673-16678.

Developing methods for assessing coral reef vitality: a tale of two scales

Phillip Dustan
Department of Biology
College of Charleston, Charleston S.C. 29424

Abstract

This contribution will discuss the population biology of reef corals off Key Largo, Florida Keys at different temporal/spatial scales It deals with a long term study of coral population distribution and abundance at Carysfort Reef and then, building on that work, discusses the development of methods designed to assess the vitality of reef coral populations over large areas in short time periods. The technique combines field information that is easily and rapidly collected in the field with multivariate statistical probing techniques.

Introduction

In 1974 I joined a team funded by the Harbor Branch Foundation and Smithsonian Insititution that was researching the ecology of the reef tract off Key Largo, Florida. My direction was to investigate man's impact on coral reefs. I found myself working in a reef system that was familar but quite different from the reefs of the North Coast of Jamaica where I had trained. The reefs were not a as diverse, as well-developed, nor as luxuriant, yet they shared common species, general structure and zonational patterns.

The reefs off Key Largo can be grouped into three broad reef types: inner patch reefs, middle reefs, and outer fringing-type reefs at the edge of continental shelf. These outer reefs achieve the structure and community zonational patterns characteristic of West-Indian reefs (Goureu 1959). In 1974 Carysfort Reef was located at the northern corner of John Pennekamp Coral Reef State Park, now the Key Largo National Marine Sanctuary. Carysfort Reef was, and still is, the richest, most diverse reef in the Florida Keys outside of the Dry Tortugas. It had a well developed reef flat, a luxuriant A. palmata zone and a rich and diverse fore reef community below 10 meters not found elsewhere in the region. I reasoned that since Carysfort was far from human population centers it would probably be the least anthropologically disturbed. It was my intention that Carysfort Reef would become our reference for comparison with other reefs in the region. If change were to occur it may be most detectable in the areas with higherst coral abundance and diversity.

Studies at Carysfort Reef

A hierarchial approach to the problem began with studies at the levels of the organism, population, and ecosystem. The underlying premise was that the condition of a coral reef community could be assesd through an examination of the coral population biology following a simplification of the logistic equation for population growth:

Coral standing stock = births (recruitment) - deaths

Coral standing stock was estimated with using line transects, recruitment rates estimated by surveying the abundance of small (baby) colonies, and mortality by investigating the causes and rates of coral deaths. We established a study grid consisting of twenty-one 25 meter long transects that traverse the reef from the back reef to the base of the fore reef at a depth of approximately 20 meters. Coral abundance was censused with taught-line transects, and then the lines were removed. For comparison, we carried out a similar study at Long Key Reef (Bird Key Reef) off Fort Jefferson in the Dry Tortugas. This work revealed that the two reefs were substantially different from each other which precluded conclusions about anthropogenic forcing functions as agents of change or differences in the zonation and species composition (Dustan, 1985)

Recruitment was investigated by following the size frequency distribution of small corals in designated plots in different reef zones. Coral diseases was examined by field experiments that measured the rates of tissue destruction, examined the susceptibilty of different species to diseases and following infected corals through periodic field observation.

As we were beginning our work we were introduced to the direct impact of man on reefs by boat groundings. The trimiram Maya with three onboard wrecked on Key Largo Dry Rocks destroying a swatch of reef that measured approximately 10 x 60 meters. We have followed the "recovery" of this area as the small boat grounding count continues to increase and has become a significant threat to the reefs in the area.

Our early results suggested that the reef tract was changing dramatically (Dustan 1977, 1978). Coral recruitment was down and small corals were becoming more difficult to find on the reef. Two coral diseases, Black Band Disease and the White Plague (not White Band Disease), were seen as the most significant "infectious" diseases, while a third condition termed algal- sediment interaction, was causing significant loss of living tissue as fine sediment became trapped by filamentus algal strands and slowly smothered tissue at the tissue border (Dustan, 1977).

Carysfort Reef was resurveyed in 1982-3, seven years after the initial survey. Coral coverage and diversity had increased in the shallow areas while the deeper, fore-reef terrace had suffered significant losses (Dustan and Halas, 1987). Change in shallow water seemed driven by the destruction of the A. palmata zone which bore the scars of boat wrecks, including pieces of propellor blades and gouges laced with antifouling bottom paint. The large colonies which formed the distinct zone were fragmented and had not regrown. The area was becoming colonized with smaller, more r-selected species such as Porites astreoides, Agaricia agaricites, and Favia fragum. On the fore reef terrace, large colonies were dying from diseases and not being replaced by recruitment. The study demonstrated that reef corals at Carysfort were in a downward spiral that continues today (Porter, 1992).

Key Largo Vitality Survey

The Carysfort survey work suggested that the reefs of South Florida were in rapid decline, but the scale of our investigation did not allow us to extrapolate from Carysfort Reef to the Key Largo Reef Tract. It was also becoming apparent that reef coral communities in the Caribbean had the potential to change dramatically in a relatively short period of time: hurricanes had ravaged Jamaica and Mexico, coral diseases were common in all parts of the basin. In 1984 I started a larger scale investigation in Key Largo which addressed the question of the overall condition of corals in the region, the Key largo Coral Vitality Study. The first surveys were conducted in collaboration with undergraduates from the College of Charleston in summer 1984. J. L. Pinckney, Jr. and D. L. Slice continued with the project and contributed significantly to data analysis and interpretation.

We reasoned that we could gain insight into coral health by surveying populations for signs of distress or tissue and/or skeletal damage. This assumes that an undamaged coral will not need to allocate metabolic energy for tissue and skeletal repair and regrowth while a "less than perfect" colony will need to allocate resources towards "repair" instead putting its resources into new growth and reproduction. In this sense, vitality will be used in reference to coral conditions which influence a colony's capacity to carry out it's natural life functions. It might even be possible to detect changes in the vitality of reef coral populations by carrying out a series of temporally spaced surveys which might provide a basis for predicting the future condition of reef coral populations.

The field technique we developed is a fast, comprehensive survey technique that would allow a group of investigators to gather data in a format that could later be subjected to multivariate statistical probing techniques. The condition of a coral is observed by a diver and described with a numerical code that provides as complete a description of the state of a colony as was possible through direct observation. We tried to generate condition codes that are non-overlapping, derived from field observation and could be updated as new conditions were encountered (Dustan, 1987).

In July of 1984 we made observations on over 9800 corals on 19 different reefs in the Key Largo region. Initial analysis revealed that almost 60 percent of the corals showed signs of physical or biological stress, 5-10 percent were "infected" with either black band disease or the "white plague", and about one third of the colonies appeared healthy (Figure 1). Surprisingly, virtually all the areas we surveyed had approximately the same levels of "unhealthy" corals. There were no "hot spots" or "problem reef areas".

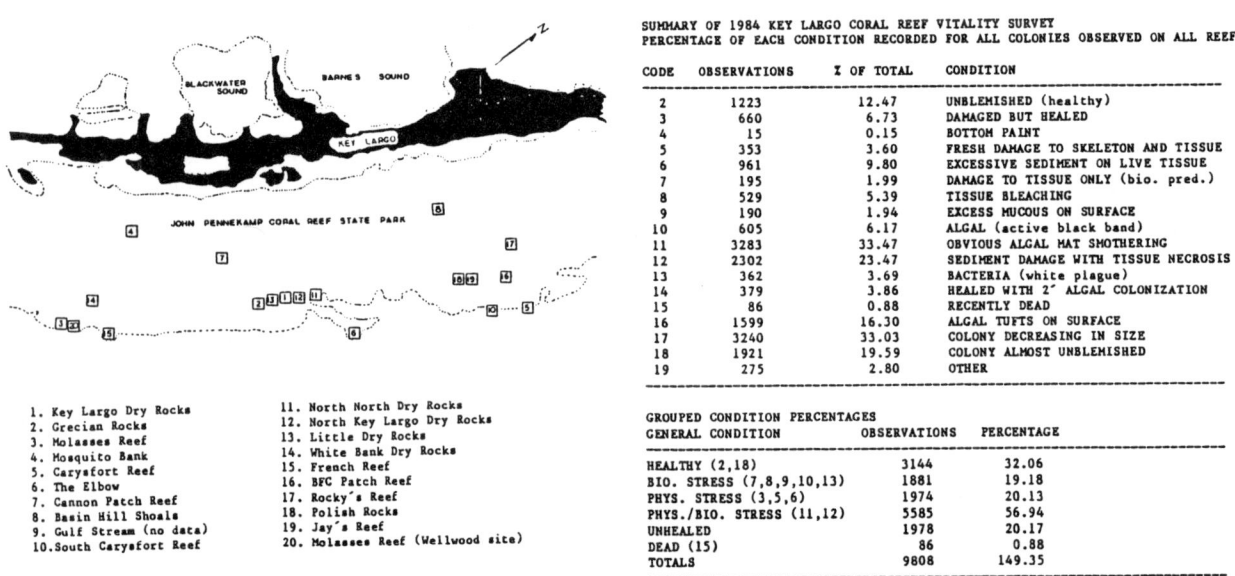

Figure 1. Location map and summary of Key Largo Vitality Survey of 1984. Total percentage is greater than 100% as colonies may have multiple conditions.

Principal components analysis revealed that 64% of the standardized variance could be explained by the first two principal components, or factors. The remainder of the variation was more or less evenly spread over the remaining sixteen eignevalues. The first factor appears to be a measure of the heterogeneity of conditions in a reef community. The second factor distingushes between reefs with respect to coral conditions. Sediment-related conditions and black band disease form a distinct group and conditions related to physical damage, predation, bleaching, and the disease "white plague" form a second, looser cluster (Fig. 2). The two processes seem largely independent of one another but seem to both have a geographic/environmental pattern which is probably due to inshore-offshore differences in species habitat range. This was confirmed by cluster analysis of reefs by species abundance and by occurences of conditions relative to total coral abundance. Both analyses separated the coral communities into inner, middle, and outer reefs which closely resembles their geographic location (Figure. 3). The geographic component may be related to terrestrial activity, or it may suggest that different species of corals are subject to different conditions.

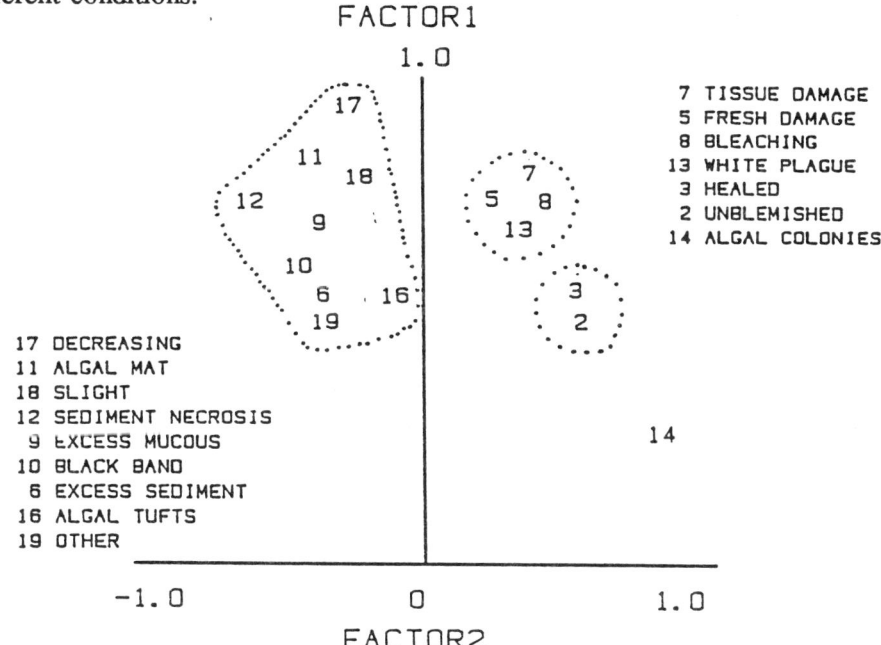

Figure 2. Plot of first two principal factors showing the separation of conditions into three main groupings.

Numerical taxonomy UPGMA clustering of species by conditions produced a series of clusters that are difficult to interpret (Fig. 3). The clusters include species from different taxonomic groups that occupy very different habitats in the reef community. The largest grouping includes most of the corals with meandroid polyps, but also includes Acropora palmata. Montastrea annularis and Acropora cervicornis group together separately. Species of Porites and Siderastrea, ecologically similar corals, group together which seems to be logical, but why should members of the genus Mycetophyllia group with species of Agaricia, or F. fragum group closely with Agaricia fragilis? These species are not very similar in morphology, habitat preference, or depth range.

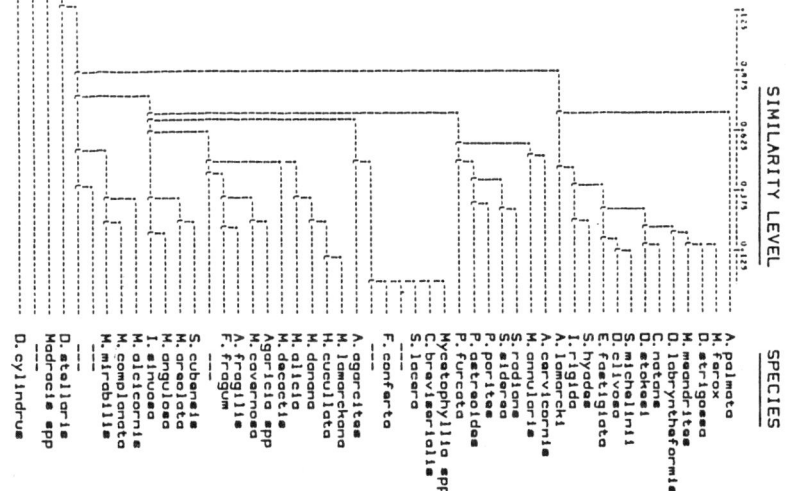

Figure 3. Phenogram of cluster analysis of coral species by conditions for Key Largo Vitality Survey data.

41

A question often raised is how to identify a control site. Ideally such a site should be pristine, remote from urbanized land masses, unexploited by the local population and have a reef system that is comparable in structure and species composition. In 1985 we surveyed reefs of San Salvador, Bahamas. The data revealed generally higher levels of "healthy" corals than found in Key Largo accompanied by a higher level of heterogeneity between reefs. We found 9 species of diseased corals, most commonly M. annularis and A. palmata. Coral conditions varied with reef site and species, 35% to 16% of the corals were unblemished (Table 1). A very small percentage showed signs of recent fresh damage to either tissue or skeleton. In Graham's Harbor white plague was common on A. palmata. Black Band Disease was easily found on M. annularis on Gaulin's Reef and the lee side of Catto Reef. The disease was absent on the seaward side of Catto, a region of intense wave energy. Black band disease was not common on M. annularis in Fernandez Bay. Curiously, these reefs, located on the lee side of the island, have suffered severe declines in coral coverage in the last ten years. A very large percentage of colonies show signs of stress from algal-sediment interactions that result from excess sediment and the growth of algae at the colonies' borders. Diseased corals were rare in deep water but the team only made 6 dives to 30m or deeper.

Condition Code	Staghorn n	Staghorn % Total	Telephone Pole n	Telephone Pole % Total	Catto Cay n	Catto Cay % Total	Description of Condition
2	49	35.5	22	25.0	12	16.0	Unblemished
3	1	0.7	3	3.4	0	0.0	Damaged but healed
4	0	0.0	0	0.0	0	0.0	Antifouling bottom paint
5	1	0.7	0	0.0	1	1.3	Fresh damage to coral
6	0	0.0	0	0.0	0	0.0	Excessive sediment
7	1	0.7	0	0.0	1	1.3	Tissue damage only
8	0	0.0	3	3.4	2	2.7	Tissue bleaching
9	0	0.0	0	0.0	0	0.0	Excess mucous
10	0	0.0	2	2.3	1	1.3	Active Black Band
11	47	34.1	26	29.6	26	34.7	Algal mat smothering
12	57	41.3	51	58.0	36	48.0	Sediment damage
13	0	0.0	0	0.0	0	0.0	White Plague
14	19	13.7	0	0.0	24	32.0	Algal islands damage
15	0	0.0	0	0.0	0	0.0	Recently dead
16	1	0.7	0	0.0	6	8.0	Algal tufts on surface
17	19	13.8	42	47.7	3	4.0	Macroalgae damage
18	28	20.3	5	5.7	31	41.3	Colony almost perfect
19	1	0.7	0	0.0	3	4.0	Other (unknown)
Totals	138	161.6%	88	175.1%	75	194.6%	

Table 1. Summary of 1986 San Salvador Preliminary Coral Reef Vitality Survey Percentage of each condition for selected species on selected reefs (data from Dustan, 1987).

Discussion

The reef corals of the Caribbean appear challenged by a number of biotic fators. Diseases are a significant factor in the mortality of A. palmata, and A. cervicornis, and M. annularis. After having first been described from the northern limits of their reefs distribution in Atlantic Ocean, coral diseases have now been reported throughout the Caribbean however, little is known about the distribution of coral diseases, species specificity, and epidemiology. The mass mortality of sea urchins on the reefs of the Bahamams and elsewhere in the Caribbean was reported in 1982-3 has caused virtually all species of coral to be challenged by algae that grow in great profusion around the borders of coral colonies. The algae colonize the dead coral skeleton substrate, which in turn results in the die back of the coral tissue which opens up more substrate for colonization.

Our investigation into the vitality of reef corals started with investigations of a single reef and have enlarged to include reefs within the reef tract of Key Largo at a reduced level of resolution. Questions raised from the Key Largo Vitality Survey of 1984 lead to a further increase in scale to include reefs in different geographical areas. The survey/statistical techniques we are developing provide a "snapshot" of coral conditions on an ecosystem scale but at a reduced level of spatial resolution over line transects. Both techniques provide valuable information and we are presently working towards a combination analysis package. Clearly more data are needed on the conditions of corals in other reef ecosystems, as is another survey of the reefs of Key Largo. Increasing the size of the data base will increase the reliability of the data while repetative surveys will allow us to probe the relation between coral conditions and community change.

The Key Largo Vitality survey demonstrates that the changes in coral we have measured on Carysfort Reef are not unique to just one reef. The widespred distribution of poor health points to a "systemic" or area wide cause rather than localized damaging events. To me, this suggests an overall degradation in habitat quality that may be the additive and cumulative result of a degradation in water quality.

While most corals in the Key Largo Reef Tract showed greater percentages of stress than in Bahamian waters, diseases and degraded coral were more common at the "control site" than predicted a priori. San Salvador, is remote from centers of civilization. There are no major sources of industrial pollution on the island and its small population size suggests that their is little anthropogenic nutrient loading of the local waters. There is little commercial fishing and most sport fishing occurs in the pelagic oceanic waters offshore. San Salvador's eastern location on the Bahamian Bank bathes it in water from the tropical Atlantic and Sargasso Sea. On an otherwise pristine island, the beaches on the eastern side of the island are littered with debris from the Atlantic fishing grounds and drift bottles from the northeast American coast and Europe have been found on East Beach. Thus oceanic drift debris, mostly plastic, forms the bulk of the pollution on the windward shoreline of San Salvador. This raises questions about the epidemiology coral diseases and possible links to mesocale or larger oceanic and atmospheric circulation patterns.

I realize that the data I have presented only describes the present state of corals in the region. It does not distingush between cause and effect, nor does it uncover the sources and/or causes of the problems. When I began to study reef it was thought that reefs were stable, climax communities that changed very slowly in ecological time. We now realize that reefs are dynamic communities that can undergo rapid change over relatively short periods of time. The studies on change due to physical and/or biological factors are now ongoing and the effects of man are taking center stage. Investigations at different spatial/temporal scales are needed to unravel the local from the global and the recent from the fossil states of coral reefs.

Acknowledgements

This research was carried out with the assistance and support of Don and Kathy Gerace of CCFL. Lorraine Dustan, J. Kostka, J. Pinckney, D. Slice, E. Woloszyn, and E. Womack assisted in diving and field data collection. Funding for aspects of this research were provided by the Jeanette and Lafayette Montgomery Foundation, College of Charleston, NOAA Sanctuary Programs, The Harbor Branch Oceanographic Institution, and the Smithsonian Institution, Ft. Pierce Branch and the NASA Jove Program. A copy of our VITAREEF software (DOS, Quick Basic) is available to interested investigators.

Literature Cited

Dustan, P., 1977. Vitality of reef coral populations off Key Largo, Florida: recruitment and mortality. Environmental Geology. 2:51-58.

Dustan, P., 1985. Community structure of reef-building corals in the Florida Keys: Carysfort Reef, Key Largo and Long Key Reef, Dry Tortugas. Atoll Res. Bull. 288

Dustan, P. 1987. Preliminary observations on the vitality of reef corals in San Salvador, Bahamas. in Curran, H.A.., ed. Proceedings of the Third Symp. on the Geology of the Bahamas: Ft. Lauderdale, Fl. CCFL Bahamian Field Station, p. 57-64.

Dustan, P. and J. C. Halas, 1987. Changes in the reef-coral community of Carysfort Reef, Key Largo, Florida: 1974-1982. Coral Reefs 6:91-106.

Porter, J.W. and O.W. Meier, 1992. Quantification of loss and change in Floridian croal reef populations. Amer. Zool. 32:625-640.

NON-INVASIVE RESEARCH AND MONITORING IN CORAL REEFS

Judith C. Lang
Texas Memorial Museum
University of Texas
Austin, TX 78705

Bassett Maguire, Jr.
Zoology Department
University of Texas
Austin, TX 78712

Allison J. King and Phillip Dustan
Department of Biology
University of Charleston
Charleston, SC 29424

ABSTRACT

Determining the ecological dynamics of coral reefs, and the effects of externally caused environmental pertubations on these dynamics, will be of great importance to our understanding and managing of coral reef ecosystems. Some new approaches to ecological monitoring and research are being developed in relatively unspoiled, reef habitats near Lee Stocking Island, The Bahamas, where zooxanthellate reef organisms have bleached periodically, at least since the fall of 1987. Our studies include abundance, distribution, recruitment, apparent health, growth and mortality of reef organisms.

Initial analyses (reported herein) are focused on :

Ecosystems level--Determining efficient methods of ground truthing for realistic interpretations of digitized aerial photographs, based on geographic information systems analyses. At present, we are comparing *in-situ* chain transect and hand-mapping techniques with high resolution videotape/point count and reef overview approaches.

Individual level--Quantitatively analysing digitized photographic images from randomly-chosen colonies of *Porites astreoides* and *Montastraea* spp. (both excellent indicators of bleaching in certain habitats) to create color indices. We are finding considerable seasonal variability in color brightness values as a function of species, habitat and year, even in colonies lacking conspicuous autumnal bleaching responses.

NON-INVASIVE RESEARCH AND MONITORING IN CORAL REEFS

Judith C. Lang, Bassett Maguire, Jr., Allison J. King and Phillip Dustan

Introduction

Most reef corals and other organisms with zooxanthellae (photosynthetic dinoflagellates) tolerate a narrow range of physical and chemical environments (1). Loss of algae and/or of photosynthetic pigments from these organisms is called bleaching. Sudden bleaching of many reef organisms throughout much of the western Atlantic and elsewhere in 1987 is evidence of widespread environmental stresses (2). Western Atlantic reefs near large human habitations are influenced by many anthropogenic perturbations (3). Regardless of location, all reef ecosystems should be affected by predicted global climate changes (4).

Long-term information on the dynamics of reef organisms and communities is needed, in part to distinguish human-induced from natural changes. Reefs distant from major sources of pollution are desirable "control sites", especially to assess the effects of any global climate changes. Resources must be catalogued at nested scales to include levels of resolution from centimeters to kilometers (4). Data on a subannual scale are required when conditions of stress, or susceptibility to infections or bleaching, vary seasonally (5, 6). Indicator species that display heightened sensitivity to a locally-important perturbation can provide critical insight into the health and functioning of an ecosystem. There are obvious moral, ethical and practical imperatives for developing non-invasive methods, particularly in marine reserves.

High-resolution photographs and videotapes are invaluable sources of information for many aspects of reef health, structure and function. Accurate color evaluation under incompletely known lighting conditions requires illumination that is even in color and intensity, and the inclusion in each image of a known gray scale. Stereo-pairs are particularly useful when the contained topographic data are used for non-invasive estimates of colony shape, size and three-dimensional growth. (Information that is readily visible to the eye underwater, like predator density, however, is better recorded *in-situ*.)

We are examining the ecological dynamics of benthic reef organisms at several spatial scales near Lee Stocking Island (23° N., 76° W.), Exuma Cays, The Bahamas. Direct human impacts on these coral reefs are minimal (3). Seawater temperatures over the reefs vary from ~ 21 to ~ 32 $^\circ$ C (7). Tidal amplitudes range up to ~1 m. Diel tidal currents are strong at our shallow sites. Autumnal mass bleaching was widespread in this area in 1987, less severe in 1990, fairly minor in 1991 and virtually non-existent in 1992 (8, 9, pers. obs.).

Ecosystem Level Studies: A. King and P. Dustan

Methods

"Traditional" transect- or quadrat- based methods, utilizing quantitative data recorded *in-situ* (10), are exceedingly labor intensive. At a far coarser scale, digital image processing techniques are used with satellite-derived information to provide baseline data for shallow reefs. Photographic quality, rather than some predetermined pixel size, is a limiting factor when low-altitude, aerial photographs substitute for satellite imagery.

Methodologies for comparing field-based measurements of community structure with remotely-sensed information are being developed at Rainbow Gardens, a shallow (3-10 m), ~3000 m^2 patch reef. The initial data set, acquired during the summer of 1991, is based on three spatial scales:

1. Chain transect techniques were used to obtain estimates of relative abundance, size (to the nearest 2 cm) and diversity in 30, regularly-spaced, permanently-marked, transects (Σ= 705 m). The visible condition (coloration, surface appearance, accumulated sediment, symptoms of disease or other soft tissue damage) of each reef coral was also recorded. Species composition and coverage have been analyzed. Visible condition of the reef corals has been coded to be compatible with the VITAREEF concept (11, Dustan this Colloquim).

2. All scleractinian reef corals larger than about 10 cm were mapped, providing a "medium perspective" of their distribution patterns on the patch reef as a whole. The reef was temporarily divided into 5 m x 5 m quadrats by a grid of lines. Hand-drawn sketches were prepared for each quadrat, then pieced together ashore. Each species was given a unique class number, and the position of each colony was entered into a digital file by tracing its polygon shape with the tablet's handpiece. The data set was gridded into a raster form image and the statistical distribution of pixels used to calculate the percentage of coral cover of the entire mapped area. These data will be used to calculate species diversity indices, zonation patterns, nearest neighbors, etc.

3. Color aerial photographs of the entire reef were taken at an altitude of about 4,600 m in a King Air turboprop airplane, using hand-held cameras. The best photograph, scanned with an Eikonix digital camera using ERDAS software, is being classified to give a geographic information systems (GIS) image that will also be analyzed for percent coral cover.

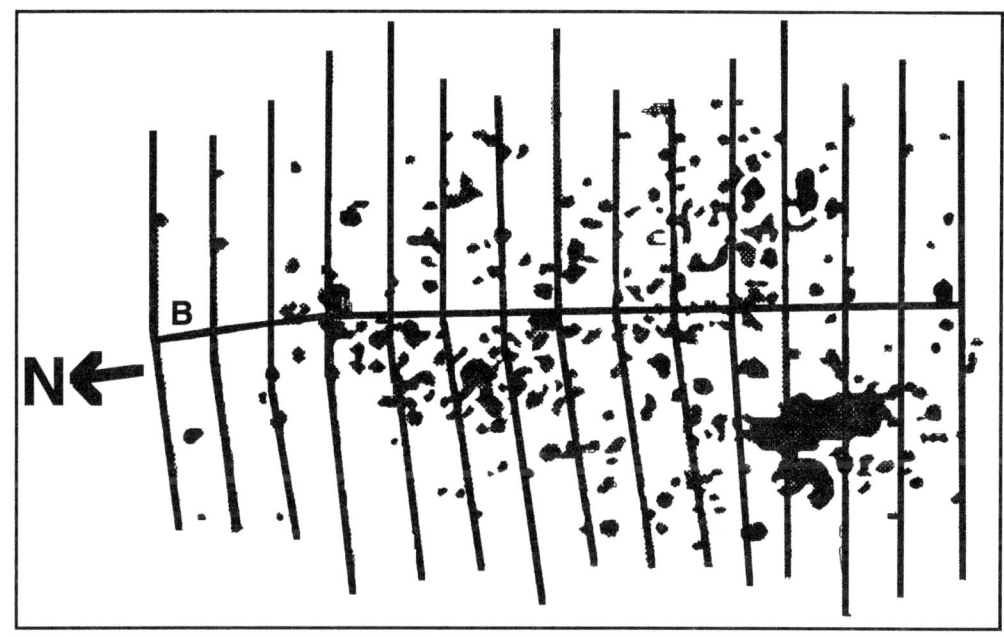

Fig. 1. Digitized map of the Rainbow Gardens patch reef, with the locations of a 70 m long baseline (B) bisecting the longer axis of the reef, the perpendicular transect lines, and the larger reef corals. The huge coral in the lower right is a *Montastraea annularis* "bommie" that has regressed after extensive bleaching in 1987 and 1991.

Results and Discussion

Dominant structural organisms at Rainbow Gardens (Fig. 1) are the reef corals *Montastraea annularis*, *Agaricia* spp., *Porites porites* and *Diploria labyrinthiformis*, along with the gorgonian *Pseudopterogorgia elisabethae*. Total live reef coral cover is estimated as 13.5% with the chain transect method ($\Sigma 705$ m), as 11.6% on the digitized map, and as 12.8% when the transects (as 1 pixel wide or as 3 pixels wide) are overlain on the digitized map. Average colony size varied from 1.0 cm for *Siderastrea radians* to 18.1 cm for *S. siderea*. About twenty species of reef corals are present at the site; eleven of which were large enough to figure in the mapping. Estimates of Shannon diversity (H') for reef corals are 1.9 (by cover) and 2.2 (by colonies), while evenness (Pielou's J) was estimated as 0.68 (by cover) and as 0.71 (by colonies).

One of our goals is to understand how to use information gathered at different spatial scales to meaningfully monitor coral reef communities. Our results to date demonstrate that underwater mapping can yield remarkably similar results with respect to overall coverage of reef corals as chain transects. The mapped colonies will also provide the ground truthing for the GIS interpretation of the digitized aerial photograph.

Another approach to ground truthing was initiated during the summer of 1992. High resolution (Hi8) color video images were obtained by swimming slowly along the major transect lines at Rainbow Gardens. Benthic cover and visible condition of reef corals are being identified at 10 cm intervals, using a point count technique, and will be compared to the results of the chain transects (12). We are also making videotapes at a larger scale to see if they can substitute for *in-situ* mapping. Advantages of video include its speed of acquisition in the field and the permanency of the record.

Aerial photographs potentially can provide information at a scale that is highly appropriate for the routine monitoring of coral reefs. There is already a large amount of archived aerial photography (color as well as black and white) that has not been well utilized as an investigatory monitoring tool. New data on "local" reefs is readily acquired using small planes. More remote regions will require the use of specialized surveillance aircraft, satellite sensors, or space shuttle imagery. Moving data sets into the GIS analytical environments opens up new areas for analysis and for cross comparisons among diverse reef systems.

Organismal Level Studies: B. Maguire and J. Lang

Methods

Little is known about "normal", within-colony variability in the colors of individual zooxanthellate organisms (see 6). Seasonal indices of color change are being developed for several western Atlantic corals that are reasonably abundant and known to be excellent, local indicators of bleaching in certain habitats (8, pers. obs.). Up to 16 randomly-chosen colonies of the *Montastraea annularis* species complex (one species/habitat) and of *Porites astreoides* were permanently tagged at duplicate "shallow "(~3 m) sites at the Norman's Pond Cay fringing reef and in "deeper" (~15 - 17 m) sites on the North Perry fringing reef in the summer of 1991. Stereo-pair photographs are being taken of each colony three times/year (Summer, Fall, Spring), based on a modification of Done's (13, pers. comm.) adaptation of the two-camera technique. There is a compass, goniometer, Macbeth gray scale and a wand of known length in front of the cameras. The coral-gray scale system is shaded to avoid effects of light "flecks" caused by surface wave refraction of sunlight.

Digitization of an image produces levels of brightness of the red, green and blue (R, G, B) of small areas of the scanned image; these levels are later used to determine the intensity of the R, G and B components of the pixels making up the image on the screen. We have analyzed such images with Photoshop® to obtain quantitative, pixel by pixel measurements of color and brightness. Blacks, all shades of gray, and white are seen when the R, G and B brightness levels have the same value. Quantitative deviations from equality of the brightness values of R, G and B of an image of an appropriate panel of the gray scale in the photograph therefore give amount and direction of the departure from white of the photographic light, effects of color distortion during film development, etc.

"Corrections" of these color artifacts to white can be made: R, G and B coral image brightness levels are each measured in terms of the brightness in R, G and B, respectively, of panels of the Macbeth gray scale in the same photograph as the coral object. We assigned the black panel a value of 1, the white panel a value of 6, and the four grays have intermediate values. The gray scale panels can be used in this way because each panel reflects the same percentage of the light regardless of the light's intensity of color. Respective optical densities of the gray scale panels (black to white) are 1.5, 1.05, 0.07, 0.44, 0.23, and 0.05; percent transmission equivalents are 3, 9, 20, 36, 59, and 89%. Coral values are used to interpolate between the two nearest gray scale panel values to increase the accuracy of the resultant data (using the brightness values in R, G and B for the coral and each panel in the gray scale--see below).

In practice, uniform, representative areas, up to ~100 cm^2 are chosen by visual examination of all the digitized images for any given coral. Histograms of the image of the chosen areas are produced by the Photoshop "histogram" analysis routine (14). Data from these histograms are then evaluated in the context of gray scale panel values. This procedure, in effect, "corrects" the image so that it is essentially as if the photograph had been taken with white light (in prep.).

Results and Discussion

Pale or whitened spots and lineations were seen in all species, and at all habitats and seasons. Some paling was clearly the result of mechanical damage by predators or commensals, in other instances differential, within-colony growth rates are suspected. Seasonal color changes are substantial and described in greater detail below. Relatively small-scale bleaching in October 1992 was restricted to several reef coral taxa (especially agariciids, *Diploria* spp., poritids) in fore-reef habitats. About half (8/18) of the marked colonies of *Porites astroeides* (N = 17), but only 15% of the *Montastraea hispidula* (N = 14) at the North Perry fringing reef were partially affected by this event. (Visual assessments are based on qualitative visual scans of the time-series photographs.) Comparable estimates the following year were 10% for *P. astroeides* and 2 % for *M. hispidula*. (N = 33 and 42, respectively). Two of the *P. astroeides* surveyed in Fall 1991 rebleached in Fall 1992: one at the opposite end of the colony from the previous year!

Representative time-series photographs of a shallow colony of *Montastraea annularis* are shown in Fig. 2. Histograms of fundamental pixel colors for a deep, bleached colony of *Porites astroeides* are given in Fig. 3. The numbers associated with the peaks give the numerical brightness levels of the gray scale panels in that color. (Black is when R, G and B are all at brightness level 0, and white is when they all are at 255. R, G and B are each 8 bit colors, giving a 24 bit image.)

Mean brightness values of unbleached parts of four shallow colonies of *Montastraea annularis* and of four deeper, darker colonies of *M. hispidula* are presented in Fig. 4. The means of the R, G and B brightness values are expressed in terms of the panel numbers (1 = black, 6 = white) of the gray scale in each image. Gray scale equivalence values are lowest in the blue and highest in the red, with green being intermediate. (Low relative brightness for any color means the coral/algal system is absorbing that color of light more effectively than it absorbs other colors. The combined higher levels of red and green, compared to the blue, produces the brown color characteristic of many reef corals.) A relatively low brightness in the blue makes sense for photosynthetic organisms, including zooxanthellate mutualists, in aquatic environments.

Fig. 2. Digitized images of *Montastraea annularis* #346 at the shallow site in Summer 1991 (Lower) and Fall 1991 (Upper). The rectangular areas marked in both images were analyzed for color brightness values. Despite image differences resulting from variations in lighting, exposure, film treatment, etc., both color and brightness were effectively evaluated.

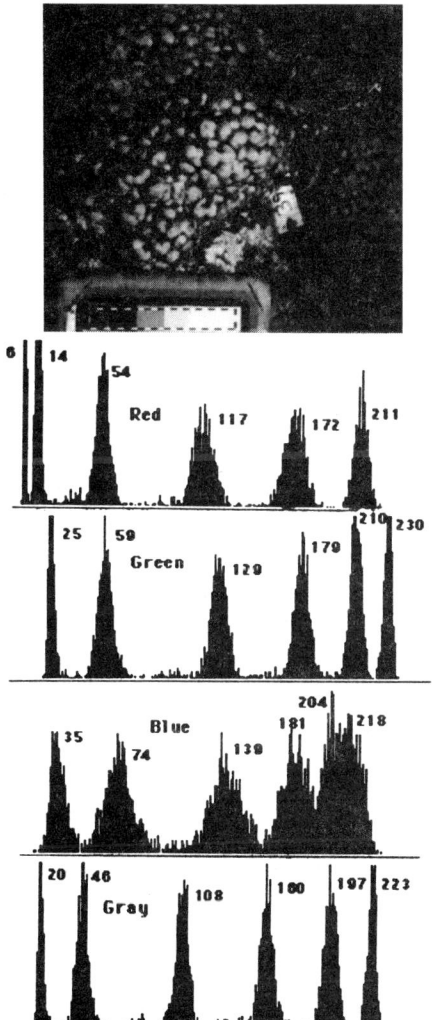

Fig. 3. Digitized image of bleached *Porites astreoides* #394 at the deeper site in Fall 1991. Each histogram is for one of the fundamental pixel colors, R, G and B (plus one for "gray"), and each has 6 peaks representing the 6 brightness levels of the gray scale in that color.

The temporal patterns exhibited by these two taxa are rather similar. All brightnesses decrease (*i.e.*, absorbances increase) between Fall 1991 and Spring 1992, then all increase, although at slightly different rates, from Spring through Fall 1992. This pattern is suggestive of a photoadaptive response, in which pigment concentrations are higher in the winter when light levels are low than in the spring and summer when light levels are higher. However, while these colonies of *M. annularis* had shown brightness increases in G and B (R was unchanged) from Summer to Fall 1991, the brightness of *M. hispidula* had decreased during this interval. Reasons for the between-year differences are not clear, but may be related to the effects of minor bleaching on the deeper site in 1991.

Non-bleached portions of *Porites astreoides* at both depths show generally similar patterns of brightness change as described in *M. hispidula* (Fig. 5). Throughout this interval, the deeper, brown-colored, unbleached *Porites* remained at almost the same brightness in the blue as did the shallow, yellowish-green colonies; however, their R and G brightness values were appreciably lower.

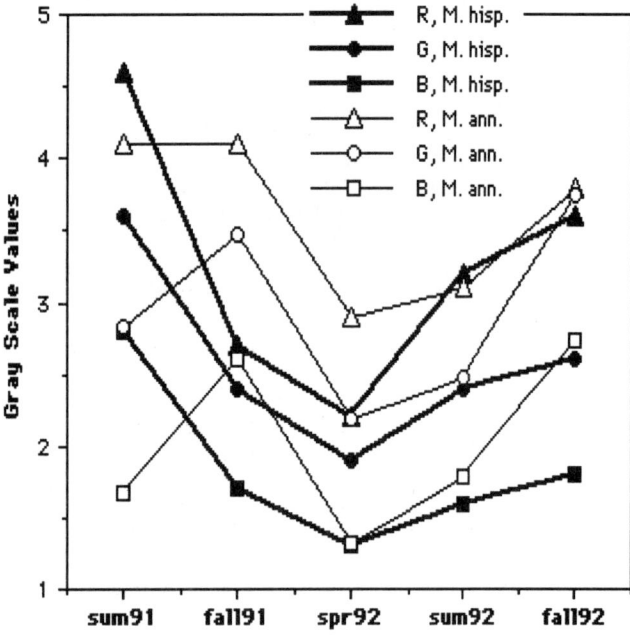

Fig. 4. Mean gray scale values for unbleached areas of *Montastraea annularis* (~3 m, thin lines) and *M. hispidula*; N = 4 colonies/species.

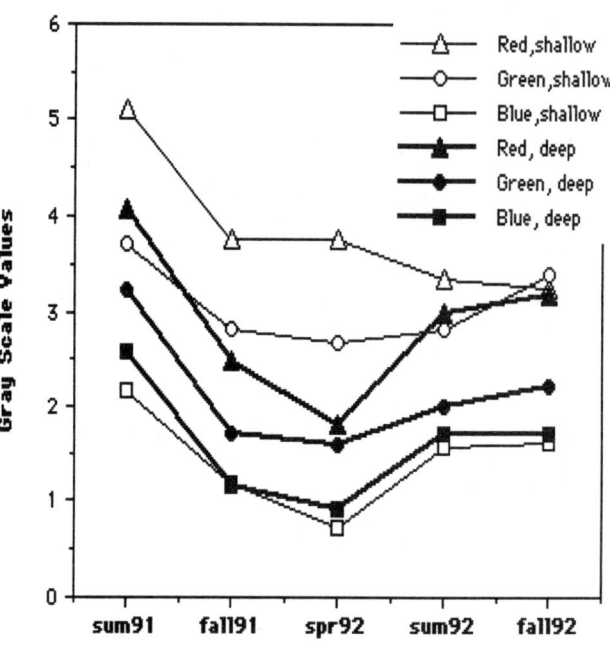

Fig. 5 Mean gray scale values for unbleached areas of *Porites astreoides* at ~3 m (thin lines) and at ~16 m (thick lines); N = 4 colonies/depth.

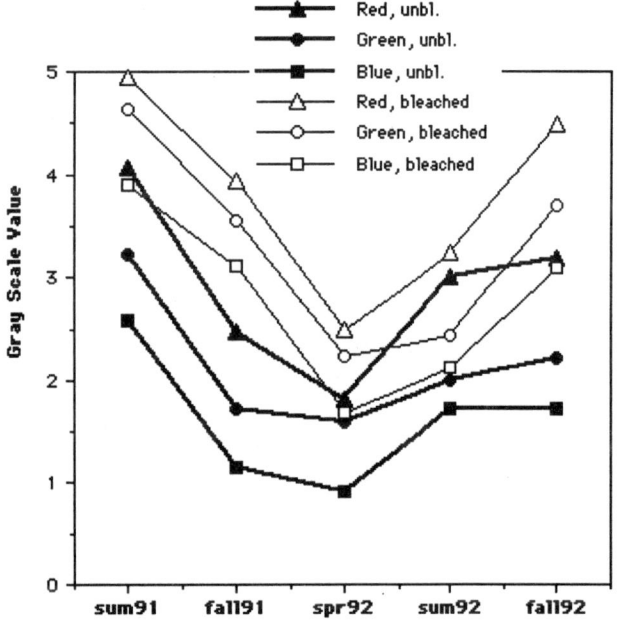

Fig. 6. Mean gray scale values for bleached (thin lines) and unbleached (thick lines) areas on colonies of *Porites astreoides* at ~16 m. N = 6 in Sum 91; 4 in Fall 91; 5 in Spr 92; 1 in Sum 92, 2 in Fall 92. Seawater temperatures in 1991 were somewhat warmer than in 1992 (7).

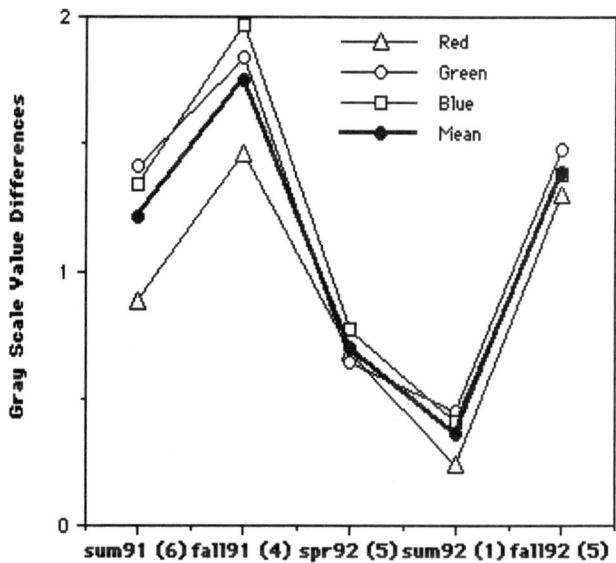

Fig. 7 Within-colony, mean gray scale difference values between bleached and unbleached parts of the colonies of *P. astreoides* shown in Fig. 6 and the mean color difference (R+G+B/3 of bleached - unbleached).

Quantitative effects of within-colony bleaching can be seen in the deeper *P. astreoides* in Fig. 6. Bleaching increased the brightness of each color, yet had little effect on coral color (the ratio between R, G and B), although the bleached areas often appeared nearly white in the photographs and to the unaided eye. Temporal differences in the brightness levels between bleached and unbleached portions of the deeper poritid colonies are shown in Fig. 7 where R, G, and B difference values and their means, (R+G+B)/3, are given. The larger difference values in parts of colonies that bleached in Fall 1991 than at any other period are consistent with macroscopic observations during this minor bleaching episode.

In the near future, we hope to address the underlying reasons for variable susceptibility to bleaching, especially in the deeper (~16 m) populations of *Porites astreoides*s. Possibilities include fine scale water circulation patterns or genetic variation of the coral hosts and/or their zooxanthellae (15, 16).

Acknowledgments

R. Dill, C. Gorham, M. Holzhausen, K. Sander and B. von Gunten are thanked for assistance in the field, R. Knight for the aerial overflight ,and E. Weil for identifications of *Montastraea*. Financial support of the Caribbean Marine Research Center and the National Undersea Research Program, NOAA, are gratefully acknowledged.

References

1. Birkeland, C. 1988. Geographic comparisons of coral-reef community processes. Proc. 6th Int. Coral Reef Symp. 1: 211-220.

2. Williams, E.H. and L. Bunkley-Williams. 1990. The worldwide coral reef bleaching cycle and related sources of coral mortality. Atoll Res. Bull. 335: 1-71.

3. Wells, S. M. (Ed.). 1988. "Coral Reefs of the World. Vol. 1: Atlantic and eastern Pacific." UNEP/IUCN.

4. D'Elia, C.F., R.W. Buddemeier and S.V. Smith, (Eds.). 1991. Workshop on Coral Bleaching, Coral Reef Ecosystems and Global Change: Report of Proceedings. Maryland Sea Grant College.

5. Peters, E.C. 1993. Diseases of other invertebrate phyla: Porifera, Cnideria, Ctenophora, Annelida, Echinodermata. pp. 393-449 in J.A. Couch and J.W. Fournie (Eds.), "Pathobiology of Marine and Estuarine Organisms". CRC Press.

6. Gates, R.D. 1990. Seawater temperature and sublethal coral bleaching in Jamaica. Coral Reefs 8: 193-197.

7. Wicklund, ,R.I., G.D. Dennis and K.W. Mueller. 1993. Summary of data from the water temperature monitoring network at Lee Stocking Island, Bahamas, 1988-1991. Caribbean Marine Research Center Technical Rept. Ser. 93-1.

8. Lang, J.C., R.I. Wicklund and R.F. Dill. 1988. Depth- and habitat- related bleaching of zooxanthellate reef organisms near Lee Stocking Islands, Exuma Cays, Bahamas. Proc. 6th Int. Coral Reef Symp., 3: 269-274.

9. Lang, J.C., H.R. Lasker, E.H. Gladfelter, P. Hallock, W.C. Jaap, F.J. Losada and R.G. Muller. Spatial and temporal variability during periods of "recovery" after mass bleaching on western Atlantic coral reefs. Amer. Zool. 32: 696-706.

10. Dustan, P. and J.C. Halas. 1987. Changes in the reef-coral community of Carysfort Reef, Key Largo, Florida: 1974 to 1982. Coral Reefs 6: 91-100.

11. Dustan, P. 1987. Preliminary observations on the vitality of reef corals in San Salvador, Bahamas. Proc. 3rd Symp. Geol. Bahamas, CCFL Bahamian Field Station: 57-64.

12. Carleton, J.H. and T.J. Done. 1992. Estimating relative abundance of coral reef benthos using video transects. 7th Int. Coral Reef Symp. Abstracts:15.

13. Done, T.J. 1982. Photogrammetry in coral ecology: a technique for the study of change in coral communities. Proc. 4th Int. Coral Reef Symp. 2: 316-320.

14. Biedny, D. and B. Monroy. 1991. The official Adobe Photoshop Handbook. Bantam.

15. Porter, J.W., W.K. Fitt, H.J. Spero, C.S. Rogers and M.W. White. 1989. Bleaching in reef corals: physiological and stable isotopic responses. PNAS 86: 9342-9346.

16. Jokiel, P.L. and S.L. Coles. 1990. Response of Hawaiian and other Indo-Pacific reef corals to elevated temperature. Coral Reefs 8: 155-162.

CONDENSED VERSION OF THIS PUBLISHED PAPER REPRINTED WITH
PERMISSION OF THE AUTHORS AND THE AMERICAN ZOOLOGIST

AMER. ZOOL., 32:625–640 (1992)

Quantification of Loss and Change in Floridian Reef Coral Populations[1]

JAMES W. PORTER AND OUIDA W. MEIER

Department of Zoology, University of Georgia, Athens, Georgia 30602

SYNOPSIS. Six coral reef locations between Miami and Key West were marked with stainless steel stakes and rephotographed periodically between 1984 and 1991. The monitored areas included two photostations in the Looe Key National Marine Sanctuary, two photostations in the Key Largo National Marine Sanctuary, and two photostations in the Biscayne National Park. Stations were monitored for species number, percent cover, and species diversity of the scleractinian and hydrozoan stony corals. Monitoring began in 1984 for photostations in the National Marine Sanctuaries and in 1989 for stations in the National Park.

All six areas lost coral species between the initial survey year and 1991. Survey areas lost between one and four species; these losses constituted between 13% and 29% of their species richness. Five of the six areas lost live coral cover. Based upon photographs taken repeatedly at these locations, net losses ranged between 7.3% and 43.9%. In the one station showing an increase in coral cover, the increase was only for the canopy branches of *Acropora palmata*; understory branches of this same species lost surface area at the same rate as canopy branches gained area. For most of the common species, there was a reduction in the total number of living colonies in the community, and a diminution in the number of large, mature colonies. Throughout the study period, there was no recruitment to any of the photostations by any of the massive frame building coral species.

Mortality of this magnitude is often associated with hurricane damage, but in this survey the losses occurred during a period without catastrophic storms. Sources of mortality identifiable in the photographs include (1) black band disease and (2) "bleaching"; other potential sources of mortality are also considered. We conclude, for our survey areas, that loss rates of this magnitude cannot be sustained for protracted periods if the coral community is to persist in a configuration resembling historical coral reef community structure in the Florida Keys.

METHODS

Monitoring methods

We use several methods to monitor each reef site. In photostation surveys, the primary goal is to identify the species of scleractinian corals and hydrocorals present and quantify their abundance. Chain transect surveys are used to determine the relative abundances of different substrate types as well as coral species. Video surveys of transects and photostations are also recorded to preserve information in digital format. Larger scale haphazard photographic surveys are used to determine whether the photostations are representative of the surrounding reef. Finally, a 1000 m² swim survey on each reef provides a virtually complete list of coral species present on the reef. Most of the data presented here are taken from photostation surveys. A major feature of our photostation method is that the boundaries of the actual areas sampled are permanently marked by stainless steel stakes cemented into holes drilled into limestone substrate so that the stations can be relocated.

---

[1] From the Symposium on *Long-Term Dynamics of Coral Reefs* presented at the Annual Meeting of the American Society of Zoologists, 27–30 December 1991, at Atlanta, Georgia.

Chain transects were established by stretching a 25-m line between two eyepins permanently cemented into the seafloor. Chains are attached to the 25-m line at the beginning of each meter, allowed to drop to the seafloor, and made to conform to the three-dimensional substrate directly below the 25-m line. The number of chain links overlying each different type of substrate are counted and recorded. This process is replicated three times for each transect. The effect is that of "slicing" through the reef and tracing the resulting outline. In this survey, all scleractinian corals and hydrocorals are identified to species. Other categories of organisms and substrate types were recorded, but are not considered in this paper. Three 25-m chain transects have been surveyed annually since 1989 in each of the Biscayne N.P. sites; one 25-m chain transect was surveyed in each of the N.M.S. sites beginning in 1991.

Photostations are set up on a four-stake system, with four stainless steel stakes cemented into the substrate defining the x- and y-coordinates of a 2.00 × 2.25 m (4.5 m^2) PVC frame which serves as a positioning grid. Rings to support the grid from underneath are slipped over the stakes and screwed in place at notches filed into the stakes so that the z-coordinates of the grid are defined as well. This grid provides the boundaries and supports for a smaller PVC camera frame) 0.50 × 0.75 m, or 0.375 m^2) with a 35 mm Nikonos V camera with a 28 mm underwater lens mounted 1.0 m above the plane of the frame. The camera frame outlines the actual two-dimensional area sampled with each photograph. Twelve photographs, each covering 0.375 m^2, are required to survey each 4.5 m^2 area. In each of the photostations at Carysfort and Looe Reefs, the 4.5 m^2 grid is laid down twice for a total area of 9.0 m^2 (24 photographs). In the photostations at Biscayne N.P., the grid is laid down three times for a total area of 13.5 m^2 (36 photographs).

Before 1991 the placement of the 4.5 m^2 grid in Carysfort and Looe Reefs was guided by two stakes that defined the corners along one side of the large frame during placement. In 1991 those photostations were improved by the implantation of stainless steel stakes that more precisely and repeatably define the z-axis, thereby bringing all photostations up to the same standard of the four-stake system for future surveys. All data presented here from Carysfort and Looe Reefs were collected from photographs using the two-stake system. The sites in Biscayne N.P. have been based since their establishment upon the four-stake system. The photostations on Looe Reef were surveyed in 1984, 1985, 1986, and 1991; Carysfort Reef photostations were photographed in 1984, 1985, 1986, 1988, and 1991; and Biscayne N.P. photostations were surveyed in 1989, 1990, and 1991.

The 0.50 × 0.75 m camera frame provides a reliable scale within each photograph that is accurate at the level of the frame. In order to create an objective measure of scale at the level of the substrate, in 1991 "scale pins" were added to all photostations: stainless steel rods measuring ¼" in diameter were driven into ³⁄₁₆" holes drilled into areas of bare, stable substrate and the distances between pins measured to the nearest 0.5 cm with tree calipers. A set of four pins was established within one frame of each set of 12 photographs.

In order to test whether our photostations are truly representative of the surrounding reef, we have conducted haphazard surveys of the areas in which our photostations are located. Using either a Hasselblad camera mounted on a 4 m^2 frame, or a Nikonos camera mounted on a 1 m^2 frame, photographs representing 60 to 100 m^2 were taken of the reef surrounding each photostation. The corals in these photographs were analyzed and quantified in the same manner as photographs from the photostations. This survey was performed once on each reef site for comparison with the coral composition of the corresponding photostation for that year, and is not repeated on a yearly basis.

Data analysis

The data collected by the chain transect method consists of an enumeration of coral species and substrate types, their sequence, and their length underneath the chain. Since there is some variation in the placement of the chain under the transect line (due to wave surge, etc.), every transect is counted three times within a one to five day period so that confidence intervals can be calculated for transect results. For each transect we calculate species richness, Shannon-Weiner species diversity, percent cover of coral species, and relative abundance of substrate types. Since we obtain three replicate counts for each transect each year, we are able to statistically compare these values between years. Since the transect length is 25 m, but the distance travelled by the chain over the length of the transect is greater than 25 m, this method also yields information about the three-dimensional topography of the reef, a parameter not directly described by our other sampling methods taken alone.

The photostation surveys are performed using Kodak Tri-X black and white negative film. Each survey is repeated with Kodak Ektachrome color slide film to produce a backup set of color photographs. Each photograph includes the outline of the camera frame, which carries identifying information on the specific reef site, frame number, and date of the photograph (see examples in Fig. 4). Coral colony and frame outlines are traced from prints onto mylar sheets, coral species are identified and assigned a unique colony number that can be followed through time, and the colonies are digitized.

Colony areas in the photographs represent projected surface area: that is, three-dimensional objects projected onto two dimensions in a non-orthographic fashion (objects closer to the camera appear to be larger than objects of the same size but further away from the camera). While orthographic surface area, the result of stereo photo images, would more accurately represent absolute percent cover (Done, 1981), both methods underestimate the biological surface area of a living coral. This is increasingly the case for colonies with greater three-dimensional relief, especially for a branching coral such as *Acropora palmata* where living tissue on the undersides of branches would not be visible at all, regardless of the photographic system employed. While projected surface area is a reasonable estimate of percent cover, it is true that estimates of change in coral cover by this method will be conservative.

The camera frame defines an area of 0.50×0.75 m at the plane of the frame, but because of the phenomenon of parallax, a photograph actually includes an area greater than 0.50×0.75 m below the plane of the frame down to the sea floor. Adjacent photographs therefore contain overlap. In order to ensure that individual colonies are counted and measured only once, the photographs are corrected for parallax. Areas of overlap in adjacent frames are removed by vertical and horizontal cut lines at the left and bottom edges of each camera frame where they overlap with the right and top edges of adjacent frames.

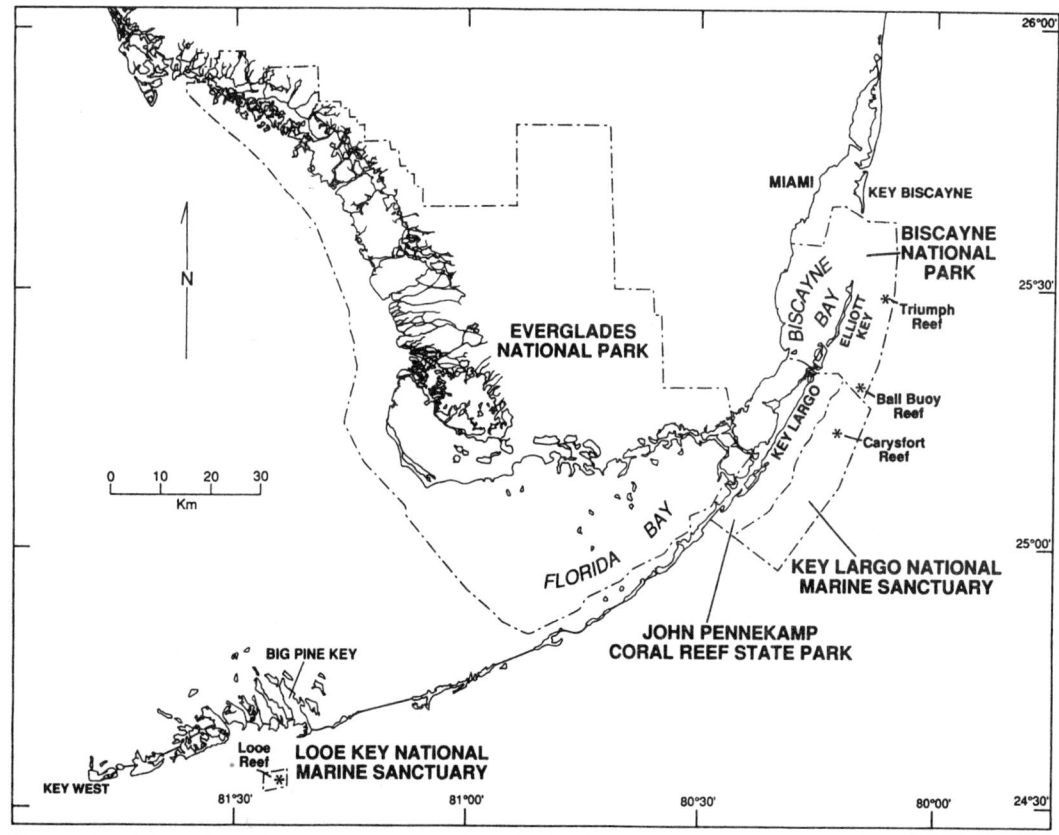

FIG. 1. Reef study sites. The locations and depths of the six photostations in this study are as follows: Biscayne National Park: Ball Buoy Reef (BP01), 3.1 m depth, and Triumph Reef (BP02), 6.0 m; Key Largo National Marine Sanctuary: two sites on Carysfort Reef, (CR01) 4.0 m and (CR02) 14.5 m; Looe Key National Marine Sanctuary: two sites on Looe Reef, (LR01) 5.5 m and (LR02) 7.7 m depth. The sites on Carysfort and Looe Reefs have been monitored since 1984, while the sites in Biscayne National Park have been monitored since 1989.

Cumulative species richness and percent cover are calculated on a frame by frame basis. Percent cover for individual species, cumulative species diversity (based either on the number of colonies of each species or the area covered by each species), and year to year comparisons for percent cover are analyzed on a colony by colony basis.

RESULTS

Changes in species number

The number of coral and hydrocoral species located in the photostations was lower in 1991 than in the initial year of sampling on every reef (Fig. 2). The rate of loss was usually higher in recent years than in earlier sampling years. The number of species lost varied between one and four; this translates into percentage losses varying between 13% and 29%.

Changes in percent coral cover

Percent cover of living coral declined in five of the six photostations and increased in one photostation between the initial year of sampling and 1991 (Fig. 3). Between 1989 and 1991, the change in projected surface area of coral in the Biscayne N.P. photostations was +30.2% (BP01) and −7.5% (BP02); in Key Largo N.M.S., coral change between 1984 and 1991 was −32.6% (CR01) and −7.3% (CR02); and in Looe Key N.M.S., coral change between 1984 and 1991 was −43.9% (LR01) and −13.2% (LR02) (Table 2).

Representative pairs of photographs from each reef site, taken in the initial sampling year and in 1991, are presented in Figure 4. The first pair of photographs, labelled "I BNP 5," is frame "5" (of 36) taken in Biscayne N.P. at site one (BP01). Evident in the photographs is increased growth of *Acropora palmata*, characteristic of that photostation alone. However, numerous protruding growths on *A. palmata* branches are also visible in 1991; it is not known whether these growths result from damselfish nips, or represent "tumors" (Peters *et al.*, 1986), or are an infestation of barnacles, polychaetes, or some other invertebrate. Two small bleached areas of *A. palmata* are also visible in the upper portion of frame 5, 1991. In the second pair of photographs, "II BNP 25" (or BP02, frame 25), a small colony of *Stephanocoenia michelinii* is present in the lower right corner in 1989; the dead skeleton of this colony is visible in 1991.

In the third pair of photographs, "I CR 4" (CR01, frame 4), cover of living *A. pal-*

mata decreases greatly from 1984 to 1991. In 1991, bared substrate has been colonized by turf algae, and numerous patches of the

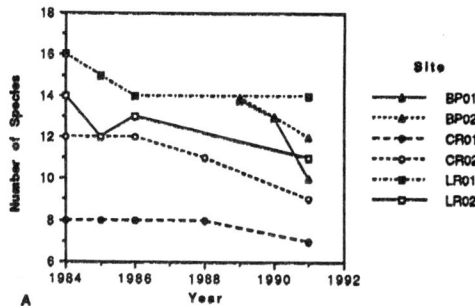

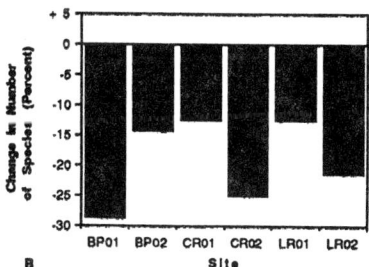

FIG. 2. Changes in species richness: number of species in each photostation during each sampling year (A) and percent change from initial survey year to 1991 (B). The initial survey year was 1989 for BP01 and BP02, and 1984 for all other photostations.

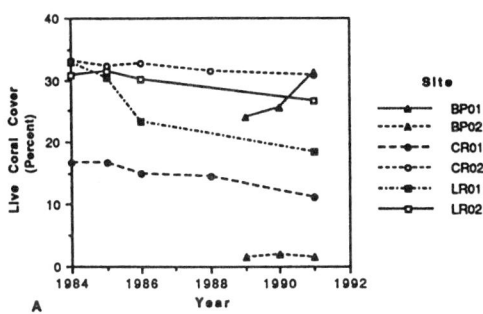

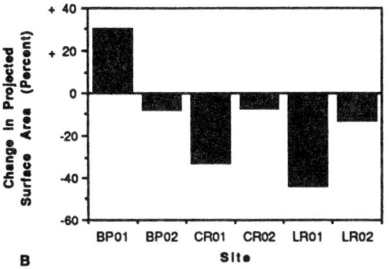

FIG. 3. Changes in percent cover of living coral: cover in each photostation during each sampling year (A) and percent change from initial survey year to 1991 (B). The initial survey year was 1989 for BP01 and BP02, and 1984 for all other photostations.

calcareous alga *Halimeda* are present. A light-colored zoanthid colony (*Palythoa*) is visible in the upper right of both frames. The primary event apparent in the fourth pair of photographs, "II CR 16" (CR02, frame 16), is partial mortality of a large colony of *Montastrea annularis*; photographs from intervening years show that the mortality occurred between 1988 and 1991. This colony "bleached" in 1987, "recovered" in 1988, but suffered partial mortality by 1991 (Fitt *et al.*, 1993).

The fifth pair of photographs, "I LR 3" (LR01, frame 3), shows the complete disappearance of a colony of *Acropora palmata*; the event occurred between 1986 and 1991. Colonies of *Montastrea annularis* and *M. cavernosa* that had been partially hidden by overtopping are visible in the 1991 photograph. The last pair of photographs, "II LR 15" (LR02, frame 15), shows partial mortality of a large *M. cavernosa* colony, which occurred between 1986 and 1991. A metal guide pin is visible in 1991; this pin was placed in 1984 into a small dead area of the coral head, but the size of the dead area remained stable through 1986, indicating that the placement of the pin was not the cause of mortality.

The map of the photostation with the greatest amount of coral loss (LR01) indicates heavy loss of the elkhorn coral, *Acropora palmata* (Fig. 5), while growth in the only photostation to exhibit overall increase in percent cover (BP01) was due primarily to growth of this same species.

Additional information from chain transects

The increase in projected surface area of *Acropora palmata* on BP01 requires examination in the context of additional information yielded by the chain transects for that site. As a measure of three-dimensional complexity, leaf area index for *A. palmata* was calculated and averaged for each year of the line transect survey on BP01 (Fig. 6). Leaf area index is calculated as the mean number of links covering living *A. palmata* tissue divided by the total number of chain links counted under meters containing *A. palmata* colonies. There was a significant decrease in leaf area index between 1989 and 1991, indicating a decrease in three-dimensional complexity during that period. Thus, while projected surface area of *A. palmata* increased on BP01 from 1989 to 1991 (Fig. 3), the leaf area index declined (Fig. 6), demonstrating that understory branches (those invisible to the camera) were lost. The total number of links covering *A. palmata* did not change during the three surveys, further demonstrating that as the canopy branches grew, the understory branches thinned. Casual observations in 1991 of fragments and broken branches of *A. palmata* lying on the seafloor support this finding.

Changes in size frequency distribution

Plots of the size frequency of selected species from Carysfort and Looe Reefs (Fig. 7) show consistent decreases in the number of large colonies of the most common species between 1984 and 1991. Total projected surface area at these sites of the species figured (*Acropora palmata, Montastrea annularis,* and *M. cavernosa*) also declined over this period. In some cases, the number of small colonies of a species increased (Fig. 7C, D), owing not to recruitment but to the death of areas within large colonies that resulted in several isolated smaller colonies. A species by species analysis of changes occurring in our study sites and the detectable events associated with these changes will be published elsewhere (Meier and Porter, in preparation).

DISCUSSION

Loss of species diversity

Changes in species number consistently indicate a loss of species diversity in each of the six reefs studied. In our plots, rare species were much more likely to suffer local extinction than common species. Since the species lost tended to be those that were relatively less abundant to begin with, their loss did not have a strong impact on total changes in percent cover. Superficially, this finding would appear to agree with models of reef development (Loya, 1976; Maguire and Porter, 1977; Connell, 1978) that predict a loss of rare species as community structure is increasingly dominated by branching corals that overtop and shade out competing understory species. This pattern was observed on shallow water reefs in Jamaica prior to Hurricane Allen (Porter *et al.*, 1981). The problem with this theoretical analysis when applied to the Florida data is that the branching corals were dying at the same time as the rare species were lost (Figs. 2, 4).

Loss of coral abundance

As Figure 3 indicates, shallow water reefs are capable of rapid increases in coral cover. The acroporid reef studied in Biscayne N.P. increased by an average of 15% of its initial abundance each year for the two year duration of the survey. The large losses identified instead for the other two acroporid reefs in the study are in striking contrast to this measured growth potential. The shallow reef surveyed on Looe Key lost 44% of its cover (Fig. 5); its counterpart on Carysfort lost 33% (Table 2). These kinds of losses among the branching coral community are normally associated with hurricanes (Stoddart, 1974; Porter *et al.*, 1981; Rogers *et al.*, 1982; Edmunds and Witman, 1991), but South Florida has been without a direct hit from a major hurricane for more than 26 years. Shinn (1989) points out that the usual frequency for hurricanes in the Keys is on average once every six to seven years. Two minor storms passed by the Florida Keys in 1985, Elena in September and Katie in November, and could have contributed to the elevated loss rates observed between 1985 and 1986. The photographs taken in 1986, however, reveal the presence of dead branches of *Acropora palmata* still standing, but without living tissue on them. The photographs also reveal living *A. palmata* that persisted through 1986 unbroken, including some large, highly branched colonies. Both of these observations suggest that storm damage was not the cause for coral loss between 1985 and 1986.

At first glance, the loss of understory branches from *Acropora palmata* in Biscayne N.P. (Fig. 6) might seem like the process of "self thinning" observed in plant populations (Harper, 1977). This process, however, has not been identified for calcium carbonate coral branches, and further, unlike trees, large coral branches "dropped" in this fashion could theoretically reattach and regrow, thus reappearing as new coral under the line transect even if invisible to an overhead camera. The line transect counts demonstrate definitively that this did not happen (Fig. 6).

Decline of both adults and juveniles

Changes in the size frequency distributions of colonies of *Acropora palmata* in Florida (Fig. 7A, B) show a decline in both large and small colonies between 1984 and 1991. In the seven years of the study, we have not identified any sexual recruitment of *A. palmata* to the population.

Like *A. palmata*, the head corals *Montastrea annularis* and *M. cavernosa* occur at depths strongly influenced by hurricanes (Woodley *et al.*, 1981; Edmunds and Witman, 1991), but since we did not record any major storms during the study period, the loss of these head corals also cannot be attributed to such physical disturbance. As with *Acropora*, there has been a steady diminution of the number of large colonies, but unlike *Acropora*, there has been an increase in the number of smaller sized colonies (Fig. 7C, D).

Increasing colony number was due entirely to "fission" events and partial mortality among larger coral colonies rather than to the appearance of sexual recruits. Observations of photographs in the sequence of sampling years indicate that most smaller colonies resulting from the breakup of larger colonies continued to decrease in size and eventually die. As with *Acropora*, no sexual recruits to the population were identified for either of the *Montastrea* species in any of our photostations.

Replacement of coral by algae

When living coral is lost from the photostations, it is replaced by substrates dominated by turf algae (Fig. 4). We have no evidence that the algae killed the coral, but rather assume that bared substrate is actively colonized by turf algae. Colonies of the blue-green alga *Lyngbya* were also present in 1991; this is the first time *Lyngbya* has been observed in any of our photostations. Black band disease, caused by another cyanobacterium, *Phormidium corallyticum* (Antonius, 1981a; Rutzler and Santavy, 1983), has also been observed in our photostations, particularly infecting *Montastrea annularis* and *M. cavernosa* colonies. In only one case was recovery from black band disease observed; in all other cases, the disease resulted in complete or partial mortality of the affected colony. Black band was much more prevalent on the southern reefs than on the northern reefs.

CONCLUSIONS AND RECOMMENDATIONS

Five of six reefs monitored declined in percent cover of living coral over the sampling period. All reefs declined in species number during this time. In some cases these losses were very high: the worst losses were 33% and 44% declines in coral cover over a seven-year period, and 25% and 29% declines in combined number of scleractinian and hydrocoral species over a seven- and two-year period, respectively. These rates of loss are obviously not sustainable over a long time period.

All research sites were located in protected areas: one national park and two national marine sanctuaries. That coral losses of the magnitude presented here occurred in protected areas indicates that current methods of protection do not prevent some significant sources of coral mortality. Even the recent expansion of the number of protected reefs with the establishment of the Florida Keys National Marine Sanctuary, for example, is not in itself adequate to halt the declines observed. Arguments for declines that occur with geological periodicity are not adequate to account for the rapid rates of decline measured here. Clearly, research is needed specifically to determine the cause or causes of coral decline. Such research programs should address: (1) the condition of corals on other reefs; (2) the role of visitor impact; (3) whether nutrient enrichment is occurring, and if so, the sources of the nutrients and their effects; (4) factors promoting infection and spread of coral disease; and (5) the status of algae and herbivores, including the sea urchin *Diadema antillarum*, other invertebrate grazers, and herbivorous fish.

The recent widespread die-off of the long-spined sea urchin, *Diadema antillarum*, (Lessios *et al.*, 1984) as well as anecdotal observations of decreases in herbivorous fish abundance, may be related to increased algal abundance that could compete with corals and their larvae for space (Birkeland, 1977; Sammarco, 1980; Carpenter, 1985). Incidents of bleaching, a response of corals to elevated sea surface temperatures, have been recorded from the Florida Keys during the past decade (including 1983, 1987, 1989, 1990, and 1991) (B. Causey, personal communication), and were occasionally observed in our photographs (Fig. 4, first plate, top); these occurrences did not necessarily result in death of the coral. Black band disease has also been observed in our photographs; this disease usually resulted in complete or partial mortality of the affected coral; in only one instance was recovery of *Montastrea annularis* from black band disease observed. Environmental stress or physical damage to corals may increase a colony's susceptibility to this disease.

Direct and indirect human impact may also be a factor in coral decline (Grigg and Dollar, 1990). Boat groundings, anchor damage, and diver damage to corals are possible sources of coral mortality, but are all controlled, at least to some extent, in our study sites by law enforcement officers and park rangers. Sources of indirect human impact resulting from development and use of the Keys include possible siltation, sediment resuspension pollution from harbors and boats, and potential problems of landfill containment and sewage disposal. The hypothesis of nutrification (Lapointe and Clarke, 1992) as a source of direct and indirect impact on coral and algal populations is certainly viable, and deserving of further study.

There is a need to monitor these reefs on multiple scales of both time and space. The processes requiring investigation occur on the level of the individual, the population, the community, the ecosystem, and the landscape; these processes have their range of variation on different temporal and spatial scales, and so sampling must occur on multiple temporal and spatial scales. In this case, one needs data of both fine-grained resolution and large scale, and the monitoring program must provide means of acquiring both if the ability to answer the most critical questions is not to be lost. Ogden *et al.* (1992) describe additional qualities desirable in an effective coral reef monitoring program. Currently even modest monitoring projects are grossly underfunded, and the long-term support essential to the success of a monitoring program is presently not within the operational time frame of funding agencies.

The current state of knowledge is inadequate to determine the long-term effects of the changes in the coral community observed in this study. Recovery times for these species at these locations are not known; neither are the community dynamics underlying processes of change and potential recovery. Though one expects that management decisions take into account information provided by studies such as this, we caution against overinterpretation of our results for management purposes: we have not measured the rates of change on other reefs, and we do not know definitively what causes are responsible for the present changes observed on these study reefs.

NOTE ADDED IN PROOF

On August 24, 1992, Hurricane Andrew passed through Biscayne National Park, producing some damage to stations BP01 and BP02 in the Park, and to CR01 in the Key Largo National Marine Sanctuary. An analysis of the effects of Hurricane Andrew will be presented elsewhere, but we note here that the loss in percent cover of living coral on some reefs over a period of seven years was much greater than losses experienced by reefs as a result of this class 4 hurricane. Every survey stake and eyepin in our photostations survived intact.

REEF FISHES AS INDICATORS OF CONDITIONS ON CORAL REEFS

Ernst S. Reese

Department of Zoology and the Hawaii Institute of Marine Biology, University of Hawaii,
Honolulu, Hawaii 96822

ABSTRACT

The abundance, distribution and behavior of coral feeding butterflyfishes, Family Chaetodontidae, serve as indicators for the assessment of ecological conditions on Pacific coral reefs. Species belonging to the corallivore feeding guild are the best indicator species. They are conspicuous, diurnally active, and their behavior is measured easily, even by relatively unskilled observers. They tend to be strongly site attached and territorial, predictable in their movement patterns, and long-lived, making them long-term, permanent residents of the living coral reef. Since they live on the reef, shelter on it at night and feed on living coral during the day, they are intimately associated with the reef. Since reef fishes are mobile, but corals are not, changes in the abundance, distribution and behavior of the coral feeders indicate changes in ecological conditions on the reef. The method is useful where perturbations to the reef are occurring slowly but chronically. A sensitive indicator method is not needed to detect massive, episodic changes to the reef. The method is useful to detect changes over time on a specific reef. It is not appropriate to compare conditions on two or more reefs at the same point in time because differences in the butterflyfishes on the reefs may be due to other processes such as recruitment. It is an inexpensive and easily implemented method which promises to be useful to assess long-term, slow but chronic changes to coral reefs. Currently studies are in progress simulating this kind of change. The application of the method to coral reefs in the Caribbean is discussed.

INTRODUCTION

The idea of using the butterflyfishes as indicators for conditions on coral reefs grew out of observations leading to the conclusion that coevolution, in the broad sense, may have occurred between corals and their predators, especially the obligate coral feeding butterflyfishes (Reese, 1977). The idea was developed further citing evidence from two species of Pacific obligate coral feeders, *Chaetodon trifascialis* and *C. trifasciatus*, which show changes in their abundance, distribution and behavior in response to conditions on coral reefs (Reese, 1981).

Continuing studies on the behavioral ecology of a number of species of butterflyfishes at Enewetak Atoll, Marshall Islands, and in Hawaii, provide a wealth of information on the social use of space, particularly territoriality, and their feeding biology including the functional morphology of their teeth and jaws and preferences for different species of corals as food (Hourigan, 1987, 1989, 1991; Irons, 1989, 1990; Kosaki, 1989; Motta, 1980, 1985, 1988, 1989a; Reese, 1975, 1989, 1991; Tricas, 1985, 1986, 1989a, 1989b). A wealth of information on butterflyfishes is available in a series of review papers edited by Motta (1989b).

From these studies the following characteristics of butterflyfish biology and behavior, relevant to the indicator hypothesis, are evident:

1. Many species of coral feeding butterflyfishes live in small areas of the reef, home ranges or territories, in heterosexual pairs.

2. Many of these species are permanent, long-lived (8 to 10 years) inhabitants of their home reefs. Thus, the time-frame is adequate to experience slow, chronic changes.

3. Within their social unit of space, they forage following predictable paths, but they occasionally make long excursions to remote locations on the reef. This is an important observation because it means that they are familiar with the reef beyond their immediate home range or territory. Thus, if conditions should become extreme, they are capable of emigration out of their home area of the reef.

4. Species which are obligate coral feeders fall into two catagories, generalists and specialists. The generalist feed on corals in the same proportion as their abundance in the environment in contrast to the specialists which feed preferentially on certain species of corals regardless of their abundance on the reef.

5. The jaws and teeth of these species are finely adapted to nip off and ingest by suction the coral polyps without damaging the calyx of the coral skeleton. This careful mode of feeding allows the coral polyp to regenerate, and thereby the fish's food resources are constantly replenished within its feeding territory.

6. The territory size is determined by two factors: food and competitor intrusion. The territory must be large enough to supply both fishes of the heterosexual pair with sufficient food yet small enough to defend against intruders.

7. Experimental removal of one member of the pair has two possible outcomes. If the male is removed, the female cannot defend the territory by herself and she disappears unless a "floater" male forms a new pair bond with her. If the female is removed, the male may try to take over the female of an adjacent pair or he abandons the territory. There do not seem to be "floater" females in the population.

8. Experimental manipulation of the food in a territory has two results. If food is removed by covering coral heads, the resident pair tries to enlarge their territory at the expense of their neighbors, and this causes the rate of agonistic encounters to increase and feeding rates to decrease. If food is added to the territory, there is no immediate result. The resident pair does not reduce the size of their territory to compensate for the additional food. But within a day or two adjacent pairs learn of the extra food and make efforts to enlarge their territories, and again we see an increase in agonistic encounter rates.

The close relationship between the coral feeding butterflyfishes and the living corals of the reef is clear. The experimental manipulations illustrate that changes result in a disruption of the *status quo* of their social behavior.

Based on these findings, the hypothesis under study can be stated as follows: coral feeding butterflyfishes respond to changes in coral quality and/or abundance by making adjustments in their abundance, distribution and behavior on the reef which are easily and rapidly quantified (Hourigan *et al.* 1988).

METHODS

Field Observations

Almost all of the research described in this paper involves direct observation of butterflyfishes on the coral reefs of Hawaii, with supplemental studies in other locations such as Enewetak Atoll, Johnston Atoll and Madang, Papua New Guinea. It is necessary to use scuba, but depths are usually about 10 m so it is possible to make up to four hour-long dives in one day. Fortunately, butterflyfishes are diurnal so all work is done during daylight hours. Since reef fishes don't "behave" under conditions of high turbulance and surge and poor visibility, most work is done under favorable weather conditions. Because the flourishing coral reefs on which we work are at depths of about 10 m, surface weather conditions directly affect the underwater conditions.

Measurements. At each study site four 30 m transects are established. The configuration depends on the reef's contour. For example, on an expansive reef of fairly uniform coral cover, a star-burst pattern is used. If the reef is a system of raised coral ridges or a narrow reef front, the transects are placed in a parallel pattern. Since we are interested in living corals and coral feeding butterflyfishes, the transects are placed in areas of high coral cover.

The next step is to count the numbers of each species of butterflyfish within 5 m of either side of the transect lines. This is followed by identifying the species of coral at 0.5 m intervals along each transect line. Abundance, distribution and diversity of the corals and the fishes are calculated.

Next, depending on which species of butterflyfish is selected as the focal species, a minimum of three pairs are chosen along the transect and their territories are measured. This is done by observing the pair during five 10-minute periods and placing nails coded with colored surveyors tape at the limits of their foraging excursions. The number of observation periods may be greater for species with large home ranges or territories. An experienced observer is able to count agonistic interactions with both conspecific intruders as well as those with other species during these 10-minute periods. Thus, territory boundries and encounter rates are measured during a single dive. On the next dive, feeding rates are measured during three 10-minute periods and the territory size is measured during the remaining portion of the dive. To measure feeding rates, the observer focuses on one member of the pair and notes each time the fish bites and the species of coral being fed upon. Feeding is recorded sequentially providing information on the rate of feeding, the corals fed upon, and the sequence of corals fed upon.

The territory is measured by stretching a surveyor's tape across the shortest axis of the territory delineated by the color coded nails, and then at each meter the lateral extensions to the territory boundry are measured. The territory size is the sum of these measurements. The method does not take into account rugosity of the reef's surface but it is appropriate for within group comparisons.

Data are recorded on sheets of plastic underwater paper attached to clipboards. Changes in absolute values of the parameters measured may indicate changes occurring on the reef. Conventional statistical analyses are used to determine whether the changes in the measured parameters are significant.

Simulation Experiments: A series of experiments are underway which attempt to simulate a slow deterioration of the condition of corals in order to determine the behavioral response of the coral feeding butterflyfishes within whose territory the corals are located. Meter square pieces of shade cloth attached to metal frames are positioned over the reef so that the corals beneath are shaded but the fish are able to swim under the shade cloth to feed. There are two independent variables: the number of frames per territory and the length of time the frames are left in place. By adding frames to a territory the amount of coral perturbed is increased and the longer the frames are left in place, the longer the corals are shaded. The two dependent variables are the behavior of the territorial pair of fishes and the condition of the corals. Feeding rates of the butterflyfishes on the shaded corals are measured directly. Corals are sampled to determine if there is a decrease in their lipid content and caloric value over time due to the shading effect.

These experiments are underway but we have no results to report. I have described this experimental approach for purposes of critical discussion of this case history at the colloquium.

RESULTS

Since much of this research currently is underway and is incomplete, the results are piecemeal, incomplete, and somewhat inconclusive. First, I will describe cases which are directly relevant to the indicator hypothesis, and then I will describe the results of the on-going research in Hawaii.

At Enewetak Atoll, Marshall Islands, the obligate coral feeder *Chaetodon trifascialis* is abundant. Individual fish hold territories which are always based on the coral *Acropora confertus* and *A. hyacinthus* (Reese, 1981). Often males and females hold territories adjacent to one another. One study site on a lagoon pinnacle supported a lush growth of *Acropora* corals and nine territories of *C. trifascialis*. In 1972 Enewetak was battered by a typhoon which destroyed the corals and no butterflyfishes were seen until five years later when a few small heads of *Acropora* and a single, small *C. trifascialis* were seen.

A similar observation was made at Yanuka Island lying off the south coast of Viti Levu, Fiji, in 1985. An abundance of dead and overturned large heads of *Acropora* and other corals attested to the devastating effects of both typhoons and predation by Crown-of-thorns. None of the obligate coral feeding butterflyfishes, known to frequent the reefs of Fiji, were seen. There is a similar story for Fagatele Bay, American Samoa (M. Crosby, personal communication). A flourishing coral area, known to support an assemblage of obligate coral feeding butterflyfishes, was ravaged by a typhoon and Crown-of-thorns and on a subsequent inspection trip very few butterflyfishes were seen.

Compared to these cases as well as other areas in the central and western Pacific such as Guam, Okinawa, the Great Barrier Reef and Tahiti, all of which have experienced damage to coral reefs from either or both typhoons and

Crown-of-thorns with a resultant decrease in the associated fish assemblages, recent storms, such as Hurricanes Iwa and Iniki, in Hawaii have not caused extensive damage to the coral reefs we are studying in Kaneohe Bay, Island of Oahu, Puako, Island of Hawaii, and sites on Kaho'olawe. Therefore, I have no first hand accounts of damage to the corals and the associated butterflyfishes. This is not to say that Hawaiian reefs were not impacted by these storms. Those more directly exposed to the full force of these storms were damaged.

Of greatest relevance to this case history is our current research at Kaho'olawe Island. This uninhabited Hawaiian island was used as a military target from World War II until about 1991 when target practice ended. Due to the effects of the bombardment and especially to the effects of overgrazing by a population of feral sheep, much of the vegetation was destroyed and wind and water eroded soil was deposited on the coral reefs along the northwest coast of the island.

We have established two study sites on Kaho'olawe. One is on the northeast coast where the effects of siltation are minimal and coral cover and diversity are relatively high. Similarly the coral feeding chaetodontids are well represented by four species (Table 1). The second study site is located in a reef area on the northwest coast of the island in an area heavily impacted by silt. Here the coral occurs on ridges perpendicular to shore. Abundance, percent coral cover, and diversity are all less than at the first site, and the coral feeding butterflyfishes are represented by a single species, *Chaetodon multicinctus* (Table 1).

TABLE 1

Comparison between two Coral Habitats at Kaho'olawe Island, Hawaii

	Hakioawa Site (low sediment)	Kuheeia Site (high sediment)
Common Coral Species	*Porites compressa* *P. lobata* *Montipora patula* *M. verrucosa* *Pavona varians* *Pocillopora meandrina*	*Porites compressa* *P. lobata* *Montipora patula* *M. verrucosa* *Pavona varians* *Pocillopora meandrina*
% Coral Cover	80-85 (N=3)	45-65 (N=3)
Common Corallivore Butterflyfishes (Genus *Chaetodon*)	*C. multicinctus* *C. ornitissimus* *C. trifasciatus* *C. unimaculatus*	*C. multicinctus*
$\bar{x}$ Territory Size (m^2) Pairs of *C. multicinctus*	84.5 (N=4)	63.3 (N=3)

Preliminary results indicate that feeding rates by the most abundant obligate coral feeding butterflyfish, *C. multicinctus*, on the most abundant species of corals, *Porites compressa* and *Montipora patula*, at both sites are comparable.

Comparisons of encounter rates for interactions between both conspecifics and other species are inconclusive. It appears that chasing rates between adjacent pairs of *C. multicinctus* at the sediment impacted site are higher suggesting that territorial boundaries are still being established. The pairs of *C. multicinctus* tend to be smaller at this site.

An interesting, unexpected, and I believe significant result of this study is that the relative absence of non-corallivore, but benthic invertebrate feeding species of butterflyfishes, such as the usually ubiquitous *Chaetodon auriga* and *C. miliaris*, indicates the scarcity of benthic invertebrates due to silt filling up the holes and crevices of the reef which under normal conditions provide shelter for these organisms. Indeed silt may be up to 30 cm deep and is fine enough to be readily suspended in the water column by a diver swimming over it. During data collection fine particulate sediment settles out on the writing slate even when the observer is working on top of the coral ridges.

Because the shading experiments are underway, we do not have results to report. Preliminary observations, however, on the behavior of the fish indicate that they rapidly habituate to covering coral heads with cloth. In fact, they behave as if they know where the coral head is located under the cloth and try to get under the cloth to feed. Therefore, we do not anticipate problems with the fish feeding under the shade-cloth frames.

DISCUSSION

A simple truth emerges: the more living coral in a habitat, the more coral feeding butterflyfishes are present. The relationship between coral diversity and butterflyfish diversity is less clear. In the Kaho'olawe study the six common species of corals are present at both sites. Coral cover is greater at the low sediment site (Hakioawa) than at the high sediment site (Kuheeia) even though the transects were placed in what appeared to be coral rich areas at both sites. Thus, the sediment filled valleys at the Kuheeia site are ignored in this study. Nevertheless, only *Chaetodon multicinctus* is common at the Kuheeia site, while four species of corallivores are present at the less disturbed site with *C. multicinctus* being the most abundant.

Surprisingly territory sizes of *C. multicinctus* are larger in the low sediment Hakioawa site in spite of higher coral cover. This may be due to the fish being larger at the low sediment site. In addition it may reflect the effect of overlapping home ranges and territories of the other coral feeders present at this site (Kosaki, 1991).

From inspection of preliminary data, agonistic chasing interactions between adjacent, territorial pairs of *C. multicinctus* appear to be higher at the high sediment site. The fish are smaller, and there are more solitary, unpaired juveniles present as well. A possible explanation is that the population of *C. multicinctus* at this site is more transitory and that newly settled recruits are forming pair bonds and trying to establish territories. Thus, at this moment in time, intruder interactions may be playing a greater role in determining territory size than food availability.

With respect to evidence from episodic events such as storms and crown-of-thorn damage to coral reefs, it is clear that these events affect the associated fish assemblages and that butterflyfishes belonging to the corallivore trophic guild are greatly impacted.

Until the results of the simulated coral damage study are in hand, it is not possible to say whether the corallivores simply stay on the reef and die because they are so strongly territorial and site attached, or whether they emigrate from the reef as it deteriorates. This result is extremely important to the use of these coral feeding butterflyfishes as indicator species, because the indicator hypothesis assumes that the fish are able to sense the deteriorating condition of the corals, possibly due to a decrease in the lipid content and caloric value of the polyps. The hypothesis further assumes that initially the fish try to expand their territories resulting in changes in feeding rates, agonistic encounter rates, and territory sizes. Eventually territorial behavior becomes unprofitable as the costs of defence exceed the trophic benefits, and as the social order of the reef breaks down, the fish emigrate from the moribund reef.

A word of caution is necessary. Even if the scenario described above proves to be true, the indicator idea is only valid when it is applied to a specific reef area, suspected to be undergoing low levels of slow, chronic perturbation. It should also be sensitive to detect recovery of a specific coral reef. The concept is not useful in comparing one coral reef with another, because differences in the assemblage of coral feeders on different reef may be due to other casual factors such as recruitment.

Within the Indo-Pacific faunal region, the use of coral feeding butterflyfishes shows great promise (Nash, 1989; White, 1989), but care must be exercised to use only those species which are obligate coral feeders and which are both abundant and common on the reef to be assessed.

How applicable is the indicator hypothesis to coral reefs outside of the Indo-Pacific faunal region? With respect to the Caribbean, butterflyishes probably are not good candidates as indicator species because they are not obligate coral feeders (Birkeland and Neudecker, 1981; Gore, 1983, 1984). Angelfishes, however, may be a good substitute since certain species feed on sponges and sponges are an important component of Caribbean reefs (Hourigan et al 1989).

CONCLUSIONS

1. Obligate coral feeding butterflyfishes are excellent candidates as indicators for ecological conditions on Pacific coral reefs.

2. The indicator hypothesis predicts that butterflyfishes respond to changes in coral abundance and quality by making adjustments in their abundance, distribution and behavior.

3. Sensitive biotic indicators are useful where changes are occurring slowly as a result of slow, chronic perturbation of the reef.

4. Once suitable indicator species are identified, the monitoring program is inexpensive and easily learned by non-specialists. Thus, it is useful in many coral reef areas of the world where funds for conservation and management may be scarce.

5. The definitive experiments to determine to what extent and how the indicator species respond to perturbations of the reef are underway.

ACKNOWLEDGEMENTS

The indicator hypothesis is based on a wealth of information about butterflyfishes collected by my graduate students, past and present. I am deeply indebted to Tom Hourigan, Darby Irons, Randy Kosaki, Javier Mendez, Phil Motta and Tim Tricas.

Support for this research has come from a variety of sources over the years: the Department of Zoology and the Hawaii Institute of Marine Biology of the University of Hawaii, the U.S. Department of Energy, the Sanctuaries and Resources Division of the National Oceanic and Atmospheric Administration, and Mauna Lani Resort, Inc. I thank Mrs. Sally Oshiro for typing the manuscript, and I thank my colleagues at the University of Hawaii and Dr. Michael Crosby of NOAA for many stimulating discussions.

LITERATURE CITED

Birkeland, C. and S. Neudecker. 1981. Foraging behavior of two Caribbean chaetodontids: *Chaetodon capistratus* and *C. aculatus*. Copeia 1981 (1):169-178.

Gore, M.A. 1983. The effect of a flexible spacing system on the social organization of a coral reef fish, *Chaetodon capistratus*. Behaviour 85:118-145.

Gore, M.A. 1984. Factors affecting the feeding behavior of a coral reef fish, *Chaetodon capistratus*. Bulletin of Marine Science 35(2):211-220.

Hourigan, T.F. 1987. The behavioral ecology of three species of butterflyfishes. Ph.D. Dissertation, University of Hawaii, Honolulu. 496 pp.

Hourigan, T.F. 1989. Environmental determinants of butterflyfish social systems. Environmental Biology of Fishes 25(1-3):61-78.

Hourigan, T.F. 1991. Dietary specialization in coral-feeding butterflyfishes: consequences for behavior and community structure. Ecology International Bulletin 19:103-118.

Hourigan, T.F., T.C. Tricas and E.S. Reese. 1988. Coral reef fishes as indicators of environmental stress in coral reefs, pp. 107-135. In *Marine Organisms as Indicators*, D.F. Soule and G.S. Kleppel, eds., Springer Verlag, New York.

Hourigan, T.F., F.G. Stanton, P.J. Motta, C.D. Kelley and B. Carlson. 1989. The feeding ecology of three species of Caribbean angelfishes (family Pomacanthidae). Environmental Biology of Fishes 24(2):105-116.

Irons, D.K. 1989. Temporal and areal feeding behavior of the butterflyfish, *Chaetodon trifascialis*, at Johnston Atoll. Environmental Biology of Fishes 25(1-3):61-78.

Irons, D.K. 1990. The natural history and behavioral ecology of the butterflyfish, *Chaetodon trifascialis*, at Johnston Atoll. MS Thesis, University of Hawaii, Honolulu. 89 pp.

Kosaki, R.K. 1989. Predation by *Chaetodon trifasciatus* and growth and distribution of *Pocillopora damicornis* at Coconut Island, Oahu, Hawaii. Pacific Science 43(2):195(abstract).

Kosaki, R.K. 1991. Patterns of resource use an aggressive interaction among three species of coral-feeding butterflyfish (Chaetodontidae). Pacific Science 45(1):94(abstract).

Motta, P.J. 1980. Functional anatomy of the jaw apparatus and the related feeding behavior of the butterflyfishes (Chaetodontidae) including a review of jaw protrusion in fishes. Ph.D. Dissertation, University of Hawaii, Honolulu, 435 pp.

Motta, P.J. 1985. Functional morphology of the head of Hawaiian and mid-Pacific butterflyfishes (Perciformes, Chaetodontidae). Environmental Biology of Fishes 13(4):253-276.

Motta, P.J. 1988. Functional morphology of the feeding apparatus of ten species of Pacific butterflyfishes (Perciformes, Chaetodontidae): an ecomorphological approach. Environmental Biology of Fishes 22(1):39-67.

Motta, P.J. 1989a. Dentition patterns among Pacific and Western Atlantic butterflyfishes (Perciformes, Chaetodontidae): relationships to feeding ecology and evolutionary history. Environmental Biology of Fishes 25(1-3):159-170.

Motta, P.J. (editor) 1989b. *The Butterflyfishes: Success on the Coral Reef*, Kluwer Academic Publishers, Boston. 256 pp.

Nash, S.V. 1989. Reef diversity index survey method for nonspecialists. Tropical Coastal Area Management 4(3):14-17.

Reese, E.S. 1975. A comparative field study of the social behavior and related ecology of reef fishes of the family chaetodontidae. Zeitschrift fur Tierpsychologie 37:37-61.

Reese, E.S. 1977. Coevolution of corals and coral feeding fishes of the family Chaetodontidae. Proceedings, Third International Coral Reef Symposium, University of Miami, Miami, Florida 1:267-274.

Reese, E.S. 1981. Predation on corals by fishes of the family Chaetodontidae: implications for conservation and management of coral reef ecosystems. Bulletin of Marine Science 31(3) 594-604.

Reese, E.S. 1989. Orientation behavior of butterflyfishes (family Chaetodontidae) on coral reefs: spatial learning of route specific landmarks and cognitive maps. Environmental Biology of Fishes 25(1-3):79-86.

Reese, E.S. 1991. How behavior influences community structure of butterflyfishes (family Chaetodontidae) on Pacific coral reefs. Ecology International Bulletin 19:29-41.

Tricas, T.C. 1985. The economics of foraging in coral-feeding butterflyfishes of Hawaii. Proceedings of the Fifth International Coral Reef Congress, Tahiti 5:409-414.

Tricas, T.C. 1986. Life history, foraging ecology, and territorial behavior of the Hawaiian butterflyfish, *Chaetodon multicinctus*. Ph.D. Dissertation, University of Hawaii, Honolulu, 247 pp.

Tricas, T.C. 1989a. Determinants of feeding territory size in the corallivorous butterflyfish, *Chaetodon multicinctus*. Animal Behaviour 37(5): 830-841.

Tricas, T.C. 1989b. Prey selection by coral-feeding butterflyfishes: strategies to maximize the profit. Environmental Biology of Fishes 25(1-3):171-185.

White, A.T. 1989b. The association of *Chaetodon* occurrence with coral reef habitat parameters in the Philippines with implications for reef assessment. Proceedings, Sixth International Coral Reef Symposium, Townsville, Australia, 2:427-431.

REEF MONITORING IN MALDIVES AND ZANZIBAR: LOW-TECH AND HIGH-TECH SCIENCE

Michael J. Risk[1], Jennifer J. Dunn[1], William R. Allison[1,2] and Chris Horrill[3]

[1]Department of Geology, McMaster University, Hamilton, Ontario, Canada L8S 4M1
[2]Marine Research Section, Male, Republic of Maldives
[3]Institute of Marine Science, Zanzibar, Tanzania

ABSTRACT

Most reefs are in tropical Third world nations, where the sophisticated technology developed by western scientists is often inappropriate. We have used a mix of low-tech and high-tech monitoring methods to evaluate the degree of stress in two Indian Ocean reef tracts: the Maldives and Zanzibar. In both countries, the most likely source of stress is sewage. Low-tech methods include community descriptions and coral growth rate determinations. Affected sites in both countries had lower coral cover and diversity, higher numbers of associates, and higher growth rates. Fish communities were very different, in Zanzibar, between stressed and unstressed reefs. High-tech methods also detected reef stress through sewage. Heavy metal values were low. Analysis of coral tissue via HPLC at Maldives showed differences in stressed sites. Stable Nitrogen isotope ratios are often elevated in areas of high sewage stress. The continuing success of such monitoring programs depends on the involvement of local counterparts, and long-term commitment by development agencies.

INTRODUCTION

The future of reefs is too important to be left to scientists. Most of the world's coral reefs lie adjacent to Third World nations, yet most of the scientists who do research on reefs live and work in the developed world. Much of the research that we do is irrelevant to reefs in the global sense, given the resources and political will required to implement the results. The real reef custodians are inhabitants of Third World countries, dependent on reefs for their livelihood. It is incumbent on them to preserve the reef resources as well as possible, but they are frequently hindered by lack of political will, financial resources, and educational levels. Over the next decade, our ability to preserve reefs will be largely dictated by the degree to which researchers can make their results useful and meaningful to the reef custodians.

At present, reef monitoring and assessment work in the Third World usually involve some combination of foreign experts working with local ministries or NGO's. The ideal situation, of course, is to train sufficient numbers of the local inhabitants in appropriate techniques that the presence of the expatriates becomes unnecessary. The most effective way to approach these programs is to combine high-tech and low-tech methodology. Low-tech in this sense does not mean lacking in rigour, or in effectiveness; instead, it refers to survey and assessment techniques that are based in sound ecological principles, require no expensive equipment, and are capable of being used by persons with little formal training. Examples would be line and transect data, organism counts, and growth rate studies. The results of low-tech measurements are uniquely useful, in that they can usually be understood by politicians and policy makers. In many cases, however, the particular problems facing a reef may be differentiated and evaluated only through the use of high-tech methods, usually some type of chemical analysis. The integration of these two approaches must be carefully done if the results are to have any impact. In this Case History, we report on two development projects, in areas where coral reefs are critically important to the wellbeing of the populace, in which both low-tech and high-tech approaches were integrated into comprehensive reef assessment schemes.

Figure 1. Location of projects in the Indian Ocean.

The Maldives is a chain of atolls stretching south in the Indian Ocean from near the southwest tip of India (Fig. 1). Of the total population of 210,000, perhaps as many as 80,000 live in the capitol, Male, an island on the rim of North Male Atoll with an area of about 2 square kilometres. Fishing and tourism are the major industries. Although the fishery is almost exclusively based on tuna, the baitfish are taken off patch reefs and the best tuna fishing is near atolls. The Maldivian diet is higher in protein than any in the world, almost all of which comes from one species: skipjack tuna. Tourists come to snorkel and dive on the magnificent coral reefs, for which the Maldives are famous. This is a nation which lives on coral and survives from coral.

Zanzibar is the largest coralline island off the coast of East Africa. Fringing reefs surround the island, and are especially well-developed on the eastern, seaward, coastline. The population of Zanzibar numbers 500,000. The economy is based on agriculture and fishing, although there is increasing emphasis on tourism. Most of the proposed tourism developments are along the coast, and will feature the lure of East African fringing reefs. Most of the fisheries are based on the reefs, and 80% of the animal protein eaten by the Zanzibaris comes from the sea. Zanzibar is a coral island, depends on the reefs for its food, and looks to reef-oriented tourism for its future.

In both study sites, there were early signs of stress on the reefs, and a growing local concern. Following requests to Canadian development agencies, we assessed the health of the reefs in both of these localities, with the help of personnel from local government agencies. To begin with, we were able to predict which of the main reef destroying agents were most likely to be operating. Probably the greatest threat to reefs, worldwide, is siltation (Cortes and Risk, 1985). The highest point on the Maldives is 2 metres above sea level, and there are no rivers. Zanzibar is only slightly less flat, having a maximum relief of just over 100m, and has a few small streams. Siltation is not likely to be a major stress on reefs, at either location. Similarly, there is some degree of concern about industrial contamination on reefs (although a cause-and-effect relationship has yet to be identified), but neither site has any industrial development to speak of. The sea water in both locales is not subject to large fluctuations in salinity or temperature. That leaves only one of the major causes for anthropogenic reef death: sewage.

All the sewage from Male is discharged, untreated, on or near the reef that forms the atoll rim. Preliminary investigations suggested that the level of coral cover at Male was lower than it should be. The atoll may have passed from a constructive to a destructive phase. Zanzibar, on the other hand, was reputed to have such a sewage based effluvium in the last century that it could be smelt long before it could be spied: its nickname among sailors was "Stinkybar". The situation has improved remarkably over the past century, but the sewage from the town is still not treated, and is discharged out to sea. Fisheries statistics suggest that the reefs are already severely overfished. The focus of the projects at both sites, therefore, was to assess the extent of degradation, and to determine whether a "smoking gun" could be found, linking this to sewage contamination. The results had to be cast in politically intelligible terms, so that they could input at the policy-making level. At all stages, the involvement of local scientists and technical staff was essential.

In this paper, we report the results from two monitoring projects that successfully combined low-tech field science with high-tech laboratory analyses. The videotapes used in all the transects, and the coral slabs used for analysis, are archived at McMaster University. The methods used are explained in more detail in Risk and Scott, 1991 and Dunn, 1993.

METHODS

Field Measurements (Low-Tech)

Coral Community Assessment.—

Coral communities were assessed with line transects, using point intercepts and plumb bobs to avoid parallax error. Sample sites were located randomly within study areas, and at each site a minimum of 4 transects were surveyed, at least 20m long. Each transect was archived on videotape after having been surveyed. Videotapes were used to verify questionable coral identifications. Standard tests were employed to assess and minimize between operator error.

Associate counts.—

Coral associates are defined as commensals, epizoans, epiphytes, and internal bioeroders. The number of coral associates increases as the corals come under increasing stress. In both countries, density of associates was counted using small quadrants placed against the corals. Only one operator performed these counts. In Zanzibar, we also estimated the density of sea urchins (Diadema) by randomly placing a meter-square quadrat frame on the bottom, and having two operators independently count all urchins with more than half their body in the frame. A minimum of twenty quadrants were scored per site. Maldives associate data were taken by P.J.B. Scott, using slightly different methodology. Although these results are less precise than those for Zanzibar, they are comparable.

Growth rates.—

In both countries, a minimum of eight colonies of Porites lobata were sampled at each study site, from the same depth and orientation. The tops of all heads were marked before removal from the substratum. Corals were rinsed in fresh water and air dried. Thin slabs were sawn down the growth axes, and X-rayed to determine growth rates. In Maldives, this was done at the local hospital; the Zanzibar slabs were brought back to Canada.

Fish community comparisons (Zanzibar only).—

Because of the concern about overfishing on Zanzibar, we assessed fish community structure by visual band transects, with corrections for operator presence. Fish assessment was done on snorkel, to avoid disturbing the subjects.

Chemical Analyses

Coprostanol.—

Coprostanol is a sterol which results from the breakdown of cholesterol. As such, it is an excellent marker for the presence of human fecal waste. Most previous studies have analyzed the coprostanol content of sediments, but in Maldives we analyzed the coral tissue. Samples were taken of Porites lobata at Male and a comparison site. There were no local freezing or freeze drying facilities, so the samples were dried in a drying oven (3-4 days at 60 degrees) and carried back to the lab. Laboratory analysis with HPLC followed the scheme outlined in Krahn et al., 1989.

Heavy Metals.—

Colonies of Porites lobata spanning at least 20 years' growth were taken at Male and also at a comparison reef. The heads were slabbed in the field with a carbide handsaw, dried, and carried back to Canada. In the lab, the corals were further slabbed with a diamond saw, X-rayed, and subsampled for metal analysis. We analyzed for Hg, Cu, U, Sn, V, Cr, Al, Cd and Zn by ICP/MS, using the method of standard addition. The same corals were analyzed for Hg in the labs of the Bedford Institute of Oceanography, and for Pb, Zn, Cd and Cu by high-precision XRF at the University of Western Ontario.

Stable Isotope Ratios: ^{15}N and ^{13}C.—

Stable isotope ratios have become an important technique in geochemistry (Arthur, 1983), but rarely have been used in a coral reef setting. Briefly, the stable isotope ratios of Carbon, ^{13}C, give an indication of the relative inputs of terrestrial and marine organic carbon. In many settings, this is also an estimate of distance from shore. The Nitrogen ratio, ^{15}N, gives an indication of trophic status. ^{15}N has been used as a sewage tracer in several marine and fresh water studies (Sweeney and Kaplan, 1980; Coakley et al., 1992), but its application to reef systems is so far limited (Allison et al., 1991). Samples of the outer parts of colonies of P. lobata were taken in both countries, at affected and comparison sites. The samples were immediately dried and carried back to Canada. In the laboratory, they were decalcified with dilute HCl, with the reaction poisoned to prevent bacterial breakdown. The resulting decalcified coral tissue was centrifuged, freeze dried, and analyzed following the methods described in LeBlanc et al. 1989.

RESULTS AND DISCUSSION

Scientific Results

In both countries, the coral diversity and cover were greatly reduced on affected reefs, as opposed to comparison reefs (Fig. 2). Coral associate densities were also much higher, in both countries, on the affected reefs (Table 1). In Zanzibar, there were particularly striking differences between the two sites in density of sea urchins. These results simply demonstrate the extent of deterioration of the affected reefs as compared to other reefs, which themselves may also be affected.

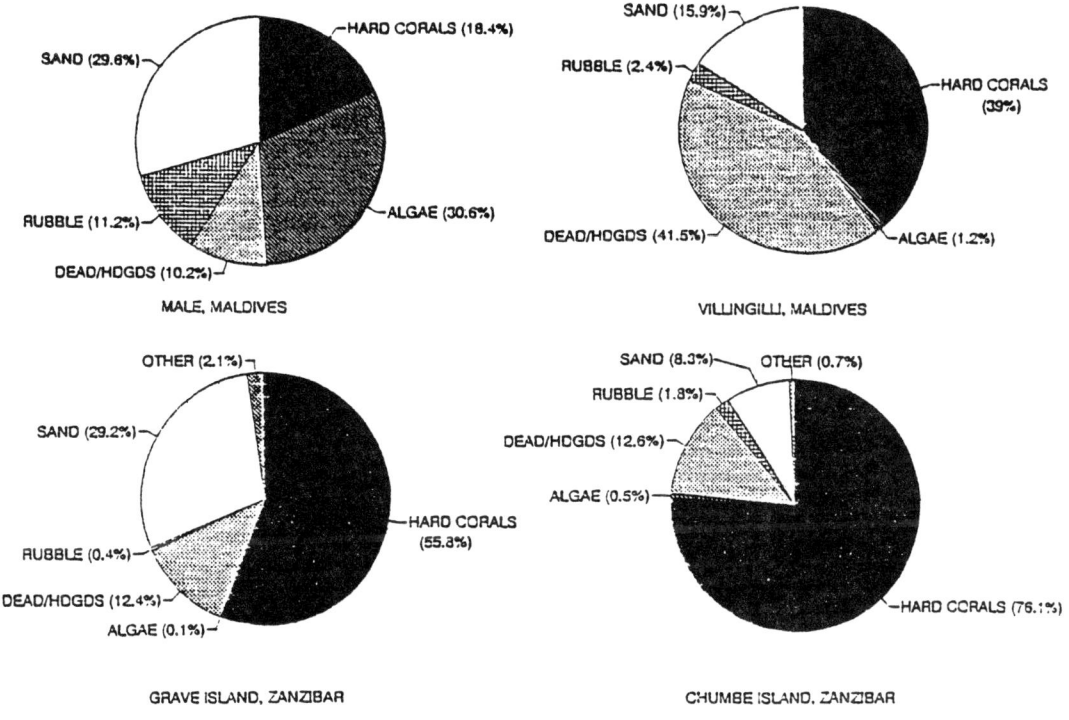

Figure 2. Pie charts of benthic communities at affected and comparison sites in Maldives and Zanzibar. In both countries, the diversity and cover of coral are less at affected sites.

	MALDIVES			ZANZIBAR	
	Affected sites (North Male Atoll)	Comparison sites (Addu Atoll)		Affected site (Grave)	Comparison site (Chumbe)
% of heads infested by associates	90%	60%	Average associate densities/m^2	2013	752
Average # of associate taxa per coral head	2.7	1.4	Average <u>Diadema</u> density/m^2	6.4/m^2	1.2/m^2

Table 1. Numbers of coral associates in <u>Porites</u> heads at affected and comparison sites in Maldives and Zanzibar. In both countries, corals at affected sites had more associates.

The growth rate data showed the same interesting trend from both sites. In a lot of previous reef monitoring work, the implicit assumption has been that coral growth rate will decrease as a function of stress. This certainly seems the case with reefs under siltation stress (Cortes and Risk, 1985; Risk et al., in press). Sewage stress, however, represents a nutrient enrichment. Corals may be largely autotrophic, but they are capable of taking up large amounts of dissolved organic matter as an additional food source. An individual coral head may be able to shift between autotrophy and heterotrophy, depending on the environment.

At both sites, the growth rate of corals at affected sites was higher than at comparison sites, although the overall coral cover was much less. The same phenomenon has also been reported by Tomascik and Sander, 1985. This may reflect what has been termed the "Janus Effect" of nutrients on corals (Edinger, 1991), in which nutrient enrichment enhances coral growth rates up to a critical level, at which the eutrophication suddenly becomes deleterious. The remaining <u>Porites</u> heads at Male may be the last, heterotrophic-prone survivors of nutrient enrichment, against which Janus has as yet to change his mask. On Zanzibar, variance in the growth rate data was very high, because the sampled population seemed made up of two sub-populations. One group of corals grew very fast, while the other grew progressively more slowly over the past decade. It may be that the slow-growing individuals were locked into autotrophy, unable to use the dissolved food source, and soon will succumb to overgrowth by algae.

On Zanzibar, the fish community at the stressed site was very different from that on the comparison site. Density of predators was very low, and there were more small herbivores.

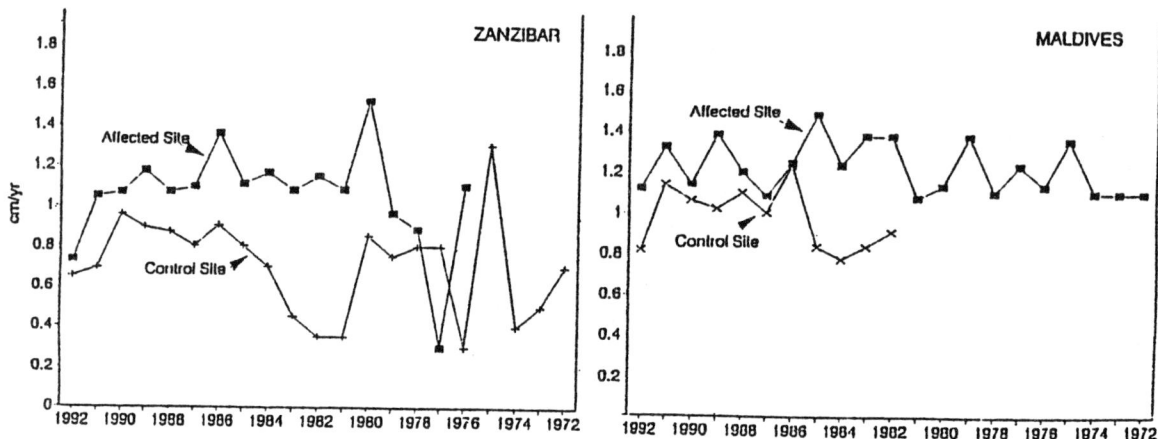

Figure 3. Coral growth rates at affected and comparison sites in Maldives and Zanzibar. The growth rates are higher at sites affected by sewage loading.

Coprostanol was not found in the corals from Male. It may be broken down by the corals' digestive processes, and hence not incorporated into the tissue. More likely, however, it wasn't there to be found. The Maldivian diet, as explained earlier, is virtually unique, in that the overwhelming proportion of the protein comes from tuna. This is almost a cholesterol-free diet. On the other hand, there were large differences in the fatty acid signatures between Male and comparison sites, and corals taken offshore form the fuel dump for the airport showed elevated hydrocarbon values.

The metal values were, in all cases, at or near detection limits, and showed no trend with time. Neither site has a lot of heavy industry, nor large concentrations of possible contamination from antifouling paint, so these results were as expected.

^{15}N values were significantly higher in Male corals than in the comparison corals (Table 2). In Zanzibar, although the average value at the affected site was higher, the difference between sites was not significant. ^{13}C values were essentially the same in all cases. These results indicate that ^{15}N has great potential for assessing sewage loading in reef ecosystems.

	δ^{13}C		δ^{15}N	
	Mean	Std.Dev.	Mean	Std. Dev.
Maldives				
Affected Site (Male)	-11.9	0.9	7.2	0.3
Comparison Sites	-11.4	0.7	5.8	0.5
Zanzibar				
Affected Site (Grave)	-9.9	0.77	4.21	0.25
Comparison Site	-10.7	0.98	4.17	0.45

Table 2. ^{15}N and ^{13}C at affected and control sites in Maldives and Zanzibar. The d^{15}N differences in Maldives are highly significant. The differences in ^{15}N between affected and comparison sites at Zanzibar are not significant.

Development Results: Sustainability

Initially, there is generally great interest in the setup and early results of monitoring programs such as we have described here. Interest in what we have termed the Low-tech methods is very high, because meaningful results can be obtained with little equipment, and in some cases relatively unskilled personnel. The largest problem is lack of taxonomic expertise.

Long term continuation is much more problematic. Most of the time, the local counterparts will be employees of government agencies with their own itineraries, which will often have to act in response to local pressures and priorities. Our counterparts have all too often been dragged off in response to real or fancied government emergencies, damaging continuity of the monitoring. Even more demoralizing is the withdrawal of support from a donor nation, partway through a project. Sustainable reef monitoring programs in the Third World can only be achieved via demonstrated long term commitment, using individuals with both scientific smarts and cultural sensitivity.

CONCLUSIONS

1. High-tech and low-tech methodologies usually complement each other in reef monitoring work, giving similar answers to the same questions.

2. Transect and growth rate data are sufficient to characterize a reef as being affected, and yield politically useful data.

3. Stable isotope ratios of Nitrogen, ^{15}N, show great promise in assessing sewage stress on a reef.

4. To institute sustainable reef monitoring projects in Third World countries requires commitment, cultural sensitivity, and scientific ability.

ACKNOWLEDGEMENTS

For help in the field, we thank Gwenn French, Gerard Faure, Hussain Zahir, Daude Mukaka, Cam Lewis, Evans Edwards and Zaha Wahid. Our work in Maldives would have been impossible without the assistance of Hassan Maniku, of the Marine Research Section, and his helpful staff; on Zanzibar, the joint McMaster-Guelph project was in conjunction with the Institute of Marine Science, whose Director, Dr. Magnus Ngoile, was a tower of strength. Partial funding of the analytical results came from NSERC Operating grants to MJR. Both the Maldives and Zanzibar projects were funded by the International Centre for Ocean Development (ICOD). This agency was abolished by the Canadian Government in March, 1992, an example of the lack of long term foresight which hinders well-conceived development projects. ICOD's administrative constipation will not be missed, but they funded some excellent work. We thank the people of Zanzibar and the Maldives, with whom and for whom this work was performed.

LITERATURE CITED

Arthur, M.A.. 1983. Stable isotopes in sedimentary geology. SEPM Short Course #10. Dallas.

Coakley, J.P., J.H. Carey and B.J. Eadie. 1992. Specific organic components as tracers of contaminated fine sediment dispersal in Lake Ontario near Toronto. Hydrobiologia 235/236:85-96.

Cortes, J.N. and M.J. Risk. 1985. A reef under siltation stress: Cahuita, Costa Rica. Bull. Marine Science 36:339-356.

Dunn, J.J. 1993. Effect of sewage on fringing reefs of Zanzibar. Unpub. B.Sc. thesis, Geology, McMaster Univ.

Edinger, E.N. 1991. Mass extinction of Caribbean corals at the Oligocene - Miocene boundary: Paleoecology, Paleoceanography, paleobiogrography. Unpub. M.Sc. thesis, Geology, McMaster Univ.

Krahn, M.M., C.A. Wigren, L.K. Moore and D.W. Brown. 1989. High-performance liquid chromatography method for isolating coprostanol from sediment extracts. J. Chromatography 481:263-273.

LeBlanc, C.G., R.A. Bourbonniere, H.P. Schwarcz and M.J. Risk. 1989. Carbon isotopes and fatty acids analysis of the sediments of Negro Harbour, Nova Scotia, Canada. Estuarine, Costal and Shelf Science 28:261-276.

Risk, M.J. and P.J.B. Scott. 1991. Final report on ICOD Contract #439: Establishment of a coral reef research unit for the Maldives. 20 p. plus 13 Appendices.

Risk, M.J., F. VanWissen and J. Carriquiry. 1993. Sclerochronology of Tobago corals: a record of the Orinoco? Seventh Int. Coral Reef Symposium, Guam. (In press).

Sweeney, R.E. and I.R. Kaplan. 1980. Tracing flocculent industrial and domestic sewage transport on San Pedro Shelf, Southern California, by nitrogen and sulphur isotope ratios. Marine Environmental Conservation 3:215-224.

Tomascik, T. and F. Sander. 1985. Effects of eutrophication on reef-building corals. Marine Biology 87:143-155.

STATUS AND RECENT HISTORY OF CORAL REEFS AT THE CARICOMP NETWORK OF CARIBBEAN MARINE LABORATORIES

Struan R. Smith[1] and John C. Ogden[2] (Editors), Pedro M. Alcolado[3], David Bone[4], Phillippe Bush[5], Jorge Cortes[6], Jaime Garzon-Ferreira[7], Richard Laydoo[8], Hazel A. Oxenford[9], Joe Ryan[10], Joth Singh[11], John Tschirky[12], Francisco Ruiz[13], Susan White[14], and Jeremy Woodley[15]

[1]Bermuda Biological Station, Ferry Reach, GE01 Bermuda, [2]**Florida Institute of Oceanography, 830 First Street South, St. Petersburg, Florida 33701 USA, [3]Instituto de Oceanologia de la Academia de Ciencias de Cuba, Calle ira. no. 18400, Playa, Habana, Cuba, [4]Instituto de Technologia y Ciencias Marinas, Universidad Simon Bolivar, Apartado Postal 89051, Caracas, Venezuela, [5]Natural Resources Unit, P.O. Box 486GT, Grand Cayman, Cayman Islands, British West Indies, [6]CIMAR, Universidad de Costa Rica, San Pedro, Costa Rica [7]Instituto de Investigaciones Marinas de Punta de Betin, Apartado 1016 Santa Marta, Colombia, [8]Institute of Marine Affairs, Hilltop Lane, Chaguaramas, P.O. Box 3160, Carenage Post Office, Trinidad and Tobago, [9]Bellairs Research Institute, Holetown, St. James, Barbados, [10]Instituto de Recursos Naturales, Apartado 5123, KM 12 1/2, Carretera Norte, Managua, Nicaragua, [11]Caribbean Environmental Health Institute, The Morne, P.O. Box 1111, Castries, St. Lucia, [12](Carrie Bow Cay, Belize) Smithsonian Institution, National Museum of Natural History, Washington, DC 20560, USA [13]Instituto de Ciencias del Mar y Limnologia, Estacion Puerto Morelos, Universidad Autonoma de Mexico, Apartado Postal 1152, Puerto Morelos 77500, Q.R., Mexico, [14]Saba Marine Park, Fort Bay, P.O. Box 18, The Bottom, Saba, Netherlands Antilles, [15]Discovery Bay Marine Laboratory, P.O. Box 35, Discovery Bay, Jamaica. **Address for correspondence.

ABSTRACT

Fourteen of 19 Caribbean marine laboratory members of the CARICOMP (Caribbean Coastal Marine Productivity) network responded to a questionnaire requesting qualitative information on the historical and present status of the coral reefs selected for long-term research in the program. Eight of the 14 sites indicated that coral cover had recently declined. While much of the loss was attributed to natural events, nutrient-loading, sedimentation, and over-fishing were also implicated. Six sites reported algal cover as medium to high (10 - >30%), the suspected result of reduced herbivory by over-fishing, Diadema mortality, and nutrient-loading. Nine of the sites reporting are located in marine parks, preserves, or areas of restricted access. Generally, coral cover has remained stable at these sites, except where threatened or damaged by direct tourist impact or distant forest clearing causing coastal sedimentation. This observation should encourage grass roots educational efforts as well as legislation to mitigate human impact on reefs. The long-term observations on these reefs sites which began in late 1992 under the CARICOMP program will help to discriminate between natural variability and human impact and assist in sustained regional coral reef management.

INTRODUCTION

There is little question that the coral reefs of the world are in decline from the impact of expanding human populations in the tropical coastal zone (Wells, 1988, Wilkinson, in press). The reefs of the Caribbean Sea and adjacent waters, about 12% of the global total area (Smith, 1978), are perhaps under the greatest threat given the small size of the Caribbean and its regional interconnection by ocean currents. Deforestation, leading to increased runoff and sedimentation, increased nutrients from sewage, over-fishing, and coastal construction and mining, have all been frequently cited as contributing causes (Ogden and Gladfelter, 1986; Rogers, 1985).

Human impacts on reefs are superimposed on long-term changes brought about by natural factors including storms and hurricanes (Woodley et al., 1981; Ogden, 1992), white- and black-band diseases (Gladfelter, 1982; Rutzler and Santavy, 1983), and coral bleaching and other suspected manifestations of global climate change (Smith and Buddemeier, 1992; Brown and Ogden, 1993). Reef herbivore populations have declined in the Caribbean, primarily through the die-off of the long-spined sea urchin Diadema antillarum in 1983-84 and over-fishing (Lessios et al., 1984; Hay, 1984; Rogers, 1985). The reduction in grazing by herbivores at some locations has resulted in increased algal abundance that inhibits coral growth and recruitment (Hughes, 1989). Clearly, the structure of a coral reef in any particular location will be the result of the long-term interplay between human-induced and natural factors. There is a growing conviction that interdisciplinary studies conducted over the full range of regional development of coral reefs will provide the best opportunity to discriminate between these two factors so that the success of management of human impact may be evaluated (Ogden, 1987).

In response to the need for long-term, region-wide comparative studies of the biodiversity and productivity of Caribbean coastal ecosystems, the CARICOMP (Caribbean Coastal Marine Productivity) program began at a workshop held at Discovery Bay Marine Laboratory in 1985 where the scientific and management rationale for a cooperative research network of Caribbean marine laboratories was established and an international Steering Committee was selected (Ogden and Gladfelter, 1986). The Steering Committee subsequently negotiated a Memorandum of Understanding (MoU) with 19 laboratories in 15 countries specifying the responsibilities of the laboratory to the network and the contribution of the program in equipment and logistical support. In 1990 and 1992 workshops were held at the University of the West Indies (UWI) in Jamaica to draft the Level I Ecosystem Monitoring Methods Manual consisting of a minimum number of observations and simple equipment which would permit all of the laboratories to participate. A Data Management Center (DMC) was established at the UWI, Kingston.

The CARICOMP program began collecting data in the fall of 1992 on the biodiversity of coral reefs, seagrasses, and mangroves as well as physical parameters according to the protocols in the Level I Methods Manual. These data are sent to the DMC and distributed to the participating laboratories on a quarterly basis. An annual program summary will be published in a regional scientific journal. The DMC also coordinates regional investigations of transient oceanographic, biological, and meteorological phenomena and serves as a clearing house for new ideas and methods.

At the December 1992 meeting of the CARICOMP Site Directors in Jamaica, it was agreed that a "snapshot" of coral reef status at the sites selected by the network and a qualitative impression of reef dynamics in the recent past would be informative both as a baseline for the start of CARICOMP program and also to indicate potential trends in Caribbean coral reefs that might help other research projects. This report was compiled from the responses received to a questionnaire sent to all 19 CARICOMP network laboratories. Five members of the network were unable to respond in time for this publication.

THE CARICOMP REEF MONITORING SITES

The locations of the CARICOMP monitoring sites range throughout the Caribbean, including low and high latitude reefs, from Barbados to Bermuda and from the Antilles to Central America (Figure 1, Table 1). Several types of reef systems in different environmental settings are represented in the program: reefs adjacent to low and high islands, reefs adjacent to continents, windward and leeward exposure conditions, and areas of frequent and rare hurricane activity. All the sites have key references that describe the coral reef communities at their sites, summarized in Wells (1988). However, very few sites had monitoring programs for reef communities or biological, physical oceanographic or climatic variables prior to the start of the CARICOMP Program (Table 1).

STATUS OF THE CARICOMP REEF SITES

Fourteen laboratories reported on the status of their reef systems and, to varying degrees, the health and status of important biological groups: (1) the abundance and constituents of the coral communities and other important sessile biota, (2) algal cover (3) abundance of the important grazer, the sea urchin Diadema antillarum, and (4) the general state of reef fish communities and the level of fishing effort. The respondents also indicated the extent of recent or historical perturbations, either natural or anthropogenic. These data are summarized in Table 2 and are discussed below.

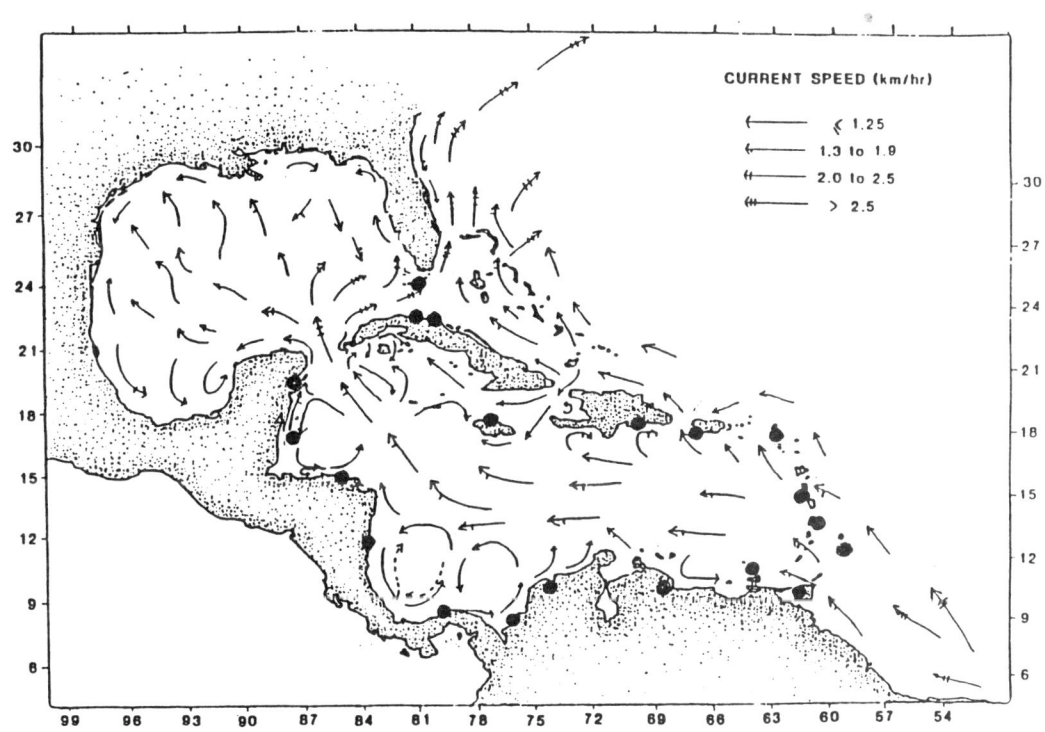

FIGURE 1: Map of the Caribbean showing the locations of the CARICOMP coral reef monitoring sites

SITE	LAT./LONG.	LOCATION	MONITORING
Barbados	13°15'N/59°30'W	Folkestone Park	N
Belize	16°47'N/88°5'W	Carrie Bow Cay	Y
Bermuda	32°27'N/64°50'W	Hog Breaker	Y
Grand Cayman	19°23'N/81°17'W	Rum Point	N
Colombia	74°08'N/11°19'W	Chenque Bay	N
Costa Rica	9°45'N/82°48'W	Parq. Nat. Cahuita	N
Cuba	22°2'N/78°12'W	Key Paredon Grande	N
Jamaica	18°13'N/77°25'W	Discovery Bay	Y
Mexico	20°56.3'N/86°50.6'W	Puerto Morelos	N
Nicaragua	12°10'N/83°W	Gr. Corn Island	N
Saba	17°38'N/63°16'W	Saba Marine Park	N
St. Lucia	13°51'N/61°5'W	Grand Caille Point	N
Tobago	11°11'N/60°51'W	Buccoo Reef	N
Venezuela	10°50'N/68°12'W	Parq. Nat. Morrocoy	.N

TABLE 1. Location of CARICOMP reef sites and status of monitoring programs.

Table 2. Status and history of changes on the CARICOMP coral reef sites.

Location	Depth (m)	Exp.[1]	Coral Community[2] (Dominant spp.)	Coral Cover	Disturbance[3] Events	Algal[4] Cover	Diadema Abund.	Fish[5] Community	Fish[6] Press	Other[7] spp.	Status[8]
Barbados	1-10	L	Ss,Pa,Aa,Ma,Mc	↓	H,S,P	L	↑	?	↑ , ↓	?	↓ , ?
Belize	11-15	W	Pp,Ma,Aa,Ac,Mm	↔	H,D	M	↓	Ac,Po,Sc	↓ , ↑	G,Sp,Z	↔
Bermuda	7-8	W	Ds,Dl,Ma,Pa,Mc	↔	B	L	↓	Sc,Ac,Ky	↑ , ↓	G	↔
Cayman	10	W	Ma,Mc,Ds,Dl,Ss	↔	H,B	L-M	↓	Sc,Ac,La	↓ , ↓	G	↔
Colombia	3-7	W	Ac,Ap,Mm,Ss,At	↓	D,Dy,B,S	M, ↑	↓	?	↓ , ↑	Sp,G	→
Costa Rica	7-10	W	Ss,Aa,Pp,Ds,Mcp	↓	B,H,S,P	H	↓	?	↓ , ↓	?	→
Cuba	10-13	W	---	---	H	---	↓	---	---	---	↔
Jamaica	10-12	W	Ma,Aa,Pp,Dl,Mc	↓	H,B,D	H	↓	Po,Sc,Ac,Sr	↓ , ↑	Sp,G	→
Mexico	0-20	W	Mal,Mcp,Mc,Dc	↓	H	H	↓	La,Ac,Sc	↓ , ↑	G,Sp,?	→
Nicaragua	14	W	Ma,Pa,At,Ap,Aa	↓?	P,Bl,H	M-H	↓	?	↑ , ↑	G	→
Saba	10	L	Ma,Ap,Ac,Mc,Ds	↔	B,H	M	↑	ScSr,Bl,Lt	↓ , ↓	Sp,G	↔
St. Lucia	10	L	Ma,Cn,Mm,Dl,Mal	↔	B	L	↓	Po,My	↑ , ↓	Z,SP,Cr	↔
Tobago	9	L	Ma,Dc,Ss,Aa,Dl,Mal	↓	D,B,H,P,S	L	↓	Ac,Bl,Sc,Lb	↓ , ↓	Sp	→
Venezuela	3-13	L	Ma,Mcp,Cn,Mc,Ap	↓	D,Bl	L	↓	?	↓ , ↓	Z,G,Sp	↔

[1]W=windward, L=leeward. [2]Corals: Ma=M.annularis, Mc=M.cavernosa, Mal=M.alcicornis, Mcp=M.complanata, Mm=M.mirabilis, Ac=A.cervicornis, Ap=A.palmata, Aa=A.agaricites, At=A.tenuifolia, Ds=D.strigosa, Dl=D.labyrinthiformis, Dc=D.clivosa, Ss=S.siderea, Cn=C.natans, Pa=P.astreoides, Pp=P.porites. [3]Disturbances: B=bleaching, H=hurricane, D=disease, Dy=dynamite, S=sedimentation, P=pollution. [4]Macro-algal coverage: L=low (<10%), M=medium 10-30%, H=high (>30%). [5]Fish families; Sc=Scaridae, Ac=Acanthuridae, Po=Pomacentridae, Sr=Serranidae, Ky=Kyphosidae, La=Labridae, Bl=Balistidae, Lt=Lutjanidae. [6]Fishing Pressure: first arrow=historical, second=present status. [7]Dominant invertebrate taxa: G=gorgonians, Sp=sponges, Z=zooanthids, Cr=crinoids. ?unknown or unreported data. [8]Status of reefs since mid 1980's. Arrows: ↔=unchanged, ↓=low or decreasing, ↑=high or increasing

Coral cover and disturbance effects

A majority of the labs (8/14) indicated that coral cover has declined recently. Much of the loss of coral was attributable to natural events such as hurricane damage, bleaching and disease effects. However, at five of the sites human-induced impacts, via nutrient loading (Barbados, Costa Rica, Nicaragua, Tobago), enhanced sedimentation (Barbados, Costa Rica, Colombia, Tobago) and dynamite fishing (Colombia), were considered major factors in the decline of coral cover.

Coral cover has remained stable at sites where human influence is low (Belize, Bermuda, Saba) or the result of protection of coral reefs through legislation, preserves, parks and education (Belize, Bermuda, Cayman Islands, Saba and St. Lucia). To some extent natural perturbations have not had severe impacts at some sites or recovery has taken place (Belize, Bermuda, St. Lucia).

Coral communities at the CARICOMP sites are roughly similar in character with massive corals (Montastrea annularis, Siderastrea siderea, Diploria spp.) dominating at most locations. Branching and foliaceous corals (Porites porites, Acropora palmata, A. cervicornis, and Agaricia spp.) were the dominant forms at only two sites (Belize and Colombia) but were important components at many other sites as well. Gorgonians, sponges and zooanthids were consistently reported as important sessile taxa. No information on the status of these reef organisms was provided, although a mass mortality of the sea fan Gorgonia ventalina has been reported recently from Columbia (Garzon-Ferreira and Zea, 1992).

Algal cover and herbivore abundance

The CARICOMP sites display various combinations of algal abundance, urchin populations and intensity of fishing effort. Five sites reported low algal abundance on their reefs (Barbados, Bermuda, St. Lucia, Venezuela, Tobago). Urchin abundance was low and fishing pressure had declined at these sites, indicating that herbivorous fish populations may be keeping algal biomass in check. Recent increases in urchin populations were noted for Barbados and may also affect algal cover at this site. Saba and Cayman Islands indicated that algal cover was low to medium, with low fishing pressure. Urchin populations have been low at both sites but also have started to increase recently.

Three sites characterized algal abundance as high (Costa Rica, Jamaica, Mexico) or medium to high (Nicaragua). In Jamaica both urchin and fish populations have been reduced sharply over the past decade (Hughes, 1989). The high algal cover on Costa Rican reefs may be the result of nutrient run-off from forest clearing on the mainland. Although urchin populations are low and fishing pressure is low on the Costa Rican reefs, the levels of herbivory may not be sufficient to control algal biomass. On the Nicaraguan reefs nutrient rich groundwaters appear to promote algal growth and this is exacerbated by intensive fish trapping on the reefs. Colombia, and Belize indicated that medium levels of algal cover were present on the study reefs. Urchin densities remain low while fishing pressure has been increasing, perhaps indicating reduced herbivory in these locations.

Fish communities were not well described from the sites. In general the damselfishes (Pomacentridae), parrotfishes (Scaridae) and surgeonfishes (Acanthuridae) were the predominant fish groups, of which the latter two are major reef herbivores. Fishing pressure was generally reduced, compared to historical trends, at three sites (Barbados, Bermuda, St. Lucia) and has remained low at six others (Cayman Islands, Costa Rica Cuba, Saba, Tobago, and Venezuela). However, fishing pressure is considered to be increasing at the other sites (Belize, Colombia, Jamaica, Mexico, and Nicaragua).

Comparisons with previous reports of the status of Caribbean reefs.

Two recent publications summarized the status of Western Atlantic reef systems in the mid 1980's (Rogers, 1985; Wells, 1988). We thought it would be instructive to compare qualitatively the present accounts of the CARICOMP sites to these earlier assessments of the status of reefs in those countries to estimate any recent changes on these reefs.

The majority of the CARICOMP reef sites are located in marine parks or preserves (Barbados, Bermuda, Colombia, Costa Rica, Saba, St. Lucia, Tobago, Venezuela) or in areas of restricted access (Belize) which may provide some degree of control over human interference. The reefs in Belize, Bermuda, Saba and St. Lucia appear to have remained stable since the mid 1980's, but the Barbadian reefs are still threatened by sedimentation and nutrient stress. The Tobago reef flat suffers from tourist-based impacts, and there has been a decline in coral cover on the reef slope, perhaps from sediment stress and nutrient loading. The Venezuelan reef site may be stabilized but coral cover is low as the entire coastal system has suffered intense human impacts for 10-15 years. Existing conservation legislation and conservation practices by dive operators in the Cayman Islands appear to be effective in maintaining the general health of the reefs. The condition of the reefs in parks at two sites (Colombia, Costa Rica) continues to decline, primarily from sedimentation stress. The CARICOMP reefs in Nicaragua and Jamaica do not have any protected status and their condition is deteriorating, due to overfishing at both sites and increased nutrient loading at the former.

ACKNOWLEDGEMENTS

The authors are grateful to the John D. and Catherine T. Macarthur Foundation, the U.S. National Science Foundation (INT-9015611 and DIR-9115368) and UNESCO for support. We particularly thank the following members of the CARICOMP Steering Committee (E. Jordan (Co-chair), P. Penchaszadeh, W. Wiebe, B.J. Kjerfve, and J.C. Zieman), the directors of the CARICOMP network laboratories, and M. Steyaert of the Division of Marine Affairs, UNESCO for their continuing support of Caribbean regional marine research.

LITERATURE CITED

Brown, B.E. and J.C. Ogden. 1993. Coral bleaching. Sci. Am. 268(1): 64-70.

Garzon-Ferreira, J. and S. Zea. 1992. A mass mortality of Gorgonia ventalina in the Santa Marta area, Colombia. Bull. Mar. Sci. 50: 522-526.

Hughes, T.P. 1989. Community structure and diversity of coral reefs: the role of history. Ecology 70: 275-279.

Hay, M.E. 1984. Patterns of fish and urchin grazing on Caribbean coral reefs; are previous results typical? Ecology 65: 446-454.

Lessios, H.A., D.R. Robertson, and J.D. Cubit. 1984. Spread of Diadema mass mortality through the Caribbean. Science 226: 335-337.

Liddell, W.D. and S.L. Ohlhorst. 1986. Changes in benthic community composition following the mass mortality of Diadema at Jamaica. J. Exp. Mar. Biol. Ecol. 95: 271-278.

Ogden, J.C. 1987. Cooperative coastal ecology at Caribbean marine laboratories. Oceanus 30: 9-15.

Ogden, J.C. 1992. The impact of Hurricane Andrew on the ecosystems of south Florida. Conserv. Biol. 6: 488-490.

Ogden, J.C. and E.H. Gladfelter (eds.). 1986. Caribbean coastal marine productivity. UNESCO Repts. Mar. Sci. 41: 59p.

Rogers, C.S. 1985. Degradation of Caribbean and Western Atlantic coral reefs and decline of associated reef fisheries. Proc. 5th Int. Coral Reef Symp., Papeete, Tahiti. 6: 491-496.

Rutzler, K. and D.L. Santavy. 1983. The black band disease of Atlantic reef corals. I. Description of the cyanophyte pathogen. P.S.Z.N.I.: Marine Ecology 4: 329-358

Smith, S.V. 1978. Coral-reef area and the contributions of reefs to processes and resources of the world's oceans. Nature May 18, 1978.

Smith, S.V. and R.W. Buddemeier. 1992. Global change and coral reef ecosystems. Annu. Rev. Ecol. Syst. 23: 89-118.

Wells, S.M. 1988. Coral Reefs of the World. Vol. 1: Atlantic and Eastern Pacific. UNEP/IUCN. 373 pp.

Wilkinson, C. in press. Coral reefs are facing widespread extinctions: Can we prevent these through sustainable management practices? Proc. 7th Intl. Coral Reef Symp., Guam, June, 1992.

Woodley, J.D., E.A. Chornesky, P.A. Clifford, J.B.C. Jackson, L.S. Kaufman, N. Knowlton, J.C. Lang, M.P. Pearson, J.W. Porter, M.C. Rooney, K.W. Rylaarsdam, V.J. Tunnicliffe, C.M. Wahle, J.L. Wulff, A.S.G. Curtis, M.D. Dallmeyer, B.P. Jupp, M.A.R. Koehl, J. Niegel, and E.M. Sides. 1981. Hurricane Allen's impact on Jamaican coral reefs. Science 214: 749-755.

GLOBAL STATUS OF SCLERACTINIA, ALCYONARIA, ANTIPATHARIA, STYLASTERINA AND MILLEPORINA IN THE TROPICAL WESTERN ATLANTIC: GUIDELINES AND ASSESSMENT

K.M. Sullivan[1], R. Roca[2], E.C. Peters[3] and M. Chiappone[1]

[1] Marine Ecology Program of The Nature Conservancy and Department of Biology, University of Miami, P.O. Box 249118, Coral Gables, FL 33124. [2] Latin American Science Program, The Nature Conservancy, 1815 N. Lynn Street, Arlington, Va 22209. [3] Tetra Tech Inc., Fairfax, VA 22209.

ABSTRACT

The methodology developed by the Nature Conservancy's Biological and Conservation Database System was applied to the ranking and assessment of benthic cnidarians of the tropical western Atlantic. One-hundred and forty-seven species of shallow-water Scleractinia, Alcyonaria, Antipatharia, Stylasterina and Milleporina coral species were evaluated for taxonomic status, distribution, habitat requirements, ecology, and susceptibility to threats. The project produced a dynamic database within the Biological and Conservation Database that applies consistent criteria to the ranking of corals and provided a methodology for setting protection priorities. The ranking of several rare corals is explained to illustrate the process.

INTRODUCTION

The Nature Conservancy has a long history of determining rarity and ranking terrestrial plants and animals. Marine ecosystems, however, have received considerably less attention. A common perception is that marine benthic invertebrates are widely distributed, occur in a number of community types, are not comparable to terrestrial plant populations, and thus are not significantly threatened by human activities (Thorne-Miller and Catena, 1991). In order to facilitate the decision-making process on what communities and species should be protected, the Nature Conservancy (TNC) developed the Biological and Conservation Data System (BCD).

Responding to the necessity of protecting a vast array of natural communities and species, TNC developed a ranking system that includes information on global, national, and sub-national (states, provinces) ranks of species and communities. The TNC ranking guidelines were primarily developed to ascertain the conservation status of terrestrial elements of biodiversity (Master, 1991). A challenge to marine conservation is to develop new methodologies for understanding how changes in marine communities can be translated into fluctuations in populations and loss of biodiversity.

Shallow-water benthic coral species (Phylum Cnidaria) found reefs in the tropical western Atlantic biogeographic province were selected for inclusion in the database. The ranking process needs to be comprehensive by comparison and inclusion of an entire taxonomic group; it is not feasible to rank only a few species of corals without consideration of all known species in a region. The list of corals developed for ranking represents such a comprehensive group, covering two classes within the phylum.

A list of scleractinian and black corals were proposed as candidates for possible addition to the List of Endangered and Threatened Wildlife and Plants by the National Marine Fisheries Service and Office of Protected Resources of the National Oceanic and Atmospheric Administration. These species were nominated to solicit information on the status of these species and to obtain further nominations of additional species of corals (*Federal Register* 56(112):26797-26798). A more extensive list of both Indo-Pacific and Atlantic coral species also exists for the Convention on International Trade in Endangered Species (CITES). While these developments are intended to protect coral populations, the reasons for listing these particular species have not been published, nor were the lists developed as a dynamic resource. Furthermore, how the species will be protected from over-collection, commercial trade, or pollution is unclear.

A goal in the ranking of coral populations is the assessment and characterization of benthic community types that are clearly linked to the long-term viability of coral species, and thus, deserve protection. The assessment of coral reef communities presents a much more daunting task and is the focus of considerable ecological research. The tracking of individual coral species that can be consistently evaluated for rareness and threats promises to provide an important tool for establishing conservation priorities and making meaningful measures of conservation success.

METHODS

A hierarchical classification design for shallow-water (< 100 m depth), benthic, continental shelf communities in the tropical western Atlantic was developed. The community classification scheme was essential to consistently interpret information on habitat requirements for coral species. The ranking of coral species included an evaluation of how many different benthic community classes a given species colonizes. Some community classes have a relatively narrow depth range (reef crests) and represent specific habitat requirements of some species. In addition to examining what benthic community classes coral species colonized, we were also interested in qualitative information on whether a species dominated a given community class or was only occasionally observed in the community. For example, some reef crest communities can be dominated by *Acropora palmata*, but back reef lagoons may be only sparsely populated with this species.

An explanation of the ranking system of The Nature Conservancy's

Heritage Program and its comparison to other ranking systems (e.g., IUCN, U.S. Fish and Wildlife) is provided in detail in Master (1991). A 1-5 scale is used for ranking elements; ranks are applied separately for elements at the global, national, and subnational (state, provincial) levels. A brief explanation of the ranks includes: G1, critically imperiled globally; G2, imperiled globally; G3, rare or uncommon but not imperiled; G4, not rare and apparently secure but with cause for long-term concern; and G5, demonstrably widespread, abundant, and secure.

The following criteria are critical in defining a population or occurrence of a given coral species, and include: 1) estimation of the size and boundary of a site with a habitat description, 2) numbers of colonies per sampling area, and 3) size range of colonies. This information allows for the assessment of the abundance and reproductive viability of coral species. For example, colonies of *Montastraea annularis* are only able to reproduce after attaining a living tissue surface area of 100 cm^2 (Szmant, 1991).

A measure of numerical abundance of a coral species alone would not be sufficient to answer the questions of what habitats are important or what abundance of critical habitats are necessary for the long-term viability of the species. For example, *Eusmilia fastigiata* is characterized as an under-story species on dome patch reefs, which are often dominated by *Montastraea annularis* in mature stages of patch reef growth and development. *E. fastigiata* depends on high three-dimensional complexity on reef communities, as it colonizes the sides of dead coral heads or is found underneath coral heads on patch reefs. The abundance of *E. fastigiata* is therefore dependent on not only the number of populations of the species, but also on the number of habitats that the species occupies and the quality of those habitats.

The tropical western Atlantic was divided into eight biogeographic regions: 1) southern Florida, 2) Gulf of Mexico, 3) Bahamian archipelago, 4) Greater Antillean, 5) Lesser Antillean, 6) Northwest Caribbean, 7) Continental Caribbean, and 8) Bermuda. The distributions of coral species were evaluated based on the number of regions in which species occurred.

RESULTS

One hundred and forty-seven valid species of hydrocorals, antipatharians, alcyonarians, and scleractinians were identified as members of shallow (< 40 m depth) reef communities in the tropical western Atlantic. There were larger gaps in information for coral species ecology compared to range and habitat information. Example information is provided in Table 1 on the scientific name, global rank, reasons for specified ranks, and taxonomic status for representative coral species.

An example of the ranking process for a G3 ranked coral is

provided. This rank would be interpreted as a rare or threatened species that warrants conservation attention. A species considered to be moderately endangered is *Acropora cervicornis*. In terms of distribution, *A. cervicornis* has a widespread distribution in the tropical western Atlantic, including southern Florida, Bahamas, Gulf of Mexico, Northwest Caribbean, Greater and Lesser Antilles, and the Continental Caribbean. Habitats where this species have been documented include: spur and groove reefs, octocoral-dominated hardgrounds, and patch reefs. In terms of fragility and threats, this species is considered to be highly threatened based on: 1) mass mortalities in the Caribbean since the 1970's; 2) susceptibility to white band disease and bleaching (Peters, 1984); and 3) anchor damage (Davis, 1977). Mass mortality events have been attributed to temperature-induced stress (Porter et al., 1982), white band disease, and damage from catastrophic events such as hurricanes. This species is characterized by high growth, but exhibits limited sexual recruitment (Rylaarsdam, 1983). Summation of abundance, range, and threats yields a global rank of G3. The conservation ranking of *A. cervicornis* represents a case where a species is widespread but is restricted to a narrower range of community classes, and is considered highly endangered due to recent population trends and documented anthropogenic impacts.

For the 147 coral species studied, three species (2.1%) are highly ranked as G2, *Lytreia plana*, *Madracis senaria*, and *Plexaurella grandiflora*. These corals appear to be endemic to the northwestern Caribbean. They have a very restricted range and occur in very few (1-2) marine communities, but no specific threats have been reported. A group of 18 species (13%) have a rank of G2G3. These species exhibited a moderate to restricted distribution, occur in few (3-5) marine hard bottom communities, and had sedimentation as the most common threat. A substantial number (42) of species (30.4%) are moderately endangered (G3), indicating a concern for long-term conservation. The set of 34 (24.6%) G3G4 species should be tracked closely because as information on threats becomes available some of the ranks might change to G3. The remaining species are not considered endangered. Only seven species (0.5%) are G5. They are widely distributed and occupy various marine communities without apparent threats.

DISCUSSION

The compilation of literature that was conducted to develop the species list of benthic reef cnidarians in the tropical western Atlantic revealed that many taxonomic questions remain. In the scleractinian corals, species and subspecies were traditionally classified on the basis of their skeletal morphology (e.g., dimensions of corallites; features of the coenosteum). Specimens with similar skeletal morphological features that intergrade in a series were considered to belong to a single species and distinct morphological gaps indicated separate species (Wells, 1956). Recent studies, however, have shown that some scleractinians may exhibit high levels of variability in skeletal characteristics that may be genetically dictated (e.g., Brakel, 1977) or that may change as the result of environmental factors such as light intensity, sedimentation rate, water movement, and food availability (Foster, 1980).

The ranking process has highlighted species that may indeed be truly rare, but require additional research on distribution and taxonomy. The application of ranking criteria to all species led to the development of a comprehensive list of research needs in coral biology. The information compiled from global ranks allows a broader assessment of resources within a given region or within national boundaries. It is often not possible in practice to distinguish between effects of climate change, anthropogenic alterations or natural variability on reef systems, thus monitoring physical parameters or water quality alone can not establish causal links to changes in reef benthos. Tracking the status of the most critical populations of corals can provide some trend data with less ambiguity of interpretation and greater management implications. There is certainly a need for continued research and monitoring of the spatial dynamics of reefs (Bythell et al., 1992), but in-depth studies will only be feasible at selected reef sites.

With the completion of global ranks, the Biological and Conservation Database in The Nature Conservancy's Heritage Network extends the methodology for determining regional, national, and sub-national ranks. The ranking process can play an important role in prioritizing to marine species for conservation attention. Combined global, national, and sub-national ranks can give an instant overview of a species' known or probable threat of extinction.

ACKNOWLEDGEMENTS

Support for this project was provided by the Caribbean Program, Latin American Division and Florida Keys Initiative of The Nature Conservancy.

LITERATURE CITED

Bayer, F.M. 1961. The Shallow-water Octocorallia of the West Indian Region. A manual for marine biologists. Martinus Nijoff, The Hague. 373 pp.

Brakel, W.H. 1977. Corallite variation in *Porites* and the species problem in corals. Pages 457-462 *in* Proceedings of the Third International Coral Reef Symposium, Miami, volume 1.

Bythell, J. C., E. Gladfelter and M. Bythell. 1992. Ecological Studies of Buck Island Reef National Monument, St. Croix, U.S. Virgin Islands: A quantitative assessment of selected components of the coral reef ecosystem and establishment of long-term monitoring sites. Island Resource Foundation, St. Thomas. 72 pp.

Davis, G.E. 1977. Anchor damage to a coral reef on the coast of

Florida. Biol. Conserv. 11: 29-34.

Foster, A.B. 1980. Environmental variation in skeletal morphology within the Caribbean reef corals *Montastraea annularis* and *Siderastrea siderea*. Bull. Mar. Sci. 30(3): 678-709.

Knowlton, N., E. Weil, L.A. Weigt, and H.M. Guzmán. 1992. Sibling species in *Montastraea annularis*, coral bleaching, and the coral climate record. Science 255: 330-333.

Master, L.L. 1991. Assessing threats and setting priorities for conservation. Conserv. Biol. 5(4): 559-563.

Peters, E.C. 1984. A survey of cellular reactions to environmental stress and disease in Caribbean scleractinian corals. Helgol. Meersunters. 37: 113-137.

Porter, J.W., J.F. Battey and G.J. Smith. 1982. Perturbation and change in coral reef communities. Proc. Natl. Acad. Sci. 79: 1678-1681.

Rylaarsdam, K.W. 1983. Life histories and abundance patterns of colonial corals on Jamaican reefs. Mar. Ecol. Prog. Ser. 13: 249-260.

Szmant, A.M. 1991. Sexual reproduction by the Caribbean reef corals *Montastrea annularis* and *M. cavernosa*. Mar. Ecol. Prog. Ser. 74: 13-25.

Thorne-Miller, B. and J. Catena. 1991. The Living Ocean. Understanding and protecting marine biodiversity. Island Press, Washington D.C. 180 pp.

Wells, J.W. 1956. Scleractinia. Pages 328-44 *in* R.C. Moore, ed. Treatise on Invertebrate Paleontology Part F, Coelenterata. Kansas University Press, Lawrence, Kansas.

Wells, J.W. 1973. New and old scleractinian corals from Jamaica. Bull. Mar. Sci. 23(1): 16-58.

Zlatarski, V.N. and N.M. Estalella. 1982. Les scleractiniaires de Cuba avec des donnees sur les organismes associes. Academic Bulgare des Sciences, Sofia, Bulgaria. 472 pp.

Table 1. Representative conservation ranking information for species of tropical western Atlantic corals. For each species, taxonomic comments, the global rank, and the reasons for specified global ranks are provided.

Species	Taxonomic Comments	Rank	Ranking Reasons
Plexaurella grandiflora		G2	May be endemic to Brazil (Bayer, 1961), but no other information found from resources consulted.
Goreaugyra memorialis	Zlatarski and Estalella (1982) considered this to be a morphological variant of *Meandrina meandrites*.	G2G3	Known only from type location from the Bahamas, but may occur in Cuba; no specific threats cited from resources consulted.
Dendrogyra cylindrus		G3	Moderately widespread distribution but restricted to shallow reef communities; characterized by slow growth and low reproductive output.
Acropora cervicornis		G3	Widespread distribution, occurs on many classes of marine hard bottom communities, but is highly susceptible to bleaching, disease, sedimentation, and mechanical damage.
Eusmilia fastigiata	Two forms have been listed for this species: forma *typica* and forma *flabellata* (Wells, 1973).	G3G4	Widespread distribution but restricted to reef communities; moderate sensitivity to sedimentation.
Montastraea annularis	This species may be composed of up to three subspecies or forms (Knowlton et al., 1992).	G5	Widespread distribution, dominates many classes of marine communities, but is susceptible to bleaching, disease, and mechanical damage.

HAZARDS AND HUMAN INTERVENTION

	PAGES
Long-term Monitoring (2.5 Years) of Effects of Short-term Field Exposure of Stony Corals to Dispersed and Undispersed Crude Oil *Richard E. Dodge and Anthony H. Knap*	87 - 93
Symbiont Loss ("Bleaching") in the Reef-Dwelling Benthic Foraminifer *Amphistegina gibbosa* in the Florida Keys in 1991-92 *Pamela Hallock and Helen K. Talge*	94 - 100
The Status of the Remnant Population of *Acropora palmata* (Lamarck, 1816) at Dry Tortugas National Park, Florida, with a Discussion of Possible Cases of Changes since 1881 *Walter C. Jaap and Frank J. Sargent*	101 - 105
Phosphorus Inputs and Eutrophication on the Florida Reef Tract *Brian E. Lapointe, William R. Matzie, and Mark W. Clark*	106 - 112
Why Conservation by Legal Fiat Does Not Work *Howard Latin*	113 - 119
Alacranes and Akumal Coral Reefs, Mexico. Their Health, Uses and Concerns *Enrique Martinez-Osegueda, Ricardo Munoz-Chagin, and Gustavo de la Cruz-Aguero*	120 - 125
Effects of Temperature and UV-B on Different Components of Coral Reef Communities From the Bahamas *Marjorie L. Reaka-Kudla, Douglas S. O'Connell, James D. Regan, and Robert I. Wickland*	126 - 131

Oil on Troubled Waters: Impacts of the Gulf War on Coral Reefs 132 - 138

Callum M. Roberts, Nigel Downing, and Andrew R.G. Price

Oil Refinery Impacts on Coral Reef Communities in Aruba, N. A. 139 - 145

C. Mark Eakin, Joshua S. Feingold and Peter W. Glynn

LONG-TERM MONITORING (2.5 YEARS) OF EFFECTS OF SHORT-TERM FIELD EXPOSURE OF STONY CORALS TO DISPERSED AND UNDISPERSED CRUDE OIL

Richard E. Dodge[1] and Anthony H. Knap[2]

[1]Nova University Oceanographic Center, 8000 N. Ocean Dr., Dania, FL 33004; [2]Bermuda Biological Station for Research, Ferry Reach, Bermuda

ABSTRACT

A field experiment was conducted to evaluate long-term effects to shallow sub-tidal coral reef species from short-term exposure to dispersed and untreated crude oil. The study location was in the northwestern Laguna de Chiriqui, Caribbean coast of Panama. Experimental sites consisted of 900 m^2 plots which were enclosed by a boom with .45 cm deep skirts. All sites contained shallow subtidal coral reefs. One site was designated as a control. One site received dispersed oil at a target concentration of 50 ppm for 24 hours, representing a high exposure. One site received only crude oil at an amount of about 1 l/m^2 for a duration of approximately 48 hours, representing a moderate exposure.

Prespill chemical and biological parameters were collected in March and mid November, 1984. The experimental spill was conducted in late November, 1984. Monitoring of parameters continued periodically until August, 1986. Biological parameters that were measured included epifaunal and epifloral coverage of the coral reef substrate utilizing plotless line transects. Skeletal growth of four selected coral species was also measured at each site. Chemical sampling involved analysis (not reported here) of large and small-volume water samples for GC and GC/MS together with large-volume water samples by pumping through XAD resin.

Results indicated that the coverage of all organisms, hard corals, all animals, and all plants was significantly depressed in the Dispersed Oil treatment compared to the Control station. Little recovery of most organisms was evident some 20 months after initial treatment. Coverage parameters of the Oil Only treatment were generally lower than, but not usually significantly different from coverage of the Control. Of the four coral species investigated for growth, two (Agaricia tennuifolia and Porites porites) showed significant effects from exposure to dispersed oil (reduced blade and tip extension rate at the dispersed oil site). These results provided useful indications of long-term effects from short-term field expsoure of corals and coral reefs to oil and dispersed oil. Information from this and other field and laboratory studies benefits marine management by providing data upon which to base informed decisions regarding dispersant use in tropical areas.

INTRODUCTION

Background

A major threat to corals and coral reefs is contamination from spilled oil. The effects of oil and oil products on corals and coral reefs is comparatively little studied, sometimes controversial, and generally poorly understood (Loya and Rinkevich, 1980; Brown and Howard, 1985). Results of field studies have suggested harmful effects from spills or from chronic oil pollution from spills or refinery operations. Loya (1975) indicated chronic exposure could affect coral reproduction and larval development. Rinkevich and Loya (1977) demonstrated a reproductive and mortality effect from repeated exposures. Cohen et al. (1977) found oil exposed corals expelled larvae more quickly than normal. Bak (1987) investigated chronic oil pollution effects from refinery operation in Aruba. Decreased coral cover, spatial structure, and juveniles were some results. Thorhaug et al. (1989), in experiments in Jamaica, found major differences in tolerances to dispersed oil products between coral species. *Acropora palmata*, the dominant reef crest species was found to be highly sensitive compared to other deeper water dominant species, such as *Montastrea annularis*. Dodge et al. (1984, 1985) monitored short-term and long-term skeletal growth of Bermuda *Diploria strigosa* and found few differences between those treated with short-term dispersed oil, oil alone, and controls. Wyers (1986) described behavioral effects of this species. Knap (1987) concluded this coral species was tolerant of short-term exposures to oil and dispersed oil.

A recent and striking example of oil spill effects on corals was the Galeta (Panama) Oil Spill. In 1986 this major oil spill of over 50,000 barrels (8 million liters) of crude occurred in Panama over a complex area of mangroves, seagrasses, and coral reefs. The oil remained a factor for many months to years due to onshore winds and depositional pooling in mangroves (for later reoiling). Only small amounts of dispersants were reported to have been used. There was extensive mortality reported of shallow subtidal reef corals. Effects were most evident at less than 9 ft (3 m), but total coral cover decreased by about 50 percent at even 27-36 ft (9-12 m) depths. Sublethal effects included bleaching, tissue swelling, partial mortality, and tissue lesions (Jackson et al., 1989). Even four years after the spill, corals displayed elevated injury frequency and depressed growth rates (Keller and Jackson, 1991; Guzman et al., 1991). Coral reproduction and recruitment was affected. Coral larval brooders recruited in much greater numbers than broadcasting species. The extensive sublethal effects to corals suggested that there may be continuing and severe long-term effects in population reproduction and structure. Coral injury has promoted algal colonization of dead skeletons and overgrowth by other organisms. Stress from oil may have made surviving corals more susceptible to such overgrowth and disease. Long-term effects of short-term exposures are less well studied and known.

Purpose of this Paper

A field experiment was conducted to assesses the long-term effects of short-term exposure of shallow coral reef, mangrove, and seagrass environments to crude oil and chemically dispersed oil (Ballou et al., 1987). Detailed results of effects to corals and reefs are reported here. Small oil spills are likely to be more common than major catastrophies. The temptation to use dispersants for cleanup is great. Therefore, it is useful to understand long-term effects of oil alone and oil plus dispersant in order to develop best spill management schemes.

METHODS AND MATERIALS

Sites

Description.-

Study sites were located on shallow subtidal coral reefs in the northwestern Laguna de Chiriqui, Caribbean coast of Panama. Each site was rectangular (30 x 30 m) and was covered approximately 50% with mangroves and 50% by seagrass and coral reefs. Water depth over the corals was approximately .6 m. Two of the sites, designated as the Dispersed Oil and Oil Only sites were approximately .5 km apart on one island. A third site, designated as the Control was located on a separate island about 5 km away. (For coral growth studies only, a replicate control site was established midway between the dispersed and oil only sites.)

Preparation and Treatment.-

Biological, chemical, and physical data were collected prior to the experimental spill in March and again in mid November, 1984. During experimental treatment of the sites (late November, 1984), each were completely enclosed within a 45 cm deep boom. For the dispersed oil treatment, dispersant was added directly to barrels of Prudhoe Bay crude oil at a ratio of 20:1. A total of 4.5 barrels of the dispersed oil mixture was released inside the boomed site over a 24 hour period. The target concentration in the water column was 50 ppm over 24 hours and the release was governed by continuous monitoring with a fluorometer. The actual concentrations fluctuated considerably due to current patterns and the difficulty of releasing the dispersed oil in an even pattern over the entire site area. Untreated oil was released at an application of 1 liter per square meter, simulating the stranding amount from a 100 to 1000 barrel spill. The oil treatment duration was two days. Four barrels were released at the start of the first day and two additional barrels were released at the start of the second day.

Sites were monitored at five or less time periods following treatment. Details of monitoring periods are given below under assessment methods.

Floral/Faunal Assessment - Transects

Ecological parameters of coral reefs in the shallow zone (0-2 m), where projected impact was expected to be greatest from experimental treatment, were monitored using the point plotless line transect method. The point plotless line method is described in detail in Dodge et al. (1982). At each assessment site, 4 locations for semipermanent line transects were established by marking ends with metal rods 1.0-1.5 m in length driven into the reef substrate. Each transect line was 10 m in length. Two transect lines were laid parallel to the reef crest in water depths of approximately 1 m. Two other lines were laid parallel to the first in depths of approximately 1.3 m. Data were collected by a diver swimming over the transect line and recording the identity of the substrate lying beneath points established at 10-cm intervals. For each transect, 100 data points were collected. Substrate was categorized as either organism or bare. In essentially all cases, bare substrate consisted of rubble formed by dead Porites porites or other coral species.

Organisms were further subcategorized. Stony corals were identified to species. Other animals were classified to Phylum, Order, or species. For plants, fleshy and calcareous algae and seagrass were distinguished. For a site, major categories were averaged over transects for a mean representation. The data set obtained allowed derivation of percentage of coverage for the various animal and plant components. These were Total Organisms, Total Corals, Total all Animals, and Total Plants.

An initial survey was conducted in March 1984 where 4 transects at each site were surveyed. In the survey immediately prior to the spill in November 1984, the initial transect marker rods of most sites could not be relocated. New markers were established which were occupied then and on each subsequent assessment (December, 1984, March, 1985, June, 1985, December, 1985, and July, 1986). During each assessment each transect line was assessed in duplicate during each site survey. Consequently, the data set of the initial survey is not directly comparable to the subsequent data in terms of transect locations and replication. Statistical analyses did not include the initial transect data (however, they are included in the figures for information purposes). Results were analyzed by repeated measures ANOVA.

Coral Growth

The coral species' Montastrea annularis, Agaricia tennuifolia, Porites porites, and Acropora cervicornis were chosen for growth assessment following treatment by oil or dispersed oil. At each site approximately 5 specimens of each species were fixed to cement blocks with underwater quick-setting cement at 1-2 m depth in the central portion of each site. Montastrea annularis and Acropora cervicornis did not occur naturally at this shallow depth and were transplanted at the same reef from approximately 4 and 3 m, respectively. Porites porites and Agaricia tennuifolia were collected from the same shallow depths in which they were cemented. At least 7 days prior to treatment with oil or dispersed oil, specimens at each site were stained with alizarin red S (Lamberts, 1978) for approximately 5 hours. Staining was accomplished by securing a clear plastic bag around corals and injecting alizarin red S at sufficient concentration.

Following treatment and allowing for a several month growth period, stained specimens at each site were collected for analysis. Additional specimens of Porites porites and Agaricia tennuifolia which were present in the confines of the area of each site were selected for additional staining and later collection during subsequent monitorings.

Remarks on the Nature of Coral Colonies

Montastrea annularis is a hemispherical-type coral forming individual heads. Porites porites, however, is a branched coral with many individual branches often radiating from a common base. Although in practice specimens consisted of several branches of the same genotype, breakage from handling and/or prior breakage from bioerosion often obscured these relationships. Therefore, for this species, the operational unit was a well-defined branch. Colony considerations for Agaricia tennuifolia were similar to those of P. porites. A. tennuifolia forms blade-like growths and therefore the operational unit of measurement was a blade which was generally distinct from other colony parts. As with P. porites, each stained cluster was composed of several blades, most of which were probably a similar genotype.

For Acropora cervicornis, transplantation was conducted by breaking branch tips (greater than 10 cm in length) from in situ living colonies, staining, and cementing branches to blocks. Transplanted branches were, in general, from different genotypes and so each block contained several branches from a different original genotype.

Growth Measurement Procedures

Measurement procedures for Montastrea annularis are described in more detail in Dodge (1982). Embedded medial skeletal surfaces were polished to a clear surface suitable for measurement under low-power microscopy. The parameter Septa Increase was measured along well cross-sectioned septa which revealed the alizarin stain line and current septa top. For Agaricia tennuifolia, when possible, individual blades were identified on each stained cluster. Five measurements per blade were made with calipers from the stain lines to the blade distal surface. Observation of the stain line was made by holding the blade in front of a strong light. The thickness of the blade at the stain line was also measured with calipers. For Porites porites, where possible, at least five branch tips were identified from each staining unit. These were cut from the branch (below the stain line) using a dentist saw. Each tip was then cut or ground to produce a medial surface suitable for stain-line observation. The linear growth (extension) from the stain line top to the branch tip top was recorded. For Acropora cervicornis, stained tips of individual branches were cut off from the main branch body using a dentist saw. Each tip was labeled by site and staining unit. Tips were carefully sectioned medially and a length measurement between stainline and tip margin was taken by caliper.

RESULTS

Floral/Faunal Assessment - Transects of Coral Reefs

Table 1. Mean Percent Coverage of organism categories at each site.

Date	3/7/84		11/25/84		12/3/84		3/28/85		6/28/85		12/6/85		7/31/86	
Time Pre/Post Spill	(8 Mos pre)		(3 Days pre)		(5 Days post)		(4 Mos post)		(7 Mos post)		(12 Mos post)		(19 Mos post)	
Replication	n=4		n=8		n=8		n=8		n=8		n=8		n=8	
DISPERSED OIL	X	s.d.	X	s.d.	X	s.d.	X	s.d.	X	s.d.	X	s.d.	X	s.d.
Total Corals	33.5	11.7	27.3	13.8	21.6	14.2	19.4	12.0	16.3	12.5	9.5	10.8	8.6	9.4
Total All Animals	50.3	8.3	54.8	7.6	42.4	9.7	32.0	10.4	29.9	8.5	22.9	8.3	27.5	10.4
Total Plants	3.8	2.2	2.0	2.9	2.5	3.0	1.1	1.6	0.3	0.5	0.3	0.5	0.9	0.8
Total Organisms	54.0	6.5	56.8	7.4	44.9	9.7	33.1	10.6	30.1	8.3	23.1	8.2	28.6	10.6
OIL ONLY	X	s.d.	X	s.d.	X	s.d.	X	s.d.	X	s.d.	X	s.d.	X	s.d.
Total Corals	30.5	18.7	27.6	13.2	24.0	9.4	23.4	12.1	25.6	7.8	21.4	9.0	18.6	11.9
Total All Animals	50.3	19.1	55.6	13.3	51.8	10.6	48.1	11.8	57.0	11.1	54.4	16.9	60.5	15.4
Total Plants	7.0	1.4	13.5	4.5	12.6	2.5	5.5	3.3	3.8	2.4	3.6	2.0	3.0	2.6
Total Organisms	57.3	18.6	69.1	11.0	64.4	10.2	53.6	10.6	60.8	12.2	58.0	17.3	63.5	17.6
CONTROL	X	s.d.	X	s.d.	X	s.d.	X	s.d.	X	s.d.	X	s.d.	X	s.d.
Total Corals	21.3	2.5	15.3	4.7	15.8	5.4	8.4	4.8	14.1	5.4	8.6	6.5	7.3	6.5
Total All Animals	49.3	7.9	53.6	3.3	53.6	3.5	42.5	7.6	46.9	10.2	43.8	10.4	37.4	11.0
Total Plants	19.3	4.1	29.6	7.5	27.4	5.0	37.6	16.1	39.6	16.2	42.0	11.9	39.8	8.6
Total Organisms	68.5	4.7	83.3	6.0	81.0	4.8	80.1	10.9	86.5	7.8	85.8	4.9	77.1	6.5

Table 1 provides percent coverage results for major categories. The November, 1984 pre-treatment values of a given ecological parameter were slightly different among sites. Consequently, values at each monitoring period were normalized to this pre-treatment value by subtraction, allowing a similar frame of reference for each site in comparison to others. Figures 1a and 1b illustrate normalized results for total organisms and hard corals. For Total Organisms, Total Corals, and Total Animals, repeated measures ANOVA of the normalized data set indicated that the Dispersed post-treatment means were significantly lower than those of the Control. Oil treatment means were lower than Control means, but not significantly, except for total Plants.

Figure 1: The mean percentage of reef substrate covered by a) all organisms and b) hard corals only at the dispersed oil, oil only, and control sites. Error bars are +/- 1 standard deviation. Percentages are normalized by substraction to the Nov., 1984 pre-treatment mean for each site.

a)   b)

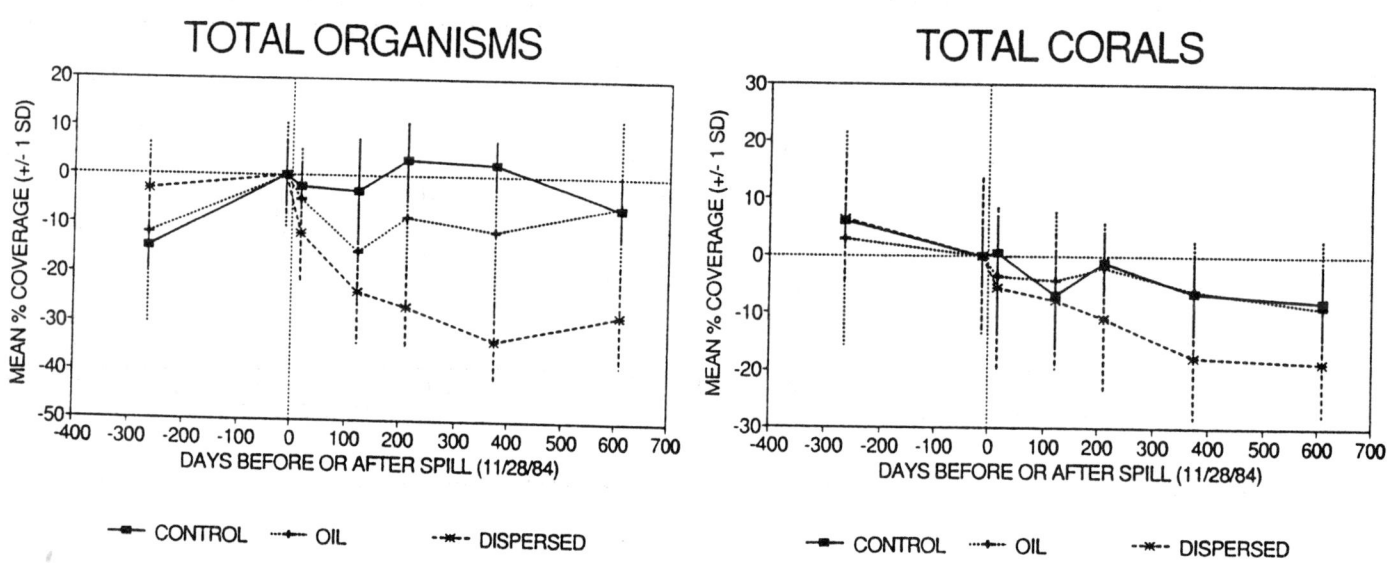

Growth:

Table 2. Coral extension growth rate (cm/yr)

Treatment	stained collected #growth days Species	Nov-84 Mar-85 126 X	s.d.	n	28-Mar 27-Jun 91 X	s.d.	n	Jun-85 Dec-85 163 X	s.d.	n	Dec-85 Jul-86 235 X	s.d.	n
DISPERSED	A.tennuifolia	1.30	0.21	4				1.01	0.28	5	1.00	0.43	3
OIL ONLY	A.tennuifolia	2.88	0.41	5				2.62	0.58	4	2.80	0.37	5
CONTROL	A.tennuifolia	2.62	0.38	6				2.63	0.56	8	2.73	0.78	5
DISPERSED	P.porites	2.47	1.00	34	2.14	1.41	12	2.47	0.59	24			
OIL ONLY	P.porites	3.64	1.08	16	3.13	1.28	17	3.13	1.12	9	2.95	1.12	36
CONTROL	P.porites	2.79	1.25	31	3.50	1.89	59	2.75	1.11	33	1.33	0.53	21
DISPERSED	M.annularis	0.90	0.17	5									
OIL ONLY	M.annularis	0.85	0.03	4									
CONTROL	M.annularis	0.83	0.07	5									
DISPERSED	A.cervicornis	6.27	3.28	31									
OIL ONLY	A.cervicornis	4.66	1.95	30									
CONTROL	A.cervicornis	5.31	2.14	34									

Table 2 presents growth results for each species, site, and time period. For M. annularis and A. cervicornis, ANOVA indicated no difference in growth between treatments within the single staining interval (November, 1984 - March, 1985) of approximately 120 days following treatment. Figures 2a and 2b, illustrate results for both A. tennuifolia and P. porites. Repeated measures ANOVA for both species indicated that extension in the dispersed oil treatment was significantly lower than in the Control. The extension rate in the oil only treatment was not statistically different from the control growth.

Figure 2: Mean extension growth of coral colonies at intervals following experimental field treament for a) A. tennuifolia and b) P. porites.

a)   b)

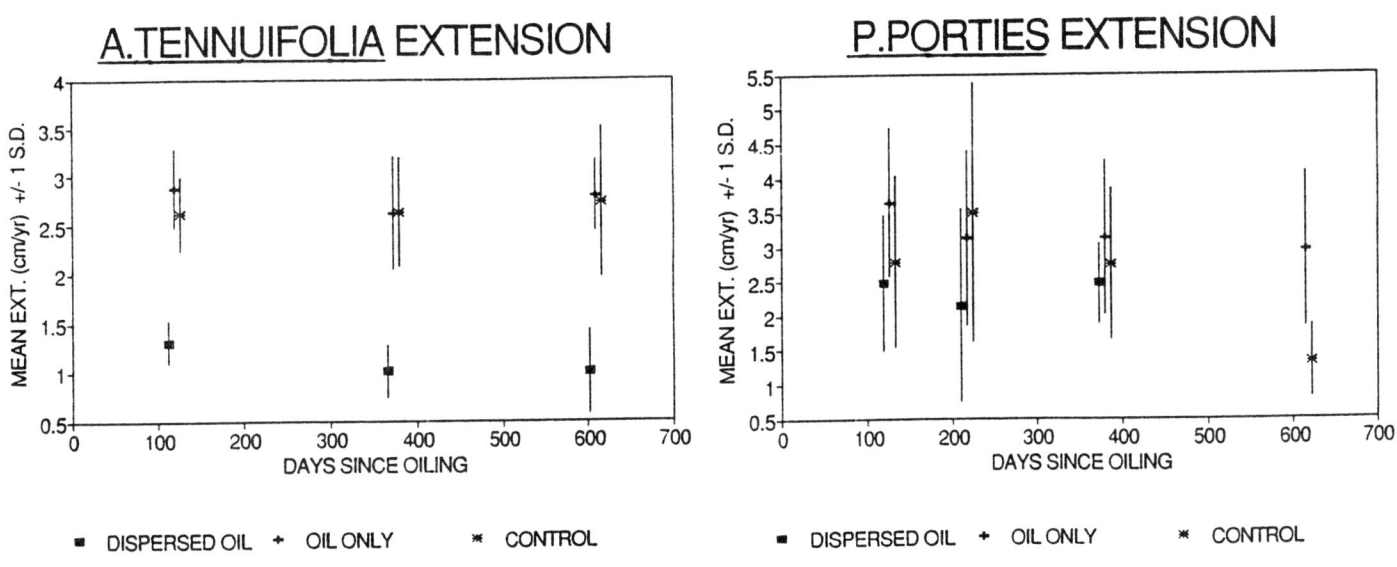

DISCUSSION

The results of this study indicate that a short-term exposure of a shallow coral reef environment to dispersed oil can have serious consequences, even over the long-term. Coverage (normalized to pre-treatment values) in the Dispersed Oil site of major categories of all organisms, hard corals, all animals, and plants were significantly depressed relative to those in the Control site. Growth of two of the most important hard coral species was significantly depressed in the Dispersed Oil site. Coverage and other parameters of the Dispersed Oil site showed little indication of recovery at the conclusion of monitoring, nearly two years after exposure. This was probably not due to chronic re-exposure because hydrocarbon monitoring revealed only very low concentratons following the experimental spill. Slow recovery may have been linked to changes in the reef structure. Many binding sponges were killed by the dispersed oil. This acted to destabilize the reef surface, perhaps killing some corals and preventing rapid successful recolonization by others. The short-term exposure of this study to Oil Only did not appear to have similar significant consequences to the coverage of reef proper. It is reasonable that short-term exposure to floating oil is less serious than a similar exposure to oil which is dispersed throughout the water column and which can come into direct contact with benthic animals and plants. Long term exposure to oil only allows for natural sinking of the oil and for soluble oil components to be leached into the water.

Jackson et al. (1989) and Guzman et al. (1991) reported significant effects of oil only on coverage and growth of affected corals. Dispersant was used in the Galeta spill; however, they speculated that dispersant amounts and location of use were not sufficient to have caused the observed effects. Because the Galeta spill was extremely large and of relatively long duration, the consequent exposure of the organisms to oil was much greater than in this study. In addition, chronic exposure has continued to occur from leaching of oil from mangrove sediments.

The degree of significnat effect on coral growth (and other responses) appears to be variable and depends upon the exposure, type of hydrocarbon pollution, duration and level of exposure, geographic location, laboratory or field setting, and species. Some species of Acropora appear to be relatively tolerant to hydrocarbon expsoure (short-term dispersed oil) as in this study and in that by Legore et al. (1989). Guzman et al. (1991), however, reported significant effects to A. palmata following exposure to a major spill (primarily oil only). Thorhaug et al. (1989) found A. palmata to be sensivite to dispersed oil concentrations. In our study we found significant growth effects from short-term dispersed oil to the extension of A. tennuifolia and P. porites, but not to M. annularis and A. cervicornis. Oil only, however, showed no significant effects to these species. Guzman et al. (1991) found significant oiling effects on three (Porites astreoides, Diploria strigosa, and M. annularis) out of four species tested (no effect on Siderastrea siderea). Dodge et al. (1984) found no substantial effects to Bermuda D. strigosa from short exposures to oil or dispersed oil.

Hydrocarbon spills of small size and short duration in tropical reef areas are likely to increase in frequency as oil shipping and usage increase. Clean up by dispersant is a management option. While this procedure may be effective in some instances (e.g., where mangroves only are involved), it should be used with caution in others cases, especially in light of detrimental response of some benthic organisms to even short-term exposure (e.g., reef organisms of this study). Oil spill management would be enhanced by more precise documentation of short and long term effects to the broad spectrum of tropical organisms which construct and reside in/or coral reefs.

CONCLUSION

Short-term exposure (24 hrs) of Panama coral reef flora and fauna to dispersed oil caused significant detrimental effects (reduced coverage of a variety of species and reduction in growth of some species of hard corals). A similar short-term exposure of oil only did not have comparable effects.

LITERATURE CITED

Bak, R.P.M. 1987. Effects of chronic oil pollution on a Caribbean coral reef. mar. Poll. Bull. 18: 534-539.

Ballou, T.G., R.E. Dodge, A.K. Knap, S.H. Hess, and T.D. Sleeter. 1987. Effects of a dispersed and undispersed crude oil on mangroves, seagrasses, and corals. API Publication No. 4460. American Petroleum Institute, Washington, D.C. 227pp.

Brown, B. E. & Howard, L.S. 1985. Assessing the effects of "stress" on reef corals. Advances in Mar. Biol 22:1-63.

Cohen, Y., A. Nissenbaum, and R. Eisler. 1977. Effects of Iranian crude oil on the Red Sea octocoral Heteroxenia fuscesens. Environmental Pollution. 12: 173-186.

Dodge, R.E., A. Logan, and A. Antonius. 1982. Quantitative reef assessment studies in Bermuda: a comparison of methods and preliminary results. Bull. Mar. Sci. 32: 745-760.

Dodge, R.E., S.C. Wyers, H.R. Frith, A.H. Knap, S.R. Smith, and T.D. Sleeter. 1984. The effects of oil and oil dispersants on the skeletal growth of the hermatypic coral Diploria strigosa. Coral Reefs. 3.: 191-198.

Dodge, R.E., A.H. Knap. S.C. Wyers. H.R. Frith, T.D. Sleeter. and S.R. Smith. 1985. The effect of dispersed oil on the calcification rate of the reef-building coral Diploria strigosa. Proc. 5th Int. Coral Reef Congress, Tahiti. 6: 453-457.

Guzman, H.M., J.B.C. Jackson, and E. Weil. 1991. Short-term ecological consequences of a major oil spill on Panamanian subtidal reef corals. Coral Reefs. 10: 1-12.

Jackson, J.B.C., J.D. Cubit, B.D. Keller, V. Batista, K. Burns, H.M. Caffey, R.L. Caldwell, S.D. Garrity, C.D. Getter, C. Conzalez, H.M. Guzman, K.W. Kaufmann, A.H. Knap, S.C. Levings, M.J. Marshall, R. Steger, R.C. Thompson, and E. Weil. 1989. Ecological effects of a major oil spill on Panamanian coastal marine communities. Science. 243. pp. 37-44.

Keller, B.D. and J.B.C. Jackson, eds. 1991. Long-term assessment of the oil spill at Bahia Las Minas, Panama, interim report, Volume I: executive summary. OCS Study MMS 90-0030. U.S. Dept. of the Interior, Minerals Management Service, Gulf of Mexico OCS Regional Office, New Orleans, LA., xii, 48pp.

Knap, A.H., T.D. Sleeter, R.E. Dodge, S.C. Wyers, H.R. Frith, and S.R. Smith. 1983. The effects of oil spills and dispersant use on corals: a review and multidisciplinary experimental approach. Oil & Petrochemical Pollution. 1: 157-169.

Lamberts, A.E. 1978. Coral grwoth: alizarin method. In. Coral reefs: research methods, edited by D.R. Stoddart & R.E. Johannes, UNESCO, Paris, pp 523-527.

LeGore, S., D.S. Marszalek, L.J. Danek, M.S. Tomlinson, J.E. Hofman, and J.E. Cuddebak. 1989. Effect of chemically dispersed oil on Arabian Gulf corals: a field experiment. 1989 Oil Spill Conference. p 375-381.

Loya, Y. 1975. Possible effects of water pollution on the community structure of Red Sea corals. Mar. Biol. 29: 177-185.

Loya, Y. and B. Rinkevich. 1980. Effects of oil pollution on coral reef communities. Mar. Ecol. Prog. Ser. 3: 167-180.

Rinkevich, B. and Y. Loya. 1977. Harmful effects of chronic oil pollution on a Red Sea scleractinian coral population. 3rd Int. Coral Reef Symp. 2: 585-591.

Thorhaug, A., F. McDonald, B. Miller, J. McFarlane, B. Carby, M. Anderson, V. Gordon, and P. Gayle. 1989. Dispersed oil effects on tropical habitats: preliminary laboratory results of dispersed oil testing on Jamaica corals and seagrass. 1989 Oil Spill Conference. pp 455-458.

Wyers, S.C., H.R. Frith, R.E. Dodge, S.R. Smith, A.H. Knap, and T.D. Sleeter. 1986. Behavioral effects of chemically dispersed oil and subsequent recovery in Diploria strigosa. Mar. Ecol. 7: 23-42.

ACKNOWLEDGEMENTS

We thank the A.P.I. for their financial support of this project. We also thank the following individuals for assisting in various aspects of the field work: T.D. Sleeter, B. Baca, S.C. Hess, M. Brown, and T. Ballou. This paper is contribution #1345 of the Bermuda Biological Station for Research.

SYMBIONT LOSS ("BLEACHING") IN THE REEF-DWELLING BENTHIC FORAMINIFER *AMPHISTEGINA GIBBOSA* IN THE FLORIDA KEYS IN 1991-92

Pamela Hallock and Helen K. Talge

Department of Marine Science, University of South Florida, 140 Seventh Avenue S., St. Petersburg, Florida 33701

ABSTRACT

The reef-dwelling benthic foraminifera, *Amphistegina* spp., are dependent upon diatom endosymbionts for growth and calcification. Symbiont loss was discovered in *A. gibbosa* in September 1991 in the Florida Keys when >80% of post-juvenile (>0.6 mm in diameter) individuals were mottled or bleached in samples collected from depths of 10-30 m. Populations at Conch Reef were sampled between September 1991 and December 1992. Normal specimens dominated during winter months; symbiont loss resumed in March, peaked in June, with normal juveniles common by autumn. Population density in September 1992 was approximately 5% of the density found in September 1991. Suppressed asexual reproduction, congenital deformities, and abnormal shell damage were observed in affected populations. Symbiont loss was also observed in *Amphistegina* spp. from Australia, Jamaica, Hawaii, and Palau in 1992.

Some aspect of radiant energy appears to contribute to symbiont loss in *Amphistegina* spp. In the laboratory, symbiont loss can be induced in post-juvenile individuals in weeks by exposure to above-optimum intensities of fluorescent lights and within days by exposure to low doses of ultraviolet radiation. The injection of large quantities of volcanic aerosols into the atmosphere at low latitudes by Mt. Pinatubo in June 1991 may have altered the spectral quality of solar radiation reaching the sea surface in 1991 and 1992. *Amphistegina* individuals, which actively seek optimal visible light intensities, may be particularly vulnerable to an increase in ultraviolet radiation relative to available visible light.

INTRODUCTION

Bleaching (symbiont loss or expulsion) in corals, and its possible relation to global environmental change, is a topic of national concern as demonstrated by U.S. Senate hearings on the subject in 1987 and 1990, and by the NSF/EPA/NOAA sponsored workshop in June 1991 (D'Elia et al., 1991). Zooxanthellate corals on the reefs of the Florida Keys and elsewhere in the western Atlantic region have experienced extensive bleaching (symbiont loss) in at least three major events over the past decade, 1982-83, 1986-88, 1990-91 (Williams and Bunkley-Williams, 1992).

Symbiont loss was first documented in field populations of the reef-dwelling foraminifer, *Amphistegina gibbosa*, in September 1991 in the Florida Keys (Hallock et al., 1992). Bleaching was extensive in nearby Cnidaria, including *Palythoa*, *Millipora* and *Agaricia*. Living individuals of *A. gibbosa* host diatom endosymbionts (Hallock et al., 1986), probably *Nitzschia frustulum* var. *symbiotica* (Lee and Anderson, 1991). Symbionts occupy the periphery of the cytoplasm and reside in tiny depressions (pore vaults) in the chamber wall (Lee and Anderson, 1991). Cytological investigations of mottled individuals revealed empty pore vaults and abnormal numbers of large vacuoles (Hallock et al., 1992). Similar mottling was previously observed in *A. gibbosa* and *A. lessonii* (an Indo-Pacific species) grown in culture at 25-26° C under fluorescent lights at photosynthetically-active radiation (PAR) intensities exceeding 6 and 14 $uE\ s^{-1}\ cm^{-2}$ respectively (Hallock et al., 1986).

Following discovery of symbiont loss in field specimens, the *A. gibbosa* population at Conch Reef in the Florida Keys was monitored from September 1991 through December 1992. This paper describes symbiont loss, population density changes, apparent suppression of asexual reproduction, congenital deformities, and several unusual kinds of shell damage that were observed in this population during this time.

Reef-dwelling foraminifera with algal endosymbionts (Lee and Anderson, 1991) are important biological (Sournia, 1976) and sedimentological (Hallock, 1981a) contributors to reef systems. *Amphistegina* is a nearly circumtropical, reef-dwelling foraminiferal genus. The shells of these protists make up nearly 25% of Hawaiian beach sands (Hallock Muller, 1976) and as much as 95% of sand-sized sediments on some Pacific atolls (McKee et al., 1959). If Pacific populations are ever impacted in the way that the *A. gibbosa* population has been at Conch Reef, the loss of sediment production could be substantial. Therefore, it is imperative for bleaching in *Amphistegina* to be thoroughly documented and that its causes be identified.

METHODS

Amphistegina gibbosa is typically found in algal turf and reef rubble at depths of at least 8 m to in excess of 40 m in densities of 10^4 to 10^5 individuals m^{-1} (Hallock et al., 1986). Sampling methods were described by Hallock et al. (1992). SCUBA divers collected rubble into plastic bags, which were taken to a shore-based laboratory where foraminifera and associated "Aufwuchs" were removed from the rubble using a toothbrush. Resultant samples were examined microscopically within three hours of collection. *Amphistegina* were picked and visually ranked as "normal", "mottled", or "bleached" (Fig. 1). To determine if visual observations could be quantified, individual specimens were measured (maximum diameter), crushed, and chlorophyll pigments were extracted using the methanol method of Holm-Hansen and Riemer (1978). Because most specimens exhibiting symbiont loss appeared "mottled" to some degree, ranging from one or more anomalous white spots to nearly bleached with a few remaining brown areas, and because very few specimens were found fully bleached, for fluorometric analysis living specimens were individually classified as

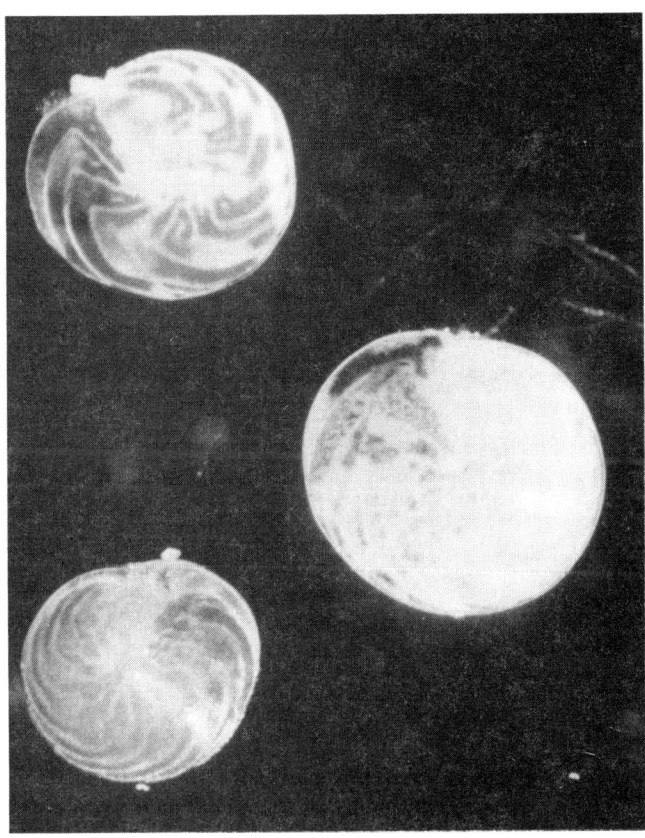

Figure 1. *Amphistegina gibbosa* (40x). Clockwise from top: mottled specimen, bleached specimen, normal specimen.

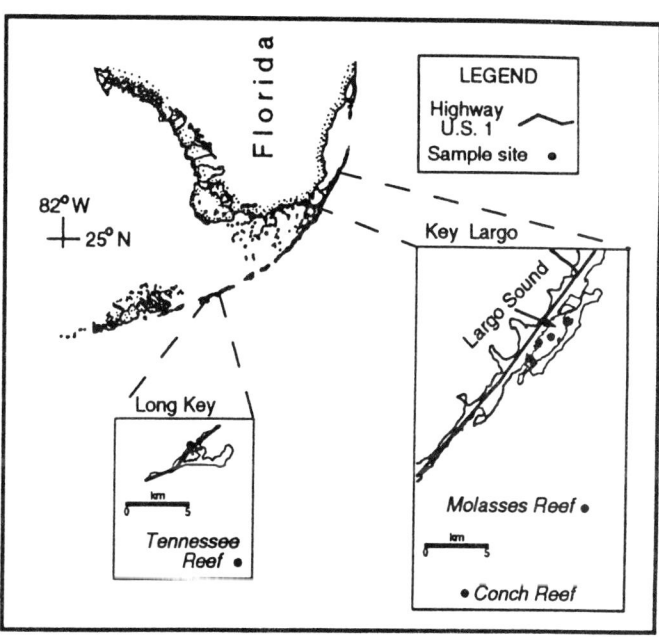

Figure 2. Sampling sites in the Florida Keys.

"normal", "some mottling", "very mottled or pale". A group of laboratory-bleached individuals were also fluorometrically analyzed for comparison with field specimens. To determine relative densities, all living *A. gibbosa* specimens from individual rubble pieces were counted and the bottom area covered by those pieces were measured to the nearest 1 cm^2.

Following the discovery of symbiont loss in *A. gibbosa* at Conch, Carysfort, and Molasses Reefs (Fig. 2) in late September 1991, a population at Conch Reef, 18 m depth, was sampled at least bimonthly through December 1992. Samples were also collected at 30 m depth between June and December 1992. After observing unexpectedly high proportions of mottled individuals in early May 1992, a preliminary shading experiment was developed to begin to test the hypothesis that some quality of solar radiation was triggering symbiont loss in these foraminifera. In June, three 0.25 m^2 UV-opaque plastic plates were placed over reef rubble at Conch Reef, 18 m depth. New plates reduce PAR by <10% and UV-B by approximately 90%. In July, one 0.25 m^2 UV-transparent plastic plate was emplaced over rubble in the vicinity of the other three. This plate reduces both PAR and UV radiation by <10%. Fouling and sediments on the plates reduced PAR by approximately 50% in 1-2 months, so plates were replaced in July and September. Rubble samples were taken from beneath those plates in July, September and October.

In May and September 1992, several hundred individuals were collected live from Conch Reef and maintained in culture for several weeks to observe reproductive activity. Culture methods were similar to those previously described by Hallock et al. (1986). When an asexual reproduction occurred, the parent diameter was measured to the nearest 50 µm, young individuals were counted, distinguishing between normal and deformed individuals, and between sinistrally and dextrally coiling individuals.

In addition to work in the Florida Keys, samples of living *Amphistegina* were collected and examined from Heron Island, Australia in early March 1992; Montego Bay, Jamaica on May 15, 1992; Palau, Western Caroline Islands, and Chuuk, Eastern Caroline Islands, in late June 1992; and Makapuu, Oahu, Hawaii in late June 1992.

RESULTS

Analysis of covariance of fluorometry data (Fig. 3) showed no significant difference between "normal"-appearing individuals and those with "some mottling" ($F=0.21$; $df=1,62$), while "very mottled and pale" ($F=7.44$; $df=2,87$) and "laboratory-bleached" ($F=17.5$, $df=3,89$) specimens have significantly reduced chlorophyll concentrations. The latter specimens contain negligible chlorophyll concentrations.

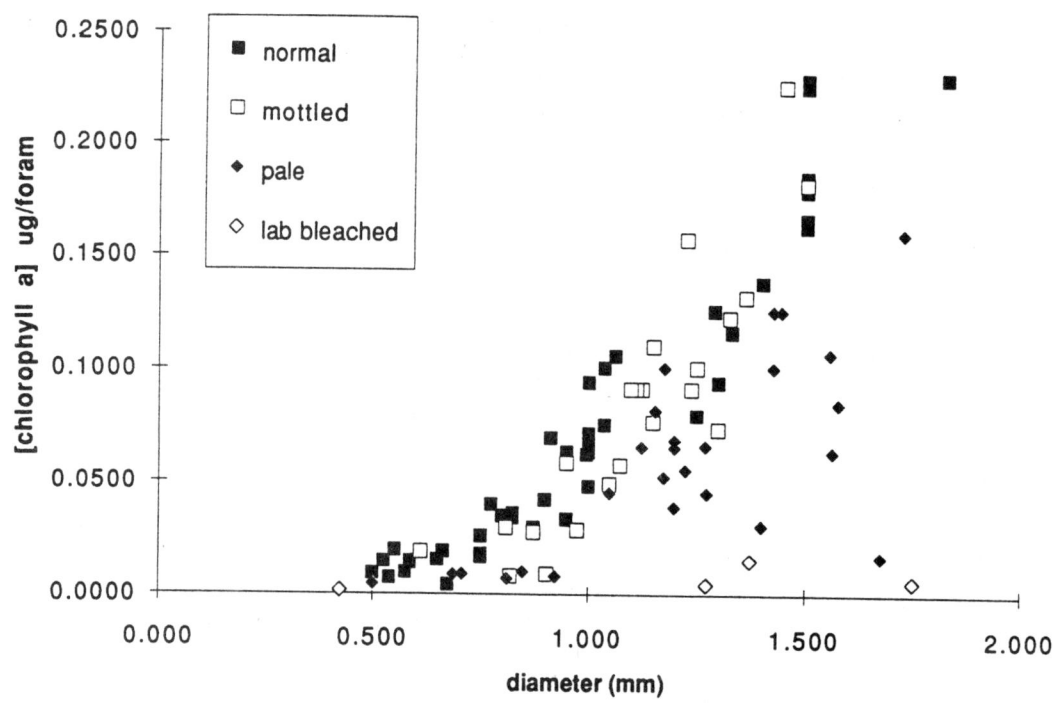

Figure 3. Fluorometry data for normal, mottled, pale (including very mottled), and laboratory-bleached specimens of *Amphistegina gibbosa*.

Data on the *A. gibbosa* population from Conch Reef, collected between September 1991 and December 1992, are presented in Table 1. In September 1991, nearly two-thirds of the population was mottled or bleached. Juveniles (≤ 0.6 mm in diameter), most normal in color, were common. Between September and January, population densities declined as did the proportion of mottled individuals. Symbiont loss resumed by March, peaked in June and July, and declined in the fall months. Population densities remained low and few juveniles were present in the population during summer months, though individuals of reproductive size (>1 mm) were common in the population. Juveniles increased in the population during the fall, as did the proportions of adults showing shell damage or appearing grainy instead of either mottled or uniform golden brown. Subpopulations shaded by both UV-transparent and UV-opaque plastic plates showed reduced bleaching by September, but only those under the UV-opaque shields substantially increased in densities during the experiment. Samples collected from 30 m were bleached in similar proportions in June and July, but maintained higher population densities and began to recover more quickly in the late summer.

By September 1992, extensive shell damage and deformities were commonly observed in the population. Breakage included margin chipping or loss, and loss of the entire row of outer chambers. Some tests were so fragile that several chambers sheared off when a test was picked up with forceps. Living individuals were found infested by filamentous algae and microborers, and a small predatory foraminifer and its bore holes were commonly seen on living individuals. Shape abnormalities included twisted and elongate tests, conjoined tests, tests with distended protoconchs (initial chambers), and tests with two apertures. Fused individuals of different sizes were also recorded. Breakage was most common, occurring in 5-20% of the individuals counted. Other types of damage together account for less than 5% of the individuals.

Data on asexual reproductions observed in culture within three weeks after field collection are shown in Table 3; 27 clones were observed from the May 6 samples and 25 clones from the September 25 samples. From previous observations of reproduction in *Amphistegina* spp. (Hallock 1981b and unpubl. observations), a "normal" *A. gibbosa* clone is produced by a parent individual at least 1.1 mm in diameter and consists of 300-800 juveniles of which less than 0.5% are nonviable, none are deformed, and <5% coil sinistrally. In the May clones, 37% of the reproducing individuals were <1.1 mm in diameter and most of those clones produced fewer than 100 young. Nearly half produced some deformed young and 6 clones contained more than 10% deformed young. In September, 84% of the asexually reproducing individuals were <1.1 mm and most produced small, damaged clones. Congenital deformities observed included addition of chambers at abnormal angles, yielding twisted-looking or elongate juveniles, specimens with distended protoconchs, and conjoined twins.

Data from other locations are presented in Table 4. At Tennessee Reef, in the middle Florida Keys, samples were collected for culture experiments on May 10 and June 23, 1991. Specimens collected in May were normal and were used for experiments. Many specimens collected in June were mottled or pale, so the collections were deemed unusable for experiments. Because the specimens had been collected on a very clear, sunny day using an open boat, overexposure to sunlight during transport was considered a possible

Table 1 Observations of the Amphistegina *gibbosa* population from Conch Reef, Florida Keys, 1991-1992.

Date	Temp. (°C)	Depth (m)	No. Counted	Density ($\#\times10^4$ m^{-2})	Percent Normal	Percent Mottled	Percent Bleached[1]	Percent Juveniles[2]
9/27/91	29	18	344	4.4	34	38	28	34
11/7/91	23	18	342	0.73	68	17	15	39
1/9/92	<23	18	17	0.28	100	0	0	29
3/27/92	<25	18	31	0.27	75	16	3	42
5/6/92	23-25	18	428	0.31	33	63	4	33
6/1/92	27	18	175	0.27	18	79	3	6
		30	222	1.1	16	76	8	5
7/6/92	28	18	101	0.25	18	33	49	15
		18*	162	1.5	25	47	28	13
		30	103	0.5	17	34	51	10
9/25/92	29	18	501	0.23	28	39	33	17
		18**	25	0.18	72	24	4	68
		18*	338	1.6	68	26	6	43
		30	490	2.4	57	33	10	42
10/30/92	27	18	394	0.87	62	28	10	48
		18**	132	0.35	80	16	4	50
		18*	602	0.85	75	22	3	52
		30	402	4.0	59	27	14	48
12/4/92	26	18	203	2.3	68	27	5	35
		30	204	2.9	71	23	6	38

[1]Very mottled, pale or bleached [2]Diameter <0.6 mm *Under UV-opaque shade **Under UV-transparent shade

Table 2. Summary of data on asexual reproductions of individuals reproducing within 3 weeks after collection in May and September 1992.

Month	Number clones	Parent <1.1 mm	<150 young	>10%* deformed	Nonviable clones	>10%** sinistral
May	27	37%	37%	22%	11%	50%
Sept.	25	84%	72%	70%	24%	84%

*Percentage of clones in which more than 10% of the juveniles showed deformities.
**Percentage of clones in which more than 10% of the juveniles coiled sinistrally.

cause of the mottling. In retrospect, this was likely the first observation of symbiont loss in *Amphistegina* in 1991. Nearly 10% of the specimens of *A. lessonii* collected from Heron Island were mottled, but virtually no specimens were normal in appearance: most appeared grainy and many tests were twisted or damaged and repaired. Corals, particularly acroporids, were extensively bleached on the Heron Reefs and elsewhere on the Great Barrier Reef in early 1992 (Oliver, 1992). In May 1992 at Jack Tar Reef in Montego Bay, about a quarter of the *A. gibbosa* population, mostly adult individuals, were mottled; normal juveniles dominated the population. Some mottling was observed in *A. lessonii* and *A. lobifera* from Oahu, Hawaii, and Palau, Western Caroline Islands, but not from

Chuuk, in the Eastern Caroline Islands. *Amphistegina radiata* collected on Palau were extensively mottled and many specimens collected were as much as 4-5 mm in diameter, more than double normal size, indicating suppression of asexual reproduction.

Table 4. Observations of *Amphistegina* spp. at Other Locations in 1991-92

Date	Location	Depth (m)	Temp. ($^{\circ}$C)	Corals Bleached?	*Amphistegina* mottled?
5/91	Tenn. Reef, FL Keys	20	26	no	no
6/91	Tenn. Reef, FL Keys	20	28	no	many, % unknown
9/91	Molasses & Carysfort Reefs, FL Keys	10-30	29	yes	80% of adults
3/92	Heron Island, Australia, GBR	8-20	25	yes	some, 5-10%
5/92	Montego Bay, Jamaica	8	27	no	26% - *A. gibbosa* 38% of >0.6 mm
6/92	Makapuu, Oahu, Hawaii	1	27	no	5% - *A. lessonii* 40%- *A. lobifera*
6/92	Ngerong, Palau	5-15	28	minor	88% - *A. radiata* 8% - *A. lessonii*
6/92	Moen, Chuuk	<3	27	minor	no
10/92	Makapuu	1 m	unknown	unknown	14% - *A. lessonii*

DISCUSSION

Hallock et al. (1992) demonstrated cytologically that color loss in *A. gibbosa* is caused by loss of its diatom symbionts. Fluorometric analysis (Fig. 3) showed measureable loss in chlorophyll concentrations within very mottled and bleached individuals. While the decline in chlorophyll in individuals exhibiting some mottling was not statistically significant, it is evident from visual observations that symbiont loss is gradual. The amount of chlorophyll in a normal *Amphistegina* is dependent upon cytoplasmic volume. Maximum diameter is a quick indicator of size, but because the shape can be quite variable (Hallock et al., 1986), diameter is a relatively poor indicator of volume. At the early stages of symbiont loss, inter specimen variability in cytoplasmic volume can mask differences in chlorophyll-to-diameter ratios. Performing detailed morphometric analysis on each specimen subjected to fluorometry would provide a more precise quantitative indicator of symbiont loss. It would also be extremely time consuming and no more useful than visual analysis.

Symbiont loss is the most obvious of several kinds of damage to this *A. gibbosa* population. Suppression of asexual reproduction in some individuals and premature reproduction of small, damaged clones by others may account for the low population density observed at Conch Reef during most of 1992. The abundant evidence of weakened tests, predation and microboring is further evidence that symbiont loss weakens affected individuals. Production of substantial proportions of sinistrally coiling juveniles in clones produced in the laboratory is not detrimental in itself, but does indicate environmental change (Hallock, 1988).

The exact cause of symbiont loss in *Amphistegina gibbosa* at Conch Reef and other locations is still uncertain. It is clear that symbiont loss in *Amphistegina* was not caused by elevated sea-surface temperatures. None of the examples of symbiont loss occurred at temperatures above 29° C except at Conch Reef in late summer 1991.

We have several reasons to suspect that above-optimum intensities of at least some wavelengths of solar radiation may be causing symbiont loss and associated damage in *A. gibbosa*. Photoinhibition was previously recognized in *Amphistegina* spp. (Lee et al., 1980; Hallock et al., 1986), but the destructive wavelengths have not been determined. Mottling and bleaching can be induced in *A. gibbosa* in the laboratory with fluorescent light at intensities >6uE s^{-1} cm^{-2}(Hallock et al., 1986). In post-juvenile individuals, mottling and bleaching can be induced more quickly by augmenting fluorescent light with low intensities of UV-A and UV-B radiation (Talge and Hallock, 1993). In field populations of *A. gibbosa* at Conch Reef in 1992, symbiont loss peaked with the solstice. Following the solstice, proportions of individuals exhibiting symbiont loss declined faster and population densities increased more quickly in the 30 m population and in shaded subpopulations at 18 m than in the unshaded 18 m population. Furthermore, cases of symbiont loss in *Amphistegina* spp. appear to have been widespread in 1992.

While we do not suggest that symbiont loss has not occurred previously in *Amphistegina* spp., we contend that it is unusual and detrimental to the population. The senior author has been studying *Amphistegina* intermittently since 1970 (e.g., Hallock Muller,

1974) and previously sampled six different populations monthly through two different years (Hallock, 1981a). Mottling has been observed in laboratory cultures under above-optimum intensities of fluorescent lights (Hallock et al., 1986), which emit some radiation in the UV-B range. Prior to the observation of damaged individuals from Tennessee Reef in late June 1991, the only known observation of mottling in a field population was in a few specimens collected at Lee Stocking Island in February 1988 by Karen Smith, who was participating in a post-bleaching coral survey.

In clear oceanic waters, UV radiation in the 280-320 nm wavelength range can reach depths of 20 m or more at intensities ($>10^{-3}$ watts m^{-2}) capable of influencing both DNA and plant chromophores (Smith and Calkins 1976; Smith and Baker 1981). Characteristic responses to UV-B radiation, including damage to chromophores, reproduction and development (Hader and Worrest, 1991), appear to be occurring in mottled *Amphistegina*. If symbiont loss is caused by damaging intensities of UV radiation, what can account for their exposure beginning in the summer of 1991? A behavioral characteristic of *Amphistegina* may provide a clue. Individuals orient to some radiation optimum. Though the spectral characteristics of that optimum have not been determined, preliminary experiments indicate response to visible wavelengths, not to UV radiation (Talge, unpublished). We postulate that, if atmospheric or water-column conditions changed such that the intensities of longer wavelengths (>400 nm) declined while shorter wavelengths (<400 nm) remained constant or increased, these foraminifera would move to more exposed positions with the possible consequences being symbiont loss and reproductive damage.

The eruptions of Mt. Pinatubo in early to mid June 1991 certainly altered intensities of solar radiation reaching the Earth's surface in 1991 and 1992. Is it possible that the spectral quality was altered as well? Ash and aerosols injected into the atmosphere by the volcano quickly circled the globe at low latitudes (Horgan, 1992). The result was sufficient decline in visible and infra-red radiation reaching the Earth to apparently disrupt global wind systems, contributing to two consecutive years of El Niño-Southern Oscillation (ENSO) conditions. Although some shorter wavelength radiation must have been reflected or absorbed by the volcanic emissions, the aerosols apparently catalyzed ozone destruction by volcanically-produced, chlorine-rich volcanic gases and by anthropogenic chlorofluorocarbons in the stratosphere. High latitude, stratospheric ozone concentrations reached record lows in 1992 (Brasseur, 1992) and ozone depletion was measured in tropical latitudes (Grant et al., 1992)

The relationship between ENSO and coral-bleaching events has been recognized since 1983 (Glynn, 1984); the relationship between ENSO events and major low-latitude volcanic eruptions has more recently been recognized. The major ENSO and coral-bleaching events of 1982-83 followed the eruption of El Chichón volcano in Mexico. The somewhat smaller, catastrophic Nevado del Ruiz eruption in Colombia in 1986 preceded the 1986-87 ENSO and coral-bleaching event. Mid-latitude ozone depletion was documented following the El Chichón eruption (Hofmann and Soloman, 1989). Glynn et al. (1992) demonstrated that some coral species are more sensitive to the combination of elevated temperature and UV radiation than to either factor alone. Is it possible that with the anthropogenic destruction of the Earth's stratospheric ozone layer, volcanic eruptions can produce sufficient shifts in the solar spectra reaching the Earth as to be damaging to photosymbiotic organisms?

Photosynthetic symbioses account for significant primary and carbonate production in both pelagic and neritic tropical oceanic realms. If these symbioses prove to be sensitive to relative or absolute increases in intensities of biologically-damaging UV radiation penetrating surface waters of the world's oceans, implications for carbonate production and the global carbon budget may be profound.

CONCLUSIONS

1. Symbiont loss was observed in *Amphistegina gibbosa* in the Florida Keys in 1991 and 1992, and in Montego Bay Jamaica in May 1992.

2. Symbiont loss was accompanied by suppression of asexual reproduction and reproductive damage in individuals that did reproduce. Congenital deformities were observed both in field populations and in clones produced in the laboratory by specimens recently collected from field populations.

3. Tests of many specimens exhibiting symbiont loss were damaged by physical or biological mechanisms, sometimes both.

4. Elevated water temperatures were not the cause of symbiont loss observed in *A. gibbosa* in 1992.

5. Evidence implicating radiant energy as a factor contributing to symbiont loss in *Amphistegina* spp. include

    a) previous observations of mottling in laboratory cultures exposed to above-optimum intensities of fluorescent light and to low intensities of biologically damaging wavelengths of ultraviolet radiation (UV-B);

    b) observations that symbiont loss in Florida Keys population peaked in June and July, corresponding to peak solar insolation; and

    c) faster recovery in shaded subpopulations at 18 m water depth and in unshaded populations at 30 m than in unshaded populations at 18 m.

ACKNOWLEDGMENTS

The initial discovery of symbiont loss in *A. gibbosa* occurred while sampling under NOAA-National Undersea Research Center/UNCW Subcontract No. 9120; subsequent research has been supported by NOAA-NURC/UNCW Subcontracts No. 9204 and 9322, and by NSF-OCE-9203278. We owe special thanks to Dr. Steven Miller, Director, Thomas Potts, Mission Coordinator, and David Ward, Divemaster, at the NOAA-NURC/UNCW Florida Keys Facility in Key Largo, for their encouragement, suggestions and invaluable field assistance. E. M. Cockey and R. G. Muller assisted in sampling and countless hours of foram picking. G.A. Vargo provided advice and facilities for the fluorometric analysis; Karen Smith assisted in the sample preparation and measurement. Tony Greco took the SEM photomicrographs. Mark Peebles provided technical assistance in computer graphics and R.G. Muller with statistics.

LITERATURE CITED

Brasseur, G. 1992. Ozone depletion - volcanic aerosols implicated. Nature 359:275-276.

D'Elia, C.F., R.W. Buddemeier and S.V. Smith. 1991. Workshop on Coral Bleaching, Coral Reef Ecosystems and Global Change: Report of Proceedings. Maryland Sea Grant College Publ. No. UM-SG-TS-91-03. 49 pp.

Glynn, P.W. 1984. Widespread coral mortality and the 198283 El Nino warming event. Environ. Conserv. 11(2):133-146.

Glynn, P.W., R. Imai, K. Sakai, Y. Nakano, and K. Yamazato. 1992. Experimental responses of Okinawan (Ryukyu Islands, Japan) reef corals to high sea temperature and UV radiation. Proceedings, 7th International Coral Reef Symposium. (in press).

Grant, W.B., J. Fishman, E.V. Browell, V.G. Brackett, D. Nganga, A. Minga, B. Cros, R.E. Veiga, C.F. Butler, M.A. Fenn and G.D. Nowicki. 1992. Observations of reduced ozone concentrations in the tropical stratosphere after the eruption of Mt. Pinatubo. Geophys. Res. Lett. 19(11):1109-1112.

Häder, D.-P. and R.C. Worrest. 1991. Effects of enhanced solar ultraviolet radiation on aquatic ecosystems. Photochem. Photobiol. 53:717-725.

Hallock, P. 1981a. Production of carbonate sediments by selected large benthic foraminifera on two Pacific coral reefs. J. Sed. Petrol. 51:467-474.

Hallock, P. 1981b. Light dependence in *Amphistegina*. J. Foram Res. 11:42-48.

Hallock, P. 1988. Notes on coiling direction in trochospiral benthic foraminifera. Rev. Paleobiol. Vol. Spec. No. 2:799-802.

Hallock, P., T.L. Cottey, L.B. Forward and J. Halas. 1986a. Population biology and sediment production of *Archaias angulatus* (Foraminiferida) in Largo Sound, Florida. J. Foram. Res. 16: 1-8.

Hallock, P., L.B. Forward and H.J. Hansen. 1986. Environmental influence of test shape in *Amphistegina*. J. Foram. Res. 16: 224-231.

Hallock, P, H.K. Talge, K. Smith and E.M. Cockey. 1992. Bleaching in a reef-dwelling foraminifer, *Amphistegina gibbosa*. Proceedings, 7th International Coral Reef Symposium, Guam. (in press).

Hallock Muller, P. 1974. Sediment production and population biology of the benthic foraminifer *Amphistegina madagascariensis*. Limnol Oceanogr. 19:802-809.

Hallock Muller, P. 1976. Sediment production by shallow water benthic foraminifera at selected sites on Oahu, Hawaii. Maritime Sed., Spec. Publ. 1:263-265.

Hofmann, D.J. and S. Solomon. 1989. Ozone destruction through heterogenous chemistry following the eruption of El Chichon. J. Geophys. Res. 94(D4):5029-5041.

Holm-Hansen, O. and B. Reimer. 1978. Chlorophyll a determination: improvements in methodology. OIKOS 30:438-447.

Horgan, J. 1992. Vocanic disruption - a giant eruption frays the tattered ozone layer. Scientific American, March:28-29.

Lee, J.J. and O.R. Anderson. 1991. *Biology of Foraminifera*. Academic Press, New York, 368 pp.

Lee, J.J., M.E. McEnery and J.R. Garrison. 1980. Experimental studies of larger foraminifera and their symbionts from the Gulf of Elat on the Red Sea. J. Foram. Res. 10:31-47.

McKee, E.D., J. Chronic and E.B. Leopold. 1959. Sedimentary belts in the lagoon of Kapingimarangi Atoll. Bull. Amer. Assoc. Petrol. Geol. 43:501-562.

Oliver, J. 1992. Coral bleaching alert. Reef Res. 2:11.

Smith, R.C. and K.S. Baker. 1981. Optical properties of the clearest natural waters (200-800 nm). Appl. Opt. 20:177-184.

Smith, R.C. and J. Calkins. 1976. The use of the Robertson meter to measure the penetration of solar middle-ultraviolet (UV-B) into natural waters. Limnol. Oceanog. 21:746-749.

Sournia, A. 1976. Primary production of sands in the lagoon of an atoll and the role of foraminiferan symbionts. Mar. Biol. 37:29-32.

Talge, H.K. and P. Hallock. (1993). Observation of symbiont loss in benthic foraminifera. Proceeding of the Association of Scanning Electron Microscopists (Scanning'93), Orlando, Florida. (in press).

Williams, E.H., Jr. and L. Bunkley-Williams. 1992. 1989-1991 Worldwide coral reef bleaching. Proceedings, 7th International Coral Reef Symposium, Guam. (in press).

THE STATUS OF THE REMNANT POPULATION OF *ACROPORA PALMATA*
(LAMARCK, 1816) AT DRY TORTUGAS NATIONAL PARK, FLORIDA,
WITH A DISCUSSION OF POSSIBLE CAUSES OF CHANGES SINCE 1881

Walter C. Jaap and Frank J. Sargent

Florida Marine Research Institute, 100 8th Ave. SE
St. Petersburg, Florida 33701-5095

ABSTRACT

Acropora palmata communities covered 44 hectares of reef habitat at Dry Tortugas in 1881. *Acropora palmata* disappeared from Long Key Reef before 1932 and from Bird Key Reef between 1932 and 1960. In 1976, a remnant population was estimated to cover less than 600 m^2, and about two-thirds of that population died in the winter of 1977. In 1993, the population perimeter enclosed approximately 1,400 m^2, and the densest aggregation of colonies covered a 728-m^2 area. The causes of the population collapse are unknown, but the most plausible cause is a combination of the effects of hurricanes and cold-water mortality.

INTRODUCTION

The Dry Tortugas area is a complex of islands, shoals, and reefs located approximately 117 km west of Key West, Florida. The geographic boundaries lie within 24°33' and 24°44' N latitude and 82°46' and 82°58' W longitude. Scientific investigations of the area, particularly with respect to coral reef research, began about 1850 with expeditions by Louis and Alexander Agassiz and continued until about 1937 (see summaries by Colin, 1980; Davis, 1982; and Jaap et al., 1989). Research on the area was renewed in the early 1970s (Davis, 1977a; 1977b), and an interdisciplinary investigation of the benthic resources was made in 1975-1976 (Davis, 1982; Jaap et al., 1989). Since 1976, Florida Marine Research Institute (FMRI) researchers have made extensive field investigations of Dry Tortugas coral reefs (e.g., Jaap et al., 1989).

The elkhorn coral, *Acropora palmata* (Lamarck, 1816), is an environmentally sensitive species that requires clear, highly saline, well-circulated water; solid substrate; and moderate water temperatures (optimally 25°C to 29°C) without extreme seasonal variation (Jaap et al., 1989). The species was first recorded (as *Madrepora palmata*) at Dry Tortugas by A. Agassiz (1882), who reported that populations were concentrated in a band seaward of Long Key and Bird Key and that they covered approximately 44 hectares (4.4 X 10^6 m^2, 108.7 acres) in 1881.

Field notes by Wells (1932) indicated that by then *A. palmata* had become restricted to depths of 6-10 feet along the seaward edge of Bird Key Reef rampart and the seaward end of Five-Foot Channel, a tidal channel with a hard bottom and strong currents. A sketch map in Wells' notes shows that the Bird Key Reef rampart was about 366 m long. Wells characterized the shallow-water reef community as a *Diploria clivosa* association in the shallower area seaward of the rampart and an *Acropora palmata* association between the *D. clivosa* association and the 20-ft (6-m) depth contour. However, Wells did not estimate the areal coverage of *A. palmata*.

Davis (1982) compared the distributions of corals at Dry Tortugas in 1976 with those described and mapped by Agassiz (1882). Davis noted that *Acropora palmata* had been virtually eliminated from Dry Tortugas by 1976, occurring only in two patches in Five-Foot Channel. He estimated that the areal coverage was slightly less than 600 m^2 in 1976 and that 60% to 70% of that population had been killed by hypothermia in January 1977; hypothermia also killed 91% of populations of *Acropora cervicornis* (Lamarck, 1816) at Dry Tortugas west of Loggerhead Key and at White Shoal (Davis, 1982). Subsequent field surveys by FMRI researchers and others have located no *A. palmata* other than the population at Five-Foot Channel.

This contribution describes the current status of the Five-Foot Channel population of *A. palmata* and briefly augments the discussions of the possible causes of the species' decline presented by Davis (1982) and Jaap et al. (1989).

METHODS

To assess changes in the distribution and abundance of *Acropora palmata*, we evaluated the report and map published by Agassiz (1882) and the map published by Davis (1979); we reviewed pertinent literature, especially that of Wells (1932), Davis (1982), and Jaap et al. (1989); and we examined aerial photographs taken in 1960, 1973, 1983, and 1991 that we obtained from the National Park Service (NPS), the National Oceanic and Atmospheric Administration (NOAA), the U.S. Fish and Wildlife Service (USFWS), and the U.S. Environmental Protection Agency (EPA).

In May 1993, we mapped the densest concentration of *A. palmata* in Five-Foot Channel using a compass and fiberglass measuring tape. At 3-m intervals along the 126-m center base line, we measured the perpendicular distances from the line to points where we no longer found dense aggregations of *A. palmata*; we then used those measurements to compute the surface area of dense stands of that species. In September 1993, we used a differential Global Positioning System (GPS) with an estimated accuracy of $\pm$ 1-2 m to map the perimeter that enclosed virtually all colonies of elkhorn coral. For GPS mapping, a boat equipped with a GPS receiver followed a snorkeler as he swam around the elkhorn thicket. The GPS receiver provided one geographic fix per second. Data were recorded on a portable computer and were later processed with Geographic Information System (GIS) software to determine the area contained within the perimeter. We then mapped the perimeter of the *A. palmata* population on a GIS version of Davis' 1979 map, which was enhanced by interpretations of 1983 aerial photographs based on Davis' 1982 map (Filbey, 1983).

The unpublished reports, maps, GIS data files, and aerial photographs used in this study are on file at FMRI.

RESULTS AND DISCUSSION

The area within the perimeter mapped by GPS in 1993 that included colonies of *A. palmata* was 1,400 m^2. Figure 1 is an enlarged image of part of the enhanced Davis (1979) map, modified to show the elkhorn coral thicket in Five-Foot Channel. The denser aggregation of colonies of *A. palmata* within the perimeter, mapped in our diving survey, covered an area of 728 m^2. The offshore point of origin of the dense aggregation was 24°37'13.7"N, 82°52'06.4"W, and the inshore terminal point was 24°37'17.8"N, 82°52'06.4"W. The principal axis was 63 m long, 150-330° magnetic. Along this axis, the width of the dense aggregation ranged from <1 m to 17.5 m. To the east and west of the dense aggregation, but within the perimeter boundary, we found approximately 20 small colonies and fragments of *A. palmata*. Presumably, these had been carried away from the dense thicket by storms and had successfully reattached to the sea floor. We could not determine from photographs whether or not *A. palmata* was present.

Loss of *A. palmata* at Dry Tortugas could have been caused by hurricanes, by hypothermia associated with winter cold fronts, by hyperthermia associated with summer doldrums, by disease, or by human activities.

Human activity at Dry Tortugas was at its zenith during the construction of Ft. Jefferson, a large fortress on Garden Key, between 1840 and 1870. Archival photographs document dredging of the moat of Ft. Jefferson during that construction. Flurries of activity continued for several decades thereafter. The United States Navy used the Dry Tortugas as a fleet staging area for the invasion of Cuba during the Spanish American War (1898). The Navy established coal-fueling docks at Dry Tortugas during World War I (1914-1918) and also deepened the harbor and channels at Garden Key at that time. On January 10, 1964, the freighter *S.S. Brother George* spilled an estimated 500 tons of Bunker C oil near Pulaski Shoal, Dry Tortugas (Haugen and Robertson, 1964; Miami Herald, 1964). A residue of this oil persisted around Bush Key and Long Key for at least five months (De Sylva and Stephens, 1964). Nevertheless, there is no evidence that any of these activities had any significant effect on the elkhorn coral populations in Five-Foot Channel.

Acropora palmata populations at Dry Tortugas reportedly were damaged by a phenomenon referred to as "Black Water" (Mayer, 1902; Feinstein et al., 1955). Evidence of this perturbation is recorded in growth bands of *Montastraea annularis*; older colonies from Florida reefs exhibit unique, narrow X-ray bands corresponding to 1878-1880, implying that growth in those years was retarded (R. B. Halley, U.S. Geological Survey, St. Petersburg, and J. H. Hudson, Key Largo National Marine Sanctuary, Key Largo, pers. comm.). However, the Agassiz map, compiled approximately three years after the black-water episode, indicated that the elkhorn coral populations remained robust after that episode, although the staghorn coral populations had collapsed (Agassiz, 1882; Davis, 1982).

Diseases affecting *A. palmata* include one called "white band disease," believed to be bacterial in nature (Peters et al., 1983), which caused morbidity and mortality in the species at Buck Island, off St. Croix, U.S. Virgin Islands (Gladfelter et al., 1977). Over a few years, the *A. palmata* populations at St. Croix, U.S. Virgin Islands, were infected and suffered epidemic mortality (Gladfelter, 1982). White band disease has occurred in *A. palmata* at other Florida reefs (W. C. Jaap, pers. obsv.), but we know of no cases of the disease in *A. palmata* at Dry Tortugas.

Hurricanes can severely damage populations of *Acropora palmata*. The passage of Hurricane Allen off Jamaica virtually extirpated *A. palmata* populations in Discovery Bay, Jamaica (Woodley et al., 1981). Twelve hurricanes passed close to Dry Tortugas during the period from 1930 to 1960 (Neumann et al., 1987). The great hurricane of 1935 passed over or near the Dry Tortugas, and four hurricanes with winds exceeding 193 km/hr passed directly over the Dry Tortugas between 1935 and 1970 (Jaap et al., 1989). Thick deposits of rubble and sediments on the shallow portions of Bird Key Reef (Shinn et al., 1977) provide circumstantial evidence that a hurricane destroyed the reef by depositing rubble and sediments on the reef; the rubble and sediment may have been derived from nearby Bird Key, which disappeared sometime after 1932.

Hypothermia generated by the passage of winter cold fronts has caused massive mortalities of populations of shallow-water corals at Dry Tortugas. A cold-water event during the winter of 1962-63 was discussed by Jaap et al. (1989), and the event of January 1977 was discussed by Davis (1982), Porter et al. (1982), and Jaap et al. (1989). These reports imply that diebacks of *Acropora* caused by hypothermia are recurrent events at Dry Tortugas. Although the remnant elkhorn coral population in Five-foot Channel that was reduced by two-thirds during the cold front in January 1977 has recovered, similar cold-water events may have contributed to the collapse of the population of *A. palmata* at Dry Tortugas between 1932 and 1974.

The precise cause of the population collapse of *Acropora palmata* at Dry Tortugas cannot be definitively determined. Effects of human activities and disease cannot be documented, but they seem to have been minimal at most. Circumstantial evidence exists that hurricanes may have contributed to the decline in three ways: by killing the coral by direct wave action, by burying the corals with sediment and coral debris, and by destroying habitat appropriate for recolonization. Two massive die-offs of *A. palmata* resulting from hypothermia have been documented. Thus, the most plausible cause of the population collapse of *A. palmata* at Dry Tortugas is a combination of hurricane damage and cold-water mortality. The existence of a small remnant population of *A. palmata* in Five-Foot Channel may indicate a lack of suitable habitat in the areas formerly occupied by the species.

CONCLUSIONS

Acropora palmata at Dry Tortugas disappeared from the Long Key area prior to 1932 and from Bird Key Reef between 1932 and 1960. Destruction of habitats by hurricanes, death by hypothermia, or both may have caused the decline of the *A. palmata* population at Dry Tortugas since 1881. The population has not recovered to original levels, probably because environments with the combination of conditions that support recruitment and growth of *A. palmata* have been virtually eliminated at Dry Tortugas, except in Five-Foot Channel.

ACKNOWLEDGMENTS

This work was supported by State of Florida general revenue funds and the Area of Critical State Concern Trust Fund; the National Park Service; and Sea Keys, funded by the John D. and Catherine T. MacArthur Foundation. We thank the staff at Dry Tortugas National Park (formerly Ft. Jefferson National Monument) for the support and encouragement they have provided over the years. We specifically thank Cliff Green, Mike and Monica Eng, Carolyn Wiley, John and Terry Gibson, and Wayne Landrum. Caroline Rogers coordinated the research program for NPS, and we appreciate her continued support. Gary Davis (NPS) provided the 1973 aerial photographs that he used to compile his map. Other aerial photographs were provided by NOAA (1960, 1991) and USFWS and EPA (1983). Larry Murphy and Tim Smith (Submerged Cultural Resources Unit, NPS) provided the Differential GPS hardware and software. Leanne J. Miller (FMRI), Linda Vandamann (NPS), and Skip Dryer, Bill Goodwin, and Richard Windgrove (all NOAA, Florida Keys Marine Sanctuary Program) assisted with the diving survey. Timothy J. Leary (FMRI) assisted with cartography and Ron Matchok (FMRI) kept our boats operating. We thank Jennifer L. Wheaton, William G. Lyons, James F. Quinn, Jr., Thomas H. Perkins, and Judith Leiby (all FMRI) for critical review of the manuscript.

LITERATURE CITED

Agassiz, A. 1882. Explorations of the surface fauna of the Gulf Stream, under the auspices of the United States Coast Survey II. The Tortugas and Florida reefs. Mem. Am. Acad. Arts Sci. Centennial Vol. 2(1): 107-132.

Colin, P. L. 1980. A brief history of the Tortugas marine laboratory and the Department of Marine Biology, Carnegie Institution of Washington. Pages 137-148 in M. Sears and D. Merriman, III, eds. Oceanography, the past. Springer, New York.

Davis, G. E. 1977a. Effects of recreational harvest on a spiny lobster, *Panulirus argus*, population. Bull. Mar. Sci. 27: 223-236.

———. 1977b. Anchor damage to a coral reef on the coast of Florida. Biol. Conserv. 1: 29-34.

———. 1979. Outer continental shelf resource map, coral distribution Fort Jefferson National Monument, the Dry Tortugas. U.S. Dept. Interior, Bureau of Land Management, Outer Continental Shelf Office, 500 Camp Street, New Orleans, LA 70130.

———. 1982. A century of natural change in coral distribution at the Dry Tortugas: a comparison of reef maps from 1881-1976. Bull. Mar. Sci. 32: 608-623.

De Sylva, D. P. and W. M. Stephens. 1964. Report on an investigation of the effects of an oil spill on the area at Fort Jefferson National Monument. Inst. Mar. Sci. Univ. Miami. 5 pp.

Feinstein, A. A., A. R. Ceurvels, R. F. Hutton and E. Snoek. 1955. Red tide outbreaks off the Florida west coast. Rep. to Fla. State Board Conserv. by the Mar. Lab. Univ. Miami. 44 pp.

Filbey, R. D. 1983. Florida Keys seagrass and coral reef inventory. Vol. 6. Dry Tortugas - January 1983. U.S. EPA, Environmental Monitoring Systems Laboratory, Las Vegas, Nevada. iii + 25 pp.

Gladfelter, W. B. 1982. White-band disease in *Acropora palmata*: implications for the structure and growth of shallow reefs. Bull. Mar. Sci. 32(2): 639-643.

_____, E. H. Gladfelter, R. K. Monahan, J. C. Ogden and R. F. Dill. 1977. Environmental studies of Buck Island Reef National Monument. Rep. to the U.S. Natl. Park Serv. 144 pp.

Haugen, R. T. and W. B. Robertson, Jr. 1964. Later report on Fort Jefferson oil spill. Memorandum W-3415, Everglades National Park and Fort Jefferson National Monument. 5 pp.

Jaap, W. C., W. G. Lyons, P. Dustan and J. C. Halas. 1989. Stony coral (Scleractinia and Milleporina) community structure at Bird Key Reef, Ft. Jefferson National Monument, Dry Tortugas, Florida. Fla. Mar. Res. Publ. 46. 31 pp.

Mayer, A. G. 1902. The Tortugas as a station for research in biology. Science 17: 190-192.

The Miami Herald. January 14, 1964. An article titled: Hundreds of birds may die in petroleum slick.

Neumann, C. J., B. R. Jarvinen and A. C. Pike. 1987. Tropical cyclones of the North Atlantic Ocean, 1871-1986. Historical climatology series 6-2. Natl. Climatic Data Center, Asheville, North Carolina and the Natl. Hurricane Center, Coral Gables, Florida. 186 pp.

Peters, E., J. Oprandy and P. Yevich. 1983. Possible causal agent of "white band disease" in Caribbean acroporid corals. J. Invertebr. Pathol. 41: 394-396.

Porter, J. W., J. Battey and G. Smith. 1982. Perturbation and change in coral reef communities. Proc. Natl. Acad. Sci. 79: 1678-1681.

Shinn, E. A., J. H. Hudson, R. B. Halley and B. Lidtz. 1977. Topographic control and accumulation of some Holocene coral reefs: south Florida and Dry Tortugas. Proc. Third Int. Coral Reef Symp. 2: 1-7.

Wells, J. W. 1932. A study of the reef Madreporaria of the Dry Tortugas and sediments of coral reefs. Unpublished manuscript, 138 pp.

Woodley, J. D., E. A. Chornesky, P. A. Clifford, J. B. C. Jackson, L. S. Kaufman, N. Knowlton, J. C. Lang, M. P. Pearson, J. W. Porter, M. C. Rooney, K. W. Rylaarsdam, V. J. Tunnicliffe, C. M. Wahle, J. L. Wulff, A. S. G. Curtis, M. D. Dahllmeyer, B. P. Jupp, M. A. R. Koehl, J. Neigel and E. M. Sides. 1981. Hurricane Allen's impact on Jamaican coral reefs. Science 214(4522): 749-755.

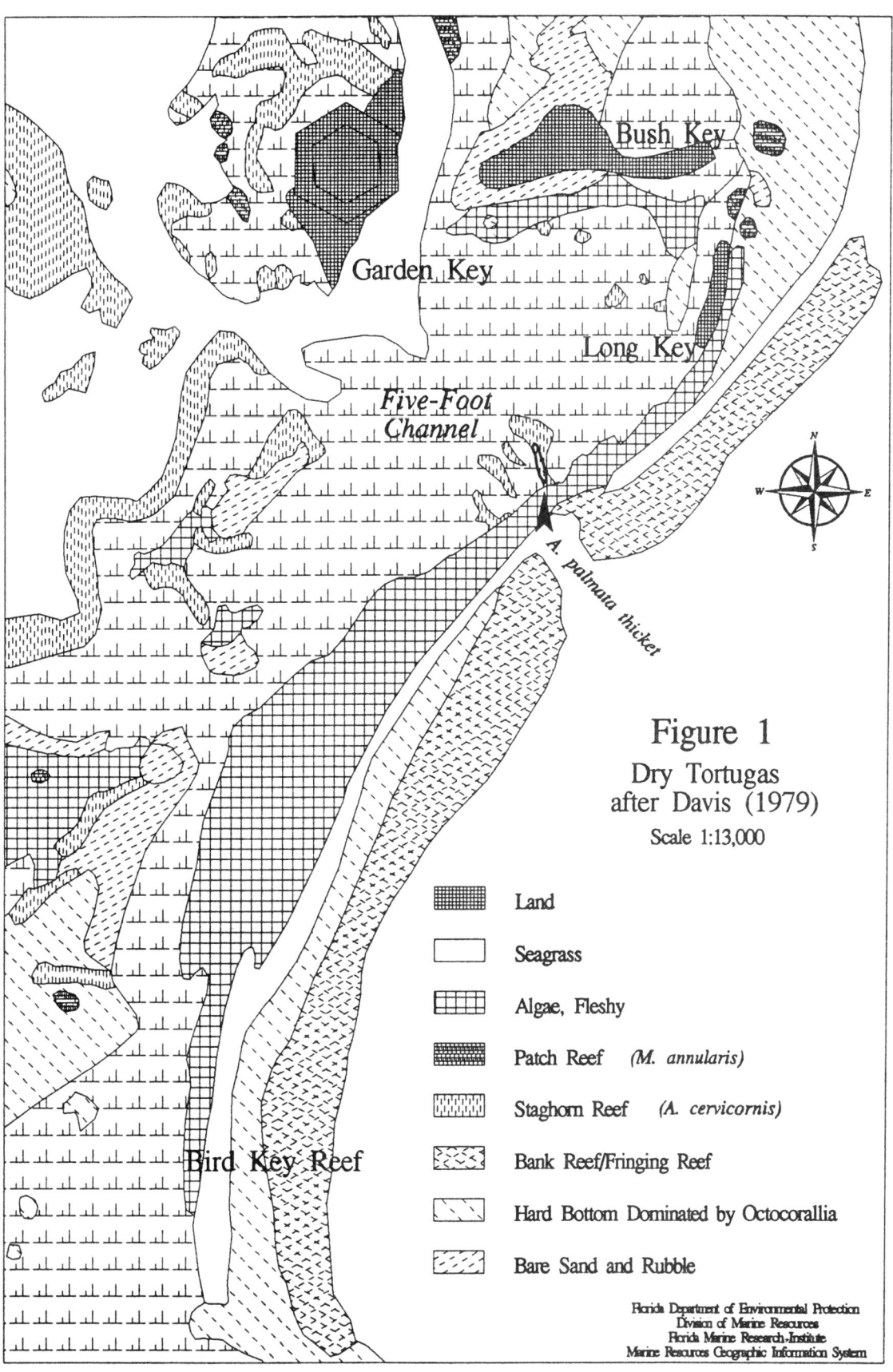

PHOSPHORUS INPUTS AND EUTROPHICATION ON THE FLORIDA REEF TRACT

Brian E. Lapointe,[1] William R. Matzie,[1] and Mark W. Clark[2]

[1] Harbor Branch Oceanographic Institution, Inc.
Rt. 3, Box 297A
Big Pine Key, FL 33043

[2] Center for Wetlands and Water Resources
University of Florida
Gainesville, FL 32601

ABSTRACT

The Florida Reef Tract (FRT) has experienced dramatic change and loss of coral cover during the past decade following many decades of intense human activities on the south Florida watershed. Comparative studies during 1990 showed that chlorophyll a, turbidity, and total dissolved phosphorus were 2-3 fold higher on bank reefs of the FRT compared to similar reefs in the less developed western Caribbean region. Sampling during summer 1992 showed high phosphorus concentrations in reduced salinity coastal waters along the eastern Gulf of Mexico, indicating land-based sources of phosphorus input. Existing data and observations also show that prevailing currents of the inner shelf waters of the eastern Gulf of Mexico move southerly, into Florida Bay, and then seaward, providing a mechanism for phosphorus transport to the FRT.

Because the carbonate-rich waters of the FRT are phosphorus-limited, cumulative phosphorus inputs from far-field sources (as well as near-field sources) mix with N-rich waters in the Florida Keys and provide a balanced nutrient supply needed to sustain nuisance algal blooms. Enrichment above a threshold of ~ 0.10 μM total dissolved phosphorus appears adequate to support nuisance algal blooms. A Landsat satellite image taken in late May 1992 showed a dense phytoplankton bloom in the same area where we observed phosphorus-rich (N-limited) waters of the eastern Gulf of Mexico flowing into N-rich (P-limited) waters of western Florida Bay. Increased phytoplankton and turbidity resulting from mixing of these water types result in widespread algal blooms, which stress reef systems by reducing submarine light while simultaneously increasing sedimentation that smothers corals, increases coral disease, and enhances coral overgrowth by benthic macroalgae. Temperature extremes have long been assumed to exert the primary stress on coral reef development along the FRT. However, our data and observations suggest that phosphorus inputs from human activities in south Florida represent an upstream source contributing to eutrophication on the FRT.

INTRODUCTION

Coastal eutrophication resulting from human nutrient inputs is considered one of the most urgent environmental signals correlating with the global decline of coral reefs (D'Elia et al., 1991; Bell, 1992). The 220-mile long Florida Reef Tract (FRT), the largest coral reef system in North America, is adjacent to rapidly growing south Florida which generates wastewater inputs from domestic, agricultural, and industrial sources. Evidence suggests that the FRT has experienced loss and change in coral populations over the past decades (Dustan and Halas, 1987; Porter and Meier, 1992). Eutrophication -- defined here as "nuisance algal blooms" (Paerl, 1988) -- has been repeatedly cited as a major threat to the FRT (Miller, 1988; USEPA, 1992). While studies have documented the role of localized domestic wastewater inputs on eutrophication of the FRT (Lapointe and Clark, 1993), more distant but significant sources of nutrient inputs from the south Florida watershed have not been assessed.

There is cause for special concern regarding nutrient inputs from the eastern Gulf of Mexico as these coastal waters are highly enriched in phosphorus (P), the primary nutrient element limiting algal growth and eutrophication in back-reef waters of the FRT (Lapointe, 1987; FDER, 1987; Lapointe, 1989). In Floridian rivers, concentrations of soluble reactive phosphorus (SRP) correlate with the distribution of phosphatic-rock formations in the watershed (Kaufman, 1969). Odum (1953) first noted the magnitude of phosphorus pollution along this coastline. Available data indicate that the greatest contribution of phosphorus to these waters is the direct result of the activity and interference by man, particularly the phosphate mining industry (Task Group Report, 1967). The inner shelf waters of the eastern Gulf of Mexico have prevailing flow to the south and southwest (Klein and Orlando, 1992), a pattern that is enhanced during the wet season (Jones et al., 1973). We have also documented very strong net cumulative flow of Gulf of Mexico/Florida Bay waters through tidal passes in the Keys towards Hawk Channel and the FRT (Lapointe et al., 1992). These data, together with observations by scientists and commercial fishermen, indicate a transport mechanism by which P inputs from the eastern Gulf of Mexico can impact the FRT. To date, no studies have been made of the dissolved P concentrations on the FRT in relation to the south Florida watershed nor have comparative studies been performed with nearby coral reefs lacking such intense human P inputs. We here provide evidence that dissolved phosphorus pools are significantly higher on the FRT than relatively pristine reefs of the western Caribbean region. Furthermore, we demonstrate that coastal waters of the eastern Gulf of Mexico may represent a significant upstream source of P contributing to algal blooms on the FRT.

METHODS

Sampling Stations and Water Analysis

FRT-Western Caribbean - These studies were performed during summer 1990 on a research expedition aboard the R/V *Cape Hatteras*. Six reef sites were selected *a priori* from navigation charts, and included three bank reefs on Banco Chinchorro, Yucatan (Cayo Norte, Cayo Centro, and Cayo Lobos), Hol Chan and Curlew Reef on the Belize Barrier Reef system, and a fringing reef on the east side of Roatan, Honduras (Fig. 1; Table 1). Six offshore bank reef sites were also sampled on the FRT, which included Carysfort Reef, Molasses Reef, Alligator Reef, Sombrero Reef, Looe Key, and Sand Key (Fig. 1; Table 1). Six water samples (three surface, three bottom) were collected with a 5.0 liter Niskin bottle at three different stations per site in 2-8 m water depth along a transect extending from the back reef to the fore reef of each site. The samples were frozen in clean high density polyethylene bottles until analysis.

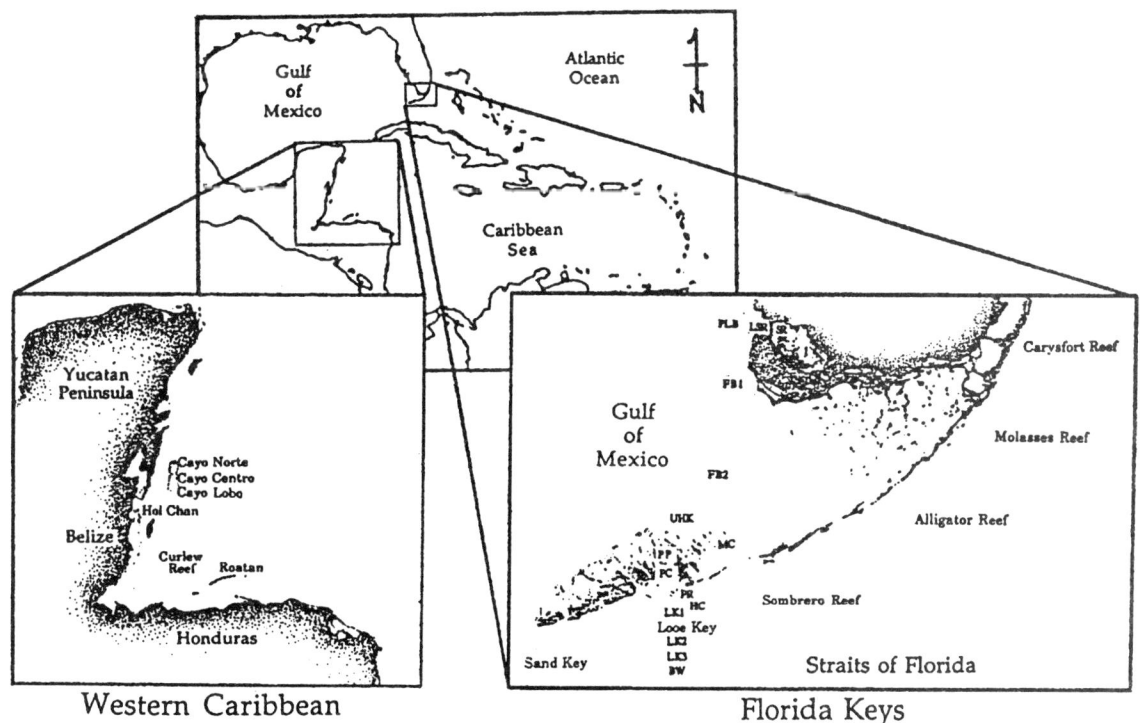

Figure 1. Maps of Florida Keys and Caribbean areas showing location of study sites.

This comparative study focused on determination of total dissolved nitrogen and phosphorus (TDN, TDP). These nutrient pools include dissolved organic nitrogen and phosphorus (DON, DOP) which are important nutrient pools supporting algal growth in oligotrophic waters (Jackson and Williams, 1985). We also measured chlorophyll a and turbidity as an index of algal response to nutrient concentrations. Chlorophyll a and turbidity are good overall indicators of eutrophication as they integrate nutrient loading over time and also had the highest negative correlation with coral growth rate along a eutrophication gradient in Barbados (Tomascik and Sanders, 1985).

Aliquots of the water samples were filtered through a GFF 0.45 µm filter prior to nutrient analysis. The filtrate was analyzed for TDN and TDP by persulfate digestion and determination of nitrate and SRP on a Technicon Autoanalyzer (D'Elia et al., 1977; Menzel and Corwin, 1965). A subsample of the filtrate was also analyzed for SRP using a Bausch and Lomb spectrophotometer fitted with a 10 cm cell; dissolved organic phosphorus (DOP) was estimated by subtraction of SRP from TDP. The filters were analyzed for chlorophyll a by extraction with DMSO and analysis on a Turner Designs Model 10 fluorometer (Burnison, 1979). Turbidity (as nephelometric turbidity units, NTU) was determined on unfiltered water samples immediately following collection on a Hach Model 2100 turbidimeter calibrated with formazin standards. Unpaired t-tests were used to statistically compare the water quality data pooled for the two regions.

Eastern Gulf of Mexico - FRT- Our study of the eastern Gulf of Mexico and the FRT was performed on July 24, 1992 and focused on the spatial distribution of total nitrogen (TN), total phosphorus (TP), and salinity measured at 17 stations along a transect extending from estuarine waters of the Shark River to oceanic blue waters offshore Looe Key National Marine Sanctuary; the station codes for the Shark River-Looe Key transect shown in Fig. 1 are as follows: Shark River (SR), Little Shark River (LSR), Ponce de

Leon Bay (PLB), Northwest Cape (NWC), East Cape (EC), Florida Bay (FB1), Florida Bay (FB2), Moser Channel (MC), Upper Harbor Key (UHK), Port Pine Heights canal (PP), Pine Channel (PC), Munson Island Patch Reef (PR), Hawks Channel (HC), Looe Key back reef (LK1), Looe Key lagoon (LK2), Looe Key fore reef (LK3), and blue water 2 km south of Looe Key (BW). GPS data were recorded for all stations.

The samples were collected at ebbing tide by coordinating movements of two small research vessels along different sections of the transect. Samples were collected from surface and bottom waters with a Niskin bottle and stored as described above. Salinity of the waters was measured using a Hydrolab Surveyor II calibrated immediately prior to use. Concentrations of total nitrogen (TN) and total phosphorus (TP) were determined on unfiltered water samples by persulfate digestion as described above. We used total N and P pools in this study because these pools include particulate fractions that are important to nutrient transport by currents and tides (Gardner et al., 1990).

RESULTS

FRT-Western Caribbean

Mean concentrations of TDN were similar between the two regions compared to 2- to 3-fold higher concentrations of TDP on the FRT (Table 1). TDN concentrations averaged ~ 3.1 µM in both regions whereas TDP averaged 0.19 µM on the FRT and 0.07 µM in the western Caribbean. The elevated TDP on reefs of the FRT was due primarily to elevated DOP concentrations (0.16 µM vs. 0.04 µM) as SRP concentrations were similar (~ 0.05 µM) between the two regions (Table 1). Because of similar TDN concentrations but elevated TDP in the Keys, TDN:TDP ratios were over 2-fold higher in the western Caribbean (~56:1) compared to the FRT (~23:1; Table 1).

TABLE 1. Concentrations of total dissolved nitrogen, total dissolved, dissolved organic, and soluble reactive phosphorus, chlorophyll a, and turbidity on coral reefs of the Florida Keys and the western Caribbean. Values represent means ± 1 standard deviation.

VARIABLE	FLORIDA KEYS	N	WESTERN CARIBBEAN	N	SIGNIFICANCE
TDN	3.11 ± 1.65	36	3.16 ± 0.58	24	NS
TDP	0.19 ± 0.12	36	0.07 ± 0.03	32	P = 0.000
SRP	0.05 ± 0.04	36	0.04 ± 0.03	32	NS
DOP	0.16 ± 0.09	36	0.04 ± 0.03	32	P = 0.000
TDN:TDP	22.5 ± 16.1	36	55.9 ± 23.9	29	P = 0.000
CHL-A	0.20 ± 0.11	37	0.11 ± 0.06	24	P = 0.002
TURBIDITY	0.35 ± 0.22	38	0.14 ± 0.04	24	P = 0.000

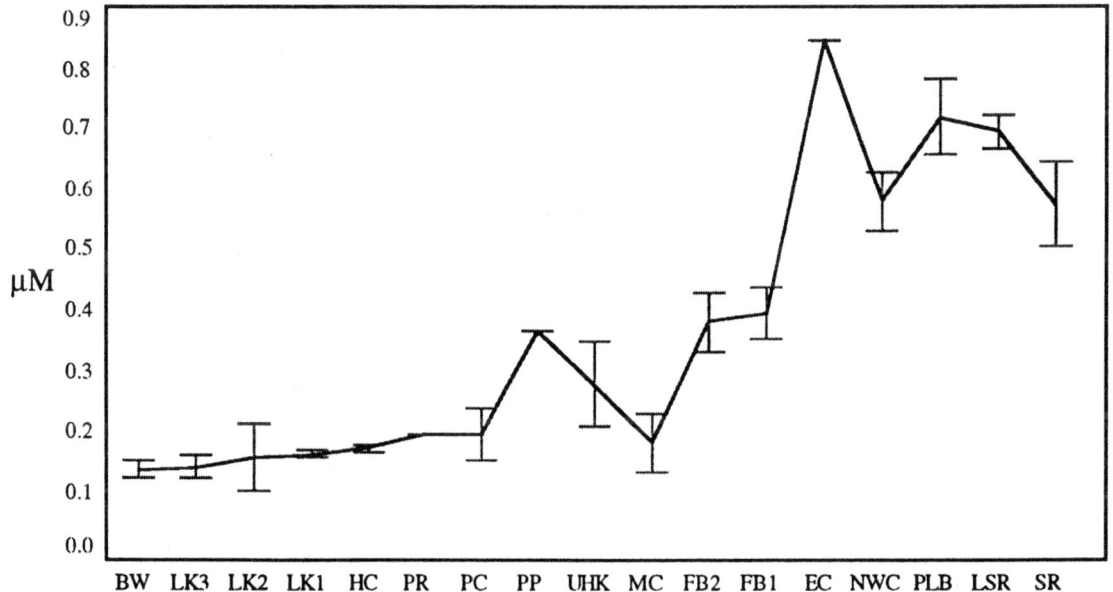

Figure 2. Total phosphorus along the Shark River-Looe Key transect. Values represent means ± 1 standard deviation.

Concentrations of chlorophyll a averaged 0.20 µg · l⁻¹ on the FRT, a value higher than the mean of 0.11 µg · l⁻¹ for the western Caribbean (Table 1). The mean turbidity was also significantly higher on the FRT, 0.35 NTU, compared to a mean of 0.14 NTU in the western Caribbean region (Table 1).

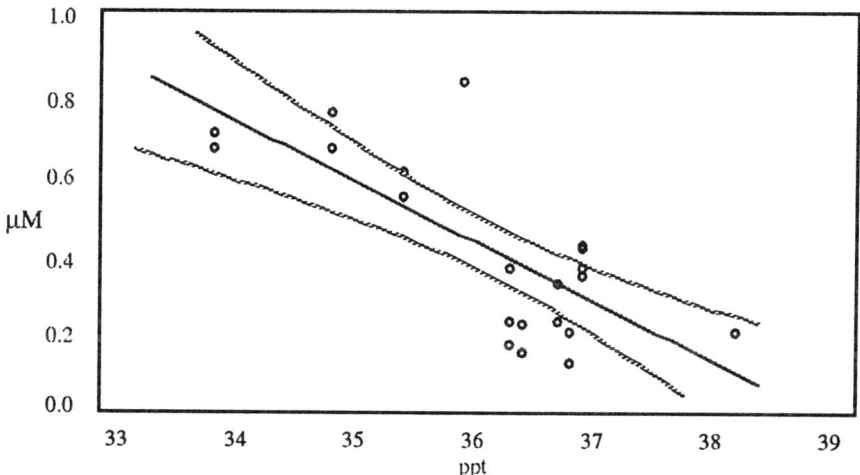

Figure 3. Regression of total phosphorus vs. salinity along the Shark River-Looe Key transect. The correlation coefficient (r) is -.71 and the regression is significant at p = .000094.

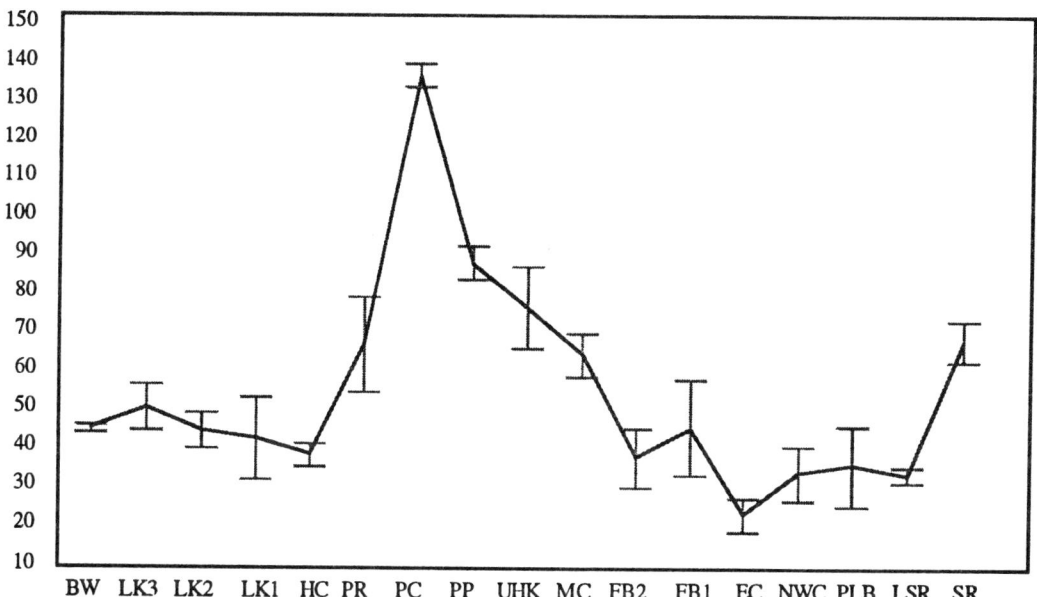

Figure 4. Water column total N:total P ratio along the Shark River-Looe Key transect.

Eastern Gulf of Mexico - FRT

Total P concentrations decreased from peak values along the eastern Gulf of Mexico, through tidal passes of the Keys and to the most offshore station south of Looe Key (Fig. 2). Total P concentrations up to 0.9 µM occurred offshore East Cape and decreased along the western edge of Florida Bay; total P concentrations increased in nearshore Keys' waters around Big Pine Key and then decreased to values of ~ 0.20 µM at Looe Key. Total P values in blue water south of Looe Key were < 0.20 µM (Fig. 2)

Regression analysis of the total P concentrations with salinity along this transect indicated a significant and negative correlation (Fig. 3). The highest total P concentrations occurred in reduced salinity water around the East Cape area and along the western edge of Florida Bay compared to the lowest P concentrations and highest salinities in more oceanic waters adjacent to Looe Key.

The total N: total P (TN:TP) ratio varied significantly along this transect from the lowest values around East Cape (< 30) to the highest values (> 100) in nearshore waters around Big Pine Key. The Shark River had a relatively high N:P ratio (~70) and the waters of Hawk Channel and Looe Key had intermediate values (~30 - 50; Fig. 4).

A Landsat satellite image (from Path 15, Row 43; Fig. 5) of south Florida recorded on May 29, 1992 shows the presence of a highly discolored, turbid zone in the East Cape area where the Shark River system discharges into the eastern Gulf of Mexico and western Florida Bay. The turbidity was caused by a dense phytoplankton bloom consisting largely of the blue-green alga *Synechococcus* and diatoms.

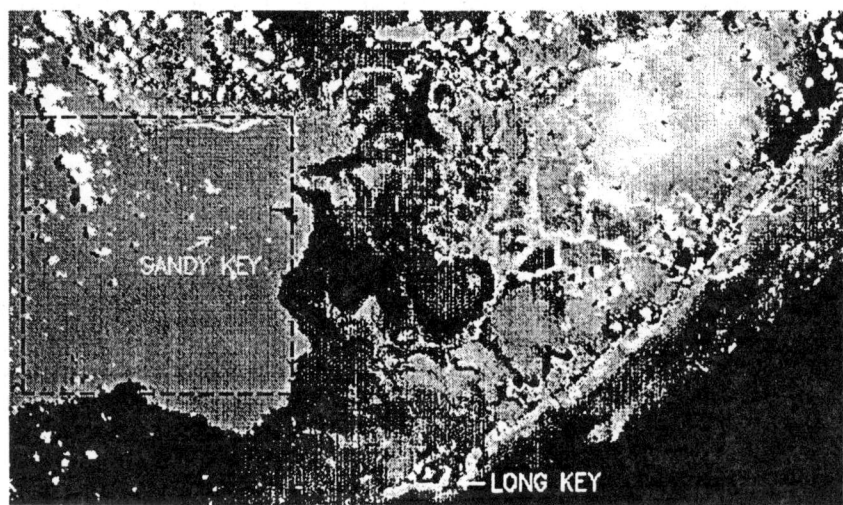

Image courtesy of Ken Haddad, Florida Marine Research Institute and EOSAT Corporation.
Figure 5. Landsat satellite image of south Florida upstream of the FRT (May 29, 1992) showing extent of algal bloom at East Cape. Boxed area is central region of algal bloom in western Florida Bay.

DISCUSSION

Our findings of higher TDP but similar TDN concentrations on the FRT compared to western Caribbean reefs suggests that algal growth on the FRT is more weakly limited by P compared to the Caribbean sites. This conclusion is directly supported by the significantly lower TDN:TDP ratio in the waters of the FRT (~23) compared to those of the Caribbean (~56); algal growth is increasingly P-limited as the N:P ratio rises above 30:1 and increasingly N-limited as the ratio decreases below this value (Ryther and Dunstan, 1971). Carbonate-rich waters of the Keys and Caribbean region tend to be P-limited in contrast to siliciclastic waters in temperate latitudes that are N-limited (Ryther and Dunstan, 1971; Lapointe et al., 1992). The carbonate sediments on tropical reefs are generally organic-poor and strongly bind phosphate (DeKanel and Morse, 1982) but not inorganic N (Rosenfeld, 1979). Along with other biogeochemical processes, the end result is a general tendency towards P-limitation of algal growth in shallow, carbonate-rich waters except where P inputs occur from either natural (e.g. guano-rich seabird rookeries, Lapointe et al., 1993) or human sources (e.g. sewage, Lapointe and O'Connell, 1989; Littler et al., 1991).

In the absence of historic data on TDP concentrations on the FRT, one might assume that TDP concentrations of the FRT were historically comparable to those that currently exist on the Caribbean sites. Globally, human activities have increased the average P concentration of river water by approximately 300% (Meybeck, 1982). Between 1974 and 1981, nitrogen and phosphorus loads entering the Gulf of Mexico increased by 46 and 55%, respectively (Smith et al., 1987). In fact, rivers along the entire southwest coast of Florida, which are upstream of the FRT with prevailing currents, have P concentrations substantially higher than most rivers in North America (data from Lovejoy et al., 1990; Flannery et al., 1991). These large P burdens result largely from phosphate mining and associated pollution that make the Alafia, Peace, and Fenholloway rivers the greatest P carriers in Florida (P concentrations in the Alafia are > 200 ppm; LaRock and Bittaker, 1973).

Additional P inputs to the FRT result from agricultural and domestic wastewater inputs in south Florida and the Keys. Over one-million acres are intensively farmed for sugarcane, sod, vegetables and cattle, practices that have increased phosphorus loads to the Everglades (Belanger et al., 1989). Freshwater wetlands like the Everglades have limited capacities for P retention and do not offer long term protection of downstream receiving waters from eutrophication (Richardson, 1985). Sewage generated by an average population of 75,000 residents (a value that approximately doubles during peak tourist periods) living within the Florida Keys also contributes significant P directly into surface waters of the FRT; specific sources include Key West's 7 MGD of secondarily-treated effluent discharged from a shallow coastal outfall. Approximately 65 % of the Key's wastewaters are disposed of by on-site sewage disposal systems (~ 30,000 septic tanks and cesspits), which elevate nutrient concentrations of groundwaters that discharge into adjacent coastal waters (Lapointe et al., 1990). An additional ~ 1,100 shallow injection wells also introduce N and P to groundwaters that could also enter surface waters via submarine groundwater discharge.

A SRP concentration of ~ 0.10 µM is considered a threshold for eutrophication on coral reefs (Bell, 1992). While this value may be useful in a general comparative sense, concentrations of other available P sources need to be considered. A threshold based only on SRP ignores the widely recognized role of DOP in supporting algal growth demands via phosphatase enzymes that allow cycling from DOP pools. For example, the shallow waters of the FRT contain extensive populations of filamentous and microfilamentous macroalgae that have high alkaline phosphatase activities (APA; Lapointe, 1989). This fact explains how eutrophication on the FRT, including macroalgal overgrowth of seagrasses and corals, can occur in waters with < 0.10 µM SRP (Lapointe and Clark, 1993; Lapointe et al., 1993). Our findings of a mean DOP concentration of ~ 0.19 µM on the FRT, together with knowledge that large labile fractions of DOP pools are important to phytoplankton growth in oligotrophic waters (Jackson and Williams, 1985), provides a kinetic mechanism by which low but significant levels of DOP enrichment can support algal blooms.

Considering that the mean concentration of TDP on relatively pristine Caribbean reefs was < 0.07 µM, we suggest that a TDP concentration of ~ 0.10 µM represents a threshold for algal development and eutrophication on the FRT. We believe that the elevated chlorophyll a and turbidity on the FRT compared to the Caribbean sites is direct evidence of a widespread algal growth response to increases in the TDP concentrations on the FRT. Many commercial fishermen, residents, and scientists alike have witnessed the increasing algal blooms and associated turbidity over broad areas of the FRT over the past decade, especially in the waters of western Florida Bay in the vicinity of East Cape where the Shark River system discharges into the eastern Gulf of Mexico and western Florida Bay. The increased burdens of P to coastal waters of the eastern Gulf of Mexico over past decades have very likely increased inputs of P into the downstream N-rich waters of Florida Bay and the FRT (Lapointe and Clark, 1993) where they would result in "balanced" algal growth and development of algal blooms. Over time, cumulative P inputs would reduce the TDN:TDP ratio -- as suggested by this study -- and shift limitation of algal growth from P-limitation towards N-limitation. The relatively low N:P ratios around East Cape suggest that cumulative P inputs may have already shifted the waters in this "mixing zone" to N-limitation.

The FRT thus appears similar to freshwater lakes that also undergo downward shifts in the N:P ratio with increasing P-enrichment and eutrophication, favoring dominance of N-fixing blue-green algae (Schindler, 1977). Several species of nuisance blue-green algae have become abundant on the FRT over the past decade, and include not only the phytoplankter *Synechococcus* but also the filamentous *Phormidium* (a coral pathogen and the causal agent of "black-band disease") and *Lyngbya* (Porter and Meier, 1992; Lapointe and Clark, 1993). Some have suggested that the upper latitudinal limits of coral reef development are often set by competition of macroalgae with corals and that macroalgae are favored at higher latitudes that have higher nutrient concentrations (Johannes et al., 1983); indeed, increased abundance of macroalgae has correlated with the decreased coral cover on the FRT (Porter and Meier, 1992), suggesting eutrophication has already enhanced macroalgal competition with reef corals.

CONCLUSIONS

Large-scale anthropogenic nutrient enrichment is widely recognized by scientists modeling the effects of eutrophication on the productivity of the continental shelves (e.g. see Walsh, 1988) and the open ocean (Fanning, 1989). Inputs of P to coastal waters of the eastern Gulf of Mexico appear to be carried downstream by prevailing currents to the N-rich, P-limited waters of the FRT. This nutrient enrichment model is a plausible mechanism that can explain the recently recognized eutrophication occurring over broad areas of the FRT. Although low temperature stress is considered a primary factor affecting coral reef growth and distribution in Florida (Porter et al., 1982; Burns, 1985), our data and observations suggest that eutrophication has recently become a major stress to reef development and may lead to further reef decline and extinction. Eutrophication is a major cause of coral-reef decline worldwide, due to interactive stresses related to phytoplankton blooms, sedimentation, epiphytic algal growth, coral disease, elevated water temperatures and coral bleaching, and light limitation (Bell, 1992). Our findings are consistent with results of a recent NSF-sponsored workshop on coral reef ecosystems that "anthropogenic stresses resulting directly from population growth and development are the strongest environmental signals and the greatest threat to coral reefs" (D'Elia et al., 1991). It appears that the threshold phosphorus concentrations for critical eutrophication in the shallow, carbonate-rich, and macrophyte-dominated waters of the FRT are quite low (e.g. TDP ~ 0.10 µM) and comparable to sensitive freshwater ecosystems.

REFERENCES

Belanger, T. V., D. S. Scheidt, and J. R. Platko II. 1989. Effects of nutrient enrichment on the Florida Everglades. Lake and Reservoir Management 5(1)101-111.

Bell, P. R. F. 1992. Eutrophication and coral reefs - some examples in the Great Barrier Reef lagoon. Water Research, 26:553-568.

Burnison, B. K. 1979. Modified dimethyl sulfoxide(DMSO) extraction for chlorophyll analysis of phytoplankton. Can. J. Fish. Aquat. Sci. 37: 729.

Burns, T. P. 1985. Hard-coral distribution and cold-water disturbances in South Florida: variation with depth and location. Coral Reefs 4:117-124

D'Elia, C. F., P. A. Steudler, N. A. Corwin. 1977. Determination of total nitrogen in aqueous samples using persulfate digestion. Limnol. Oceanogr. 22: 760-764.

D'Elia, C. F., W. Buddemeier, S. V. Smith. 1991. Workshop on coral bleaching, coral reef ecosystems, and global change: Report of Proceedings, Maryland Sea Grant Publication UM-SG-TS-91-03.

DeKanel J. and J. W. Morse. 1982. The chemistry of orthophosphate uptake from seawater onto calcite and aragonite. Geochim. Cosmoschim. Acta. 42:1335-1340.

Dustan, P. and J. Halas. 1987. Changes in the reef-coral community of Carysfort Reef, Key Largo, Florida, 1974-1982. Coral Reefs 6:91-106.

Fanning, K. A. 1989. Influence of atmospheric pollution on nutrient limitation in the ocean. Nature 339:460-463.

FDER, 1987. Florida Keys monitoring study. Water quality assessment of five selected pollutant sources in Marathon, FL.

Flannery, M.S., H.C. Downing Jr., G. A. McGarry, and M.O. Walters. 1991. Increased nutrient loading and baseflow supplementation in the Little Manatee watershed. Proc. Tampa Bay Area Scientific Information Symposium 2 369-396.

Gardener, W. D., M.J. Richardson, I. D. Walsh, and B.L. Bergland. 1990. In-situ optical sensing of particles for determination of oceanic processes. Oceanography 3:2 11-17.

Jackson, G. A. and P. M. Williams. 1985. Importance of dissolved organic nitrogen and phosphorus to biological nutrient cycling. Deep-Sea Research 32: 223-225.

Johannes, R. E., W. J. Wiebe, C. J. Crossland, D. W. Rimmer, and S. V. Smith. 1983. Latitudinal limits of coral reef growth. Marine Ecology Progress Series 11:105-111.

Jones, J. I. et al. 1973. Physical oceanography of the Gulf of Mexico and Florida continental shelf. The Eastern Gulf of Mexico 1973, The State University System of Florida Institute of Oceanography IIB-1-6.

Kaufman, M. I. 1969a. Generalized distribution and concentration of orthophosphate in Florida streams. U. S. Geological Survey Map Series 33. The Eastern Gulf of Mexico 1973, The State University System of Florida Institute of Oceanography IIC-46.

Klein C. J. III and S. P. Orlando Jr. 1993. A spatial framework for the water quality management in the Florida Keys National Marine Sanctuary. Technical Report of Strategic Environmental Assessments Division, NOAA, Rockville, Md.

Lapointe, B. E. 1987. P and N-limited photosynthesis and growth of *G. tikvahiae* in the Florida Keys. Mar. Biol. 93:561-568.

Lapointe, B. E. 1989. Macroalgal production and nutrient relations in oligotrophic areas of Florida Bay. Bull. Mar. Sci. 44:312-323.

Lapointe, B. E. and M. W. Clark. 1993. Nutrient inputs from the watershed and coastal eutrophication in the Florida Keys. Estuaries 15: 465-476.

Lapointe, B. E., M. M. Littler and D. S. Littler. 1992. Nutrient availability to marine macroalgae in siliciclastic versus carbonate rich coastal waters. Estuaries 15:75-82.

Lapointe, B. E., M. M. Littler and D. S. Littler. 1992. Modification of benthic community structure by natural eutrophication: The Belize Barrier Reef. Proc. 7th Int. Coral Reef Symp. in press.

Lapointe, B. E. and J. D. O'Connell. 1989. Nutrient-enhanced growth of *Cladophora prolifera* in Harrington Sound, Bermuda: Eutrophication of a confined, phosphorus-limited marine ecosystem. Estuarine, Coastal, and Shelf Science 28:347-360.

Lapointe, B. E., J. D. O'Connell, and G. S. Garrett. 1990. Nutrient couplings between on-site sewage disposal systems, groundwaters and nearshore surface waters of the Florida Keys. Biogeochemistry 10: 289-307.

Lapointe, B. E., N. P. Smith, P. Pitts, and M. W. Clark. 1992. Baseline characterization of chemical and hydrographic processes in the water column of Looe Key National Marine Sanctuary. Final Report (contract # NA 86AA-H-CZ071) to National Oceanic and Atmospheric Administration, Marine Sanctuaries Division, Washington, D. C.

LaRock, P. and H. L. Bittaker. 1973. Chemical data of the estuarine and nearshore environments in the Eastern Gulf of Mexico. The State University System of Florida Institute of Oceanography IIC-8.

Littler, M. M., D. S. Littler, and E. A. Titlyanov. 1991. Comparisons of N- and P-limited productivity between high granitic islands versus low carbonate atolls in the Seychelles Archipelago. Coral Reefs 10:199-209.

Lovejoy, S.B., B. Dunkelberg, and J. G. Lee. 1990. Sources and quantities of nutrients entering the Gulf of Mexico. The environmental and economic status of Gulf of Mexico. Gulf of Mexico Program 41-43.

Menzel, D. W. and N. A. Corwin. 1965. The measurement of total phosphorus in seawater based on the liberation of organically bound fractions by persulfate oxidation. Limnology and Oceanography 10:280-282.

Meybeck, M. 1982. Carbon, nitrogen and phosphorus transport by world rivers. Am. Journ. Sci. 282:401-450.

Miller, J. 1988. Results of a workshop on coral reef research and management in the Florida Keys: A blueprint for action. NOAA Technical Report, National Undersea Research Program, Washington, D.C.

Odum, H. T. 1953. Dissolved phosphorus in Florida waters. Fla. Geol. Surv. Report of Investigation 9, Par. 1: 1-40.

Paerl, H. R. 1988. Nuisance phytoplankton blooms in coastal estuarine, and inland waters. Limno. Oceanogr. 33(4):823-847.

Porter, J. W., J. F. Battey, and G. J. Smith. 1982. Perturbation and change in coral reef communities. Proc. Natl. Acad. Sci. 79:1678-1681.

Porter, J. W. and O. W. Meier. 1992. Quantification of loss and change in Floridian reef coral populations. American Zoologist 34:625-640.

Rosenfeld, J. 1979. Ammonium adsorption in nearshore anoxic sediments. Limnol. Oceanogr. 24:356-364.

Richardson, C. J. 1985. Mechanisms controlling phosphorus retention capacity in freshwater wetlands. Science 228:1424-1427

Ryther, J. H. and W. M. Dunstan. 1971. Nitrogen, phosphorus, and eutrophication in the coastal marine environment. Science 171:1008-13.

Schindler, D. W. 1977. Evolution of phosphorus limitation in lakes. Science 195:260-262.

Smith, R. A., R. B. Alexander, and M. G. Wolman. 1987. Water quality trends in the nation's rivers. Science, 235:1607-1615.

Task Group Report, 1967. Sources of nitrogen and phosphorus in water supplies. J. AWWA 59: 344-366.

Tomascik, T. and F. Sander. 1985. Effects of eutrophication on reef-building corals. Marine Biology, 87:143-145.

USEPA, 1992. Water quality protection program for the Florida Keys National Marine Sanctuary: Phase I report.

Walsh J. J. 1988. On the nature of continental shelves. Academic Press, Inc.

WHY CONSERVATION BY LEGAL FIAT DOES NOT WORK

Howard Latin[1]

Rutgers Law School, 15 Washington St., Newark, N.J. 07102
Ph: (201) 966-1911; FAX: (201) 648-1445.

ABSTRACT

Environmental laws are only hortatory words unless they are implemented; yet, non-implementation, non-enforcement, and violations of conservation laws are so common that they must be viewed as the norm rather than exception in the great majority of nations. Current biodiversity protection measures are inherently inadequate and environmental law by itself is too frail a mechanism to achieve the many fundamental changes in human behavior necessary to ensure worldwide protection of endangered ecosystems and wildlife. In place of highly general, utopian conservation mandates now imposed by legal fiat, effective biodiversity conservation programs must be tailored to the particular social, economic, political, and ecological characteristics of varied resource exploitation problems. These conservation programs must integrate particularized laws, scientific research on specific ecological hazards, environmental education campaigns, economic incentive or assistance measures designed to make conservation "profitable" for affected groups, and economic disincentives or realistic legal sanctions to curtail harmful activities.

INTRODUCTION

In recent decades, hundreds of environmental treaties and national conservation laws have been enacted.[2,3] During this same period, humanity has caused greater ecological destruction than in any comparable era in recorded history.[4] If the treaties and supporting national laws subsumed under the label of "International Environmental Law" (IEL) are evaluated on the basis of actual conservation accomplishments--not political rhetoric, media attention, conferences held, or documents drafted--there can be no doubt that IEL is failing to protect most threatened ecosystems and species.[5] Most conservation laws embody lofty aspirations without commensurate international or national implementation commitments. Once this pattern of illusory IEL is recognized and contrasted with the severity and urgency of global ecological degradation problems, implementation of better biodiversity conservation strategies should be considered perhaps the most critical need in the environmental policy field.

No short paper could provide a systematic assessment of the tangible effects of hundreds of environmental laws, much less of their intangible consciousness-raising ramifications.[6] Nevertheless, the evidence appears overwhelming: Conservation programs in developing nations lack adequate institutional frameworks, political commitments, financial support, and personnel; enforcement is rare to nonexistent; and compliance is haphazard at best. The biodiversity preservation record of many developed nations is little better. Yet, most environmental officials, scientists, lawyers, and NGO activists do not yet recognize that the implementation and compliance problems they routinely observe reflect a worldwide phenomenon, not just isolated instances of environmental law failures. This paper describes common patterns of IEL failures and then identifies some underlying causes of these deficiencies. The final section briefly discusses the need for particularized, integrated conservation strategies.

RECURRING PATTERNS OF NON-IMPLEMENTATION AND NON-COMPLIANCE

It may be impossible to prove on a quantitative basis that IEL is failing abjectly relative to the magnitude and urgency of global ecological problems, but several widespread patterns of inadequate implementation and compliance should be familiar to people working in environmental fields.

"Paper" Parks

A 1992 World Conservation Monitoring Centre report on environmental conditions estimated that there are more than 8,500 large legally protected areas including national parks, biosphere reserves, and other categories, covering about 5 percent of the world's land area and some marine waters.[7] Yet, creating protected area boundaries on paper does not ensure that ecosystems and wildlife in those areas will actually be protected.

Bunaken National Park.--Indonesia has established 23 marine conservation areas including 17 with coral reefs.[8] Bunaken and nearby islands off the coast of North Sulawesi were first formally protected in 1980 and were declared a National Park in 1989.[9] Yet, a late-1992 draft management plan for the Park identified continuing damage from mangrove and forest cutting throughout the park;

coral mining for roads and other structures; over-exploitation of marine fisheries; use of traps, nets, and other harmful fishing methods; fuel and oil spills; and reef damage from divers and boats anchoring on the reefs.[10] A recent survey conducted by an Indonesian marine scientist found that "[m]ost damaging of all are fishing by explosive and muroami . . . practised by non-resident fishermen who moved from one island to the other."[11] This survey concluded that proper management has never been implemented due to inadequate funding, inadequate personnel and training, and the failure to zone areas within Bunaken Park for different activities.[12] A 1992 report by a USAID consultant found "almost half" of the respondents surveyed "have not as yet heard about the park" and other people are "unclear" about its boundaries and functions.[13] This sociologist also noted that: "The [development] literature abounds with examples of continued natural resource exploitation by local peoples seeking revenue and/or subsistence from protected areas despite regulation, boundaries, fines, and other restrictive measures."[14]

Ecuadorian Parks.--The World Conservation Monitoring Centre estimated that 5.62 percent of Ecuador's land, about 10M hectares, is "totally protected" in terms of legal status.[15] However, the most recent available figure for state financing of protected area management programs in Ecuador was only $250,000 US.[16] With regard to oil extraction within Amazonian protected areas, one study concluded: "Although Ecuadorian law unambiguously recognizes the public interest in a clean and healthy environment, . . . the national government has shown little or no willingness to comply with the law and establish meaningful environmental controls over the nation's most powerful industry."[17]

Indian Parks.--Virtually all primary forests in India have been destroyed except those in national parks. Village populations on the periphery of the parks have grown rapidly and livestock grazing, fodder collection, and fuelwood collection within the parks remain very common, resulting in steady deterioration of ecological conditions and wildlife levels.[18] Park wardens seldom interfere with subsistence-level exploitation of park resources and their lives may be threatened when they do attempt to perform their legal responsibilities.[19]

Mining in a Tasmanian Park.--Australia classifies many areas as national parks, state parks, and World Heritage Sites. Yet, the protections offered by these legal designations may be partly or wholly illusory when resource exploitation conflicts arise. For example, the Tasmanian state government recently announced it will redefine property boundaries in the Douglas-Apsley National Park to a maximum depth of 50m to enable "unobtrusive" mining by allowing shafts drilled below 50m to extend into the park.[20]

"Paper" Plans

Most IEL agreements require implementation of systematic planning and resource management programs. The Convention on Biological Diversity adopted in 1992 by the United Nations Conference on Environment and Development (UNCED) provides that each state shall "[d]evelop national strategies, plans or programmes for the conservation and sustainable use of biological diversity . . ."[21] Yet, many nations lack the expertise and financial support necessary to develop meaningful plans and others lack the political commitment to enforce compliance with whatever plans are created.

Ningaloo Park Management Plans in Western Australia.--For about six weeks each year, Ningaloo Marine Park in Western Australia is the site of the world's largest known concentration of whale sharks. The W.A. Wildlife Conservation Act forbids harassment of wildlife and the Conservation and Land Management Act requires parks and public lands to be administered pursuant to official management plans. The 1989 Ningaloo Park Plan prohibits commercial activities and aerial overflights without a license issued by the W.A. Department of Conservation and Land Management (CALM).[22] In the past three years, a whale shark tourism industry has developed in Ningaloo Park--commercial tourist boats use low-flying planes to spot and chase the whale sharks and then allow divers or swimmers to touch and "ride" the animals. CALM has never issued any license for these activities nor imposed any regulatory controls despite patent violations of state law and Ningaloo Plan provisions. CALM cited funding constraints as the reason for its inaction, but an even more significant factor is its reluctance to limit lucrative tourism while W.A. is in a recession.[23] The federal Australian National Parks and Wildlife Service has joint responsibility for wildlife protection because Ningaloo Marine Park extends into Commonwealth waters. Yet, ANPWS has no game wardens or enforcement personnel in Western Australia, the nation's largest state. Five years after Ningaloo National Park was created, ANPWS is still soliciting comments on its proposed management plan--the ANPWS draft plan has only one picture on the cover, showing a diver riding a whale shark.[24]

Tropical Forest Action Plans (TFAPs).--Clear-cutting of tropical rainforests is generally recognized as a very destructive practice from a biodiversity conservation perspective. Under FAO and International Tropical Timber Organization standards, each nation is supposed to develop a TFAP that will ensure exploitation of forest resources on an ecologically sustainable basis. Yet, a review of the TFAPs of several developing nations found that most allow wwidespread clear-cutting and anticipate substantially increased timber yields in the near future despite the absence of institutional frameworks, expertise, personnel, and funding necessary to administer a sustainable forest management program.[25]

Fisheries in United States Waters.--The National Marine Fisheries Service (NMFS) is responsible for developing regional plans to conserve fisheries stocks, but NMFS lacks the funding, political support, and bureaucratic commitment necessary to regulate uncontrolled fishing practices that may waste more than 90 percent of the total catch. One fisheries consultant cited this waste as a "national scandal and an unconscionable disgrace."[26] After more than a decade of falling productivity in commercial fisheries, NMFS still has not implemented management plans that will stem the decline. The Georges Bank, for example, was once among the most productive fishing areas in the world, but precipitous decreases have occurred in many species populations and the New England Fishery Management Council recently proposed reducing the allowable catch by a further 50 percent.[27]

International Trade in Endangered Species

The Worldwatch Institute has estimated that 30 percent of the annual $5-8 billion international trade in wildlife is illegal.[28] A few years ago, a merchant in Cairo tried to sell the author a crocodile-skin belt by noting that crocodiles are endangered and this fine belt would no longer be available once the species becomes extinct. In 1992, the author presented a paper in Singapore and found hundreds of stores selling ivory figurines. One shopkeeper explained that Singapore merchants can sell large quantities of ivory because: "Ivory illegal to come in. Not illegal to go out." A week later, a businessman from Indonesia's Maluku Province displayed two birds of paradise, a legally protected species, and said anyone with the "right contacts" could buy them in his country. The illicit trade in ivory, turtle shells, bear parts, parrots, animal furs, rhinoceros horn, orangutans, and many other ostensibly protected species continues because there is little enforcement of international treaties against suppliers and even less effort has been made to restrict activities of importing and merchant states.[29,30]

Destructive Forestry Practices

UNCED's Preparatory Committee approved a "non-legally binding" statement of forestry principles that says: "[f]orest resources and forest lands should be sustainably managed to meet the social, economic, ecological, cultural and spiritual human needs of present and future generations" and "[n]ational policies and strategies should provide a framework for increased efforts, including the development and strengthening of institutions and programmes for the management, conservation and sustainable development of forests and forest lands."[31] These general IEL mandates characteristically fail to address specific economic, social, political, and ecological circumstances that underlie different patterns of deforestation and are crucial for the implementation of realistic conservation strategies.

Consider the varied mechanisms leading to deforestation: Many states, such as Brazil and Malaysia, have adopted explicit policies promoting timber cutting as a means to earn foreign exchange and increase development.[32] Brazil also has the world's largest reforestation program, but poor people frequently follow the logging roads and destroy newly planted seedlings in order to use the land for marginal agriculture and livestock grazing.[33] In Papua New Guinea, corrupt public officials and international logging companies have conspired to circumvent PNG laws against deforestation and to undervalue timber exports, which reduces national and local revenues and thus increases pressure for further forest cutting.[34] In India, locals villagers often invade park boundaries to obtain fuelwood and livestock fodder. The U.S. government allows logging of old-growth public forests at below-market prices to subsidize timber companies and retain jobs in areas that may have few other employment opportunities.[35] If the U.S. government fosters non-sustainable deforestation on economic grounds, it cannot be surprising that many developing nations make similar choices. Readers should note that unauthorized clearing of reforested lands, denuding of trees in national parks, and political corruption are illegal under national laws and incompatible with the provisions of several international conventions, but environmental law has not stopped these practices.

Destructive Exploitation of Marine Resources

Enforcement of marine protection laws is especially difficult because property rights to ocean resources are normally diffuse, close monitoring of exploitative activities is usually infeasible, and the resulting ecological damage may be difficult to see and even harder to document on a scientific basis. Under these conditions, destructive and illegal uses of marine resources are common. "Dynamite fishing" is a serious problem in Papua New Guinea, Indonesia, and dozens of other nations. Indonesians consume tens of thousands of turtles each year despite national and international laws protecting endangered turtle species. Greater availability of motorboats in Fiji has enabled exploitation of remote turtle nesting grounds, though turtles are also protected under Fijian national law.[36] "Flashlight fishing" in Yap enables outsiders to encroach on traditional fishing grounds because the probability of apprehension is greatly reduced at night.[37] Cyanide is widely used in the Philippines for collection of ornamental fish for the private aquarium trade.[38] Coral is mined for construction purposes and collected for jewelry.[39] Unauthorized fishing vessels frequently invade the territorial waters of coastal nations.[40] All of these practices violate environmental treaties or laws.

UNDERLYING CAUSES OF IEL FAILURES

In many respects, the causes of IEL failures are also the causes of inadequate progress in more traditional domains of public international law (PIL). The inability to obtain consensus on anything but a lowest-common-denominator basis, the insistence of most states on retaining unrestricted sovereignty, and the absence of meaningful sanctions for non-compliance are familiar PIL problems that arise in other realms of international policy as often as in environmental conflicts. Biodiversity protection does, however, present distinctive problems with respect to the time-frames and required particularity of potential solutions.

Common Imperfections in International Law

IEL is first and foremost international law: Its fundamental unit is the state, not the ecosystem; its primary principle is state sovereignty, not conservation of nature. The large IEL "community" is comprised of politicians, bureaucrats, lawyers, interest-group lobbyists, and scholars who work mainly in national capitals and large cities. IEL activities focus primarily on the preparation, criticism, revision, and interpretation of documents drafted in the specialized terminologies of law and diplomacy. Most IEL efforts are directed at consensus-building among governments and international organizations, not among the people who actually own, use, or damage ecological resources. If the IEL community recognizes that an existing conservation law is inadequate, the customary "solution" is to invoke international law processes in an attempt to obtain voluntary government acceptances of better laws. When sovereignty conflicts with environmental protection requirements, sovereignty prevails. There is a striking discontinuity between this enterprise, which operates primarily at international and national levels, and the myriad activities that threaten diverse ecosystems and species in disparate areas.

Excessive Generality.--International agreements tend to be framed in highly general terms because greater specificity would require the PIL community to pass judgment on the appropriateness of the behavior of many states--states that would then be less likely to ratify the negotiated treaties. For example, the UNCED biodiversity convention provides that states should "regulate or manage biological resources important for the conservation of biological diversity whether within or outside protected areas, with a view to ensuring their conservation and sustainable use."[41] This vague mandate is altogether different from telling nation A that it must conserve ecosystem B to protect species C and D.

Failure to Make "Hard Choices".--Every IEL treaty or declaration requiring states to protect ecosystems and species also includes provisions that are facially incompatible with the goal of biodiversity conservation. For example, UNCED's Convention on Biological Diversity stipulates that states have "the sovereign right to exploit their own resources pursuant to their own environmental policies" and that "economic and social development and poverty eradication are the first and overriding priorities of developing countries".[42] The UNCED Forestry Principles similarly stress that: "States have the sovereign and inalienable right to utilize, manage and develop their forests in accordance with their development needs and level of socio-economic development . . ., including the conversion of such areas for other uses within the overall socio-economic development plan and based on rational land-use policies."[43]

These clauses authorize states to exploit "their" natural resources in whatever fashion they deem appropriate if they justify destructive resource exploitation on developmental grounds. However sincere or cynical the state's reasons may be, there is no mechanism in UNCED agreements or PIL for other states and international organizations to dispute each nation's environmental decisions on the merits. As long as international and national laws avoid making hard choices that impose specific conservation duties on states, and as long as implementation depends wholly on voluntary efforts by each state, IEL is unlikely to contribute much to biodiversity protection.

Consensus-Based Compromises.--A central principle of PIL is that states are not bound by any international obligation unless they voluntarily consent to it. This principle imposes great pressure on IEL proponents to pursue a consensus representing as close to unanimous agreement as they can attain. While complete unanimity may not be necessary, non-participation by a major nation or significant group of lesser states is likely to undermine support for an environmental treaty. This happened when the United States refused to accept the United Nations Convention on the Law of the Sea (UNCLOS).[44] In the same vein, threats each year by a few nations to withdraw from the International Whaling Commission jeopardize the present moratorium on whaling and prevent the Commission from adopting stricter protections.[45] The need for a nearly universal consensus clearly leads to dilution of IEL conservation initiatives until few nations object to them.

A more subtle effect flows from the general language adopted in most international law agreements: It is hard for states to predict how they will be affected by new IEL obligations. Rather than focussing on the specific characteristics of particular natural resources issues, states under the current approach envision the worst possible scenarios or contingencies as threats to their national self-interest. The United States, for example, refused to ratify UNCLOS because we possess the leading technology for deep sea-bed mining, which might prove valuable in some unspecified place at some unspecified time if mineral prices and extraction costs cooperate. The Bush Administration also rejected the Biodiversity Convention because we excel in biotechnology science and our profit from scientific innovations might be reduced if other nations can claim some form of legal interest in previously unknown genetic or biological materials. Thus, the typical IEL effort to draft agreements in terms so idealized and general that few nations will feel threatened by them has the paradoxical effect of inducing states to imagine abstract, hypothetical infringements on their sovereignty that may never materialize in any practical form.

Inadequate Sanctions for Non-Compliance.--Under accepted principles of PIL, sovereignty is the preeminent concern and international sanctions are never imposed except in the most extreme circumstances, as in the cases of Iraq, South Africa, and Serbia. In the absence of sanctions for non-compliance with international obligations or their own national laws, many states openly flaunt and others tacitly condone violations of legal conservation requirements. The IEL community surely knows but seldom admits that many governments facilitate "illegal" actions producing economic benefits, that governments and international organizations often sponsor environmentally destructive projects in pursuit of development, and that governing elites in some countries pursue private gains regardless of the harms inflicted on nature or local populations.

In response to U.S. legal controls on tuna imports derived from fishing methods that kill dolphins, the UNCED Rio Declaration provided that states should not impose trade restrictions to promote environmental objectives. Thus, most states participating in UNCED rejected use of trade sanctions to discourage ecologically destructive practices and no UNCED agreement imposes any sanctions for violations of international or national environmental laws. The typical PIL requirement for unanimity or widespread consensus is clearly incompatible with the imposition of meaningful sanctions for environmental damage, and the Rio Declaration condemnation of trade restrictions suggests that sanctions for violations of conservation laws would seldom be acceptable even if majority-rule processes were somehow instituted for international lawmaking.

Inadequate Implementation Resources.--No principle of international law precludes states from adopting elaborate legal obligations without having the administrative resources or political commitments to implement those laws. Whether the context is international arms control, enforcement of human rights, or implementation of environmental protection programs, "words are cheap" but effective administration is not. Biodiversity conservation is an inherently difficult and costly enterprise, and the implementation burdens are especially severe in developing countries that typically lack comprehensive information about their natural resources and a cadre of experienced environmental scientists and managers. Moreover, developing countries ordinarily place higher priorities on economic growth and public health measures than on ecosystem conservation and would be reluctant to allocate substantial financial resources to biodiversity preservation even if they had them. Governments may achieve "the best of both worlds" from a political perspective by enacting strict conservation laws to placate environmentalists and then not administering or enforcing those laws to reduce administrative costs and to accommodate pressures from economic interests.

Distinctive IEL Problems

Several inherent characteristics of biodiversity conservation issues create special difficulties for environmental lawmaking: Most current laws are framed in general terms, but natural systems are extremely diverse and usually unique. Most laws are developed in response to human needs, human time-frames, and human institutions, but these criteria may not suitable or sufficient for programs designed to preserve endangered ecosystems and species. Most environmental issues are complex and subject to extensive scientific uncertainties, but the presence of uncertainty allows affected interest groups and politicians to defer effective action on the grounds that it is bound to be expensive and may be premature.

Decentralization of Resource Exploitation Activities.--Unlike war and peace issues or other common international law problems, ecological degradation is a decentralized process involving hundreds of thousands of disparate groups and activities. Many people whose actions damage natural resources do not understand the long-term harmful consequences of their activities, the feasibility of alternative modes of behavior, or the relevant national and international environmental laws. In many developing nations, people often view conservation laws enacted in remote capitals as far less compelling than their social, cultural and historical traditions of resource use. Even when people understand conservation laws and want to comply, they often lack alternative income sources or economic aid that would enable them to modify ecologically harmful behavior without reducing their standard of living. It is obvious that people will not let their families starve to save trees or tigers, whatever the laws may mandate. The sobering reality is that many people living far above subsistence levels will also refuse to comply with biodiversity protection laws that may diminish their prosperity.

Irreversibility of Ecosystem and Species Destruction.--However desirable peace, democracy, and libertarian rights may be and however frequently they are imperiled, there is no finite deadline for them to be achieved. When people are oppressed or economies depressed, these conditions produce much suffering but our descendants will have their own opportunities to overcome human folly or replicate it. In contrast, if we do not protect ecosystems and species before they are lost, and often before they become endangered, there will seldom be a second chance to undo the damage. Science cannot recreate species that become extinct. In most instances the same point applies to vulnerable ecosystems: even when every species in an ecosystem exists in other places, ecosystems involve so many complex interactions that attempts to resurrect them would seldom succeed. This constraint imposes countless separate deadlines on efforts to prevent further biodiversity destruction.

Irreversible Trends in Natural Resources Exploitation.--World population growth, rising aspirations for material welfare, increasing marketization of ecological resources, and wider diffusion of exploitation technologies represent "ratchet effects," in the sense that they are irreversible unless some form of Armageddon occurs. In recent decades, many people who once consumed natural resources only for subsistence purposes have become participants in local, national, and international commodity markets that provide incentives for increased resource exploitation. At the same time, expanded access to technologies such as chain saws, guns, refrigeration units, motorboats, and synthetic-fiber fishing nets have enabled increased resource exploitation. Even if resources consumption can be reduced in the wealthier nations, as it must be, these irreversible trends in developing countries will inescapably impose greater pressures on natural systems. Thus, the time-frame for conservation efforts must be regarded as critical because incentives and capabilities for further ecological degradation are increasing every day. Indeed, E.O. Wilson has argued that this is the "make-or-break decade" for biodiversity preservation.[46] Other scientists contend that "time is rapidly running out for the terrestrial ecosystems of the tropics. At the present rate of degradation, there will be little of the natural environment remaining for scientists to study ten years from now."[47]

THE NEED FOR PARTICULARIZED, INTEGRATED CONSERVATION STRATEGIES

Space constraints allow only a brief sketch of the comprehensive conservation measures the author believes are necessary to make progress toward global biodiversity protection.

Particularized Biodiversity and Hazard Inventories

Current IEL agreements require nations to try to preserve as much biodiversity as possible consistent with sustainable development, and yet many states do not know which distinctive biodiversity resources they possess or which activities are endangering those resources. We cannot protect every endangered ecosystem or species, and we cannot protect many of them unless we understand in detail the distinctive characteristics of particular ecological systems and the threats to their existence. While scientists are studying many relevant issues, research efforts are seldom aimed at answering the specific policy-oriented questions that environmental decisionmakers must resolve.[48] Scientists usually seek knowledge of interest to science rather than information tailored directly to conservation needs. Scientists also tend to suspend judgment when faced with significant uncertainty without acknowledging that many biodiversity conservation issues have critical short-term time horizons--thus, from an environmental protection perspective, much present scientific research exemplifies the adage that "Nero fiddled while Rome burned."[49]

Particularized Conservation Priorities and Resource Allocations

Different conservation strategies are required to prevent further ecological damage in dissimilar locations and exploitation contexts. With regard to coral reef protection, for example, some harmful activities are motivated by subsistence needs and others by trading in international or national commodity markets, some result from ignorance and others from selfish calculation, some have the potential for widespread destruction and others have limited spatial effects. What could a conventional IEL treaty say on this topic except: "Calling all nations--Protect your coral reefs!" Marine conservation laws must be tailored to the specific characteristics of diverse sources of ocean degradation. In the realm of biodiversity protection, one size of remedy emphatically does not fit all problems.

In many settings, there is no realistic prospect that biodiversity can be protected in the face of intense exploitation pressures.[50] Countless "hard choices" will be necessary to decide whether the chances of long-term success warrant the investment of scarce financial support and personnel in each specific case. These choices need not be made on a monolithic basis: different nations, multilateral organizations (such as the World Bank), and environmental NGOs can pursue conservation of diverse resources in disparate settings. There are, however, ample opportunities for better coordination among conservation efforts: many groups have produced educational materials and environmental assessment methodologies that could be adapted to serve in a variety of conservation contexts, and there may be economies of scale in some conservation financing, lawmaking, and enforcement activities. We must be more creative in devising new biodiversity protection strategies, in determining what kinds of programs are most likely to succeed in varied resource exploitation settings, and in disseminating this knowledge.

Particularized Educational and Public Awareness Campaigns

Environmental education and public awareness programs must be targeted at the groups that damage specific ecological features and at people in affected areas who could benefit from conserving those natural resources. It may be essential in the long run to educate the entire population of nations, but first priority programs should be aimed at those who have the most to lose from ecological destruction and the most to gain from biodiversity conservation. Because most environmental education efforts have been undertaken without simultaneously addressing the economic needs and motivations of the actors whose behavior must be changed, the campaigns often failed to attain adequate conservation and "back sliding" has been a common phenomenon.[51]

Economic Incentive Mechanisms to Promote Conservationist Behavior

Society cannot ensure lasting biodiversity protection and sustainable development unless we devise ways to make conservation profitable or to provide equivalent benefits for groups that otherwise will exploit natural systems in a destructive manner. Economic incentives for conservation can include direct payments in the form of rents, royalties, subsidies, or bribes; new employment opportunities in non-destructive or ecologically sustainable activities; or indirect mechanisms such as trade preferences and international debt reductions. There is little chance of widespread biodiversity preservation unless developed nations agree to "pay" for conservation in developing states, but these direct or indirect payments cannot be effective in most instances unless they are targeted at specific natural resources exploitation problems and unless they reach the people who are actually affected.

Legal and Economic Penalties for Environmentally Harmful Behavior

There will always be some groups that can gain more by destroying ecological features than by conserving them, and other people will "hold out"[52] in ways that undermine social support for biodiversity protection. Economic incentives may increase the willingness of many groups to support active conservation efforts, but incentive schemes would be more effective when combined with legal and economic sanctions applied to environmentally destructive activities. Imposition of legal sanctions for harmful behavior may also be more equitable in some cases than subsidies for protective behavior.

These elements must be *integrated* into comprehensive conservation programs targeted at protecting selected natural resources. Scientific research can seldom prove useful in terms of environmental policy unless it is tailored to the characteristics of specific environmental hazards. Conservation laws can seldom function if affected peoples do not understand the benefits and values of biodiversity protection. Education can seldom achieve the desired behavioral modifications when intended recipients lack feasible economic alternatives. Education also cannot eliminate selfish or uncooperative behavior that may frustrate a social consensus on the need for conservation. Economic incentive programs could seldom work without laws to create and enforce new environmental entitlements. Moreover, given practical limits on financial support for conservation programs, economic incentive mechanisms are unlikely to provide sufficient inducements for biodiversity protection unless they are supplemented by realistic legal and economic disincentives to deter destructive activities. The importance of combining these various elements--targeted education, non-destructive natural resources entitlements, economic incentives, economic disincentives, and legal sanctions--into integrated conservation programs cannot be stressed too strongly. Previous efforts to accomplish one or another of these functions have often failed because of inattention to, or the inability to accomplish, other required elements.

CONCLUSION

The standard for comparison among alternative conservation strategies should not be whether new programs will attain perfect results, but rather whether particularized, integrated approaches can perform substantially *better* despite their imperfections. It will not be easy to persuade governments or multilateral organizations to implement the comprehensive and expensive measures necessary to promote biodiversity protection on a global scale. Yet, past experience has shown that conventional conservation-by-legal-fiat approaches cannot be successful, and the severity of worldwide ecological degradation problems requires comparably urgent remedial measures. Environmental law, environmental science, and environmental economics are all essential for implementing conservation programs that can work. At present, however, these disciplines for the most part function independently, and each is failing to achieve widespread biodiversity protection.

ALACRANES AND AKUMAL CORAL REEFS, MEXICO. THEIR HEALTH, USES AND CONCERNS

Enrique Martínez-Osegueda, Ricardo Muñoz-Chagín and Gustavo de la Cruz-Agüero

Centro de Investigación y de Estudios Avanzados del IPN Unidad Mérida
Apdo. Postal 73-Cordemex, Mérida Yucatán, 97310 MEXICO.

ABSTRACT

We deal with a general ecological diagnostics of Alacranes and Akumal coral reefs, Mexico, based on benthic community components, present reef use, and prospects. Both systems are similar in composition; although, some coral species were recorded only in one site or the other. Benthic coverage is dominated by algae. Among scleractinian corals, *Montastrea annularis* is the dominant species, with *M. cavernosa* and *Siderastrea radians* as codominants in Alacranes. Alacranes supports important fisheries, while Akumal is subject to touristic-related activities. At present, Alacranes and Akumal are in good health conditions. Alacranes is on the way of being the first Mexican marine biosphere reserve protected by Federal laws, while Akumal will be subjected to higher development pressure from huge touristic project and related human settlements along the Mexican Caribbean coast. Certainly, such potential risks are growing faster than any other regional or global changes.

INTRODUCTION

Coral reefs in the Mexican waters, have only developed significantly in the Gulf of Mexico and in the Caribbean Sea. In the Gulf of Mexico, Alacranes Reef, with almost 500 km^2 in area, is the largest reef of the Gulf. In the Mexican Caribbean, besides Chinchorro Bank and Cozumel reefs, there is a coastal barrier of more than 250 km length, starting at Contoy Island, Quintana Roo and continuing toward the south to Belize. Akumal Reef belongs to this reef system.

This paper deals with the status of Alacranes and Akumal reefs, based on prevalent benthic reef components. It also includes a review of the factors that could threaten their integrity.

Alacranes Reef is circa 140 km to the north of Puerto de Progreso, Yucatan; Akumal Reef is 105 km south of the City of Cancun, Q. Roo (Figure 1).

The information in this contribution comes from the works of Martínez-Osegueda (1989) and Martínez-Osegueda, et al. (in preparation) for Alacranes, and Muñoz-Chagín (1992) for Akumal. The sampling methods used in Alacranes were linear transects 10 m long with a chain of synthetic material, as proposed by Porter (1972), and 9 m long photo-transects taking a photograph each 0.5 m with 0.9 m constant focal distance. In Akumal, underwater photography with a picture every 1.6 m approximately and 0.8 m constant focal distance was used. Absolute and relative frequency values are utilized following Dodge *et al.* (1982).

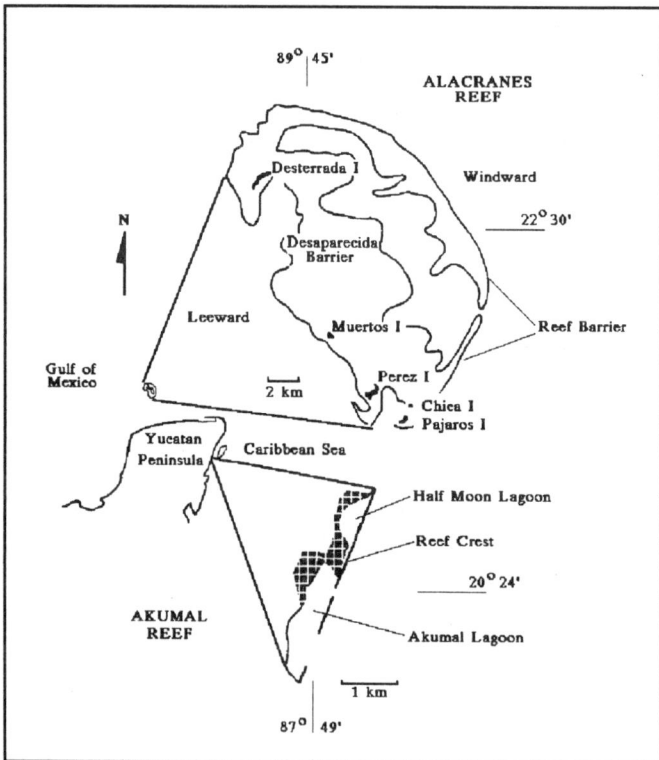

Figure 1. Location of Alacranes and Akumal coral reefs.

RESULTS

As both Alacranes and Akumal Reefs belong to the Caribbean Province (Briggs, 1974), their benthic communities are very similar (Table 1). Composition agrees with those reported for Cozumel Reefs by Muckelbauer (1990) and for Jamaica by Liddell and Ohlhorst (1981, 1987).

TABLE 1. Principal benthic components in Alacranes and Akumal coral reefs, Mexico. (indet. = indeterminated; Al. = algae). Scleractinian naming convention is after Zlatarski and Martinez-Estalella (1982).

Udotea spp.	Encrusting Sponge	*Isophyllia sinuosa* f. *typica*
Halimeda spp	Branching Sponge	*I. sinuosa* f. *rigida* +
Caulerpa spp.	*Palythoa caribbea*	*Micetophyllia lamrckiana*
Dictyota spp.	Colonial Anemone indet.	*Dendrogyra cylindrus* +
Padina spp.	*Gorgonia ventalina*	*Dichocoenia stokesi*
Ventricaria ventricosa?	*Pseudopterogorgia americana*	*Meandrina meandrites* f. *typica*
Lobophora variegata	Octocorals indet.	*M. meandrites* f. *brasiliensis*
Sargassum hystrix +	*Millepora alcicornis* f. *alcicornis*	*M. meandrites* f. *memorialis*
Amphiroa spp.	*M. alcicornis* f *complanata*	*Eusmilia fastigiata*
Stypopodium zonale	*Stylaster roseus*	*Agaricia agaricites* f. *massiva*
Halimeda/Dictyota	*Acropora cervicornis*	*A. agaricites* f. *unifaciata*
Halimeda/Filament Al.	*A. palmata*	*A. agaricites* f. *bifaciata* +
Halimeda/Blue-green Al.*	*A. prolifera* *	*Helioseris cucullata*
Dictyota/Lobophora	*Madracis decactis* f. *typica*	*Siderastrea radians* f. *siderea*
Dictyota/Caulerpa *	*M. decactis* f. *mirabilis*	*Siderastrea radians* f. *radians*
Dictyota/Amphiroa	*Favia fragum*	*Porites porites* f. *typica*
Dictyota/Filament Al.	*Colpophyllia natans*	*P. porites* f. *divaricata*
Dictyota/Calcareous Al. *	*Diploria labyrinthiformis*	*P. astreoides*
Lobophora/Filament Al.	*D. strigosa*	*Spirobranchus giganteus*
Amphiroa/Filament Al.	*Montastrea cavernosa*	*Nemaster rubiginosa*
Calcareous Al.	*M. annularis*	*Clavelina* spp.
Filament Algae	*Stephanocoenia intersepta*	Benthic Fauna indet.
Blue-green Algae	*Oculina diffusa* *	Coral Rubble
Indetermined Algae	*Scolymia lacera*	Calcareous Substrate
Masive Sponge	*Mussa angulosa*	Sand

* Recorded only in Alacranes   + Recorded only in Akumal

According to structural features in Alacranes, four types of community are defined and compared with that observed in Akumal: I. Reefs dominated by Algae, Stony Corals and Substrate; II. Reefs with Sponges and Other Cnidarians, reaching their highest values; III. Reefs dominated by Algae and Substrate; and IV. Reefs where Algae and Scleractinians are dominant. Akumal Reef has both characteristics of types II and IV of Alacranes (Figure 2).

The Other Cnidarians assemble, includes soft corals, *Palythoa caribbea* and colonial anemones; Stony Corals group is formed by scleractinians and the hidrozoans *Millepora alcicornis* f. *alcicornis*

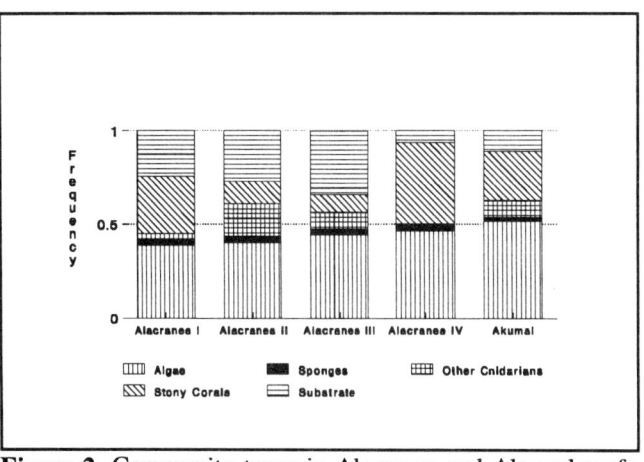

Figure 2. Community types in Alacranes and Akumal reefs

and *M. alcicornis* f. *complanata*. Substrate includes calcareous substrate, sand, and coral rubble.

Dictyota spp, *Lobophora variegata* and Filament Algae, dominate in both reefs. In Akumal, as well as in many Caribbean reefs, *Halimeda* spp is a subdominant component, but scarcely represented in Alacranes. Incrusting Calcareous Algae are also dominant in Akumal, but not in Alacranes (Table 2). However, it should be noted that, due to limitations in resolution, the frequency of Incrusting Algae that covers part of the coral rubble, was underestimated in Alacranes.

TABLE 2. Relative frequency of dominant benthic components in Alacranes and Akumal reefs, Mexico.

	ALACRANES		AKUMAL
	LEEWARD	WINDWARD	
Calcareous algae			0.3506
Filament algae	0.2967	0.2988	0.2218
Dictyota spp	0.1855	0.2337	0.1602
Lobophora variegata	0.1534	0.2964	0.1281
Lobophora/Dictyota	0.1274		
Halimeda spp			0.0982
Palythoa caribbea		0.4872	
Pseudopterogorgia spp		0.3184	
Montastrea annularis	0.4266		0.4321
M. cavernosa		0.2317	
Siderastrea radians f. *siderea*		0.2016	
Calcareous substrate	0.5949	0.7953	0.6454
Sand	0.2047		
Coral rubble	0.2005		

Note: Only taxa with an absolute frequency larger than 0.05 are included.

A distinctive feature of Alacranes windward reef barrier is the subdominant frequencies of *Palythoa caribbea* and the octocoral *Pseudopterogorgia americana* with *P. caribbea* being the dominant species in the shallow barrier, between 0.5 and 3 m depth, reaching a frequency of 0.7

DISCUSSION

From 75 components of benthic biota recorded, only 9 are not common to both reefs, prevailing the scleractinians *Acropora prolifera* and *Oculina difussa*, found in Alacranes but not in Akumal. *Dendrogyra cylindrus*, *Isophyllia sinuosa* f. *typica*, *Meandrina meandrites* f. *brasiliensis*, *M. meandrites* f. *memorialis*, and *Agaricia agaricites* f. *bifaciata*, were found only at Akumal Reef (Table 1). *D. cylindrus* is also absent in the other Campeche Bank and Veracruz reefs (i.e. Chávez, 1973; Külmann, 1975; Villalobos, 1971).

An interesting fact about the reef barrier in Alacranes, is that presently *Acropora palmata* is not so frequent as reported by Kornicker and Boyd (1962) which they identified as the principal barrier builder. Among scleractinian corals, the most important species in both systems is *Montastrea annularis* being the dominant one in Akumal and in Alacranes leeward, with similar absolute frequency of 0.1143 and 0.1028, respectively. In the windward barrier of Alacranes, *M. annularis* is subdominant, while *M. cavernosa* and *Siderastrea radians* f. *siderea* are the dominant. The dominance of *M. annularis* is a common feature of the reefs all along the Caribbean (Milliman, 1973; Szmant, 1991). It is pertinent to say that *Millepora* represents 0.0647 and 0.0107 of the Stony Coral relative frequency in Alacranes and Akumal, respectively.

Calcareous Substrate distribution is important in both systems, although its absolute frequency in Alacranes is a little more of the double than that of Akumal. This component is the same which Porter (1991), calls Calcareous Pavement. Coral Rubble and Sand Substrate, representing more than 0.05 of the absolute frequency in Alacranes, comes mainly from the destruction of *Acropora cervicornis* and *Porites porites* colonies and can measure the damage on the reefs from tropical storms and hurricanes. It serves not only as a suitable substrate for recruitment of scleractinian larvae, but contribute significantly to the formation of islands in Alacranes.

Thousands of birds inhabit or visit these islands, mostly during their winter migration through the Gulf of Mexico (Howell, 1989). *Sula dactylatra* predominates as resident species, with around 3,000 individuals, as well as *Sterna fuscata* that reproduces, nests and breeds in Perez Island during five or six months of the year. The number of individuals of *S. fuscata* has been estimated in 25,000 which arrives to nest every year from a total of 38,000 migrants (Edda González, pers. comm.). The birds in Alacranes are an important part of the ecosystem and they provide an additional indicator of its health condition.

Alacranes is one of the most well preserved reef in Mexico; the only human activity is commercial fishing including finfishes of high commercial value, lobsters and snails (*Pleuroploca* and *Strombus*) as the main target species; gastropod populations have been overexploited in spite of prohibition. Their existence in Alacranes is in danger, as it happened with seal monk *Monachus tropicalis*, presently extinguished not only in Alacranes but also in the Caribbean (Andrews, 1984). Petroleum exploration and exploitation is another permanent hazard because Campeche Bank is the main oil field in the country. Oil spill is another risk for whole Yucatan Peninsula marine environment due the intensive oil traffic through Yucatan Strait.

Alacranes Reef will be in the near future designated as the first Mexican Marine Biosphere Reserve and be provided with a Management Plan based on protection and monitoring programs, such as those proposed by Kenchington & Hudson (1988).

Akumal Reef has different problems, since it is included in the megaproject named "Cancun-Tulum Touristic Corridor" that, although it is in its initial stage, includes extending the touristic facilities along this corridor and the construction of a 130 km coastal highway. At the present time, there are 4 hotels, resorts with several summer houses, restaurants, stores and a small village associated with the development in Akumal. Sewage goes to septic sink holes, constituting a potential problem, due to the high permeability of the karstic soil of the Yucatan Peninsula.

At Akumal there is one of the best coral reef developed in the area; it has two shallow and small reef lagoons (Figure 1), that could be easily affected by urban pollution. Moreover, sport diving may add to the impact on the reef.

Benthic community structure in Akumal Reef resembles that of Alacranes which is less influenced by man, a fact which permits us to infer that Akumal is in good health condition. However, we have to mention its increasing use without any kind of regulation.

In Akumal lagoon, the richness of scleractinians is higher than that of algae, while in Half Moon lagoon the opposite is true, indicating that in this lagoon, natural conditions are less suitable for stony corals development. It is a shallow and turbid lagoon, and its continuous reef crest does not allow a good water exchange. Furthermore, outside the reef crest we recorded five times more *Dictyota* coverage than in other sites at the same depth. Although, these evidences are not a proof of organic pollution, they support the necessity of continuous monitoring of the reef health through water quality and other oceanographic parameters.

Coral bleaching is one of the main issues related to reef health and global changes (Brown and Ogden, 1993). Although, after extensive surveys we never found such event in Alacranes. In Akumal there was a single sighting of bleaching on *Mendrina meandrites* and several more on the same species and *Agaricia agaricites* in Cozumel reefs. We do not know the present extent of bleaching along the Mexican Caribbean.

CONCLUSIONS

Protecting biodiversity in the tropical zones is a high priority task worldwide. Coral reefs are high diversity ecosystems of a limited global distribution. It is urgent to carry out the necessary research and take actions that may assure their physical and functional integrity. Protection of Alacranes reef is a feasible action to assure in some extent the conservation of its biodiversity.

Tourism activities in Quintana Roo coast, are the main economic drive, generating employment as well as domestic and foreign investment. Unfortunately, tourism development grows faster than generation of biological and ecological information badly needed for management purposes.

The present level of economic development in Akumal is a serious constraint for designating this area as a protected zone; however it is necessary to determine the environmental impact as well as to undertake studies for its management. To carry on this task it is indispensable to rely on the joint work of the people and state and federal governments, in order to attain sustainable coastal development. The cost of this research is a lot less than its long term benefits (Spurgeon, 1992).

ACKNOWLEDGEMENTS

We are very gratful to Dr. Luis Capurro for advice and permanent academic support. We thank Dr. Gerardo Gold for his suggestions and critical review of an earlier version of the manuscript. We also appreciate the involvement and help from Gonzalo Arcila and Akumal Dive Shop. We whish to thank to Secretaría de Marina-Armada de México (Mexican Navy) for providing continuous field support in Alacranes and other Mexican reefs.

LITERATURE CITED

Andrews, A.P. 1984. La extinción de la foca (*Monachus tropicalis*) en Yucatán. Escuela de Ciencias Antropológicas de la Universidad Autónoma de Yucatán, Boletín 12. 3-12 pp.

Briggs, J.C. 1974. Marine Zoogeography. McGraw-Hill, New York. 380 pp.

Brown, B.E. and J.C. Ogden. 1993. Coral bleaching. Scientific American, January 1993: 44-50

Chávez, E.A. 1973. Observaciones generales sobre el arrecife de Lobos, Veracruz. An. Esc. Nal. Cienc. Biol., México 20: 13-21

Dodge, R.E, A. Logan and A. Antonius. 1982. Quantitative reef assessment studies in Bermuda: a comparison of methods and preliminary results. Bull. Mar. Sci. 32(3): 745-760

Howell, S.N.G. 1989. Additional information of the birds of the Campeche Bank, Mexico. J. Field Ornithol. 60(4): 504-509.

Kenchington, R.A. and B.E.T. Hudson (Eds.) 1988. Coral Reef Management Handbook. UNESCO. 321 pp.

Kornicker, L.S. and D.W. Boyd. 1962. Shallow water geology and environment of Alacran Reef complex, Campeche Bank, Mexico. Am. Ass. Petr. Geol. Bull 40: 640-673.

Külmann, D.H.H. 1975. Charakterisierung der korallen riffe von Veracruz/Mexico. Int. Revue ges. Hydrobiol. 60(4): 495-521.

Liddell, W.D. and S.L. Ohlhorst. 1981. Geomorphology and community composition of two adjacent reef areas, Discovery Bay, Jamaica. J. Mar. Res. 39(4): 791-804.

Liddell, W.D. and S.L. Ohlhorst. 1987. Patterns of reef community structure, North Jamaica. Bull. Mar. Sci. 40(2): 311-329

Martínez-Osegueda E. 1989. Estudio comparativo de los escleractínios de sotavento y barlovento del Arrecife Alacranes. Folletos de Divulgación. Dirección Gral. de Oceanografía Naval. México. 18 pp.

Milliman, J.D. 1973. Caribbean coral reefs. Pages 1-50 *in* O. A. Jones and R. Endean, eds. Biology and Geology of Coral Reefs. Academic Press, N. Y. 1-50 pp.

Muckelbauer, G. 1990. The shelf of Cozumel, Mexico: topography and organisms. Institut für Paläontologie. Erlangen. Facies 23: 185-240.

Muñoz-Chagín, R. F. 1992. Estructura de la comunidad bentónica del Arrecife de Akumal, Quintana Roo, México. M. Sc. Thesis. Centro de Investigación y de Estudios Avanzados del IPN. Mérida, Yucatán, México. 90 pp.

Porter, J.W. 1972. Ecology and species diversity of coral reef in opposite sides of the Ithsmus of Panama. The Panama Biota Symp. prior to the Sea Level Channel. Bull. Biol. Soc. Wash. 2: 89-116.

Porter, J.W. 1991. Methods for the analysis of coral reef community structure. Dept. of Zool. University of Georgia. Athens, GA U.S.A. 40 pp.

Spurgeon, J.P.G. 1992. The economic valuation of coral reefs. Mar. Poll. Bull. 24(11): 529-536.

Szmant, A.M. 1991. Sexual reproduction by the Caribbean reef corals, *Montastrea annularis* and *M. cavernosa*. Mar. Ecol. Prog. Ser. 74: 13-25.

Villalobos, A. 1971. Estudios ecológicos de un arrecife coralino en Veracruz, México. Symp. on Invest. and Res. of the Caribbean Sea and Adjacent Regions: 531-545 pp.

Zlatarski, V.N. and N. Martinez-Estalella. 1982. Les Scléractiniaires de Cuba. Editions de l'Académie bulgare des Sciences, Sofia. 472 pp.

EFFECTS OF TEMPERATURE AND UV-B ON DIFFERENT COMPONENTS OF CORAL REEF COMMUNITIES FROM THE BAHAMAS

Marjorie L. Reaka-Kudla[1], Douglas S. O'Connell[1], James D. Regan[2], and Robert I. Wicklund[3]

[1]Department of Zoology, University of Maryland, College Park, Maryland 20742. [2]Claude Pepper Institute, Florida Institute of Technology, 150 West University Blvd., Melbourne, Florida. [3]Caribbean Marine Research Center, 4905 Indian Draft Road, Covington, Virginia 24426.

ABSTRACT

Temperature and UV-B have been some of the most consistently implicated factors in coral bleaching episodes, and projections of current trends indicate that anthropogenic elevations of these 2 factors (if unabated) may pose environmental threats during the 21st century and beyond. We undertook a 4 week experimental evaluation of the effects of 3 different temperatures (27°, 29°, and 31°C) and 3 different intensities of UV-B flux (ambient, +10%, +20%) for coral, algae, and solitary invertebrates living in shallow reef environments at Lee Stocking Island, Bahamas. While several workers have investigated the interactive effects of temperature, UV, and in come cases salinity or other factors on corals, no research has analyzed how these factors might differentially impact different components of the community and therefore impose unforeseen long term shifts in community structure. We found that bleaching of Acropora prolifera increased with temperature and UV-B exposure; 95% of the branchlets bleached after 3 weeks in the high temperature/high UV condition. The algae we examined (Microdictyon sp.), however, grew in all of the experimental conditions, and this response was greatest at high UV/low temperature and high temperature/ambient UV conditions. The motile invertebrates tested (brittle stars, hermit crabs, urchins, bivalves) showed little mortality in any condition. If these results hold in other species of corals, fleshy algae, and solitary invertebrates, they suggest that corals will be more adversely affected than one would predict from the physical factors alone.

INTRODUCTION

Reports of mass bleaching episodes in the West Atlantic and around the world have caused considerable international concern in the last 5 years (Brown and Ogden 1993). In addition, data from monitoring studies indicate a decline in size of colonies or live coral cover for a number of reef tracts (e.g., Porter and Meier 1992, Goreau 1992). The causes of this decline in reef health usually have not been determined with certainty. Numerous West Atlantic reefs are subject to both warm and cold water intrusions, as well as marked salinity and turbidity variations (Robertson et al. 1982, Jaap 1984). A number of reef tracts suffer from natural and anthropogenic nutrient enrichment, which probably enhances disease and directly or indirectly suppresses reef growth (Hallock and Schlager 1986, Hallock et al. 1988, LaPointe and O'Connell 1988). Accelerated bioerosion also is likely to occur in corals that have been weakened by partial bleaching, disease, or environmental stress (Reaka-Kudla pers. obs.).

Bleaching episodes have been correlated most consistently (although not exclusively) with temperature deviations (Glynn 1988, 1990, 1991; Roberts 1990). Tropical organisms are known to live near their upper temperature tolerances (Jokiel and Coles 1990), and even the relatively small increases in temperature that are predicted for tropical seas during the next several hundred years due to "greenhouse" warming (IPCC 1992) are likely to exert large effects upon the vitality and growth of reef corals. When superimposed upon higher mean temperatures, intervals of warmer conditions (such as those of future El Ninos) could impose catastrophic effects upon reef communities. Even today, Glynn and deWeerdt (1991) have reported that 2 reef-building hydrocorals were largely eliminated from their ranges in the East Pacific by the elevated temperatures of the 1982-83 El Nino event.

Ambient UV-B light intensities (280-320nm) also are increasing in some parts of the world as a result of anthropogenic depletion of stratospheric ozone. Researchers using different data sets have estimated that total column ozone has decreased from 2-5%/decade in recent years (Kerr 1991). Even when cyclic solar effects and reflectivity errors in backscattered data are corrected, Herman et al. (1991) show that the global average for total column ozone declined by 2.9 $\pm$ 1.3% over an 11-year period from 1978-1989. Since the % decrease in ozone is associated with approximately double increases in UV-B penetration (Vogelmann and Ackerman 1993), these values suggest that globally averaged UV-B penetration increased by about 5.8% over this period; this in turn implies a potential increase of approximately 50% per century if the conditions of the 1980s were to persist. Although the ozone effect was at first thought to be limited largely to polar latitudes, ozone destruction has been detected over northern mid-latitudes (Kerr 1991; Stolarski et al. 1991, 1992; Madronich 1992), and some information suggests that ozone depletion could reach the tropics (Crawford 1987). Madronich (1992) has calculated amounts of biologically active UV-B (using DNA action specra) at different latitudes; tables and graphs in this work suggest that, while the greatest increases in DNA damage are occurring at 30° N/S and above, all trends are positive even in low latitudes, and biologically active UV-B appears to increase significantly during July and August at the equator. Also, after the 1991 eruption of Mt. Pinatubo, depletions of total column ozone of 5-8% (implying 10-16% increase in UV-B) were observed above the tropics (Brasseur 1992, Vogelmann and Ackerman 1993). Even if ozone depletion in tropical regions results in a relatively small **percentage** increase in UV-B penetration, the **absolute** increase in UV intensity could be large and biologically significant because of the high intensities of radiant energy received there already.

Relatively few workers have examined the implications of changes in UV-B intensities for aquatic organisms, especially in clear tropical waters that are most likely to transmit UV. Some coral reef studies indicate that increased intensities of both UV and visible light can cause bleaching and reduced growth, photosynthesis, or calcification in corals and related organisms (Jokiel 1980; Jokiel and York 1982; Siebek 1981, 1988; Hoegh-Gulfberg and Smith 1989; Jokiel and Coles 1990; Lesser et al. 1990; Glynn et al. 1993).

Because temperature and UV have been some of the most consistently implicated (although controversial) factors in bleaching episodes and because projections of current trends indicate that anthropogenic elevations of these 2 factors pose potentially grave environmental threats for the 21st century and beyond, we undertook an experimental evaluation of the effects of 3 different temperatures (27°, 29°, 31°C, which represent approximate winter and summer ambient and above-average but encountered summer temperatures in the Exumas) and 3 different intensities of UV flux (ambient shallow water [1.5m] = 2160 joules/m^2/day as quantified by Regan et al.'s (1992) summer field observations at these depths near Lee Stocking Island, and 10% and 20% above ambient, 2376 and 2592 joules/m^2/day) upon a coral, an alga, and several species of solitary invertebrates. We simulated a shallow reef environment because field observations (Regan et al. 1992) suggested that shallow reef environments would be most affected by potential changes in UV-B exposure and it is here that reef organisms would be most likely to experience interactions between UV-B, visible light, and temperature. Data in the studies cited above suggest that levels of UV-B could increase to 10-20% greater than now over the next century when current decadal trends in ozone depletion, the long life of CFCs already in the atmosphere, and the effects of the Montreal Protocol all are taken into consideration.

METHODS

The organisms included in the study were collected at about 1.5m depth from a patch reef on a cay near Lee Stocking Island. The coral, Acropora prolifera, is a fast growing species that was flourishing on the patch reef; it also provided a comparison for a study evaluating the effects of temperature and UV-B on a West Pacific congener, Acropora valida (Glynn et al. 1993). Branchlets were taken from the same colony or from colonies in as close proximity to each other as possible in order to avoid genetic differences among experimental subjects. The alga, Microdictyon sp., is a bubble-like green alga that was observed overgrowing coral heads in shallow reef habitats near Lee Stocking Island, and the solitary invertebrates used included brittle stars (Ophionereis reticulata, Ophiocoma echinata), hermit crabs (Calcinus tibicens, Paguristes sp.), urchins (Echinometra viridis), and bivalves (Arca sp.). Clumps of algae and solitary invertebrates also were taken from as restricted an area as possible in the vicinity of the patch reef.

We used an outdoor laboratory setting covered with transparent mylar (which filters out UV-B) and a neutral density screen (black nylon netting that reduces intensity but does not alter spectral composition) so that natural visible light was maintained at intensities equivalent to those measured in these shallow water environments (1.5m) in the Exumas. To modify UV-B independently from visible light, we used solar simulators constructed of GEFS40 sunlamps surrounded by Kodacel filters (the latter screen emissions <295nm from the lamps; these wavelengths do not penetrate earth's atmosphere). These solar simulators produce wavelengths and intensities approximately equivalent to the solar spectrum (Rupert 1978, Regan and Parrish 1982, Regan 1991). Twenty-seven individual aquaria with recirculating water systems that rested in 3 separate water bath tanks were sustained at the 3 respective temperatures; the 3 UV conditions, maintained by longitudinal banks of solar simulators overhead, trisected the temperature conditions. Black plastic curtains were hung between the 3 UV conditions to prevent diffusion. UV intensities emitted by the lamps in each of the 3 conditions were confirmed during the day and night (when there was no interference from visible light) with a UV radiometer (Jagger meter calibrated against a Yellow Springs International thermopile; Jagger 1961) prior to the experiment. Temperatures, which were monitored at regular intervals throughout the day and night, were maintained at 27.15 $\pm$0.36°(standard error), 29.03 $\pm$0.23°, and 30.94 $\pm$0.26°C in the 3 respective conditions. We report only major trends here because logistic constraints prevented randomization of placement of our temperature and UV conditions. A more detailed analysis, where these constraints are rectified and additional species are included, will be forthcoming. We feel that the relatively large sample sizes used, clear patterns in the data, and the simultaneous comparisons of the 3 major taxa within each experimental condition justify the primary conclusions about how different components of the community respond to the variables tested and warrant further work on additional species.

All samples were placed into and recovered from tanks using a random number table. A 1cm mesh screen (held 2cm above the bottom by a frame) supported the branchlets of coral and the clumps of algae (tied onto the top of upright glass rods with monofilament line). The motile invertebrates were allowed to crawl about at the bottom of the aquarium. We attempted to protect the clumps of algae from any urchins that might escape from under the screen, climb the glass rods, and graze on the algae by placing small plastic shields resembling "squirrel shields" around the rod below the algae, but we observed that during the last week of the experiment several urchins emerged and outmaneuvered the shields, resulting in damage to the algae; consequently, algal weights from the last week of the experiment were discarded. For the coral, we report direct observations of bleaching (to the white condition) in branchlets that were collected and frozen for further analysis at the end of 1,2,3, or 4 weeks (other dependent variables measured will be reported elsewhere). The samples of algae were weighed individually at the beginning of the experiment and after collection of samples at either 1,2,3, or 4 weeks, at which times each set of samples was frozen for further analysis. The solitary invertebrates were observed throughout and collected and frozen at the end of the experiment.

RESULTS

The results of these experiments demonstrate negative effects of both temperature and UV-B on the coral. No coral branchlets had bleached white by the end of 1 week, but by the end of 2 weeks bleaching had begun at high temperature (10% bleached at 31°/ambient UV) and at high UV (3% bleached at 27°/+20% UV), and especially at high temperature/high UV (60% bleached). These patterns continued and intensified, culminating in the patterns seen in Table 1 at week 4. By then, the branchlets had bleached and died at high temperatures, especially 31°. Those in higher UV conditions bleached more than those at lower UV in the same temperature condition, even at 27°. An interaction between temperature and UV-B is apparent in these data, although we await data from our more stringent experimental design (above) to evaluate these trends more rigorously. The results suggest that the highest temperature (31°) exerted a more detrimental effect upon the coral than the highest UV intensity (+20%) that we tested.

In constrast, the algae grew in all conditions (Table 2). We include data only through 3 weeks because by that time the urchins had become hungry and several escaped from under the mesh frame, outmaneuvered the plastic guards, and damaged the algae. Algal growth is enhanced at high temperature (31°) at ambient levels of UV. Increased exposure to UV-B appears to enhance growth at low (27°) temperature but inhibit growth at high temperature (31°). Similar patterns in growth among conditions were seen over the first 3 weeks. Further studies will analyze these trends more stringently.

We observed minimal effects (in no particular pattern) of the levels of UV-B tested upon the solitary invertebrates (Table 3). This result may have occurred because the invertebrates could escape the UV-B by hiding under the edges of the frame (which we observed), and because the coral, algae and mesh overhead shaded them from some of the UV. The solitary invertebrates tested, like the algae, also appear to be more temperature tolerant than the corals.

Table 1. Coral bleaching at week 4. Data represent % of Acropora prolifera branchlets that were bleached white (N=40 branchlets in each condition). J=joules, d=day.

	Temperature (°C)		
	27°	29°	31°
Ambient UV (2169 J/m²/d)	0%	4%	77%
+10% UV (2376 J/m²/d)	12%	23%	78%
+20% UV (2592 J/m²/d)	32%	50%	95%

Table 2. Mean increases in algal weight through week 3. Data are % increases in weight for pieces of Microdictyon sp. tied to the top of vertically oriented glass rods (N=9 measurements in each condition).

	Temperature (°C)		
	27°	29°	31°
Ambient UV (2169 J/m²/d)	9.4%	9.1%	23.3%
+10% UV (2376 J/m²/d)	19.6%	10.5%	15.0%
+20% UV (2592 J/m²/d)	25.3%	7.5%	12.6%

Table 3. Percentage survival in solitary invertebrates. Data are derived from deaths among all taxa in each condition (1 brittle star died at ambient UV/27°, 1 urchin at ambient UV/29°, and 1 bivalve at +10% UV/29°); 21 invertebrates were placed in each condition, including 6 brittle stars (<u>Ophionereis reticulata</u>, <u>Ophiocoma echinata</u>), 6 hermit crabs (<u>Calcinus tibicens</u>, <u>Paguristes</u> sp.), 6 urchins (<u>Echinometra viridis</u>), and 3 bivalves (<u>Arca</u> sp.).

	Temperature (°C)		
	27°	29°	31°
Ambient UV (2169 J/m^2/d)	95.2%	100%	100%
+10% UV (2376 J/m^2/d)	95.2%	100%	100%
+20% UV (2592 J/m^2/d)	100%	95.2%	100%

DISCUSSION

These results, the first of their kind as far as we know, suggest that if ozone depletion causes increases in tropical UV-B intensities by as much as 10 or 20%, shallow water corals could be significantly negatively affected. This impact would occur not only because of the direct effects of UV-B upon the coral, but also because growth of algae (the corals' primary competitors for space on the reef) could be facilitated by higher levels of UV (as long as temperatures do not increase) and because solitary invertebrates (such as bioeroders) generally do not appear to be adversely affected by elevated UV-B. One other study (Dohler 1984) has reported that, in phytoplankton (diatoms), moderate doses of UV-B caused an increase in biomass production, while higher dosages of UV-B caused lower productivity and depressed protein content in the diatoms. Data in the present study also suggest that persistently warmer conditions (in the absence of elevated UV-B) could favor dominance of algae over corals, both because high temperature inflicts more damage upon corals than UV (at the levels we tested) and because high temperature did not adversely affect the algae (as long as it was not superimposed with high UV). Relationships between algae and solitary invertebrates (some of which graze algae) will be complex, depending upon the combinations of environmental temperature and UV-B that they experience. Solitary invertebrates (some of which scrape and bore coral) appear to be less affected by either UV-B or temperature than the corals, probably because most hide under structures or in crevices during the day and emerge only in crepuscular or nocturnal periods (Dominguez and Reaka 1988). The lack of an effect of temperature on solitary invertebrates in our experiments is somewhat surprising, since experiments by Glynn and D'Croz (1990) showed that survival of symbiotic crustaceans associated with corals declined at higher temperatures. However, this may have been due to the declining health of their obligate coral hosts (Glynn et al. 1985) rather than temperature alone.

Consequently, corals may suffer more than predicted by the straightforward effects of temperature and UV-B upon them, and an ensuing breakdown of the physical structure of reefs could have a devastating effect upon these high diversity systems. Our final interpretations will await more rigorous statistical analyses of these effects and studies of a number of the dependent variables that we have measured. Also, more species of corals, algae, and solitary invertebrates (particularly grazers and bioeroders) must be included before definitive conclusions about the impact of changing thermal and UV-B environments upon reef communities can be made. For example, <u>A</u>. <u>prolifera</u> is a rapidly growing species of coral and may be more prone to bleaching than some of the more slowly growing massive species of corals, and other species of algae may be more damaged by the environmental conditions imposed than was the opportunistic <u>Microdictyon</u> sp. We are pursuing additional comparisons, but we believe that the above patterns are provocative.

CONCLUSIONS

1. The branching coral, Acropora prolifera, is negatively impacted by exposure to increasing dosages of UV-B (to 20% above ambient) and elevated temperatures (from 27° to 31°C). These effects began at week 2 and were much amplified by the end of the 4 week experiment.

2. The opportunistic "bubble-like" alga, Microdictyon sp., survives and grows when exposed to the increased levels of UV-B and temperature tested here (growth is highest at ambient temperature/high UV and ambient UV/high temperature).

3. The solitary invertebrates tested (brittle stars, hermit crabs, urchins, and bivalves) are little affected by the environmental conditions we tested for 4 weeks.

4. If the results obtained for these species hold for other corals, algae and solitary invertebrates, this experiment suggests that altered environmental conditions potentially could induce long term changes in shallow reef communities which are unforeseen on the basis of present knowledge of the effects of temperature and UV-B on one group of organisms such as corals.

ACKNOWLEDGEMENTS

The work was supported by a grant from NOAA's National Undersea Research Center and the Caribbean Marine Research Center.

LITERATURE CITED

Brasseur, G. 1992. Volcanic aerosols implicated. Nature 359: 275-276.
Brown, B. E., and J. C. Ogden. 1993. Coral bleaching. Sci. Amer. 268: 64-70.
Crawford, M. 1987. Landmark ozone treaty negotiated. Science 237: 1557.
Dohler, G. 1984. Effect of UV-B radiation on the marine diatoms Lauderia annulata and Thalassiosira rotula grown in different salinities. Mar. Biol. 83: 247-253.
Dominguez, J. H., and M. L. Reaka. 1988. Temporal acticity patterns in reef-dwelling stomatopods: A test of alternative hypotheses. J. Exp. Mar. Biol. Ecol. 117: 47-69.
Glynn, P. W. 1988. El Nino-southern oscillation 1982-83: Nearshore population, community and ecosystem responses. Ann. Rev. Ecol. Syst. 19: 309-345.
Glynn, P. W. 1990. Coral mortality and disturbances to coral reefs in the tropical Eastern Pacific. Pages 55-126 in P. W. Glynn, ed. Global ecological consequences of the 1982-83 El-Nino-Southern Oscillation. Elsevier Press.
Glynn, P. W. 1991. Coral reef bleaching in the 1980s and possible connections with global warming. Trends Ecol. Evol. 6: 175-179.
Glynn, P. W., and L. D. D'Croz. 1990. Experimental evidence for high temperature stress as the cause of El Nino-coincident coral mortality. Coral Reefs 8: 181-192.
Glynn, P. W., and W. H. deWeerdt. 1991. Elimination of two reef-building hydrocorals following the 1982-83 El Nino warming event. Science 253: 69-71.
Glynn, P. W., M. Perez, and S. L. Gilchrist. 1985. Lipid decline in stressed corals and their crustacean symbionts. Biol. Bull. 168: 276-284.
Glynn, P. W., R. Imai, K. Sakai, Y. Nakano, and K. Yamazato. 1993. Experimental responses of Okinawan (Ryukyu Islands, Japan) reef corals to high sea temperature and UV radiation. Proc. 7th Internat. Coral Reef Symp. (in press).
Goreau, T. J. 1992. Bleaching and reef community change in Jamaica: 1951-1991. Amer. Zool. 32: 683-695.
Hallock, P., and W. Schlager. 1986. Nutrient excess and the demise of coral reefs and carbonate platforms. Palaios 1: 389-398.
Hallock, P., A. C. Hine, G. A. Vargo, J. A. Elrod, and W. J. Jaap. 1988. Platforms of the Nicaraguan rise: Examples of the sensitivity of carbonate sedimentation to excess trophic resources. Geology 16: 1104-1107.
Herman, J. R., R. Hudson, R. McPeters, R. Stolarski, Z. Ahmad, X.-Y. Gu, S. Taylor, and C. Wellemeyer. 1991. A new self-calibration method applied to TOMS and SBUV backscattered ultraviolet data to determine long-term global ozone change. J. Geophys. Res. 96(D4): 7531-7545.
Hoegh-Gulfberg, O., and G. J. Smith. 1989. The effect of sudden changes in temperature, light and salinity on the population density and export of zooxanthellae from the reef corals Stylophora pistillata Esper and Seriatopora hystrix Dana. J. Exp. Mar. Biol. Ecol. 129: 279-303.
Jaap, W. C. 1984. The ecology of the South Florida coral reefs: A community profile. U. S. Fish Wildl. Serv. FWS/OBS-82/08: 1-138.
Jagger, J. 1961. An inexpensive meter for measuring UV. Radiation Res. 14: 394-403.
Jokiel, P. L. 1980. Solar ultraviolet radiation and coral reef epifauna. Science 207: 1069-1071.

Jokiel, P. L., and S. L. Coles. 1990. Response of Hawaiian and other Indo-Pacific reef corals to elevated temperature. Coral Reefs 8: 155-162.

Jokiel, P. L., and R. H. York, Jr. 1982. Solar ultraviolet photobiology of the reef coral Pocillopora damicornis and symbiotic zooxanthellae. Bull. Mar. Sci. 32: 301-315.

IPCC. 1992. Climate change: The Intergovernmental Panel on Climate Change impacts assessment, 1992 Supplement. IPPC Secretariat, Geneva.

Kerr, R. A. 1991. Ozone destruction worsens. Science 252: 204.

LaPointe, B. E., and J. O'Connell. 1988. The effects of on-site sewage disposal systems on nutrient relations of groundwater and nearshore waters of the Florida Keys. Monroe Co. Planning Dept., Key West, Fla., Tech. Rept.: 1-67.

Lesser, M. P., W. R. Stochaj, D. W. Tapley, and J. M. Schick. 1990. Bleaching in coral reef anthozoans: Effects of irradiance, ultraviolet radiation, and temperature on the activities of protective enzymes against active oxygen. Coral Reefs 8: 225-232.

Madronich, S. 1992. Implications of recent total atmospheric ozone measurements for biologically active ultraviolet radiation reaching the earth's surface. Geophys. Res. Let. 19(1): 37-40.

Porter, J. W., and O. W. Meier. 1992. Quantification and loss and change in Floridian reef coral populations. Amer. Zool. 32: 625-640.

Regan, J. D. 1991. So who goes sunbathing in Antarctica? J. Nat. Inst. Health Res. 3: 52-54.

Regan, J. D., and J. A. Parrish. 1982. The science of photomedicine. Plenum Press. 658 pp.

Regan, J. D., W. L. Carrier, H. Gucinski, B. C. Olla, and R. I. Wicklund. 1992. DNA as a solar dosimeter in the ocean. Photochem. Photobiol. 56: 35-42.

Rupert, C. S. 1978. Biological effectiveness of ultraviolet light. Nat. Cancer Inst. Monogr., DHEW Pub., NIH 78-1532, 50: 85-90.

Siebeck, D. 1981. Photoreactivation and depth-dependent UV tolerance in reef coral in the Great Barrier Reef, Australia. Naturwissenschaften 68: 426-428.

Siebeck, D. 1988. Experimental investigation of UV tolerance in hermatypic corals (Scleractinia). Mar. Ecol. Progr. Ser. 43: 95-103.

Stolarski, R., P. Bloomfield, and R. McPeters. 1991. Total ozone trends from Nimbus 7 TOMS data. Geophys. Res. Let. 18(6): 1015-1018.

Stolarski, R., R. Bojkov, L. Bishop, C. Zerefos, J. Staehelin, and J. Zawodny. 1992. Measured trends in stratospheric ozone. Nature 356: 342-349.

Vogelmann, A. M., and T. P. Ackerman. 1993. Harmful UV radiation may increase after volcanic eruptions. Eos 74(2): 25.

OIL ON TROUBLED WATERS: IMPACTS OF THE GULF WAR ON CORAL REEFS

Callum M. Roberts[1], Nigel Downing[2], and Andrew R.G. Price[3,4]

[1]Eastern Caribbean Center, University of the Virgin Islands, St Thomas, US Virgin Islands, 00802, USA. [2]Ashcroft, Rotherfield Peppard, Henley-on-Thames, Oxon, RG9 5LB, UK. [3]Ecosystems Analysis and Management Group, Dept of Biological Sciences, University of Warwick, Coventry, CV4 7AL, UK. [4]Coastal and Marine Programme, IUCN (World Conservation Union), Rue Mauverney 28, CH-1196 Gland, Switzerland.

ABSTRACT

During the 1991 Gulf War some 6-7 million barrels of oil were dumped into the Arabian Gulf. For 10 months an oily soot from blazing wells rained onto the region, obscuring the sun. These acts of environmental terrorism raised great fears for the future of the Gulf's marine life, especially since it is naturally an extreme environment and has been subjected to unprecedented coastal development pressures over the past 2-3 decades. Some inshore patch reefs covered by oil for several weeks suffered no more than an initial loss of mobile fauna. Offshore islands of Saudi Arabia were oiled but escaped lightly. Three surveys in 1991 and 1992 suggest that these reefs remain remarkably unscathed. A survey of Kuwaiti island reefs in July 1991 also suggested an absence of subtidal effects. However, by May 1992 Kuwaiti reefs were showing signs of stress with extensive coral bleaching reported. In December 1992 they were resurveyed and data compared with surveys made before the war. Whilst there had been mortalities of *Acropora* and *Porites* at two of three islands visited, these were no greater in magnitude than kills prior to the Gulf War. Only on an inshore patch reef close to the source of the largest oil spill was a more widespread coral mortality noted. A significant decline in fish populations was also detected at Kubbar Island. Whilst Gulf War pollution may be implicated in these effects, it is not necessarily the only cause. Environmental stresses coupled with escalating human pressures make the long-term future for corals reefs in the Gulf very uncertain.

INTRODUCTION

Environmental conditions in the Arabian Gulf stretch the tolerance limits for the existence of coral reefs Sheppard et al. 1992). This near-enclosed, shallow sea has high sediment loads and salinities and is subject to extremes of temperature at both ends of the scale which exceed those experienced by reefs elsewhere. Nevertheless, this high latitude setting does support some relatively well-developed reefs, uniquely able to tolerate these marginal conditions.

In early 1991 some 6-7 million barrels of oil were discharged into the northern Gulf as a result of the Gulf War (Earle 1992), the largest known oil spill in human history. Above water, the sun lay partially hidden for several months in Kuwait and northern Saudi Arabia until the last of the oil fires were extinguished in November 1991, and the oily soot fallout smothered sea and land alike. The area affected contains some of the richest coral reefs in the Gulf. Yet this was not the first environmental disaster to hit the region. The Iraq-Iran war had already emptied an estimated two million barrels of oil into the Gulf during the 1980s. Added to this, human pressures on the coastal zone have been increasing dramatically over the past two decades. For example, recent estimates indicate that on the Saudi Arabian coast 50% of mangroves have been lost and 40% of the coast infilled over this period (IUCN/MEPA 1987). Has Gulf War pollution been the barrel which broke the camel's back for coral reefs?

CORAL REEFS IN THE GULF

Environmental profile

The Gulf is a shallow basin covering some 226,000 km^2 and lies between the Arabian peninsula and the mountains of Iran. Covering a latitudinal range of about 24° to 30°N it is perhaps best described as sub-tropical. During past ice ages it dried out and the Tigris and Euphrates rivers meandered through a low lying valley to empty directly into the Indian Ocean through the present day Strait of Hormuz. The recent history of the Gulf as a near-enclosed sea thus began some 10,000 years ago when rising sea levels connected it again with the Indian Ocean. The present day fauna and flora have recolonised since then.

The Gulf is a sea where extremes prevail. With an average depth of only 35m and a maximum of 165m, the sea has little capacity to buffer changes in temperature which occur in this high latitude setting. As a consequence coral reefs experience some of the greatest extremes of temperature of reefs anywhere in the world (Downing 1985, Coles and Fadlallah, 1991). Sea surface temperatures routinely fall below 14°C often for many days. At the other end of the scale, summer temperatures can soar to over 40°C in shallow coastal areas.

The shallowness of the Gulf also promotes high turbidity due to resuspension of bottom sediments by waves. "The desert continues below the sea" is an apt phrase coined to describe the Gulf's vast area of soft bottomed habitats, although an inappropriate description for their rich biological productivity. Turbulence typically keeps horizontal visibility between 1 and 10m and reduced light levels are thought to be one of the mains reasons that coral growth peters out below 10m deep (Basson et al. 1977).

Enclosed by deserts and connected to the Indian Ocean only by the narrow Strait of Hormuz, high summer temperatures and huge areas of shallows turn the Gulf into an efficient evaporation basin. As there is little rain, most of this is replaced by inflowing seawater raising ambient salinities to between 40 and 44ppt and to over 70ppt in enclosed bays and Gulfs such as the Gulf of Salwah.

Reef distribution and development

In such a high stress environment it is remarkable that coral reefs occur at all. Not surprisingly, they cover only a tiny area and much of the coral growth in the Gulf does not contribute to development of a carbonate framework but only coats older geological structures with a thin veneer. Nevertheless, well-developed reefs do occur, especially in the north western Gulf along the Saudi Arabian coast. Although there have been reports of good reef development off the Iranian coast (Harrington 1976, Harger 1984) little is known of this area. Consequently, this paper will focus on the well-studied reefs of the western Gulf. In Saudi Arabia, reef coral biotopes have been estimated to cover an area of 390km^2 (<1% of subtidal habitat; IUCN/MEPA 1987) and in Kuwait less than 4km^2. Most of these reefs are small inshore patch reefs lying between 2 and 20km from the coast. The best developed reefs lie further offshore (40-60km) and in many cases have associated low-lying coral cays.

The pattern of reef development appears to be closely linked to the effects of environmental extremes (Sheppard 1988). Temperature, salinity and turbidity appear to be the main controls. Moving south reef-development is poorer although the area covered by coral communities is larger. Off the coasts of Bahrain and Qatar there are extensive shallow banks of hard substrata (Pleistocene limestone) which support corals and, at their margins, a relatively rich coral reef fauna. Moving south into the Gulf of Salwah, increasing salinity progressively eliminates coral species until beyond about 55ppt only algal vegetation remains. The waters of the United Arab Emirates support numerous small patch reefs and some fringing reefs around low-lying islands, but coral diversity is low (Sheppard et al. 1992).

Figure 1: Map of the north-western Arabian Gulf showing the locations of places mentioned in the text.

Whilst the effects of salinity act in a progressive fashion, reefs are subject to periodic mass coral mortalities due to low temperature throughout their present range (Downing 1985, Shinn 1976). However, despite suffering heavy losses in terms of coral cover, the reefs seem very resilient to such kills. Mortality appears to be concentrated on fast-growing species such as *Acropora* spp., and in two well-documented cases recovery was probably complete within six years for reefs in Qatar (Shinn 1976) and in Kuwait (Downing 1991).

Compared to the adjacent Indian Ocean coral reef communities of the Gulf are depauperate. Of the groups most closely studied, there are only 52 species of corals known, at least 183 species of reef-associated fishes and 99 species of echinoderms (Downing 1985, McCain et al. 1984, Price 1982, Sheppard and Sheppard 1991, Smith et al. 1987). Although no corals are restricted to the Gulf, around 6% of reef associated fishes and 12.1% of all echinoderms are endemic. Speciation is likely to have been enhanced by the isolated nature of the Gulf but it is unlikely that all have evolved since its most recent reconnection with the Indian Ocean (Sheppard et al. 1992). Gradients in species richness closely follow those of reef development, increasing moving offshore from the north-western Gulf and decreasing moving north and south from this.

HUMAN PRESSURES ON GULF CORAL REEFS

Effects of the 1991 Gulf War

The Gulf War was only the most recent of a series of human pressures on Gulf reefs (Sheppard et al. 1992). In the aftermath of the war, greatest concern was focussed on the effects of oil and pollution from the burning oil wells of Kuwait (McKinnon and Vine 1991). The best reefs lay within the path of the oil slick and the smoke plume covered the whole area, the latter being most dense over the north-west Gulf coast (Figure 1). Aside from direct chemical effects, scientists feared that reduced sunlight from the smoke would chill the Gulf's waters below levels which could be tolerated by corals (Downing 1991, Sheppard et al. 1993). An additional stress resulted from discharge of untreated sewage into Kuwait's waters for over one year after the war ended.

Extent of pollution

Heavy soot fallout was reported on three islands off the coast of Kuwait, Kubbar, Qaru and Umm al Maradem, shortly after the end of the war in July 1991 (Downing 1991). Soot was also transported much further south, affecting coastal and offshore areas of Saudi Arabia. Most of the oil released floated south by-passing the above Kuwaiti islands (Downing 1991, Downing and Roberts 1992). Oiling was heaviest in inshore areas of Saudi Arabia lying to the north of the island of Abu Ali. This island acted as a natural boom, preventing most of the oil from travelling further south. Some inshore patch reefs north of Abu Ali were reported to have been covered in oil for several weeks (Y. Fadlallah pers. comm.). Further offshore, the island reefs escaped more lightly. Even so, 14,200m^3 of oil were removed from the beaches of Karan Island and all the other Saudi Arabian coral islands were also oiled (McKinnon and Vine 1991).

By the time oil reached Saudi Arabian waters, much of the lightest, most toxic fractions had evaporated. However, several inshore patch reefs along the Kuwaiti coast were probably exposed to high concentrations of these fractions for several weeks.

Present status of reefs

There have been several surveys of reefs in the Gulf since the war ended to determine how much damage was caused by pollution (Downing 1991, Downing and Roberts 1993, Fadlallah in press a,b, Greenpeace 1992, IUCN 1992). Early reports suggested that offshore island reefs had escaped virtually unscathed (Downing 1991, Greenpeace 1992). A survey of island reefs of Saudi Arabia in November 1992 has confirmed this (Roberts 1993).

Inshore reefs of Saudi Arabia which were covered by floating oil lost many of their fishes (which either quit the reefs or perished *in situ*), but there has been substantial recolonisation since then (J. McCain pers. comm.). However, corals on these reefs apparently remain healthy, with no bleaching or unusual mortality observed (Y. Fadlallah pers. comm., Roberts 1993).

In April to May 1992 the National Oceanic and Atmospheric Administration (NOAA) of the US made a research cruise through the Gulf on the R/V Mt Mitchell. Although they were unable to detect any effects of the war on offshore reefs of Saudi Arabia, Bahrain or Qatar, the scientists on board reported widespread bleaching of corals in Kuwait. It was even suggested that some of the reefs had been so heavily impacted as to be virtually dead implying a major perturbation by Gulf War pollution. However, scientists in Kuwait who were familiar with these reefs were unconvinced by the results of this cruise (B. Habashi pers. comm.).

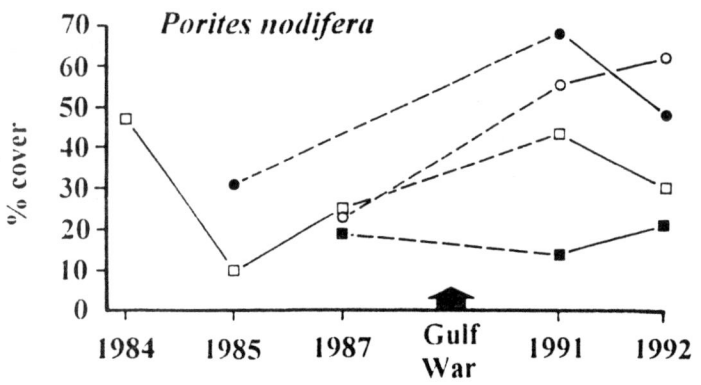

Figure 2: Changes in the % cover of live *Porites nodifera*, one of the main reef-building coral species, on Kuwaiti reefs. (O) Kubbar, (■) Qaru east reef, (●) Qaru west reef, and (□) Umm Al Maradem. Data are from Downing and Roberts (1993).

In November and December of 1992 a further survey was made of Kuwaiti reefs by two of us. One of us (ND) spent eight years at the Kuwait Institute of Scientific Research studying the ecology of these reefs (Downing 1989 a,b,c) and had established a monitoring programme. Key sites were resurveyed in 1991 shortly after the war (Downing 1991) and again in 1992 (Downing and Roberts in press). The results of the 1992 survey, six months after the NOAA cruise showed that the reefs were far from dead. Although there had been coral mortalities at several sites, these had occurred in a complex pattern. Since 1991, at Kubbar Island about 50% of the tabular *Acropora* sp. had died, whilst *Porites nodifera* continued its recovery from a 1985 kill. At Qaru there had been relatively recent death of about 10% of the reef-flat *Porites nodifera* in one area of the reef (Figure 2). At Umm al Maradem both species of

Acropora, A. sp. and *A. valida*, had suffered a combined mortality of approximately 40% and approximately 6% of reef-flat *Porites nodifera* had died (Figure 2). Inshore, at Getty Reef, no evidence of any coral mortality was found. By contrast, further north the reef at Qita't Urayfijan, just 15km south of the Mina Al Ahmadi terminal from which much of the oil was released, had evidently suffered substantial coral mortality. This was concentrated on *Porites nodifera* and *Platygyra lamellina*. At all sites studied there was no evidence of current coral bleaching and recovery was well underway with many new recruits present and regrowth from partially killed colonies.

Fish counts were made at Kubbar, Qaru and Umm al Maradem in both 1991 and 1992 and compared with pre-war censuses (Downing and Roberts in press). Those at Kubbar showed a significant decrease in abundance across species (26 of 37 species showed decreases in abundance between pre- and post-war censuses; $p < 0.05$). However, although trends of decrease were apparent at Qaru (30 of 46 species decreased) and Umm al Maradem (21 of 34 species decreased) these differences were not significant. Surveys of fishes were not made at the inshore sites.

Despite the above evidence of post-war decline in Kuwait's reefs, they were far from being dead. Indeed, Getty Reef was in excellent condition, and even at Qita't Urayfijan, qualitatively, the densities of commercially important fishes (mostly large predators) appeared high suggesting a relatively healthy reef.

Is the Gulf War to blame for damage to Kuwait's reefs?

The most obvious explanation for damage to Kuwait's reefs is Gulf War pollution, but is this the correct one? Fadlallah et al. (in press) suggested that reduced water temperatures from the smoke plume had caused the observed coral mortalities. McCain et al. (in press) found that during the height of the oil fires, summer water temperatures at Manifa, 110km south of Kuwait, were

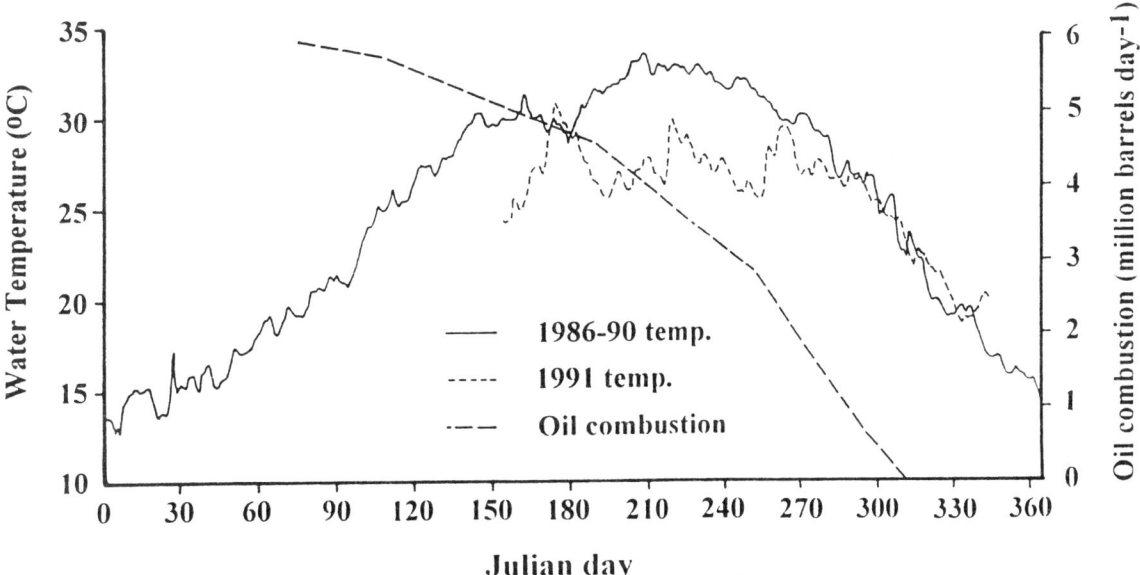

Figure 3: Mean daily water temperature at Manifa pier, Saudi Arabia, for 1991 and for the period 1986-90, in relation to the production of smoke from burning Kuwaiti oil wells. Modified from McCain et al. (in press) with permission.

reduced up to 7°C over the average of the previous five years (Figure 3). However, the oil fires had been extinguished several months before bleaching was observed and water temperatures had apparently recovered their normal pattern (McCain et al. in press). It was also suggested that toxic effects of oil, particularly at Qita't Urayfijan had caused coral death (Downing and Roberts in press), or that discharges of untreated sewage had played a role (Fadlallah in press).

Reductions in population densities of fishes at Kubbar may have been due to reduced recruitment, and/or increased post-settlement mortality. McCain and Hassan (in press) have recently shown a reduction in the abundance of ichthyoplankton in the vicinity of oil sheens in Saudi Arabian Gulf waters. The collapse of the penaeid shrimp fishery in Saudi Arabia following the war (Carpenter 1992) is probably at least partly due to mortality of pelagic larvae (C. Mathews, unpublished report). By contrast, the 1992/93 shrimp season in Kuwait has produced a bumper harvest, probably because Kuwaiti nursery grounds were not impacted by oil and shrimp were not fished for the previous 18 months.

However, the complex pattern of mortalities observed does not lend itself well to simple explanations based on single factors. Nor is it easy to determine whether mortalities were effects of the war or due to natural environmental fluctuations. As noted above, mass coral mortalities are frequent on Gulf reefs. The magnitudes of mortality observed were in keeping with those recorded on Kuwaiti reefs in the mid 1980s (Downing 1987b), and further south (Shinn 1976). We have argued elsewhere that only a cocktail of stresses could have caused the observed changes in Kuwait's reefs (Downing and Roberts in press). These could include war-related, natural and other human stresses. However, partitioning the effects of stresses based on the available data would be pure speculation.

THE GULF: A SEA UNDER INCREASING HUMAN PRESSURE

The Gulf War has focussed world attention on a sea which was until then little known outside the region. However, as a result of the vast oil wealth of the area the Gulf has undergone rapid changes over the past few decades. Rapidly escalating human pressures have had widespread effects. The sea into which Saddam Hussein emptied Kuwait's oil was far from pristine.

Oil has been part of the Gulf's environmental profile since pre-history, with many natural seepages occuring (Downing 1985, McKinnon and Vine 1991). However, oil input to the Gulf now takes place on a massive scale. More than 30% of the world's tanker traffic passes through this sea (Linden et al. 1990), and with an estimated 10,000 oil related structures (Y. Fadlallah pers. comm.), it is thought that at least 250,000 barrels of oil enter the Gulf each year, the equivalent of the Exxon Valdez oil spill of 1989 (Earle 1992). Other estimates put the annual oil input to the Gulf much higher than this with up to 2 million barrels discharged annually (P. Litheraty pers. comm.)!

The coast of the Gulf has undergone development on a grandiose scale, especially in the west. An idea of the level of this development can be gained by examining the investment per kilometre of coast. In an early study of Gulf pollution, Walgate (1978) estimated that industrial investment averaged \$40 million km^{-1} on the Arabian coast and \$20 million km^{-1} on the Iranian coast. In Saudi Arabia it reached up to \$100 million km^{-1}. Whilst falling oil revenue led to a later drop in the rate of expansion, present levels of investment will be far higher than this.

Massive expansion of coastal infrastructure has caused widespread damage to coastal habitats such as mangroves and seagrass beds (IUCN/MEPA 1987). Effects on reefs have lagged those on inshore soft bottomed habitats because most reefs lie offshore. However, in the long term infilling and water pollution present a major threat to the Gulf's coral reefs.

Infilling of shallow coastal areas to create new land has two main origins. It creates cheap land and is a convenient dumping ground for dredge spoil. Since most of the Gulf coast is shallow, extensive dredging has been necessary to provide access to ports and loading facilities. By the mid 1980s the dredged area of shallow Saudi Arabian waters had reached an estimated 46.5km^2 (IUCN/MEPA 1987).

Despite the presence of enormous stretches of unused land, overpricing by landowners has led to pressure to infill (Oakley 1989). In Qatar for example, a suitable inland site for a new international airport has been rejected because the local Emir refused to sell the land at a reasonable price (Dunn and Roberts 1986). Plans to infill over a large area of coral reef to the south of Doha are now well advanced.

In Bahrain many nearshore areas have been infilled over the years. However, much more ambitious infilling over reefs to the east and north has been contemplated (Price et al. 1983) although so far resisted. Coastal modifications from causeway construction have also added to effects on marine habitats, including reefs (Vousden and Price 1985, Oakley 1989). In most cases, the consequences for marine life of altering current regimes have been inadequately assessed.

Pollution in the Gulf is also a growing problem. The vast industrial and petrochemical complexes which line the shores produce huge quantities of effluents contaminated with many compounds damaging to marine life. Desalination plants, for example, add chlorine and chromic acid to cooling water to prevent fouling of pipes, often at concentrations which are toxic to life in the discharge areas (Oakley 1989). One Saudi Arabian fertiliser plant alone releases 5.8 million m^3 of waste water containing ammonia and heavy metals into the Gulf annually (IUCN/MEPA 1987). Evaluating the effects of effluents is made much more difficult since most industrial plants are veiled in secrecy and discharges cannot be sampled (Oakley 1989). In Saudi Arabia, even the country's own environmental protection agency, MEPA, are not permitted to sample from most oil refinery outfalls (MEPA Dhahran, pers. comm.). Oakley (1989) reported that the one Saudi Arabian refinery which would allow sampling, Petromin on the Red Sea coast, discharged effluent containing 7500 tonnes of hydrocarbons per year!

Domestic pollution adds to the Gulf's problems. Populations along the coast have expanded as rapidly as industrial infrastructure and with urban populations increasing at 6-10% per year (Walgate 1978), inputs of sewage have escalated. In many places this has been inadequately treated or not treated at all. At Al Khobar, on the Saudi Arabian coast, over 10 million m^3 of untreated sewage were being released directly into the sea annually in the mid 1980s (IUCN/MEPA 1987). The pollution problem is compounded by the low volume of water in the Gulf, which limits it buffering capacity, and a low turnover rate, estimated to take 3-5.5 years for complete turnover of water (Hunter 1986). Little is known of the long-term effects of pollutant build-up on Gulf reefs or other biota. However, a recent study confirmed that contamination is becoming a problem, showing that Saudi Arabian shrimp contained arsenic levels exceeding international guidelines (J. McCain pers. comm.).

Direct impacts on reefs are also beginning to be felt, even on the offshore islands. In the lee of Jurayd Island heavy anchoring by fishing dhows has reduced large areas of reef to rubble, and anchor damage is also evident at the other islands (Roberts 1993). Increasing use is also being made of reefs for recreational fishing and diving.

The Gulf War has alerted the world to the plight of coral reefs in the Gulf. However, war-related pollution has only been one more in a catalogue of stresses impinging on marine life, albeit a highly visible one. Whilst the tolerance limits of reef organisms toward particular stressors may not yet have been exceeded, we should worry about the fact that reefs are being subjected simultaneously to multiple stresses. The combined effects of different stresses may reduce the abilities of organisms to withstand human impacts and the natural hazards they face in this extreme environment. For example, studies elsewhere have shown that temperature tolerances of corals may be reduced where populations are exposed to other sources of stress (Jokiel and Coles 1990). Little by little, life in a difficult place has been getting harder for marine organisms in the Gulf.

It is to be hoped that current efforts to reverse the tide of degradation of Gulf marine habitats will not be too little too late. However, it will take a major change in the attitudes and policies of states bordering the Gulf to provide a secure future for the region's coral reefs.

CONCLUSIONS

Studies soon after the Gulf War suggested that offshore coral reefs had virtually escaped damage, although some inshore reefs were affected. In 1992 however, some Kuwaiti reefs showed signs of serious stress which were blamed on the Gulf War. While some of these effects may have been due to war-related pollution, the reefs exist in an naturally stressful environment and the causes of coral and fish mortalities cannot be determined with certainty. By late 1992 recovery of affected reefs appeared well under way. However, increasing human pressures on Gulf reefs make their future very uncertain.

ACKNOWLEDGEMENTS

We would like to thank the World Conservation Union (IUCN), the World Wide Fund for Nature (WWF), the Meteorology and Environmental Protection Administration (MEPA)(Saudi Arabia), the "Marine Sanctuary for the Gulf Region" project of the National Commission for Wildlife Conservation and Development (Saudi Arabia)/Commission of the European Community, The Regional Organisation for the Protection of the Marine Environment (ROPME)(Kuwait), the Environmental Protection Department (Kuwait) for supporting our work in the Arabian Gulf.

LITERATURE CITED

Basson, P.W., J.E. Burchard, J.T. Hardy and A.R.G. Price 1977. Biotopes of the western Arabian Gulf: marine life and environments of Saudi Arabia. ARAMCO, Dhahran, Saudi Arabia.

Carpenter, K.E. 1992. Preliminary observations on the effects of the 1991 Gulf War on fisheries. Mar. Poll. Bull.

Coles, S.L. and Y.H. Fadlallah. 1991. Reef coral survival and mortality at low temperatures in the Arabian Gulf: new species-specific lower temperature limits. Coral Reefs 9: 231-237.

Dipper, F. 1991. The oil, the Gulf, the impact. BBC Wildlife March 1991: 190-193.

Downing, N. 1985. Coral reef communities in an extreme environment: the northwest Arabian Gulf. Proc. 5th Int. Coral Reef Congress, Tahiti 6:343-348.

Downing, N. 1989a. Final report on "A study of the corals and coral reef fishes of Kuwait". Volume I: Project outline, summary and recommendations. Kuwait Institute for Scientific Research, Kuwait. 18pp.

Downing, N. 1989b. Final report on "A study of the corals and coral reef fishes of Kuwait". Volume II: The reef building corals. Kuwait Institute for Scientific Research, Kuwait. 156pp.

Downing, N. 1989c. Final report on "A study of the corals and coral reef fishes of Kuwait". Volume III: The coral reef fishes. Kuwait Institute for Scientific Research, Kuwait. 151pp.

Downing, N. 1991. A survey of the coral islands of Kubbar, Qaru and Umm Al Maradem. Kuwait, 13th-19th July 1991. IUCN, Gland, Switzerland. 22pp.

Downing, N. and C.M. Roberts. 1993. Impact of the Gulf War on the coral reefs of Kuwait: results of the Nov/Dec 1992 survey. IUCN, Gland, Switzerland. 33pp.

Downing, N. and C.M. Roberts. In press. Effects of the Gulf War on coral reefs: an analysis of long-term data. Mar. Poll. Bull.

Dunn, I.G. and C.M Roberts 1986. Doha West Bay Lagoon development: environmental studies. Parts 1 & 2. ABCS Ltd, Chatham, UK.

Earle, S.A. 1992. Persian Gulf pollution. Assessing the damage one year later. National Geographic February 1992, 122-134.

Environmental Protection Council 1991. State of the environment report. A case study of crimes against the environment. Environmental Protection Council, Kuwait. 164pp.

Fadlallah, Y.H., C.M. Eakin, K. Allen, S.A. Rahim, J. Jaubert, A. Al-Sofyani, M. Reaka-Kudla, S.A. Earle, J. Randall, S. Kayal and F. Cava. In press. Assessment of coral reef ecosystems in the ROPME Sea Area following the 1991 Gulf War oil spill. Abstract.

Fadlallah, Y.H., C.M. Eakin, S.A. Rahim, K. Allen and M.L. Reaka-Kudla. In press a. Distribution, community structure and reproduction of reef corals in the western ROPME Sea Area, with special reference to *Acropora* following the 1992 Gulf War oil spill. Abstract.

Greenpeace. 1992. The environmental legacy of the Gulf War. Greenpeace International, Amsterdam. 42pp.

Harger, J.R.E. 1984. Rapid survey techniques to determine distribution and structure of coral communities. UNESCO Reports in Marine Science 21: 83-91.

Harrington, F.A. 1976. Iran: surveys of the southern Iranian coastline with recommendations for additional marine reserves. Pages 50-75 in Promotion of the establishment of marine parks and reserves in the northern Indian Ocean including the Red Sea and Persian Gulf. IUCN Publ. New Series, No. 35, IUCN, Gland.

Hunter, J.R. 1986. The physical oceanography of the Arabian Gulf: a review and theoretical interpretation of previous observations. Pages 1-23 in R. Halwagy et al., eds. First Gulf conference on environment and pollution, Kuwait, February 7-9th, 1982. University of Kuwait.

IUCN/MEPA. 1987. Arabian Gulf. Saudi Arabia: an assessment of biotopes and coastal zone management requirements for the Arabian Gulf. MEPA Coastal and Marine Management Series, Report No. 5, IUCN, Gland. 248pp.

IUCN. 1992. IUCN's response to the 1990-91 Gulf War. Unpublished report, IUCN, Gland, Switzerland.

Jokiel, P.L. and S.L. Coles 1990. Response of Hawaiian and other Indo-Pacific reef corals to elevated temperature. Coral Reefs 8: 155-62.

Linden, O.M., M.Y. Abdelraheem, M.A. Gerges, I. Alam, M. Behbehani, M.A. Borhan and L.F. Al-Kassab. 1990. State of the marine environment of the ROPME Sea Area. UNEP Regional Seas Reports and Studies. No 112, Rev. 1. UNEP, Nairobi, 34pp.

McCain, J.C., A.B. Tarr, K.E. Carpenter and S.L. Coles. 1984. Marine ecology of Saudi Arabia. A survey of coral reefs and reef fishes in the northern area, Arabian Gulf, Saudi Arabia. Fauna of Saudi Arabia 6: 102-120.

McCain, J.C. and M. Hassan. In press. The effects of the Gulf War on the planktonic stages of fishes and shrimp. Mar. Poll. Bull.

McCain, J.C., D.W. Beard and Y.H. Fadlallah. In press. The influence of the Kuwaiti oil well fires on seawater temperature in the western Arabian Gulf. Mar. Poll. Bull.

McKinnon, M. and P. Vine. 1991. Tides of war. Eco-disaster in the Gulf. Immel Publishing, London. 192pp.

Oakley, S.G. 1989. Ecological factors affecting the management of marine resources. *In* Proc. of a workshop on the ecological imperatives for sustainable resource use, 20-21 June 1989, National Commission for Wildlife Conservation and Development, Riyadh, Saudi Arabia.

Price, A.R.G. 1982. Echinoderms of Saudi Arabia. Comparison between echinoderm faunas of Arabian Gulf, SE Arabia, Red Sea and Gulfs of Aqaba and Suez. Fauna of Saudi Arabia 4: 3-21.

Price, A.R.G., D.H.P. Vousden and R.F.G. Ormond. 1983. Ecological study of sites on the coast of Bahrain, with special reference to the shrimp fishery and possible impact from the Saudi-Bahrain Causeway under construction. IUCN Report to the UNEP Regional Seas Programme, Geneva.

Roberts, C.M. 1993. Impact of the Gulf War on the coral reefs of Saudi Arabia: Results of the November 1992 survey. Report to The World Conservation Union (IUCN), Gland. 18pp.

Sheppard, C.R.C. 1988. Similar trends, different causes: responses of corals to stressed environments in Arabian seas. Proc. 6th Int. Coral Reef Symp., Townsville 3: 297-302.

Sheppard, C.R.C. and A.L.S. Sheppard. 1991. Corals and coral communities of Arabia. Fauna of Saudi Arabia 12: 3-170.

Sheppard, C.R.C., A.R.G. Price and C.M. Roberts. 1992. Marine ecology of the Arabian region. Patterns and processes in extreme tropical environments. Academic Press, London. 359pp.

Shinn, E.A. 1976. Coral reef recovery in Florida and the Persian Gulf. Environ. Geol. 1: 241-254.

Smith, G.B., M. Saleh and K. Sangoor. 1987. The reef ichthyofauna of Bahrain (Arabian Gulf) with comments on its zoogeographic affinities. Arab. Gulf J. Sci. Res. B5: 127-146.

Vousden, D.H.P. and A.R.G. Price. Bridge over fragile waters. New Scientist 1451: 33-35.

Walgate, R. 1978. Pollution in the Persian Gulf. Nature, London 272: 573.

OIL REFINERY IMPACTS ON CORAL REEF COMMUNITIES IN ARUBA, N.A.

C. Mark Eakin[1], Joshua S. Feingold[2] and Peter W. Glynn[2]

[1]National Oceanic and Atmospheric Administration, Office of Global Programs, 1100 Wayne Ave., Suite 1225, Silver Spring, MD 20910. [2]University of Miami, Rosenstiel School of Marine and Atmospheric Science, Marine Biology and Fisheries, 4600 Rickenbacker Cswy., Miami, FL 33149

ABSTRACT

From 1925 to 1985, Lago Oil and Transport Co. operated a transshipping terminal and refinery on the southeastern coast of Aruba, N.A. This facility has affected the nearshore marine ecosystem through both oil contamination at the harbor and tanker berths, and from disturbance related to shipping, dredging and construction. The impact of this facility on nearby coral reef communities was studied from January 1987 to August 1989. This included an analysis of reef community structure comparing sites adjacent to the refinery with those upstream and downstream, the modern and historical growth of the predominant coral species, and recruitment of new corals. Both upstream and downstream control sites were in good health and exhibited high diversity. In contrast, reefs adjacent to the refinery exhibited low density and diversity of live corals and abundant dead coral rubble. Additionally, periods of construction in the inner harbor and on surrounding spoil islands and high refinery activity corresponded well with periods of reduced coral growth near the refinery. Although the relative importance of oil contamination, sedimentation and other anthropogenic effects is uncertain, our observations suggest that sedimentation and other physical stress resulted in substantial reductions in environmental quality at the disturbed sites. Coral recruitment at the highly impacted sites showed hope for recovery if these environments are protected from renewed perturbation.

INTRODUCTION

While studies have discussed the short-term effects of oil on corals and reef communities, there have been few investigations of the impacts of chronic exposures. As reviewed in Vandermeulen & Gilfillan (1984) and Loya & Rinkevich (1987) several studies have reported healthy reefs in chronically oiled areas, while others have shown dramatic effects on coral reproduction and physiology. However, the potential for disturbance of coral reefs by oil drilling, production, refining and transport facilities goes beyond the influence of oil release. Operation of such facilities can reduce ecosystem health through mechanical damage, sedimentation and turbidity, and the release of other pollutants. Sedimentation and other effects of dredging and marine construction can seriously impair coral health (Loya, 1976; Marszalek, 1981; Yamazato, 1987; Salvat, 1987).

Here we discuss the impact of an oil refinery on coral reef communities in the southeastern Caribbean Sea. The Lago Oil and Transport Company operated a transshipping and refining facility on the island of Aruba from 1925-1985. From Lago records (Harcharik, pers. comm.), Lago began transshipping in 1925, and refining in 1929. Operations were expanded through the 1930s, followed by major activity during World War II. Further expansion occurred in the 1950s, with dredging and other harbor improvements around 1959. Dredging was again carried out in 1967, and supertanker berths were installed in 1975. After that, operations quickly dropped and the facility closed in March, 1985. Besides oil contamination, nearshore environments have been impacted by dredge and fill operations in the refinery harbor in the western end of Sint Nicolaas Baai (including augmentation of fill on a spoil island) and the construction of deep water berths to accommodate supertankers. The greatest oil impacts have originated as leakage from oil holding tanks into Sint Nicolaas Baai and Commandeurs Baai and operational losses from the transshipping facilities.

METHODS

Data were collected during three periods. Initial community analyses and collections were conducted during January 1987; coral staining and further collections during August 1987; and collection of stained corals and other samples during August 1989.

Site Descriptions

The island of Aruba is located in the southeastern Caribbean Sea, 29 km north of Venezuela. Strong northeast trade winds and the Caribbean Current produce a steady longshore current along the southern coast and heavy surf along the eastern and northeastern coasts. Corals are common in lagoons along the eastern shore, and reefs are well developed along the southern coast. Individual sites, described below, are shown in Figure 1. Sites were selected to include one upstream "control" site (Dog Cemetery), two disturbed sites (Refinery Reef and Reef Berths), and one downstream "control" (Pos Chikitu). Sampling locations within the selected treatment groups were chosen based on two criteria: 1) the presence of coral habitat, and 2) the ability to be relocated using shore reference marks.

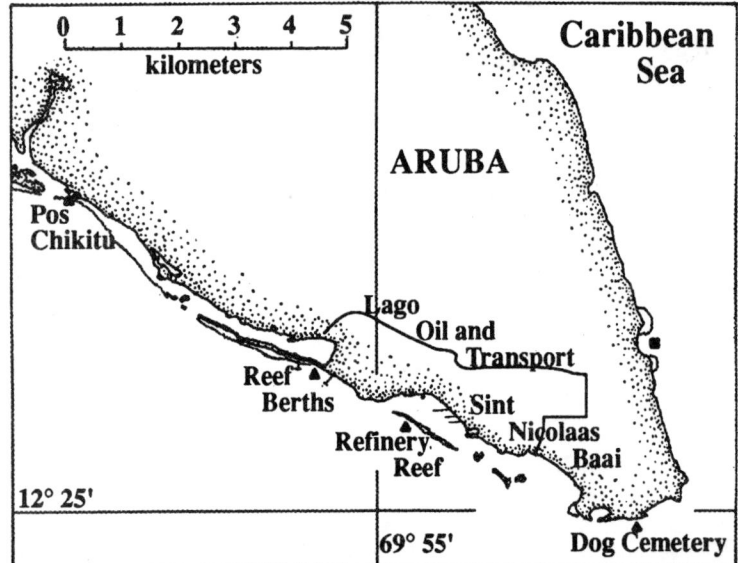

Figure 1. Chart of southeastern Aruba. Locations of study sites denoted by triangles. Note approximate outline of Lago Oil and Transport Co. facility.

Dog Cemetery.–Located to the east of Sint Nicolaas Baai, this reef was strongly influenced by prevailing currents, high wave stress and surge. Coral cover was high, and zonation well developed, with a nearshore crest of live *Acropora palmata*, a steep slope predominated by lobate *Montastrea annularis* and *Dendrogyra cylindrus*, a base of massive *M. annularis*, *D. cylindrus*, *Diploria* spp. and *Colpophyllia natans*, and fields of *Acropora cervicornis* at 10 m depth. Dead *A. palmata* in growth position were common on the reef crest.

Refinery Reef.–The reef extended the length of a spoil island built up through harbor construction and maintenance, and consisted of dead massive coral framework and sandy bottom, with some live coral. The reef sloped gradually from the surface to 10 m, followed by a steep, mostly sandy slope. Sediments contained small accumulations of dark petroleum-based particulates beneath the surface. Small *Diploria strigosa* predominated, primarily growing on dead corals. Formations of recently killed *Montastrea annularis* and *Dendrogyra cylindrus* were evident. Copious debris was found here, primarily in shallow water near the filled island.

Reef Berths.–Located between the supertanker berths immediately downstream of the refinery, this site was similar to Refinery Reef. The site gradually sloped from the surface to about 10 m, but then dropped rapidly, partly the result of underwater blasting for the dockage of deep draft vessels. Here too, the sediment contained fine, black petroleum-based particulate, as well as surface tar balls. Many small colonies of massive species were seen growing on old framework. Nearshore corals had suffered much mechanical damage from the dumping of large debris.

Pos Chikitu.–Located 5 km downstream of the refinery, coral cover and diversity were high along the relatively steep slope. Large colonies of *Montastrea annularis*, *Dendrogyra cylindrus*, *Colpophyllia natans* and *Diploria strigosa* and stacks of *Acropora cervicornis* were present. The growth form of *M. annularis* changed from massive in the shallow backreef to lobate on the upper slope and to more flattened plates on the lower wall (*M. annularis* morphotypes III, I and II respectively, sensu Knowlton et al., 1992). The reef crest was poorly developed, consisting primarily of dead framework, with some live *A. palmata*.

Community Surveys

Each site was sampled at both the 5 and 10 m depth contours. A 100 m line was laid down approximately parallel to shore along each permanently marked isobath. Ten, 10 m chain transects were centered on the 100 m line, placed perpendicular to the shore at randomly selected intervals along this line. The substratum or organism directly beneath each link of a loosely laid chain was tallied and identified to the genus or species. Percent live and dead coral cover were calculated from the transects. Data were arcsin transformed, tested for assumptions of ANOVA and analyzed with a two way ANOVA for differences among sites and depths. Differences among site means were tested by a *posteriori* Student-Newman-Keuls (SNK) tests (Sokal and Rohlf, 1969). Three transects along the 10 m isobaths at the Refinery Reef and Reef Berths sites were randomly chosen for resurvey and comparison 30 months later. The percent cover of each bottom type was compared between the original (1987) and subsequent surveys (1989).

Recruitment was assessed by measuring the basal circumference of small colonies of *Diploria strigosa*, *Montastrea annularis*, *Meandrina meandrites* and *Siderastrea siderea* at Reef Berths and Pos Chikitu. Size data and the time required to measure the colonies (colonies per diver-minute = Col./d.min) were analyzed for differences between sites. Additionally, the numbers and sizes of small corals were determined in alternate 1 m^2 sections of transects at the 10 m isobath of Reef Berths and Pos Chikitu during periods 24 months apart.

Sclerochronological Analysis

Approximately 10 colonies of *Diploria strigosa* and *Montastrea annularis*, were tagged and stained *in situ* with alizarin red-s stain (Lamberts, 1978) at Reef Berths and Pos Chikitu. After 24 months, 28 of these colonies were recovered (Reef Berths: 8 *D. strigosa*, 7 *M.annularis*; Pos Chikitu: 7 *D. strigosa*, 6 *M. annularis*). The corals were sectioned, x-rayed, and measured for growth beyond the stain lines at three points along the skeleton. Mean growth was tested for between site differences.

Columnar colonies of *Montastrea annularis* (morphotype I sensu Knowlton et al., 1992) collected at each of the four study sites were cut, x-rayed and analyzed for growth. High-low density band doublets were marked independently by two examiners (blinded). The markings were compared, final marks were placed on the prints and annual linear growth was measured. Annual growth rates were plotted by year for all colonies; unusually large or small increments were reexamined, and adjusted when appropriate. Five year running means of annual growth were graphed by year and examined visually for trends (modified from Hudson, 1981). Changes in coral growth rate were then compared with refinery activity during the colonies' life.

RESULTS
Community Surveys

The four study sites differed significantly in their live coral cover (Table 1, two-way ANOVA, $p<0.0001$). Neither depth, nor the interaction between location and depth significantly influenced live coral cover. The SNK multiple comparisons test showed that the disturbed sites, Refinery Reef and Reef Berths, were not statistically different, and had less coral cover than both Dog Cemetery and Pos Chikitu. Also, Pos Chikitu had significantly more live coral than Dog Cemetery. Statistical analysis of the dead coral cover (ANOVA) showed no significant differences among the sites or between the two depths (5 m and 10 m). Conversely, sand and dead coral rubble were significantly higher at the disturbed sites.

Table 1. Percent of live coral cover in transect lines (n=10 transects at each site and depth). Values listed as mean and 95% confidence interval. Vertical lines denote sites that did not differ significantly (SNK test, p>0.05).

Site	Depth	% Cover Mean	C.I.	ANOVA Source	df	p
I Refinery Reef	5 m	3.01	2.23	Subgroups	7	
I (disturbed)	10 m	1.46	0.71	location	3	< 0.0001
I				depth	1	ns
I Reef Berths	5 m	5.55	4.21	interaction	13	ns
I (disturbed)	10 m	2.62	2.72	error	71	
				Total	79	
Dog Cemetery	5 m	23.16	17.03			
(control)	10 m	22.64	9.55			
Pos Chikitu	5 m	28.89	7.56			
(Control)	10 m	39.12	7.98			

Some portions of the shallow and deep reef at Dog Cemetery were composed of nearly monotypic stands of acroporid corals. Typically, these corals are found in well flushed environments and do not tolerate turbid conditions. The greatest coral diversity was observed at this site -- 26 of 34 total species were present. The comparison of community transects revealed a slight increase in live coral cover from 1987 to 1989. Mean coral cover in these transects increased from 1.6 to 7.5% at Refinery Reef and 0.5 to 3.7% at Reef Berths. Although evocative of change, the differences were too slight to be significant with the small sample sizes.

Reef Berths and Refinery Reef were characterized by many small colonies of the corals *Diploria strigosa*, *Montastrea cavernosa*, *Siderastrea siderea* and *Meandrina meandrites*. Size-frequency analysis showed that significantly smaller corals were present at Reef Berths than at the downstream site (Pos Chikitu). Comparisons of the densities of young colonies found far more colonies at Reef Berths (2.67 Col./d.min) than Pos Chikitu (1.21 Col./d.min). Data on the recruit coral colonies found in these surveys are summarized in Table 2. *Diploria strigosa* recruits were smaller and more numerous at Reef Berths than at Pos Chikitu. This may have resulted from greater availability of substrata suitable for settlement at Reef Berths, perhaps from mechanical damage of corals at that site. The higher coral cover at Pos Chikitu may have limited recruitment by reducing substrate availability. Large mean coral recruit size at Pos Chikitu suggests an earlier recruitment event or more rapid growth than at Reef Berths.

Table 2. Sizes of small corals measured at each site in January 1987. Values are expressed as mean basal circumference (±95% confidence interval), tested with t' test (Sokal and Rohlf, 1969).

Coral Species	Site	n	Size (cm) Mean	C.I.	t' Test
Diploria strigosa	Reef Berths	100	11.6	1.16	
	Pos Chikitu	100	32.2	3.12	P << .001
Montastrea cavernosa	Reef Berths	100	11.1	1.78	
	Pos Chikitu	25	39.9	5.57	P << .001
Meandrina meandrites	Reef Berths	100	16.6	0.57	
	Pos Chikitu	49	50.9	7.51	P << .001
Siderastrea siderea	Reef Berths	100	5.2	1.45	
	Pos Chikitu	56	25.9	7.06	P << .001

Comparisons of the number and sizes of recruits in 1987 and 1989 surveys revealed no changes through time (t-test), indicating that any new recruitment during this period was minor. The slight increase in mean colony sizes at Reef Berths (1987: 19.4 ± 3.1, 1989: 21.0 ± 1.5) is consistent with the growth that would be expected of similarly aged colonies. The presence of young colonies at Reef Berths suggests recovery of the reef community from past disturbance. Yet, the paucity of recruitment since 1987 indicates that full recovery will require a considerable amount of time.

Sclerochronological Analysis

Stained corals confirmed that regular seasonal banding, with a winter high density band and summer low density band, occurs in the two species examined. The growth rate of the brain coral *Diploria strigosa* was almost identical between Reef Berths and Pos Chikitu, while *Montastrea annularis* growth was significantly lower at Reef Berths (Table 3). As *M. annularis* is somewhat susceptible to sediment stress this may indicate that this disturbance was greater near the refinery. Similar growth rates of *D. strigosa* at the two sites indicates that this species was not significantly affected by disturbances near the refinery.

Table 3. Two year growth of stained corals Aug. 1987-Aug. 1989. Mean values (mm/y ± 95% confidence intervals) are compared using a one-tailed t-Test.

	Diploria strigosa		*Montastrea annularis*	
	Reef Berths	Pos Chikitu	Reef Berths	Pos Chikitu
Mean	4.3±0.4	4.6±0.7	7.1±1.0	12.4±1.0
n	8	7	7	6
t-Test	ns		p<0.05	

Growth values for *Montastrea annularis* in Aruba are among the highest reported in the Caribbean, and varied from 1.04 cm/yr at Refinery Reef to 1.36 cm/yr at Pos Chikitu (Figure 2). Annual growth rates varied significantly among years and among colonies (nested ANOVA, p<0.001 and 0.01 respectively), and were significantly slower at the disturbed than the control sites (SNK test, p<0.01). Growth at Dog Cemetery fluctuated dramatically around 1920, and slowly increased after the mid 1950s (Figure 2). At Pos Chikitu, growth was remarkably consistent, with a slight decline in growth throughout the records. Changes in growth rates at the disturbed sites frequently coincided with major refinery activities. Growth rates began to decline at Refinery Reef one year after the installation of the refinery and continued down until after expansion and dredging in the 1960s. Growth at Reef Berths was more variable, but began a rapid decline shortly after World War II and around the time that facility expansion began. Growth rate recovery at Reef Berths coincided with that at Refinery Reef in the late 1960s, but began a dramatic drop again shortly after the installation of the supertanker berths and initiation of dispersant use around 1975. It should be noted that some lag between stress and growth rate changes results from the smoothing function used.

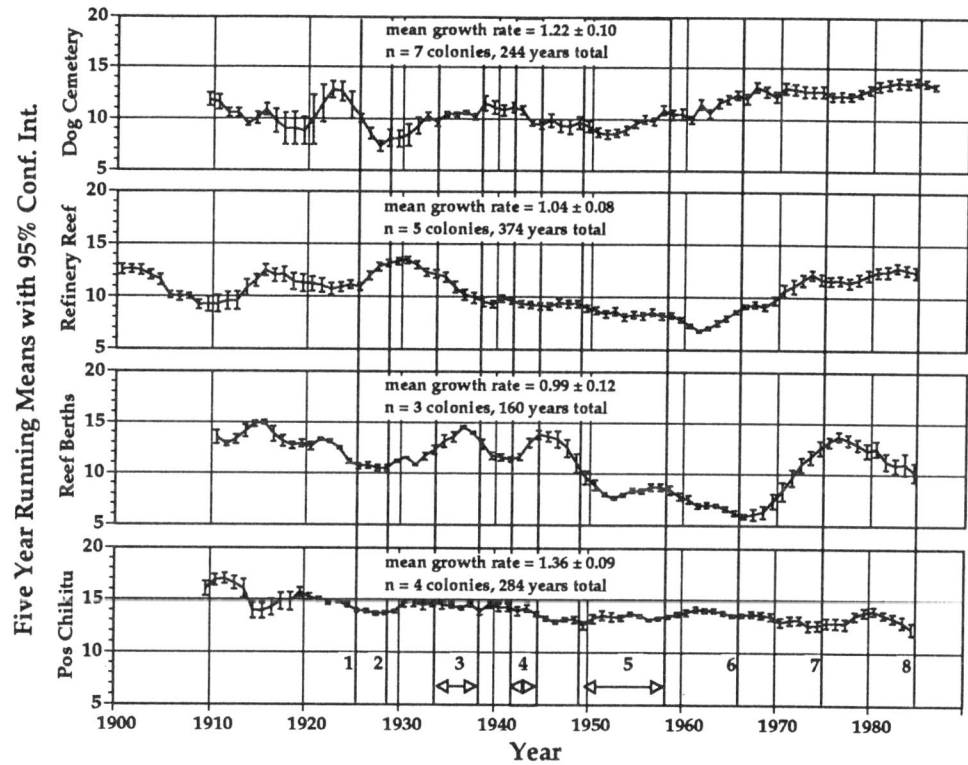

Figure 2. Five year running means of skeletal growth rates (± 95% confidence interval), of *Montastrea annularis* collected at four sites in Aruba. Relevant historical events noted on figure are: [1]transshipping terminal constructed, [2]refinery operations begun, [3]first expansion, [4]World War II, [5]second expansion and harbor improvements, [6]inner harbor dredging, [7]supertanker berth constructed, dispersant use initiated (Bak, 1989), [8]refinery and transshipping terminal closed.

DISCUSSION

There is little question that Lago operations damaged nearby coral reefs. Coral mortalities resulted from some combination of direct mechanical damage, siltation stress, and oil and other petrochemical stress. Correlation of periods of reduced growth with periods of high activity, especially construction, support the hypothesis that refinery activity reduced coral health. The lack of such correlation at either Dog Cemetery or Pos Chikitu indicates that the stress was localized. This also suggests that the main cause of stress was related to mechanical damage and sedimentation, as oil contamination of surface waters often extended downstream beyond Pos Chikitu.

At both disturbed sites, Reef Berths and Refinery Reef, new corals recruited following the death of old reef-building corals. Smaller colony size can be due to a younger age (indicating a recent recruitment pulse) or slower growth (indicating stress). As growth of *Diploria strigosa* was similar all sites (Table 3), small colonies of *D. strigosa* at Reef Berths are recent recruits. The higher coral cover at Pos Chikitu may limit recruitment by reducing the availability of substrata. Numerous larvae did recruit to available substrata at the disturbed sites -- substrata made available as a byproduct of adult coral mortalities and the addition of construction debris.

While the growth rate of *Diploria strigosa* did not differ between Pos Chikitu and Reef Berths, recent growth of stained *Montastrea annularis* was significantly slower at Reef Berths (Table 3). Decreased growth often results from increased stress (Highsmith, 1979). Corals are sensitive to sediment loading because of direct and indirect effects on coral physiology (Marszalek, 1981; Yamazato, 1987). Decreased water clarity from suspended sediments affects corals and their symbiotic zooxanthellae, which like most plants require sunlight for energy production. As corals derive up to 90% of their energy from these photosynthetic endosymbiotes (Muscatine, 1973), they suffer when light levels are attenuated (Maragos, 1972). Suspended sediments also reduce the foraging efficiency of polyps, hindering capture of important planktonic prey. Sediment that settles directly on exposed tissue further stresses corals that must expend energy in its removal. Loya (1976) reported that *Diploria strigosa* was relatively sediment tolerant, especially compared with *Montastrea annularis*. The differences in growth rate as a response to sedimentation stress allows the use of *M. annularis* as an indicator of reef environmental quality.

Sclerochronological analysis of corals at the refinery sites revealed that growth tracked many changes in Lago's activity. Growth at Refinery Reef responded rapidly to the initiation of refinery activity and continued to decline with increased activity. The increase in growth in the mid-1960s is a bit puzzling, as refinery activity continued at a high level until the early 1970s. While growth at Reef Berths was more variable, the same long period of low growth was seen from the mid 1940s to the late 1960s. Only a slight decline was exhibited from 1940 to 1960 at Pos Chikitu, but a slight, long-term decline may represent slight decreases in environmental quality along the entire coast. The upstream site, Dog Cemetery, showed high variability in growth rates with a slight overall increase. In fact, there was no indication of any response among Dog Cemetery corals to oil spills in the 1960s and 1970s when oil released around Curaçao coated the eastern shores of Aruba.

The sites most disturbed by refinery operations exhibited low live coral cover, low growth rates of stained *Montastrea annularis*, recruit-skewed coral populations, and periodic reductions in coral growth. It is safe to conclude that the construction and operation of the Lago Oil refinery have degraded living conditions for corals in the area around the refinery. Severe siltation and mechanical damage could have been wholly responsible for the disturbance observed. Unfortunately, our work can only document the influence of these stresses on coral health, and cannot differentiate among sources of the stress. Both acute and chronic exposure to oil can be stressful to shallow subtidal corals (Vandermeulen & Gilfillan, 1984; Loya & Rinkevich, 1987; Jackson et al., 1989) and perhaps even reduce skeletal growth (Guzmán and Jackson, 1991). In addition, the use of dispersants often places corals at greater risk by exposing subtidal corals to oil that would otherwise remain at the surface and to chemicals that are themselves toxic (Dodge et al., 1985). This could explain the long term declines in growth seen at both the refinery sites and the slight decline at Pos Chikitu. However, the presence of apparently healthy coral reefs in areas subjected to chronic surface oil slicks raises uncertainty about the effect of surface oil on deep subtidal corals (Loya & Rinkevich, 1987; Fadlallah et al., 1993; NOAA, 1993). Our results are consistent with those of Bak (1987), who found dramatic declines in reef health along 10-15 km of coastline near the refinery. However, his conclusion that oil pollution had major lethal effects downstream of the refinery was speculative since the losses of species that he reported were predominantly found within the region of refinery operations rather than in areas considerably downstream.

It is most likely that the refinery's primary impact on reefal organisms was sediment related. Sedimentation and mechanical damage associated with dredging and construction have been shown to impact both short term coral health and long term growth (Hudson, 1981; Marszalek, 1981). Marine construction, especially during dredging and blasting, can introduce large quantities of sediment into the reefal environment. Once introduced, other forces may exacerbate the effects of sediments. Shipping activities resuspend particles and scour corals with propwash, while debris and fill added to artificially enhance islands may slump onto reefs. Reef damage is somewhat self-perpetuating. Unlike healthy reefs in which the cover of stony and horny corals reduces the transport of sediments into the water column, heavily disturbed reefs have little topographic complexity to baffle water flow at the sediment water interface and prevent sediment resuspension.

As is true with any activity that impacts the environment, economic gains of development and industry must be balanced against environmental losses. In Aruba, the destruction of reefs has resulted in the loss of habitat for artisanally harvested fishes, and diminished tourism value. Reefs can recover, given sufficient time under favorable environmental conditions. In 1989, the reefs near the refinery appeared to be recovering from the disturbances of the past. However, transshipping and refinery operations have resumed at the Lago site. Enthusiasm for renewed refinery activity should be tempered by the need to protect these nearshore habitats. We only hope that care will be taken to protect recovering reefs from renewed environmental insult.

CONCLUSIONS

1. Coral reefs located adjacent to the refinery (Refinery Reef, Reef Berths) have been disturbed by the presence of the refinery. This is supported by reductions in growth rates associated with refinery operations, skewed size distributions, reduced live coral cover, and the ubiquitous anthropogenic and coral rubble at the disturbed sites.

2. The presence of large amounts of dead corals, some in growth position, at the disturbed sites indicates that these reefs previously supported well developed reefs.

3. Conditions conducive to coral reef growth are not diminished downstream from the refinery, relative to conditions upstream.

4. Recruitment of young colonies to the disturbed sites suggests that environmental conditions improved during recent periods of reduced activity at Lago. Proper protection of the marine environment should lead to recovery at these reefs.

ACKNOWLEDGEMENTS

Logistical support for sampling in Aruba was provided by H. vanBerkel, various personnel of Lago Oil and Transport, and the captain and crew of the M/V Rainbow. Sampling was aided by the efforts of M.A. Coffroth, J.M. Eakin, A. George-Ares, H. Guzmán, R. Lemaitre, D. Perrine, H. vanBerkel, G.L. Voss, A. Yedid. We thank D. Harcharik, of ESSO Caribbean and South America, for supplying information on Lago activity and H. Hudson, U.S. Geological Survey, for the use of equipment for sclerochronological analysis. This paper is dedicated to the memory of G.L. Voss who continues to inspire our work.

LITERATURE CITED

Bak, R.P.M. 1989. Effects of chronic oil pollution on a Caribbean coral reef. Mar. Poll. Bull. 18(10): 534-539.

Dodge, R.E, T.D. Jickells, A.R. Kanap, S. Boyd, R.P.M. Bak. 1985. The effect of dispersed oil on the calcification rate of the reef-building coral *Diploria strigosa*. Proc. 5th Intl. Coral Reef Conr. Tahiti 6: 453-457.

Fadlallah, Y.H., C.M. Eakin, K.W. Allen, R.A. Estudillo, S.A. Rahim, M. Reaka-Kudla, S.A. Earle. 1993. Distribution and community structure of scleractinian corals in Qatar, Bahrain, eastern Saudi Arabia, and Kuwait - collections and surveys of the Mt. Mitchell Cruise, May 1992. Proceedings of the scientific workshop on results of the R/V Mt. Mitchell cruise, Regional Organization for Protection of the Marine Environment. Kuwait. in press.

Guzmán, H.M. and J.B.C. Jackson. 1991. Chapter 5: Subtidal Reef Corals. Pages 121-151 *in* Keller, B.D. and J.B.C. Jackson eds. Long-term assessment of the oil spill at Bahía Las Minas, Panama, interim report, volume II: technical report, U.S. Dept. of Interior, Minerals Management Service.

Highsmith, R.C. 1979. Coral growth rates and environmental control of density banding. J. Exp. Mar. Biol. Ecol. 37: 105-125.

Hudson, J.H. 1981. Growth rates in *Montastrea annularis*: a record of environmental change in Key Largo Coral Reef Marine Sanctuary, Florida. Bull. Mar. Sci. 31(2): 444-459.

Jackson, J.B.C., J.D. Cubit, B.D. Keller, V. Batista, K. Burns, H.M. Caffey, R.L. Caldwell, S.D. Garrity, C.D. Getter, C. Gonzalez, H.M. Guzmán, K.W. Kaufman, A.H. Knap, S.C. Levings, M.J. Marshall, R. Steger, R.C. Thompson, and E. Weil. 1989. Ecological effects of a major oil spill on Panamanian coastal marine communities. Science, 243: 37-44.

Knowlton, N., E. Weil, L.A. Weigt, H.M. Guzmán. 1992. Sibling species in *Montastraea annularis*, coral bleaching, and the climate record. Science 255: 330-333.

Lamberts, A.E. 1978. Coral growth: alizarin method. Pages 523-527 *in* Stoddart, D.R. and Johannes, R.E., eds. Coral reefs: research methods, UNESCO.

Loya, Y.L. 1976. Effects of water turbidity and sedimentation on the community structure of Puerto Rican corals. Bull. Mar. Sci. 26(4): 450-466.

Loya, Y.L. and B. Rinkevich. 1987. Effects of petroleum hydrocarbons on corals. Pages 91-102 *in* B. Salvat, ed. Human impacts on coral reefs: facts and recommendations. Antenne Museum E.P.H.E., French Polynesia.

Maragos, J.E. 1972. The study of the ecology of Hawaiian reef corals. Ph.D. thesis, Univ. of Hawaii. 290 pp.

Marszalek, D.S. 1981. Impact of dredging on a subtropical reef community, southeast Florida, U.S.A. Proc. Fourth Intl. Coral Reef Symp. 1: 147-153.

Muscatine, L. 1973. Nutrition of corals. Pages 77-115 *in* Jones, O.A. and R. Endean eds. Biology and Geology of Coral Reefs, Vol. II, Biology 1, Academic Press, New York. 480 pp.

National Oceanic and Atmospheric Administration, Office of the Chief Scientist. 1993. Mt. Mitchell expedition to the ROPME Sea Area February-June 1992, IOC/UNESCO. 58 pp.

Salvat, B. 1987. Dredging in coral reefs. Pages 161-184 *in* B. Salvat, ed. Human impacts on coral reefs: facts and recommendations, Antenne Museum E.P.H.E., French Polynesia.

Sokal, R.R. and F.J. Rohlf. 1969. Biometry., W.H. Freeman and Co. 776 pp.

Vandermeulen, J.H. and E.S. Gilfillan. 1984. Petroleum pollution, corals and mangroves. MTS Journal 18(3): 62-72.

Yamazato, K. 1987. Effects of deposition and suspension of inorganic particulate matter on the reef building corals in Okinawa, Japan. Galaxea 6: 289-309.

REEFS OF FLORIDA, BAHAMAS, BERMUDA AND GULF OF MEXICO

	PAGES
The Health and Short-Term Change of Two Coral Patch Reefs, Fernandez Bay, San Salvador Island, Bahamas *H. Allen Curran, Durelle P. Smith, Lucy Chambers Meigs, Ann E. Pufall, and Mary Lisa Greer*	147 - 153
Twenty Years of Change in Coral Communities over Deep Reef Slopes along Leeward Coasts in the Netherlands Antilles *R.P.M. Bak and G. Nieuwland*	154 - 159
Fifty Years of Impacts on Coral Reefs in Bermuda *C.B. Cook, R.E. Dodge, and S.R. Smith*	160 - 166
The Relationship Between Environmental Factors and Coral Bleaching at Lee Stocking Island, Bahamas in 1990 *George D. Dennis and Robert I. Wicklund*	167 - 173
The M/V Wellwood and Other Large Vessel Groundings: Coral Reef Damage and Recovery *Stephen R. Gittings, Thomas J. Bright, and Derek K. Hagman*	174 - 180
Protection and Monitoring of Reefs on the Flower Garden Banks, 1972-1992 *Stephen R. Gittings, Thomas J. Bright, and Derek K. Hagman*	181 - 187

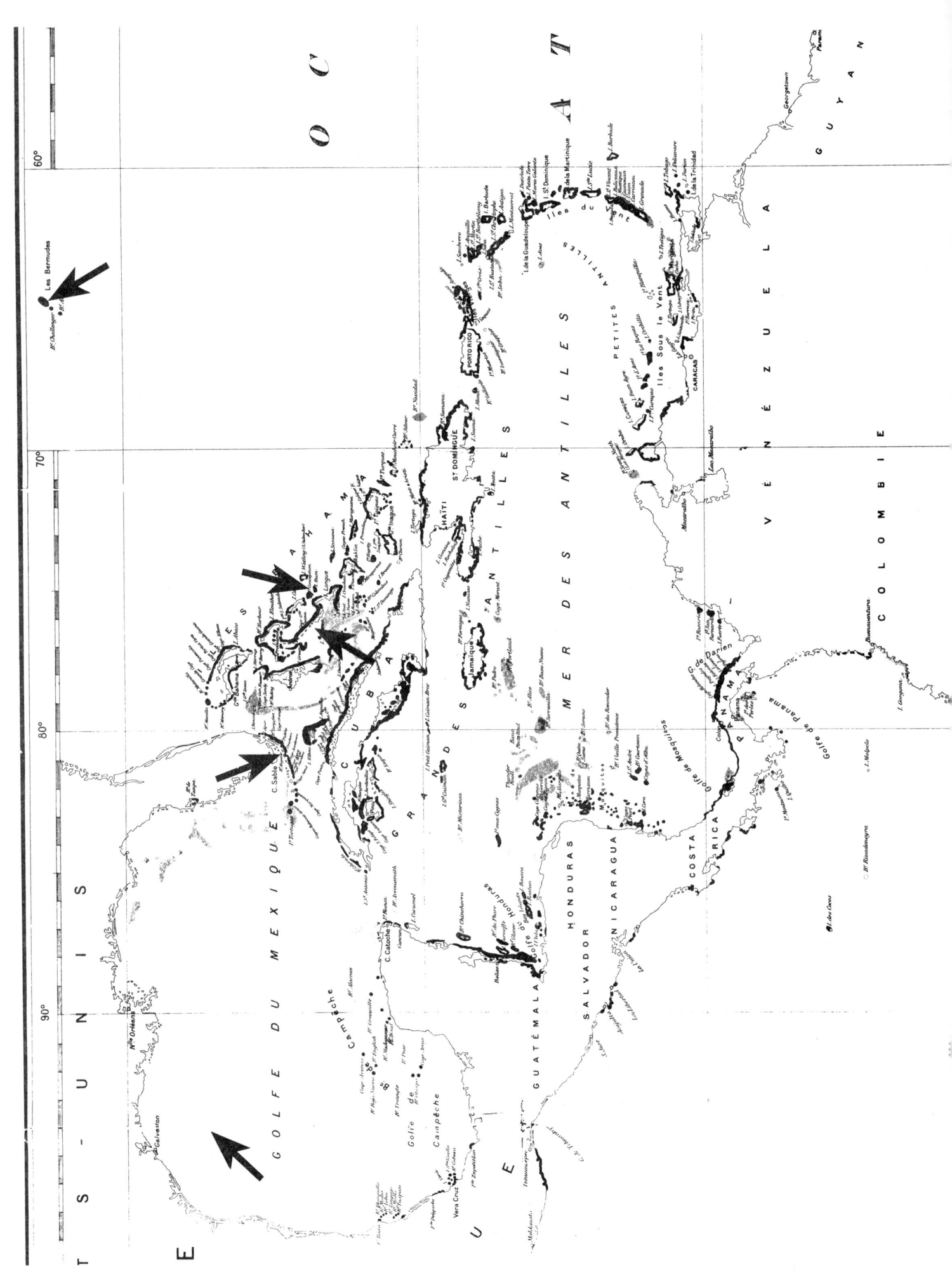

THE HEALTH AND SHORT-TERM CHANGE OF TWO CORAL PATCH REEFS, FERNANDEZ BAY, SAN SALVADOR ISLAND, BAHAMAS

H. Allen Curran[1], Durelle P. Smith[1], Lucy Chambers Meigs[2],
Ann E. Pufall[1], and Mary Lisa Greer[3]

[1] Department of Geology, Smith College, Northampton, Massachusetts 01063. [2] Department of Geology and Geophysics, University of Wisconsin-Madison, Madison, Wisconsin 53706. [3] Department of Geology, Colorado College, Colorado Springs, Colorado 80903

ABSTRACT

Two coral patch reefs on the leeward shelf of San Salvador Island have been studied with surveys in 1983-84 and 1992 to monitor their ecologic health and short-term change. Snapshot Reef covers an area of 50 x 50 m and is dominated by *Montastrea annularis*. The reef was mapped in detail to show the position and size of its coral heads and 64 of these heads were studied in detail. To describe the reef, measurements were made of the height of each head, percent live coral coverage, the dominant coral species, total number of coral species present, *M. annularis* morphotypes present, and the relative occurrence of algae, sponges, octocorals, and dead coral surface. Several types of statistical analyses were performed, indicating a direct relationship between height and number of coral species and also between relative abundance of octocorals and number of coral species. An inverse relationship was observed between relative abundance of algae and amount of bare coral surface. There was a strong correlation between height in 1992 and a combination of percent living coral and number of coral species. An average increase in size of the coral heads of 13 cm from 1984 to 1992 was determined, and there were significantly more coral species, less algae, and less sponge on each head in 1992 than 1984. However, there was not a significant change in the percentage of live coral on the heads. The overall picture is one of a reef in at least a steady state condition. There also is a strong correlation between coral head height in 1992 and a combination of the number of coral species and relative abundance of algae. This relationship may provide a useful means of predicting the future "health" of a given coral head.

The nearby Telephone Pole Reef has been studied by comparisons of transects and photographs made in 1983 and 1992, and they reveal that significant recent change has occurred. In 1983, this reef consisted largely of *M. annularis* heads with dense thickets of *Acropora cervicornis* in its outer parts. Today the *M. annularis* heads remain seemingly unchanged, but virtually all of the *A. cervicornis* has died and collapsed to form layers that now are being covered by rapidly growing heads of *Porites porites*. These surveys have established a baseline for monitoring of the health and short-term change on both of these reefs in the future.

INTRODUCTION

Most previous studies of modern coral reefs have focused on barrier, bank-barrier, and fringing reefs. Surprisingly, there have been few studies devoted to coral patch reefs, although patch reefs commonly are a prominent element of modern reef complexes (Brown and Dunne, 1980). Nonetheless, relatively little is known about the ecologic health and short-term change on such reefs. This study was concerned with two *Montastrea annularis*-dominated patch reefs, Snapshot Reef and Telephone Pole Reef, located in Fernandez Bay on the leeward shelf of San Salvador Island, Bahamas (Figure 1). The purpose of the study was to document the state of the two patch reefs with respect to physical setting, community structure, diversity, and short-term change. Initial surveys of the two reefs were conducted in June of 1983 and 1984, and follow-up surveys using similar methods were made in June, 1992. Analysis of the data from the two surveys has permitted recognition of some short-term changes on the reefs and gives an indication of the present health of the reefs. In addition, a baseline of observations now is in place to permit monitoring of future natural and human-induced change on these two patch reefs, both of which are popular sites for visitation by sport scuba divers. With the recent opening of a large Club Med on San Salvador, possibly the biggest news on the island since its "discovery" by Columbus, these reefs likely will be more heavily used for recreation in the future, and they may provide good test sites for monitoring the effects of sport scuba diver visitation.

San Salvador is located about 600 km ESE of Miami on an isolated carbonate platform, well east of the Great Bahama Bank (Figure 1). The island is bordered by a narrow shelf with an abrupt shelf-edge break leading to a very steep slope. The eastern and southeastern coasts of the island typically are windward to the prevailing trade winds. A well-developed *Acropora palmata*-dominated bank-barrier reef lies off the north coast of the island, and smaller bank-barrier reefs occur along the southeast and southern coasts. Hundreds of small patch reefs dot the

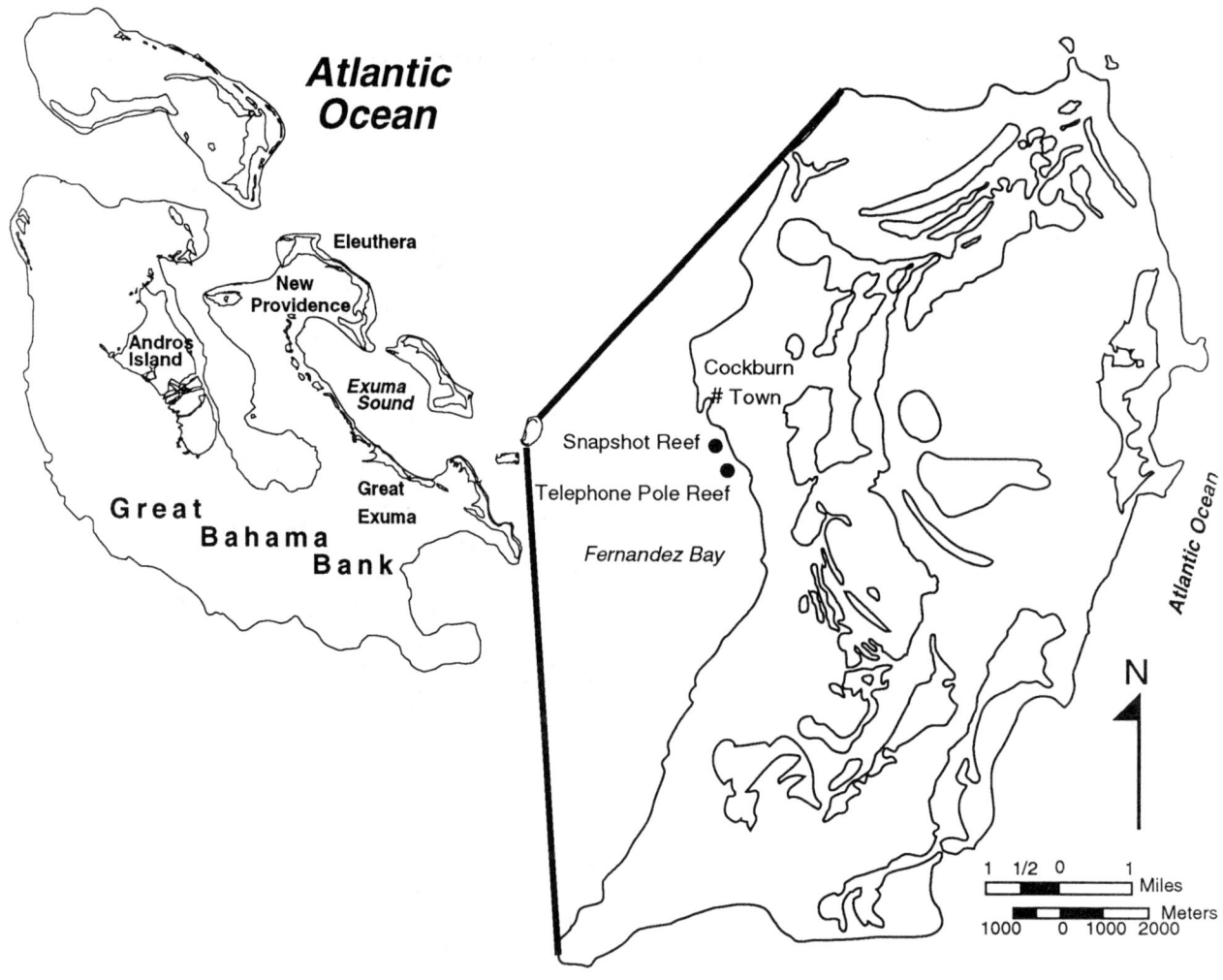

Figure 1. Location of San Salvador Island, Bahamas and Snapshot and Telephone Pole reefs in Fernandez Bay, off the island's leeward coast.

island's eastern shelf, and on the leeward western shelf larger patch reefs occur in the broad embayments of the coast. The Snapshot and Telephone Pole reefs of Fernandez Bay are two of the better developed patch reefs along the island's west coast. Both reefs lie about 200 to 250 m offshore in water depths of 4 to 5 m and are well-bathed by fully oceanic waters. No significant bleaching events have been reported for these reefs. The landward margin of Fernandez Bay is bordered by a road, but the area is only sparsely populated. Both patch reefs can be reached by swimming from the beach or by small boat.

METHODS

The Field Surveys

Snapshot Reef.—Consisting of an aggregation of individual coral heads dominated by *M. annularis*, this patch reef occupies an area of about 50 x 50 m. A detailed, plan view map of the reef (Figure 2) was made by Chambers (1984), with minor revisions made during June, 1992. A set of 64 coral heads were identified, numbered, and studied in some detail in both surveys. A protocol was used during both surveys (modified and expanded in 1992) to provide a means for systematic observations of each head as follows: 1) accurate measurement of coral head height; 2) visual estimate of the percentage of live coral coverage (1=0-20%, 2=21-40%, 3=41-60%, 4=61-80%, 5=81-100%); 3) dominant coral species present; 4) total number of coral species present; 5) relative abundance of non-scleractinian components, i.e. algae, sponges, octocorals, and dead coral surface (1=rare, 2=minor, 3=common, 4=dominant); 6) presence of *M. annularis* morphotypes, as described by Knowlton et al. (1992).

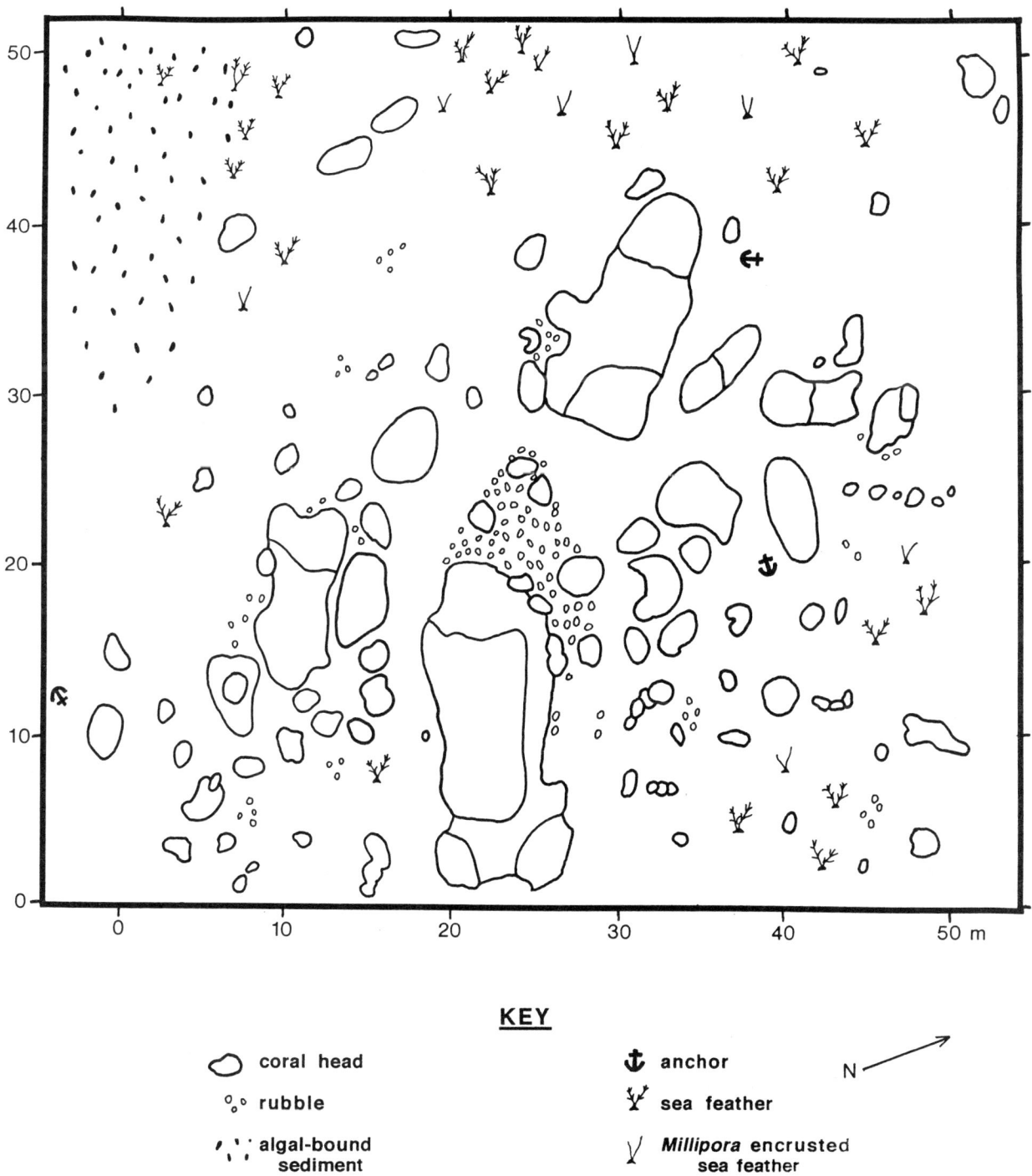

Figure 2. Plan view map of Snapshot Reef. Sixty-four coral heads were identified and described for this study.

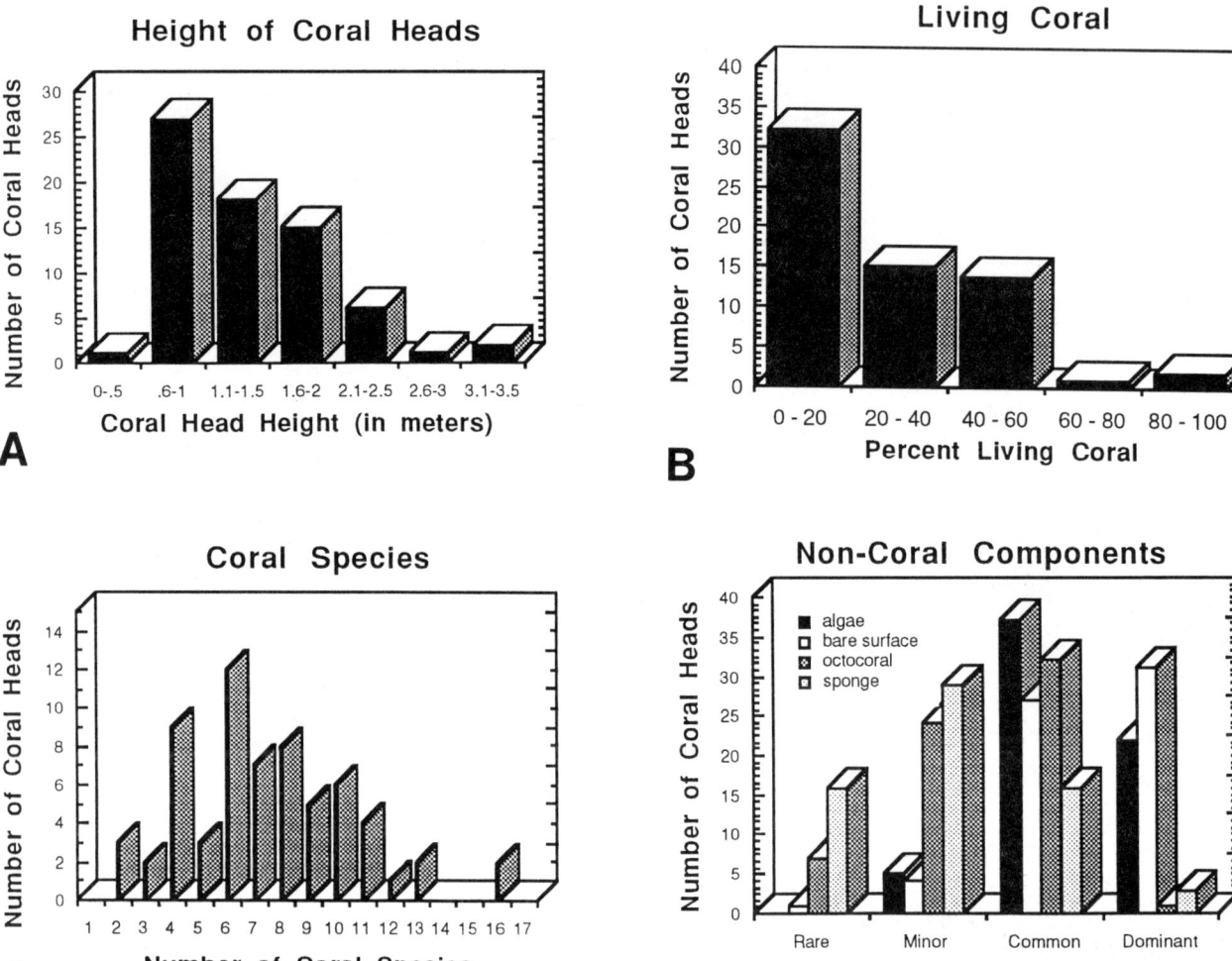

Figure 3. Frequency histograms showing A) height of the coral heads; B) percent living coral; C) number of coral species present; and D) relative abundances of non-coral components.

Telephone Pole Reef.—This is a larger, somewhat irregularly shaped patch reef dominated principally by large *M. annularis* heads separated by areas of smaller corals growing on layers of dead *Acropora cervicornis*. Heads of *Porites porites* now are rapidly spreading over the beds of dead *A. cervicornis*. Because of its larger size, it was not feasible to make a plan map, and this reef has been studied by constructing a series of transects (too lengthy to be reproduced here), beginning with a master transect (Erickson, 1985) that runs from the beach to a distance of 400 m offshore, seaward of the reef proper. Three shorter transect lines paralleling the master transect were constructed in June, 1992, over the main part of the reef to provide more complete coverage of the reef proper. The purpose of these transects was primarily to establish a baseline for the measurement of future change on this reef. A similar protocol as described above was used for collection of data from 32 *M. annularis* heads.

Data Analysis

For Snapshot Reef, frequency histograms (Figure 3) were drawn from the 1992 survey data to illustrate general trends and to form a descriptive definition of the present state of the reef. General descriptive statistics including means, medians, standard deviations, and variances of the variables were calculated. Pearson product-moment correlation coefficients were used to assess relationships between pairs of variables. Multiple regression was used to determine if any of the measured variables were predictors of height or percent living coral on a given coral head. Height and percent living coral were chosen as the dependent variables for the multiple regressions because these variables appear to be our best indicators of the health of the reef. We think that the ability to predict either of these variables may prove to be a useful tool in predicting the health of a given reef. T-tests were used to compare the 1984 survey data with that of 1992 to see if any significant short-term changes on the reef could be

Figure 4. Photographs from Telephone Pole Reef: A) thicket of living *Acropora cervicornis*, 1983, bar scale = 15 cm; B) dead *A. cervicornis*, largely collapsed, 1992, bar scale = 15 cm; C) small head of *Porites porites* growing on *A. cervicornis*, 1983, bar scale = 15 cm; D) large heads of *P. porites*, commonly growing on a layer of dead *A. cervicornis*, 1992, bar scale = 25 cm.

detected. Data histograms similar to those of Figure 3 also have been made for Telephone Pole Reef using 1992 data, but they are not reported here because we have no earlier survey data. Our analysis of Telephone Pole Reef reported here is based on qualitative comparison of transects and photos from 1983 and 1992 surveys.

RESULTS

Present State and Short-term Change of Snapshot Reef

From the histogram data of Figure 3, it can be determined that the mean coral head height for this reef was 1.36 m, mean percent living coral was 37%, mean number of coral species per head was 7, with algae and bare coral surface being the dominant non-coral components and morphotype 1 as the dominant morphotype of *M. annularis*. There was a strong direct relationship between height and number of coral species, r (df=52) = 0.703, and also between relative abundance of octocorals and number of coral species, r (df=52) = 0.488. A fairly strong inverse relationship was observed between relative abundance of algae and amount of bare coral surface, r (df=52) = -0.527. There was a strong relationship between height in 1992 and a combination of the percent living coral and the number of coral species, R = 0.732, R^2 = 0.535. An average growth of the coral heads of 13 cm from 1984 to 1992 was significant, t (df=60) = 4.968, p < .0001. There were significantly more coral species, t(df=56) = 2.679, p < .01, less algae, t(df=58) = -2.585, p < .01, and less sponge, t(df=58) = -5.543, p < .0001, on each head in 1992 than in 1984. However, there was not a significant change in the percentage of live coral on the heads. We also found a strong correlation between height in 1992 and a combination of the number of coral species and the relative abundance of algae in 1984, R = 0.928, R^2 = 0.860.

Short-term Change on Telephone Pole Reef

Comparisons of transects and photographs made on this reef in 1983 and 1992 clearly indicated that in the intervening years all of the *A. cervicornis* originally present and seemingly healthy has died (Figure 4). Today there are only two or three small branches of living *A. cervicornis* on this reef. *P. porites* heads, most appearing healthy and many 1 m in diameter or larger, now are common on this reef, and often are growing on the layer of dead *A. cervicornis*. We now have baseline data on many of the large *M. annularis* heads of this reef but cannot yet make historical comparisons. Visually, these heads appear to be in the general same state of health as those of Snapshot Reef.

DISCUSSION

Data from the frequency histograms reveal a picture of Snapshot Reef in 1992. Most of the 64 coral heads are between 0.5 to 2 m tall and have less than 60% living coral, 4 to 11 coral species are found on each head, *M. annularis* morphotype 1 is dominant and 3 is common, and *Agaricia agaricites*, algae, and bare coral surfaces all are common on the heads. Our measurements indicated that the coral heads are growing (mean 13 cm/8years). If calculated as a growth rate, our rate would be somewhat higher than previously reported growth rates for *M. annularis* (10.7 mm/yr., Hoffmeister & Multer, 1964; 10 mm/yr., Hudson, 1979; 7.8 mm/yr., Knowlton et al., 1992), but we were measuring the heights of coral heads, not the true growth rate of individual coral heads, so we suspect that operator measurement error would account for our larger number. Nonetheless, we do believe that the coral heads truly have grown during the study period. We interpret Snapshot Reef to be in at least a steady state condition given that the mean of percent living coral on the heads has not changed and that species diversity is increasing. A recent study of the crinoids on Snapshot Reef (Meyer et al., 1991) indicates that the populations of the two species of *Nemaster* that reside on the large *M. annularis* heads are holding their own or even slightly increasing, and this might also be taken as a sign of the steady health of the reef as a whole. In addition, 86% of the variability of the present height of the heads in 1992 can be predicted from the number of coral species and relative abundance of algae found on each head in 1984. In other words, if the number of coral species and relative abundance of algae is known for a given coral head, 86% of the variability of the height of that coral head can be predicted. This relationship may be a useful means of predicting the future "health" of a given coral head.

Clearly, Telephone Pole Reef is in a state of significant change. The thickets of *A. cervicornis* that were luxuriant here in the late 1970's-early 1980's (and, in fact, gave the reef its other local name, Cervicornis Reef) have died and largely become layered. The cause of death is unknown; we are not aware of any major storm that may have adversely affected the reef, and no disease or bleaching event has been reported. A successional event is taking place with the advent and rapid growth of *P. porites* heads and some other corals over the areas of dead *A. cervicornis*, and we recently have initiated a study to monitor the growth of *P. porites* in a selected area of this reef.

CONCLUSIONS

Through synthesis of field observations and statistical analyses of survey data gathered in the early 1980's and 1992, the ecologic health and short-term changes on two coral patch reefs was determined. Snapshot Reef, dominated by large *M. annularis* heads, has shown the following trends over an eight-year period: 1) overall growth of the coral heads; 2) increase in species diversity of the heads; and 3) a constant percentage of live coral on the heads. This reef has not shown signs of deterioration over the study period and appears to be in at least a steady state. Telephone Pole Reef has undergone rapid change in the past decade. Thickets of *A. cervicornis*, apparently healthy in the late 1970's-early 1980's, have died, and they now are being overgrown by rapidly growing heads of *P. porites*. The large *M. annularis* heads of this reef appear to be in a similar state to those of Snapshot Reef. A data baseline now is in place for the continued monitoring of these two coral patch reefs as they face an uncertain future of accelerating development on San Salvador Island and increased diver visitation.

ACKNOWLEDGMENTS

We thank the directors and staff of the Bahamian Field Station for full logistical support of our field work on San Salvador Island. The Keck Geology Consortium provided funding for the summer 1992 research from a grant from the W. M. Keck Foundation. Patricia Pierce Erickson is acknowledged for earlier research and an unpublished report on Telephone Pole Reef. David White helped greatly with the underwater field work, and Jennifer Christiansen assisted with preparation of the figures.

LITERATURE CITED

Brown, B.E. and R.P. Dunne, 1980. Environmental controls of patch reef growth and development. Marine Biology 56: 85-96.

Chambers, L., 1984. Snapshot Reef: A study of patch reef coral abundance and distribution, San Salvador Island, Bahamas. Smith College, Department of Geology, Special Studies Report. 77 pp. (unpublished).

Erickson, P.P., 1985. Field guide to Telephone Pole Reef (*Acropora cervicornis* Reef), San Salvador Island, Bahamas. Smith College, Department of Geology. 27 pp. (unpublished).

Hoffmeister, J.E. and H.G. Multer, 1964, Growth-rate estimates of a Pleistocene coral reef of Florida. Geol. Soc. America Bull. 75(4): 353-357.

Hudson, J.H., 1979. Absolute growth rates and environmental implications of Pleistocene *Montastrea annularis* in southeast Florida. Geol Soc. America Abstracts with Programs 7(1): 24 (abstract).

Knowlton, N., E. Weil, L.A. Weigt and H.M. Guzman, 1992. Sibling species in *Montastraea annularis*, coral bleaching, and the coral climate record. Science 255: 330-333.

Meyer, D.L., B.J. Greenstein and G. Llwellyn, 1991. Population stability of crinoids at Snapshot Reef, San Salvador, Bahamas. Pages 181-184 *in* R.J. Bain, ed. Proceedings of the fifth symposium on the geology of the Bahamas, Bahamian Field Station, San Salvador, Bahamas.

TWENTY YEARS OF CHANGE IN CORAL COMMUNITIES OVER DEEP REEF SLOPES ALONG LEEWARD COASTS IN THE NETHERLANDS ANTILLES

R.P.M. Bak[1,2], and G. Nieuwland[1]

[1] Netherlands Institute for Sea Research, (NIOZ), P.O. Box 59, 1790 AB Den Burg, Texel, The Netherlands. [2] University of Amsterdam, Institute for Systematics and Population Biology, P.O. Box 4766, 1009 AT Amsterdam, The Netherlands.

ABSTRACT

Thirty-six m^2 of reef slope communities were analysed at each of four depths, 10, 20 30 and 40 m, for changes in the time intervals between the years 1973, 1983 and 1992. Comparisons over the twenty year period are based on photographic records of large, 3 x 3 m, quadrats along four transects on the leeward coasts of Curaçao and Bonaire. We compared coral cover numbers of coral colonies and species richness at each data point.

There was a significant decrease in coral cover and colony number in both periods in the upper part of the reef (10-20 m). In the deep reef (30-40 m) this decrease was not observed and coral cover was maintained or increased. Species richness decreased at all depths in both ten-year periods.

INTRODUCTION

Curiosity and interest in the linkage between the biology of individual coral species, expressed in their respective ecological strategies, and the development of benthic reef communities, prompted us to start monotoring permanent quadrats on the reef bottom in 1973 (Bak and Luckhurst 1980). Our first analysis of the changes occurring in the quadrats after five years indicated that ecological strategies of coral species, which show an enormous range (e.g. Bak and Engel 1979, Bak 1983, Porter 1987), are clearly reflected by the changes in the coral community (Bak and Luckhurst 1980). A second result was that we found processes and phenomena on the deep reef (30, 40 m) to differ significantly from those in the shallower parts of the reef (10, 20 m).

Because we saw changes in the development of the coral communities and observed that these changes differed significantly in magnitude between depths, we became intrigued by the long-term development of our communities. At that time the only long-term monitoring we were aware of was the Connell study of quadrats in very shallow reef habitats on the Great Barrier Reef (Connell 1976, 1978) and it seemed expedient to continue our surveys. Consequently our quadrats were photographed at least yearly between 1973 and 1992 (except 1984/1985).

In this case study we compare the communities in 1973, 1983 and 1992 in view of the subject of the Colloquim: Health, Hazards and History. We focus on health and history and report on changes in species number, coral cover and numbers of colonies over a twenty-year time interval.

METHODS

We studied four transects on the leeward coasts of the Netherlands Antilles. Transects I and II are at Carmabi Buoy 1, transect III is at Carmabi Buoy 2 (Curaçao), transect IV is at Karpata (Bonaire, for details on all locations see van Duyl 1985). Along each transect four quadrats (3x3 m) are situated at depths of 10, 20, 30 and 40 m. Quadrats are marked at corners with stainless steel bars.

The quadrats were photographed using a Nikonos camera, equipped with a UW Nikkor 15 mm f/2.8, picture angle 94°. Kodak 400 ASA film was used in all surveys. The photograph of the complete quadrat was supplemented by a series of detailed, overlapping photographs of the bottom. Negatives were printed to obtain contrasty 20x26 cm photographs. Photographs were analysed for number and cover of coral species (projected surface area) using a CalComp DrawingBoard II and a digitizer program (EDC, Agricultural University Wageningen).

All coral species were identified to species level except *Madracis decactis* and *M. pharensis*, which were grouped. Because both species are common, species richness presented in the Result section is a minimum value. Two of the *Montastrea annularis* morphs (Knowlton et al. 1992, Van Veghel and Bak 1993) are common in the permanent quadrats (the columnar and the massive morphs). The third morph, 'bumpy' is very rare and it is grouped with the massive morph.

In addition to a description of the changes over time there is the need for summary statistics to understand the main trends in the data set. We used a three-way factorial analysis of variance model with year, depth and transect main effects and first order interactions: (y = constant +depth +transect +year +depth*transect +depth*year +transect*year) as a descriptive summarizing tool for changes in coral cover and numbers of colonies. Coral cover data were approximately normally distributed. Coral colony numbers were approximately normally distributed after one outlier was reduced to the next maximum value.

RESULTS

Species number.- The initial number of coral species in the permanent quadrats varied from 16 to 5 from shallow to deep water. Numbers for each quadrat and changes in species richness are shown in Fig.1. Compared with 1973 the number of species is down in 1983 and in 1992 in all quadrats (but two) and at all depths. Abundant species (density >20 colonies each depth) generally showed a decrease in number of colonies but did not suffer species extinction in the quadrats. All species that had disappeared between 1973 and our 1992 census belonged to species that had been relatively rare (density <10 colonies each depth). There is no obvious difference in patterns between depths (Fig. 1).

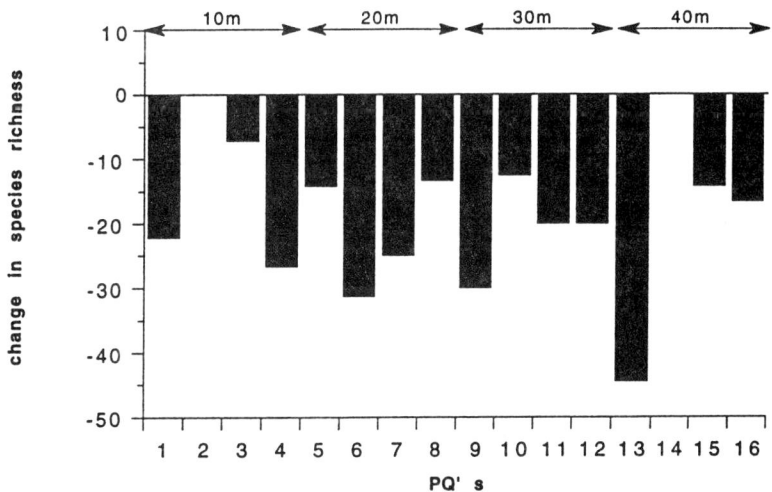

Fig. 1. Percentage change in species richness for each quadrat (1-16) at 10, 20, 30 and 40 m between 1973 and 1992

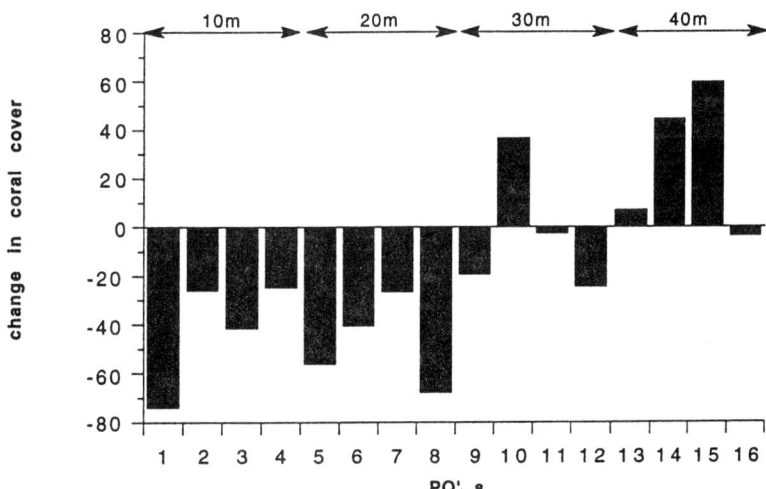

Fig. 2. Change in oral cover, for each quadrat (1-16) at 10, 20, 30 and 40 m between 1973 and 1992, expressed as percentage of 1973 cover.

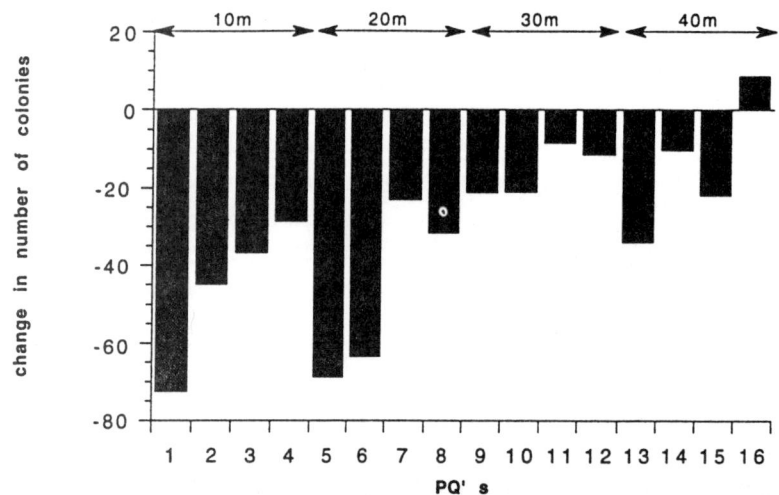

Fig. 3. Change in number of coral colonies for each quadrat (1-16) at 10, 20, 30 and 40 m between 1973 and 1992

Coral cover-. Coral cover varied initially from 27-77% in the 10 m quadrats, from 37-84% in the 20 m quadrats, from 22-66% in the 30 m quadrats and from 14-42% in the 40 m quadrats. There are enormous changes in coral cover over time. Differences in coral cover between the 1973 and 1992 surveys are shown in Fig. 2. There is a clear difference between the shallow and the deep quadrats. At 10 and 20 m cover has decreased in all quadrats but at 30 and 40 m cover was the same or increased. This pattern was the same for the 1973-1983 and the 1983-1992 time interval.

As for differences among the various coral species: all species declined in the shallower part of the reef (10-20 m), except *Colpophyllia natans*, which showed an increase. Some species decreased in proportion to the overall decrease in coral cover (e.g. *Madracis mirabilis*), some decreased more than average (e.g. *Agaricia agarticites*). At the deep reef there was a clear increase of *A. lamarcki*.

Number of colonies. - There was a decrease in number of colonies at all depths but less so in the deep reef (30, 40 m, Fig. 3). Abundant species (density >20 colonies each depth) generally declined in numbers (77%) though abundance was maintained in 18% of the species and increased in 4%.

DISCUSSION

Although the reefs of the Netherlands Antilles are fairly rich in species for a Caribbean reef, species lists giving approximately 55 species, quantitative surveys over the reef slope from 10-40 m give typically 15-19 species for 5 m wide belt transects (Bak 1977). Apparently our permanent quadrats, with a species richness of up to 17 species in 1973, reflected the diversity of the area. The data show that there is a consistant decrease in species in the time interval 1972-1992. Rare species became extinct in the quadrats, abundant species became less abundant (except for deep *Agaricia lamarcki*). Quadrats at all depths lost 3-5 species while only one species shows up as a new recruit in 1992 (*A. lamarcki* at10 m). Similar loss of rare species from coral reef permanent quadrats has been reported for shallow reefs in the Florida Keys (Porter and Meier 1992).

The change in cover over time for each depth is summarized in Fig. 4. Bak and Luckhurst (1980) noticed that over the period 1973-1978 cover of reef bottom components was remarkably constant. After a period of twenty years our conclusion must be different. There is a significant decrease in coral cover at 10 and 20 m depth (ANOVA F p<). Is this simply because our perspective has changed or is there a change in processes and mechanisms? Bak and Luckhurst noticed that change, in terms of spatial rearrangement of bottom components, is much more a phenomenon of the shallow (10, 20 m) than the deep reef (30, 40 m). Fig. 4 demonstrates that change in cover is limited to the shallower part of the reef.

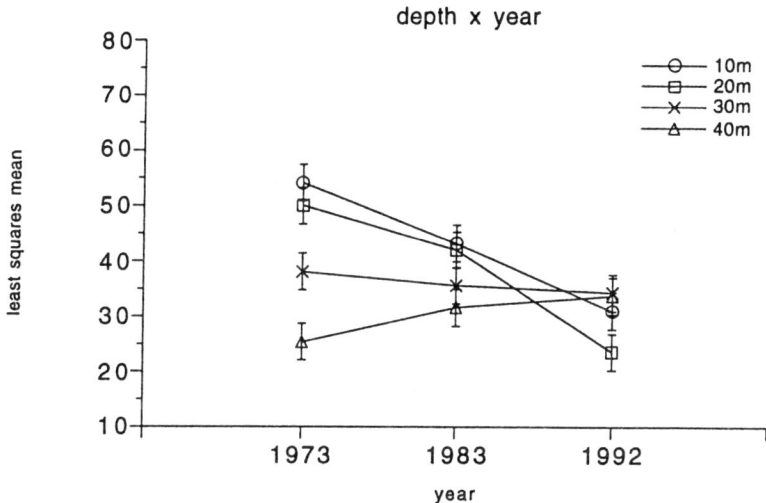

Fig. 4. Model of the change in coral cover at each depth from 1973 to 1992 (R^2= 0.954, p < 0.001)

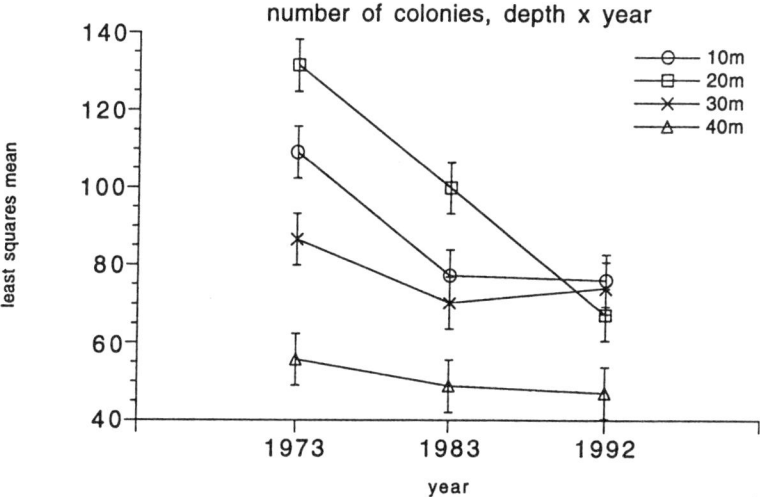

Fig. 5. Model of the change in number of corel colonies at each depth from 1973 to 1992 (R^2= 0.940, p< 0.010

The decrease in number of coral colonies at each depth is summarized in Fig. 5. Again the large differences are restricted to the shallower depths. It appears that mortality is overshadowing growth and settlement especially at 10 and 20 m. Mortality is reflected in loss of coral cover and decreasing numbers of colonies.

There are a series of well-known/hypothetical causes for the degradation of coral reefs. These include coral bleaching, competition, diseases and environmental change. Coral bleaching only occasionally occurs on reefs at depths greater than 10 m, e.g. in Curaçao it has been seen in *Agaricia lamarcki* as deep as 40 m. The species most susceptible to bleaching in the Netherlands Antilles is *Montastrea annularis* (Meesters and Bak 1993) which was only common in quadrats at 10 m. Here cover in *M. annularis* changed from 10% to 12% to 7% (1973 to 1983 to 1992) and we conclude that coral bleaching was no major cause of mortality in our permanent quadrats.

Mass mortalties of *Diadema antillarum* on reefs (Lessios et al. 1983, Bak et al. 1984) resulted in increase of thallose algae (Carpenter 1985, de Ruyter van Steveninck and Bak 1986) and this ultimately can result in the demise of coral communities (Hughes et al. 1987). Algae such as *Lobophora variegata* and *Dictyota spp.* may have increased on our reefs and algal cover will be analysed in the photographs.

Another common competitor for space on our reefs is the compound ascidian *Trididemnum solidum* (Bak et al. 1981, van Duyl et al. 1981). We hypothesize that a possible increase in the abundance of the ascidian is related to eutrophication and are in the process of investigating changes in abundance of this organism along the leeward Curaçao coast since 1981.

Hurricanes are rare in this area of the Caribbean, but hurricane Joan swept the islands in 1988. The impact of this storm can be analysed in our photigraphs records from 1986 and 1989. However, for our purpose here it is sufficient to note that we observe the same pattern in the 1973/1983 and the 1983/1992 intervals. The hurricane has not been decisive in setting the pattern of decreasing coral cover and colony density.

Factors such as diseases are unlikely to be important. White-band disease is practically limited to the *Acropora* speceis and these are only common at shallower depths than 10 m along these coasts (Bak and Criens 1981, van Duyl 1985). Black-band disease is rare on our reefs. The most likely factor in the degradation of the shallow part of the reef is 'coastal development', including eutrophication (role unknown but under study) and artificial beach construction.

Theoretically the possibility remains that the changes we observed in the upper part of the reef are not anthropogenic in origin but are part of natural, cyclic phenomena. On a geological scale reefs wax and wane. Comparative studies of our quadrats and similar quadrats at the untouched reefs at the upcurrent, eastern tip of the islands will help to address this point. It is clear, however, that even though on a geological scale we may see part of a cycle, in terms of coral community dynamics the development appears completely unbalanced.

CONCLUSIONS

Coral cover and number of coral colonies significantly decreased in quadrats studied in the upper part (depths 10 and 20 m) of the reefs of Curaçao and Bonaire.
At the deep reef (30, 40 m) there is no decrease in coral cover.
Species richness decreased over all quadrats at all depths.
The same trend was observed during the time intervals 1973-1983 and 1983-1992.

ACKNOWLEDGEMENTS

We thank the Carmabi staff and dive buddies (on Curaçao), Kalli de Meyer, Roberto Hensen (Stinapa Bonaire), Franklin Winklaar and Eric Newton (on Bonaire) for their support, each at his own depth. For help with data processing and statistical analysis we are indebted to Rob Dapper and Jaap van der Meer (NIOZ).

LITERATURE CITED

Bak, R.P.M. 1977. Coral reefs and their zonation in the Netherlands Antilles. AAPG Studies in Geology 4: 3-16.
Bak, R.P.M. 1983. Aspects of community organization in Caribbean stony corals (Scleractinia). UNESCO Rep. Mar. Sci 23: 51-68
Bak, R.P.M. and S. Engel. 1979. Distribution, abundance and survival of juvenile hermatypic corals (Scleractinia) and the importance of life history strategies in the parent coral community. Mar. Biol. 54: 341-351.
Bak, R.P.M. and B. Luckhurst. 1980. Constancy and change in coral reef habitats along depth gradients at Curaçao. Oecologia (Berl.) 47: 145-155.
Bak, R.P.M., F.C. van Duyl and J. Sybesma. 1981. The ecology of the tropical compound ascidian *Trididemnum solidum*. II. Abundance, growth and survival. Mar. Ecol. Prog. Ser. 6: 43-52.
Bak, R.P.M., M.J.E. Carpay and E. D. de Ruyter van Steveninck, 1984. Densities of the sea urchin *Diadema antillarum* before and after mass mortalities on the coral reef of Curaçao. Mar. Ecol. Prog. Ser. 17: 105-108.
Carpenter, R.C. 1985. Sea urchin mass mortalities: effects on reef algal abundance, species composition, and metabolism and other coral reef herbivores. Proc. Fifth Coal Reef Congr. Tahati 4: 53-60
Connell. J.H. 1976. Competitive interaction and the species diversity of corals. Pages 51-58 *in* G.O. Mackie. ed. Coelenterate ecology and behaviour. Plenum Press. New York.
Connell, J.H. 1978. Diversity in tropical rain forests and coral reefs. Sci. 199: 1302-1310.
Duyl, F.C. van. 1985. Atlas of the living reefs of Curaçao and Bonaire, Netherlands Antilles. Publ. Foundation Scient. Res. Caribbean Region 117: 1-13
Duyl, F.C. van., R.P.M. Bak and J. Sybesma. 1981. The ecology of the tropical compound ascidian *Trididemnum solidum*. I. Reproductive strategy and larval behaviour. Mar. Ecol. Prog. Ser. 6: 35-42
Hughes, T.P., D.C. Reed and M.J. Boyle. 1987. Herbivory on coral reefs: community structure following mass mortalities of sea urchins. J. Exp. Mar. Biol. Ecol. 113:39-59
Knowlton, N., E. Weil, L.A. Weight and H.M. Guzman. 1992. Sibling species in *Montastrea annularis*, coral bleaching and the coral climate record. Sci. 255: 330-333
Lessios, H.A., P.W. Glynn and D.R. Robertson. 1983. Mass mortalities of coral reef organisms. Sci. 222: 715

Meesters, E. and R.P.M. Bak. in press. Effects of coral bleaching on tissue regeneration potential and colony survival. Mar. Ecol. Prog. Ser.

Ruyter van Steveninck, E. D. de and R.P.M. Bak. 1986. Changes in abundance of coral-reef bottom ccomponents related to mass mortality of the sea urchin *Diadema antillarum*. Mar. Ecol. Prog. Ser. 34: 87-94

Porter, J.W. 1987. Species profiles: life histories and environmental requirements of coastal fishes and invertebrates (South Florida). Reef building corals. U.S. Dept Interior. Biol.Rep. 82

Porter, J.W. and Q.W. Meier. 1992. Quantifiation of loss and change in Floridan reef coral populations. Amer. Zool. 32: 625-640

Van Veghel, M.L.J. and R.P.M. Bak. 1993. Intraspecific variation in a dominant Caribbean reef building coral, *Montastrea annularis* : genetic, behavioral and morphometric aspects. Mar.Ecol. Prog.Ser. 92: 255-265

FIFTY YEARS OF IMPACTS ON CORAL REEFS IN BERMUDA

C. B. Cook[1], R. E. Dodge[2], and S. R. Smith[3]

[1]Harbor Branch Oceanographic Institution, 5600 US 1 N., Ft. Pierce, FL 34946
[2]Nova University Oceanographic Center, 8000 N. Ocean Drive, Dania, FL 33004
[3]Bermuda Biological Station for Research, Inc., 17 Biological Station Lane, Ferry Reach GEO1, Bermuda

ABSTRACT

The high latitude coral reefs of Bermuda have been impacted by two major kinds of events since the early 1940's. The first was the dredging operation in Castle Harbour which led to the construction of Kindley airfield (now the Bermuda Air Terminal.) The associated sedimentation, turbidity and altered hydrology caused a mass mortality of corals, especially of the major reef-building genus *Diploria*. While there has been post-dredging recruitment of corals, *D. strigosa*, a species sensitive to sedimentation, has been particularly slow to recover and is less prevalent at this site than elsewhere in Bermuda. Ship groundings comprise the second class of event: since 1940, thirteen major ship groundings have occurred on the reefs which have destroyed an estimated 1% of the outer reefs. Studies of the recovery and recruitment of corals at a major grounding site indicate that these processes occur very slowly in Bermuda. It is estimated that 100 - 150 years would be required to restore coral coverage and species diversity, with species of *Diploria* being particularly slow to recover. Recent episodes of coral bleaching in Bermuda are considered to have had very little effect on coral populations and reefs.

INTRODUCTION

Located between latitudes 32° 15' and 32° 30' N, Bermuda has the highest latitude coral reefs in the Western hemisphere. The surface waters of the Sargasso Sea around Bermuda are warmed by Gulf Stream circulation, so that Bermuda is the northern limit of distribution for numerous species of Caribbean corals. During the winter, surface waters of the Sargasso Sea around the islands typically fall to 18-19°C and occasional cold fronts may drop inshore reef water temperatures as low as 14° (Morris et al., 1977). Hence, Bermuda's reef corals, which are Caribbean in origin, grow at slow rates relative to conspecifics elsewhere (Logan and Tomascik, 1991), and may be more sensitive to elevated temperatures (Coles et al., 1976; Cook et al., 1990). Since recruitment of corals is probably *only* through local reproduction (e.g., Smith, 1992), it would appear that Bermuda's corals, being at the limits of their range and likely temperature tolerances, would be slow to recover from mass mortality events.

As we shall discuss, the major events that have impacted Bermuda's corals and coral reefs over the past fifty years have been associated with human activities. Hurricanes have had relatively little effect: unlike Caribbean reefs that are dominated by relatively fragile, branching species of *Acropora* (unknown in Bermuda), Bermuda's reefs are dominated by massive boulder corals (Dodge et al., 1982; Logan, 1988) that are more resistant to storm wave energy. Rather, socio-political considerations underlie the potential for reef disturbance. The island's land mass of 20 square miles is home to a resident human population of 58,000, and attracts over half a million tourists annually. Situated at a crossroads in the North Atlantic, Bermuda's strategic position in the North Atlantic (Figure 1) has made it a focus of military operations. A major development was the construction of Kindley Airfield during World War II (now the site of the Bermuda Air Terminal). Dredging for the airfield and associated sedimentation and turbidity had immediate effects on the reefs of Castle Harbor, while the long-term impacts of this operation include the continued sedimentation effects and the use of Castle Harbor as a metal waste dumping site. Bermuda's location also makes the island's reefs vulnerable to ship groundings, with the potential for physical damage and pollution from spillage. At least one hundred vessels are known to have struck Bermuda's reefs since the time of colonization (1609).

In this paper we review the impacts of the Castle Harbor dredging operation, of the various ship groundings that have occurred since 1940, and the possible effects of recent elevated temperatures on coral bleaching in Bermuda. The effects of the Castle Harbor dredging are based largely on the study by Dodge and Vaisnys (1977) comparing corals in Castle Harbor with those from other Bermuda reefs. Coral losses associated with post-1940 ship groundings are compared with estimates of coral recolonization and growth on a recent ship grounding site (Smith, 1992). The effects of coral bleaching are based on the work of Cook et al. (1990), and subsequent surveys by Cook and Smith.

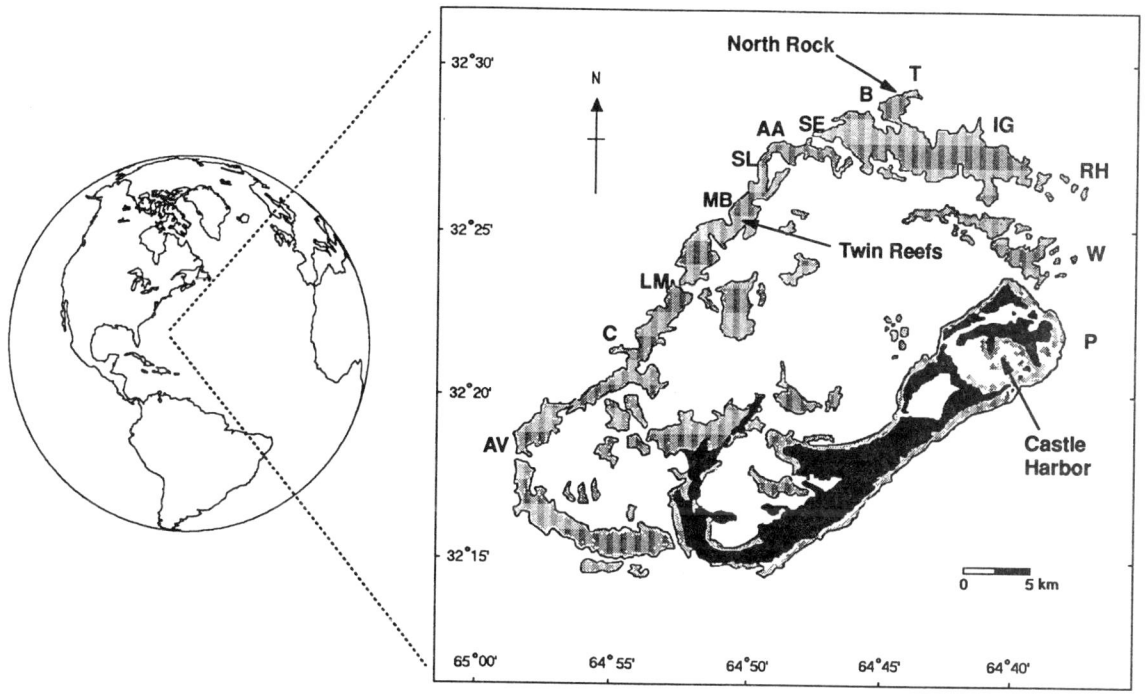

Figure 1. The location of Bermuda. The detailed map indicates the location of study sites (North Rock, Twin Reefs) and major ship groundings discussed in the text and Table 1. Black areas are land mass, while the stippled areas indicate reefal shoals (5m depth contour). (Modified from Logan, 1988)

MATERIALS AND METHODS

Castle Harbor Studies

Castle Harbor is a semi-enclosed basin, averaging 9 m in depth, and contains many reefs of 1-3m depth. These reefs range from shoal-like near shore and pinnacle or knoll-like in more open water (Figure 1). Kindley Airfield, a major geomorphologic feature surrounding the northern portion, was constructed by dredging Castle Harbor from 1941-1943 when 16-20 million cubic yards of fill were pumped to form the hard-packed airfield foundation. To assess the effects of sedimentation and turbidity on the corals of the Harbor, analyses were made between 1974 and 1976 of abundance, species distribution, growth patterns and age distribution of both living and dead coral assemblages from Castle Harbor reefs and from other undisturbed reefs external to the Harbor. Observations were made on living specimens of *Diploria* spp., and live specimens were collected from Castle Harbor as well as at a variety of stations representing reef types of the Bermuda platform.

Skeletal analysis. Dead coral specimens were collected from the harbor and sectioned with a diamond bit saw to obtain thin medial slabs. Slabs were X-radiographed and negatives printed to reveal annual density bands. Dates of density band formation were assigned by counting back from the known age of the living growth surface. Extension of each band was measured by calipers. Growth patterns were evaluated by plotting and comparing the yearly extension of colonies versus time, and colony age was estimated using the number of available growth bands and colony shape. Bioerosion and a pronounced lowering of extension rate at the death surface were factors in creating uncertainty about the uppermost bands, which represented the several years prior to death.

Ship Groundings

Occurrences of ship groundings. The major ship groundings on Bermuda's reefs over the past 53 years are listed in Table 1. Their location is given in Figure 1.

Estimation of reef damage from ship groundings. The size of the impact zone for each ship grounding was estimated by doubling the hull area (length * width). This is a conservative estimate because vessels that remain aground can be moved by storm waves causing additional reef damage, and larger vessels impacting at high speed are likely to have a larger impact area. Also, rubble and sediments created by the initial impact can be later mobilized by storm waves, and prop wash effects generated when the ship attempts to free itself can create significant additional impact, although this impact is difficult to estimate on an areal basis.

Estimation of recovery rates of ship grounding sites. Rates of recovery of reefs following ship groundings were estimated from the patterns of re-colonization and growth of juvenile corals following the grounding of the Mari Boeing in 1978 (Smith 1985, 1990, 1992). Coral surveys were conducted at two locations (ED and WD) at this site in 1986, 1989 and 1992. Twenty 0.25 m^2 quadrats were randomly deployed at each location in 1986 and 1989, and 10 0.25 m^2 quadrats were used in 1992. The maximum diameter or two most significant axes of each coral colony in a quadrat were measured with calipers and the two dimensional area of the colony was calculated.

Coral Bleaching

Transect surveys. Transect sites were set up at two northern rim reefs, North Rock and Twin Reefs (Figure 1). Colonies of scleractinian corals and *Millepora alcicornis* were surveyed using the point method (Dodge et al., 1982) along 20m transects. Five transects were made at each survey, with corals being scored along 10 cm points for bleaching condition ("normal", "pale", "blotched", "white", with the latter being live colonies with no evident coloration). For the purposes of this paper, all bleaching categories were combined. Random swim surveys were also taken at North Rock at other times to assess bleaching of *M. alcicornis*. Temperature records were made both on-site and from air / seawater records of the Oceanographic Command of the US Naval Air Station (NAS Bermuda).

RESULTS

Impacts on Castle Harbor Reefs

Species composition and abundance. Qualitative observations coupled with collection information revealed that in 1974 *Diploria strigosa* and *D. labyrinthiformis* were similar in abundance on reefs outside the Harbor, or that *D. strigosa* was predominant (q.v. Dodge et al., 1982). However, *D. labyrinthiformis* predominated in the Harbor, with virtually no *D. strigosa* older than fifteen years. Among the dead Castle Harbor corals, the two species were evenly split.. Living coral cover within the harbor was much less than outside, while the proportion of easily recognizable dead corals was much greater within the Harbor.

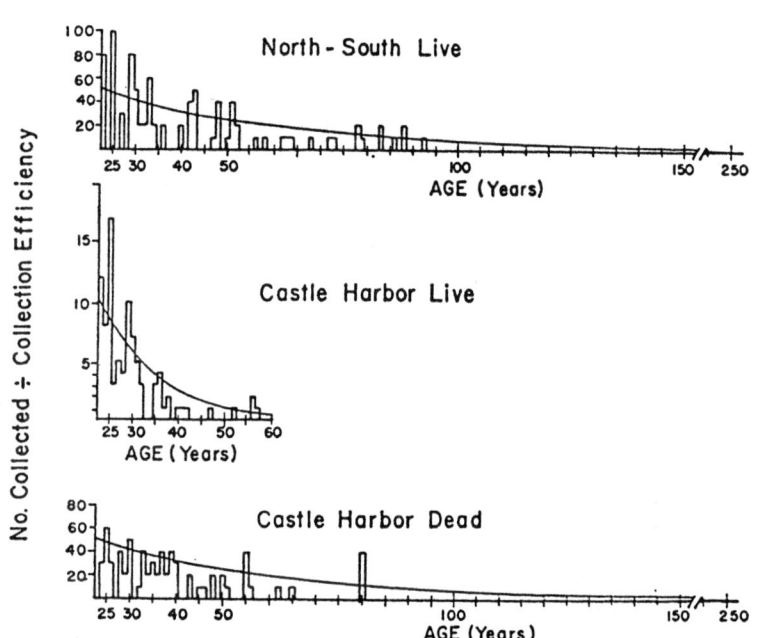

Figure 2. Age distributions of collected corals; "North and South live" refers to Bermuda corals collected from reefs outside of Castle Harbor. (From Dodge and Vaisnys, 1977)

Age distribution: The age structure of collected dead corals from Castle Harbor was similar to that of live corals outside the harbor (Figure 2, corrected for collection efficiency; Dodge and Vaisnys, 1977) while the living corals in the Harbor had a strikingly lower longevity and a higher rate of intrinsic increase than did the live corals from outside the harbor (Figure 2). Particularly evident is the absence of larger living corals from the harbor.

Growth Pattern Analysis: Specimens of contemporary Bermuda *Diploria* spp. had similar patterns of extension growth from year to year. For many of the dead corals of Castle Harbor the growth patterns also had common features. Particularly obvious was a decline in extension rate prior to death, suggesting a stress period preceding mortality.

Recovery from Ship Groundings

Extent of ship groundings in Bermuda since 1940. Table 1 summarizes the estimated impact zone for the major ship groundings since 1940. By our conservative estimates, 73 hectares of reef, or 1% of the total outer reef area, have been damaged by these vessels and attendant salvage operations. Most of these vessels were stranded on shallow reefs (< 10m) but two oil tankers, *Tifoso* and *Aquila Azteca*, grounded on the deeper outer terrace at 18-20 m. Site visits to recent groundings (*Mari Boeing*, *Tifoso* and

Sealuck; Smith 1985 and unpubl.) confirmed that coral was devastated in the areas under the hulls of the ships, leaving virtually no viable fragments, and that extensive peripheral areas adjacent to the grounded vessels were also severely disturbed.

After 14 years, only 3-4% of the reef surface is covered by live coral at the *Mari Boeing* site (Figure 3). This is in contrast to the more typical values of 20-40% seen on undisturbed reefs such as North Rock (Dodge et al., 1982). The current rate of coral re-colonization and growth is about 25 $cm^2\ m^{-2}\ yr^{-1}$, and is very similar to estimates of re-growth at the site from 1980-84 (Smith, 1985). Given coral coverage on undisturbed Bermuda reefs of 20-40% (Dodge et al., 1982), it would take 80-160 years before coral coverage would be similar to that prior to the accident.

Table 1. Major ship groundings on Bermuda's reefs 1940-1993. Specific information about some groundings, such as movement of a ship on a reef or later sinking at a site different from the site of grounding was used to increase estimates of impact, usually by a factor of 2. 4-6 additional groundings occurred during W.W.II but were never reported for security reasons (T. Tucker, pers. comm.). Groundings by smaller yachts were not tabulated.

Vessel	Date	Site[1]	Length of ship (m)	Estimated area of impact (m^2)
Pelinaion	16 Jan 1940	St. David's Head (P)	117	3500
Constellation	July 43	Western Blue Cut (C)	60	1200
Whychwood	9 Nov 1955	Mill's Breaker (W)	95	9000
Ivan Gorthon	25 Nov 1958	NE Breaker (IG)	~75	500
Safina Ejamoorijat	25 Mar 1961	Leghorn Rock (SE)	135	100,000
Baltika	31 August 1973	W. of North Rock (B)	~136	7000
Rio Haina	30 Dec 1976	Kitchen Shoals (RH)	~60	2500
La Maria	29 Sep 1977	E. Blue Cut (LM)	153	9000
Mari Boeing	27 Dec 1978	Hog Breaker (MB)	160	400,000
Arcadian Victory	24 Feb 1980	Chubb Heads (AV)	63	1200
Tifoso	20 Jan 1983	E. of North Rock (T)	225	100,000
Sealuck	15 Sep 1984	W. of North Rock (SL)	~181	4000
Aquila Azteca	10 Jan 1984	W. of North Rock (AA)	302	90,000

Estimated area of damaged reef (total) 73 hectares
Total of outer reef: ~101,000 hectares
Estimated amount of reef area lost (%): ~1%

[1] Number in parentheses refers to location on Figure 1.

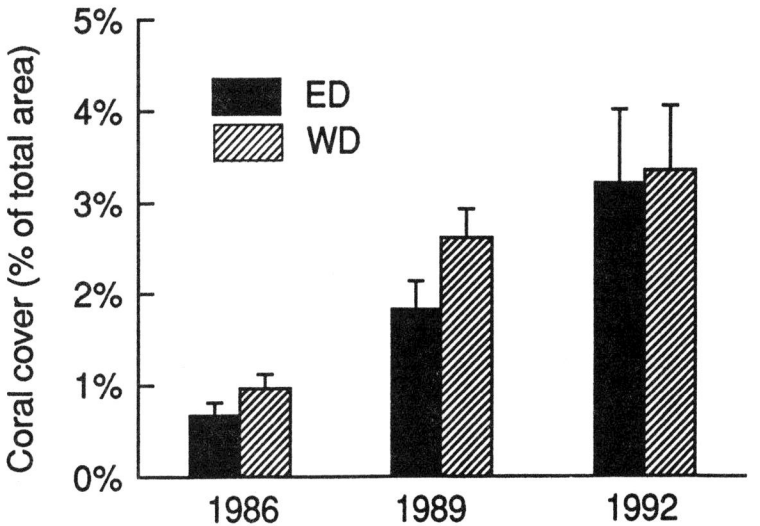

Figure 3. Mean percentage coral cover (± SEM) at two study locations on the *Mari Boeing* site in 1986, 1989 and 1992, showing recruitment and growth since the 1977 grounding incident.

The dominant recruiting coral is *Porites astreoides* and the largest colony observed to date is about 100 cm^2 in size. Other common coral recruits were *Favia fragum* and *Siderastrea radians*. The dominant corals on Bermuda's reefs, *Diploria strigosa* and *D. labyrinthiformis*, have recruited very slowly to the grounding site and the largest observed colonies of these species are only about 20 cm^2 in size (Smith 1990, 1992; unpubl. data.)

Coral Bleaching

Bermuda has had two summers with record warm temperatures since 1986, according to NAS Bermuda records. 1988 had the longest period of prolonged warmth, both in air temperatures (NAS Bermuda) and sea surface temperatures (Cook et al., 1990). 1991 was the second warmest summer in NAS records. Reef water temperatures exceeded 29°C during much of these periods. During both of these periods (August through September 1988, July - August in 1991) bleached corals were evident on Bermuda's reefs, with *Millepora alcicornis* being the species most affected (Figure 4). Although the transect data of Figure 4 were taken from different sites in 1988 and 1991, random swim surveys during this period at the North Rock showed less but still significant bleaching (24 July 91: 22.6% of 53 colonies bleached, T = 27.8°; 6 August 91, 47.3% of 87 colonies bleached, T = 29.4°; 21 October 1991, 13.6% of 83 colonies bleached, T = 26.7°).

Neither the 1988 nor 1991 events produced known coral mortality at our sites, and recovery was evident within 3-4 months (Figure 4). The prevalent white patches of *M. alcicornis* during these periods were evident even to casual observers, but not during cooler summers or during any fall through winter periods, when surveys revealed little if any bleaching.

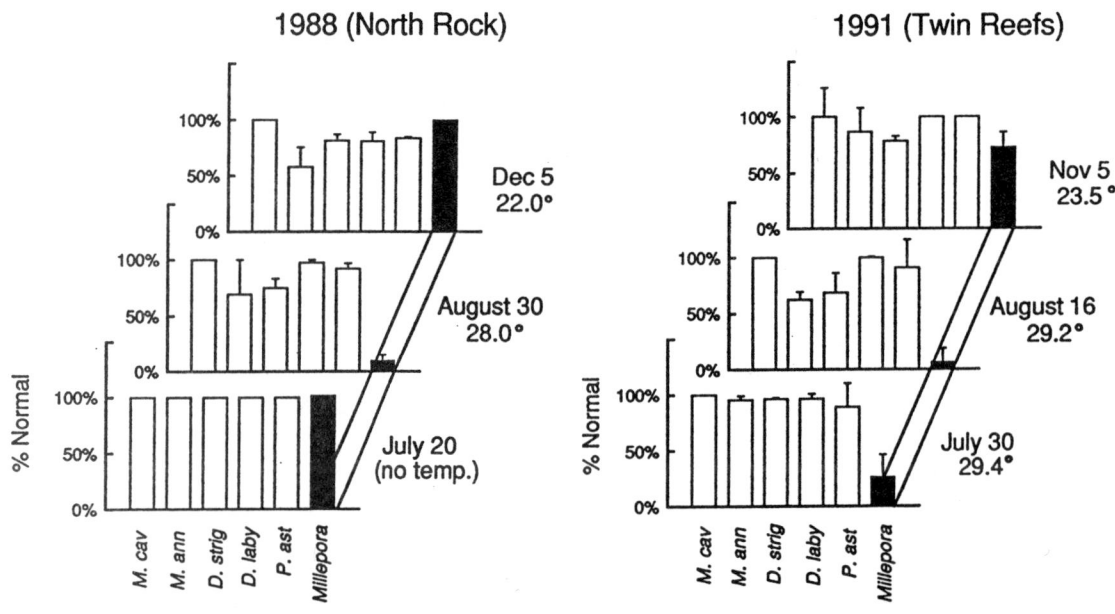

Figure 4. Coral bleaching by species at North Rock and Twin Reefs sites, 1988 and 1991. 1988 data from Cook et al. 1990. Solid bars represent data for *Millepora alcicornis*; scleractinian species are indicated by open bars. Temperatures at 7-9m depth are indicated. Vertical bars are ± SEM.

DISCUSSION

Impact of Dredging on Castle Harbor Reefs

The striking differences in the age structures of living corals inside and outside Castle Harbor, and between living and dead corals in the harbor, still exist today (cf. Logan, 1988, p. 54). The greater longevity of corals from reefs other than Castle Harbor and the higher r (intrinsic rate of increase) of the Castle Harbor population (Dodge and Vaisnys, 1977) suggested a recovering coral population in the harbor. The low maximum age of corals in the harbor suggested a past event had occurred which had eliminated most of the harbor's older corals; the reduced coral coverage and abundance in the harbor supported this conclusion. In addition, there has been a change in the species composition of Castle Harbor corals. Prior to the dredging activities, *D. strigosa* and *D labyrinthiformis* were equally abundant; in the 1974 surveys, *Diploria labyrinthiformis* was the predominant species. On other reefs in Bermuda, the two species are of equal abundance, or *D. strigosa* predominates (Dryer and Logan, 1978; Dodge et al. 1982;

data of Cook et al., 1990). *D. labyrinthiformis* is better adapted for sediment rejection than *D. strigosa* (Hubbard and Pocock, 1972).

Thus, dredging for airfield construction in 1941-43 is concluded to have caused a major disturbance in Castle Harbor. The actual dredging activities increased sedimentation and turbidity, both of which can have detrimental effects on corals (Rogers, 1990). These effects together with subsequent changes in circulation were instrumental in causing a catastrophic mass mortality of corals. Analysis of growth patterns supports this conclusion. Dead corals showed a similar pattern of growth but with a marked decline prior to death. This is consistent with a population which suffered mass mortality

Today there is a relatively sparse population of various hermatypic corals on the Castle Harbor reefs, . Species composition and abundance indicate that the reef ecology has not returned to pre-dredging conditions, even after 50 years from the initial disturbance. Yet these corals still cope with sedimentation problems. The airport site is now the location of the metal dump for the island, although it is not clear that Castle Harbor corals are impacted by metal pollution (Jickells and Knap 1984). The effects of a proposed toxic ash disposal plan for the harbor and its reefs have yet to be determined.

Ship Groundings

Damage and recovery of reefs after ship groundings A significant area of Bermuda's outer reefs has been severely damaged by ship groundings in the past 53 years. The physical effect of these groundings has been the complete elimination of all living coral over varying spatial scales, from a few hundred m^2 to hectares. The re-growth of coral at the Mari Boeing grounding site indicates that coral recovery rates are very low on Bermuda's outer reefs, on the order of at least a century for the re-establishment of typical coral coverage. Thus the relatively high frequency of groundings on Bermuda's reef over the past 50 years has produced a cumulative effect on coral populations due to this very slow recovery rate.

The semi-quantitative estimate for recovery does not take into account the species composition and size frequency distribution of corals that constitute normal reef assemblages. This consideration is important because of the great contribution large colonies make to the reproductive output of the entire population (Hughes et al., 1992) The two dominant reef-building corals in Bermuda (*D. strigosa* and *D. labyrinthiformis*) appear to be very poor recruiters, presumably because of their broadcast mode of spawning (Smith 1992). These two species also have slow growth rates in Bermuda, with <0.5 cm radial growth per year (Dodge, 1978). Thus, it may take much longer for these corals to repopulate damaged reefs and reach sufficient size to initiate sexual reproduction. It is noteworthy that *D. strigosa* has been also slow to recover in Castle Harbor, emphasizing the sensitivity of this major reef-building species to mass mortality events in Bermuda.

Associated effects of ship grounding. The loss of reef structure and topography that accompanies a ship grounding appears to have a significant effect on reef fish activity. Smith (1988, 1990) monitored the grazing activity of fishes at the Mari Boeing site and found that grazing rates were reduced. He attributed these observations to the lack of refuge from predators and the size of the area that had been disturbed. The implication is that the reefs damaged by ship groundings have reduced secondary productivity and this situation would remain in effect for decades until sufficient coral re-growth would take place to provide fishes with sufficient shelter from predation.

Fortunately there has been little impact of oil spills from any of these grounding incidents. A summary of the oiling incident associated with the grounding of *Tifoso* and the Bermuda government's contingency plan are reviewed by Knap et al. (1985).

Coral Bleaching

In comparison to other areas that have been affected by coral bleaching. the few events associated with warm temperatures in Bermuda have been relatively minor, with no long-lasting effects; there are no confirmed instances of coral mortality. *Millepora alcicornis* appears to be the most sensitive species in Bermuda, and we now believe that is species is an indicator for warm-temperature bleaching events in Bermuda. Other species of *Millepora* are also sensitive to elevated temperatures (*e.g.* Glynn and de Weert, 1991), so that members of the genus may be appropriate indicator species on other reefs.

ACKNOWLEDGMENTS

We wish to thank Eric Annis, Andrea Jones and Deborah Hayward for assistance, and Lt. Cmdr. Jim Bancroft of the Oceanographic Command, NAS Bermuda for providing temperature data. Some of this work was supported by grants from ONR (#N00014-91-J-1408 to CBC) NSF (OCE-7517618, to RED for the dredging study) and the Highland Fidelity Graduate Fellowship and the Bermuda government (to SRS). This is Contribution # 954 of the Harbor Branch Oceanographic Institution, and # 1344 of the Bermuda Biological Station for Research, Inc.,

CONCLUSION

Both the dredging of Castle Harbor in the early 1940's and ship groundings over the past 53 years have deleteriously affected Bermuda's reefs. Sedimentation, turbidity and altered hydrology resulting from the dredging operation produced mass mortality of corals, and the major reef-building species in Bermuda (*Diploria strigosa*) has been very slow to recover. On ship grounding sites coral recovery is slow because of poor recruitment and slow growth by *Diploria* spp.. Reef fish populations are reduced on grounding sites and may remain depressed until sufficient coral growth has occurred. Coral bleaching has had little impact on Bermuda reefs.

LITERATURE CITED

Coles, S. L., P. L. Jokiel and C. R. Lewis. 1976. Thermal tolerance in tropical versus subtropical reef corals. Pacif. Sci. 30:159-166.

Cook, C. B., A. Logan, J. Ward, B. Luckhurst and C. J. Berg. 1990. Elevated temperatures and bleaching on a high latitude reef: the 1988 Bermuda event. Coral Reefs 9:45-49.

Dodge, R. E., and J. R. Vaisnys. 1977. Coral populations and growth patterns: responses to sedimentation and turbidity associated with dredging. J. Mar. Res. 35:715-730.

Dodge, R. E. 1978. The Natural Growth Records of Reef-building Corals. Ph. D. Dissertation, Yale University.

Dodge, R. E., A. Logan , and A. Antonius. 1982. Quantitative reef assessment studies in Bermuda: a comparison of methods and preliminary results. Bull. Mar. Sci. 32:745-760.

Dryer, S. and A. Logan. 1978. Holocene reefs and sediments of Castle Harbor, Bermuda. J. Mar. Res. 36:399-425.

Glynn, P. W. and W. H. de Weert. 1991. Elimination of two reef-building hydrocorals following the 1982-83 el Niño event. Science 253:69-71.

Hubbard, J. H. and Y. Pocock. 1972. Sediment rejection by recent scleractinian corals: a key to paleo-environmental reconstruction. Geol. Rundsch. 61:598-626.

Hughes, T. P., D. Ayre, and J.H. Connell. 1992. The evolutionary ecology of corals. Trends in Ecol. Evol. 7:292-295

Jickells, T. D. and A. H. Knap 1984. The distribution and geochemistry of some trace metals in the Bermuda coastal environment. Est. Coastal Shelf Sci. 18:245-262.

Knap, A. H., T. D. Sleeter and I. W. Hughes 1985. Case history: the grounding of the *M/T Tifoso*, 1983 -- a test of Bermuda's contingency plan. Proceedings of the 1985 Oil Spill Conference, EPA/API/USCG, pp. 289-291.

Logan, A. 1988. Holocene Reefs of Bermuda. Sedimenta IX , Univ. of Miami, pp. 1-63.

Logan, A., and T. Tomascik. 1991. Extension growth rates in two coral species from high-latitude reefs of Bermuda. Coral Reefs 10:155-160.

Morris, B., J. Barnes, F. Brown and J, Markham 1977. The Bermuda Marine Environment, Vol.1. Bermuda Biological Station Special Publication No. 15, pp. 1-120.

Rogers. C. S. 1990. Responses of coral reefs and reef organisms to sedimentation. Mar,. Ecol. Progr. Ser. 62:185-202.

Smith, S. R. 1985. Reef damage and recovery after ship groundings in Bermuda. Proc. 5th Int. Coral Reef Symp. 4:497-502.

Smith, S. R. 1988. Recovery of a disturbed reef in Bermuda: influence of reef structure and herbivorous grazers on algal and sessile invertebrate recruitment. Proc. 6th Int. Coral Reef Symp. 2:267-272.

Smith, S. R. 1990. The influence of herbivorous grazers on the recovery of a disturbed coral reef in Bermuda. Ph. D. Dissertation, Univ. of Georgia.

Smith, S. R. 1992. Patterns of coral recruitment and post-settlement mortality on Bermuda's reefs: comparisons to Caribbean and Pacific reefs. Amer. Zool. 32:663-673.

THE RELATIONSHIP BETWEEN ENVIRONMENTAL FACTORS AND CORAL BLEACHING AT LEE STOCKING ISLAND, BAHAMAS IN 1990

George D. Dennis and Robert I. Wicklund

Caribbean Marine Research Center
805 East 46th Place
Vero Beach, Florida 32963

ABSTRACT

Following the Caribbean-wide bleaching event of 1987 we instituted monitoring of environmental factors that might contribute to stress on coral reefs at our marine laboratory in the Bahamas. Once again in 1990 extensive bleaching occurred from shallow water to 33 m. Elevated water temperatures were closely associated with the start of this bleaching. Periods of calm wind with little rain and high insolation in the summer preceded these elevated water temperatures. The extensive nature of the bleaching in 1990 may be attributable to the long duration of elevated temperatures, atypical for this site. Density cascading of warm hypersaline water on to the shelf in the summer may be an additional stress on deeper reefs at this location.

INTRODUCTION

The apparent decline of coral reefs worldwide has prompted the Caribbean Marine Research Center (CMRC) to establish a long-term study of reefs in the Exuma Cays, Bahamas. During the fall of 1987 scientists observed bleached hard and soft corals, sponges, and anemones from shallow water to 95 m (Lang et al., 1988). This Caribbean-wide bleaching event of 1987 was believed to be associated with elevated water temperatures but we could find no long-term in-situ seawater temperature data set anywhere in the Caribbean to address this question. At that time CMRC started monitoring more closely environmental conditions on reefs near our marine laboratory at Lee Stocking Island (LSI), Bahamas. The site is particularly interesting because: 1) coral reefs are well monitored, thus the timing of bleaching can be well documented, 2) there is little anthropogenic contribution to environmental stress (e.g., sewer discharge, heavy metal, or pesticide pollution), 3) turbidity stress is very low due to the lack of river runoff, and 4) a range of depths and habitats are in close proximity to the laboratory facilitating the study and comparison of reef systems. Other unique physical characteristics of the site include: 1) extreme temperature range experienced by shallow-water coral reefs in the Bahamas (18-32°C), and 2) reefs are situated on the edge of a large shallow-water bank that rapidly responds to local meteorological conditions and generates density currents (masses of warm saline water) that might affect deeper reefs on the shelf.

Lang et al. (1988) hypothesized that elevated water temperature in 1987 resulted in coral bleaching and that the cause of this warm water was local calm wind conditions. Other contributing factors proposed include density cascading of warm saline water off the bank and clear skies resulting in synergistic light-related effects. Following the 1987 coral bleaching event, CMRC instituted continuous water temperature monitoring and measurement of meteorological parameters might that influence water temperature. Elevated water temperatures at our site could be due to a regional rise in temperature (i.e., an ENSO event) or simply localized conditions such as calm winds and clear skies or a combination of the two. Past events in the Florida Keys (Jaap, 1979; 1985) and locally (Lang et al., 1988) have suggested that doldrum periods contribute to warm water events resulting in bleaching. Duration of the thermal stress also may be a factor in determining the magnitude of a bleaching event. Here we address the hypothesis that elevated water temperature resulted in the coral bleaching event of 1990 in the Bahamas and identify the potential cause of thermal-related stress on corals.

METHODS

Visual observations on coral reefs were made by divers on a weekly basis and more frequently after the start of bleaching. Three locations were monitored: Rainbow Garden (on the bank), Perry Reef (shallow fringing reef, 20 m), and Adderley Dropoff (shelf-edge reef, 33 m) (Figure 1). Thermographs, recording water temperature every 30 min, were deployed at several locations on the bank, as well as, at Perry reef and the shelf edge off Adderley Cut (Figure 1)(see Wicklund et al., 1993 for other locations). A General Oceanic current meter with conductivity probe was used to determine salinity in Adderley Cut (1990) and at Adderley Dropoff (1992). A Campbell Scientific meteorological station summarized hourly measurements of air temperature, relative humidity, insolation (pyranometer, cal/cm^2), rainfall, wind speed and direction from 1990-1992.

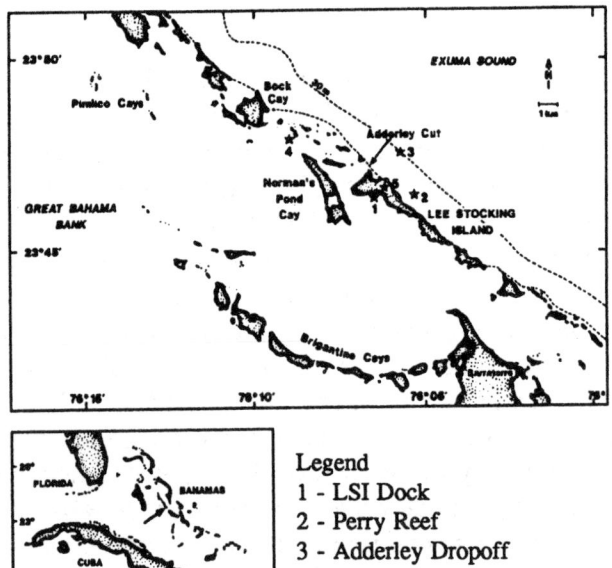

Figure 1. Map of Lee Stocking Island and Sampling Locations.

RESULTS

Bleaching Observations

Following the massive bleaching event of 1987, little bleaching was observed in 1988 and 1989 and cannot be attributed to any specific environmental cause. Widespread bleaching was again observed in mid-August 1990 at 20-25 m on the shelf-edge fringing reef and involved 1-2% of the reef. By mid-September bleaching was observed in a depth range of 2-46 m. Bleaching at 20 m consisted of about 25% of the reef. Bleached organisms included stony coral, gorgonians, and sponges (see Table 1 for list of species). Bleaching continued to increase in number of colonies affected through the first week of October. Several colonies of *A. cervicornis* and *P. porites* that bleached and survived in 1987 died in 1990. One loggerhead sponge (*Spheciospongia vesparia*) at 35 m, reduced in size through tissue loss in 1987, bleached again in 1990. No further bleaching was observed in 1991 or 1992.

Table 1. List of species bleached in 1990 at Lee Stocking Island.

Porifera (sponge)	Scleractinia (hard coral)	Gorgonacea (soft coral)
Aplysina spp.	*Acropora cervicornis*	several unidentified species
Spheciospongia vesparia	*Agaricia agaricites*	
Xestospongia muta	*Diploria strigosa*	
	Montastrea annularis	
Hydrozoa (fire coral)	*Montastrea cavernosa*	
Millepora alcicornis	*Porites porites*	

Environmental Observations

Hydrographic.— Bank (3 m)

Coral bleaching occurred at Lee Stocking Island following a short period (18 days) of daily average water temperatures above 30.5°C on the bank in July-August 1990 followed by another temperature peak in mid-September (Figure 2). A maximum temperature of 32.5 was reached on 23 September 1990. The July monthly average for 1990 did not differ from surrounding years, but August and September were significantly warmer in 1990 (Table 2). The 5-yr record at the LSI dock distinctly shows a longer-term maxima in 1990 (Figure 3); this trend needs to be substantiated.

We examined two trends in water temperature in detail. One hypothesis was that a more rapid rate of warming in the spring might result in a pool of warm water upon which singular events in the summer could react. Spring water temperature increase is relatively linear from April through June, so we compared the rate of spring temperature rise for 1988-1992 (Table 3). In 1990 the rate of spring water temperature increase was not exceptional, in fact in most years the temperature rose more rapidly than in 1990.

Typically by the end of August water temperature starts its annual decline. Examination of plots of the yearly data suggest that the warm period was prolonged in 1990 (Figure 2). To test this hypothesis we examined the temperature trends from July through September. Our hypothesis of prolonged warming would be confirmed if the slope of the trend was significantly less than in other years. For bank waters 1990 was the only year with a significant positive slope for this period confirming the prolonged warming period in 1990 (Table 3).

Great Bahama Bank salinities are typically 38 ppt and can reach 43 ppt (Pitts and Smith, 1993), thus adding a synergistic stress factor to the local environment (Marcus and Thorhaug, 1981). During July and August 1990 pulses of warm (to 31.2°C) saline (to 40 ppt) water exited through island passes onto the shelf. Bank patch reefs previously studied by Lang et al. (1988) are bathed in these water masses without apparent detrimental effects.

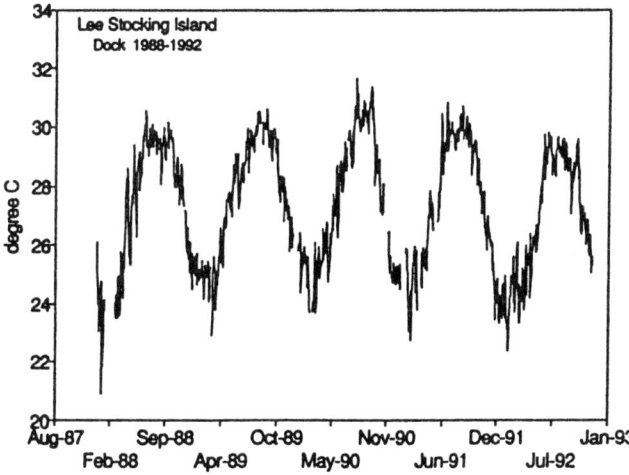

Figure 2. Five-year record of water temperature at the LSI Dock.

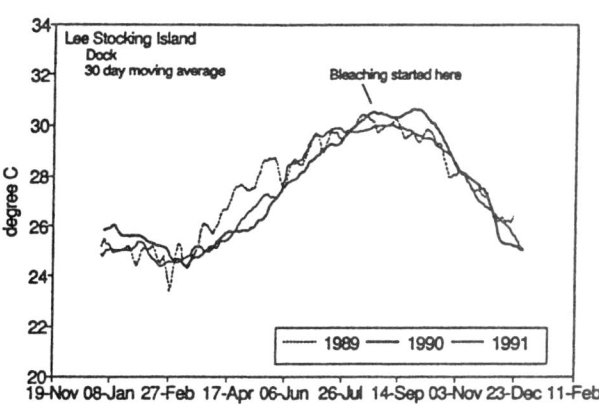

Figure 3. Annual water temperature record for 1989-1991 at the LSI Dock.

Hydrographic.— Fringing Reef (20 m)

Perry reef also exhibited two temperature peaks in July/August and at the end of September in 1990 with the second being higher. In addition the longer-term maxima in 1990 is evident. Warming by month paralleled that observed on the bank with September being significantly warmer than other years (Table 2). Increasing temperature through the summer also is evident at this location (Table 3). No salinity data is available from this area, though Perry Reef is upstream from the pass at the north end of the island. Given the prevailing currents, hypersaline waters would not be expected to reach this reef on a regular basis, though they are known to occur there.

Hydrographic.— Shelf-edge Reef (33 m)

The deepwater basin of Exuma Sound acts as a buffer to water temperature change, being warm in the winter and cooler in the summer than shallow bank waters. Instrument failure resulted in missing most of July and August 1990 for this location. Early July was no warmer than other years but by the last week in September temperature was elevated and comparable to the fringing reef (Table 2). Though our data are more fragmented at the shelf-edge reef, the longer-term trend is still evident and indicates that in 1990 water temperatures at 33 m were the highest of the 5-yr record; even at 98 m this warming was evident.

There was no conductivity recorder on the shelf in 1990, but data from a near-bottom recorder in 1992 showed that high salinity pulses can reach the bottom at this site, a mechanism for carrying warm water to the deep reefs.

Table 2. Comparison of average monthly water temperature for summer months by year. Means compared by ANOVA followed by Tukey's HSD test. Underlined years are not significantly different.

		Tukey's HSD Test for Differences Among Years LOW<--------------------->HIGH					Monthly Average Temperature (°C)				
							1988	1989	1990	1991	1992
July											
	Dock	1992	1989	1990	1988	1991	29.70	29.52	29.61	29.74	29.16
	Perry Reef	1989	1990	1988	1992		28.23	27.86	28.17	---	28.78
	Adderley (2-21 Jul)	1990	1988	1989	1991	1992	26.97	27.02	26.78	27.39	28.15
August											
	Dock	1992	1988	1991	1989	1990	29.34	30.10	30.49	29.96	29.27
	Perry Reef (21-31 Aug)	1988	1989	1992	1990	1991	28.44	28.68	29.53	29.53	28.80
September											
	Dock	1992	1988	1991	1989	1990	29.56	29.74	30.59	29.62	28.48
	Perry Reef	1992	1988	1989	1991	1990	28.57	28.94	29.79	29.45	28.44
	Adderley (28 Sep - 10 Oct)	1992	1989	1988	1991	1990	28.72	28.71	29.65	28.99	28.65

Table 3. Comparison of water temperature trends for spring and summer at two locations. Slopes compared by ANCOVA followed by Tukey's HSD test. Underlined years are not significantly different.

```
                     Tukey's HSD Test for Differences Among Years
                                     Trend Slope
                     LOW<--------------------------->HIGH
Spring (April-June)
  Dock                1989   1990   1988   1991   1992
                      ----          ----
  Perry Reef          1991   1990   1989   1992   1988
                      ----   ----   ----   ----   ----

Summer (July-September)
  Dock                1992   1988   1991   1989   1990
                      ----   ----   ----   ----   ----
  Perry Reef          1991   1992   1988   1989   1990
                      ----   ----   ----   ----   ----
```

Meteorological.—

Wind data at Lee Stocking Island are available for 1990-1992; typically July-October is the calmest period of the year. There is no significant difference in number of days of low winds (≤ 3 m/s) between 1990 and 1991, but 1992 was significantly more windy (Table 4). In addition 1992 had significantly fewer days with above average insolation (Table 4). There was no difference in the number of summer days with rainfall between 1990 and 1991, though 1990 had only about 60% of the total summer rainfall of 1991.

When examined in detail the prolonged warm water period from 24 July to 3 October 1990 was the result of three rises in temperature closely related to declines in wind speed (Figure 4). Over a 14-day period in late July water temperature increased from a daily average of 28.6° to 31.7°C, concurrent with a period of low winds, little   The second small rise is related to a short period of reduced winds (28-31 Aug) and no increase in insolation (Figure 4). The final temperature rise is associated with a 12-day calm period (14-30 Sept) with an increase in insolation followed by rain and declining water and air temperature.

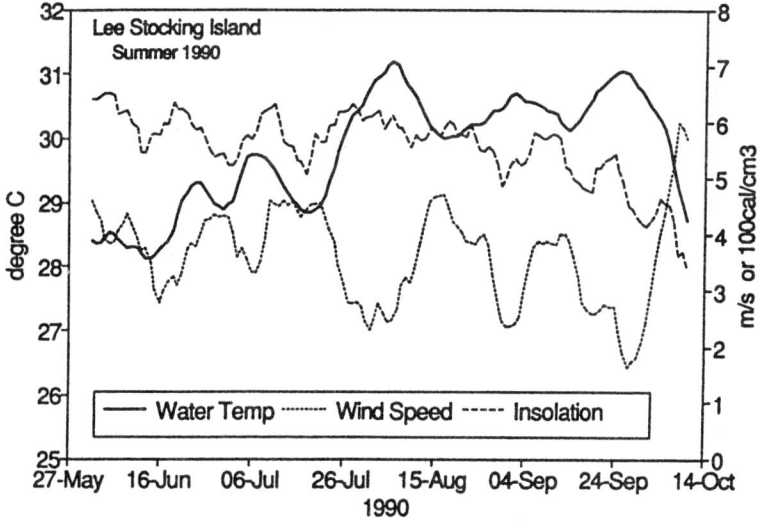

Figure 4. Daily average bank water temperature, wind speed, and insolation for the summer of 1990.

Table 4. Frequency of calm days (≤ 3 m/s), days with rain, and calm days with above average insolation in the summer at Lee Stocking Island. Arrows indicate significant differences based on chi-square test.

Number of days with calm winds					Number of Days with Rain				Total Summer
Year	JUL	AUG	SEP	Total	JUL	AUG	SEP	Total	Rainfall (mm)
1990	8	9	13	30	8	12	8	28	63.85
1991	6	9	13	28	11	10	9	30	106.83↑
1992	0	4	5	9↓	5	10	15	30	83.92

Number of calm days with above average insolation

Year	JUL	AUG	SEP	Total
1990	6	6	6	18
1991	4	3	6	13
1992	0	1	2	3

DISCUSSION

Corals thrive near their upper thermal tolerance level in summer prompting claims that global warming might cause more frequent thermal stress (Williams and Bunkley-Williams, 1990). There were no sea-surface-temperature (SST) anomalies in 1990 (Atwood et al., 1992, but see Strong and McCormick, 1990), though a trend in increasing SST through the 1980's for the Caribbean has been suggested (Goreau et al., 1992). Certainly no irrefutable evidence of SST anomalies in the Caribbean exists such as found in the 1982/83 ENSO event for the eastern Pacific (Glynn, 1990). Our whole range of thermographs (3-98 m) indicates that 1990 was warmer than the surrounding years. The 1990 bleaching event at Lee Stocking Island is correlated with elevated water temperatures, possibly a result of favorable weather conditions on top of a longer-term maxima in temperature. Bleaching might have been negligible but for a late September calm period that prolonged the period of elevated water temperatures. Rainfall appears to have a mitigating influence on the effect of solar heating on bank waters as there was little rise in water temperature when a calm period was associated with substantial rainfall.

Rather than deeper waters staying cooler in the summer, shelf-edge water temperature rose close to levels at shallow-water fringing reefs. Deeper-water reefs must be adapted to lower temperatures based on the lower maximum temperature causing bleaching as has been proposed for Bermuda corals (Cook et al., 1990).

Bank waters are typically hypersaline, ranging from 38-44 ppt and corals must be adapted to these conditions as well developed patch reefs exist in the Bahamas (Newell et al., 1959). The intrusion of these warm hypersaline conditions on shelf habitats is not as well documented. Basin waters have typical oceanic salinities (36-37 ppt) (US Navy, 1967; Schroeder, 1977; this study), thus shelf-edge reefs should not be acclimated to hypersaline conditions. Periodic density cascading of warm hypersaline water off the bank may be an additional stress on shelf reefs especially around passes. The role of salinity stress cannot be accurately evaluated without further information on the frequency, duration, and areal extent of density cascading.

CONCLUSIONS

Elevated water temperature around Lee Stocking Island was closely related to a significant coral bleaching event in 1990. Bleaching was not the result of a single upper level temperature threshold, as bleaching occurred over a range of depths and temperatures suggesting a large pool of water with elevated temperature. Elevated temperatures in 1990 were related to local climatological phenomena, including calm wind conditions, high insolation, and low rainfall that occurred on top of a longer-term maxima in water temperature. Rainfall, not previously considered an important factor, can have a substantial influence on water temperature. Exposure to elevated water temperature (>31°C on the bank) in 1990 appeared to take more than a couple of days, but less than three weeks, to initiate bleaching. Prolonged elevated temperatures may be the primary contributing factor to the magnitude of the bleaching event in 1990.

ACKNOWLEDGEMENTS

J. Lang and R. Dill provided additional information on bleaching organisms and N. Smith provided salinity data. K. Mueller maintained the water temperature database and provided quality control. Review by G. Wenz helped improve the paper. The NOAA National Undersea Research Program provided support for this project.

LITERATURE CITED

Atwood, D.K., J.C. Hendee and A. Mendez. 1992. An assessment of global warming stress on Caribbean coral reef ecosystems. Bull. Mar. Sci. 51: 118-130.

Cook, C.B., A. Logan, J. Ward, B. Luckhurst and C.J. Berg. 1990. Elevated temperatures on a high latitude coral reef: the 1988 Bermuda event. Coral Reefs 9: 45-49.

Glynn, P.W. 1990. Coral mortality and disturbances to coral reefs in the Tropical Eastern Pacific. Pages 55-126 *In* P.W. Glynn, ed. Global Ecological Consequences of the 1982-83 El Niño-Southern Oscillation, Elsevier Oceanogr. Ser.

Goreau, T.J., R.L. Hayes, J.W. Clark, D.J. Basta and C.N. Robertson. 1992. Elevated satellite sea surface temperatures correlated with Caribbean coral bleaching. *In* R.A. Geyer, Ed. Geophysical/Geochemical Aspects of Global Warming. CRC Press

Jaap, W.C. 1979. Observations on zooxanthellae expulsion at Middle Sambo Reef, Florida Keys. Bull. Mar. Sci. 29: 414-422.

Jaap, W.C. 1985. An epidemic zooxanthellae expulsion during 1983 in the lower Florida Keys coral reefs: hyperthermic etiology. Proc. 5th Inter. Coral Reef Congr. Tahiti 6: 143-148.

Jokiel, P.L. and S.L. Coles. 1990. Response of Hawaiian and other Indo-Pacific reef corals to elevated temperature. Coral Reefs 8: 155-162.

Lang, J.C., R.I. Wicklund and R.F. Dill. 1988. Depth- and habitat-related bleaching of zooxanthellate reef organisms near Lee Stocking Island, Exuma Cays, Bahamas. Proc. 6th Inter. Coral Reef Symp. Townsville, Aust. 3: 269-274.

Marcus, J. and A. Thorhaug, 1981. Pacific versus Atlantic responses of the subtropical hermatypic coral *Porites* spp. to temperature and salinity effects. Proc. 4th Inter. Coral Reef Symp. Manila 2: 15-20.

Newell, N.D., J. Imbrie, E.G. Purdy and D.L. Thurber. 1959. Organism communities and bottom facies, Great Bahama Bank. Bull. Amer. Mus. Nat. Hist. 117(4): 177-228.

Pitts, P.A. and N.P. Smith. 1993. Annotated summary of temperature and salinity data from the vicinity of Lee Stocking Island, Exuma Cays, Bahamas. CMRC Tech. Rept. No. 93-3, Vero Beach, FL

Schroeder, W.W. 1977. Current and hydrographic characterization of the south central insular shelf of Grand Bahama Island. Proc. 3rd Inter. Coral Reef Symp., Miami 2: 517-523.

Strong, A.E. and R.C. McCormick. 1991. Coral bleaching and sea surface temperatures. Proc. Oceanogr. Soc. Conf. St. Petersburg, FL.

U.S. Navy. 1967. Environmental Atlas of the Tongue of the Ocean Bahamas. U.S. Naval Oceanographic Office, Spec. Publ. SP-94, 74 p.

Wicklund, R.I., G.D. Dennis and K.W. Mueller. 1993. Summary of data from the Water Temperature Monitoring Network at Lee Stocking Island, Bahamas, 1988-1991. CMRC Tech Rept. No. 93-1, Vero Beach, FL

Williams, E.H. and L. Bunkley-Williams. 1990. The world-wide coral reef bleaching cycle and related sources of coral mortality. Atoll Res. Bull. No. 335, 71 p.

THE M/V WELLWOOD AND OTHER LARGE VESSEL GROUNDINGS: CORAL REEF DAMAGE AND RECOVERY

Stephen R. Gittings[1], Thomas J. Bright[2] and Derek K. Hagman[2]

[1] Flower Garden Banks National Marine Sanctuary, 1716 Briarcrest Dr., Suite 702, Bryan, Texas, 77802
[2] Texas A&M Sea Grant College Program, 1716 Briarcrest Dr., Suite 702, Bryan, Texas, 77802

ABSTRACT

The characteristics of reef community damage caused by three large vessel groundings in the Florida Keys were investigated between 1984 and 1991. Damage at each site included impact to living resources, framework alteration and fracturing, reef rock displacement, and sediment production. These were caused by vessel contact with the bottom, by propwash and cable dragging during attempts by operators and/or salvagers to refloat the ships, and by subsequent movement of destabilized substrates. None of the groundings were accompanied by significant cargo or fuel spills. Coral community recovery was followed for five years on Molasses Reef after the grounding of a 122 m freighter. Repetitive and random photographic methods, and diver counts were used to assess coral populations, cover, recruitment, and the fate of damaged coral colonies. Substantial population recovery occurred in the five years following the grounding, but colonies remained small. Hard coral recruitment was dominated by species that brood larvae. These species were also numerical dominants in undamaged communities nearby. Though, in time, complete recovery would occur naturally, transplantation could be used to increase the relative abundance of species found only rarely as recruits. These include primarily the large massive corals conspicuous in mature reef communities. Most are broadcast spawners, and have long planktonic stages, low recruitment rates, and low relative abundances in mature communities. Following large vessel groundings that cause extensive flattening of portions of the reef surface, transplantation could also serve to restore lost habitat complexity, and enhance the rate of development of associated invertebrate and reef fish assemblages.

INTRODUCTION

On August 4, 1984, the 122 m freighter M/V WELLWOOD ran aground on Molasses Reef, in the Key Largo National Marine Sanctuary (Fig. 1). Damage occurred where the vessel made contact with corals along its inbound path, at the site where the vessel was hard aground, and during ship salvage efforts (Bright and Andryszak [1984]; Curtis [1985]; Gittings and Bright [1988]). In the area of initial contact (approximately 8 meters depth), large corals were abraded, toppled or fractured (within and seaward of Area BS in Fig. 1). The final resting site (6-8 m depth) was the most heavily impacted portion of the reef. Under the bow and amidships (Area BB in Fig. 1), the broad tops of forereef spurs were ground flat by the ship hull, and linear piles of boulders were formed by the plowing of the port side of the ship as it pivoted on the reef. Nearly all corals were destroyed in the 1500 m^2 flattened area. Corals in some depressions survived, but were shaded during the 12 days the ship remained aground, and lost zooxanthellae. This also occurred in toppled colonies. Substantial tissue loss occurred on colonies with severe bleaching. During ship salvage, many corals and large barrel sponges seaward of the grounding site were damaged by tug cables used to haul the vessel off the reef.

Damage assessments were also conducted at two other ship grounding sites in the Sanctuary. On October 25, 1989, the 47 m oil field supply vessel M/V ALEC OWEN MAITLAND ran aground in a reef coral community in 2-3 meters of water approximately 2.5 km southwest of Carysfort Light (Gittings, 1991a). Along the 156 m grounding track, at least two community types were affected, one of high relief and dominated by gorgonians and the hydrozoan Millepora spp., and the other a low relief hard bottom with lower coral abundance. Damage on the 88 m inbound path included toppling, fracturing, and crushing of coral colonies. At the end of and perpendicular to the inbound path, was an area 64 m in length where the vessel apparently turned during initial freeing efforts. Damage there consisted of grinding by the ship's hull, removal and overturning of corals, and excavations caused by propwash. The final resting site measured 68 m in length, contained two large excavations totaling over 25 m in length, the remains of detacted corals, and rubble and sediment accumulations. The two excavation (or blowout) craters were formed by propwash during attempts by the crew to free the vessel.

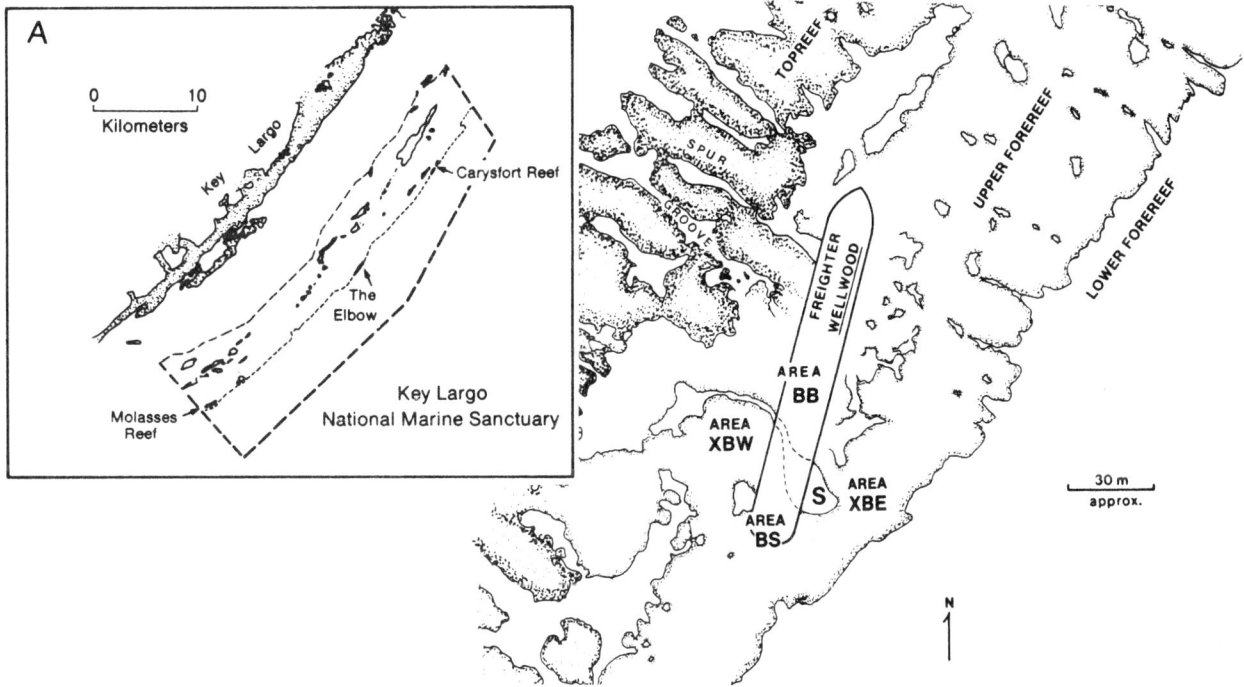

Figure 1. Study areas at the grounding site of the M/V WELLWOOD. Inset (A) shows the locations of reefs in the Key Largo National Marine Sanctuary near the grounding sites discussed here.

On November 11, 1989, the 143 m freighter M/V ELPIS ran aground in a reef coral community in 8.5-10.0 meters of water 0.5 km northeast of the Elbow Reef Light. This vessel caused over 3,000 m² of damage. It produced intermittent damage over nearly 100 m of reef before coming to rest and flattening an area nearly 40 m in length. Propwash apparently caused by forward and reverse thrust resulted in craters 18 m and 11 m in diameter, respectively, each 2-3 m deep. After coming to rest, the vessel pivoted 230° and drifted into shallower water, flattening roughly 700 m² of additional sea bottom over an 80 m length. Upon removal, vessel propwash produced a 75 m long trench that, together with rubble accumulations, covered over 1400 m² (Gittings, 1991b).

While coral communities affected by ship groundings vary considerably, the collective characteristics of damage identified at the three sites discussed here distinguish large vessel grounding damage from other forms of human or natural impact. This paper focuses on the characteristics of mechanical damage caused by ship groundings. We also discuss the physical and biological processes affected by groundings that, in turn, affect reef community recovery. Finally, implications for mitigation and recovery enhancement efforts are discussed.

METHODS

At the shallow water grounding site of the ALEC OWEN MAITLAND, damage occurred in more than one coral community type. The probable pre-grounding boundaries between different communities were determined using post-grounding aerial photography and ground truthing. Probable pre-grounding coral population levels at the site were determined using underwater video, and quantitative photographic and survey techniques in undamaged areas. The extent of destruction to the coral community was then assumed to be the difference between the existing populations at the site and population levels in similar, but undamaged communities nearby.

Similar techniques were used at the two deeper sites as well, but aerial photography was not as heavily relied upon. Divers surveyed the grounding sites and determined, based on topography, depth, and observed reef zonation, the probable pre-grounding community types at each grounding site.

Damage assessments required between three and seven days at each site using two to three dive teams. Field sampling at the WELLWOOD site, where coral community recovery was monitored, was conducted quarterly between August 1984 and November 1986, then again in September 1988 and August 1989. Each sampling trip lasted four to five days.

Similar quantification techniques were used at all sites. Random photographic techniques were used to assess hard coral and gorgonian abundance and distribution in damaged and undamaged (control) areas (Gittings et al., 1990). Randomly located photos were taken in each area, each providing coverage of either 0.5 m^2 or 1.0 m^2, depending on the nature of the coral community (e.g., average size and abundance). They were analyzed to determine sizes and numbers of scleractinians, gorgonaceans, hydrozoans, and zoanthideans by species for each area. Percent cover was considered the vertical projection of a colony onto the substrate (like canopy cover in terrestrial ecosystems) and was calculated for scleractinians using a digital planimeter. For upright gorgonians, relative size was determined ("small" being 0-10 cm height, "medium" 10-30 cm, and "large" over 30 cm). Gorgonian canopy cover at the WELLWOOD site, and all coral cover at the other sites was measured using the random point-intercept method. Clear acetate overlays containing 100 randomly located points were laid over photos, and cover was estimated by counting points covering each coral species.

At the WELLWOOD site, recruitment was assessed from random photographic data, and underwater counts of juvenile corals in the area of greatest destruction (Area BB). Numerical abundances on random photographs were compared between sampling periods. Recruitment rates were determined in terms of net increases in individual groups (gorgonians, scleractinians, and hydrozoans) and species, where possible. In November 1986, September 1988, and August 1989, underwater counts in eighteen 1 m^2 quadrats were made in Area BB to determine the population of scleractinians, gorgonians, hydrozoans, zoanthideans, and selected associated invertebrates in the area. Samples were spaced approximately 1 m apart on a line from the southernmost to the northernmost portion of Area BB. This visual method was employed because many juvenile corals are found predominantly on the undersides or sides of reef surfaces, and may not be accounted for using down-looking photographic techniques.

Another technique used to evaluate population changes (recruitment and loss) was repetitive photography of three 15 m x 0.5 m transects. For two of the three transects (107 and 110), half of each was located in Area BB and half in areas beyond the direct impact of the ship hull. For the third transect (102), the impacted half was in an area only partially damaged by the vessel (i.e., adult colonies and considerable topographic relief remained).

Lateral coral growth on damaged and undamaged Montastrea annularis colonies at the WELLWOOD site was measured using repetitive photographic techniques described by Gittings et al., (1988). Eighty-four permanent stations were established and photographed from 1984 to 1989. Tissue growth and retreat rates were compared to determine the fate of damaged colonies and the influence of colony displacement (e.g. damaged colonies displaced into sand vs. those remaining on the reef following fracture).

RESULTS

Gittings et al. (1990) reported the results of five years (1984-1989) of population studies at the WELLWOOD grounding site. Coral populations had increased by 1989 from virtually 0% in an area of major impact to 65% and 78% of supposed pre-impact populations for hard corals and gorgonians, respectively. They also found that recruitment rates increased with time, and estimated that population levels could approach pre-grounding levels after six years of recovery. But coral cover, particularly for scleractinians, had not increased as fast as populations levels. Gorgonian cover increased from virtually 0% of that in the control area (Area XBE in Fig. 1) to approximately 40% of cover in the control area by 1989. Hard coral cover increased from an average of 12.4% of cover in the control area during the first two years after the grounding to 22.1% in 1988 and 1989.

Diver counts in square meter quadrats in Area BB indicated that coral populations in 1989 were roughly 20 m^{-2} (less than 4 m^{-2} existed in the first counts in 1986). Gorgonians and scleractinians had approximately equal populations (nearly 10 m^{-2} each), and accounted for 95% of all corals. Millepora spp. represented 5% of the hard coral population in the area.

Coral recruitment on repetitive transects was dominated by gorgonian corals (45% of all recruits), followed by scleractinians (36%) and Millepora spp. (19%). Gorgonian recruitment was dominated by Pseudopterogorgia spp. (75%), Gorgonia ventalina (14%) and Briareum asbestinum (7%). Scleractinian recruitment was dominated by Favia fragum (38%), Agaricia agaricites (32%), and Porites sp. (10%). Though these taxa accounted for over 90% of all corals in the Area BB by 1989, richness (the number of coral taxa) increased gradually, primarily due to an increase in the number of scleractinian species.

Massive corals such as Montastrea spp., Diploria spp., and Dichocoenia stokesi, which were conspicuous in surrounding habitats, were only rarely encountered in Area BB. Their relative abundances, however, were similar in both areas. Though conspicuous due to their larger size in undisturbed habitats, these corals did not represent numerically dominant species in any area.

Fig. 2 shows cumulative coral recruitment on the impacted portions of repetitive transects between 1984 and 1989. Gittings (1988) showed that recruitment on Transect 102 (in the partially damaged area) was significantly higher than that on the other transects through 1986. In fact most recruitment on Transect 102 occurred in the first two years after the grounding; most recruitment on Transects 107 and 110 (in the heavily damaged area) occurred after 1986. Recruitment on the undamaged portions of the transects was similar between 1984 and 1989 (Gittings and Bright, 1990).

Gittings et al. (1988) and Gittings and Bright (1990) showed that coral colonies displaced into sandy habitats during or after the grounding had greater tissue retreat rates than those not displaced from the reef. Between 1988 and 1989, however, stations in sand and on the reef had virtually identical rates of advance and retreat. Fig. 3 compares growth at stations on three coral colonies, one damaged and displaced into sand (Head S; 10 stations), one damaged but not displaced (Head D; 8 stations), and an undamaged colony (Head C; 12 stations). The ternary diagrams show the proportions of marginal tissue growing, retreating, and remaining stable between sample periods. Prior to 1988 (Periods A-I), data indicated that damaged colonies displaced into sand had comparatively high proportions of retreating margins. Damaged colonies that remained on the reef exhibited high retreat only during the first three months following the grounding (Period A). In 1989, all colonies had proportions of advancing margins of at least 50%.

DISCUSSION

Damage Characteristics

The principal forms of damage observed at all three grounding sites can be divided into four categories: impacts to living resources, framework fracturing, reef rock displacement, and sediment production. Impacts to living resources included obliteration, fracture, or abrasion of coral colonies (and associated reef invertebrates), displacement of colonies, and bleaching (primarily at the WELLWOOD site, where the vessel remained aground for nearly two weeks). Unique to the WELLWOOD site was the shearing of many corals and sponges over a large area seaward of the grounding site by cables used to remove the vessel from the reef. This damage could have been avoided by keeping the cables off the bottom.

Reef framework damage varied with the size of the vessel, the nature of the grounding, and the configuration of the reef surface on which the grounding occurred. At each site, however, some portion of the reef surface was flattened (ranging from several to over 1500 m^2) and large cracks in the reef surface appeared, particularly where the ship's hull rested on the bottom.

Reef rock displacement at each site was caused by movement of loose material either by the ship hull (i.e., plowing, which formed a long pile of rubble along the west side of the WELLWOOD site; Curtis, 1985), by propwash during attempts of remove the vessel from the reef, or by storms following the grounding. Rubble movement caused by propwash and storms was exacerbated in areas with reef framework damage. The large craters at each site attest to the destructive power of propwash in mechanically damaged habitats. In each case, fallout from propwash caused the burial of corals in the vicinity of the craters, as well as abrasions on surviving colonies. "Secondary" damage was documented on repetitive transects at the WELLWOOD site, where storm-tossed rubble, generated by the grounding, damaged and destroyed a number of colonies adjacent to the grounding site during Hurricane Kate in 1985 (Gittings, 1988).

At each site, areas flattened by the ship hull also contained fine sediments that formed as the vessel pulverized corals and rock on the reef top. These sediments were generally found packed by the weight of the vessel into depressions on the reef surface. Removal required storms at the deeper grounding sites, or less energetic events at the shallower water site.

The effect of the generation of both loose material and sediments is to inhibit recruitment or survival of benthic fauna and flora (e.g., Bak and Engel, 1979). Data at the WELLWOOD site substantiated this effect; recruitment was low in the first year following the grounding in Area BB compared to less damaged areas, and increased significantly thereafter.

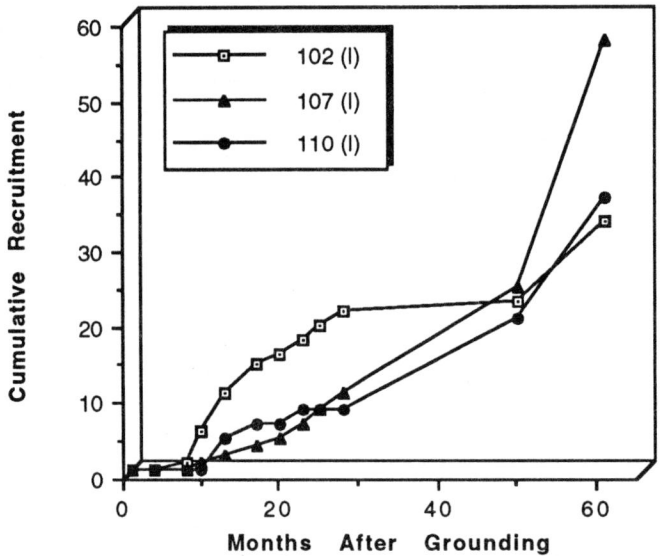

Figure 2. Cumulative coral recruitment (all species combined) on the impacted portions of repetitive transects 102, 107 and 110 between 1984 and 1989.

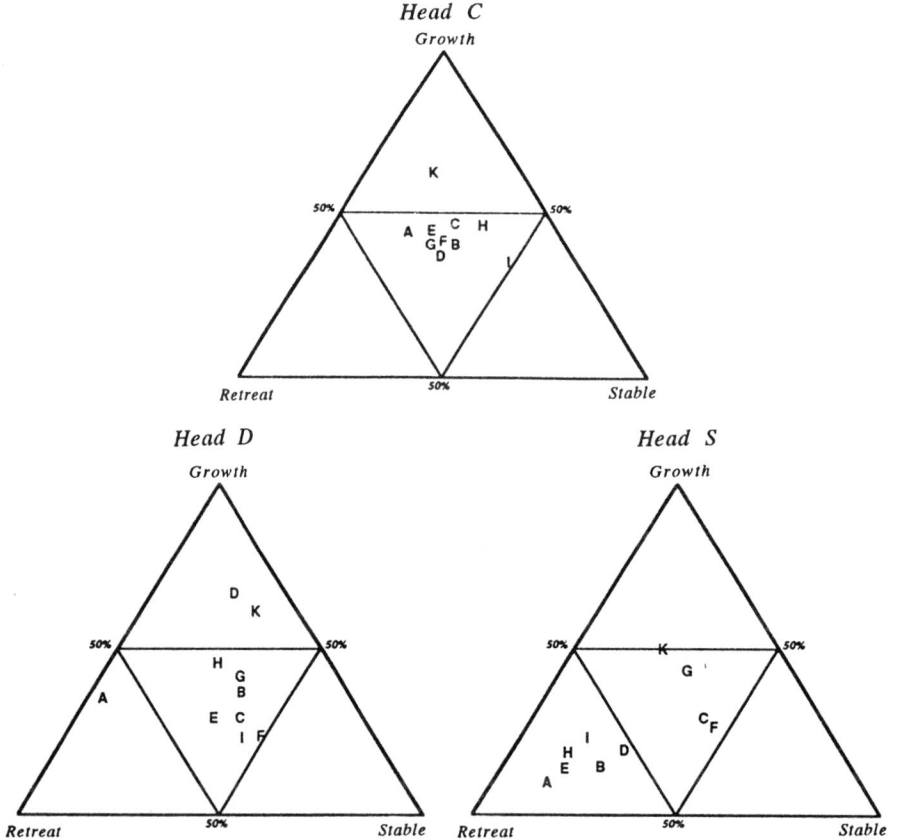

Figure 3. Ternary diagram showing the proportions of growing, retreating, and stable coral margins during each sample period on three different coral heads. Letters indicate sample period as follows: **A**=Aug 84-Nov 84, **B**=Nov 84-Mar 85, **C**=Mar 85-May 85, **D**=May 85-Aug 85, **E**=Aug 85-Dec 85, **F**=Dec 85-Mar 86, **G**=Mar 86-Jun 86, **H**=Jun 86-Aug 86, **I**=Aug 86-Nov 86, **J**=Nov 86-Sep 88 (no data), **K**=Sep 88-Aug 89.

Coral Community Recovery

Recovery of a reef coral community requires the replenishment of populations as well as the restoration of age-class structure. Recovery of the reef habitat must also include the regeneration of pre-existing three-dimensional structure. The disparity between the increases in population levels and coral cover at the WELLWOOD site in the first five post-grounding years is attributable to the lack of large colonies in the recovering community. This reflects the lack of age-class structure recovery.

As suggested by the percent cover estimates at the WELLWOOD site, gorgonian corals, which grow much faster in area than stony corals, contributed most significantly to the increase in coral cover at the site. Gittings et al. (1990) predicted that gorgonian cover would approach control levels much faster than stony coral cover. Extrapolation of best fit curves on percent cover data suggested that control community percent cover could be reached in Area BB at approximately seven years for gorgonians ($r^2=0.965$; second order polynomial), and over 12 years for hard corals ($r^2=0.192$).

Nevertheless, complete community recovery would still require the development of species diversity, age-class structure and three-dimensional habitat structure in the area comparable to that in control areas, and development of a diverse community of associated reef algae, invertebrates and fishes.

Species dominating the recovery community in Area BB were those dominating mature communities in control areas, but relative abundances changed considerably over the course of the study. The scleractinian coral species dominating Area BB (F. fragum, Porites sp., and A. agaricites) were described by van Moorsel (1983) and Szmant (1986) as larval brooders. Planulae released from brooding adults are able to settle soon after release and may colonize areas near parent colonies. Generally, these species produce small colonies, have multiple reproductive cycles per year, have high recruitment rates, and are often found in unstable habitats. They are analogous to r-selected, opportunistic species in some respects (Pianka, 1970), especially in their ability to colonize substrates made available through removal of other organisms, as occurs during ship groundings. Thus, a high relative abundance of these species in the early recovery community should be expected.

Broadcast spawners in surrounding habitats, such as M. annularis, M. cavernosa, Diploria strigosa, Acropora spp., and Siderastrea siderea would be expected to colonize the grounding site at a slower rate and reach maximum abundance in later recovery phases. These species were found only occasionally in Area BB. As adults, they are usually larger than brooding species and have only one spawning period per year (Szmant, 1986). They become conspicuous in mature communities due to their size, and contribute substantially to coral cover and three-dimensionality on the reef, but are not numerical dominants.

Implications for Recovery Enhancement

Gittings et al. (1988) discussed potential ameliorative measures that could minimize secondary damage and enhance recovery following mechanical disturbance to reef communities. These included fine sediment removal, rubble removal or stabilization, and coral transplantation. Sediment removal could enhance recruitment by facilitating substrate conditioning (Crisp and Ryland, 1960) and by increasing habitat complexity. Rubble removal, or stabilization using cement, could reduce secondary damage caused by resuspension during storms and increase bottom stability (Endean and Stablum, 1973; Wulff, 1984). Coral transplantation may increase recruitment in denuded areas (Gittings et al. 1988), increase habitat complexity (Maragos, 1974; Gabrie et al., 1985), and has aesthetic value (Shinn, 1976).

Because corals displaced into sandy habitats by the grounding had higher tissue loss than other damaged colonies, transplantation programs should utilize these colonies. But survival of dislodged coral colonies on the reef surface is also threatened due to their instability (Hudson and Diaz, 1988). These dislodged corals could be re-secured by cementing them either in their original position or as transplants.

Coral reproductive strategies should be considered in decisions regarding transplantation. It probably would not be prudent to include most brooding species in a transplantation program. Some of these species recruit fairly rapidly in denuded habitats (Agaricia spp., F. fragum, Porites spp., and Pseudopterogorgia spp.), and recruits probably arise primarily from nearby adults.

Corals that should be considered for transplantation are those that form large, massive colonies, which on the Florida Reef Tract include M. annularis, M. cavernosa, D. strigosa, S. siderea, and possibly Acropora spp., among others. These corals generally broadcast gametes into the water column, where external fertilization takes place (Gittings et al., 1992), and dispersal is often over long distances (Szmant, 1986). Recruits are rarely observed, but survival of colonies, once a safe size is reached, can be high. As with other massive corals, these species are slow growing (except Acropora spp.). These characteristics make them good candidates for restoration programs.

It should be recognized, however, that even without transplantation, the relative abundance of these species in denuded areas at the WELLWOOD grounding site was comparable to control areas after only five years. They would, therefore, be expected to recover naturally to pre-impact age-class structure, but natural recovery time would be considerable. Transplantation of large colonies of broadcasting species offers the recovering community sexually reproductive individuals and, perhaps more importantly, provides the habitat complexity necessary for recovery of the full complement of reef invertebrates and fishes that characterize these diverse communities.

LITERATURE CITED

Bak, R.P.M. and M.S. Engel. 1979. Distribution, abundance, and survival of juvenile hermatypic corals (Scleractinia) and the importance of life history strategies in the parent coral community. Mar. Biol. 54:341-352.

Bright, T.J. and B.A. Andryszak. 1984. Coral population recovery following grounding of the freighter WELLWOOD on Molasses Reef, Key Largo National Marine Sanctuary I. Preliminary damage assessment and experimental design. Rept. of NOAA Office of Ocean and Coastal Resource Management, Sanctuary Programs Division. 35 pp.

Crisp, D.J. and J.S. Ryland. 1960. Influence of filming and surface texture on the settlement of marine organisms. Nature 185 (4706):119.

Curtis, C. 1985. Investigating reef recovery following freighter grounding in the Key Largo National Marine Sanctuary (Florida Keys, USA). Proc. 5th Int. Coral Reef Cong. 6:471-476.

Endean, R. and W. Stablum. 1973. The apparent extent of recovery of reefs of Australia's Great Barrier Reef devastated by the crown-of-thorns starfish (*Acanthaster planci*). Atoll Res. Bull. 168:1-26.

Gabrie, C., M. Porcher and M. Masson. 1985. Dredging in French Polynesian coral reefs: towards a general policy of resource exploitation and site development. Proc. Fifth Int. Coral Reef Symp. 4:271-277.

Gittings, S.R. 1988. The recovery process in a mechanically damaged coral reef community. Ph.D. Dissertation, Texas A&M University, Dept. of Oceanography, College Station, TX. 228 pp.

Gittings, S.R. 1991a. Coral reef destruction at the M/V ALEC OWEN MAITLAND grounding site, Key Largo National Marine Sanctuary. Rept. to U.S. Dept. of Justice, Torts Branch, Civil Division. Texas A&M Research Foundation Project No. 6795. 28 pp.

Gittings, S.R. 1991b. Reef coral destruction at the M/V ELPIS grounding site, Key Largo National Marine Sanctuary. Rept. to U.S. Dept. of Justice, Torts Branch, Civil Division. Texas A&M Research Foundation Project No. 6795. 28 pp.

Gittings, S.R. and T.J. Bright. 1988. The M/V WELLWOOD grounding: A sanctuary case study. The Science. Oceanus 31(1):35-41.

Gittings, S.R. and T.J. Bright. 1990. Coral recovery following grounding of the freighter M/V WELLWOOD on Molasses Reef, Key Largo National Marine Sanctuary. Report to NOAA Office of Ocean and Coastal Resource Management. Contract No. NA88AA-H-CZ037. 73 pp.

Gittings, S.R., T.J. Bright, and B.S. Holland. 1990. Five years of coral recovery following a freighter grounding in the Florida Keys. Proc: American Academy of Underwater Sciences, 10th Annual Symposium. pp. 89-105.

Gittings, S.R., T.J. Bright, A. Choi, and R.R. Barnett. 1988. The recovery process in a mechanically damaged coral reef community: recruitment and growth. Proc. 6th Int. Coral Reef Symp. 2:225-230.

Gittings, S.R., G.S. Boland, K.J.P. Deslarzes, C.L. Combs, B.S. Holland, and T.J. Bright. 1992. Mass spawning and reproductive viability of reef corals at the East Flower Garden Bank, northwest Gulf of Mexico. Bull. Mar. Sci. 51(3):420-428.

Hudson, J.H. and R. Diaz. 1988. Damage survey and restoration of M/V WELLWOOD grounding site, Molasses Reef, Key Largo National Marine Sanctuary, Florida. Proc. 6th Int. Coral Reef Symp. 2:231-236.

Maragos, J.E. 1974. Coral transplantation: a method to create, preserve, and manage coral reefs. Sea Grant Advisory Rep. UNIHI-SEAGRANT-AR-74-03 CORMAR-14. Univ. of Hawaii, Honolulu.

Pianka, E.R. 1970. On "r" and "K" selection. Am. Nat. 104:592-597.

Shinn, E.A. 1976. Coral reef recovery in Florida and the Persian Gulf. Env. Geol. 1:241-254.

Szmant, A.M. 1986. Reproductive ecology of Caribbean reef corals. Coral Reefs 5:43-54.

von Moorsel, G.W.N.M. 1983. Reproductive strategies in two closely related corals (*Agaricia*, Scleractinia). Mar. Ecol. Prog. Ser. 13:273-283.

Wulff, J.L. 1984. Sponge-mediated coral reef growth and rejuvenation. Coral Reefs 3:157-163.

PROTECTION AND MONITORING OF REEFS ON THE FLOWER GARDEN BANKS, 1972-1992

Stephen R. Gittings[1], Thomas J. Bright[2], and Derek K. Hagman[2]

[1] Flower Garden Banks National Marine Sanctuary, 1716 Briarcrest Dr., Suite 702, Bryan, Texas, 77802
[2] Texas A&M Sea Grant College Program, 1716 Briarcrest Dr., Suite 702, Bryan, Texas, 77802

ABSTRACT

Escalating oil and gas production on the outer continental shelf of the Gulf of Mexico in the 1970's stimulated monitoring programs to document any related long-term changes in coral populations and growth rates on the reefs of the Flower Garden Banks. Regulations prohibiting industrial development on the banks, and those requiring the shunting of discharges to deep water within four miles of the banks have been in place since 1974. Repetitive and random photographic techniques and direct measurements have been used to measure coral population parameters and growth rates since 1972. In the subsequent 20 years, no significant changes have been observed in coral cover, population levels, diversity, evenness, or accretionary and encrusting growth. However, demonstrable impacts have resulted from vessel anchoring and natural catastrophes such as the mass mortality of the sea urchin, Diadema antillarum. The installation of mooring buoys, the notification on charts of anchoring restrictions, and the designation of the Flower Garden Banks National Marine Sanctuary have greatly reduced anchor damage. Future research needs to address threats posed by increasing use of the reefs by recreational divers and boaters.

INTRODUCTION

The East (EFG) and West (WFG) Flower Garden Banks are located on the outer continental shelf (OCS), 195 km south of the Texas/Louisiana border (Fig. 1). The banks are topographic expressions of seafloor uplift caused by vertically migrating salt originating from Jurassic evaporite deposits 15 km below the seafloor (Rezak et al., 1985). The bank crests, 19 km apart, support coral reefs that rise to within 15 m of the surface (Bright et al., 1984). Bank zones containing the highest diversity coral reefs (above 36 m) cover over 1.3 km^2. Hard bottom areas covering over 87 km^2 occur to over 100 m depth and contain zones dominated by low diversity reefs, coralline algae, sponges, antipatharians, and octocorals. Drowned reefs that probably formed during lower sea level stands occur in the deeper zones of the banks (Rezak et al., 1985).

The Flower Garden Banks, at nearly 28°N, are near the northern physiological limits for tropical reef-building corals in the Gulf of Mexico (Rezak et al., 1990). These isolated reefs are over 600 km from reefs in the southwestern Gulf and on the Yucatan Shelf. Only 18 of the approximately 65 Western Atlantic reef-building coral species occur here (Bright et al., 1984). Yet, reported abundance and growth rates rival those in more tropical locales at similar depths (Hudson and Robbin, 1980).

Resource Protection

Increasing oil and gas development on the northwest Gulf OCS in the 1970's coincided with the first rigorous examinations of the unusual biological communities on a number of offshore banks in the region. The Department of Interior, Minerals Management Service (MMS; formerly the New Orleans Outer Continental Shelf Office of the Bureau of Land Management [BLM]) regulates offshore development and recognized that tropical marine communities on some of the banks could be vulnerable to water quality changes caused by unusual levels of sedimentation under drill mud plumes and other discharges.

In 1974, the BLM promulgated protective lease stipulations around a number of OCS banks (Fig. 1). At each of the Flower Garden Banks, a "No-Activity Zone" out to approximately 100 m depth (roughly the edge of the banks) prohibited all industry activity. A "1-Mile Zone" beyond the "No-Activity Zone" was established wherein the BLM required shunting of drill cuttings and discharges to within 10 m of the seafloor. It was assumed, and later confirmed, that the local currents at these depths would preclude sediments and other discharges from reaching the shallow reef communities (Rezak et al., 1985). Monitoring studies were also required in conjunction with drilling in the "1-Mile Zone." A "4-Mile Zone" was established in which shunting, but not monitoring, was required.

Another significant threat during this period to reefs at the Flower Gardens came from vessel anchoring. Though the BLM/MMS could regulate anchoring by industry vessels, increasing recreational

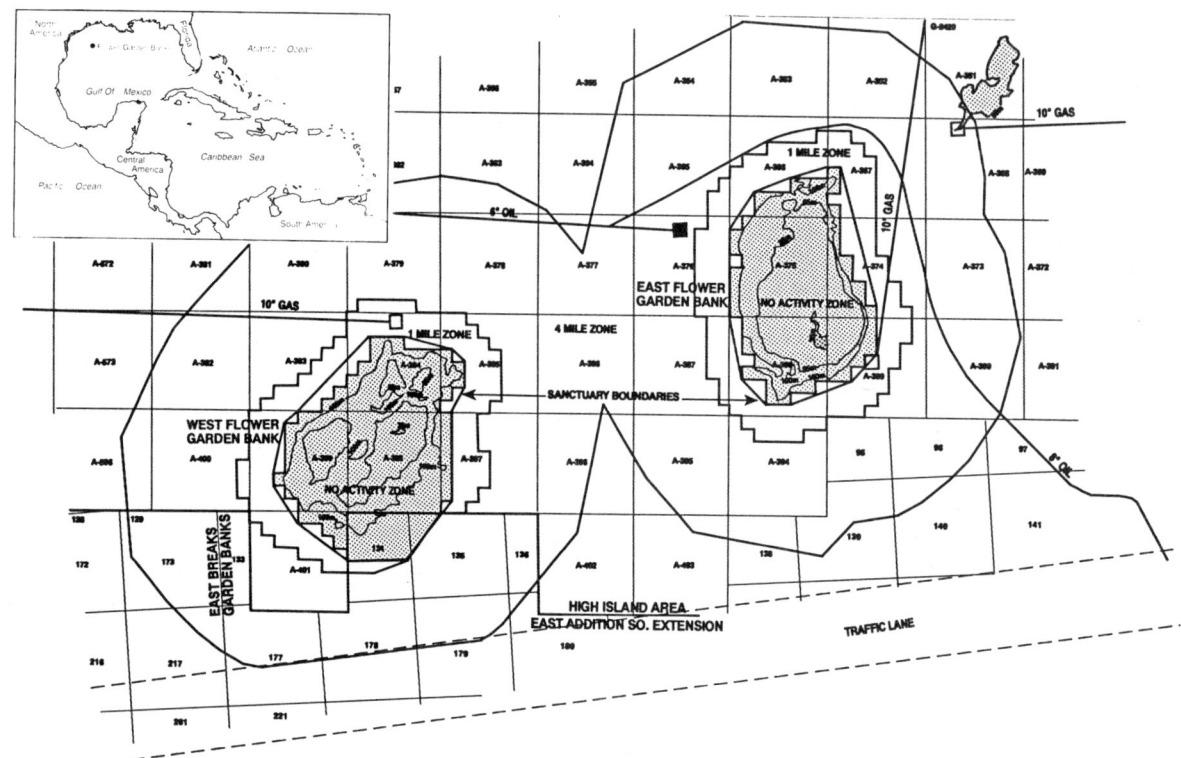

Figure 1. Location of the East and West Flower Garden Banks (inset), MMS regulatory zones, pipeline and platform locations, lease blocks, and Sanctuary boundaries.

use of the reefs, as well as occasional anchoring by large freighters and tankers went unregulated. An attempt was made in 1982 to restrict anchoring through the Coral Fishery Management Plan for the Gulf of Mexico. This failed, however, because it was determined that anchoring was not a fisheries issue. In 1986, a notation first appeared on navigation charts labeling the Flower Gardens a "Protected Area." No large vessel anchoring has been reported since this notation appeared. In 1990, volunteers from a number of environmental organizations installed 12 mooring buoys on the Flower Gardens, effectively deterring further damage by small vessel anchors.

In January 1992, the Flower Garden Banks National Marine Sanctuary was designated by the National Oceanic & Atmospheric Administration. Sanctuary regulations prohibit oil and gas development; anchoring in coral; possessing, collecting, injuring and altering Sanctuary resources; all types of fishing except hook-and-line; most types of discharges; possessing or using explosives; and releasing electrical discharges.

Monitoring

A wide range of human activities can be blamed for the many cases of coral reef demise worldwide (see Salvat, 1987). At the Flower Gardens, human-related threats to reefs include the continued presence of the oil and gas industry, high levels of large vessel traffic in the region (Rainey, 1991), and the expected increases in the levels of recreational use following the Sanctuary's designation (Tilmant, 1987). Thus, the primary objective of ecological and monitoring studies at the Flower Gardens has been to document the condition of the reefs, and the level of temporal variation in benthic communities.

Studies on coral populations and growth rates at the Flower Gardens began in 1972 with funding from BLM (e.g., Tresslar, 1974) and continued until 1980. BLM later required operators to fund reef monitoring studies during exploratory drilling near these ecologically sensitive communities. Funding for surveys in 1982, 1983, and 1988 was provided by industry; from 1988 to 1992, the MMS funded monitoring. These studies have allowed the development of a long-term database, and standardized data collection and analysis techniques.

METHODS

Coral growth rates and population levels have been measured on both banks using repetitive or random photography (Viada, 1980; Kraemer, 1982; Bright et al., 1984; Gittings et al., 1992) as well as direct measurements (Hudson and Robbin, 1980; Deslarzes, 1992; Gittings et al., 1992). Since 1980, stations for measuring encrusting growth of Montastrea annularis and Diploria strigosa have been established by implanting stainless steel nails 23 cm apart near colony borders allowing periodic photography of a repeatable 13.3 by 19.7 cm area (Kraemer, [1982] used 16 stations; Gittings et al., [1992] used 240 stations). Encrusting growth and retreat are determined by first projecting repetitively photographed margins in close-up photographs onto the same surface using an image enlarging/reducing map projector. Areas of growth and retreat, as well as border lengths over which the changes occurred, are measured by planimetry.

Long-term records of accretionary growth have been obtained from 16 colony cores at the Flower Gardens (Hudson and Robbin, 1980; Deslarzes, 1992). Accretionary growth rates from 1910 to 1989 have been determined by measuring the thickness of annual bands on X-radiographs of core slabs.

Visual estimates of percent cover on the WFG were made in 1972 by divers in 26, 10 m^2 circular quadrats (Tresslar, 1974). Since then, reef coral population parameters have been obtained using random transect photography (Bright et al., 1984; Gittings et al., 1992). Prior to 1988, percent cover data were acquired for all coral species using the line intercept method (Bright et al., 1984). Recent studies have used planimetric methods (Gittings et al., 1992). Other measurements include relative dominance (percent cover relative to total coral cover), species diversity (based on cover and on coral counts), and evenness (the apportionment of individuals among species) (Gittings et al., 1992). Spatial and temporal comparisons are made using analysis by variance techniques and multiple range tests.

Monitoring since 1988 has included the use of repetitive photography of 8 m^2 quadrats to detect and quantify short-term changes on the reefs (Gittings et al., 1992). Periodically, photographs are taken at 40 stations on each bank. Stations are marked by posts, and photographed from directly above the station center using a T-shaped camera frame equipped with a down-looking camera maintained at 2.0 m above the bottom (Gittings et al., 1992). Slides of each station are examined sequentially; the first slide is used as a template against which consecutive slides are compared. Incidences of growth and retreat (mortality) are enumerated, and the apparent cause of mortality noted (e.g., bleaching, disease).

RESULTS

Cover on the WFG Bank was estimated at 38 ± 7% (95% confidence interval) in 1972 (Tresslar, 1974). Data collected from 1978-1980 (Viada, 1980; Kraemer, 1982) and analyzed using the line intercept method suggested cover of 50.4 ± 5.3% and 55.2 ± 7.9% for the EFG and WFG, respectively. In neither case were cover data significantly different than those acquired in the 1988-1991 study (46.0 ± 2.2% on the EFG and 46.5 ± 2.0% on the WFG), nor were differences detected in measures of diversity and evenness. In addition, cover and relative dominance for individual species reported in the 1978-1980 period were close to those found in the 1989-1991 period (Fig. 2), though significant differences in relative dominance were found for two species on the EFG.

The accretionary growth rate of M. annularis, measured in cores from 1910 to 1989 averaged 6.6 mm/yr (range of 5.1 to 8.2). A decrease in growth rates, and a concurrent increase in year-to-year variability was evident between 1957 and 1980 (see also Hudson and Robbin, 1980). Annual growth rates (Fig. 3) since 1980 have been consistently near the mean growth rates prior to 1957 (Gittings et al., 1992).

Net encrusting growth rates along colony margins at the Flower Gardens averaged 3.0 mm/yr for M. annularis, and 2.0 mm/yr for D. strigosa. Net encrusting growth rates differed from data collected on Molasses reef in the Florida Keys, which exhibited growth rates of essentially zero on apparently healthy adult M. annularis colonies (Gittings et al., 1988). Encrusting growth of M. annularis at the Flower Gardens averaged 7.6 mm/yr and retreat averaged -8.6 mm/yr (Gittings et al., 1992). Respective rates for D. strigosa were 8.4 and -8.0. The rates of growth and retreat reported by Kraemer (1982) at the Flower Gardens did not differ significantly from the 1989-1991 estimates.

Measurements of cumulative areas of advance and retreat showed that for every square centimeter of D. strigosa tissue lost between 1989 and 1991, approximately 1.5 cm^2 grew. For every square centimeter of M. annularis lost, approximately 1.8 cm^2 grew. Data from 10 encrusting growth stations on Molasses Reef showed that for every 1.0 cm^2 of M. annularis lost between 1984 and 1986, 0.93 cm^2 grew (Gittings et al., 1988).

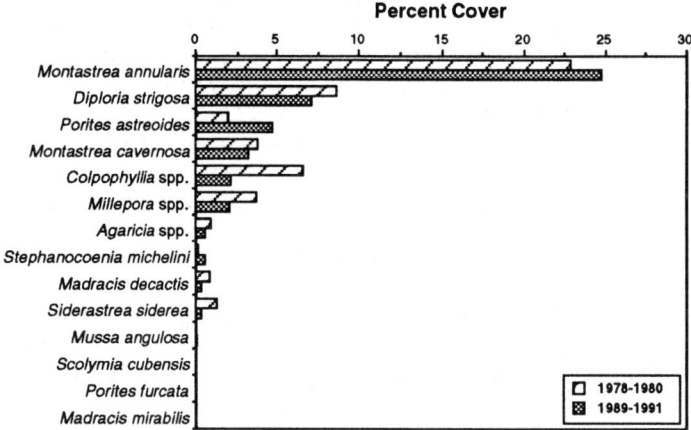

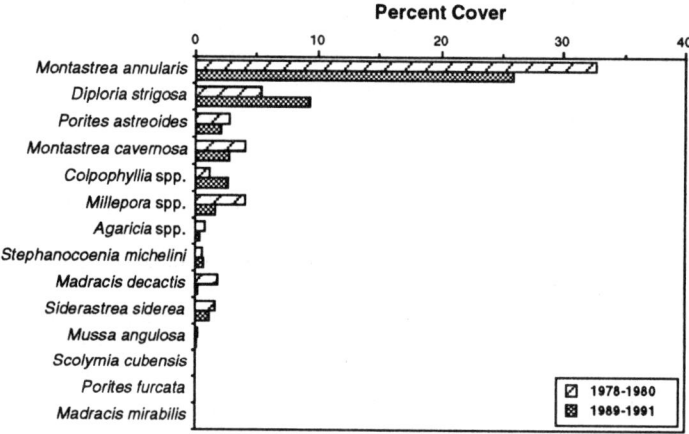

Figure 2. Comparison of percent cover of coral species at the East and West Flower Garden Banks between the 1978-1980 and 1989-1991 sampling periods. Data from 1978-1980 were taken from Viada (1980) and Kraemer (1982).

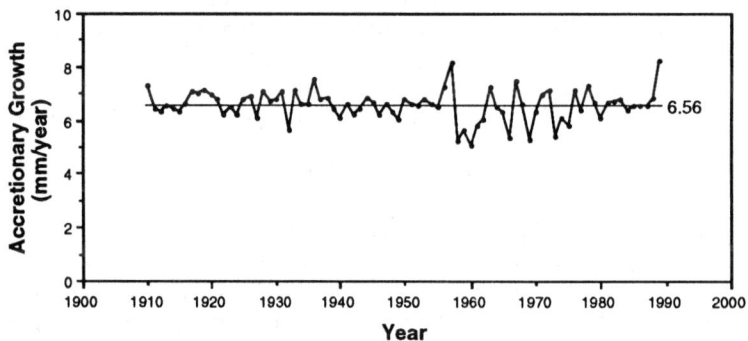

Figure 3. Accretionary growth (mm/yr) of four <u>Montastrea annularis</u> colonies estimated from 1910 to 1989 at the Flower Garden Banks. Growth was estimated from annual band areas measured on X-radiographs of sections from 10 cm diameter cores. Mean of all estimates was 6.56 mm/yr.

Coral growth was clearly identifiable at 8 m² repetitive stations, but was difficult to quantify because areas of growth were small relative to the large scale of the photographs (4,566 occurrences at all stations). Mortality was not as frequent and was generally minor; 2,657 observations of tissue loss were made, the majority of which were due to undetected causes. In a few instances however, tissue loss was extensive and in some cases entire colonies died; apparently as a result of infection by disease. For the most part, the infection rate was low. Less than 2% of corals analyzed over a three-year period at repetitive stations were infected. Approximately 69% of diseased coral colonies (46 of 67) exhibited some level of mortality. Coral bleaching, observed predominantly in the summer of 1990, occurred in nearly 5% of the coral colonies, but only 7% of these (14 colonies) exhibited measurable tissue loss (Hagman and Gittings, in press). Tissue loss was much more significant on diseased colonies than on bleached colonies.

DISCUSSION

Since coral population studies at the Flower Gardens began in 1972, no statistically significant changes in coral populations or growth rates have been documented. With the exception of the time period between 1957 and 1980, no upward or downward trends in accretionary growth have been seen during the 1900's. In addition, high levels of coral reproduction have been documented using artificial settlement plates (Baggett and Bright, 1985) and by annual observations of mass spawning of corals (Gittings et al., 1992). Data increasingly suggest that the Flower Gardens contain fully functional, healthy coral communities.

No substantial tissue mortality resulted from recent coral bleaching at the Flower Gardens. Temperature data obtained between 1989-1991 suggest a bleaching threshold temperature of nearly 30°C for the most sensitive coral species at the Flower Gardens. During the 1990 bleaching event, temperature at the WFG Bank peaked at 30.1°C and remained above 29.8°C for 92 hours (Hagman and Gittings, in press). Elsewhere, severe coral bleaching has been shown to cause substantial mortality (Glynn, 1984). Apparently, temperature excursions at the Flower Gardens have not been of sufficient intensity or duration to induce substantial mortality.

At present, diseases may be the most significant natural threat to corals on the Flower Garden Banks. The only substantial tissue mortality observed at repetitively photographed stations occurred as a result of "ridge-mortality" (Abbott, 1979) or other diseases. However, disease is not considered to be prevalent, since only 2% of colonies analyzed at repetitive stations appeared to be affected during the three year period between 1989 and 1991.

Coral disease incidence may increase with deteriorating environmental conditions (Antonius, 1981a). Unfortunately, rates of occurrence of disease and bleaching were not obtained in early surveys of reef corals at the Flower Gardens, making long-term comparisons impossible. Continued investigation of the frequency of disease and its effects will be an important component of long-term monitoring. In addition, research on identification of diseases at the Flower Gardens will be conducted so that the occurrence of exotic infestations might be detected. Neither "black band" nor "white band" diseases (Antonius, 1981b) have been documented at the Flower Gardens.

Natural changes that have been observed at the Flower Gardens include the mass mortality of black-spined sea urchins (<u>Diadema antillarum</u>), between 1983 and 1984, and subsequent increases in algae cover, which rose from very low levels to over 14% in less than a year (Gittings and Bright, 1987). Coral cover did not change. Algae cover diminished after 1985 and has remained relatively low. Video transect data collected between 1989 and 1991 suggested an increase in abundance of the herbivorous stoplight and queen parrotfishes (<u>Sparisoma viride</u> and <u>Scarus vetula</u>; Gittings et al., 1992) over 1980-1982 levels (Boland et al., 1983). This may have been a result of the abundance of algae following the sea urchin die-off and may explain the lack of continued high algae cover on the reefs.

CONCLUSION

Reef monitoring at the Flower Gardens has had a relatively long history, primarily as a response to the perceived threat of environmental degradation caused by offshore industrial development. Regulations and other protective measures imposed by the Federal Government have been, in part, similar responses. The level of effectiveness of protection is assumed to be measured by the amount of ecosystem change observed. On this basis, monitoring data suggest that strict regulation of vessel anchoring and industry operations near the Flower Gardens has effectively eliminated environmental impact to the reefs. But factors also contributing to the lack of reef deterioration include the isolation of the reefs by nearly 200 km from onshore and nearshore development, and the sheer volume of water masses separating the reefs from offshore production facilities.

While industrial activity in the region has declined recently, recreational use of the Flower Garden reefs is increasing rapidly. Roughly 2,000 divers visit the reefs each year on charter boats and personal crafts. An estimated 10,000 dives are made annually (Capt. Gary Rinn, pers. comm.). Monitoring studies need to consider additional environmental threats posed by humans. These include mechanical damage caused by boaters and divers, the effects of sewage and garbage discharges on the reefs, trash accumulations, and perhaps the effects of fish feeding and molestation (e.g. riding manta rays and turtles) on behavior patterns. While Sanctuary regulations address some of these concerns, increasing levels of use by humans are likely to pose unforeseen challenges in resource protection and management.

LITERATURE CITED

Abbott, R. E. 1979. Ecological processes affecting the reef coral population at the East Flower Garden Bank, northwest Gulf of Mexico. Ph.D. Dissertation, Dept. of Oceanography, Texas A&M Univ., College Station, TX. 154 pp.

Antonius, A. 1981a. Coral reef pathology: a review. Proc. 4th Int. Coral Reef Symp. (Manila) 2:3-6.

Antonius, A. 1981b. The "band" diseases in coral reefs. Proc. 4th Int. Coral Reef Symp. (Manila) 2:7-14.

Baggett, L. S. and T. J. Bright. 1985. Coral recruitment at the East Flower Garden Reef (northwestern Gulf of Mexico). Proc. 5th Int. Coral Reef Cong. 4:379-384.

Boland, G. S., B. J. Gallaway, J. S. Baker and G. S. Lewbel. 1983. Ecological effects of energy development on reef fish of the Flower Garden Banks. Final Report. National Marine Fisheries Service, Contract No. NA80-GA-C-00057. 466 pp.

Bright, T. J., G. P. Kraemer, G. A. Minnery and S. T. Viada. 1984. Hermatypes of the Flower Garden Banks, northwestern Gulf of Mexico: a comparison to other western Atlantic reefs. Bull. Mar. Sci. 34: 461-476.

Deslarzes, K. J. P. 1992. Long-term monitoring of reef corals at the Flower Garden Banks (northwest Gulf of Mexico): reef coral population changes and historical incorporation of barium in Montastrea annularis. Ph.D. Dissertation, Dept. of Oceanography, Texas A&M Univ., College Station, TX, 170 pp.

Gittings, S. R. and T. J. Bright. 1987. Mass mortality of Diadema antillarum at the Flower Garden banks, northwest Gulf of Mexico: effect on algae and coral cover. Benthic Ecology Meetings, Raleigh, North Carolina. (abstract)

Gittings, S. R., G. S. Boland, K. J. P. Deslarzes, C. L. Combs, B. S. Holland and T. J. Bright. 1992. Mass spawning and reproductive viability of reef corals at the East Flower Garden Bank, northwest Gulf of Mexico. Bull. Mar. Sci. 51(3):420-428.

Gittings, S. R., G. S. Boland, K. J. P. Deslarzes, D. K. Hagman and B. S. Holland. 1992. Long-term monitoring at the East and West Flower Garden Banks. OCS Study/MMS 92-006, U.S. Dept. of Interior, Minerals Management Service, Gulf of Mexico OCS Regional Office, New Orleans, LA, 206 pp.

Gittings, S. R., T. J. Bright, A. Choi and R. R. Barnett. 1988. The recovery process in a mechanically damaged coral reef community: recruitment and growth. Proc. 6th Int. Coral Reef Symp. 2: 225-230.

Glynn, P. W. 1984. Widespread coral mortality and the 1982/1983 El-Niño warming event. Env. Conserv. 11:133-146.

Hagman, D. K. and S. R. Gittings. (in press) Coral bleaching on high latitude reefs at the Flower Garden Banks, NW Gulf of Mexico. Proc. 7th Int. Coral Reef Symp.

Hudson, J. H. and D. M. Robbin. 1980. Effects of drilling mud on the growth rate of the reef-building coral, Montastrea annularis. Pages 455-470 in R. A. Geyer, ed. Marine environmental pollution, Vol. 1: Hydrocarbons. Elsevier, New York.

Kraemer, G. P. 1982. Population levels and growth rates of the scleractinian corals within the Diploria-Montastrea-Porites zones of the East and West Flower Garden Banks. MS Thesis, Texas A&M Univ., College Station, TX, 138 pp.

Rainey, G. 1991. The risk of oil spills from the transportation of petroleum in the Gulf of Mexico. Proc.: 11th Ann. Gulf of Mexico Information Transfer Meeting. U.S. Dept. of Interior, Minerals Management Service. MMS Contract No. 14-35 -0001-30499. OCS Study MMS 91-0040. pp. 298-317.

Rezak, R., T. J. Bright and D. W. McGrail. 1985. Reefs and banks of the northwestern Gulf of Mexico: their geological, biological, and physical dynamics. John Wiley and Sons, New York, 259 pp.

Rezak R., S. R. Gittings and T. J. Bright. 1990. Biotic assemblages and ecological controls on reefs and banks of the northwest Gulf of Mexico. Am. Zool. 30: 23-35.

Salvat, B. 1987. Human impacts on coral reefs: facts and recommendations. Antenne Museum E.P.H.E., French Polynesia, 253 pp.

Tilmant, J. T. 1987. Impacts of recreational activities on coral reefs. In: B. Salvat (ed.) Human impacts on coral reefs: facts and recommendations. Antenne Museum E.P.H.E., French Polynesia, pp 195-214.

Tresslar, R. C. 1974. Corals. Pages 116-139 In: T. J. Bright and L. H. Pequegnat (eds.) Biota of the West Flower Garden Bank. Gulf Publishing Co., Houston, 435 pp.

Viada, S. T. 1980. Species composition and population levels of scleractinian corals within the Diploria-Montastrea-Porites zone of the East Flower Garden Bank, northwest Gulf of Mexico. MS Thesis, Dept. of Oceanography, Texas A&M Univ., College Station, TX, 96 pp.

REEFS OF THE CARIBBEAN

	PAGES
Hurricane Hugo's Impact on Salt River Submarine Canyon, St. Croix, U.S. Virgin Islands *Richard B. Aronson, Kenneth P. Sebens, and John P. Ebersole*	189 - 195
The Impacts of Fishing on Coral Reefs *James A. Bohnsack*	196 - 200
Comparison of Biological and Geological Perspectives of Coral-Reef Community Structure at Buck Island, U.S. Virgin Islands *Dennis K. Hubbard, Elizabeth H. Gladfelter, and John C. Bythell*	201 - 207
Coral Reef Degradation: A Long-Term Study of Human and Natural Impacts *Terence P. Hughes*	208 - 213
Hurricanes and Anchors: Preliminary Results From the National Park Service Regional Reef Assessment Program *Caroline S. Rogers*	214 - 219
Is Herbivore Loss More Damaging to Reef Than Hurricanes? Case Studies From Two Caribbean Reef Systems (1978-1988) *Robert S. Steneck*	220 - 226
Structural Changes and Vulnerability of a Coral Reef (Cayo Enrique) in La Parguera, Puerto Rico *Vance P. Vicente, Ph.D.*	227 - 232

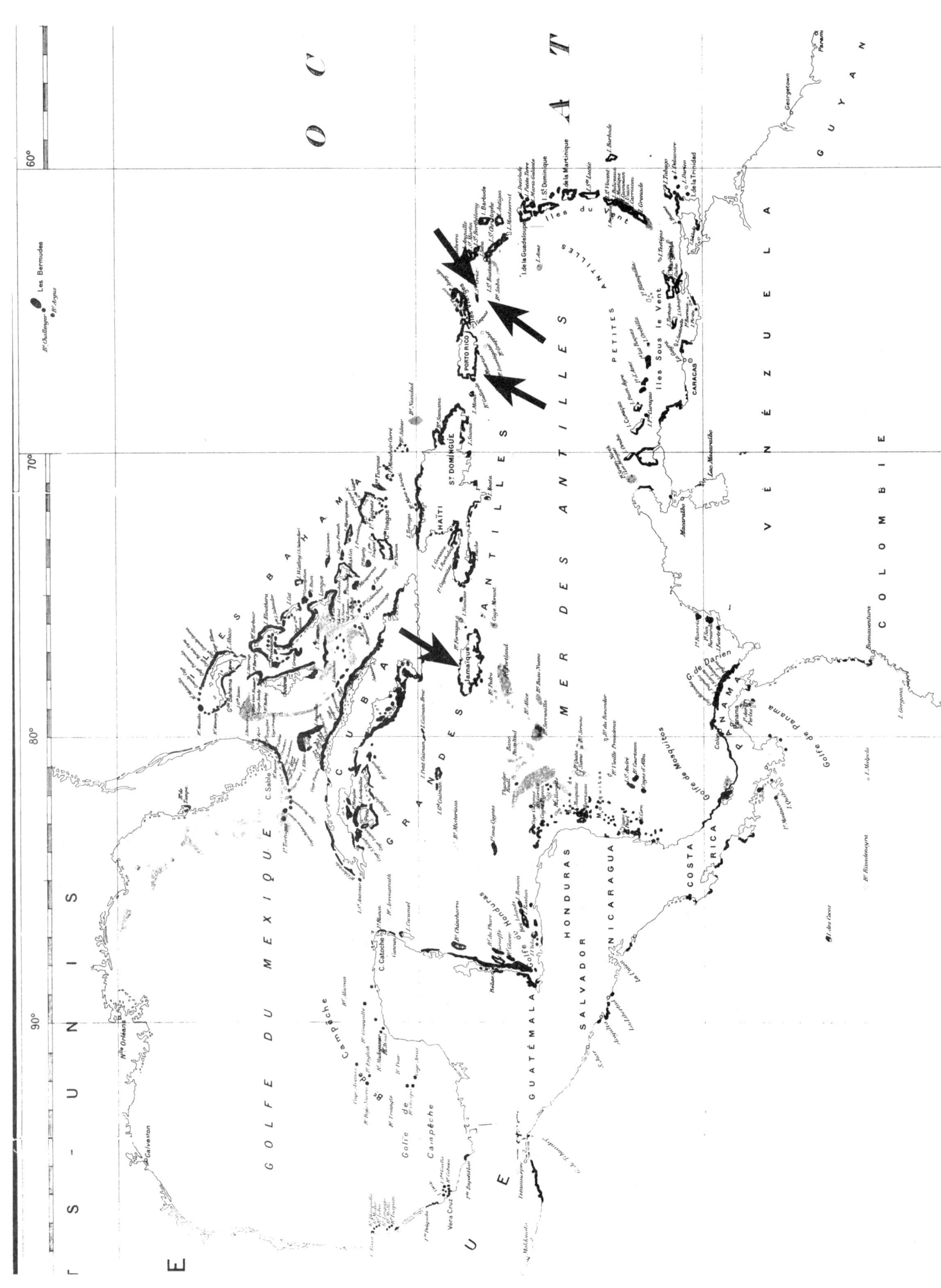

HURRICANE HUGO'S IMPACT ON SALT RIVER SUBMARINE CANYON, ST. CROIX, U.S. VIRGIN ISLANDS

Richard B. Aronson[1], Kenneth P. Sebens[2], and John P. Ebersole[3]

[1]Department of Invertebrate Zoology, National Museum of Natural History, Smithsonian Institution, Washington, DC 20560; and Institute of Marine and Coastal Sciences, Rutgers University, New Brunswick, New Jersey 08903. [2]Department of Zoology, University of Maryland, College Park, Maryland 20742. [3]Department of Biology, University of Massachusetts-Boston, Harbor Campus, Boston, Massachusetts 02125.

ABSTRACT

This study examined the effects of Hurricane Hugo (1989) on the biota of Salt River Canyon, St. Croix. Although fish assemblages were not drastically altered, there were some changes in species composition after Hurricane Hugo. These differences were related primarily to changes in sedimentary distribution during the storm. An order of magnitude decline in the abundance of echinoderms was also apparently related to sediment movement. Videotaped transects showed a decline in coral cover after the storm at six depths between 8 and 33 m. The greatest effect on a coral species population occurred at greater depths, where the fragile, foliaceous *Agaricia lamarcki* experienced considerable damage from strong oscillatory flows during Hurricane Hugo. It appears that the observed, hurricane-induced changes in fish, coral, and echinoderm assemblages can be directly related to physical processes.

INTRODUCTION

Large-scale disturbances provide opportunities to observe community responses over a range of habitats at multiple sites. Despite their fortuitous nature and inherent statistical difficulties, the generalizations derived from 'natural experiments' can be more robust than conclusions based on smaller-scale field and laboratory experiments (Diamond, 1986). Hurricanes have aroused considerable interest among coral reef ecologists since Connell (1978) suggested their role in maintaining the diversity of sessile reef biotas. That role, and the importance of other natural and anthropogenic perturbations, remain controversial (Jackson, 1991). How important hurricanes are to the balance between corals and benthic macroalgae, how hurricanes interact with mass mortalities of the sea urchin *Diadema antillarum*, and how these processes will affect community dynamics over the next several decades are pivotal questions in the ecology of Caribbean coral reefs (Hughes, 1989; Knowlton, in press).

In 1980, Hurricane Allen devastated the reef at Discovery Bay, Jamaica (Woodley et al., 1981). Eight years later, Hurricane Gilbert reset fore reef communities there to the conditions that prevailed immediately after Allen. Long-term studies at Discovery Bay and nearby sites (Knowlton et al., 1990; Hughes et al., 1987; Liddell and Ohlhorst, 1987; Precht, in press) have enhanced our knowledge of hurricane effects. However, the pre-Allen ecology of these Jamaican reefs may have been atypical. Hurricanes pass close to the north coast of Jamaica more frequently than once per decade on average, but none had affected Jamaica for several decades preceding Hurricane Allen (Kjerfve et al., 1986). Moreover, Discovery Bay is heavily fished, a condition that, along with the *Diadema* dieoff, has contributed to post-hurricane alterations (Hughes et al. 1987). Studies elsewhere in the Caribbean have shown moderate to severe hurricane effects (Rogers et al., 1991; Mah and Stearn, 1986; Edmunds and Witman, 1991; Fenner, 1991).

Similar physical destruction was noted on some reefs in St. Croix, U.S. Virgin Islands following Hurricane Hugo, but, as with Hurricane Allen, the severity of the impact varied from place to place (Woodley et al., 1981; Hubbard et al., 1991). The submarine canyon at Salt River, St. Croix (Figure 1) experienced currents up to 5 m • sec^{-1} and wave heights of at least 3.5 m during Hurricane Hugo (Hubbard et al., 1991). Hard substrata were scoured by an enormous quantity of sediment that was transported down Salt River Canyon and off the shelf. Yet post-storm visual assessments suggested that fore reef damage at Salt River Canyon, as elsewhere along the north shore of the island, was less severe than at south-facing sites, which received greater wave energy (Hubbard et al., 1991). The fortuitous existence of pre-Hugo data on the composition of demersal fish, sessile benthic, and echinoderm assemblages provided an opportunity to examine hurricane effects at a site where the biota initially appeared not to have been radically altered by the storm.

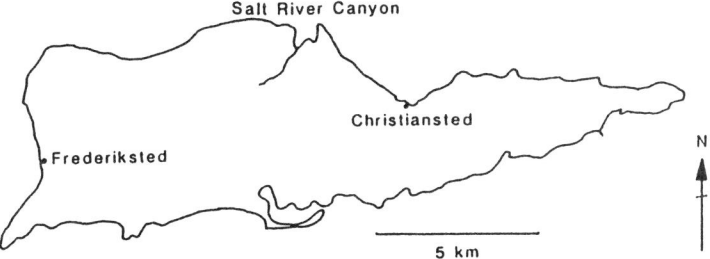

Figure 1. Map of St. Croix showing location of Salt River Canyon.

METHODS

Salt River Canyon

Hubbard (1989) described the geology of Salt River Canyon (64°45'N, 17°47'W). The sediment-covered Canyon floor runs roughly north-northwest from its shoreward boundary to its seaward opening on the north coast of St. Croix. The East Slope and the West Wall, which delimit Salt River Canyon, differ markedly in physical structure. Details of the Canyon environment are presented below as part of particular site descriptions (based on Hubbard (1989, 1992) and our own observations).

Fishes

Repeated counts of fish species were made on the East and West sides of Salt River Canyon before and after Hurricane Hugo. Both sites were at 15.2-18.3 m depth and ran horizontally for ≈ 50 m. Along the study site on the West Wall, the reef framework is steep--vertical in some places--and physically complex, with living and dead corals, buttresses, sand chutes, and many cavities and crevices. By contrast, the East Slope study area consists, over most of its length, of a gradually sloping limestone pavement, with lower coral cover and lower topographic complexity. The East Slope rises from the sand-covered Canyon floor at angles of 15-45°. At its seaward (northern) end, the East Slope site is covered in places by sediment flows, ending at the "Pinnacle Area", with foliose corals, high coral cover, and high physical complexity. Here the East Slope steepens and becomes similar to the West Wall in its microhabitat features. Before Hurricane Hugo, the study sites on both sides were in contact with the sandy floor of the Canyon over some portion of their length. However, large quantities of sediment were transported out of the Canyon during the hurricane, so that most of the West Wall site became separated from the sandy bottom by a 1-2 m vertical section of freshly exposed wall (Hubbard et al., 1991; Hubbard, 1992). Despite that net export, sediment was also imported from the shelf east of the Canyon, and some portions of the East Slope pavement were buried by sand.

Counts of fish species were made during 18-23 August 1989, one month before Hurricane Hugo, by four saturation divers working from NOAA's *Aquarius* undersea habitat. Fish species were counted by the same divers 38 days after the hurricane, during 26-30 October 1989, by three surface-based scuba divers. There were thus four sets of counts: (East and West Sides) X (Before and After Hugo). Ten counts of fish species were made on each side of the Canyon before the hurricane, and four counts were made on the West Wall and five counts on the East Slope after the hurricane. The counting method, described by Kaufman and Ebersole (1984), accumulates species over time until no new species are seen for 10 min.

Jaccard's Coefficient of Community (number of species shared/total number of species) was calculated for each pair of counts, and unweighted pair-group cluster analysis was performed on the matrix of similarity values. For further examination of how the hurricane affected species composition of the two fish assemblages, mean similarity for all possible pairwise combinations was calculated for four comparisons: East Before vs East After and West Before vs West After to determine which assemblage was affected more strongly by the hurricane, and East Before vs West Before and East After vs West After to determine whether the hurricane had reduced or enhanced the differences in species composition between the fish assemblages on the two sides of the Canyon. When all possible similarity values are computed, the same counts are included in several similarity values. To prevent problems of independence in statistical tests, subsets of similarity values with no counts in common were constructed by randomly drawing species counts from the four sets, without replacement.

Corals

Sebens and Johnson (1991) videotaped corals on the East Slope during an *Aquarius* saturation mission in August 1988, along six depth contours: 8, 12, 15, 21, 27, and 33 m, ± 1 m. One of us (RBA) videotaped those transects by surface-based scuba diving after Hurricane Hugo, in July 1990. The transects ran 100-150 m linear distance along the isobath.

The serendipitous nature of this study gave rise to a flaw in sampling design. Since the exact locations of the pre-hurricane transects were not marked, the post-hurricane transects could not be videotaped along identical tracks. Post-hurricane transects were situated within 2 m horizontal distance of the corresponding pre-hurricane transects. The only exception was at 15 m. At that depth, the post-hurricane transect covered a similar, adjacent area of reef. We therefore interpret our video results with caution, particularly the 15 m depth transects.

The transects were videotaped using a Sony V9 (8 mm) camcorder with video lights. A diver swam slowly above the reef along the depth contour, videotaping from a height of 30 cm above the reef surface. A 15 cm plastic ruler was attached to a metal rod that projected 30 cm forward from the camera housing. The ruler provided scale on the videotapes and standardized the distance from camera to reef substratum. This procedure produced clear stop-action frames that covered a width of 30-50 cm.

The videotapes were analyzed by playing them back on a monitor with ten random dots on a plastic screen overlay. The tapes were stopped blindly approximately every three seconds, and the identity of substratum occupants under each dot was recorded for that frame. Three seconds was long enough to assure that the tape had moved to a new, non-overlapping area of substratum. In this way, percent cover values for hard coral species (Scleractinia plus Milleporina) were calculated for hard substratum. Each transect was quantified by 1000-2000 random dots, of which half or fewer fell on living coral.

Echinoderms

One of us (RBA) censused echinoderms in a talus slope along the East Slope. The talus slope, which is shoreward (southeast) of the East Slope fish and video transect area described above, is composed of loose coral rubble covered with crustose coralline algae and algal turf. The echinoderms, which were almost exclusively ophiuroids, were sampled by swimming a randomly-determined number of fin kicks at 15 m depth, placing a 0.11 m^2 quadrat in the loose rubble habitat, turning over the cobbles, and identifying and counting the animals underneath. Ophiuroids down to a disk diameter of 5 mm were censused, and the ophiuroids and cobbles were placed back in their original positions. A pre-hurricane census (n=10 quadrats) was conducted in June 1989 during an *Aquarius* saturation mission. Eight post-hurricane censuses were conducted by surface-based scuba diving from November 1989 to September 1991 (n=25 in all cases).

RESULTS

Fishes

Before Hurricane Hugo, 129 fish species were counted in the Salt River Canyon study areas, and the two sides of the Canyon had roughly equal species richness (Table 1A). Asymptotic species accumulation curves (number of species *versus* time) indicate adequate sampling during the counts, and 79 of the 129 species were seen in at least half the censuses for one or both of the study sites. Species accumulation curves for counts after the hurricane are not qualitatively different from those for pre-hurricane counts. The variances in species richness are similar for all four sets of counts (Table 1A), obviating the need to test the homogeneity of variances. A two-way ANOVA, with Side and Hurricane as independent variables, shows that the hurricane had no effect on the average number of fish species per count in the Canyon as a whole (Table 1B). There is no statistically significant Before- vs After-hurricane difference in the number of species present on either side, although the average loss of more than six species per count on the West Wall, representing a reduction of nearly 10 %, is suspect at p=0.065. A significant Hurricane X Side interaction term in the ANOVA indicates that the loss of species on the West Wall does differ significantly from the gain on the East Slope (Table 1B).

Cluster analysis (Figure 2) indicates that differences between species counts are most strongly related to differences between Canyon sides, with the first branching of the dendrogram completely separating all East Slope counts from all West Wall counts. Later branchings indicate effects of the hurricane on species composition. The second major branching in the dendrogram separates all Before Hugo from After Hugo counts on the West Wall. Before and After counts on the East Slope also separate early in the dendrogram, but not as clearly, with one Before Hugo count clustering with the After Hugo group.

The earlier and more complete separation between Before and After Hugo counts on the West Wall suggests that the hurricane had more impact on species composition on the West Wall than on the East Slope. Direct comparison of Before and After similarity values for the two sides bears this out: the mean Coefficient of Community for the 50 possible East Slope Before vs After comparisons (0.605 ± 0.048 SD) is greater than that for the 40 possible Before vs After comparisons for the West Wall (0.529 ± 0.094 SD).

Table 1. Summary of fish data for Salt River Canyon. A. Mean number of fish species per count ± standard deviation, and (in parentheses) number of counts for East Slope and West Wall, Before and After Hurricane Hugo. B. ANOVA table with orthogonal contrasts for number of fish species per census.

A.	East Before	East After	West Before	West After
	62.7 ± 5.19 (10)	67.0 ± 5.96 (5)	62.9 ± 5.70 (10)	56.5 ± 5.45 (4)

B. Source of variation	df	SS	MS	F	p
Main Effects	3	73.845	36.923	1.172	0.326
Hurricane	1	72.188	72.188	2.292	0.143
Side	1	2.967	2.967	0.094	0.765
Hurricane X Side	1	172.862	172.862	5.488	0.027
Residual (Error)	25	787.500	31.500		
Total	28	1034.207			
A priori tests among means					
West Before vs After	1	117.029	117.029	3.715	0.065
East Before vs After	1	61.633	61.633	1.950	0.174

A two-tailed t-test of randomly-selected independent subsets (5 similarity values for East Slope, 4 similarity values for West Wall; no counts in common) indicates a significantly greater difference between Before and After counts on the West Wall than on the East Slope ($t_s=2.412$, df=7, p=0.047).

Comparing similarity values between counts indicates that Hurricane Hugo reduced the difference between sides in the species composition of fish assemblages. The mean Coefficient of Community for the 100 possible East vs West comparisons before the hurricane (0.524 ± 0.047 SD) is less than that for the 40 possible East vs West comparisons after the hurricane (0.575 ± 0.040 SD), but a t-test of randomly-selected independent subsets (no counts in common) falls just short of significance ($t_s=2.106$, df=12, two-tailed p=0.067), perhaps due to the small number of counts on the West Wall after the hurricane.

Examination of Before and After species lists for the two study sites reveals great changes in the occurrence of species associated with sandy substrata, while species associated with consolidated substrata exhibited only minor changes. These changes are associated with the most striking physical change in Salt River Canyon caused by Hurricane Hugo: sediment export and import, which raised the West Wall site from the sandy floor of the Canyon and increased the amount of sand substratum at the East Slope. The changes in species occurrence help account for the respective relative gains and losses in species richness on the East and West sides of the Canyon. However, they cannot account for the increased similarity between sides following the hurricane; rather, the sedimentary changes should have enhanced the differences between sides.

A second trend is a drastic post-hurricane decline of all cardinalfish (Apogonidae) on the West Wall. These nocturnal planktivores had been very common on the West Wall and relatively rare on the East Slope prior to Hurricane Hugo. It is not obvious why apogonids should have been so heavily reduced on the West Wall, but that reduction helps explain both the relative loss of species on the West Wall, and the slight reduction of differences between the East and West sides after Hurricane Hugo.

Corals

The video transects before and after Hurricane Hugo show substantial and significant declines in total coral cover at each depth: the 95 % confidence intervals about the before and after percent cover values do not overlap for any depth (Figure 3). For individual species, there were some changes after the hurricane, although few of these were dramatic.

At the shallowest depth, 8 m, coral species richness dropped from 14 before to 7 after Hurricane Hugo. The most common coral, *Montastrea cavernosa*, occupied 11.5 percent cover before but only 7.0 percent cover after. The second most common species was *Diploria strigosa*, at 8.8 percent cover before and 2.0 percent cover after. All but one of the other coral species declined in abundance. At 12 m depth, there were 14 species in the transect before the hurricane and 12 after. The same two species were the most abundant, with *M. cavernosa* at 7.3 percent cover before and 3.7 after, and *D. strigosa* at 2.9 percent cover before and 2.2 after. All but three of the other species declined.

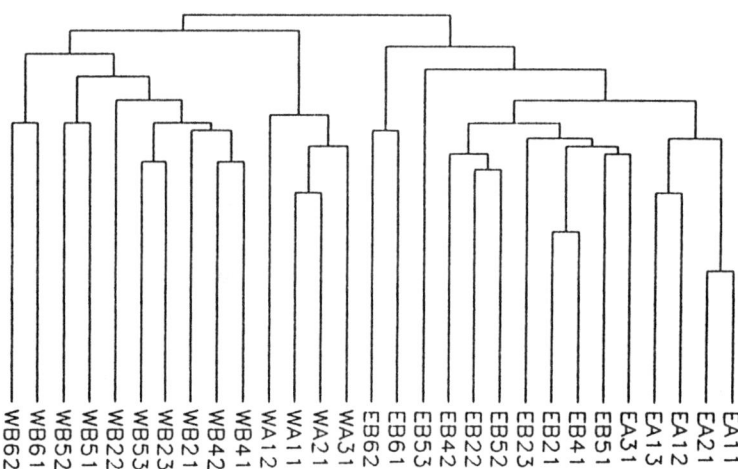

Figure 2. Dendrogram from cluster analysis of fish species counts. EB = East Slope before Hurricane Hugo, EA = East Slope after, WB = West Wall before, WA = West Wall after.

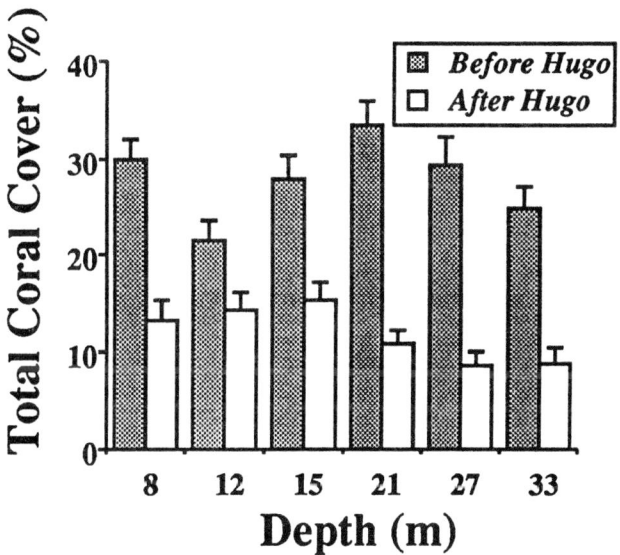

Figure 3. Percent cover of hard corals (Scleractinia plus Milleporina) before and after Hurricane Hugo. Error bars represent 95 % confidence intervals.

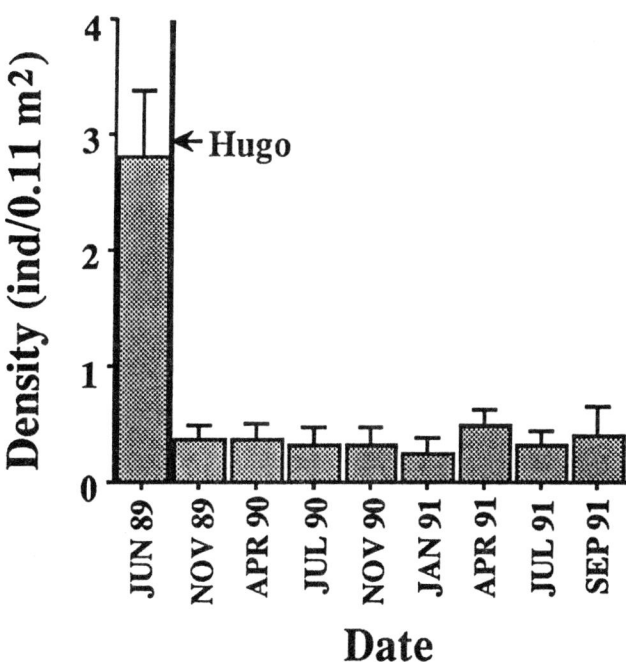

Figure 4. Ophiuroid abundance in the talus slope before and after Hurricane Hugo. Error bars represent standard errors.

At 15 m depth, all but one of the 14 species present before the hurricane declined. At 21 m depth, *Agaricia lamarcki* and *A. agaricites* were the most common corals. The former declined from 15.7 to 4.9 and the latter from 6.1 to 0.94 percent cover. *Montastrea annularis* decreased from 3.8 to 0.1 percent cover, and all other species either remained similar or declined after the storm. At 27 m depth, *A. lamarcki* was the only common coral prior to Hurricane Hugo, at 23.6 percent cover. This species declined to 7.1 percent cover after. The 7 other species present before the storm declined. At 34 m depth, *A. lamarcki* declined from 21.9 to 8.3 percent cover. Five other species declined, and *A. agaricites* increased from 0.1 to 0.4 percent cover.

Echinoderms

Echinoderms were the most abundant mobile benthic invertebrates under the rubble comprising the talus slope, and ophiuroids comprised 98 % of the 99 echinoderms counted. The remaining two individuals were regular echinoids, which appeared in post-hurricane censuses. Total ophiuroid density declined by approximately 90 % in Salt River Canyon after Hurricane Hugo (Figure 4), and ophiuroid populations did not recover during the two years of post-hurricane monitoring (ANOVA on log-transformed quadrat counts, $p < 0.0005$). Observations of sediment movement explain the ophiuroid decline on the East Slope. In the talus habitat, imported sediment filled in most of the interstices of the rubble, excluding the ophiuroids. Those holes and crevices remained filled for the two years over which the post-hurricane censuses were conducted.

DISCUSSION

At the three shallower depths along the East Slope, almost all coral species declined in percent cover after Hurricane Hugo, although none of the changes was of great magnitude. Because the post-hurricane transects were not in exactly the same positions as the pre-hurricane ones, differences were expected on that basis alone. However, the observed differences are large enough and the direction of change is consistent enough among coral species and depths to suggest a hurricane effect on the coral assemblage. The largest overall change occurred at 8 m depth, where species richness was halved and where the common species showed substantial reductions in percent cover. On the deeper reef, the one common species was severely affected. The large plating coral *Agaricia lamarcki* declined drastically at all depths below 15 m. The deep zones of the East Slope are normally exposed to very slow, unidirectional currents, on the order of ≤ 5 cm·sec^{-1} (Sebens and Johnson, 1991), but they must have received strong oscillatory flows during the hurricane. It is likely that the large, fragile plates of *A. lamarcki* broke at that time.

Ophiuroids experienced an order of magnitude decline in abundance in the talus slope. Movement of sediment out of the talus slope presumably will permit ophiuroid immigration and recruitment. Likewise, many of the fish species most affected by the storm are closely associated with the sandy substratum that was so profoundly altered. The link between the observed changes in fish and ophiuroid assemblages and the impact of Hurricane Hugo on the physical environment reinforces earlier work on the importance of habitat structure (Kaufman and Ebersole, 1984; Moran and Reaka-Kudla, 1991).

Unlike Hurricane Allen's impacts in Jamaica, there is no evidence for great structural alteration or mass mortality of corals, with the exception of *Agaricia lamarcki*. Hughes and Jackson (1985) measured a maximum net recovery rate of 1 % growth in area per year for *A. lamarcki* in Jamaica. Applying this estimate to the drop in *A. lamarcki* cover observed in Salt River Canyon, complete regeneration of this population could take longer than 100 yr. Reversal of the hurricane-generated changes in fish assemblages are likely to depend on the reaccumulation of 2×10^6 kg of sediment in the Canyon and the redistribution of sediment away from the East Slope. Barring another major storm, the reaccumulation process could also take as long as 100 yr (Hubbard, 1992).

CONCLUSION

Hurricane Hugo caused changes in the fish, coral, and ophiuroid assemblages of Salt River Canyon. Despite the initial, qualitative impression that the storm had only minor effects on the biota, some large changes occurred. Those changes were attributable to sediment movement (fish and ophiuroids) and water movement (corals) during Hugo. We do not yet know how typical our results are of sites experiencing "non-catastrophic" levels of hurricane damage.

ACKNOWLEDGEMENTS

This research was funded by the NOAA National Undersea Research Program and the Smithsonian Institution Scholarly Studies Program. We thank J. Beets, W. Cleveland, A. Friedlander, L. Kaufman, T. Maney, H. Martel, C. McIvor, S. Rhoades, and J. Woodley for assistance with the field work. L. Savina and A. Johnson helped analyze the videotapes. We are grateful to S. Miller and the *Aquarius* operations staff for logistical support on St. Croix during the chaotic months following Hurricane Hugo.

LITERATURE CITED

Connell, J. H. 1978. Diversity in tropical rain forests and coral reefs. Science 199: 1302-1310.

Diamond, J. 1986. Overview: laboratory experiments, field experiments, and natural experiments. Pages 3-12 *in* J. Diamond and T. J. Case, eds. Community ecology, Harper and Row.

Edmunds, P. J. and J. D. Witman. 1991. Effects of Hurricane Hugo on the primary framework of reefs along the south shore of St. John, U. S. Virgin Islands. Mar. Ecol. Prog. Ser. 78: 201-204.

Fenner, D. P. 1991. Effects of Hurricane Gilbert on coral reefs, fishes and sponges at Cozumel, Mexico. Bull. Mar. Sci. 48: 719-730.

Hubbard, D. K. 1989. Depositional environments of Salt River estuary and submarine canyon, St. Croix, U.S.V.I. Pages 181-196 *in* D. K. Hubbard, ed. Terrestrial and marine geology of St. Croix, U.S. Virgin Islands. West Indies Laboratory Spec. Pub. 8, St. Croix, United States Virgin Islands.

Hubbard, D. K. 1992. Hurricane-induced sediment transport in open shelf tropical systems--an example from St. Croix, U. S. Virgin Islands. J. Sedim. Petrol. 62: 946-960.

Hubbard, D. K., K. M. Parsons, J. C. Bythell and N. D. Walker. 1991. The effects of Hurricane Hugo on the reefs and associated environments of St. Croix, U. S. Virgin Islands--a preliminary assessment. J. Coast. Res. Spec. Issue 8: 33-48.

Hughes, T. P. 1989. Community structure and diversity of coral reefs: the role of history. Ecology 70: 275-279.

Hughes, T. P. and J. B. C. Jackson. 1985. Population dynamics and life histories of foliaceous corals. Ecol. Monogr. 55: 141-166.

Hughes, T. P., D. C. Reed and M.-J. Boyle. 1987. Herbivory on coral reefs: community structure following mass mortalities of sea urchins. J. Exp. Mar. Biol. Ecol. 113: 39-59.

Jackson, J. B. C. 1991. Adaptation and diversity of reef corals. BioScience 41: 475-482.

Kaufman, L. S. and J. P. Ebersole. 1984. Microtopography and the organization of two assemblages of coral reef fishes in the West Indies. J. Exp. Mar. Biol. Ecol. 78: 253-268.

Kjerfve, B., K. E. Magill, J. W. Porter and J. D. Woodley. 1986. Hindcasting of hurricane characteristics and observed storm damage on a fringing reef, Jamaica, West Indies. J. Mar. Res. 44: 119-148.

Knowlton, N. In press. Thresholds and multiple stable states in coral reef community dynamics. Am. Zool.

Knowlton, N., J. C. Lang and B. D. Keller. 1990. Case study of natural population collapse: post-hurricane predation on Jamaican staghorn corals. Smithsonian Contrib. Mar. Sci. 31: 1-25.

Liddell, W. D. and S. L. Ohlhorst. 1987. Patterns of reef community structure, north Jamaica. Bull. Mar. Sci. 40: 311-329.

Mah, A.J. and C. W. Stearn. 1986. The effect of Hurricane Allen on the Bellairs fringing reef, Barbados. Coral Reefs 4: 169-176.

Moran, D.P. and M. L. Reaka-Kudla. 1991. Effects of disturbance: disruption and enhancement of coral reef cryptofaunal populations by hurricanes. Coral Reefs 9: 215-224.

Precht, W. F. In press. Variations in sediment and biofacies distribution patterns (1978-1990), west Discovery Bay, Jamaica. Bull. Mar. Sci.

Rogers, C. S., L. N. McLain and C. R. Tobias. 1991. Effects of Hurricane Hugo (1989) on a coral reef in St. John, USVI. Mar. Ecol. Prog. Ser. 78: 189-199.

Sebens, K. P. and A. S. Johnson. 1991. Effects of water movement on prey capture and distribution of reef corals. Hydrobiologia 226: 91-101.

Woodley, J. D. and 19 others. 1981. Hurricane Allen's impact on Jamaican coral reefs. Science 214: 749-755.

THE IMPACTS OF FISHING ON CORAL REEFS

James A. Bohnsack

National Marine Fisheries Service, Southeast Fisheries Science Center,
Miami Laboratory, 75 Virginia Beach Dr., Miami, FL 33149

ABSTRACT

Fishing is a widespread activity that can damage habitat, remove organisms, and indirectly alter community balance on coral reefs. Fishing has significantly reduced populations of some reef species, particularly larger species which are often top predators. Reef organisms tend to be vulnerable to overfishing because of life history characteristics that are not adapted to high adult mortality associated with fishing. Reduced fish populations can indirectly impact coral reefs particularly by changing patterns of predation and herbivory which are important structuring forces in coral reef ecosystems. Indirect effects of fishing have received little scientific investigation although some evidence exists supporting their importance. Marine fishery reserves, areas protected from all fishing activities, offer opportunities to better understand the impacts of fishing on coral reef health and function by serving as experimental controls.

INTRODUCTION

The purpose of this paper is to review the potential of fishing as significant factor capable of influencing coral reef ecology. Reef fisheries include fishes, invertebrates, and turtles where they are not protected. Many of the targeted species are major components of reefs in terms of biomass and function. The influence of fishing on reef systems has not been well documented, appreciated, nor understood. I review what is and is not known about the impacts of fishing on reefs and suggest approaches for gaining a better understanding.

METHODS

I reviewed available literature concerning reef fisheries and ecology to identify general patterns and deficiencies in knowledge. Emphasis was on the Caribbean region, although examples were drawn from other areas where appropriate. Examples are representative but not exhaustive because of space limitations.

RESULTS

Fishing directly and indirectly impacts coral reefs (Russ, 1991). Direct impacts include the removal of organisms and habitat damage from destructive fishing practices. Use of dynamite, chemicals, and bottom trawls, for example, can directly damage reefs. Indirect impacts can result from the removal of important components of the ecosystem, such as predators and herbivores, which could disrupt ecological relationships. The balance of competition for space between corals, sponges, and algae, for example, could be indirectly shifted by a changes in densities of herbivores and grazers due to fishing.

Reef fishing occurs worldwide and is perhaps the single most pervasive direct human activity affecting coral reefs (Grigg and Dollar, 1990). Even remote areas receive periodic fishing visits that can have lasting impacts. Unfortunately, few reef fisheries data exist from most areas of the world for documenting direct changes in fish assemblages, let alone documenting indirect effects on corals and reefs. Indirect changes are often subtle, difficult to document, and impossible to measure over small scales of space and time.

Fishing can change species composition, reduce population abundance, and lower average fish size and age structure. Population declines have been dramatic in many instances, although often long-term data are not available from which to document historical changes (Munro and Williams 1985; Russ, 1991). Populations of sea turtles, once a common reef inhabitants, have declined to a point that they are now considered threatened or endangered over much of the world. In the Caribbean, declines in the abundance of Nassau grouper (Epinephelus striatus) and jewfish (Epinephelus itajara) have led to their protection in some areas. Significant differences in fish composition have been shown between reefs under different levels of exploitation in Jamaica (Munro, 1983; Koslow et al. 1988), in Florida, U.S.A. (Bohnsack, 1982), and elsewhere (Alcala and Russ, 1990). In Bermuda, grouper (Serranidae) disappeared between 1975 and 1981 due to commercial fishing (Bannerot, et al., 1987). Reef fish landings declined in Puerto Rico from a high of 2.5×10^6 kg in 1979 to 0.8×10^6 kg by 1988 (Appeldoorn et al., 1992). Nassau grouper, once the major targeted species, has effectively disappeared. Total Gulf of Mexico landings of red snapper (Lutjanus campechanus) traditionally the most important reef species, declined from 7.7×10^6 kg in 1981 to 1.9×10^6 kg in 1990 due to a combination of directed exploitation and bycatch mortality of juveniles caught in shrimp trawls (Goodyear, 1992). Similar declines have been reported for reef fishes from reefs around the world (Munro and Williams, 1985). In Hawaii, for example, nearshore fishery resources declined approximately 85% since the turn of the century (Shomura, 1987). Preliminary results from long-term research suggests that overfishing was the most significant factor causing this decline (Grigg, 1992).

Fishing tends to selectively remove larger organisms because of their greater value for food, income, and sport. Thus, average size often declines before total numbers of fish as has been shown for commercial fisheries in Bermuda (Bannerot, et al., 1987), Australian recreational charterboats (Craik, 1981), and for recreational party boats in the southeastern U.S. (Huntsman and Willis, 1989; Huntsman, 1992).

Even when fishery landings are sustained, dramatic population changes are possible. Florida spiny lobster (Panulirus argus) landings, for example, have been stable since the 1960's despite an almost total annual removal of the reproductive stock (Davis, 1977; Harper, 1991). The stock is probably maintained by larvae arriving from upstream sources. However, no information exists about what impacts, if any, the removal of such an abundant and major organism has on reef ecology. The reduced presence of large lobster could have significant impacts on their prey and predators. Presumably lobster are important predators on mollusks and an important food resources for other species such as jewfish and nurse sharks (Ginglymostoma cirratum).

Reef organisms are considered vulnerable to overfishing because of their behavior and life history characteristics (U.S. Department of Commerce, 1990; Russ, 1991). Many fishes are naturally curious, unwary, or aggressive which makes them vulnerable. Grouper, a favored target of fishermen, will readily approach spearfishermen, enter traps, and aggressively take bait. Many species are easily exploited because reefs are geographically limited and fish occurrence is highly predictable in space and time. The life history characteristics of reef organisms include long life, slow growth, low natural mortality, delayed reproduction, multiple reproductions, sex changes, and large body size. These are considered adaptations for conditions where adult mortality is low and recruitment is uncertain because offspring have low survival probability. Long life with many reproductive events, for example, increases the chances that sufficient offspring will be produced and survive to replace adults in the next generation. Fishing could greatly decrease reproductive output by reducing the average life span and individual fecundity. Overfishing can reduce total fecundity or abundance to a point where a population may not produce enough offspring to replace adults.

Many harvested reef organisms have important ecological functions, such as the transfer energy and nutrients in the reef food web. Although most reef fishes are carnivores, herbivorous fishes, particularly surgeonfishes (Acanthuridae) and parrotfishes (Scaridae), can be locally important (Goldman and Talbot 1976). Herbivorous grazing can open settlement sites for coral larvae. Meyer, et al. (1983) showed that fishes can influence coral growth by transferring nutrients to reefs from surrounding forage areas. While some species attack corals, others benefit corals by feeding on coral predators (mollusks, polychaetes, other fishes) and competitors (sponges and algae)(Glynn, 1990). Fishes are also major planktivores forming a "wall of mouths" on many reefs (Hamner, et al., 1988). These species are sources of larval predation and nutrient acquisition.

Predation and herbivory are important structural forces on coral reefs (Ogden and Lobel, 1978; Hay, 1981, 1984; Lewis and Wainwright, 1985; Lewis, 1986; Glynn, 1990; Hixon and Beets, 1993). Fishing could potentially disrupt natural ecosystem function by changing relationships competitors and between predators and prey, particularly by the removal of larger top predators that act as keystone species. Keystone species are well documented in marine systems (Paine, 1966). Sea otters, for example, promote kelp forests on the west coast of North America by controlling sea urchin grazing (Estes and Palmisano, 1974; Palmisano and Estes, 1976; Estes et al., 1982). Interestingly, the importance of sea otters to the ecosystem was recognized after populations recovered from hunting (Dayton, 1975; Simenstad et al., 1978). Goeden (1982) noted that piscivorous fishes could be keystone species in coral reefs. Several studies have shown indirect changes in reef communities related to fishing. Hay (1984) suggested that patterns of increased sea urchin density and grazing in the Caribbean may be artifacts of fishing. McClanahan and Muthiga (1988) correlated differences in coral cover with sea urchin densities and sizes and fisheries exploitation from Kenya. McClanahan and Shafir (1989) concluded that "removal of top invertebrate-eating carnivores appears to have cascading effects on the entire coral reef ecosystem." Knowlton, et al. (1990) reported that predation from a snail (Coralliophila), a polychaete (Hermodice), and damselfish (Pomacentrus) prevented the recovery of staghorn corals (Acropora), after a hurricane on reefs in Jamaica. They also developed a threshold model showing how predation on corals prevents recovery. Fishing potentially could have aggravated coral mortality by reducing the natural predators for these species. Although the precise role of fishing in these events is unknown, Jamaica is considered to be intensively exploited (Munro, 1983; Koslow et al. 1988). Knowlton (1992) modeled mechanisms in which various levels of human exploitation could influence fish and urchin populations and lead to multiple stable states of coral reef existence.

DISCUSSION

Although the direct impacts of fishing on reef organisms has been documented and acknowledged from a fisheries perspective, the ecological consequences and indirect effects on the ecosystem have not been well studied. Many potential mechanisms have been suggested to explain how fishing could affect coral reefs. However, empirical evidence and testing are limited. Most evidence showing indirect effects is at best anecdotal, although some correlations and experimental evidence suggests that changes in levels of predation and herbivory are likely to be important.

I suggest seven reasons for a lack of progress. (1) Clearly, there is a lack of long term data showing changes in fishing effort, harvest, and ecosystem dynamics. (2) Researchers tend to focus on traditional disciplines (e.g. fisheries, coral biology, geology, ichthyology, taxonomy) resulting in a lack of multidisciplinary approaches to reef problems. Too often coral researchers ignore fishes and fishery workers ignore other taxa (Sale, 1991) which hinders scientific progress. (3) Coral research tends to concentrate on proximate problems while ignoring ultimate causes. For example, coral mortality from predation and algal competition may be mediated by fishes and fishing. (4) The importance of predation has often been ignored or dismissed. For example, Knowlton, et al. (1990) noted a general dismissal of predation as being important in Caribbean reefs. Often fishing effects are ignored because fishing can not be measured and controlled (see Hay, 1984). Also, some scientists deliberately avoid working on species targeted by fisheries because of the human interference. (5) Fishing effects are often directly confounded with other human activities (Goeden, 1982) which makes distinguishing the importance of fishing difficult. Examples of confounding factors include proximity to coastal development, pollution, sedimentation, diver impacts, and habitat loss and degradation. (6) Relatively few experimental studies exist. This is partly because of the complexity of the problems and potential interactions. (7) Lastly, there has been a lack of opportunity to study fishing effects because of a lack of valid scientific controls sites. It is essential to be able to compare fished and unfished areas.

Our understanding of fishing and its ecological effects on reefs is growing rapidly. Probably one of the most important and exciting scientific developments is the increased establishment of marine protected areas. Marine fishery reserves, areas with no fishing, offer the best chance to have scientifically valid controls in which the system can operate with minimal fishing interference (McClanahan and Muthiga, 1988; McClanahan and Shafir, 1989; Ballantine 1991). Because fishes can achieve a more natural level of abundance and size structure in reserves, we can differentiate effects of fishing from other human activities. For example, if harvested species are more abundant and coral health better in reserves than in adjacent fished areas, then fishing is the likely ultimate cause of the difference, rather than pollution, habitat loss, or other human activity. If fishes influence corals and reef function, then the reef performance will differ between reserves and other areas. Factors like air and water pollution are more likely to affect all areas.

CONCLUSIONS

Fishing is potentially a major direct and indirect structuring force on modern coral reefs. Much of the research on ecological mechanisms on corals reef has ignored the potential impact of fishing. Many studies of "natural processes" may have produced results that are artifacts of exploitation. Although it is premature to conclude what role fishing has had in reported declines of coral reefs on either a local (e.g. Porter and Meier, 1992) or global scale, considerable circumstantial evidence exists that excessive fisheries exploiation can be a problem. Further investigation is badly needed. Marine reserves offer a means to distinguish effects of fishing from other factors impacting coral reef ecology. The increased use of marine reserves around the world offers a unique scientific opportunity to learn basic and applied knowledge about coral reef systems.

LITERATURE CITED

Alcala, A.C. and G.R. Russ. 1990. A direct test of the effects of protective management on abundance and yield of tropical marine resources. J. Cons., Cons. Int. Explor. Mer. 46: 40-47.

Appeldoorn, R., J. Beets, J. Bohnsack, S. Bolden, D. Matos, S. Meyers, A. Rosario, Y. Sadovy, and W. Tobias. 1992. Shallow water reef fish stock assessment for the U.S. Caribbean. NOAA Technical Memorandum NMFS-SEFSC-304, 70 p.

Ballantine, B. 1991. Marine reserves for New Zealand. University of Auckland, Leigh Laboratory Bulletin No. 25: 1-196.

Bannerot, S.P., W.W. Fox, Jr., and J.E. Powers. 1987. Reproductive strategies and the management of snappers and groupers in the Gulf of Mexico and Caribbean. Pages 561-603 in J.J. Polovina and S. Ralson, (eds). Tropical snappers and groupers: Biology and fisheries management. Westview Press. Boulder, Colorado. 659 p.

Bohnsack, J.A. 1982. The effects of piscivorous predator removal on coral reef fish community structure. <u>1981 Gutshop: Third Pacific Technical Workshop Fish Food Habits Studies</u>. Washington Sea Grant Publication. pp 258-267.

Craik, G.J.S. 1981. Recreational fishing on the Great Barrier Reef. Proceedings of the Fourth International Coral Reef Symposium, Manila, Vol. I: 47-52.

Davis, G.E. 1977. Effects of recreational harvest on a spiny lobster, <u>Panulirus argus</u>, population. Bull. Mar. Sci. 27: 223-236.

Dayton, P.K. 1975. Experimental studies of algal canopy interactions in a sea otter-dominated kelp community as Amchitka Island, Alaska. U.S. National Marine Fisheries Service Fishery Bulletin 73:230-237.

Estes, J.A. and J.F. Palmisano. 1974. Sea otters: Their role in structuring nearshore communities. Science 185: 353-355.

Estes, J.A., R.J. Jameson, and E.B. Rhode. 1982. Activity and prey election in the sea otter: Influence of population status on community structure. Am. Nat. 120: 242-258.

Goeden, G.B. 1982. Intensive fishing and a 'Keystone' predator species: Ingredients for community instability. Bio. Conserv. 22: 273-281.

Goodyear, C.P. 1992. Red snapper in the U.S. waters of the Gulf of Mexico. A report to the Gulf of Mexico Fishery Management Council by the Miami Laboratory, Southeast Fisheries Science Center, NOAA, U.S. Department of Commerce. MIA 91/92-70.

Glynn, P.W. 1990. Feeding ecology of selected coral-reef macroconsumers: patterns and effects on coral community structure. Pp 365-400 in Z. Dubinsky (ed.), Coral Reefs. Ecosystems of the World 25. Elsevier. New York. 550 p.

Goldman, B., and F.H. Talbot. 1976. Aspects of the ecology of coral reef fishes. Pages 125-154 in O.A. Jones and R. Endean, (eds.). Biology and geology of coral reefs. Vol 3. Academic Press, New York. 435 p.

Grigg, R. 1992. Coral reef resource management: a ten year research program in the main Hawaiian Islands, 1990-2000. Pp 91-98 in M. Ricard, (ed). Comptes Rendus du Congres de l' International Society for Reef Studies (Nomea, 14-18 novembre 1990).

Grigg, R.W. and S.J. Dollar. 1990. Natural and anthropogenic disturbance on coral reefs. Pages 439-452 in Z. Dubinsky (ed.), Coral Reefs. Ecosystems of the World 25. Elsevier. New York. 550 p.

Hay, M.E. 1981. Herbivory, algal distribution, and the maintenance of between-habitat diversity on a tropical fringing reef. Am. Nat. 118: 520-540.

Hay, M.E. 1984. Patterns of fish and urchin grazing on Caribbean coral reefs: Are previous results typical. Ecology 65: 446-454.

Hamner, W.M., M.S. Jones, J.J. Carleton, I.R. Hauri, and D.M. Williams. 1988. Zooplankton, planktivorous fish, and water currents on a windward reef face: Great Barrier Reef, Australia. Bull. Mar. Sci. 42: 459-479.

Harper, D.E. 1992. Spiny lobster monitoring report on trends in landings, CPUE, and size of harvested lobster. A report to the Gulf of Mexico Fishery Management Council by the Miami Laboratory, Southeast Fisheries Science Center, NOAA, U.S. Department of Commerce. MIA 91/92-85.

Hixon, M.A. and Beets, J.P. 1993. Predation, prey refuges, and the structure of coral-reef fish assemblages. Ecol. Monogr. 63: 77-101.

Huntsman, E.R. and P.W. Willis. 1989. Status of reef fish stocks off North Carolina and South Carolina as revealed by headboat catch statistics. North Carolina Coastal Oceanography Symposium. NOAA, National Undersea Research Program. NOAA-NURP Rept. 89-2: 387-454.

Huntsman, G. 1992. Reef species. Pp 4-10 in J. Murray and J. Faris (eds.). Proceedings of the First Annual North Carolina Marine Recreational Fishing Forum: An Overview of the Fishery. University of North Carolina Sea Grant College Program UNC-SG-92-08.

Knowlton, N. 1992. Thresholds and multiple stable states in coral reef community dynamics. Amer. Zool. 32: 674-682.

Knowlton, N., J.C. Lang, and B.D. Keller. 1990. Case study of natural population collapse: Post-hurricane predation on Jamaican staghorn corals. Smithsonian Contr. Mar. Sci. 31: 1-25.

Koslow, J.A., F. Hanley, and R. Wicklund. 1988. Effects of fishing on reef fish communities at Pedro Bank and Port Royal cays, Jamaica. Mar. Ecol. Prog. Ser. 43: 201-212.

Lewis, S.M. and P.C. Wainwright. 1985. Herbivore abundance and grazing intensity on a Caribbean coral reef. J. Exp. Mar. Biol. Ecol. 87: 215-228.

Lewis, S.M. 1986. The role of herbivorous fishes in the organization of a Caribbean reef community. Ecological Monographs 56: 183-200.

Meyer, J.L., E.T. Schultz, and G.S. Helfman. 1983. Fish schools: An asset of corals. Science 220: 1047-1049.

McClanahan, T.R. and N.A. Muthiga. 1988. Changes in Kenyan coral reef community structure and function due to exploitation. Hydrobiologia 166: 269-276.

McClanahan, T.R. and S.H. Shafir. 1989. Causes and consequences of sea urchin abundance and diversity in Kenyan coral reef lagoons. Oecologia 83: 361-370.

Munro, J.L. 1983. Caribbean coral reef fishery resources. ICLARM Studies and Reviews 7. International Center for Living Aquatic Resources Management, Manila, Philippines. 276 p. Munro, J.L. and D.M. Williams. 1985. Assessment and management of coral reef fisheries: Biological, environmental, and socio-economic aspects. Proc. Fifth Intern. Coral Reef Congress. Tahiti. 4: 544-578.

Ogden, J.C. and P.S. Lobel. 1978. The role of herbivorous fishes and urchins in coral reef communities. Env. Biol. Fish. 3: 49-63.

Palmisano, J.F. and J.A. Estes. 1976. Sea otters: Pillars of the nearshore community. Nat. Hist. 1976: 46-53.

Paine, R.T. 1966. Food web complexity and species diversity. Amer. Natur. 100: 65-75.

Russ, G.R. 1991. Coral reef fisheries: Effects and yields. Pp 601-636 in Sale P.F. (ed.). The ecology of fishes on coral reefs. Academic Press, Inc. San Diego. 754.

Sale, P.F. 1980. The ecology of fishes on coral reefs. Oceanogr. Mar. Biol. Ann. Rev. 18: 367-421.

Sale, P.F. (ed.). 1991. The ecology of fishes on coral reefs. Academic Press, Inc. San Diego. 745 p.

Shomura, R.S. 1987. Hawaii's marine fishery resources: yesterday (1900) and today (1986). National Marine Fisheries Service, U.S. Department of Commerce, Honolulu Laboratory Administrative Report H-87-21: 14 pp.

Simenstad, C.A., J.A. Estes, and K.W. Kenyon. 1978. Aleuts, sea otters, and alternate stable-state communities. Science 200: 403-411.

U.S. Department of Commerce. 1990. The potential of marine fishery reserves for reef fish management in the U.S. southern Atlantic. Snapper-Grouper Plan Development Team Report for the South Atlantic Fishery Management Council. J.A. Bohnsack (ed.). NOAA Technical Memorandum NMFS-SEFC-261 45 p.

COMPARISON OF BIOLOGICAL AND GEOLOGICAL PERSPECTIVES OF CORAL-REEF COMMUNITY STRUCTURE AT BUCK ISLAND, U.S. VIRGIN ISLANDS

Dennis K. Hubbard[1], Elizabeth H. Gladfelter[2] and John C. Bythell[3]

[1]VI Marine Advisors, 5046 Cotton Valley, St. Croix, USVI 00820-4519. [2]5006 N. Grapetree, St. Croix, USVI 00820-4549, [3]Dept. of Marine Sciences, The University, Newcastle upon Tyne NE1 7RU, United Kingdom

ABSTRACT

Both distribution and abundance of corals in seven cores from Buck Island National Reef Monument are similar to the patterns quantified by 16 years of repeated surveys. In addition, differences in accretionary styles in the northern versus southern reefs over the past 7000 years mimic differences in present coral-community structure. Along the northern reef, protected from most major storms, the zonation pattern is very clean with few corals from one zone being found in others. Along the more-frequently disturbed southern reef, coral zonation was mixed. The distribution of *Acropora palmata* in cores compares best with the 1976 survey conducted before the devastation of the *A. palmata* community by White Band Disease. This may suggest that such afflictions are relatively new to Caribbean coral reefs. The general agreement between the core data and averaged patterns seen over the duration of the survey, contrasted with the disagreement with many individual surveys, points out both the short-term plasticity of the reef community and the importance of a well-constrained and longer-term data base when addressing questions about either long-term reef stability or the importance of recent changes seen on reefs throughout the Caribbean.

INTRODUCTION

In his plenary address to the Sixth International Coral Reef Symposium, Peter Davies contrasted the biases of researchers examining coral reefs from biological and geological perspectives. Despite the heavy dependence of geological models on modern biological principles, the differing temporal and spatial scales at which the two disciplines focus have on more than one occasion produced contrary ideas about the stability of coral reefs through time. Jackson (1992) elaborated upon the difficulty in separating signal from noise in modern reefs, in which the types of changes that define their "stability" may occur over a time period that is greater than the span between the classic works of Charles Darwin and the convening of this Colloquium.

The significance of this problem has come into clear focus with recent discussions of the "health" of modern coral reefs and the possible effects that man's presence might have upon it. While the impetus for the most-recent debate has been the sudden and dramatic changes witnessed in several individual reef systems (e.g., the Caribbean-wide die-off of *Diadema antillarum*: Lessios *et al.*, 1984; outbreaks of *Acanthaster planci* along the Great Barrier Reef: Endean and Cameron, 1985; Wilkinson, 1990; and, most-recently, coral bleaching: Brown, 1990), the underlying questions have been with us for some time. From a more theoretical perspective, are coral reefs stable ecological entities or are they inherently unstable communities subject to frequent change? With regard to recent events that have focused the public eye on coral reefs, perhaps the answer is both. From a more-applied perspective, are the changes that we are now witnessing in modern coral reefs largely due to the presence of man or are they simply part of a boom-and-bust cycle that operates outside the temporal scale that we can address with our present biological-survey base?

Goreau (1992) has provided us with an impressive but descriptive narrative of coral-reef change around Jamaica since the earliest studies of his father in 1951. Similarly, a growing record of "reef decline" is being amassed from the Florida Keys and elsewhere in the greater Caribbean region. Identifying the causes of this decline and, by extension, remedial management strategies is of critical importance if the driving mechanisms are indeed anthropogenic.

Jackson (1992) proposed that the answer to questions of "stability" may be better addressed in fossil reefs where the shorter-term perturbations seen by a single generation of researchers are averaged out over time. Using the relative abundance of *Acropora palmata*, *A. cervicornis* and *Montastrea annularis*, he argued for long-term stability of major coral populations within the Pleistocene reefs of Barbados. He further pointed out the disappointingly sparse list of long-term ecological monitoring sites that might be used for comparison with information derived from the more-recent fossil record. In this vein, a more collaborative approach among reef workers from multiple disciplines may hold the key to unraveling questions about the effects of both temporal and spatial scale on the questions discussed above (Hubbard, 1988).

This paper builds upon these earlier arguments by comparing 16+ years of biological monitoring data from Buck Island Reef National Monument (St. Croix, U.S. Virgin Islands; Fig. 1) to patterns of reef accretion revealed in seven cores that record the 7,000-year geologic history of the same system. The following discussion addresses two questions. First, are ecological patterns seen in reef cores comparable to those seen on the reef surface and, if so, what length of monitoring is required to affect a reasonable match? And second, can comparison of these two data bases provide any insight into the geologic recurrence of the kinds of events that we are now witnessing?

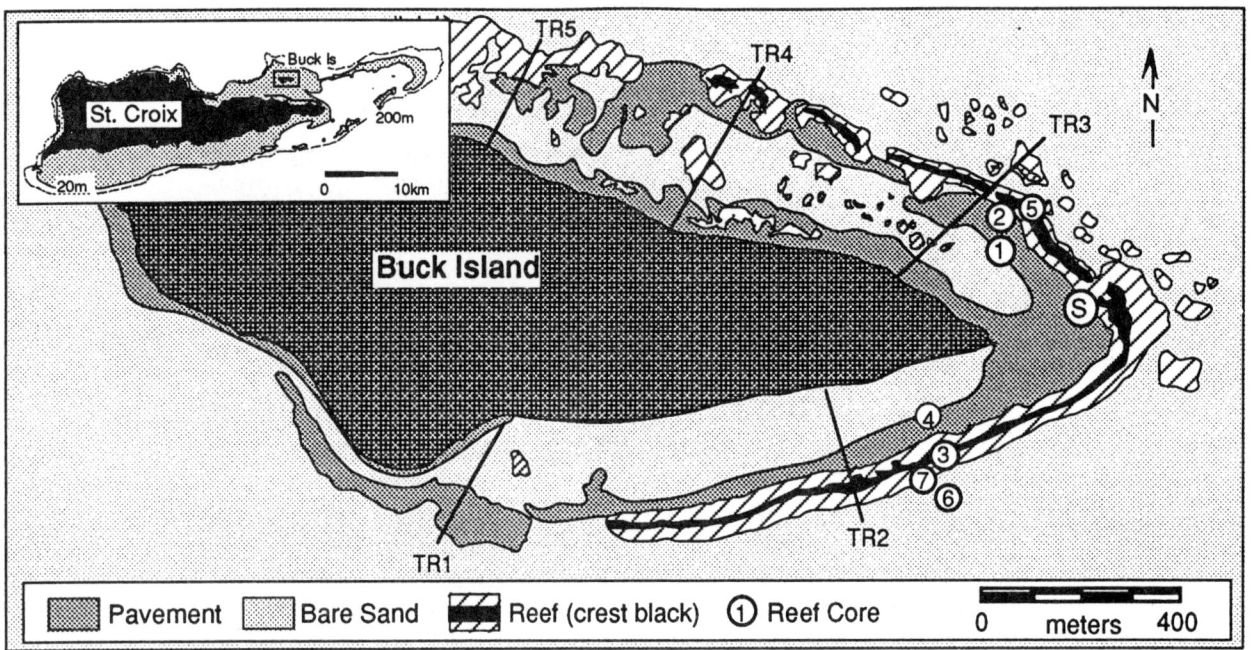

Figure 1. Map showing the locations of transects (TR1-TR5) and core sites (circled numbers) around Buck Island. The location relative to St. Croix is shown in the inset.

METHODS

Biological Surveys

Over a 16-year period, the reefs surrounding Buck Island have been monitored by researchers at West Indies Laboratory, under the supervision of two of the authors (EHG, JB). The initial survey was conducted in the fall of 1976 as part of a resource-assessment program for the U.S. National Park Service. Five radial transects were extended from shore to beyond the base of the forereef (TR1-TR5; Fig. 1). Using 10-m chain transects and between 15 and 35 haphazardly thrown 1-m^2 quadrats in each reef zone, the distribution of major coral species was measured. Surveys were repeated in 1988, 1989, 1990 and 1993, along with numerous spot observations and measurements in the interim. Details can be found in Bythell et al. (1989).

Reef Coring

Seven cores were recovered from the main reef surrounding Buck Island. The SCARID drill that was used in the coring operation was similar in principle to an earlier version described in Macintyre (1975). It was operated by divers and powered through hydraulic hoses from a 21-hp diesel pump on the surface. A double-walled, wire-line core barrel recovered core in 151-cm sections. Drilling character was monitored by the divers relative to a permanent scale mounted on the drill. Using this information and the samples recovered from each core interval, a detailed log of sample position was maintained. Radiocarbon dates from clean coral samples and the patterns of coral occurrence were used to constrain the temporal patterns of reef development.

Based on patterns identified in cores, each coral sample was assigned to either a backreef, shallow forereef (<7m) or a deep forereef/bank facies. Paleo-water depth was derived from the position of each sample within a core, its radiocarbon age and sea level at that time (note - based on nearly 100 *A. palmata* dates from St. Croix and Puerto Rico, the curve of Lighty et al., 1981 for Florida and the Caribbean Sea reasonably applies to these reefs: Hubbard, unpubl. data). Coral recovery within each zone was averaged from all core intervals that were interpreted to fall within a specific environment.

THE MODERN BUCK ISLAND SYSTEM

A continuous reef crest forms an arcuate barrier around the eastern end of Buck Island (Fig. 1). The position and character of the reef reflects the dominant easterly trade winds. Generally, the reefs exhibit the "typical" zonation patterns seen on many Caribbean reefs. The reef crest is dominated everywhere by algal-covered pavement along with *Millepora* spp. and, in protected grottos along the northern reef, isolated patches of large head corals - especially *Diploria strigosa*. The forereef community usually grades from branching corals in water less than 5 meters deep to head corals below. The dominant constituents of the benthic community are summarized in Table 1 and Figure 2.

Table 1. Benthic-community structure along Buck Island Reef - 1976 to present.

Benthic Cover	Percent Cover on North (South) Reefs				
	Fall 76	Fall 88	Fall 89	Fall 90	Winter 93
Backreef					
Live Coral (total)	n/a	4.0 (1.3)%	4.0 (5.2)%	4.3 (1.5)%	7.8 (3.2)%
A. palmata	n/a	0.0 (0.8)%	0.0 (0.5)%	0.0 (0.0)%	0.0 (0.0)%
A. cervicornis/prolifera	n/a	0.0 (0.0)%	0.0 (0.0)%	<.1 (0.0)%	0.1 (0.0)%
Agaricia spp.	n/a	0.6 (0.3)%	<.1 (0.1)%	0.3 (0.1)%	0.5 (0.0)%
Diploria spp.	n/a	0.6 (0.2)%	1.5 (2.3)%	0.3 (1.0)%	2.1 (1.7)%
M. annularis	n/a	0.0 (<.1)%	1.5 (0.3)%	0.5 (0.0)%	0.8 (1.2)%
Porites spp.	n/a	2.8 (<.1)%	1.0 (0.1)%	2.9 (<.1)%	1.9 (0.0)%
Other head corals	n/a	0.0 (0.0)%	0.0 (1.9)%	0.3 (0.4)%	2.4 (0.3)%
Turf/macroalgae	n/a	75.7 (91.1)%	73.3 (91.3)%	63.6 (83.3)%	48.5 (69.6)%
Other live cover	n/a	19.7 (7.1)%	16.1 (0.0)%	30.4 (6.5)%	29.1 (0.3)%
Sand	n/a	0.6 (0.5)%	6.0 (3.5)%	1.7 (8.7)%	14.6 (26.9)%
Shallow Forereef					
Live Coral (total)	52.3 (n/a)%	12.0 (31.4)%	12.7 (8.5)%	6.8 (0.6)%	14.6 (1.3)%
A. palmata	30.8 (n/a)%	0.3 (4.5)%	1.8 (0.5)%	1.0 (0.0)%	2.1 (<.1)%
A. cervicornis/prolifera	0.0 (n/a)%	0.0 (0.0)%	0.0 (0.0)%	0.0 (0.0)%	0.0 (0.0)%
Agaricia spp.	4.6 (n/a)%	4.6 (2.1)%	4.6 (0.3)%	3.1 (0.1)%	4.0 (0.2)%
Diploria spp.	<.1 (n/a)%	0.0 (<.1)%	2.0 (<.1)%	<.1 (0.0)%	<.1 (<.1)%
M. annularis	0.0 (n/a)%	0.0 (4.2)%	<.1 (2.4)%	<.1 (0.0)%	0.0 (<.1)%
Porites spp.	6.5 (n/a)%	5.4 (17.9)%	1.0 (3.8)%	1.9 (0.4)%	6.4 (0.5)%
Other head corals	10.4 (n/a)%	1.7 (2.7)%	3.3 (1.5)%	0.8 (0.1)%	2.1 (0.6)%
Turf/macroalgae	n/a	69.0 (68.2)%	70.5 (91.5)%	88.0 (95.8)%	82.3 (96.3)%
Other live cover	2.9 (n/a)%	19.0 (0.4)%	6.5 (0.0)%	5.2 (0.0)%	3.1 (0.1)%
Sand	n/a	0.0 (0.0)%	10.3 (0.0)%	0.0 (3.7)%	0.0 (2.3)%
Lower Forereef/Bank					
Live Coral (total)	n/a	8.9 (48.0)%	12.8 (41.8)%	4.3 (25.2)%	10.8 (22.2)%
A. palmata	n/a	0.6 (0.0)%	2.6 (0.0)%	0.0 (0.0)%	0.0 (0.0)%
A. cervicornis/prolifera	n/a	0.0 (1.5)%	0.0 (0.5)%	0.0 (<.1)%	0.0 (0.0)%
Agaricia spp.	n/a	2.2 (2.1)%	2.5 (1.5)%	1.0 (0.5)%	2.9 (1.1)%
Diploria spp.	n/a	<.1 (1.6)%	1.4 (0.5)%	0.3 (<.1)%	1.0 (<.1)%
M. annularis	n/a	3.8 (23.8)%	2.9 (27.2)%	0.9 (19.2)%	3.8 (11.9)%
Porites spp.	n/a	0.4 (14.8)%	3.2 (5.3)%	1.3 (3.6)%	1.7 (7.6)%
Other head corals	n/a	1.9 (4.2)%	0.2 (6.8)%	0.8 (1.9)%	1.4 (1.6)%
Turf/macroalgae	n/a	76.6 (24.4)%	49.0 (34.0)%	47.5 (46.5)%	58.3 (20.7)%
Other live cover	n/a	10.7 (4.1)%	26.9 (2.2)%	26.7 (1.2)%	21.6 (2.8)%
Sand	n/a	3.8 (23.5)%	11.3 (22.0)%	21.5 (27.1)%	9.3 (54.3)%

Differences in forereef zonation around Buck Island are largely the result of differing wave regimes on the north versus the south side. The northern reef faces into the 40-km wide channel between St. Croix and the Leeward Islands. Wave energy is generally higher during both prevailing conditions and the passage of smaller storm fronts. Open-Atlantic ground swell passing through the Anegada Passage to the northeast strike the northern reefs, often with heights of 2-4 meters and periods near 10 seconds (pers. obsn.). The area is protected from most hurricanes, however (Hubbard et al., 1991). As a result, a well-developed *Acropora palmata* community dominated the northern reef at the beginning of the monitoring period. Along the base of the precipitous forereef (d = 7 - 9m), colonies of *Agaricia* spp., *Porites astreoides* and other head corals have typically covered 5 to 10% of the bottom.

The southern forereef is sheltered by all but direct-hit storms by the larger island of St. Croix. In 1976, *A. palmata* was important constituent on the upper forereef but did not dominate to the extent seen on the opposite side of Buck Island. Various species of head (*Porites astreoides*) and branching *Porites porites* and *P. furcata* were of equal or greater importance, resulting in a more mixed community (Table 1). Near the base of the forereef slope and onto the adjacent shallow bank (d~10m), a dense assemblage of primarily *Montastrea annularis* is the major reef former, locally exceeding 50% in its coverage.

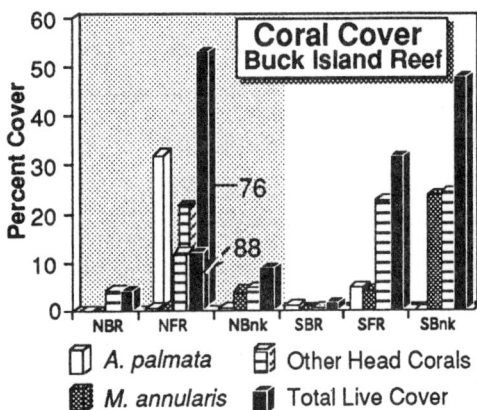

Figure 2. Reef cover along the northern (shaded, left) and southern reef (right) at Buck Island. Reef zones include the backreef (BR), shallow forereef (FR) and deep forereef/adjacent bank (Bnk). Data for the northern forereef (NFR) were collected in 1976 (rear bars) and 1988 (front bars). Monitoring at other sites started in 1988. Note the high total cover and the dominance of *A. palmata* along the northern forereef. Also, zonation is clearly defined between NFR and NBnk. In contrast, the southern reef zones are much more mixed.

Changes Through Recent Time

In general, the benthic community shows remarkable stability - with two notable exceptions (Table 1). Along the northern forereef, a rich *A. palmata* existed along the entire northern reef in 1976. Total live cover exceeded 50% with over half of that being *A. palmata* (Fig. 2). This was a strong consideration in siting the permanent snorkel trail ("S" on Figure 1), still a popular attraction among both locals and tourists. While quantitative data do not exist, the southern reef had healthy stands of this branching coral, but in lower abundance (pers. obsn.). During the latter part of the decade, "White Band Disease" struck the reefs of Buck Island and many other areas throughout the Caribbean Sea (Gladfelter, 1982). By the mid-1980's, *A. palmata* populations on Buck Island had decreased to less than 1% of their 1976 levels (compare the 1987 and 1988 surveys in Table 1). During the same period, the remainder of the coral population was unchanged (i.e. this event affected only *A. palmata*, but the remaining corals have yet to take advantage of the space provided by the extirpation of this once-dominant branching coral).

The other significant event in the recent history of Buck Island reefs is the passage of Hurricane Hugo in September, 1989. The north-facing reefs that normally receive the brunt of the wave energy were spared as the storm approached along its southerly path. Once the storm was close enough for waves to come from the northeast, the short fetch between St. Croix and the northern islands limited wave heights to 3-4 meters (Hubbard *et al.*, 1991). As a result, damage to the north reef was minimal and most of the dead *A. palmata* along the northern shelf was standing after the storm, despite its already weakened condition due to bioerosion.

In contrast, the southern reefs are usually sheltered from near-miss hurricanes that pass to the south, but received the brunt of Hurricane Hugo. Based on hindcasting, Hubbard *et al.* (1991) suggested that 7-m waves with periods exceeding 10 seconds likely reached the area. Coral in water shallower than 10 meters was obliterated by the strong wave surge. In the lower forereef, however, coral damage was light, due to the protection afforded by the water column and the massive character of the dominant corals.

The fate of the reef debris was dictated by the slope of the south-facing forereef. To the west, the forereef slope was more gradual; coral ripped from the forereef was deposited in a broad debris apron along the backreef (Hubbard *et al.*, 1991) where an ephemeral increase in live coral was measured after Hugo (see Fall89; Table 1). To the east, rubble slipped down the steeper reef face and was deposited among the live *M. annularis* heads at the base of the slope.

COMPARISON WITH CORES

The geologic history of Buck Island reef has been one of both vertical and lateral accretion over the past 7,000 years (Hubbard, 1991; ms in prep). The types of corals and their relative abundances over that time period (Table 2) parallel what exists along the reef surface today (Fig. 3). The northern forereef cores are dominated by *A. palmata*, and to a lesser degree by *M. annularis*. The 28.8% average recovery of *A. palmata* from northern-forereef cores is considerably higher than the average cover by the same coral over the past decade and a half. It compares favorably, however, with the abundance of *A. palmata* before the outbreak of White Band Disease in the late 1970's (30.8%, Fall76: Table 1). Species dominance along the southern upper forereef is poorly defined, with roughly equal cover by *A. palmata*, *M. annularis* and "other" corals (Fig. 3).

The differences in accretionary style from north to south mimic patterns seen on the present reef. In 1976, the shallow northern forereef was clearly dominated by *A. palmata* while head corals comprised most of the lower forereef community. In core, the upper and lower forereef facies are clearly dominated by *A. palmata* and *M. annularis*, respectively. Few head corals are found in the *A. palmata* facies and *vice versa*. In contrast, the more-mixed coral assemblage on the present-day southern forereef is clearly reflected in the southern cores which show significantly greater mixing of corals within all facies.

Table 2. Coral recovery from seven cores through the main Buck Island reef.

Reef Facies	N*	Coral	Average Recovery	Range of Recovery	Reef Facies	N*	Coral	Average Recovery	Range of Recovery
Backreef (North)	2	No corals recovered; accretion stopped after the reef crest formed to the north.			Backreef (South)	1	No corals recovered; accretion stopped after the reef crest formed to the south.		
Shallow Forereef (North)	3	*A. palmata* *M. annularis* "Other" corals	28.82% 5.75% 0.06%	18.01-46.36% 0.00-9.65% 0.00-0.18%	Shallow Forereef (South)	3	*A. palmata* *M. annularis* "Other" corals	9.53% 5.50% 2.30%	6.50-10.80% 0.00-10.00% 0.00-5.10%
Deep Forereef/Bank (North)	2	*A. palmata* *M. annularis* "Other" corals	5.37% 18.37% 5.22%	2.52-8.22% 15.77-20.96% 2.64-7.79%	Deep Forereef/Bank (South)	2	*A. palmata* *M. annularis* "Other" corals	0.00% 10.83% 3.78%	0.00-0.00% 5.80-15.85% 1.46-6.10%

* Number of cores penetrating this environment of deposition

DISCUSSION

The agreement between core and quadrat data is good news for geologists trying to use the present to model the past. Conversely, patterns that are discernible in the fossil record can have valuable applications to questions that address a longer temporal framework than is possible from our monitoring records from modern reefs. Also, the differences that do occur between cores and quadrats may provide some insight into the geologic occurrence of some of the dramatic events we are witnessing today.

Storms as Controls of Reef Character

Observations of the Buck Island reef community after the passage of Hurricane Hugo in 1989 may hold an important clue to the differences between the northern and southern forereef communities in both core and quadrat data. The northern reef is protected from higher-latitude storms by St. Thomas and the British Virgin Islands. During the southerly passage of storms, it sits in a lee position. Even Hurricane Hugo, which passed directly over St. Croix, was less effective than might be presumed due to the limited fetch to the north. As a result, conditions that affect zonation are stable, allowing a clear separation to develop between shallow-water branching acroporids and deeper-water head corals.

While the southern reefs are normally protected from near-miss storms by St. Croix, they receive the brunt of an approaching storm aimed directly at the island. As Hurricane Hugo passed overhead, the southerly facing reefs were devastated, leaving a homogenized suite of rubble that was ultimately deposited in environments that were different than the one from which it was derived. Given a 100-year return frequency for a Hugo-type hurricane, these major storms have probably exerted a profound impact on the stability of southern Buck Island reefs. The more-mixed coral assemblage seen throughout the southerly Buck Island cores probably reflects these processes.

Similarities between the *M. annularis* community on the present-day southern forereef/bank and in cores from the same area likely reflect long-term stability in this deeper environment. This is reinforced by the high survivorship of the lower-forereef *M. annularis* community when other areas on the reef were totally destroyed. It is worth noting that the southern *M. annularis* community has steadily declined from 27.2% cover just after Hurricane Hugo to only 11.9% earlier this year. This is not a result of latent mortality of small fragment left by the storm as appears to have occurred in Discovery Bay, Jamaica after the Passage of Hurricane Allen (Knowlton *et al.*, 1990). The *M. annularis* colonies along the base of the southern Buck Island forereef were intact well after the storm and showed no signs of damage. The causes of this recent decline are still unknown.

White Band Disease

Unlike the storm effects just discussed, frequent extirpation of shallow-water branching corals by disease do not appear to be reflected in the core record at Buck Island. The occurrence of *A. palmata* in the northern cores closely mimics the 1976 community, but is at least two orders of magnitude greater than anything seen in subsequent surveys. The strong variance between the *A. palmata* population found in the later surveys and what is seen in cores may support the idea that White Band Disease (WBD) is a relatively new force driving the population dynamics of this and other reefs. While this conclusion requires an enormous leap of faith, the striking similarity between the core data and pre-WBD conditions is difficult to ignore. Whether this reflects a recent emergence of WBD as a control of coral "health" or is simply the result of selective preservation of *A. palmata* in the shallow-forereef cores begs for closer examination.

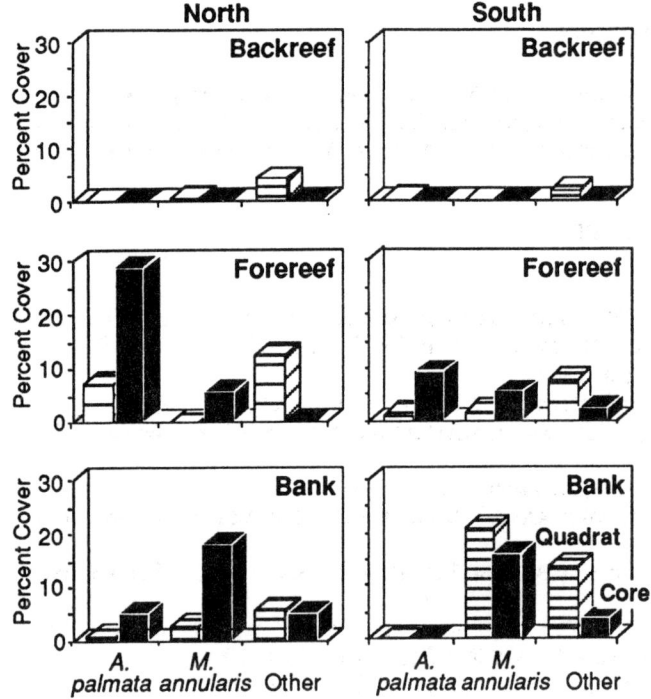

Figure 3. Coral recovery in Buck Island cores. Like on the present-day reefs, cover in the backreef is low. The northern shallow forereef is dominated by *A. palmata*. The 28.8% recovery is nearly identical to the 30.8% cover by this coral at the same site in 1976. Agreement is poor with the 1988 survey, taken after the *A. palmata* community was decimated by White Band Disease in the late 1970's and early 1980's. The strong division between upper forereef branching corals and lower forereef/bank head corals is apparent in both cores and quadrats. Along the southern forereef, the coral community is similarly mixed in both modern and fossil data. The consistent differences between the north and south reefs imply that the conditions responsible for well-defined zonation to the north and mixing of coral assemblages in the south have been constant over the past 7,000 years. Susceptibility to hurricane damage is proposed as a likely controlling mechanism.

Coral Taphonomy

This discussion has drawn somewhat on the assumption that what is preserved within a reef in some way approximates what lived on it through time. There are numerous and dangerous pitfalls to this assumption. First, different coral colonies grow at different rates, depending on species and their position within the normal range of occurrence. Thus, a core comprised of equal parts of rapidly growing *A. palmata* and more-slowly growing *M. annularis* is not necessarily evidence for equal cover by the two species throughout the period of time recorded in the cores. In addition, colony shape can exert an important control on the preservability of particular corals or groups of corals. *Agaricia* spp. is particularly susceptible to post-mortem removal by bioerosion (Hughes and Jackson, 1985). Similarly, finely branching corals like *P. porites* and *P. furcata* are easily broken and bioeroded. Interestingly, the greatest disagreement between the quadrat data and what was found within the reef cores involves these species. Before we can quantitatively compare core and quadrat data, the effects of preservation bias need to be better understood. Nevertheless, the patterns described above illustrate the value of long-term (greater than a decade) biological monitoring, whether the purpose is to interpret ancient reefs or to understand the temporal changes in their modern counterparts.

CONCLUSIONS

Despite the tenuous assumptions that must be made to quantitatively compare quadrat data to coral abundance in cores, a remarkable similarity exists between the two at this site. Specifically:

1. Shallow versus deeper-water zonation patterns that are discernible in the cores mimic what is seen on the present-day reefs.

2. Variations in exposure to both prevailing wave conditions and periodic storms have left a recognizable geologic signature in the Buck Island reefs that parallels the pattern seen today. Zonation along the northern reef is distinct with little mixing between shallower branching corals and deeper head corals. In contrast, the southern-reef community is a more-mixed assemblage, often with no clear species dominance.

3. The geologic record of *A. palmata* is more consistent with conditions in 1976 than with those from any subsequent survey. This may indicate that "White Band Disease" and similar coral afflictions have been less important in the geologic past. This may be further supported by the recent decline on *M. annularis* along the southern forereef for no apparent reason.

ACKNOWLEDGMENTS

The authors wish to acknowledge the support of the National Park Service, the National Science Foundation and the National Undersea Research Office of NOAA. In the field, the staff of the National Park Service provided invaluable assistance with logistics and many of the biological surveys. Finally, we want to thank the staff, students and researchers of West Indies Laboratory for the support and creative ideas that made this project possible.

LITERATURE CITED

Brown, B.E. (ed.) 1990. Coral bleaching. Coral Reefs 8: 153-232.

Bythell, J., E. Gladfelter, W. Gladfelter, K. French and Z. Hillis. 1989. Buck Island National Monument - changes in modern reef-community structure since 1976. Pages 145-154 in D.K. Hubbard, ed. Terrestrial and Marine Geology of St. Croix, U.S. Virgin Islands. Spec. Pub. No. 8, West Indies Laboratory, St. Croix, U.S. Virgin Islands.

Endean, R. and A.M. Cameron. 1885. Ecocatastrophe on the Great Barrier Reef. Proc. 5th Int. Coral Reef Symp. 5: 309-314.

Gladfelter, W.B. 1982. White band disease in *Acropora palmata*: implications for the structure and function of shallow reefs. Bull. Mar. Sci. 32: 639-643.

Goreau, T.J. 1992. Bleaching and reef community change in Jamaica: 1851-1991. Amer. Zool. 32: 683-695.

Hubbard, D.K. 1988. Controls of modern and fossil reef development: common ground for biological and geological research. Proc. 6th Int. Coral Reef Symp. 1: 243-252.

Hubbard, D.K., 1991. Geologic development of Buck Island Reef National Monument. Report to the National Park Service, West Indies Laboratory 36p.

Hubbard, D.K., K.M. Parsons, J.C. Bythell and N.D. Walker. 1991. The effects of Hurricane Hugo on the reefs and associated environments of St. Croix, U.S. Virgin Islands - a preliminary assessment. J. Coastal Res. Spec. Issue No. 8: 33-48.

Hughes, T.P and J.B.C. Jackson. 1985. Population dynamics and life histories of foliaceous corals. Ecol. Monogr. 55: 141-166.

Jackson, J.B.C. 1992. Pleistocene perspectives on coral reef community structure. Amer. Zool. 32: 719-731.

Knowlton, N., J.C. Lang and B.D. Keller. 1990. Case study of a natural population collapse: post-hurricane predation on Jamaican staghorn corals. Smithsonian Contr. Mar. Sci. 31: 1-25.

Lessios, H.A., D.R. Robertson, J.D. Cubit. 1984. Spread of the *Diadema* mass mortality through the CAribbean. Science 226: 335-337.

Lighty, R.G., I.G. Macintyre and R. Stuckenrath. 1982. *Acropora palmata* reef framework: a reliable indicator of sea level in the western Atlantic for the past 10,000 years. Coral Reefs 1: 125-130.

Macintyre, I.G. 1975 A diver operated hydraulic drill for coring submerged substrates. Atoll Res. Bull. 336: 1-7.

Wilkinson, C.R. (ed.) 1990. *Acanthaster planci*. Coral Reefs 9: 93-172.

CORAL REEF DEGRADATION: A LONG-TERM STUDY OF HUMAN AND NATURAL IMPACTS

Terence P. Hughes

Department of Marine Biology, James Cook University, Townsville, QLD 4811, AUSTRALIA

ABSTRACT

Long-term annual monitoring of coral reef communities on the north coast of Jamaica has revealed dramatic changes over the past two decades caused by natural and human stresses. Coral cover at replicate sites and depths has declined from 27-77% in the 1970's to less than 5% at most locations in 1990. Conversely, macroalgal cover has increased sharply from 1-3% cover before 1983 to >90% today. The species composition of coral, algal and herbivore assemblages has also changed markedly. Several major reef zones, described earlier in pioneering studies by T.F. Goreau and colleagues, no longer exist (e.g. those formerly dominated by *Zoanthus* spp., *Acropora palmata* and *A. cervicornis*).

Damage from two hurricanes (in 1980 and 1988) has been exacerbated by overfishing, which along with mass-mortalities of sea urchins (1983) has resulted in a sustained algal bloom that continues to prevent normal recovery of corals. Monitoring techniques alone were not always sufficient to uncover the mechanisms causing shifts in species composition. A parallel program of experiments, demographic analysis and life history studies has clarified why some species have declined while others have increased, and suggests some management options. The prospects for recovery of coral abundances in the short- and medium-term are poor. These results have numerous implications for the design of global reef-monitoring programs.

INTRODUCTION

Long-term studies of coral populations and communities are useful for many reasons. First, many ecological processes are slow and cannot be detected in the short-term. Many corals are long-lived, and it is appropriate that we scale our studies in relation to their lifetime. Second, most ecological processes have high annual variability (e.g. coral recruitment), so that results from one or a few years can be misleading. Third, long-term monitoring reveals the recent history of a reef community, which can help to explain the impact of events occuring now. For example, the effect on a reef of a hurricane today depends in part on how long it has been since the previous disturbance and what effect it had. Fourth, monitoring studies are essential for investigations of rare or episodic events, such as outbreaks and die-offs of predators, or hurricanes. Fifth, long-term monitoring allows us to assess the impact of man's activities in relation to the background dynamics of a reef.

Coral reef communities in the vacinity of Discovery Bay, Jamaica, have been studied intensively for more than 35 years, and therefore provide a rare opportunity to quantify changes in species abundances over a considerable length of time. I show here that patterns of coral abundance have been altered drastically over the past 2 decades, with coral cover declining by up to 90%. The distinctive *Zoanthus*, *Acropora palmata* and *A. cervicornis* zones (Goreau 1959) are no longer recognizable, since these dominant species have suffered sharp reductions in abundance. Most of these changes can be related to 3 events; Hurricane Allen (1980), an algal bloom caused by overfishing and mass-mortalities of sea urchins (1983) and Hurricane Gilbert (1988). My aims here are (1) to briefly describe changes in coral communities during this recent turbulent history, (2) to summarize what these perturbations tell us about processes important to the community structure of tropical reefs, (3) to discuss the prospects for recovery of Jamaican coral reef communities, and (4) to outline implications of these results for future monitoring programs in Jamaica and elsewhere.

METHODS

I censused sessile communities using line transects and permanently marked plots for the last 6-14 years at 9 locations that were chosen to include major reef zones and habitats typical of Jamaican reefs. Accordingly, 3 of the sites were in the lagoonal backreef of Discovery Bay (Crosby Patch Reef, Stills Patch Reef, and the inner reef crest or *Zoanthus* zone), 3 more were nearby on gently sloping forereefs (at depths of 2m, 10m, and 20m), and 3 were at Rio Bueno 4km to the west (on a shallow platform at 7m, and on an adjacent vertical cliff at 10m and 15-20m depths). Many of these sites have been the locations of earlier studies which provide additional temporal comparisons (see Results).

All transects consisted of replicate 10m lengths of tape that were positioned haphazardly each year to ensure statistical independence. Ten replicate transects were run at 7m, 10m and 15-20m depths at Rio Bueno in 1977 and 1981. These were done again in 1986 along with the 3 backreef and 3 forereef sites at Discovery Bay, using 15 transects (to compensate for declining coral cover). In 1988, 1989, 1990 and 1993, these 9 sites were surveyed once more, using 20 transects per site. In addition to transects, coral and algal communities at 7m, 10m and 15-20m at Rio Bueno were censused annually since 1977 by photographing 28-42 permanently positioned 1m² quadrats. All corals in the photographs were traced to form maps, which were then digitized to calculate relative abundances, diversity, etc. and to follow survival and growth of individual colonies for life-history and demographic analysis (see Hughes 1989 for further details). Algal cover was measured by superimposing a grid of regularly-spaced dots onto photographs of unmanipulated quadrats, and counting those in contact with algae. I also measured densities of the most conspicuous Jamaican herbivore (and occasional predator of corals), the echinoid *Diadema antillarum*, at 14 locations along 100km of coast over 14 years (a total of 90 estimates).

RESULTS

Coral cover has declined significantly at all sites over the past ten or more years, coinciding with major changes in the species composition of corals. Most of these changes are related to two hurricanes (1980 and 1988), and to a prolonged algal bloom (from 1984 to the present) following mass-mortalities of *Diadema antillarum* in 1983. I describe first the changes which have occurred at Rio Bueno where monitoring has been carried out most intensively, and then summarize similar changes which have occurred on other reefs.

In 1977 coral abundance at Rio Bueno was very high, with an average of 62%, 70% and 47% cover recorded in transects and permanent quadrats at depths of 7m, 10m and 15-20m, respectively (Fig. 1). However, in 1980 hurricane Allen inflicted moderately heavy damage especially to shallow reefs at this site. Coral cover by 1981 had fallen to 22-38% (Fig. 1), and the relative abundances of species had changed significantly. In particular, tall branching *Acropora* species were virtually eliminated. By contrast, massive moundlike species did not change significantly, while bushy and platey corals declined by intermediate amounts (Porter et al., 1981, Woodley et al. 1981, Hughes 1989).

For 3-4 years following hurricane Allen, coral cover increased slowly, rising by one-third at 7m from 22% in 1981 to 29% in early 1984 (Fig. 1). However, some species increased greatly, while others showed little or no change. Two weedy species, *Agaricia agaricites* and *Briarium asbestinum*, more than doubled their cover from 1981 to 1983 at 7m and 10m, following copious larval recruitment onto areas bared by hurricane Allen. In comparison, massive corals that survived the hurricane well (e.g. *Montastrea annularis, Colpophyllia natans*) changed little, while branching *Acropora* species remained rare.

Three years after Hurricane Allen, the echinoid *Diadema antillarum* suffered mass-mortalities from disease, in 1983 (Hughes et al., 1987). Beforehand, from 1976 to July 1983, densities of *D. antillarum* on Jamaican forereefs were an average of $7.5 \pm 2.1 m^{-2}$ (mean ± S.D). This high density may have been partially caused by a paucity of predatory and herbivorous fish, due to chronic overfishing. *Diadema* population sizes fell abruptly by mid-August 1983 by almost 2 orders of magnitude. There has been virtually no recovery since, with average densities on forereefs from 1983-1993 of only $0.09 \pm 0.02m^{-2}$.

The die-off of *Diadema* (and the prior removal of fish) began an unprecedented algal bloom which soon cut short the recovery of corals from the 1980 hurricane (Fig. 1). Macro-algal cover at Rio Bueno rose from close to zero prior to 1983 to 61-94% at different depths by 1990. The algal bloom has caused a long-term recruitment failure of corals since 1984 (Hughes 1989). As a result, short-lived coral species (e.g. *Agaricia agaricites, Leptoseris cucullata*), which rely on continuous recruitment inputs have declined disproportionately (ibid).

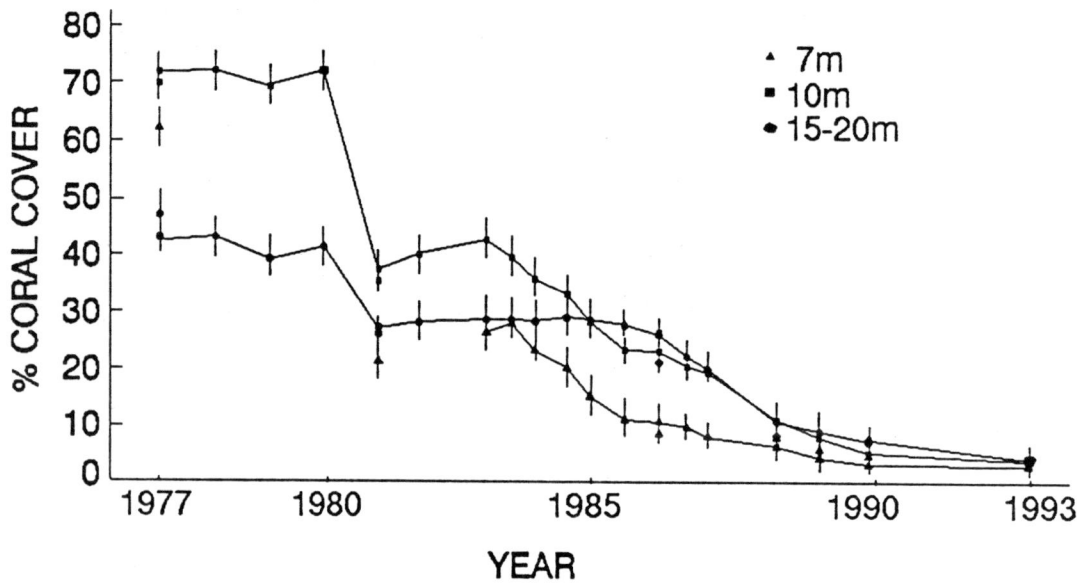

Figure 1. Percent cover (mean ± S.E.) of corals at 7m, 10m and 15-20m depths at Rio Bueno, Jamaica from 1977-1990. Connected points are replicate m² permanent plots. Unconnected points represent replicate 10m line-transects.

Table 1. Coral cover (mean ± S.E.) before 1980 and in 1993 on Jamaican Reefs.

BACKREEF	<1980	1990
Zoanthus Zone (0-1m)	77.0[a] (1976)	0.26 ± 0.11
Crosby Patch Reef (1-3m)	39.0[b] (1975)	7.64 ± 1.03
Stills Patch Reef (1-3m)	36.0[b] (1973)	2.55 ± 0.39
FOREREEF		
A. palmata zone (1m)	56.7 ± 9.4[c] (1978)	0.25 ± 0.06
A. cervicornis zone (10m)	42.0 ± 7.6[c] (1978)	2.82 ± 0.55
20m	7.0 ± 7.6[c] (1978)	1.84 ± 0.46

Sources:- a: Karlson (1980). b: Sammarco (1982). c: Huston 1985

In 1988, Hurricane Gilbert reduced algal cover and biomass substantially, but the decline was short-lived. In marked contrast to the destruction of Hurricane Allen in 1980, coral abundance at 7m was virtually unaffected by Hurricane Gilbert (Fig. 1). However, deeper sites at 10m and 15-20m lost almost half their coral cover during 1988. To date there are no signs of recovery. Indeed, from 1984 to the present, coral cover at Rio Bueno has declined inexorably at every annual census, to only 5-6% at all 3 depths (Fig 1).

Other sites on the fore- and back-reef of Discovery Bay have also undergone extensive changes (Table 1). Prior to 1980 coral cover varied from 27-77% (Table 1; data from Karlson 1983, Carpenter 1981, Sammarco 1982, Huston 1985). However by 1993, coral cover was less than 3% at all forereef and 2 of the 3 backreef sites, while algal cover was everywhere greater than 90%. No *Zoanthus* spp. were found in twenty 10m transects on the shallow backreef (the *Zoanthus* zone described by Goreau (1959)). Similarly, *Acropora palmata* was not detetected on the fore reef at 2m (the *palmata* zone), while cover by *A. cervicornis* at 10m in 1993 was only 0.4 ± 0.3 % (the *cervicornis* zone).

DISCUSSION

Community Dynamics

The study clearly shows the important role of physical disturbances in coral reef dynamics. The high coral cover prior to 1980 (Figure 1, Table 1) indicates that a major hurricane had not substantially affected sites on the north coast of Jamaica for at least several decades (Woodley, in Press). The effects of the two hurricanes in 1980 and 1988 varied among locations (from reef to reef, along depth-gradients), in time (Hurricane Allen vs Hurricane Gilbert), and among species. For example, corals on the vertical wall at Rio Bueno were damaged relatively little by Hurricane Allen (Fig. 1), compared to the amount of destruction to the gently sloping reefs at Discovery Bay, 4km away (e.g. Porter et al., 1981, Woodley et al., 1981). Shallow reefs were affected more than deep ones in 1980, but the opposite occurred in 1988, probably because susceptible species had been virtually wiped out in shallow water by the first hurricane and no regeneration had yet taken place (Fig. 1). The differences observed in rates of hurricane mortality among species and morphological types are presumably due primarily to varying susceptibilities to wave damage, sedimentation, etc. (e.g Woodley et al. 1981, Hughes 1989).

The effects of the *Diadema* die-off highlight the role of herbivory and algal-coral competion in the dynamics of reef communities. The lack of herbivory due to the loss of *Diadema* and chronic overfishing has prevented normal recovery from recurrent hurricanes. Further changes in the species composition of corals have occurred since 1984 due to differences in their susceptibility to algal overgrowth (Hughes 1989). The net result is a coral assemblage strikingly different from those described in Goreau's (1959) pioneering studies.

Prospects for recovery

The main impediment to recovery of coral assemblages on Jamaican reefs today is the presence of dense algal mats which preempt space and overgrow coral recruits. Severe storms can remove much of the algal biomass, as occurred during Hurricane Gilbert in 1988, but the algae recovers much too quickly to allow corals a foothold. Therefore, herbivory is the most likely process that could once more reduce algal abundance. However, Jamaican reefs are chronically overfished, and are likely to remain so in the future. Other invertebrate macroherbivores have not increased in numbers sufficiently to reduce algal biomass even after almost a decade since the *Diadema* crash (Hughes et al., 1987, unpubl. data). Consequently, the best prospect for a return to a high coral cover seems to lie with recovery of *Diadema antillarum* itself. However, analysis of *Diadema* population structures shows that recruitment has been negligible at most sites and densities remain at very low levels (Hughes, unpubl. data).

The removal of algae would most likely result in colonization by a few early successional coral species, i.e. those with high rates of recruitment, particularly brooding agaricids. Branching acroporids and long-lived massive corals are likely to increase much more slowly, because they typically recruit in much smaller numbers (e.g. Hughes 1985). It is unlikely that coral assemblages in Jamaica will resemble the descriptions of earlier workers (e.g. Goreau 1959) for several decades or longer.

Design of Monitoring Programs

A number of lessons have emerged from this study, concerning the design of long-term programs. First of all, monitoring efforts have to be flexible to account for changing conditions. For example, changes in coral cover can be detected with much less sampling effort when cover is uniformly high than when it is low and patchy. Therefore, it is essential that the amount of replication (number of sites, transects, photo-quadrats, etc.) is responsive to change in order to avoid over- and under-sampling. In this study, I had to increase the number of transects used to follow coral cover twice (from 10 to 15, and later to 20 transects per site) to maintain a high precision (Fig. 1). Secondly, this ability to respond means that at least some information has to be analyzed between every sampling period, and not allowed to accumulate in a raw data-bank to the point where analysis becomes overwhelming or occurs too late. The design of monitoring programs must take account of the substantial time, effort and expense involved in *analysis* of the data. Thirdly, a monitoring program should have enough flexibility to add and drop variables in response to new conditions. This study focussed initially on coral dynamics, *Diadema* abundances, and algal cover. Later other variables were added because they were likely to show interesting responses to new circumstances (e.g. following the *Diadema* die-off, I monitored algal biomass and densities of other sea urchins and snails, see Hughes et al., 1987). It would be a mistake to gather the same data year after year if conditions warrent a change of focus. Fourthly, monitoring protocols on their own are often incapable of revealing the underlying mechanisms of change in abundance, and a parallel program of experimentation or demographic analysis is required to explain why these alterations occur. For example, the algal bloom most affected short-lived corals (e.g. *Agaricia agaricites*) because they rely on availability of substrate for continuous recruitment, as shown by clearance experiments (Hughes 1985, 1989). Fifthly, Figure 1 shows a decline in coral abundance over time, a pattern common to virtually all other long-term monitoring studies of reef communities (e.g. Bak and Luckhurst 1980, Dustan and Halas 1987, Glynn 1990, Liddell and Ohlhurst 1986, Porter et al., 1981). Some of these declines have been related to events such as hurricanes, *Acanthaster* outbreaks, the *Diadema* die-off, and El Nino. However, in other cases, this pattern may simply reflecting a systematic bias in some monitoring programs, where the initial surveys were carried out at locations that have unusually high coral cover or diversity. Obviously, if coral cover is, say, 80-90%, then it is much more likely that local abundances will decline over time than increase. This decline is of little concern if other nearby areas show the opposite pattern. However, we will never detect increases if we ignore areas that have the capacity to do so, and instead concentrate our efforts only at locations with high coral cover. This bias in site selection will have to be avoided in the future in order to detect any large-scale changes by coral communities due to global warming.

ACKNOWLEDGEMENTS

I thank H. Choat, B. Willis and the Coral Ecology Group at JCU for comments on the manuscript. Field and lab assistance was provided by numerous colleagues, particularly M.J. Boyle, G. Bruno, M. Carr, L. Dinsdale, F. Jeal, and D. Reed. F.Jeal, J.B.C. Jackson and J.H. Connell provided much encouragement and support. This research was funded by the National Sciences Foundation (USA), National Geographic, the Whitehall Foundation, and the Australian Research Council.

REFERENCES

Bak, R.P.M., and B.E. Luckhurst. 1980. Constancy and change in coral reef habitats along depth gradients at Curacao. Oecologia. 47: 145-155.

Dustan, P. and J.C. Halas. 1987. Changes in the reef-coral community of Carysfort Reef, Key Largo, Florida: 1974 to 1982. Coral Reefs 6: 91-106.

Glynn, P.W. 1990. Coral mortality and disturbances to coral reefs in the Tropical Eastern Pacific. Pp. 55-126 in Glynn, P.W. (Ed.), Global ecological consequences of the 1982-83 El Nino-Southern Oscillations. Elsevier, Amsterdam.

Goreau, T.F. 1959. The ecology of Jamaican reefs. I. Species composition and zonation. Ecology 40: 67-89.

Hughes, T.P. 1985. Life histories and population dynamics of early successional corals. Proc. 5th International Coral Reef Symposium, Tahiti, Vol. 4: 101-106.

Hughes, T.P. 1989. Community structure and diversity of coral reefs: the role of history. Ecology 70: 275-279.

Hughes, T.P., D.C. Reed, and M.J. Boyle. 1987. Herbivory on coral reefs: community structure following mass mortalities of sea urchins. J. exp. mar. Biol. Ecol. 113: 39-59.

Huston, M. 1985. Patterns of species diversity in relation to depth at Discovery Bay, Jamaica. Bull. Mar. Sci. 37: 928-935.

Karlson, R.H. 1983. Disturbance and monopolization of a spatial resource by *Zoanthus sociatus* (Coelenterata, Anthozoa). Bull. Mar. Sci. 33: 118-131.

Liddell, W.D., and S.L. Ohlhurst. 1986. Changes in benthic community composition following the mass mortality of *Diadema* at Jamaica. J. exp. mar. Biol. Ecol. 95: 271-278.

Porter, J.W., J.D. Woodley, G.J. Smith, J.E. Neigel, J.F. Battey, and D.G. Dallmeyer. 1981. Population trends among Jamaican reef corals. Nature 294: 249-250.

Sammarco, P.W. 1982. Echinoid grazing as a structuring force in coral reef communities: whole reef manipulations. J. exp. mar. Biol. Ecol. 61: 31-55.

Woodley, J.D. (In Press). The incidence of hurricanes on the north coast of Jamaica since 1870: are the classic reef descriptions atypical? Hydrobiologica Reviews.

Woodley, J.D. and 19 others. 1981. Hurricane Allen's impact on Jamaican coral reefs. Science 214: 749-755.

HURRICANES AND ANCHORS: PRELIMINARY RESULTS FROM THE NATIONAL PARK SERVICE REGIONAL REEF ASSESSMENT PROGRAM

Caroline S. Rogers
Virgin Islands National Park, St. John, USVI 00830

ABSTRACT

The U.S. National Park Service (NPS) began a Regional Assessment Program for coral reefs in the U.S. Virgin Islands and Florida in 1988. Scientists from NPS and six other institutions have now established long-term monitoring sites at Virgin Islands National Park (St. John, USVI), Buck Island Reef National Monument (St. Croix, USVI), Biscayne National Park (Florida) and Fort Jefferson National Monument (Florida). Hurricane Hugo passed through the USVI in 1989, causing severe destruction in some reef areas while leaving others untouched. Patchy damage to reefs in Florida was also noted after Hurricane Andrew; damage from this August 1992 storm is still being assessed. Fort Jefferson National Monument escaped the onslaught of Andrew. No significant recovery in live coral cover has been evident at the Buck Island or Virgin Islands National Park (VINP) study sites 3.5 years after Hurricane Hugo. Similarly, no recovery was evident at another site in St. John which was destroyed by a large anchor 4.5 years ago.

INTRODUCTION

In 1988, the U.S. National Park Service (NPS) began a Regional Assessment Program for coral reefs in the U.S. Virgin Islands and Florida. The goal of this ongoing program is to establish effective long-term research and monitoring programs at each of these four sites: Virgin Islands National Park (St. John, USVI), Buck Island Reef National Monument (St. Croix, USVI), Fort Jefferson National Monument (Florida, now Dry Tortugas National Park), and Biscayne National Park (Florida). The objectives of the program include: 1) development and evaluation of standardized methods for assessment of trends on coral reefs and preparation of a Coral Reef Monitoring Manual; 2) collection of environmental data; and 3) collection of baseline data and determination of rates of change in abundance of reef organisms. Scientists from NPS and six other institutions have participated in this program: the Principal Investigators are James Beets, James Bohnsack, John Bythell, Peter Edmunds, Virginia Garrison, Elizabeth Gladfelter, William Gladfelter, Dennis Hubbard, Walter Jaap, Joseph Kimmel, James Porter, Caroline Rogers, Jennifer Wheaton, and Jon Witman. Some of the research from this program was presented at the 7th International Coral Reef Symposium in June 1992, and several reports and publications are already available (e.g., Edmunds and Witman, 1991; Hubbard et al., 1991; Rogers et al., 1991; Porter and Meier, 1992; Rogers 1992).

During the course of this program, two major storms have affected the study reefs. Hurricane Hugo passed over the USVI sites in September 1989 causing severe destruction in some areas.

The effects of Hurricane Andrew (August 1992) on reefs in Florida are still being assessed.

This case history briefly highlights some of the overall findings of the Regional Assessment Program while focussing on work done by NPS scientists to quantify the effects of Hurricane Hugo on the long-term monitoring site established in Virgin Islands National Park. Recovery at this site since the storm is compared to recovery at another reef in the park which suffered severe damage from a large anchor. The emphasis is on the effects these stresses have had on hard coral cover with limited data on sponges and gorgonians.

RESULTS AND DISCUSSION

Anchor Damage: Virgin Islands National Park

Many of the approximately 1 million people who visit Virgin Islands National Park (VINP) each year arrive by boat. An increase in the number of boats visiting the park has resulted in increased damage from anchors. In October 1988, a 440' ship dropped its anchor on a coral reef within the park, creating a scar 122 m long and 3 m wide, and smashing about 283 square meters of the reef. This reef slopes gradually from a depth of 6 m (20') to 12 m (40') and then steeply drops off to 22 m (71') where it ends abruptly in a sand bottom. The shallower portion of this reef is a gorgonian-dominated pavement while in deeper water, especially on the steep slope, several species of hard corals occur. Damage was estimated in Nov./Dec. 1988 using 1 m square quadrats placed inside and outside the scar. The assumption was that areas adjacent to the scar were representative of the area destroyed by the anchor. Total live cover (excluding algae) was 25.8% outside the scar and 1.3% inside. The percent of live coral cover within quadrats outside the scar ranged from 0 to 79.5% (mean 21.9%, n = 8). Within the scar, percent live cover ranged from only 0.7 to 2.0% (mean 1.2 %, n = 3).

In April 1991, 2.5 years after the anchor destruction occurred, nine permanent quadrats were established inside the scar at depths from 9 m (30') to 12 m (40') deep. These quadrats were surveyed in April 1991, June 1992, and December 1992. No substantial recovery in terms of total live cover (excluding algae) or cover by hard corals, sponges and gorgonians is evident (ANOVA, p< 0.05). Mean hard coral cover is only about 2% (Table 1). Note that some of the live cover within these permanent quadrats is from organisms which escaped damage by the anchor, not newly settled recruits.

Assessment of changes at NPS sites in the USVI and Florida

Permanent long-term monitoring sites have now been established at each of the four NPS sites in the U.S.V.I. and Florida. A brief description of the results of research conducted at these sites follows (see also Rogers et al., 1991, Bythell et al., 1992; Bythell et al., 1992).

Table 1. Percent cover of hard corals, sponges, and gorgonians and total live cover at anchor damage site (mean +/- SD)

	APRIL 1991	JUNE 1992	DECEMBER 1992
HARD CORALS	0.95 +/- 0.93	1.71 +/- 1.30	2.07 +/- 1.56
SPONGES	0.67 +/- 0.48	2.84 +/- 1.38	1.30 +/- 0.94
GORGONIANS	2.34 +/- 2.32	5.43 +/- 5.80	2.75 +/- 4.65
TOTAL LIVE COVER	4.00 +/- 3.20	10.08 +/- 6.6	6.27 +/- 6.49

Virgin Islands National Park.- In January 1989, five 20 m long transects were installed at a depth of about 12 m off Yawzi Point in Lameshur Bay, St. John. Hurricane Hugo passed over the Virgin Islands eight months later, in September 1989. Total live coral cover along study transects decreased significantly as a result of this major storm, dropping from about 21% to 12% (a change of 40%) (Rogers et al., 1991). Cover by the dominant species <u>Montastrea annularis</u> decreased as a result of Hurricane Hugo (Sept. 1989) from about 8% to about 5% (a 35% change), but it remained the most abundant coral at the study site, and neither diversity (H') nor evenness increased. The permanent transects have been surveyed eight times since Hurricane Hugo, most recently in March 1993, and no detectable increase in total live coral cover or cover by <u>Montastrea annularis</u> is evident (Figure 1).

Cover by sponges along permanent transects averaged 2.3% (range 0.5 to 5.9%) before Hugo, decreasing to 0.7% after the storm (range 0 to 2.7). Cover by sponges has consistently increased reaching maximum average values of about 5% in November 1992 (higher than before the storm).

Gladfelter (1993) examined sponges and gorgonians in quadrats along the permanent transects at Yawzi in July 1991 and July 1992. He suggests that sponges are recovering somewhat faster than gorgonians, but points out that his data are not from permanent quadrats and should be interpreted cautiously. He found more gorgonian and sponge species, and more gorgonian colonies in 1992 than in 1991.

Buck Island Reef National Monument.- Hurricane Hugo devastated portions of the reef at Buck Island Reef National Monument but left other areas intact. The storm caused statistically significant decreases in percent total live coral cover at some permanent study sites but no significant changes in cover by the dominant species (<u>Montastrea annularis</u>, <u>Porites porites</u>). (Percent cover by <u>P.</u>

porites did drop substantially in 3 out of 4 transects at one site.) No significant recovery in the amount of hard coral cover along transects had taken place two years after Hugo (Bythell and Bythell, 1992). Populations of Acropora palmata which appeared to be recovering slowly from white band disease were decimated by the storm, and cover fell from 5% to 0.8% (Gladfelter 1992). Resurveys of permanent transects indicate that total live coral cover has not increased substantially as of February 1993 but that significant recruitment of Diploria strigosa, Porites spp., and Agaricia spp. has occurred in some very shallow areas (pers. comm., J. Bythell, E. Gladfelter).

Biscayne National Park.- Porter and Meier (1991) reported on changes from 1989 - 1991 at two shallow "photostations" within Biscayne National Park. Ball Buoy Reef exhibited an increase in projected surface area (primarily Acropora palmata) of 30.2%. However, transects through this same area indicated no net loss or gain of this species because of loss of living tissue on understory branches. At Triumph Reef, a decrease of 7.5% in projected surface area of live coral was observed. Hurricane Andrew caused damage within the photostation at Triumph Reef but not the one at Ball Buoy Reef (pers. comm., J. Porter).

Figure 1. Percent live coral cover at Yawzi Point, St. John.

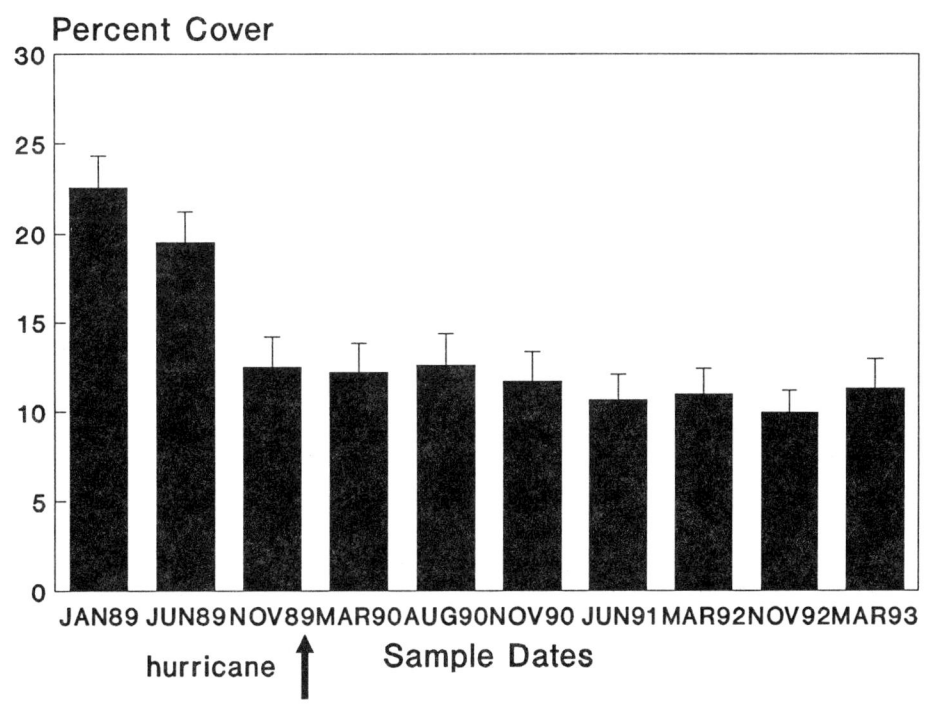

Fort Jefferson National Monument.- Extensive research at Fort Jefferson National Monument has indicated an overall stability in abundance of octocorals and hard corals at this site as estimated from several methods (Jaap et al., 1992). For example, k-dominance curves indicate no shifts in coral species diversity. This site escaped the onslaught of Hurricane Andrew and is relatively free from many of the stresses which affect Biscayne National Park. It is a critical comparative site for long-term monitoring.

CONCLUSIONS

Even extremely powerful storms such as Hurricane Hugo and Hurricane Andrew can leave some reef areas intact. Where significant losses of coral occur, recovery may be slow. Within Virgin Islands National Park, no significant recovery is apparent at the long-term study site in Lameshur Bay 3.5 years after Hurricane Hugo or at a reef damaged by a large anchor 4.5 years ago. The reefs within this park are protected from many of the stresses causing degradation of other reefs in the Caribbean, and the recovery rates reported here probably reflect natural rates following physical disturbances. None of the scientists in the Reef Assessment Program have reported significant recruitment of hard coral colonies at any of the long-term study sites. Values for mean percent coral cover at these sites in Florida and the USVI in the beginning of the program were comparable to those for many other reefs in the Caribbean and ranged from < 5% at one site in Biscayne National Park to a maximum of 40% at one zone in Buck Island. Live coral cover is now lower at three of the four long-term study sites because of damage from Hurricane Hugo and Hurricane Andrew.

LITERATURE CITED

Bythell, J.C. and M. Bythell. 1992. Benthic reef community dynamics at selected sites at Buck Island Reef National Monument, 1988-1991. Monitoring fixed linear transects using the chain transect technique. Chapter 1. Ecological studies of Buck Island Reef National Monument, St. Croix, U.S. Virgin Islands: a quantitative assessment of selected components of the coral reef ecosystem and establishment of long term monitoring sites. Part II. NPS Coral Reef Assessment Program. 24 pp.

Bythell, J.C., E.H.Gladfelter, and M. Bythell. 1992. Ecological studies of Buck Island Reef National Monument, St. Croix, U.S. Virgin Islands: A quantitative assessment of selected components of the coral reef ecosystem and establishment of long-term monitoring sites. Part II. NPS Coral Reef Assessment Program. 72 pp.

Edmunds, P.J. and J.D. Witman. 1991. Effect of Hurricane Hugo on the primary framework of reefs along the south shore of St. John, U.S. Virgin Islands. Mar. Ecol. Prog. Ser. 78: 201-204.

Gladfelter, W.B. 1991. Population structure of Acropora palmata on the windward forereef, Buck Island Reef National

Monument: seasonal and catastrophic changes 1988-1989. Chapter 5. Ecological studies of Buck Island Reef National Monument, St. Croix, US Virgin Islands: a quantitative assessment of selected components of the coral reef ecosystem and establishment of long term monitoring sites. Part 1. NPS Coral Reef Assessment Program. 22 pp.

Gladfelter, W.B. 1993. Annual change in sponges and gorgonian communities at Newfound Bay: comparison with Yawzi Point. Report to the National Park Service. 18 pp.

Hubbard, D.K., K.M. Parsons, J.C. Bythell, and N.D. Walker. 1991. The effects of Hurricane Hugo on the reefs and associated environments of St. Croix, U.S. Virgin Islands--a preliminary assessment. Journal of Coastal Research. Special Issue No. 8: 33-48.

Jaap, W.C., J.L. Wheaton, K.B. Donnelly, B.L. Kojis, and J.E. McKenna, Jr. 1992. A three-year evaluation of community dynamics of coral reefs at Fort Jefferson National Monument, Dry Tortugas, Florida, USA. In: Proc. Seventh International Coral Reef Symp. (in press). Guam.

Rogers, C.S. 1992. A matter of scale: damage from Hurricane Hugo (1989) to U.S. Virgin Islands reefs at the colony, community, and whole reef level. In: Proc. Seventh International Coral Reef Symp. (in press). Guam.

Rogers, C.S., L.N. McLain, and C.R. Tobias. 1991. Effects of Hurricane Hugo (1989) on a coral reef in St. John. Mar. Ecol. Prog. Ser. 78: 189-199.

Porter, J.P. and O.W. Meier. 1991. Quantification of loss and change in Floridian reef coral populations. Symposium on Long-Term Dynamics of Coral Reefs. American Society of Zoologists 32 (6):625-640.

IS HERBIVORE LOSS MORE DAMAGING TO REEFS THAN HURRICANES?
CASE STUDIES FROM TWO CARIBBEAN REEF SYSTEMS (1978 - 1988)

Robert S. Steneck

University of Maine, Department of Oceanography, Darling Marine Center, Walpole, Maine 04573

ABSTRACT

Case studies of reefs at Discovery Bay, Jamaica (1978 - 1987) and Teague Bay and Salt River Canyon, St. Croix (1982 - 1988) focus on physical and biotic changes that occurred in forereefs resulting from hurricanes Allen in Jamaica (1980), and David and Federic in St. Croix (1979) and the Caribbean-wide mass-mortality in the sea urchin *Diadema antillarum* (1983 - 1984).

Severe hurricanes reduce both architectural complexity of reefs and the abundance of living coral by differentially fracturing branching (acroporid) corals. This impact is greatest at shallow depths ($\leq$ 3m) where branching acroporid corals dominate. Abundances of other corals, algae (fleshy and coralline) and herbivores remained unchanged. Hurricane impact is relatively short lived because it can be reversed through the growth and regenerative capacity of corals.

Four years after the urchin die-off, macroalgal biomass remained high at all depths in Jamaica and St. Croix. Macroalgae and reef-building organisms such as corals and coralline algae were inversely correlated at all depths and stations studied. At one 3m site coral abundance declined to zero following the urchin die-off. The sudden loss of sea urchins when subtracted from the fishing-induced decline in megaherbivorous fishes, may have created an unprecedented decline in total herbivory. Without constructive elements for reef growth to counteract bioerosion, reefs will degenerate. Clearly other factors could contribute to the loss of corals but the close temporal correlation seen at two distinct sites argues for herbivory playing a major role in reef growth by facilitating recruitment, growth and survival of reef building organisms.

INTRODUCTION

Case histories of Caribbean reefs may provide the best argument against the outdated concept that diversity begets stability. Highly diverse coral reefs throughout the Caribbean have proven to be highly unstable with large-scale changes in community dominance and physical structure widely observed. Unfortunately, even striking changes in reefs are often difficult to quantify because data for the pre-disturbed state are lacking. My case studies focus on two different reef systems in St. Croix and Jamaica, both of which were affected by two different and unrelated natural events: hurricanes and changes in herbivory.

All reefs were periodically studied between 1978 and 1988 (see Recent Reef Histories). However, the timing of the studies fortuitously gave me an opportunity to evaluate the relative importance of hurricanes and the mass mortality of the herbivore, *Diadema antillarum*. For the purpose of these case studies, I will focus on changes in the reef's architectural complexity, population densities of the dominant grazing sea urchin, *Diadema antillarum*, and resultant changes in algal biomass and the abundances of dominant reef building organisms such as scleractinian corals, *Millapora* sp and encrusting coralline algae. I focus most of my attention on shallow forereef zones because they have the highest organic and calcium carbonate productivity. Further, I show that consequences of the mass mortality in *D. antillarum* could have long-lasting consequences because the subsequent increase in algal biomass may negatively impact the major carbonate producing organisms and thus affect the regenerative capacity of the reef.

METHODS

Recent Reef Histories

The Discovery Bay reef on the north shore of Jamaica was the site of some of the earliest reef research in the Caribbean (Goreau, 1959). My quantitative reef surveys were conducted during July of 1978, 1982 and 1987. Hurricane Allen hit the reef August 1980 (Woodley et al., 1981), and the mass mortality of the sea urchin *Diadema antillarum* occurred July 1983 (Lessios, 1988).

The Teague Bay and Salt River Canyon reefs on the north shore of St. Croix have been intensively studied since the early 1970s (e.g., Sammarco et al, 1974). My quantitative surveys were conducted during April 1982 and 1988. Hurricanes David and Frederic struck St. Croix in August and September of 1979 (Rogers et al., 1982). The mass mortality of *Diadema antillarum* occurred January 1984.

Study Sites and Quantitative Sampling Regime

Both reef locations, Jamaica and St. Croix, were surveyed at distinct depth zones. Nine depth zones were studied in St. Croix at two locations (Teague Bay and Salt River Canyon, site details in Steneck 1983). In St. Croix, shallow sites on the Teague Bay reef between 1 and 5 meters were pooled (i.e., "3 m" zone), and sites at both Teague Bay and Salt River Canyon at 10 m were pooled (i.e.,

"10 m" zone). The deep reef zone at Salt River Canyon pooled stations between 20 and 40m (i.e., "30 m" zone). Two forereef sites were monitored on the Discovery Bay reef in Jamaica (details in Hughes et al., 1987) at depths of 3, and 10m.

Percent cover of reef-dwelling organisms and reef architectural complexity were quantified using linear transects (Rogers et al., 1982, 1983). The "spatial index" represents the meters of substratum measured all reef components following surface contours along the substratum in a plane under a linear meter length stretched straight just over the reef surface. This results in data represented as meters of reef component per linear meter measured. On planar or featureless surfaces the spatial index =1 but values over 5 m/m were recorded.

Diadema antillarum abundance was recorded at each sampling site by haphazardly tossing a meter square quadrat. Previous work determined that a minimum sufficient sample size for urchin densities is ≥ 20 quadrats per site.

Algal biomasses were determined from substratum samples collected in each zone. Macroalgae were plucked, subdivided by species, dried and weighed. Then substratum was again subsampled to determine the abundance of minute turf algae. For this 13, three mm-wide gouges, each one mm deep and one cm long, were collected for a total sampling area of 3.9 cm^2. Species-level biomasses were pooled for total fleshy algal biomass.

RESULTS

Hurricane Impacts

Three hurricanes are involved with the two case studies. Jamaica's Discovery Bay reef was most severely hit by Hurricane Allen when it passed within 50 km on 6 August 1980. Maximum winds up to 285 km/h were recorded for this hurricane and 110 km/h winds were recorded on Jamaica. Twelve meter high waves struck the Discovery Bay reef (Woodley et al., 1981). In contrast, the two hurricanes which affected St. Croix in rapid succession, Hurricanes David and Federic, were less intense and had much smaller storm-induced waves. Hurricane David passed 204 km south of St. Croix on 30 August 1979 with winds of 86 km/h and waves up to 5.7 m. Hurricane Federic passed 137 km north of St. Croix on 4 September 1979 with winds of 56 km/hr gusting to 80 km/h and waves up to 3 m.

Jamaica

Reef Architectural Complexity, and Coral Abundance

In 1978, the forereef at Discovery Bay was highly complex (Fig. 1 a). Average spatial indices ranged from 3.8 m/m at 3m to 2.8 m/m at 10m. This translates to 14.8 m2 and 7.7 m^2 of reef surface area per planar m^2 area for 3m and 10, respectively. High architectural complexity resulted from the abundance of branching acroporid corals. *Acropora palmata* dominated at 3 m (30.9 % cover $\pm$ 19.8 standard deviation, hereafter "SD", n = 34) and *A. cervicornis* dominated at 10 m (10.7% $\pm$ 13.1, n = 22). These two species comprised between 80 and 34% of all live coral at 3 and 10m forereef zones, respectively (Fig. 1b).

Hurricane Allen (1979) reduced reef architectural complexity to 1.6 and 1.4 m/m when measured in 1982 at 3 and 10 m, respectively (Fig. 1a). This translated to surface areas of 2.6 and 2.0 m^2 of reef surface area per planar m^2 for the 3 and 10m zones respectively. Thus, the 3m site was reduced to less than 18% of the pre-hurricane reef surface area. The nearly flattened 3m zone resulted from damage sustained by the branched coral, *A. palamata*. Architectural complexity remained at post-hurricane levels at both the 3 and 10 m zones through 1987.

Live coral cover decreased significantly following the hurricane (Fig. 1b) due to declines in the relatively delicate *Acropora palmata* and *A. cervicornis* at 3 and 10m, respectively. Coral cover continued to decline between 1982 to 1987 at 3m but remained constant at 10m. This difference in mortality trends between the two depths may reflect the abundance of unbranched corals at 10m. Robust mound forming corals such as *Montastrea annularis, M. cavernosa, Diploria strigosa, D. labyrinthiformis* and *Porites astreoides* were significantly more abundant at 10m and their abundance changed little from 1978 (12.6%) to 1987 (9.8%). The acroporid species never regained their prehurricane abundance and ranged between 0 and 0.5% cover at the 3 and 10m zones in 1987.

Urchins and Algal Abundance

In 1978, the urchin, *Diadema antillarum*, was abundant at both forereef sites (Fig. 2a). The abundance and depth patterns were virtually unchanged in both zones in 1982, two years after Hurricane Allen. In 1983, the urchins suffered a mass mortality which killed over 98% of the population (see Recent Reef Histories). Four years later (1987) urchin population densities ranged from 0.04/m^2 ($\pm$ 0.9, n = 66 quadrats) at 3m to 0.0/m^2, (n = 28) at 10m.

The biomass of fleshy algae (i.e., erect, non-encrusting, turfs and macroalgae; *sensu* Steneck, 1988) were low at both zones from at least 1978 through 1982 (Fig. 2b). Hurricane Allen had little lasting impact on them. However, following the mass

Jamaica

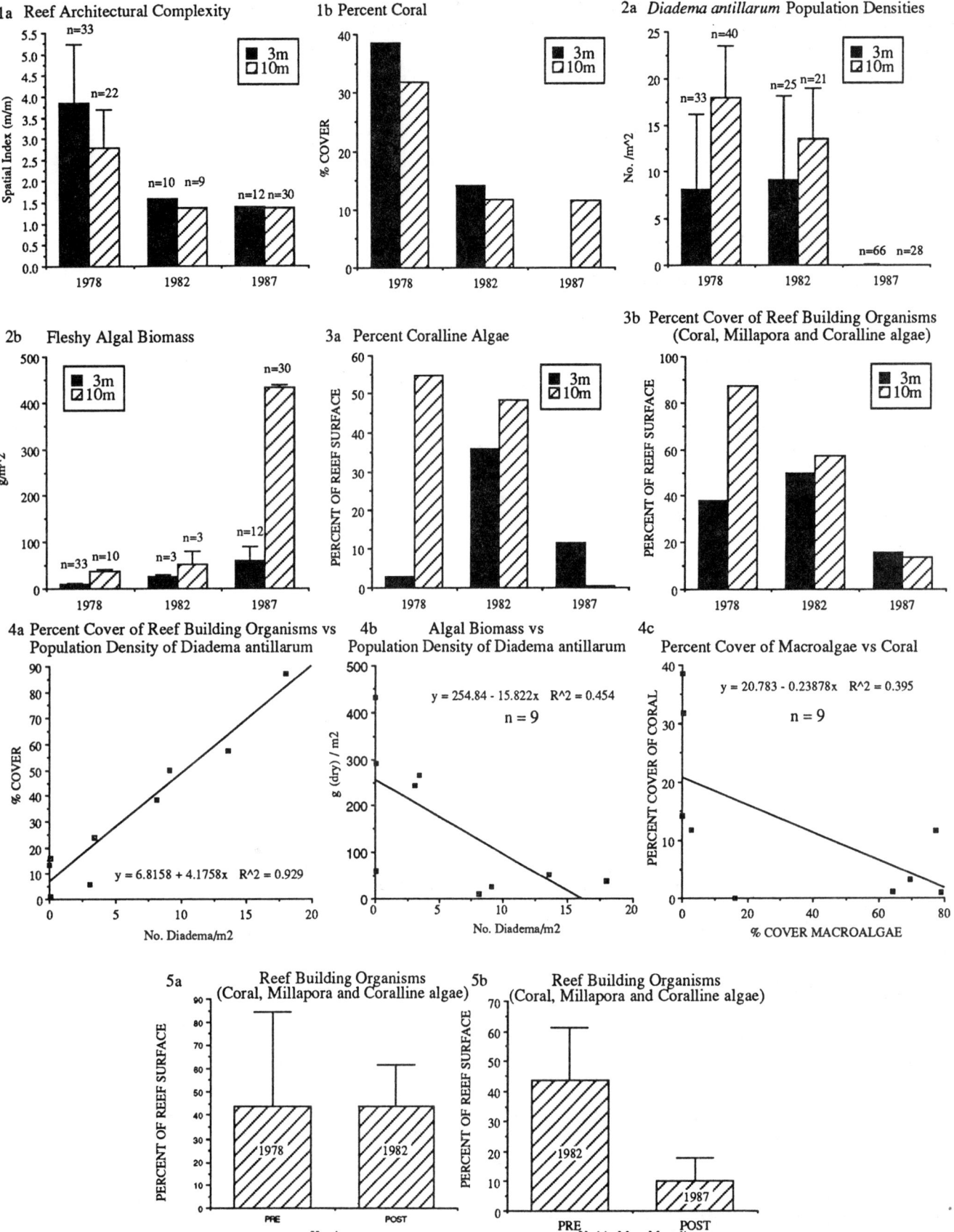

mortality of *Diadema antillarum*, algal abundance increased at both depths. The increase in algal biomass at the 10 m zone was most conspicuous due to the change in algal dominance from a low canopy algal turf to large stands of macroalgae. Macroalgal abundance rose from 2.4 and 1.8 g/m^2 in 1978 and 1982 to 400.6 g/m^2 in 1988. Although the magnitude of increase in algal biomass at 3m was not great, macroalgae which was absent in 1978 and 1982, rose to 46.3 g/m^2 in 1988.

Patterns of abundance among encrusting coralline algae (Fig. 3a) were opposite those of erect algae (Fig. 2b). Corallines were significantly more abundant at 10 m in 1978 and 1982 than in 1987 (Fig. 3a). There they declined most precipitously (Fig. 2b) following the mass mortality in urchins (Fig. 2a).

Abundance of Reef-building Organisms with Herbivores and Hurricanes

The abundance of all major reef-building organisms (i.e., scleractinian corals, *Millapora* spp. and encrusting coralline algae), remained relatively constant between 1978 and 1982 but declined in 1987 at both the 3 and 10m zones (Fig. 3b). Taken together, over all years and both zones, the percent cover of all calcareous reef-building organisms correlates directly with *Diadema* densities (Fig. 4a). In contrast, *Diadema* and algal biomass are inversely correlated (Fig. 4b), as are macroalgae and coral abundance (Fig. 4c). Reef-building organisms were not reduced in abundance two years after Hurricane Allen (Figs. 3b, 5a)

The percent cover of reef-building organisms compared before and after Hurricane Allen (Fig. 5a), were unchanged. The same analysis with respect to the mass mortality in *Diadema* indicated a strong effect. (Fig. 5b)

Fish grazing rates were relatively low in Jamaica (i.e., compared with St. Croix) but the highest values were recorded at 3m . At both depths fish grazing rates increased after the mass mortality in sea urchins. Grazing by herbivorous fishes was monitored using visual bite-rate counts (methods in Steneck, 1983). Fishes with the greatest impact include the "scraping" parrotfish (*Scarus* and *Sparisoma*), and the "denuding" tangs (*Acanthurus*) and some damselfish such as the yellow-tail damsel (*Microspathodon chrysurus*) (scraping and denuding designations in Steneck 1988). In 1982 at 3m, grazing rates were 0 for denuding fishes and 215 bites/m^2/h for parrotfishes. In that zone, following the mass mortality of *Diadema*, fish grazing rates increased to 50.6 for denuding grazers and 364.5 for the scraping parrotfishes. Grazing rates were lower at 10 m and 0 and 98.4 bites/m^2/h were recorded for denuding and scraping fishes. These rates increased to 12.5 and 155 bites/m^2/h in 1988.

St. Croix

Reef Architectural Complexity and Coral Abundance

Hurricanes Federic and David passed near St. Croix in rapid succession in August and September of 1979 but had little impact on the architectural complexity of the Teague Bay reef. Surveys conducted by Rogers et al. (1982) immediately after the hurricanes in November of 1979 recorded relatively high architectural complexity for the Teague Bay reef (i.e., 2.7 m/m spatial index, Rogers et al 1982). In 1982 I recorded a lower architectural complexity (i.e., 1.7 m/m, Fig. 6a) at the 3 m zone which may reflect the patchy nature of the hurricane disturbance on the Teague Bay reef (Rogers et al., 1982). Linear transects in 1988 recorded reef architectural complexity at 3m of 2.5 m/m (Fig. 6a).

The percent cover of live coral was 33.6 to 20.7% at 3 and 10 m, respectively in 1982 (Fig. 6b). This was more than twice the 10% reported just following the hurricanes by Rogers et al. (1982) and supports their conclusions that coral regeneration was rapid on the Teague Bay reef. At greater depths and over both sampling periods, the percent of live coral averaged between 14 and 20%. Coral morphologies were zoned with depth. The branching *Acropora palmata* dominated at 3 m, mound corals (e.g., *Montastrea cavernosa, Dichocenia stellaris,* and *Diploria* spp.) dominated at 10 m and platy corals (e.g., *Agaricia* spp) dominated zones between 20 and 40 m.

Urchins and Algal Abundance

Diadema antillarum population densities were greatest at 3 m and lowest below 20 m in 1982 (Fig. 7a). Populations declined dramatically following the mass mortality in 1984. They remained low four years later in 1988 when they reached their maximum abundance again at 3m but it was only 2.5% of their original population density.

Algal biomass was low at all depths in 1982 but increased significantly by 1988 (Fig. 7b). The most dramatic increase occurred at 10 m depth. Most of the change was due to increases in the abundance of macroalgae (primarily *Dictyota* spp, *Laurencia*, sp. and *Lobophora* sp.) which were virtually nonexistent in 1982.

Encrusting coralline algae dominated the 3m zone at Teague Bay in 1982 but decreased to less than half that abundance in 1988 (Fig. 8a). Only slight changes occurred at 10 and 30 m.

St. Croix

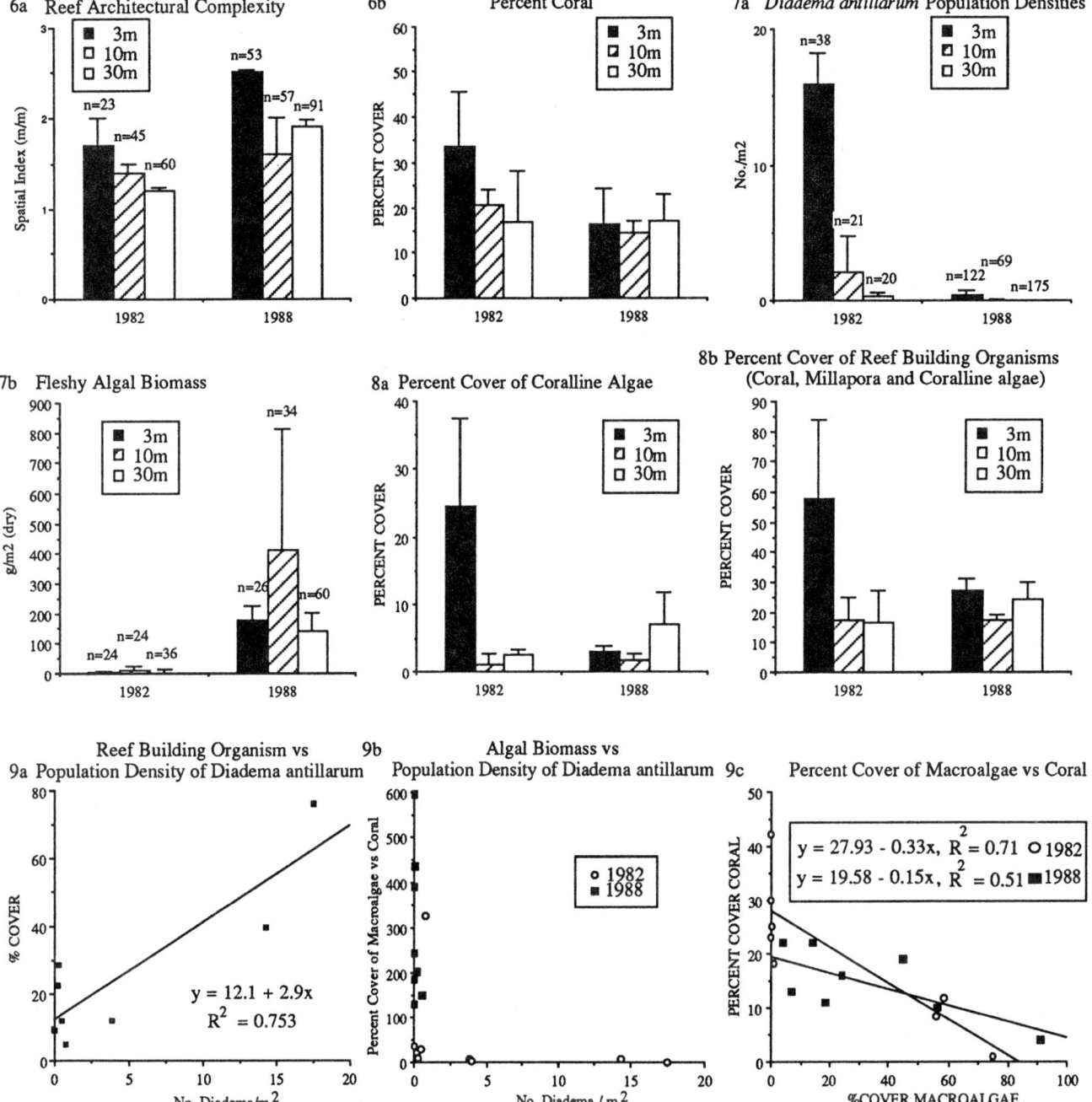

Abundance of Reef-building Organisms with Herbivores and Hurricanes

Reef building organisms declined significantly at 3 m between 1982 and 1988 (Fig. 8b). There were no significant changes at the other depth zones between years. Reef building organisms were also positively correlated with *Diadema antillarum* abundance in 1982 (Fig. 9a). Urchin densities were too low in 1988 to include them in this analysis. Macroalgal biomass was high only where *Diadema* abundance was low (Fig 9 b). Since urchin densities were low in all zones in 1988, macroalgal abundances were high (Figs 9b, 7b). Coral cover was inversely correlated with macroalgal abundance during both sampling periods (Fig. 9c).

Impact of the hurricanes on the St. Croix reefs were relatively minor and short lived. My personal experience on the Teague Bay reef dates back to 1972, and from then to 1982 no conspicuous differences were evident to me. Throughout that period, *Diadema* were annoyingly abundant, macroalgae were rare and coral was conspicuous. Therefore, the 1982 data may indicate long-persistent patterns of reef composition prior to the mass mortality.

Fish grazing was greatest in the 3 m zone in 1982 but increased at 10 m after the mass mortality in sea urchins. Grazing rates of 12.5 bites/m^2/h ($\pm$ 0.7 SD) and 625.8 ($\pm$ 884 SD) were recorded at 3 m for denuding and scraping fishes, respectively. Following the mass mortality, grazing rates at 3m were 553.0 bites/m^2/h ($\pm$ 242 SD) and 510.0 ($\pm$ 721 SD) for denuding and scraping fishes, respectively. Although lower values were recorded at 10 m for these two groups of grazing fishes in 1982 (i.e., 9.5 $\pm$ 9.2 SD, 39.5 $\pm$ 55.9 SD), significantly higher values were recorded in 1988 (i.e., 236.5 $\pm$ 87.0 SD, 1913.0 $\pm$ 1224.7 SD). At even greater depths around 30 m, grazing rates were moderately low (8.3 $\pm$ 2.3 SD, 172.3, $\pm$ 151.1 SD) from denuding and scraping herbivores, respectively).

DISCUSSION

Reefs grow most rapidly in shallow wave-exposed zones and thus the dynamics occurring there will have the greatest consequences. Reef communities living in shallow water (i.e., $\leq$ 10 m) have the greatest rates of organic (Adey and Steneck, 1985) and inorganic (i.e., calcium carbonate, Smith and Buddemeier, 1992) production. It is also where herbivory and the potential for physical disturbances are greatest.

Branching coral morphologies often dominate shallow forereef environments and comprise a significant proportion of coral framework in growing reefs (e.g., Adey and Burke, 1976, Macintyre et al., 1977). Further, branching coral morphologies are capable of most rapid growth (Gladfelter et al., 1978) and regeneration (Rogers et al., 1982) but they are also most susceptible to hurricane impacts (Porter et al., 1981).

Hurricane impact appears to be very limited both spatially and temporally. In St. Croix, the north-shore reefs (i.e., Teague Bay and Salt River Canyon) were spared by Hurricanes David and Federic whereas the south shore "Robin" reef suffered a dramatic reduction in architectural complexity (Rogers et al., 1982). Jamaica's Hurricane Allen reduced architectural complexity by more than 80% in the shallowest zones by fracturing the branching acroporid corals (Fig. 1a). However, because acroporids are capable of very rapid growth and regeneration (although this can be delayed by post hurricane diseases [Knowlton et al., 1981]), and because most of the other coral components were unchanged, hurricane impact is likely to be rather short lived. Similar conclusions were reached by Rogers et al., 1982, 1983. Finally, hurricane impacts are limited to shallow reefs of usually less than 10 m (Woodley et al., 1981, Rogers et al., 1982).

The loss of *Diadema* appears to be much more significant than hurricanes because its impact on algal abundance is very widespread (e.g., reviewed in Lessios., 1988) and relatively long-lasting. In Jamaica and St. Croix, algal biomass increased at all depths but to the greatest extent at 10 m (Figs 2b, 7b). Similar reports have been made for these reefs (e.g., Jamaica: Liddell and Ohlhorst, 1986, Hughes et al., 1987; St. Croix: Carpenter, 1990) and other reefs throughout the Caribbean (e.g., St. John, Levitan 1988; Curacao, Ruyter van Steveninck and Bak, 1986). Accumulations of macroalgae have long been known to affect the recruitment (Birkland 1977), and survival of corals (e.g., Figs. 4c, 9c; Fishelson 1973) as well as limit the abundance of encrusting coralline algae (Steneck, 1986, Liddell and Ohlhorst, 1986, Ruyter van Steveninck and Bak, 1986). Thus when considered together, reef building organisms are dependent on and positively correlated with grazers such as *Diadema antillarum* (Fig. 4a, 9a).

Herbivory from fishes may have been much more important before they were harvested by humans. In Jamaica, the fishing pressure on the reef is greater than it is in St. Croix because the human population is great and the reef area small (Stevenson and Marshall, 1974, Smith and Buddemeier, 1992). During the course of the study, only in Jamaica were herbivorous fishes served at local restaurants. I found that not only were herbivore grazing rates lower in Jamaica (see Results), but the fish body sizes were smaller as well. On both islands, fish grazing rates were highest at 3 m and thus the magnitude increase in algal biomass following the mass mortality was lower than it was at 10 m (Figs 2b, 7b). Since herbivorous fishes and *Diadema* compete for the same algal trophic resources (Carpenter, 1990), the loss of abundant, large bodied herbivorous fishes may have been compensated by increases in urchin populations. If so, that reduction in herbivore diversity may have directly contributed to cascading effects that destabilized the structure of Caribbean reefs.

Acknowledgments

Funding for this research was provided by NOAA's National Undersea Research Program grants (82 - 6, 87-5) and from NSF OCE 8315136, OCE 8600262 and OCE9116961) Facilities were provided at the Discovery Bay Marine Laboratory in Jamaica by J. Woodley and several classes from the Coral Reef Ecology Course (including R. Olsen, S. Lewis, P. Wainwright of the class of 1978) helped generate these data. Help came from C. Pfister, K. Moody, R. Wahle, S. Hacker, D. Low, B. Carpenter, J. Porter, D. Estler, T. Miller, B. Milliken, K. Nielsen, E. Fleishman. To all I am grateful.

LITERATURE CITED

Adey, W. H. and R. B. Burke. 1976. Holocene bioherms (algal ridges and bank-barrier reefs) of the eastern Caribbean. Geol. Soc. Am. Bull. 87: 95 - 109.

Adey, W. H. and R. S. Steneck 1985.Highly productive eastern Caribbean reefs: synergistic effects of biological, chemical, physical and geological factors. In Reaka M. L. (ed.).The Ecology of Deep and Shallow Coral Reefs. Symposia Series for Undersea Research, Vol. 2. Office of Undersea Research, NOAA, Rockville, Maryland.

Birkeland, C. 1977. The importance of rates of biomass accumulation in early successional stages of benthic communities. Proc. 3rd. Int. Coral Reef Symp. 1: 15 - 21.

Carpenter, R. C. 1990. mass mortality of *Diadema antillarum* 2. effects on population densities and grazing intensity of parrotfishes and surgeonfishes. Marine Biology. 104: 79 - 86.

Fishelson, L. 1973. Ecology of coral reefs in the Gulf of Aqaba (Red Sea) influenced by pollution. Oecologia 12: 55 - 67.

Gladfelter, E. H., R. K. Monahan, and W. B. Gladfelter. 1978. Growth rates of five reef-building corals in the northeastern Caribbean. Bull. Mar. Sci. 28: 728 - 734.

Goreau, T. F. 1959. The ecology of Jamaican coral reefs I. Species composition and zonation. Ecology. 40: 67-90

Hughes, T. P., D. C. Reed and M. Boyle. 1987. Herbivory on coral reefs: community structure following mass mortalities of sea urchins. J. Exp. mar. Biol. Ecol. 113: 39 - 59.

Knowlton, N. J. C. Lang, M. C. Rooney, P. Clifford. 1981. Evidence for delayed mortality in hurricane-damaged Jamaican staghorn corals. Nature. 294: 251 - 252.

Lessios, H. A. 1988. Mass mortality of *Diadema antillarum* in the Caribbean: what have we learned? Ann. Rev. Ecol. Syst. 19: 371 - 393.

Levitan, D. R. 1988. Algal-urchin biomass responses following mass mortality of *Diadema antillarum* Philippi at Saint John, U. S. Virgin Islands. J. Exp. Mar. Biol. Ecol. 119: 167 - 178.

Liddell, W. D. and S. L. Ohlhorst. 1986. Changes in benthic community composition following the mass mortality of *Diadema* at Jamaica. J. Exp. Mar. Biol. Ecol. 95: 271 - 278.

Macintyre, I. C., R. B Burke and R. Stuckenrath. 1977. Thickest recorded Holocene reef section, Isla Perez core hole, Alacran Reef, Mexico. Geology. 5: 749 - 754.

Porter, J. W., J. D. Woodley, G. J. Smith, J. E. Neigel, J. F. Battey, D. G. Dallmeyer. 1981.Population trends among Jamaican reef corals. Nature. 294: 249 - 250.

Roger, C. S., T. H. Suchanek, F. A. Pecora. 1982. Effects of hurricanes David and Frederic (1979) on shallow *Acropora palmata* reef communities: St. Croix, U.S. Virgin Islands. Bull. of Mar. Sci. 32: 532 - 548.

Rogers, C. S., M. Gilnack and H. C. Fitz III. 1983. Monitoring of coral reefs with linear transects: a study of storm damage. J. Exp. mar. Biol. Ecol. 66: 285 - 300.

Ruyter van Steveninck, E. D. and R. P. M. Bak 1986. Changes in abundance of coral-reef bottom components related to mass mortality of the sea urchin *Diadema antillarum*. Mar. Ecol. Prog. Ser. 34: 87 - 94.

Sammarco, P.W., J. S. Levinton, and J. C. Ogden. 1974. Grazing and control of coral reef community structure by *Diadema antillarum* Philippi (Echinodermata: Echinoidea): a preliminary study. J. Mar. Res. 32: 47 - 53.

Smith, S. V. and R. W. Buddemeier. 1992. Global change and coral reef ecosystems. Ann. Rev. of Ecol. Syst. 23: 89 - 119.

Steneck, R. S. 1983. Adaptations of crustose coralline algae to herbivory: Patterns in space and time. Pages 352 - 366. In Toomy, D and M. Nitecki (eds). Paleoalgology. Springer - Verlag. Berlin.

Steneck, R. S. 1986. The ecology of coralline algal crusts: convergent patterns and adaptive strategies. Ann. Rev. Ecol. Syst. 7: 273 - 303

Steneck, R. S. 1988. Herbivory on coral reefs: a synthesis. Proc. 6th International Coral Reef Symposium, Australia. 1: 37 - 49.

Stevenson, D. K., and N. Marshall. 1974. Generalizations on the fisheries potential of coral reefs and adjacent shallow water environments. Proc. Int. Coral Reef Symp. 2nd 1: 147 - 156.

Woodley, J. D., E. A. Chornesky, P. A. Clifford, J. B. C. Jackson, L. S. Kaufman, N. Knowlton, J. Lang, M. Pearson, J. Porter, M. Rooney, C. Rylaarsdam, K. Tunnicliffe, C. Wahle, J. Wulff, L. Curtis, M. Dallmeyer, B. Jupp, M. Koehl, J. Neigel, E. Sides. 1981. Hurricane Allen's impact on Jamaican coral reefs. Science 214: 749 - 755.

STRUCTURAL CHANGES AND VULNERABILITY OF A CORAL REEF (CAYO ENRIQUE) IN LA PARGUERA, PUERTO RICO

Vance P. Vicente, Ph.D.

Southeast Fishery Science Center, Caribbean.
c/o CFMC, 268 Munoz Rivera Avenue, Suite 1108
Hato Rey, Puerto Rico 00918-2577

ABSTRACT

Over the last five decades, Cayo Enrique reef has been exposed to local extinctions, warm sea surface temperatures, hurricanes, competitive displacements of hermatypic corals by sponges, and coral bleaching. The overall effects of these disturbances have been a decrease in coral cover and an increase in algal biomass. Filamentous algae, articulated coralline red algae and calcareous green algae are causing the displacement of intrinsic reef front components: corals and sponges. At present, Cayo Enrique may be considered as vulnerable. Coral reefs with low coral cover and/or high bioerosion rates cannot cope with expected sea level rise scenarios. If management measures oriented towards the restoration and enhancement of coral reefs are not implemented promptly, the ecological integrity of many reefs may be lost.

INTRODUCTION

Cayo Enrique forms part of a reef system which began to develop between 6,000 and 9,000 ybp. Eustatic sea level rise, shallow water, high water transparency, and proper substrata allowed the development of extensive coral reefs and seagrass beds within the shelf of La Parguera, Puerto Rico. Like other coral reefs along the southern coast of the island, Cayo Enrique reef is built on a light topographic high, which may represent drowned eolianitic structures (Kaye, 1959) deposited parallel to shore during the Wisconsian glacial period (see Goenaga, 1988). The reef is located 1.6 km from shore and extends 1.32 km along a northeast southwest axis (Figure 1). At present, Cayo Enrique bounds the southern limit of the inner shelf (Morelock et al., 1977).

Qualitative and quantitative assessments of benthic community structure have been conducted by Dr. Goenaga and myself at Cayo Enrique, since 1970. Several disturbances have significantly modified the structure of this reef at different scales of time, space, and intensity. The response of the reef to these disturbances, and the vulnerability of this reef is discussed.

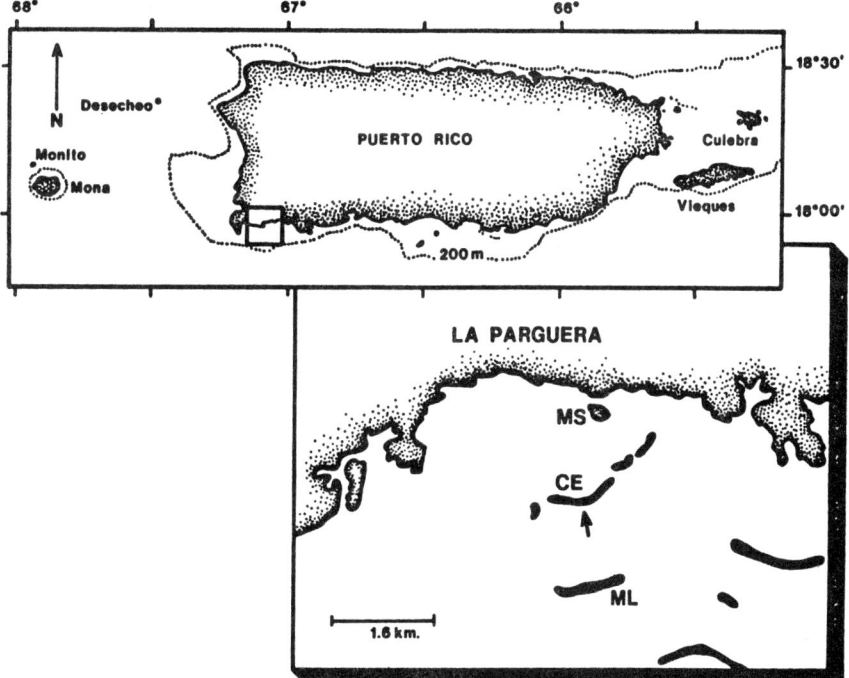

Figure 1. Location of Cayo Enrique Reef in La Parguera, southwest coast of Puerto Rico. CE = Cayo Enrique; ML = Media Luna Reef; MS = Marine Science Laboratory (Magueyes island).

METHODS

Most of the methods utilized in this study have been published in the literature. Methods to evaluate the ecological impacts of sea surface temperature anomalies are given in Vicente (1989a, 1989b). The methodology utilized to evaluate the impacts of interspecific interactions, extinctions, and bleaching events within Cayo Enrique is given in Vicente (1987; 1990a); Vicente and Goenaga 1984; Goenaga et al., 1989; and , Vicente 1990b).

RESULTS

Sea Surface Temperatures

The warmer sea surface temperatures during the 1950's (see Figure 2) are suspected to have had considerable impact on the benthic community structure of Cayo Enrique Reef. For example, species which are not truly tropical in origin are believed to become locally extinct during warm periods (Vicente, 1989a). This appears to be the case of two commercial sponge genera (Spongia and Hippospongia), which were abundant but became extinct within the Puerto Rican shelf during the 1950's (Vicente, 1989b).

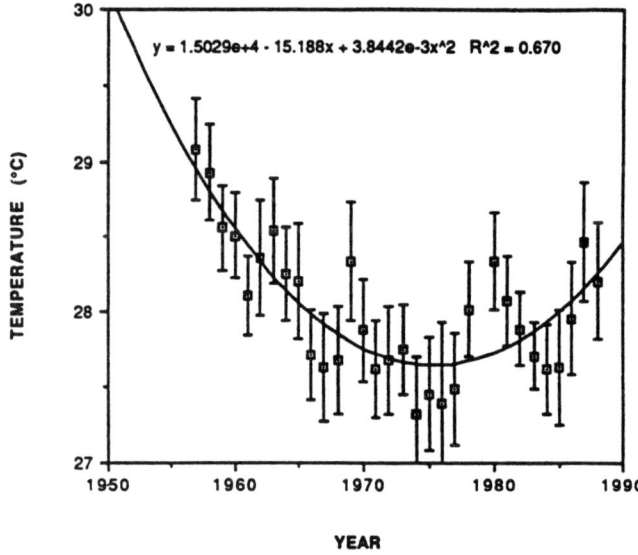

Figure 2. Sea surface temperatures at La Parguera (from Vicente, 1989b). Bars represent the Standard Error (SE). SST readings have been taken by personnel of the Department of Marine Sciences since 1958.

Hurricanes

Hurricane David (in 1979) had devastating effects on the reef front community of Cayo Enrique (and on other reef systems along the south coast of Puerto Rico). Almost all live colonies of elkhorn and staghorn corals (Acropora palmata and A. cervicornis) were broken loose and killed. Cemented elkhorn slabs were torn loose from the reef front and moved onto the reef flat. The populations of other benthic components (e.g. demosponges) within the A. palmata zone were also significantly impacted.

Competitive Displacement

Quantitative data obtained from permanent quadrat observations within the study site since September 1983 demonstrated that all scleractinian corals at the study site were becoming competitively displaced by encrusting taxa (e.g. by the demosponge Chondrilla nucula and by the encrusting alcyonarian Erythropodium caribbaeorum (Figure 3). Overgrowth displacements of corals by sponges were progressive (Figure 4).

All 13 species of hermatypic corals found within the grid became competitively displaced by C. nucula including species with defense mechanisms such as extracoelenteric digestion, sweeper tentacle formation or morphological adaptations. The competitive superiority of C. nucula over scleractinian corals did not change significantly as a function of depth or time (Vicente, 1987; 1990).

Extinction of Diadema antillarum.

During January 1984, the sea urchin Diadema antillarum became locally extinct at the study site, and throughout most reefs within the Puerto Rican shelf. This extinction had three major effects on the reef: significant mortalities of competitively dominant species; interference of overgrowth competitive processes; and an increase in filamentous algal biomass. Filamentous and articulated coralline red algae such as Gellidium pucillum, Coelothrix irregularis, and Amphiroa sp., became particularly abundant following the extinction event (Vicente, 1987).

Bleaching Event

An unprecedented Caribbean bleaching event occurred in the summer of 1987 (Williams et al., 1987) which impacted the reef front community of Cayo Enrique. About 22% (n = 326) of the monitored coral colonies became bleached of which 44% showed tissue necrosis (Goenaga et al., 1989). Light exposed bleached coral surfaces died and became colonized by filamentous algae. The overall impact of the bleaching event on Cayo Enrique was a reduction of live coral cover and an increase of filamentous algae.

Recent Observations

Between 1987 and 1990, qualitative observations at Cayo Enrique indicated that algal overgrowth has increased and coral cover has decreased. Furthermore, a calcareous green algae Halimeda opuntia (Chlorophyta: Caulerpales) have expanded its range from the reef flat onto the reef front causing extensive mortality of sessile coral reef invertebrates including hermatypic corals.

Cayo Enrique is being revisited in 1993. Permanent quadrats placed in 1983 are being photographed again and new in site information is being obtained. A preliminary, qualitative analysis of photographs taken within the study site during March 1993 indicate the following: there has been no successful recruitment of D. antillarum since its local extinction in January 1984; although Echinometra viridis have increased in abundance, the vacant niche of D. antillarum has not been filled; filamentous algae continue to be the dominant benthic component throughout the reef front community; coral cover is at its lowest level; and new damselfish territories (Stegastes albifrons) have been established over remaining live coral colonies (e.g. Colpophyllia natans).

DISCUSSION

There has been widespread national and international concern over the state of coral reefs worldwide with the increasing awareness of the intrinsic functional values of socioeconomic importance of coral reefs(e.g. shoreline protection, fisheries production, ecotourism). One of the concern is whether modern reefs will be able to cope with predicted climate change (e.g. an eustatic sea level rise of 6mm/yr over the next century). Buddemeier and Smith (1988) and Smith and Buddemeier (1992) state that this climatic scenario is well within the range of reef accretion rates (a rate of 10mm/yr is the consensus value for maximum sustained reef vertical accretion rates). This cannot hold true for Caribbean coral reefs with low coral cover (e.g. Cayo Enrique). Furthermore Caribbean reefs may be more prone to bioerosion than reefs elsewhere (Highsmith, 1980).

Cayo Enrique is a reef system under constant change. Over the last few decades natural stress factors have caused significant changes in community structure. Many coral colonies have died, coral diversity is low, live coral cover has been reduced, and filamentous algae have overgrown many corals and sponges. These factors have made Cayo Enrique reef vulnerable to any further sources of disturbance whether they be climatic or anthropogenic in origin.

Because the relative impact of the disturbances mentioned vary from reef to reef, the vulnerable state of Cayo Enrique reef may at least be representative of some other reef situations in the Caribbean. Regional characteristics of the Caribbean Sea which may be of direct relevance to the assessment of coral reefs within the West Indian Region are listed in Appendix I.

CONCLUSIONS

During the last few decades, Cayo Enrique reef has been exposed to local extinctions, warm sea surface temperatures, hurricanes, competitive displacements of hermatypic corals by sponges, and coral bleaching. The effects of these disturbances on the reef have been a decrease in coral cover and an increase in algal biomass. Many reefs within the Caribbean Region have been exposed (but some perhaps have reacted differently) to the same disturbances that have impacted Cayo Enrique. Therefore, the vulnerability of Cayo Enrique reef may be representative of, at least, some other reefs within the Region.

Management measures oriented towards conservation, restoration, and enhancement of Caribbean coral reefs may become necessary to preserve their functional values as well as their ecological integrity. Otherwise, the resistance of coral reefs to natural or enhanced climatic changes, or to any additional external sources of stress (whether natural or anthropogenic) may continue to decline. Meanwhile, some Caribbean reefs such as Cayo Enrique may be classified as vulnerable.

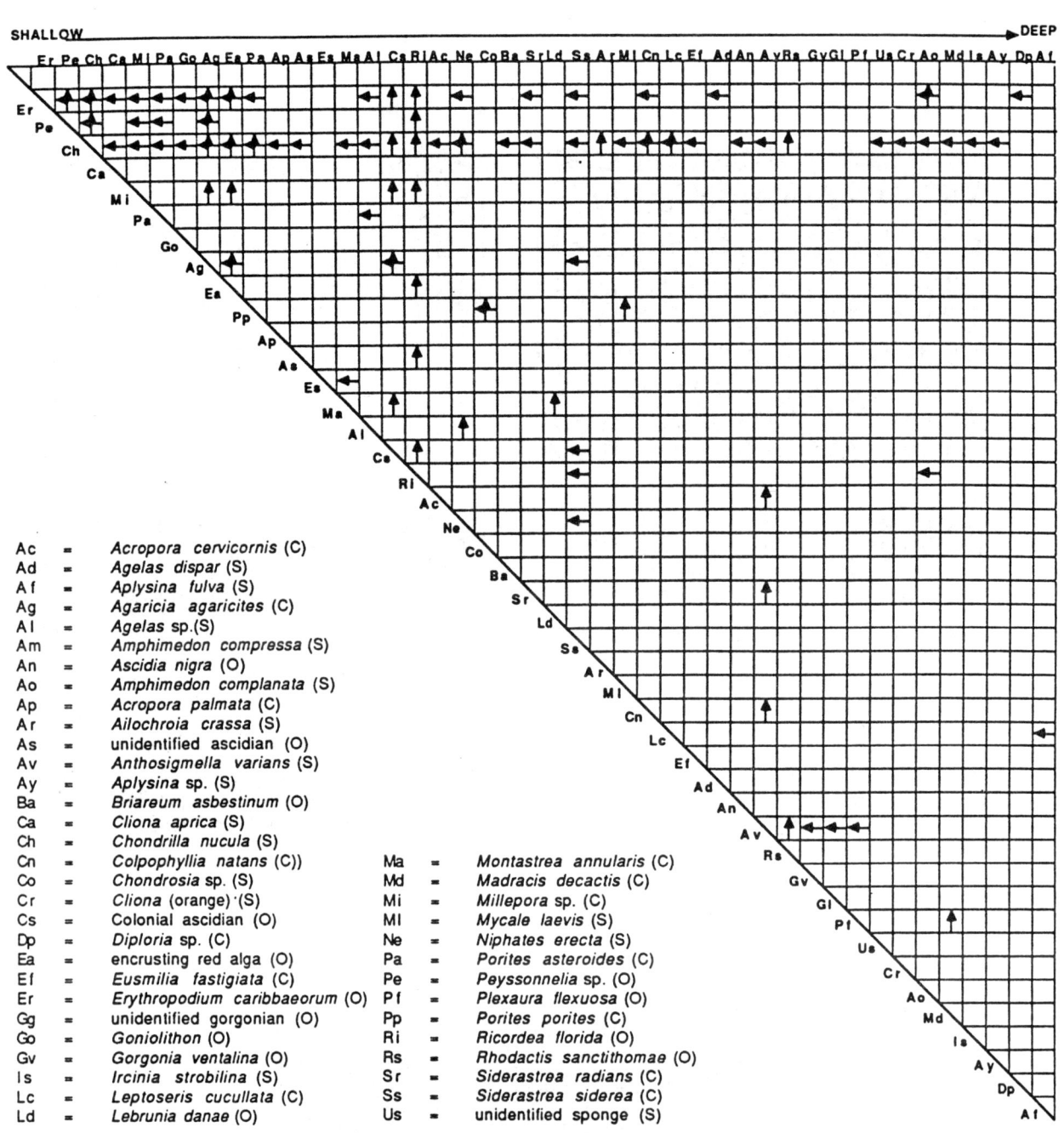

Figure 3. Contact data matrix of specific interactions found in the front reef of Cayo Enrique (from Vicente, 1990a). Arrows in each square point to winning species. Two arrows within a single square signify that either species may win (C. nucula was always the net winner in two arrow situations with corals).

Figure 4. Progressive competitive displacement of the hermatypic coral <u>Montastrea</u> <u>annularis</u> by the encrusting sponge <u>Chondrilla</u> <u>nucula</u> (September 1983 - March 1986). Arrow marks a contact area where filamentous algae interferes with the displacement process.

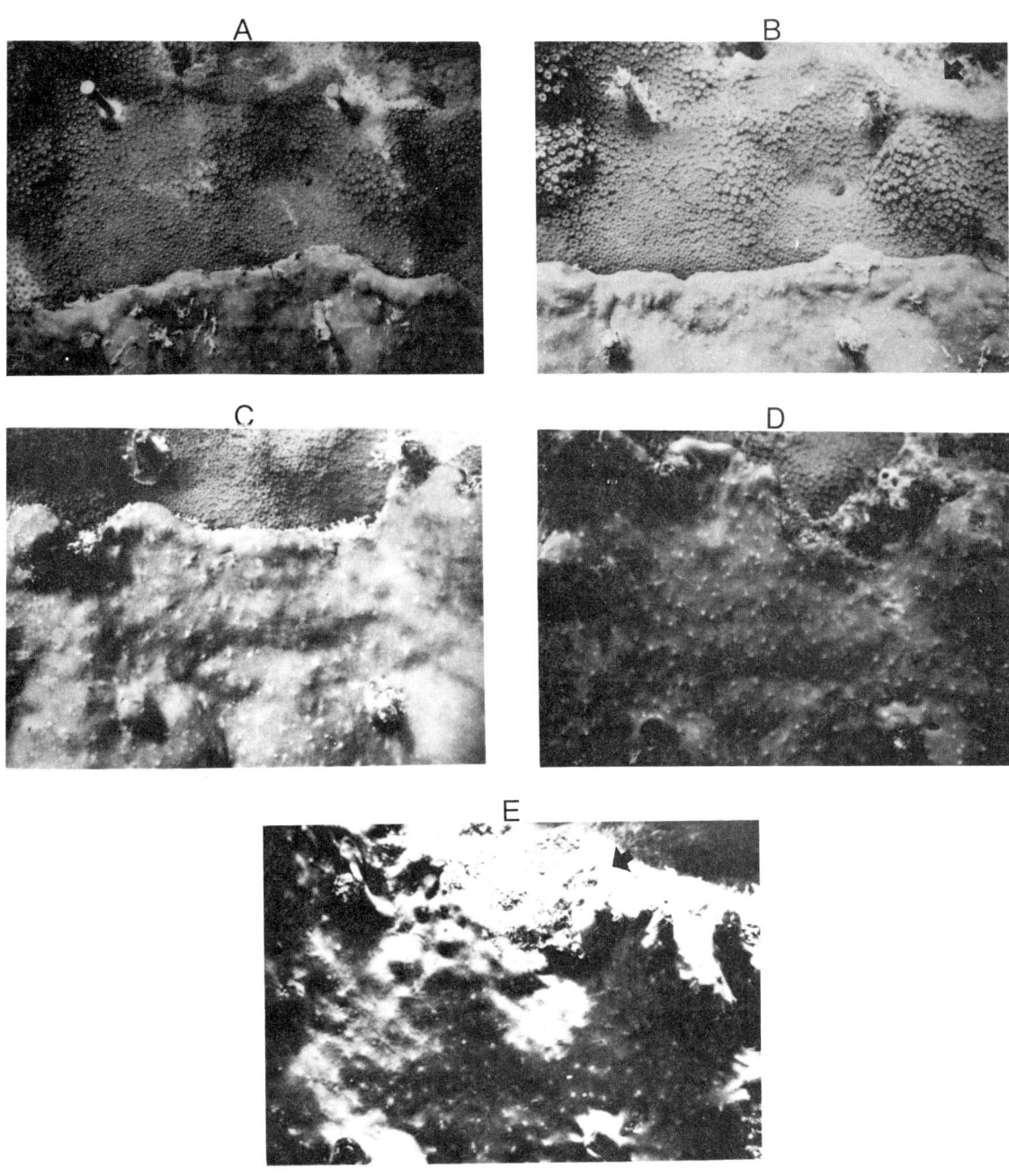

231

LITERATURE CITED

Buddemeier, R.W. and S.V. Smith. 1988. Coral reef growth in an era of rapidly rising sea level: predictions and suggestions for long term research. Coral Reefs, 7: 51-56.

Connell, J. 1978. Diversity in tropical rain forests and coral reefs. Science, 199: 1302-1310.

Goenaga, C., V.P. Vicente and R.A. Armstrong. 1989. Bleaching induced mortality in reef corals from La Parguera, Puerto Rico: a precursor of change in the community structure of coral reefs? Carib. Jour. Sci., 25(1-2): 59-65.

Goenaga, C. 1988. The distribution and growth of Montastrea annularis (Ellis and Solander) in Puerto Rican inshore platfor reefs. Ph.D. Thesis, University of Puerto Rico, Mayaguez Campus. 214pp.

Highsmith, R.C. 1980. Geographic patterns of coral bioerosion: A productivity hypothesis. J. Exp. Mar. Biol., 46: 77-96.

Kaye, C.A. 1959. Shoreline features and Quaternary shoreline changes, Puerto Rico. U.S. Geol. Survey Prof. Paper 3317-B: 49-139.

Morelock, J.,N. Schneidermann and W.R. Bryant. 1977. Shelf reefs, southwestern Puerto Rico. Pages 17-25 in Reefs and related carbonates-ecology and sedimentology. 4: 17-25. The American Association of Petroleum Geologists, Oklahoma.

Muller-Karger, F.E., C.R. McClain, and P.L. Richardson. 1988. The dispersal of the Amazon's water. Nature, 333: 56-59.

Peters, E.C. 1984. A survey of cellular reactions to environmental stress and disease in Caribbean scleractinian corals. Helgolander Meeresunters, 37: 113-137.

Smith, S.V. and R.W. Buddemeier. 1992. Global change and coral reef ecosystems. Annu. Rev. Ecol. Syst. 23: 89-118.

Vicente, V.P. 1987. The ecology of the encrusting demosponge Chondrilla nucula (Schmidt) in a coral reef community in Puerto Rico. Ph.D. Thesis. Department of Marine Sciences, University of Puerto Rico, Mayagüez, Puerto Rico. 118 pp.

Vicente, V.P. 1989a. Regional commercial sponge extinctions in the Caribbean: Are recent climatic changes responsible? Marine Ecology, 10(2): 179-191.

Vicente, V.P. 1989b. Ecological effects of sea level rise and sea surface temperatures on mangroves, coral reefs, seagrass beds and sandy beaches of Puerto Rico: A preliminary evaluation. Science-Ciencia, 16(2): 27-39.

Vicente, V.P. 1990a. Overgrowth activity by the encrusting sponge Chondrilla nucula on a coral reef in Puerto Rico. In: New Perspectives in Sponge Biology. K. Rtzler (ed.). Smithsonian Press. 525 pp.

Vicente, V.P. 1990b. Response of sponges with autotrophic symbionts during the coral-bleaching episode in Puerto Rico. Coral Reefs, 8: 199-202.

Vicente, V.P. 1992. Expected response of Caribbean coral reefs to disturbances associated with sea level rise. Paper presented at the International Workshop (WMO/UNEP/IPCC) "The Rising Challenge of the Sea". Margarita Island, Venezuela, SA.

Vicente, V.P. and C. Goenaga. 1984. Mass mortalities of the sea urchin Diadema antillarum (Philippi) in Puerto Rico. CEER-- M-195: 1-30.

Williams, E.H., Goenaga, C., V.P. Vicente. 1987. Mass bleachings on Atlantic coral reefs. Science, 238: 877-878.

APPENDIX I

There are several regional characteristics of the Caribbean Sea and certain episodes which have affected, and some are still affecting, much of the Caribbean Region as whole. These need to be discussed when assessing the status of Caribbean reefs. Some of them are listed below.

1. The Tropical Surface Water of the Caribbean Sea may not be the ideal water mass for maximum coral reef development (Vicente, 1992), since this water mass receives immense amounts of nutrients and sediments. It is believed that over 20% of the fresh water discharged annually by the world's rivers enters the Caribbean Sea. The dispersal of the Amazon's discharge alone, affects surface salinity, phytoplankton concentration, and phytoplankton species composition throughout the western tropical Atlantic (Muller-Karger et al., 1988). These factors do not necessarily promote maximum reef development, since coral reefs grow best in oligotrophic waters with low primary production rates.

2. A large portion of the Caribbean reef tract lies within the hurricane belt. This may weaken the reef structure and may cause extensive mortalities of the Acropora palmata zone and of other reef zones as well. At times however, density independent events (such as storms and hurricanes) may enhance local reef diversity when they disturb the system at an intermediate level (Connell, 1978).

3. Caribbean biological diversity is low when compared to the Indo-Pacific (there are about 80% more genera and species of corals in the Pacific than in the Caribbean).

4. The massive demise of D. antillarum which spread throughout the Caribbean from January 1983-84, and the major coral bleaching event of 1987, have probably decreased coral cover within many Caribbean reefs since both events impacted the Region as a whole.

5. Caribbean corals are frequently subjected to various forms of diseases (e.g. Black band and white band disease) and stresses as reviewed by Peters (1984).

REEFS OF SOUTH AND CENTRAL AMERICA

	PAGES
Contamination Gradient and Its Effect on the Coral Community Structure in the Santa Marta Area, Colombian Caribbean *Alberto Acosta M.*	233 - 239
A Reef Under Siltation Stress: A Decade of Degradation *Jorge Cortes*	240 - 246
Extensive Mortality of Corals in the Colombian Caribbean During the Last Two Decades *Jaime Garzon-Ferreira and Margriet Kielman*	247 - 253
Impact of Tourism Development on the Coral Reefs of the Abrolhos Area, Brazil *Zelinda M.A.N. Leao, Marcelo D. Telles, Roberto Sforza, Helio A. Bulhoes, and Ruy K.P. Kikuchi*	254 - 260
Anatomy of a Dying Coral Reef: Punta Islotes Reef, Golfo Dulce, Costa Rica *Ian Macintyre, Jorge Cortes, and Peter W. Glynn*	261 - 266
The Coral Reefs of the San Blas Islands Revisited After 20 Years *John C. Ogden and Nacy B. Ogden*	267 - 272
History of a Fringing Reef on the West Coast of Barbados 1974-1992 *Terence P. Scoffin*	273 - 278

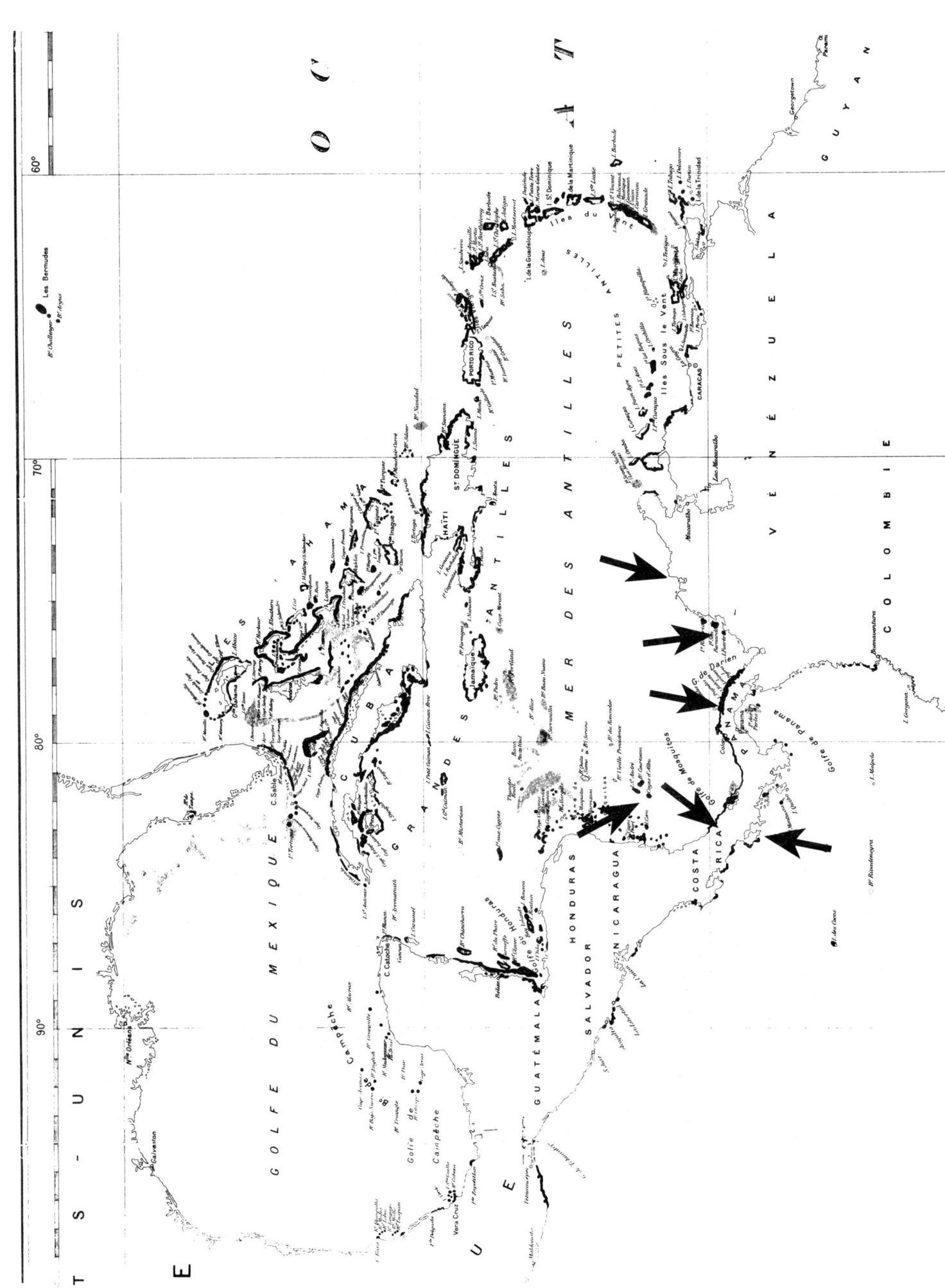

CONTAMINATION GRADIENT AND ITS EFFECT ON THE CORAL COMMUNITY STRUCTURE IN THE SANTA MARTA AREA, COLOMBIAN CARIBBEAN.

Alberto Acosta M.

Corporation for the Development, Investigation and Aplication of Biology (CORPOBIOTICA), A.A. 59629 Bogotá, Colombia.

ABSTRAC

During the last decades the marine contamination in the area of Santa Marta has increased, due specially to sources of organic matter. This has generated a deterioration of the reef ecosystem, which evidences a contamination gradient. The effects caused by contamination and stress are reflected both in time and space, changing the reefs composition and structure. These effects are seen specially in the Punta Betin reef, which is directly but moderately exposed to sources of contamination. Such effects were quantified at community level in the reefs of Punta Betin, Morro Grande Island, Granate Cove, and Gayraca Bay, where a gradual increment was found from SW to NE in the abundance, diversity (richness and covering), and structural complexity.

At population level, a comparison was made between the Punta Betin and Gayraca Bay reefs to determine the effects of reproduction in the *Montastrea cavernosa* species, prevailing in the area. Thus, the reproductive effort decreases following a gradient, the nearer to the sources of contamination.

A global study program on the sources and types of polluting agents, and their effects on the organisms is required. It is important take the appropiate control and surveillance measures which would help avoid the loss of the reef ecosystem.

INTRODUCTION

The 1700 Km-long Colombian Caribbean coast has diverse areas with reef ecosystem, among those, the area of Santa Marta stands out due to it's extension (Acero et al., 1992), which includes the Bay of the same name and the Tayrona National Natural Park (Fig. 1). These coral communities are characterized being simple coastal reef type and having a poor developed reef structure, that does not exceed a depth of 35 m (Acosta, 1989).

As from 1975, the researchers found deterioration in the Santa Marta Bay reef (Punta Betin and Morro Grande Island), showing a decrease in the number of species and the loss of coral cover, due to the increase of sediment discharges, runoff water and other pollutants. Only towards the end of the 80's, quantitative studies were made to evaluate the reef condition and to determine the natural and anthropogenic factors that would influence their development (Solano, 1987; Acosta, 1989).

The reefs in the area are of great ecological and economic relevance, nevertheless, there is little basic information about their structure, their present state, and their response to anthropogenic pressure generated by contaminating sources, such as the harbor, the coal transportation, and the runoff water from the city, the Manzanares river, and the Cienaga Grande of Santa Marta estuary.

My case history contributes to the Colloquium, since it presents the basic information about some natural and anthropogenic factors that hazards the reefs, and about the effects of contamination on the corals' physiology.

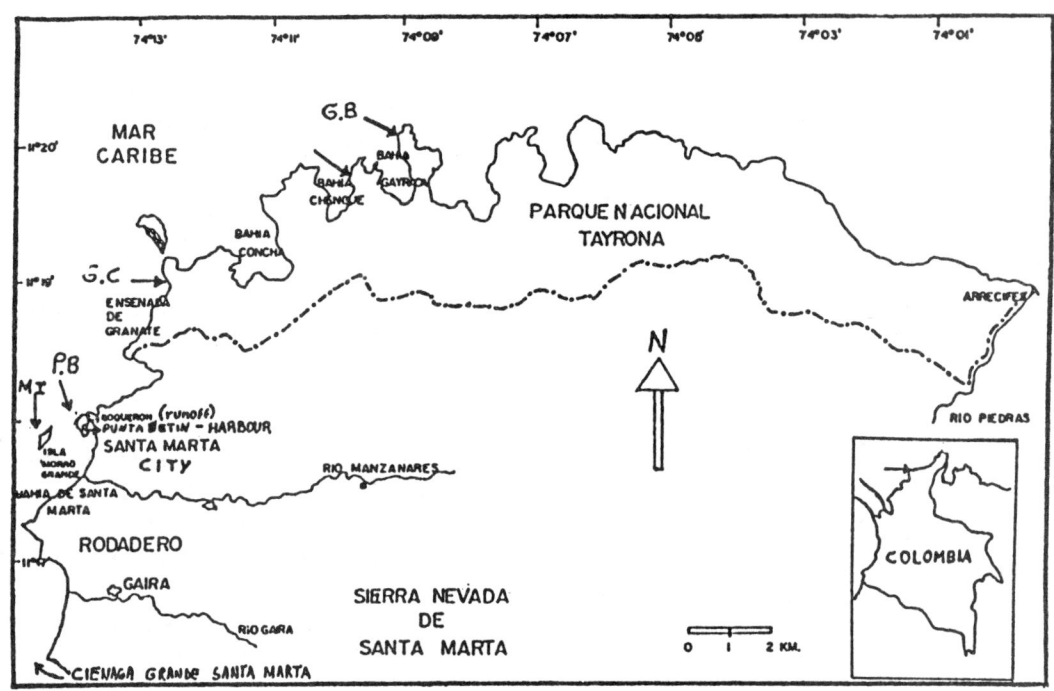

Figure 1. Map showing the location of the studied reefs in the area of Santa Marta, and the sources of contamination.

Here I am sumarizing my research at the Institute of Marine Investigations of P.Betin (INVEMAR) between 1987 and 1992. The preliminary observations indicated that a reef deterioration gradient could exist, which would decrease from SW to NE, the farther away from the continental contamination sources. In order to prove this hypothesis, the structure of the reef community was quantified along the gradient in four reefs. Specifically at population level, the reproductive effort of *Montastrea cavernosa*, the most important reef builder in the area, was quantified in two reefs so as to be able to determinate the contamination effect at the beginning and at the end of this gradient.

METHODS

The structure of the coral community was determined at Punta Betin, Morro Grande Island, Granate Cove and Gayraca Bay, using intersected length chain transects (Porter, 1972). In each reef, 10-16 of 20 m-long transects were quantified. Several categories were established such as corals, sponges, octocorals, substrate type (sand, rock), and percentage of dead coral. Based on the data of coral cover, the diversity, zonation and affinity of the reefs was determined. The biotic information was related, for each reef during the rainy season (september-november), with abiotic factors such as temperature, salinity, light penetration, downward fluxes of sediments and suspended solids.

Between october 1990 and october 1991, eight fragments from the same number of *Montastrea cavernosa* colonies were collected monthly from the Punta Betin and Gayraca Bay reefs. The samples were histologically processed in order to determine the cycle of sexual reproduction (oogenesis, espermatogenesis), the time for spawning, and the sexual ratio. Also in order to compare the reproductive effort of the species (gonadal index and fertility) between a deteriorated reef, exposed to direct contamination like Punta Betin, and a well preserved reef like Gayraca Bay. The information obtained was related to the climatic seasons.

RESULTS

The results show that the reefs located nearby the sources of contamination (Punta Betin, Morro Grande Island) have a lesser structural complexity (lower number of species, lower cover, lower diversity index) and greater reef deterioration (higher percentage of dead coral, lower abundance and smaller colony sizes due to partial mortality) in comparative to the reefs less exposed to such sources, located to the NE of the National Natural Park Tayrona (Table 1). This spatial variability in the coral structure reflects a deteriorating gradient which corresponds directly to the proximity to the contamination sources.

Table 1. A. Changes in the composition and coral community structure along a gradient of contamination in the Santa Marta area, Colombian Caribbean. B. Variation range of some abiotic factors during the raining season and the bleaching response in the coral community. C. Temporal changes in the coral composition and zonation in the P.Betin reef, directly expose to the effect of contamination.

A.		P.BETIN	MORRO I.	GRANATE	CHENGUE	GAYRACA (Unpub.)
Number of transects		11	11	16	7	10
Total species		19	20	24	26	24
Coverage percentage of live coral		19	26	37	39.5	49.4
Coverage percentage of dead coral		25	21	22	25.4	20.2
Diversity (Ln)		0.68	0.98	1.1	1.6 (Lg2)	1.7
Coral Abundance (per linear meter)		1.61	1.78	2.04		2.21
Average diameter of colonies		12	17	17		13
Dominant species in the reef		Mc	Mc	Ma-Mc	Ap,Dc,Aa,Md Mc, Ma, Ds	
Reef composition	Surface	Mc	Ds-Mc	Mc	Dc, Ap	Sr,Ds,Ca,Mc,Mal,P
	Middle	Mc	Mc	Mc-Aa	Mc,Ca,Ma,Md Ma,Ca,Mc,Sl,Mal	
	Bottom		Mc		Mc, Mc	

B.		P.BETIN	MORRO I.	GRANATE
Temperature	Range	26.2-29.5	26-31	26-31
	Average/SD.	27.8/0.7	28.6/0.8	28.2/0.6
Salinity (‰)	Range	26-37.7	26.9-34.6	26-37.7
	Average/SD.	33/0.5	32.8/0.4	33.5/1
Resuspention-sedimentation rates (mg/cm2/day)	Range	0.3-15.2	0.1-3.7	0.2-25.4
	Average/SD.	3.74/30.8	1.13/1.6	3.68/0.7
Light penetration (m)	Range	0.6-12	3-14	3.6-20
	Average/SD.	6.1-1.5	8.1-1.7	11.8/1.5
Percentage decolorated coral community		12	13	29
Percentage partially bleached coral community		15	15	24.6
Percentage totally bleached coral community		4	2	2.6
Species most sensitive to bleaching		Ma - Aa - Sr		

C.		PUNTA DE BETIN REEF			
		Erffa y Geyster 1976 HOLOCEN	Antonius 1972	Erhardt y Werding 1975	This study 1989
REEF COMPOSITION	Surface (0-15m)	Sr, Dc, Ds, Pp	Ca, Ds, Sa, Dc, Ma		Mc
	Middle (15-25m)		Mc, Aa, Sl, Ds, Ma, Sl, Ca, Mc, Sa	Mf, Ca, Dst, Ds, Ma	Mc
	Bottom (>25m)		Mc	Sl, Aa	
Total species		n=14	n=33	n=27	n=19

Aa:Agaricia agaricites; Ap:Acropora palmata; Ca:Colpophyllia natans; Dc:Diploria clivosa; Ds:Diploria strigosa; Dst:Dichocoenia stokesii; Mc:Mellocerie cucullata; Mf:Eusmilia fastigiata; Ma:Montastrea annularis; Mal:Millepora alcicornis; Mn:Meandrina meandrites; Mc:Montastrea cavernosa; Md:Madracis decactis; P:Porites astreoides; Pp:Porites porites; Sl:Stephanocoenia intersepta; Sl:Scolimia lacera; Sr:Siderastrea radians; Sa:Siderastrea siderea. Chengue reef data from Solano (1987).

The effects of contamination and stress can not only be seen in space, the structural complexity of the reefs diminishing the closer to the impact zones, but there is also evidences of changes over the time as to the composition and structure of the coral community in the Santa Marta Bay reef, as shown in Table 1.

For 1987, the best developed coral (number of species, cover and diversity) was located in the middle portions of the reef at a depht of 9-15 m, the most important reef building species the being *Montastrea cavernosa*, *M. annularis*, *Diploria strigosa*, and *Agaricia agaricites*.

The rainy season (september-november) generated stress conditions that exceeded the tolerance limits of the coral species (increments in temperature, high sedimentation, and decrease in salinity and light penetration, Table 1). This was reflected in the partial bleaching of half of the coral community, *Agaricia agaricites*, *M.annularis* and *Siderastrea radians* being the species with the lowest resistance.

At population level, *Montastrea cavernosa* showed a significantly lower reproductive effort (gonadal index, fertility) in the reef of highest deterioration and exposure to direct sources of contamination (Punta Betin), compared to the well conserved reef located in Gayraca Bay, at the other end of the gradient. This fact evidences of the physiological response of the species to direct contamination and stress (Tabla 2). The response of the Punta Betin reef includes: asynchronism in the gametogenic cycle specially in males, and an early spawning with less number of gametes released into the sea; this may possibly decrease the probability of fecundity and the reproductive success of the species, explaining partially why -although a large number of eggs and spermatozoids are released into water- there are few juvenil corals (less than 1cm in diameter) seen in the area of the Santa Marta reefs.

On the other hand, the spawning took place during two consecutive years (1990-1991) at the months of september-october, coinciding with the rainy season and the highest annual water temperature recordings.

Table 2. Variation of the reproductive effort (gonadal index and fertility) during the time of spawning in the species *Montastrea cavernosa*, as a result of contamination. Punta Betin degraded reef, Gayraca Bay reef in good conservation state,

Montastrea cavernosa			PUNTA DE BETIN					GAYRACA BAY		
		Ag	Sep	Oct	Nov	Dic		Sep	Oct	Nov
Month of spawning	Male		X	X	X	X		X	X	X
	Female	X	X	X	X			X	X	X

		PUNTA BETIN	GAYRACA BAY
Gonadal index	Male	0.71	2.8
(mm3 eggs or spermaries/cm2/year)	Female	6.6	9.28
Fertility	Male	1184	1550
(Number eggs or spermaries/cm2 area)	Female	395	581
Annual release	Male	4.560.000 spermaries/year	
a colony 50 cm diameter	Female	900.000 eggs/year	

DISCUSSION

The establishment, structure and development of reefs in the area of Santa Marta is conditioned by natural factors, such as the geomorphology of the coast, which presents a narrow continental shelf and a slope, deriving from the highest mountainous coastal formation in the world (Sierra Nevada of Santa Marta); oceanographic and climatic factors such as the proccess of upwelling and the trade winds from the NE during the dry season (december-march), and the eutrophication during the rainy season (september-november), the latter favoured by the countercurrent from Panama, and the contribution of matter and energy from neighbouring ecosystems (mangroves, estuaries, etc). These natural factors, which have remained constant through time, act in conjuction with new anthropogenic variables. As a result from this interaction, at present these is limitation in the degree of development that can be achieved by the reefs of the area. The urban, tourist, harbour and industrial activities on the coast have increased during the last decades and consequently it has modified the marine enviroment due to heavier load of various pollutants released into the sea. Even though the contamination in the area of Santa Marta could be considered of moderate intensity, annual periodicity and seasonal frecuency, it's effect is often not very noticeable at short term. During the rainy season a generation of stress conditions is seen due to the temperature increments, the upward fluxes of sedimentation, the decrease in salinity and light penetration, which can even be lethal if they exceed the degrees of tolerance of the coral species, leading to the elimination of sensitive species, and to the replacement of these by species with greater tolerance. Even the species of greater tolerane have started to show partial mortality, bleaching and susceptibility to diseases. As a consequence, the ecosystem shows a lower complexity and diversity. As a result, at the long term, spatial - temporal changes are seen in the reef composition and structure, as has likewise been registered in the reefs of Puerto Rico (Loya, 1976), Bermuda (Dodge y Vainsnys, 1977), Costa Rica (Cortes y Risk, 1984) and Jamaica (Dodge et al., 1974).

After some years of impact on P.Betin, only some species with a high degree of tolerance remain, such as *Montastrea cavernosa*, presently the dominant one in the area of Santa Marta. If the human activities and the increment of pollutants persist such as intolerable environment would be created that the subsistance of the reef would be imposibly.

It has been determined that there exist a contamination and sublethal stress effect, but nothing is known about which pollutants and in what concentration are being released from the different sources, nor about the effects on the organisms and clearance rates.

Until now, it has only been established that there is a gradient of contamination and of sublethal stress in the area of Santa Marta that affects the reef community. Also, this gradient affects the physiological processes of the *Montastrea cavernosa* especies, such as sexual reproduction, and probably growth (study in process). Even this species (dominant, and with a greater degree of tolerance and adaptability to this type of environments) shows the effects on it's gametogenic cycle, on it's spawning time, and it's reproductive effort is show to be considerably diminished, almost to its half. Tomascik and Sander (1987) also found differences in the reproductive effort comparing reefs by a eutrophication gradient. This is the reason why Harrison and Wallace (1990) propose the use of the diminishing reproductive effort as a sensitive indicator of the sublethal stress.

In the long run, the effects on reproduction would result in the decrease in the probability of fertility and larval assesment, preventing the reef from regulating itself and repopulating itself with genetically different individuals.

All this leads us to consider whether the reefs will be able to survive and adapt to the new conditions, as the vital processes of the corals are being altered.

Programs of International Cooperation could provide the scientific basis that would allow us to develop management plans on the ecosystem. The priority research area could be the paleoclimatic reconstruction starting from retrospective studies, complementing the sources, type and concentration of the pollutants released into the sea, their effects on the organisms (accumulation, cleareance), and the clearance rate in the environment. Only in this way we could establish concrete policies to establish the admissable amounts of pollutants to be released into the sea, and could propose the control and surveillance measurements needed to prevent this important natural resource from desappearing.

CONCLUSIONS

The effects of contamination and sublethal stress on the benthic species are still not well understood. Their effect is reflected at community level in spatial-temporal changes of the reef structure, as seen in the replacement of species achieving a more simple funtional structure.

At population level the effects are revealed in the alteration of the gametogenic cycle and the decrease of the reproductive effort, fundamental processes in the life history of the coral species. Possibly, part of the energy arriving at the reef is used by the species rather for its survival, than for it's reproduction or growth.

ACKNOWLEDGMENTS

I want to thank INVEMAR, and COLCIENCIAS. Especially Argenis Bonilla for her observations and comments, and Adriana Pereira and Margarita Zea for help in the English Version.

LITERATURE CITED

Acosta, A. 1989. Composition and Structure community hermatipic coral reef at three sites of the Santa Marta area. Colombian Caribbean. Thesis Biology, Department of Biology, University National of Colombia. Bogota, Colombia. 250 pp.

Acosta, A. 1992. Sexual reproduction of the reef coral Montastrea cavernosa in the Santa Marta area, Colombian Caribbean. Thesis M.Sc. Marine Biology, Department of Biology, National University of Colombia. Bogota, Colombia. 115 pp.

Acero, A. et al. 1992. Workshop of reef corals, Investigation and Management. *in* E. Alvarado. ed. Boletin Ecotropica: Ecosistemas Tropicales, Suplemento 1. Universidad Jorge Tadeo Lozano, Museo del Mar. Bogota, Colombia. 85 pp.

Antonius, A. 1972. Occurrence and distribution of stony corals in the vicinity of Santa Marta, Colombia. Mitt. Inst. Colombo-Aleman Invest. Cient. 6:89-103.

Cortes, J. and M. Risk. 1984. Reef corals in the National Park Cahuita, Costa Rica. Rev. Biol. Trop. 32(1): 109-121.

Dodge, R. and R. Vaisnyz. 1977. Coral population and growth patterns: responses to sedimentation and turbidity associated with dredging. Jor. of Mar. Sci. Res. 35(4): 715-730.

Dodge, R., R. Aller. and J. T.homsom. 1974. Coral growth related to

    resuspension of bottom sediments. Nature. 247: 574-577.
Erffa, A. und J. Geister. 1976. Uber ein holozanes korallen und mangroven vorkommennake Santa Marta, Kolumbien. Mitt. Inst. Col. Aleman. Invest. Cient. 8: 165-186.
Erhardt, H. and B. Werding. 1987. Corals of the Santa Marta Bay, Colombia. Bol. Museo del Mar. 7:19 pp.
Harrison, P. and C. Wallace. 1990. Coral reproductive biology. Pages 132-207 *in* Z. Dubinsky. ed. Ecosystems of the World 25. Coral Reefs. Elsevier Press, New York.
Loya, Y. 1976. Effects of water turbidity and sedimentation on the community structure of Puerto Rican corals. Bull. Mar. Sci. 26(84): 446-450.
Porter, J. 1972. Patterns of species diversity in Caribbean reef corals. Ecology. 53(4): 745-748.
Solano, O. 1987. Structure and diversity of the hermatipical corals in Chengue Bay, National Natural Park Tayrona. Thesis M.Sc. Marine Biology. Department of Biology, University National of Colombia. Bogota, Colombia. 110 pp.
Tomascik, T. and F. Sander. 1987. Effects of eutrophication on reef building coral. Mar. Biol. 94:77-94.

A REEF UNDER SILTATION STRESS: A DECADE OF DEGRADATION

Jorge Cortés

CIMAR and Escuela de Biología, Universidad de Costa Rica
San Pedro, Costa Rica

ABSTRACT

The coral reef at Cahuita National Park, Caribbean coast of Costa Rica, has been stressed by sediments from watersheds of rivers that flow to the sea near the Park. High sediment loads in these rivers are due to deforestation on the highlands and to inappropriate agricultural practices on the coastal plains. During the last decade natural disturbances -- coral bleaching in 1983, *Diadema antillarum* die-off in 1983 and 1992, a 7.5 earthquake in 1991 -- and other anthropogenic stresses -- pollution, tourism -- have contributed to the degradation of the coral reef.

A comparison of the reef between the late 1970's - early 1980's and 1993 revealed the following: suspended sediments and the non-carbonate fraction of bottom sediments have increased from 8 to 9 mg/l, and from 40 to 48%, respectively; live coral cover has decreased, from 40 to 11%, while dead coral, algae covered carbonate substrate and coral rubble have increased from 60 to 89%. These changes are attributed to the increase in sediment loads in the reef, increased visitation to the reef, and to natural disturbances. It is possible that the reef will recover if sediment loads in the rivers are reduced.

INTRODUCTION

The Cahuita coral reef is located on the Caribbean coast of Costa Rica, Central America (9°45'N - 82°48'W) (Fig. 1). The fringing reef is part of Cahuita National Park. The reef was characterized in the early 1980's as being under siltation stress because of high suspended sediment loads and resuspension of bottom sediments. As a result, it had low live coral coverage, diversity and coral growth rates (Cortés 1981; Cortés and Risk, 1984, 1985).

Several natural disturbances have affected the reef since 1980. In 1983 a bleaching event associated with high temperatures, was responsible for the death of corals, mainly *Acropora palmata* (Cortés et al., 1984). Also in 1983, there was massive mortality of the sea urchin *Diadema antillarum* (Murillo and Cortés, 1984), due to a water-borne pathogen (Lessios et al., 1984). In 1991 a 7.5 earthquake (Richter scale) affected the entire Caribbean coast of Costa Rica (Cortés et al., 1992). Finally, there was another die-off of *Diadema* in 1992 (unpubl. data). Parallel to these natural disturbances, visitation to the

Park increased 3 fold between 1982 and 1991. Additionally, during this entire period, siltation has continued.

In this paper I compare data on coral cover and sediments collected in 1993 with the results obtained by Cortés (1981), and put forth possible causes for the degradation of this coral reef.

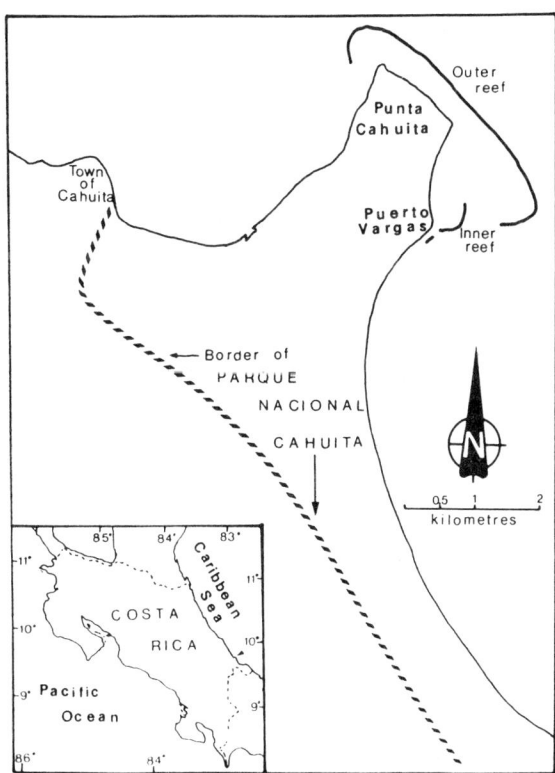

Figure 1: Location of the study reef.

METHODS

To provide comparable data, the methods used by Cortés (1981) to study the reef at Cahuita were employed in 1993. Transects were done and samples were collected, in both periods, in the same area and depth range. Sixteen line transects (10 m long) were done and the distance covered by each coral species and other substrates was recorded. Coral colony sizes (length) were calculated from the transect data. In the late 70's and early 80's the density of *Diadema antillarum* was determined using 1 m^2 quadrats. In 1993, all of the individuals encountered were counted and the area covered was calculated. Surface suspended sediments were determined by filtration of 1 liter samples onto preweighed Millepore 0.45 μm HA filters. The non-carbonate fraction of bottom sediments was determined by dissolution of carbonates with diluted HCl. Finally, records of visitation to the park expanding from 1982 to 1991 (Bermúdez, 1992) were analyzed.

RESULTS

Table 1 summarizes the data from Cortés (1981) and the results obtained in this study. Percent live coral coverage is significantly lower in 1993 than in previous surveys by Cortés (1981), while other substrates increased, including dead coral, algae covered carbonate substrate and coral rubble. The number of coral species encountered in the transects surveyed was the same (Table 1). However, *Acropora cervicornis* was recorded in 1980, but not in 1993, while the opposite occurred with *Colpophyllia natans* (Table 2). The size of *Porites astreoides* during both surveys is not significantly different (Table 1), but *P. astreoides* is more abundant now than 10 years ago (Tables 2). The average size and abundance of *Agaricia agaricites* have decreased (Tables 1 and 2), but it is still the predominant coral species at Cahuita (Table 2). *Siderastrea siderea* is currently represented by larger colonies (Table 1) and its abundance has increased (Table 2). The abundance of *Porites porites* has decreased (Table 2).

The density of *Diadema antillarum* was about 3 orders of magnitude lower in 1993 (Table 1). Suspended sediments are significantly higher in 1993 (Table 1). Percentage of the non-carbonate fraction of bottom sediments is also higher (Table 1).

Visitation to Cahuita National Park increased from just over 31,000 in 1982 to over 100,000 persons in 1991.

DISCUSSION

High sediment loads is associated with less live coral and reduced coral recruitment (Rogers, 1990). At Cahuita, live coral cover declined in the last decade while sediments loads have increased (Table 1). Also, very few recruits were encountered at Cahuita, except for *P. astreoides*. In some localities, e.g. Fanning Island (Maragos, 1974), larger colonies are found in more turbid areas. Cortés (1981) noted that colonies of some massive species at Cahuita were larger than in other areas. In 1993, *Siderastrea siderea* colonies were larger than in the earlier survey (Table 1).

Other factors may also contribute to the degradation of the coral reef at Cahuita. The bleaching event in 1983 caused close to 40% coral mortality, especially of *Acropora* spp. (Cortés et al., 1984). *A. palmata* abundance is lower now and *A. cervicornis* has not been observed recently (Table 2). Other species have recovered from the bleaching event. The massive die-offs of *Diadema antillarum* in 1983 and 1992 (Murillo and Cortés, 1984; unpublish. data) have resulted in the small surviving populations (Table 1). The reduction in urchin numbers has resulted in an increase in macroalgae cover near or on coral colonies (unpublish. data), as was observed, after 1983, in other Caribbean reefs (Carpenter, 1990). The increase in macroalgal cover has a negative effect on corals (Liddell and Ohlhorst, 1986; Lapointe, 1989). At Cahuita, macroalgae are smothering

Table 1

Comparison between data collected at Cahuita National Park in the late 1970's - early 1980's and in 1993.

	Cortés 1981	This study
1. Percent Cover		
Live coral[a]	40.4 ± 5.6 (4 - 80)	11.2 ± 2.4[b] (0 - 34)
Other substrate[c]	59.6 ± 5.6 (20 - 96)	88.8 ± 2.4[b] (66 - 100)
2. Corals		
Number of species in transects	10	10
Colony sizes (cm)		
P. astreoides	9.3 ± 1.1 n = 48	9.4 ± 5.4 n = 21
A. agaricites	21.0 ± 1.1 n = 105	14.8 ± 12.2 n = 45
S. siderea	26.6 ± 1.2 n = 32	32.6 ± 24.0 n = 17
3. Density of *Diadema*		
Diadema antillarum	4 - 33 ind/m^2	10 ind/1,000 m^2
4. Sediments		
suspended sediments (mg/l)	8.4 ± 1.6 (0.8 - 54.0) n = 34	9.1 ± 2.8[b] (3.6 - 22.1) n = 18
% non-carbonate fraction of bottom sediments	40.1 ± 10.4 (2.8 - 68.9) n = 7	47.8 ± 8.9[d] (4.9 - 81.1) n = 9

a. mean ± standard error of the mean and range in parentheses. n = 16 linear transects (10 m long)
b. Differences between years are significant (ANOVA $p < 0.05$)
c. Mainly dead coral, algal-covered carbonate substrate and coral rubble
d. Differences between years are not significant (ANOVA $p > 0.05$)

Table 2

Percentage of each species of the total live coral encountered in 16 transects.

	Cortés 1981	This study	% change
Agaricia agaricites	54.6%	39.7%	- 14.9
Siderastrea siderea	15.6	31.1	+ 15.5
Porites porites	13.0	3.8	- 9.2
Porites astreoides	6.5	11.0	+ 4.5
Diploria strigosa	3.4	0.8	- 2.6
Acropora palmata	3.1	1.9	- 1.2
Millepora complanata	2.4	3.7	+ 1.3
Diploria clivosa	0.7	2.8	+ 2.1
Montastrea annularis	0.4	2.8	+ 2.4
Acropora cervicornis	0.1	0	- 0.1
Colpophyllia natans	0	2.2	+ 2.2

corals and may affect larval settlement. The April, 1991 earthquake caused coastal uplift and slumping of part of the reef front (Cortés et al., 1992). Two of the most affected species were *A. agaricites* and *P. porites*, because of their predominance on the reef front (Cortés and Risk, 1984). Densities of both species have dropped (Table 2). Large areas of the reef are now covered by rubble of these two species, that is serving as a substrate for *P. astreoides*, which explains its increase in density (Table 2).

The above natural disturbances have affected other reefs on the Caribbean coast of Costa Rica, which are not under siltation stress. These reefs seem to have recovered from these disturbances (Cortés and Guzmán, 1985; Cortés, 1992; pers. obs.).

Recreational activities may have a deleterious impact on coral reefs. Coral trampling by reef walkers, voluntary or involuntary physical contact with corals, and boat damage are causes of coral stress and death (Tilmant, 1987; Neil, 1990). In the Florida Keys a significant linear correlation of reef use and incidence of physical damage was found (Tilmant and Schmahl, 1981). The number of visitors to Cahuita National Park has increased dramatically and they walk on the reef, break corals and cause boat damages.

Other problems have been detected recently in Cahuita. Heavy metal concentrations in coral and sediments are higher at Cahuita than at other coral reefs surveyed in both Panama and Costa Rica (Guzmán and Jiménez, 1992). These metal pollutants are associated with natural (soil erosion) and anthropogenic (domestic and industrial sewage, oil, pesticides) sources (Guzmán and Jiménez, 1992).

The sediment problem at Cahuita was found to be significant (Cortés 1981), and it is now obvious that on top of the siltation stress there are natural disturbances and other anthropogenic disturbances degrading the reef. But there is still hope for the Cahuita reef, since there is still some live coral cover and a relatively large number of coral species. Recruitment onto artificial substrate raised above the reef have been obtained (unpublish. data), herbivorous fish are present (Phillips and Pérez-Cruet, 1984), and *Diadema* has demonstrated that its populations may recover (pers. observ.). It is possible that the reef will recover if sediment loads in the rivers are reduced by re-establishing the riverine forest and by reducing deforestation on the highlands.

CONCLUSION

The coral reef at Cahuita has been continually stressed by high sediment loads. During the last decade, degradation of the reef has continued, compounded by acute natural events -- coral bleaching, *Diadema* die-offs and earthquake -- and to other anthropogenic stresses -- pollution and tourism. Because of the chronic siltation stress at Cahuita, this reef has not been able to recover from natural disturbances as has been observed in other reefs in the area. If sediment loads at Cahuita are reduced, the reef may recover.

ACKNOWLEDGEMENTS

Work at Cahuita National Park has been possible thanks to the economic support of CONICIT (1979-1981 and 1992-1993), Universidad de Costa Rica (1979 to the present) and McMaster University (1979-1981). A.C. Fonseca, C. Jiménez and E. Ruiz helped with data collecting and sample analysis. Critical reviews by G. Muller-Parker, C. Jiménez and R. Soto improved the manuscript. Logistic support over the years by the Servicio de Parques Nacionales is greatly appreciated.

LITERATURE CITED

Bermúdez, F. 1992. Evolución del turismo en las áreas silvestres: período 1982 - 1991. Servicio de Parques Nacionales, Ministerio de Recursos Naturales, San José, Costa Rica. (Internal report).

Carpenter, R.C. 1990. Mass mortality of *Diadema antillarum*, I. Long-term effects on sea urchin population dynamics and coral reef algal communities. Mar. Biol. 104: 67-77.

Cortés, J. 1981. The coral reef at Cahuita, Costa Rica: a reef under stress. MSc thesis, McMaster Univ., Hamilton, Ontario. 176 pp.

Cortés, J. 1992. Los arrecifes coralinos del Refugio Nacional de Vida Silvestre Gandoca-Manzanillo, Limón, Costa Rica. Rev. Biol. Trop. 40: 325-333.

Cortés, J. and H.M. Guzmán. 1985. Arrecifes coralinos de la costa Atlántica de Costa Rica. Brenesia 23: 275-292.

Cortés, J. and M.J. Risk. 1984. El arrecife coralino del Parque Nacional Cahuita, Costa Rica. Rev. Biol. Trop. 32: 109-121.

Cortés, J. and M.J. Risk. 1985. A reef under siltation stress: Cahuita, Costa Rica. Bull. Mar. Sci. 36: 339-356.

Cortés, J., M.M. Murillo, H.M. Guzmán and J. Acuña. 1984. Pérdida de zooxantelas y muerte de corales y otros organismos arrecifales en el Atlántico y Pacífico de Costa Rica. Rev. Biol. Trop. 32: 227-231.

Cortés, J., R. Soto, C. Jiménez and A. Astorga. 1992. Earthquake associated mortality of intertidal and coral reef organisms (Caribbean of Costa Rica). Proceedings of the 7th International Coral Reef Symposium, Guam: in press.

Guzmán, H.M. and C.E. Jiménez. 1992. Contamination of coral reefs by heavy metals along the Caribbean coast of Central America (Costa Rica and Panama). Mar. Pollut. Bull. 24: 554-561.

Lapointe, B.E. 1989. Caribbean coral reefs: are they becoming algal reefs? Sea Frontiers, March-April 1989: 83-91.

Liddell, W.D. and S.L. Ohlhorst. 1986. Changes in benthic community composition following the mass mortality of *Diadema* at Jamaica. J. Exp. Mar. Biol. Ecol. 95: 271-278.

Lessios, H.A., D.R. Robertson and J.D. Cubit. 1984. Spread of *Diadema* mass mortality through the Caribbean. Science 226: 335-337.

Maragos, J.E. 1974. Reef corals of Fanning Island. Pac. Sci. 28: 247-255.

Murillo, M.M. and J. Cortés. 1984. Alta mortalidad en la población del erizo de mar *Diadema antillarum* Philippi (Echinodermata: Echinoidea), en el Parque Nacional Cahuita, Limón, Costa Rica. Rev. Biol. Trop. 32: 167-169.

Neil, D. 1990. Potential for coral stress due to sediment resuspension and deposition by reef walkers. Biol. Conserv. 52: 221-227.

Phillips, P.C. and M.J. Pérez-Cruet. 1984. A comparative survey of reef fishes in Caribbean and Pacific Costa Rica. Rev. Biol. Trop., 32: 95-102.

Rogers, C.S. 1990. Responses of coral reefs and reef organisms to sedimentation. Mar. Ecol. Prog. Ser. 62: 185-202.

Tilmant, J.T. 1987. Impacts of recreational activities on coral reefs. Pages 195-214 *in* B. Salvat, ed. Human impacts on coral reefs: facts and recommendations. Antenne Museum E.P.H.E., French Polynesia.

Tilmant, J.T. and G.P. Schmahl. 1981. A comparative analysis of coral damage on recreationally used reefs within Biscayne National Park, Florida. Proceedings of the 4th International Coral Reef Symposium, Manila 1: 187-192.

EXTENSIVE MORTALITY OF CORALS IN THE COLOMBIAN CARIBBEAN DURING THE LAST TWO DECADES

Jaime Garzón-Ferreira and Margriet Kielman

Instituto de Investigaciones Marinas de Punta de Betin, INVEMAR,
A. Aereo 1016, Santa Marta, Colombia

ABSTRACT

Evidence is presented that reefs of the Colombian Caribbean have suffered considerable coral mortality in the last 20 years, mostly during the last decade. Live coral cover has declined to about 20-30 % of the hard substrate. The most affected species are branching and foliose corals from shallow waters, of which Acropora cervicornis, A. palmata, Agaricia tenuifolia Porites porites, P. furcata and Millepora complanata have reached mortality levels of nearly 100% at several sites. Massive corals have also been seriously affected, in shallow as well as in deep waters, specially Colpophyllia natans, Diploria strigosa, Montastrea annularis, Siderastrea siderea and Stephanocoenia intersepta. Sea fans (Gorgonia) have also suffered a recent mass mortality of more than 90%. Evidences suggest that coral mortality in the Colombian Caribbean has had its origin principally from agents of wide distribution (i.e., bleaching events and pathogenic diseases like BBD and WBD) as a part of a generalized reef deteriorarion process occurring in the wider Caribbean. Nevertheless, local agents of stress (i.e., increasing sedimentary load from rivers, fishing with explosives, sewage pollution and nautical activities) have contributed to increase the problem.

INTRODUCTION

Due to continental influence (i.e. terrestrial run-off and major river discharges) the Caribbean coast of Colombia is dominated by sedimentary and estuarine systems and less than 8% of its coastal areas support coral reef communities. The Colombian insular territories in the Western Caribbean (San Andrés and Providencia islands and nearby cays and atolls) make about half of this ammount (CORPES C.A., 1992). Distribution, composition, zonation, environmental conditions and conservation of coralline formations from Colombia were recently reviewed by Prahl and Erhardt (1985) and Wells (1988). Apart from some local damage related to human activities and a minor bleaching event, no extensive mortality of corals was reported in these reviews from the Colombian Caribbean. From the beginning of the 1980's, considerable work has been done to quantify the structure of Colombian Caribbean coral communities, most of which is not published. Since then, also, extensive mortalities of corals and other organisms became evident at these communities. The purpose of the present work is to review recent information and document the occurrence of these mortalities at the two main coralline areas of the Colombian Caribbean, discussing on possible causes and dates of occurrence.

STUDY AREAS

The Cartagena area, located south of the city of Cartagena, has the most extensive shelf reefs of the continental Colombian Caribbean, mainly at the coralline archipelagos of Islas del Rosario (10°04-14'N, 75°37-53'W) and Islas de San Bernardo (9°40-50'N, 75°45-55'W) (Fig. 1). The two archipelagos have

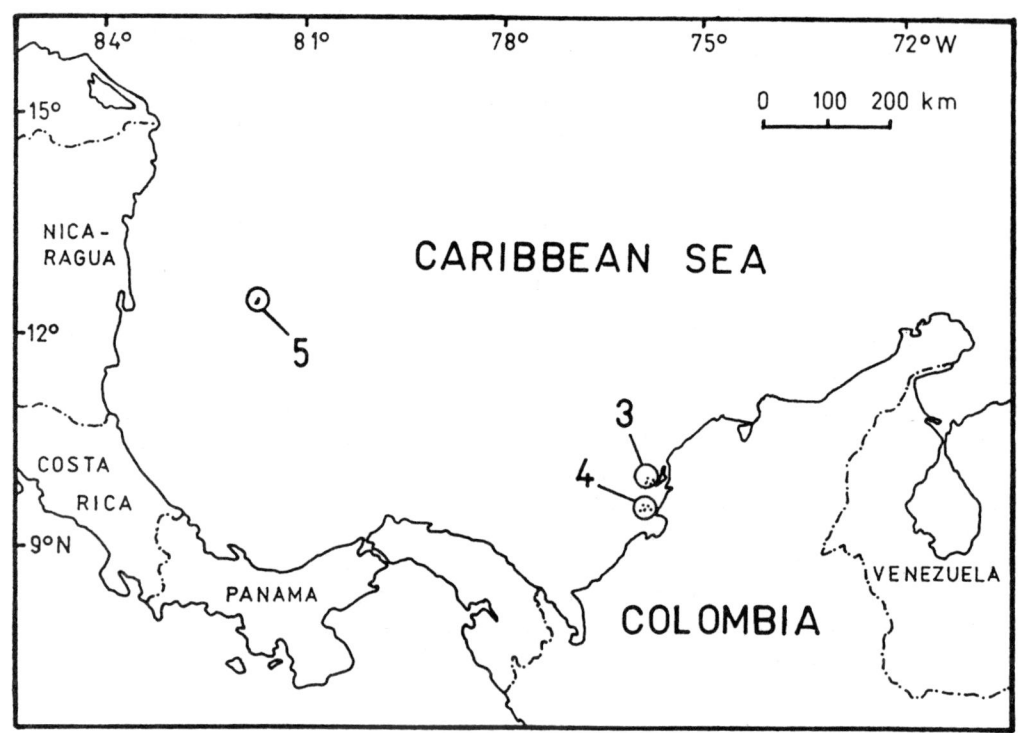

Figure 1. Location of study areas in the Colombian Caribbean: Islas del Rosario (3), Islas de San Bernardo (4) and San Andrés Island (5).

very similar geological origin, environmental conditions and reefs (Prahl and Erhardt, 1985), with warm (not lower than 26°C) and predominantly clear marine waters, although river discharges influence both archipelagos during rainy months. Fifty-seven species of stony corals have been reported from Islas del Rosario and the coral growth extends down to more than 50 m.

The oceanic island of San Andrés is located in the Western Caribbean (12°28-36'N, 81°40-44'W), lying 150 km off the coast of Nicaragua and some 800 km WNW of the Colombian coast. The island, as well as the surrounding shelf, is basically coralline in origin. Marine water is very clear all the year and has a surface temperature higher than 26°C. Coral reefs are well developed, diverse and extensive, and coral growth has been observed deeper than 50 m. Forty-seven species of stony corals are known from San Andrés (Geister, 1975; Prahl and Erhardt, 1985; Diaz et al., 1992).

METHODS

Two basic methods have been employed to estimate percent cover of corals and other components of the substrate in studies done at Colombian Caribbean reefs. The linear-quadrat method has been used in the Cartagena area. Planar surface areas were visually estimated as percentages within a 1x1 m quadrat placed every consecutive meter on a transect line. The chain-transect method has been used in San Andres. A chain was drapped over the contour of the substrate, along a transect line, and the number of links covering each bottom category was recorded. Specifications on number, length (or covered area), location, and depth of transects is given below when presenting data.

Cualitative observations and visual estimates of mortality and reef community structure during fast surveys provide additional information.

RESULTS

Cartagena Area

The first evidence of recent coral reef deterioration in the area came from observations made on May 1977 at Islas del Rosario by Werding and Sánchez (1979). They reported a significant extension of dead Acropora cervicornis near the southern coast of Rosario island. No more coral mortality was mentioned at that time, except for local damage caused by dynamite fishing, boat traffic, anchoring and coral mining. Otherwise, coral communities were apparently in a rather healthy condition and great extensions of Acropora palmata, A. cervicornis, Porites porites and Agaricia tenuifolia stands were described from many sites around the islands.

The first quantitative assessment of coral community structure in the Cartagena area was done in 1980 by Ramírez and De La Pava (1981), who studied two stations at the West coast of Isla de Tierra Bomba (10°19-23'N, 75°35-36'W). This island is situated adjacent to the Cartagena Bay and is affected by turbid and polluted waters from the bay. Nearly 560 m² of fore reef surface were sampled between 5 and 10 m depth, finding a live coral cover of 29-38% (mean 32.2%). No information was given on cover of other dead or live components of the reef bottom. Acropora cervicornis was reported as dominant (more than 50% of coral cover) at two zones and scattered patches of A. palmata were found at one station, but the authors did not mention any mortality on these two species. On the other hand, fore reef slopes were found mostly dead and very eroded (live coral cover less than 10%), suggesting the occurrence of old mortality events.

From observations made during 1982 at Isla Grande (Islas del Rosario) came the first report about extensive coral mortalities in the Colombian Caribbean (Coral and Caicedo, 1983). These authors sampled 800 m² of reef bottoms from 0 to 40 m depth, and found a live coral cover of 6.2-75.9% (mean 28.1%). Unfortunatelly, they did not give information on cover of dead coral and the other components of the substrate nor on mortality proportions of affected species. Great ammounts of dead Acropora palmata and A. cervicornis still in place were noted at the reef crest and the inner fore reef, respectively, in the northern side of the island. Live A. palmata cover at the crest ranged from only 8.2% in the NE to 51.6% in the NW (mean 29.9%). No live A. cervicornis was recorded at transects surveyed in these side of the island. On the other hand, dense stands of live A. cervicornis were found in the southern side of the island, covering 65.4% of the substrate at 2-10 m depth. One year after, Ramírez et al. (1986) estimated visually that less than 10% of populations of both species were alive at 10 stations sampled across the archipelago.

Table 1 summarizes data on mean cover of major components of the reef surface (relative to hard substrate), obtained at Islas del Rosario and Islas de San Bernardo by several authors between 1983 and 1990. Apparently, a decline in relative live coral cover from 1983 to 1988, and a stabilization since this year at a value that represents only 20.6-24.6% of the available hard substrate, occurred in the area (including both archipelagos). Changes in relative algal cover are very difficult to evaluate due to seasonality of algal communities and because filamentous algae were apparently included within the dead coral category by some authors. If it is assumed that dead coral was covered by an algal carpet, then relative algal cover may reach mean values of 52.3-75.6% (mean 68.3%) for 1983-1990 at the islands. Within the macroalgae, Dyctiota and Halimeda were strongly dominant and were observed in

Table 1. Mean percentage cover of major components of the reef surface (relative to total hard substrate), recalculated from estimations made at three coralline areas of the Colombian Caribbean by Linear quadrat (LQ), chain transect (CT) and fast survey (FS) methods. Sources: A: Ramirez et al (1986); B: Sarmiento et al. (1989); C: Penereiro et al. (1990); D: this work; E: Laverde-Castillo et al. (1987); F: Ramirez and Viña (1991); G and H: Diaz et al. (1992).

	Islas del Rosario				Islas de San Bernardo		San Andres Island	
Live hard coral	41.8	20.6	24.9	21.3[1]	31.1	22.5	29.9	26.5
Dead coral	39.5	61.0	58.0	--	31.5	28.7	--	--
Algae	17.6	14.6	16.5	52.3	37.4	41.5	62.0	67.8
Other organisms	1.1	3.8	0.5	26.4	--	7.3	8.1	5.7
Source	A	B	C	D	E	F	G	H
Depth (m)	1-6	1-20	1-30	5-25	1-10	5-10	1-20	0-22
# of stations	10	89	5	3	7	10	14	50
Method	LQ	LQ	LQ	LQ	LQ	LQ	CT	FS
Sample size[2]	495	8560	200[3]	90	670[4]	660[5]	420	5000
Date	1983	1988	1989	1990	1987	1989	1992	1992

1: excluding Millepora; 2: all in square meters except G that is given in meters; 3: channel zone data excluded; 4: coastal zone data excluded; 5: community 1 data excluded.

Table 2. Recent mortality of hard corals species at Islas del Rosario (IR) and San Andres I. (SA). Values are maximum and mean (below) percentages of dead cover relative to total cover (live + dead) of the species [recalculated from (1) Sarmiento et al., 1989; (2) Galvis, 1989; and (3) Diaz et al., 1992]. Species: Acr. cervicornis (ACE); A. palmata (APA); A. agaricites (AAG), A. tenuifolia (ATE), Col. natans (CNA), Den. cilindricus (DCI), Dic. stokesi (DST); Dip. clivosa (DCL); D. labyrinthiformis (DLA); D. strigosa (DIS); Eus. fastigiata (EFA); Mea. meandrites (MME), Mill. complanata (MCO), Mont. annularis (MAN), M. cavernosa (MCA), Por. astreoides (PAS), P. furcata (PFU), P. porites (PPO), Sid. radians (SRA), S. siderea (SSI), Ste. intersepta (SIN).

AREA	ACE	APA	AAG	ATE	CNA	DCI	DST	DCL	DLA	DIS	EFA	MME	MCO	MAN	MCA	PAS	PFU	PPO	SRA	SSI	SIN
IR (1)*	100	100	-	92	-	-	-	18	-	-	-	-	-	-	100	-	-	-	100	26	12	-
	80	89	-	31	-	-	-	<1	-	-	-	-	-	-	4	-	-	-	37	<1	<1	-
IR (2)*	100	80	-	64	-	-	-	100	-	22	-	-	-	-	63	100	23	-	100	-	100	-
	78	80	-	24	-	-	-	3	-	6	-	-	-	-	10	9	1	-	40	-	12	-
SA (3)+	100	95	80	-	70	30	70	30	40	60	80	40	90	90	90	70	100	70	80	50
	75	59	7	-	53	8	14	5	17	16	53	9	31	38	22	26	22	32	17

*: see Table 1 (B and H) for information on methods. +: 30 stations, linear-quadrat, 943 m2, 1-12 m depth, 1987.

dense patches on coral skeletons as well as covering live coral tissue (Alvarado et al., 1986; Sarmiento et al., 1989; Ramírez and Viña, 1991).

Table 2 lists 14 hard coral species that have suffered considerable recent mortality in the Cartagena area. The most affected are A. palmata and A. cervicornis, which have lost about 80-90% of their live cover, and secondly A. tenuifolia and P. porites that reached mean mortality of 20-40% at Islas del Rosario by 1987-88. These four species (and also D. clivosa, M. annularis, M. cavernosa and S. siderea) reached mortality levels of 100% at some locations, excepting A. tenuifolia that had a maximum of 92% (Sarmiento et al., 1988). Diploria strigosa, M. annularis and S. siderea were reported to have intermediate mean mortality values (6-12%). From Islas de San Bernardo, information was given about great extensions of dead A. palmata and A. cervicornis still in place, observed in 1989 at the northern side of the islands (Ramírez and Viña, 1991). Laverde-Castillo et al. (1987) reported also noticeable mortality in P. porites and Tubastrea aurea in 1987 at San Bernardo. Another mass mortality event involving a reef organism was reported from the Cartagena area by Garzón-Ferreira and Zea (1992). Hundreds of eroded skeletons of Gorgonia, still attached to the bottom, were found in 1990 at the inner fore reef in the northern coast of Isla Tesoro (Islas del Rosario).

San Andrés Island

Coral reefs of San Andrés were qualitatively surveyed in detail between 1968 and 1973 by Geister (1975). At the end of this period, a great proportion of A. cervicornis and P. porites stands in the NE reef lagoon were found dead. Also, some degree of deterioration at a shallow P. furcata patch reef of the lagoon was noted since 1968. Aside from this, coral formations around the island seemed to be in good healthy condition.

No more studies on coral reefs of San Andrés were done until 1992, when Díaz et al. (1992) carried out an intensive survey to evaluate health and present community structure. High levels of recent coral mortality (visually estimated at 47 fast survey stations) were found between 0.5 and 22 m depth, resulting in a overall mean of 52%. More than half of the stations had mortality values higher than 50%. Table 1 presents data on mean cover of major components of the reef surface (relative to hard substrate), estimated by two methods. Both produced very similar results, with mean relative live coral and algae covers of about 28% and 65% respectively. Proliferations of algae (mainly Dyctiota, Halimeda, Lobophora and Padina) were commonly found covering dead coral, as well as adjacent portions of live coral tissue. Thallous algae represented a 26% of the reef surface cover at San Andrés, estimated in chain transects.

Nineteen hard corals species were identified as affected noticeably by recent mortality in San Andrés (Table 2). Among them, 14 species reached maximum mortality levels of at least 50% and A. cervicornis, A. palmata, A. agaricites, E. fastigita, M. complanata, M. annularis, P. furcata and Siderastrea siderea of at least 80%. The most affected species is A. cervicornis, of which probably less than 1% of its recent populations survive at present; only isolated small colonis were found alive at fore reefs and the extensive patches examined at the lagoon were totally dead and fragmented. Two of the most important species in shallow reef construccion in San Andrés, A. palmata and M. complanata, showed very high mortalities in the lagoon and adjacent to the inner side of the barrier reef, while at the exposed side of the barrier their mortality levels were comparatively much lower. Furthermore, all populations of the sea fans (Gorgonia) were found mostly dead (60-100%, mean 91.4%) (Díaz et al., 1992; Garzón-Ferreira and Zea, 1992).

DISCUSSION

This review on changes of coral reefs of the Colombian Caribbean, suggest that extensive recent mortality of corals began sometime between the end of 1980 and the begining of 1982, at least for the continental coast. Previous damage reported by Geister (1975) from 1968-1973 in lagoonal reefs of San Andrés Island were related to hurricane impacts. Colombian mortality events may be part of a generalized process of coral decline, which is occurring in the Wider Caribbean from the begining of the 1980's (Williams and Bunkley-Williams, 1990).

The Rosario and San Bernardo archipelagos are seasonally influenced by turbid waters. Increased sedimentation (resulting principally from anthropogenic modifications in river drainages) has been implicated as the main cause of recent extensive mortality of corals at the islands (Alvarado et al., 1986; Ramírez et al., 1986; Laverde-Castillo et al., 1987; Ramírez and Viña, 1991). The occurrence of a mortality event of similar characteristics at the oceanic island of San Andrés, where marine waters are clear and sedimentation rates very low (Díaz et al., 1992), may indicate that another agent (or several agents) of wide distribution could be responsible. Epidemic diseases and bleaching have been related to high mortality of corals in the Caribbean and other seas during the 1980's (Williams and Bunkley-Williams, 1990). White band disease was probably the main cause of massive die-offs of Acropora spp. in Colombia, as in other Caribbean areas. Black band and other diseases are still commonly observed killing massive corals at San Andrés (Díaz et al., 1992) and in the Santa Marta area (pers. observ.). Bleaching events have been reported in San Andrés since 1969 (Geister, 1992) and in the Cartagena area from 1983, 1987 and 1990 (Ramírez et al., 1986; Sarmiento et al., 1989; Solano et al., 1993). Other agents that surely have contributed to increase coral mortality in the Colombian Caribbean during the last 20 years are: hurricanes (only at the San Andrés area), algae proliferation, seawage pollution, eutrophication, over-fishing, boat traffic, anchoring, coral mining, increased sedimentation and dynamite fishing (the last two only at the continental coast) (Werding and Sánchez, 1979; Alvarado et al., 1986; Alvarado and Corchuelo, 1992; Ramírez and Viña, 1991).

ACKNOWLEDGEMENTS

We are grateful to Elvira Alvarado (Univ. Jorge Tadeo Lozano), Francisco Arias (CIOH) and Juan Laverde-Castillo for providing unpublished information. Francisco Borrero made important comments and reviewed English text. Rosario Madera was helpful in the edition.

LITERATURE CITED

Alvarado, E.M. and M.C. Corchuelo. 1992. Efecto del Canal del Dique sobre el Parque Nacional Natural Corales del Rosario, Cartagena, Colombia (1990-1991). Final Rep. Project, Centro Invest. Cient., Univ. Jorge Tadeo Lozano, Bogotá, 23 p.

Alvarado, E.M.; F. Duque; L. Flórez and R. Ramírez. 1986. Evaluación cualitativa de los arrecifes coralinos de las Islas del Rosario (Cartagena-Colombia). Bol. Ecotrop. Ecos. Trop., 15: 1-30.

Coral, A. and A. Caicedo. 1983. Descripción de la formación arrecifal de Isla Grande (Islas del Rosario) con anotaciones ecológicas. Thesis Biol. Mar., Univ. Jorge Tadeo Lozano, Bogotá, 110 p.

CORPES C.A. 1992. El Caribe colombiano, realidad ambiental y desarrollo. Cons. Reg. Planif. Costa Atlant., Santa Marta, 275 p.

Díaz, J.M.; J. Garzón-Ferreira and S. Zea. 1992. Evaluación del estado actual del arrecife coralino de la Isla de San Andrés. Final Rep. Project, INVEMAR/CORPES, Santa Marta, 147 p.

Galvis, N.H. 1989. Evaluación cuantitativa de las llanuras arrecifales de las Islas Pavitos, Parque Nacional Natural Corales del Rosario, Cartagena, Colombia. Bol. Ecotrop. Ecos. Trop., 19: 27-54.

Garzón-Ferreira, J. and S. Zea. 1992. A mass mortality of Gorgonia ventalina (Cnidaria: Gorgoniidae) in the Santa Marta area, Caribbean coast of Colombia. Bull. Mar. Sci.,50(3): 522-526.

Geister, J. 1975. Riffbau und geologische Entwicklungsgeschichte der Insel San Andrés (westliches Karibisches Meer, Kolumbien). Stuttg. Beitr. Naturk. (Geol. Palaeont.), 15: 203 p.

Geister, J. 1992. Modern reef development and cenozoic evolution of an oceanic island/reef complex: Isla de Providencia (W Caribbean Sea, Colombia). Facies, 27.

Laverde-Castillo, J.J.A.; R. Araujo; G. Vargas and E. Patiño. 1987. Plan de monitoreo del Golfo de Morrosquillo. Primera parte: aspecto biológico. Final Rep. Project, Asoc. Cravo Norte, Ecopetrol, Bogotá, 125 p.

Penereiro, J.L.; G.R. Navas; R.A. Montoya; F. Cleves and L.T. Moreno. 1990. Cartografía ecológica de los fondos submarinos adyacentes al conjunto de islas Latifundio-Minifundio, Parque Nacional Natural Corales del Rosario, Caribe colombiano. Mem. VII Semin. Nal. Cienc. Tecnol. Mar., CCO, Bogotá: 184-194.

Prahl, H. von and H. Erhardt. 1985. Colombia corales y arrecifes coralinos. FEN, Bogotá, 295 p.

Ramírez, A. and M.L. De La Pava. 1981. Corales hermatípicos de la Isla de Tierra Bomba, Cartagena (Colombia). Estimación de algunos factores de incidencia en la sucesión vertical con anotaciones ecológicas. Thesis Biol. Mar., Univ. Jorge Tadeo Lozano, Bogotá, 138 p.

Ramírez, A. and G. Viña. 1991. Estructura de las formaciones coralinas de las Islas de San Bernardo (Mar Caribe, Colombia). Taller Arrecif. Coral. Colombia (Doc. Guía), Unpubl. Rep., Univ. Jorge Tadeo Lozano, Bogotá, unpag.

Ramírez, A.; I.B. de Ramírez and J.E. Correal. 1986. Ecología descriptiva de las llanuras madreporarias del Parque Nacional Submarino Los Corales del Rosario (Mar Caribe, Colombia). Fondo Protec. Medio Amb., FEN Colomb., Bogotá, 71 P.

Sarmiento, E.; F. Flechas and G. Alvis. 1989. Evaluación cuantitativa del estado actual de las especies coralinas del Parque Nacional Natural Corales del Rosario (PNNCR), Cartagena, Colombia. Thesis Biol. Mar., Univ. Jorge Tadeo Lozano, Bogotá, 144 p.

Solano, O.D.; G.N. Suárez and S.K. Moreno-Forero. 1993. Blanqueamiento coralino de 1990 en el Parque Nacional Natural Corales del Rosario (Caribe colombiano). An. Inst. Invest. Mar. Punta Betín, 22: in press.

Wells, S.M. (ed.). 1988. Coral reefs of the world. Vol. 1: Atlantic and eastern Pacific. UNEP/IUCN, Gland, 373 p.

Werding, B. and H. Sánchez. 1979. Informe faunístico y florístico de las Islas del Rosario en la costa norte de Colombia. I. Situación general y estructuras arrecifales. An. Inst. Invest. Mar. Punta Betín, 11: 7-20.

Williams, E. H. and L. Bunkley-Williams. 1990. The world-wide coral reef bleaching cycle and related sources of coral mortality. Atoll. Res. Bull., 335: 1-71.

IMPACT OF TOURISM DEVELOPMENT ON THE CORAL REEFS OF THE ABROLHOS AREA, BRAZIL

Zelinda M.A.N.Leão[1], Marcelo D.Telles[2], Roberto Sforza[2], Hélio A.Bulhões[3]
and Ruy K.P.Kikuchi[1]

[1] Universidade Federal da Bahia (IGEO-PPPG), Campus da Federação, 40210-340, Salvador, Bahia, Brasil
[2] Centro de Pesquisa e Manejo de Abrolhos, Rua Barão do Rio Branco 277, 45900-000, Caravelas, Bahia, Brasil.
[3] PARNAM de Abrolhos, Praia do Quitongo, 45900-000, Caravelas, Bahia, Brasil.

ABSTRACT

The reefs of the Abrolhos area, on the east coast of Brazil, are the southernmost coral reefs in the Atlantic. They have an undoubtedly importance for scientific studies, as they are ecologically unique and rich in endemic species. They are also economically valuable for fisheries. Deterioration of the Abrolhos area is not yet measured, but people pressure on the reefs has largely increased in the last years. Great part due to the tourism industry. A five years survey on the effects of the marine tourism in the offshore reefs of the Abrolhos Marine Park, revealed that the regional tourism is the most active one, and although severely controlled, visitors activity has been hazardous to the reefs. In the nearshore zones, the reefs are not under any kind of environmental control. They have been, for a long time, impacted by high sedimentation influx, caused by deforestation of the Atlantic rainforest for agriculture purposes. This is now reinforced with the fast growth of urban centers in the coastal zones. To avoid degradation of the Abrolhos reefs and to ensure their appropriated use, authorities, private developers and the community must compromise on a long term program for effective management of the reefs.

INTRODUCTION

The Abrolhos coral reefs have a characteristic growth form of mushroom-shaped pinnacles (1-25 m high and 2-50 m in diameter) called *chapeirões*, which may coalesce at their tops forming bank and platform reefs 1-20 km long and with varied shapes (Leão, 1982; Leão et al., 1988). These reef structures form two separated arcs located on the northern part of the Abrolhos Bank (Fig. 1). The platform reefs of the inner arc are almost all emergent at low tide. Their exposed reef flats are the result of reef erosion due to fluctuations of Holocene sea level along the coast of Eastern Brazil (Martin et al., 1985). In the outer arc that borders the volcanic islands of the Abrolhos Archipelago the reefs, in waters 15-20m deep, are formed by giant submerged *chapeirões* that do not coalesce.

The reefs are built by a coral fauna that has long been considered of interest on account of its high proportion of endemic species (Laborel, 1969 a and b), and particularly because the major reef builders are arcaic forms remnant of an ancient coral fauna dating back in the Tertiary (Leão, 1983).

Although deterioration of the Abrolhos area is not yet measured, people pressure on the reefs has been largely increasing in the last years, and it is primary associated with tourism development. In the whole area of the reefs (about 4,000 km^2), effective protection has only been done within the limits of the Abrolhos Marine Park (912 km^2) (IBAMA FUNATURA, 1991).

This report presents available data of a five years survey on the marine tourism in the area of the Abrolhos Park, which is already causing adverse effects on the reefs. These data are based on information about the number of visitors and the origin of the boats that come to the Abrolhos Park area, recorded on standard forms filled out by the park staff from 1988 to 1992.

The rate of urban expansion of the adjacent coastal zone in the last fourty years, is also evaluated through comparison of aerial photographs.

RESULTS

The Rate of Tourism Development

The Abrolhos Marine Park was designated in 1983, but only in 1987 it was installed by the Brazilian Government Environmental Agency (the IBAMA). The Park is subdivided into two areas; one smaller, located within the coastal arc of the reefs (the Timbebas Reef), and the other that covers the islands of the Abrolhos Archipelago and the coral reefs of the outer arc (Fig. 1). The largest area is better controlled because the marine station of the Park is located in one of the islands. The records of the activities on the Park, since its installation, reveal that the marine tourism is the most active.

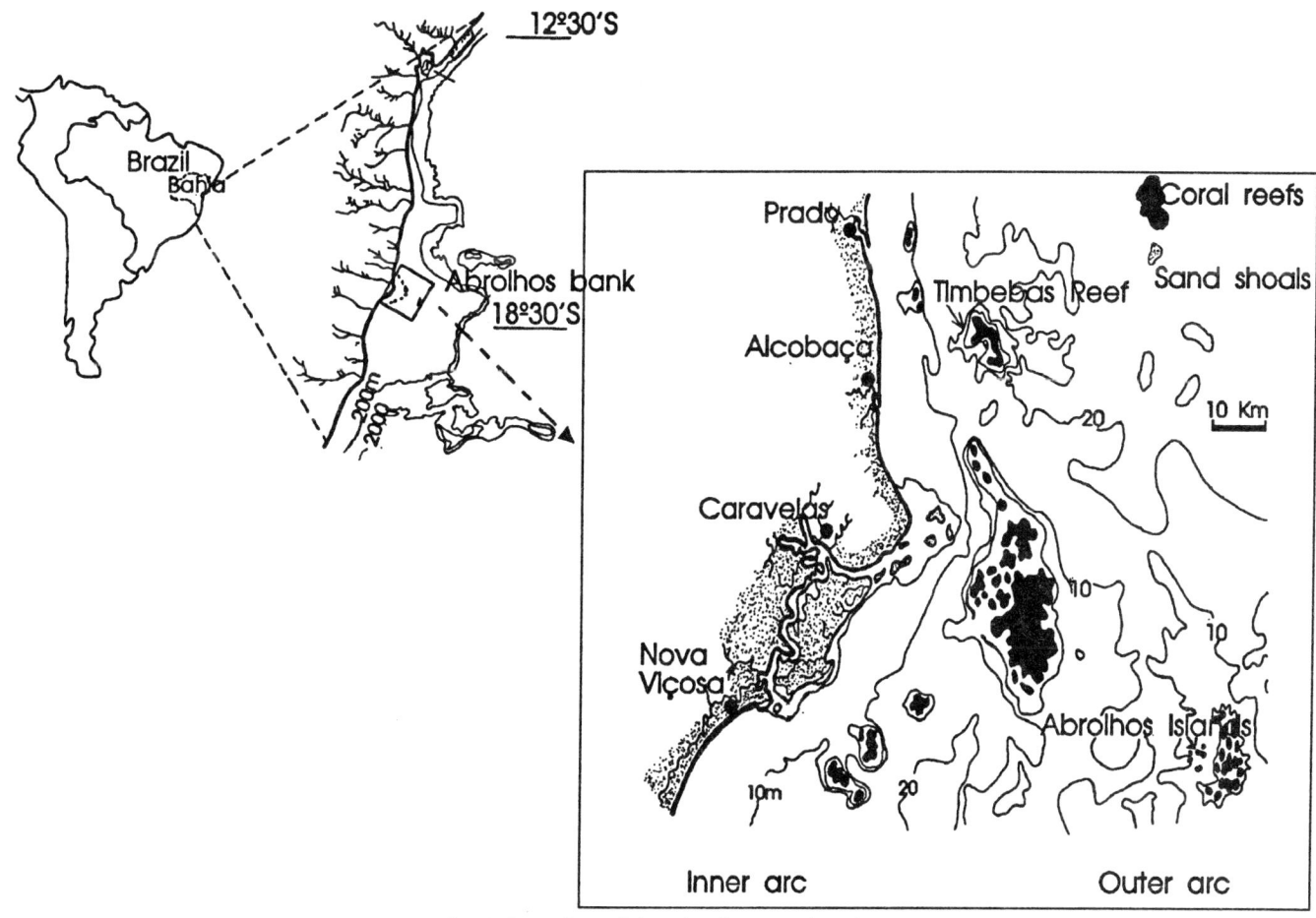

Fig. 1. Location of the Abrolhos coral reefs.

Three categories of boat visited the Park in the last five years: a) regional boats coming from the neighboring cities of the coastal area; b) national private boats commonly from the most developed states of Southern Brazil, and c) boats from foreign countries.

The regional tourism is either the largest and the most frequent (Fig. 2). It carries to the Park both domestic and international visitors through local tourism agencies that promote short trips to the reef area. During the first two years of the survey (1988-1989), it is observed that this type of tourism occurred dominantly during summer time (December to March) (Fig. 3). From 1990 to 1992, however, the visits of boats coming from the adjacent coastal cities, besides showing a great increase, it also extended to almost the whole year (Fig. 4)..

The total number of visitors arriving each year in the area of the Park augmented 407% from 1988 to 1992 (from 705 persons in 1988 to 3573 in 1992). This increasing rate was relatively continuous, though in 1991 it had a light decrease of 10% (Fig. 5).

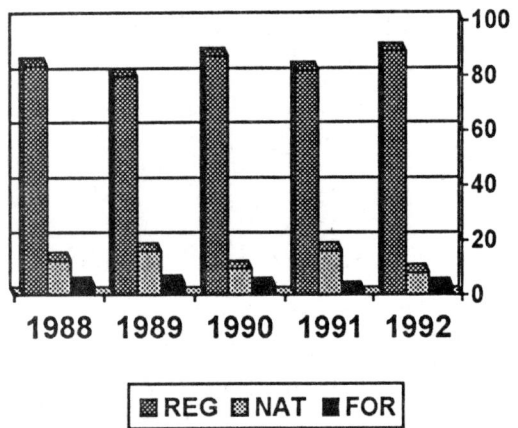

Fig 2. Relative percentage of the major categories of boats coming to the Abrolhos Marine Park from 1988 to 1992.

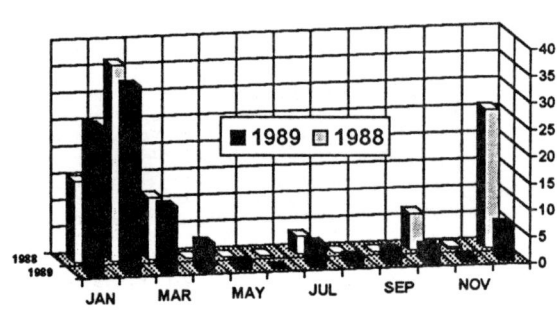

Fig. 3. Monthly percentage of visitors arriving in the Abrolhos Park through local tourism during 1988 and 1989

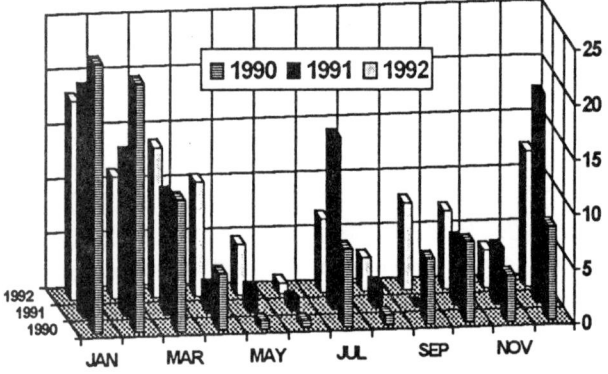

Fig. 4. Monthly percentage of visitors arriving in the Abrolhos Park through local tourism from 1990 to 1992.

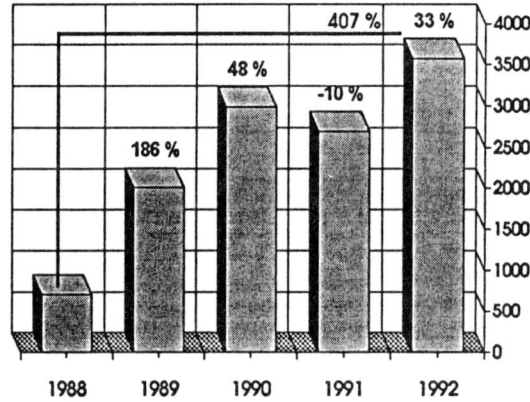

Fig. 5. The tourism increasing rate in the Abrolhos Park, based on the total number of visitors. From 1988 to 1992.

The Major Reef Disturbances

After the installation of the Abrolhos Park, the major activities of its administrative personnel have been the establishment and the maintenance of the park stations, as well as the control of visitors and fishermen arriving within the reef area. A monitoring program for evaluating impacts on the reefs is underway. Preliminary unpublished reports show that the major reef disturbances caused by the presence of visitors on the reefs are related to:

a) unappropriated boat anchorage and boat grounding, particularly on the area of the fringing reefs bordering the island of the Abrolhos Archipelago. The major effects are breakage of coral heads (Fig.6), disturbance of sea grass beds (Fig. 7) and overturning of isolated corals such as the *Meandrina braziliensis* (Fig. 8);

b) boat littering, which is introducing into the reef environment, slowly degraded plastic bottles and rubber products;

c) demand for souvenirs of reef animals, which has been intensifying the collection of corals that are locally sold (Fig. 9);

d) reef walking on the exposed surface of the poorly developed fringing reefs during low tide, which has been the major reason for localized reef damages;

Fig. 6. Broken heads of *Mussismilia braziliensis* caused by boat grounding on the reefs of the outer arc.

Fig. 7. Anchoring on grass beds in the surroundings of the islands of the Abrolhos Archipelago.

Fig. 8. Heads of the coral *Meandrina braziliensis* overturned by boat anchorage. Fringing reefs of the Abrolhos Islands.

Fig. 9. The yet primitive commerce of reef animals on the southern coast of the State of Bahia.

e) oil spill from the operation of motorized boats in the surroundings of the islands, and

f) occasional, but not so unfrequent shipwrecks that is usually caused by the presence of unexpected giant coral pinnacles.

The Urban Expansion of the Adjacent Coast

A comparison of aerial photographs from some of the cities adjacent to the reefs (Prado, Alcobaça and Nova Viçosa), taken in 1955 and 1989, shows that these urban areas expanded more then 1,000% during thirty four years. The city of Nova Viçosa for example, was in 1955 a small fishing village with an urban area of approximately 0.25 km². In 1989, its occupied territory was about 3.0 km² (Fig. 10). More than 50% of this new development is due to recreational activities.

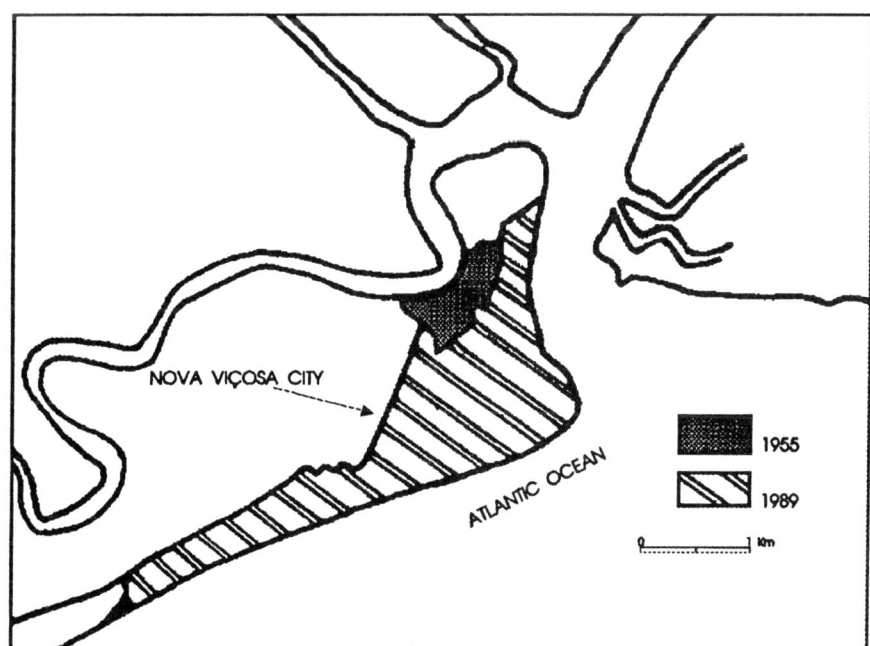

Fig. 10. The urban expansion of Nova Viçosa City based on aerial photographs from 1955 and 1989.
(For location see figure 1).

DISCUSSION

Not very long ago, the main factors that may have caused stress on the Abrolhos area, were the sediment load of rivers, the fishing using explosives and the mining of corals for lime and building purposes.

Dynamite fishing and coral extraction are now prohibited and severely controlled. The input of terrestrial sediment carried by rivers, that was in the past mainly due to deforestation of the Atlantic rainforest for agricultural use, is nowadays reinforced with the fast growth of the urban centers on the coastal zone. The water in Abrolhos is mostly turbid throughout the year.

Coastal development and its related human impacts appear to be increasing on many reefs elsewhere, and they are hardly affecting the adjacent systems (Acevedo & Morelock, 1988; English et al. 1988; Van't Hof, 1985, 1988). In the coastal area of Abrolhos, the effects of the highly accelerated urban development on the adjacent reefs are not yet measured. Offshore, in the area of the Park where there is a restrictive control, and where the only human activity is the marine tourism, preliminary observations reveal that the reefs are already under pressure.

What are, then, the levels of reef degradation within the not controlled area of the inner arc of reefs? It represents three fourths of the total reefs of Abrolhos. Besides being located closer to the urban centers, there is not any restriction for recreational or even commercial use of these reefs.

And what will happen in the near future if these conditions persist? This picture of Abrolhos is also seen in all the coral reef areas in Brasil.

An appropriate use of the coral reefs in Brazil is urged. But this will only succeed when and if authorities, private developers and the community were formely engaged on a long term program involving political, socio economic, scientific and technical aspects. This project will certainly assess an environmental monitoring program, as well as generate support for a sustained management of the reefs.

CONCLUSION

- The coral reefs of Abrolhos have been stressed for a long time, mostly due to the high sedimentation load of rivers.

- The current coastal development reinforced environmental pressure from human activity. Most of the cities along the coast have been growing at an alarming rate, more than 1,000% in the last fourty years. Great part due to the tourism industry.

- In the Abrolhos Park the marine tourism is rapidly expanding. Although being severely controlled, the activity of the park visitors is already affecting the reefs. Anchoring, boat grounding, littering, reef flat walking and the coral trade are the major causes of damages on the reefs.

- The reefs of the nearshore zone, that comprise three fourths of the total area of reefs, are not under any kind of control. The levels of degradation are completely unknown.

- The entire area of the Abrolhos reefs urges to be maintained. More specific impacted sites may warrant useful monitoring approaches. An integrated program involving authorities, administrators, educators and scientists is essential to develop effective management.

LITERATURE CITED

Acevedo, R. and Morelock, J.1988. Effects of terrigenous sediment influx on coral reef zonation in Southwestern Puerto Rico. Proceedings of the Sixth International Coral Reef Symposium, Australia, vol. 2 :189-194.

IBAMA FUNATURA 1991. Plano de Manejo: Parque Nacional Marinho de Abrolhos, Brasilia 96 p.

English, S. A., Bradbury, R. H. and Reichett, R. E. 1988. Management of large marine ecosystems - A multinational approach. Proceedings of the Sixth International Coral Reef Symposium. Australia, vol. 2 :369-374.

Laborel, J. L. 1969a. Les peuplements de madreporaires de côtes tropicales du Brésil. Annales de l'Université d'Abdijan, Serie E II, Fasc. 3, 260p.

Laborel, J. L. 1969b. Madreporaires et hidrocoralliaires recifaux des côtes brésiliennes. Systematique, ecologie, repartion verticale et geographie. Annales de l'Institute Oceanographique de Paris, 47 :171-226.

Leão, Z. M. A. N. 1982. Morphology, geology and developmental history of the southernmost coral reefs of Western Atlantic, Abrolhos Bank, Brazil. Ph.D. Dissertation, Rosenstiel School of Marine and Atmospheric Science, Miami, Florida, 218p.

Leão, Z. M. A. N. 1983. Abrolhos: O refúgio pleistocênico de uma fauna terciária de corais. Revista Ciências da Terra, 8 : 22-24.

Leão Z. M. A. N., Araujo, T. M. F. and Nolasco, M. C. 1988. The coral reefs off the coast of Eastern Brazil. Proceedings of the Sixth International Coral Reef Symposium, Australia, vol. 3 :339-347.

Martin, L., Flexor, J. M. Blitzkow, D. and Suguio, K. 1985. Geoid change indications along the Brazilian coast during the last 7,000 years. Proceedings of the Fifth International Coral Reefs Congress, Tahiti, vol. 3 :85-90.

Van't Hof, T. 1985. The economic benefits of marine parks and protected areas in the Caribean region. Proceedings of the Fifth International Coral Reef Congress. Tahiti, vol. 6 :551-556.

Van't Hof, T. 1988. Management of coral reefs and associated systems and resources in the Western Atlantic : A status review. Proceedings of the Sixth International Coral Reef Symposium, Australia, vol. 1 :89-95.

ANATOMY OF A DYING CORAL REEF: PUNTA ISLOTES REEF, GOLFO DULCE, COSTA RICA

Ian G. Macintyre[1], Jorge Cortés[2], and Peter W. Glynn[3]

A well-developed fringing coral reef in Golfo Dulce, off the Pacific coast of Costa Rica, is being smothered with fine sediment and has a present-day live coral cover of less than 2%. This reef, off Punta Islotes, has a surface area of about 12 ha, and can be divided into four distinct zones; back-reef sediments, reef-flat branching corals, fore-reef slope massive corals, and fore-reef slope talus. Data from rock and sediment cores collected along four short transects across the outer edge of this reef reveal that it was once a flourishing reef that was established 5,500 years B.P. on a basalt terrace and is up to 9m thick. This reef, well isolated from the open-ocean temperature fluctuations that restrict most reef growth in the eastern Pacific, was exposed to heavy sedimentation in the past. It recovered, however, about 2,500 years BP to have a period of vigorous reef growth before succumbing, within the last 500 years, to fresh-water and sedimentation stress following a change in local river outflow patterns. The present-day final stage of degradation is related to heavy sedimentation associated with a recent increase in human activity along the adjacent shores.

INTRODUCTION

Recent studies (see Macintyre et al. in press) have shown that significant reef accumulation in the eastern Pacific is limited to those inshore coastal areas that are protected from oceanic thermal anomalies related to both warm El Niño events and cool upwelling episodes. The semi-enclosed waters of Golfo Dulce is one such area (Fig. 1), however, the reefs in this gulf are being exposed to extensive siltation related to terrestrial runoff, and all reefs are suffering various stages of degradation (Cortés, 1990a).

In an effort to understand the history of reef growth in Golfo Dulce, the best-developed reef in terms of size and relief, off Punta Islotes, was selected for study (Cortés, 1990b). Rock cores were drilled and sediment cores vibrocored along four transects across the outer edge of this reef (Fig. 1). Sedimentological studies of these cores, including 26 radiocarbon dates, have allowed us to reconstruct the growth history of this reef and to assess the effects on its development by both natural and anthropogenic disturbances.

RESULTS

Present-day Reef Community

Although most corals are still in their original growth position, they are almost entirely dead and covered by fine sediment trapped in a filamentous algal mat. The overall live cover is less than 2% and consists primarily of large colonies of Porites lobata, a stress-resistant coral (Cortés 1990b). The zonation can be limited to four basic zones.

"Back-reef sediments" - This narrow zone that is adjacent to and parallels the shoreline is generally 1m to 1.5m deep at mean low tide. The bottom consists of fine terrigenous sediment with less than 10% carbonate. No live corals occur in this zone.

"Reef-flat branching corals" - This zone ranges in depth from 0m to 1m at mean low tide. A meshwork of dead branching corals Pocillopora damicornis and Psammocora stellata form the basic substrate (Fig. 2a) that supports scattered live and dead microatolls of Porites lobata.

"Fore-reef slope massive corals" - This zone dips gently seaward from the reef flat to about 2m where it becomes almost vertical in some areas. Large overlapping colonies of Porites lobata cover most of this zone (Fig. 2b) that extends down to depths of 10m to 12m. The uppermost gently sloping section has the highest live coral cover

---

[1] Smithsonian Institution, National Museum of Natural History, Department of Paleobiology, Washington, D.C. 20560.
[2] Universidad de Costa Rica, Centro de Investigación en Ciencias del Mar Y Limnologiá and Escuela de Biologiá, San Pedro, Costa Rica. [3] University of Miami, Rosenstiel School of Marine and Atmospheric Science, Miami, Florida 33149.

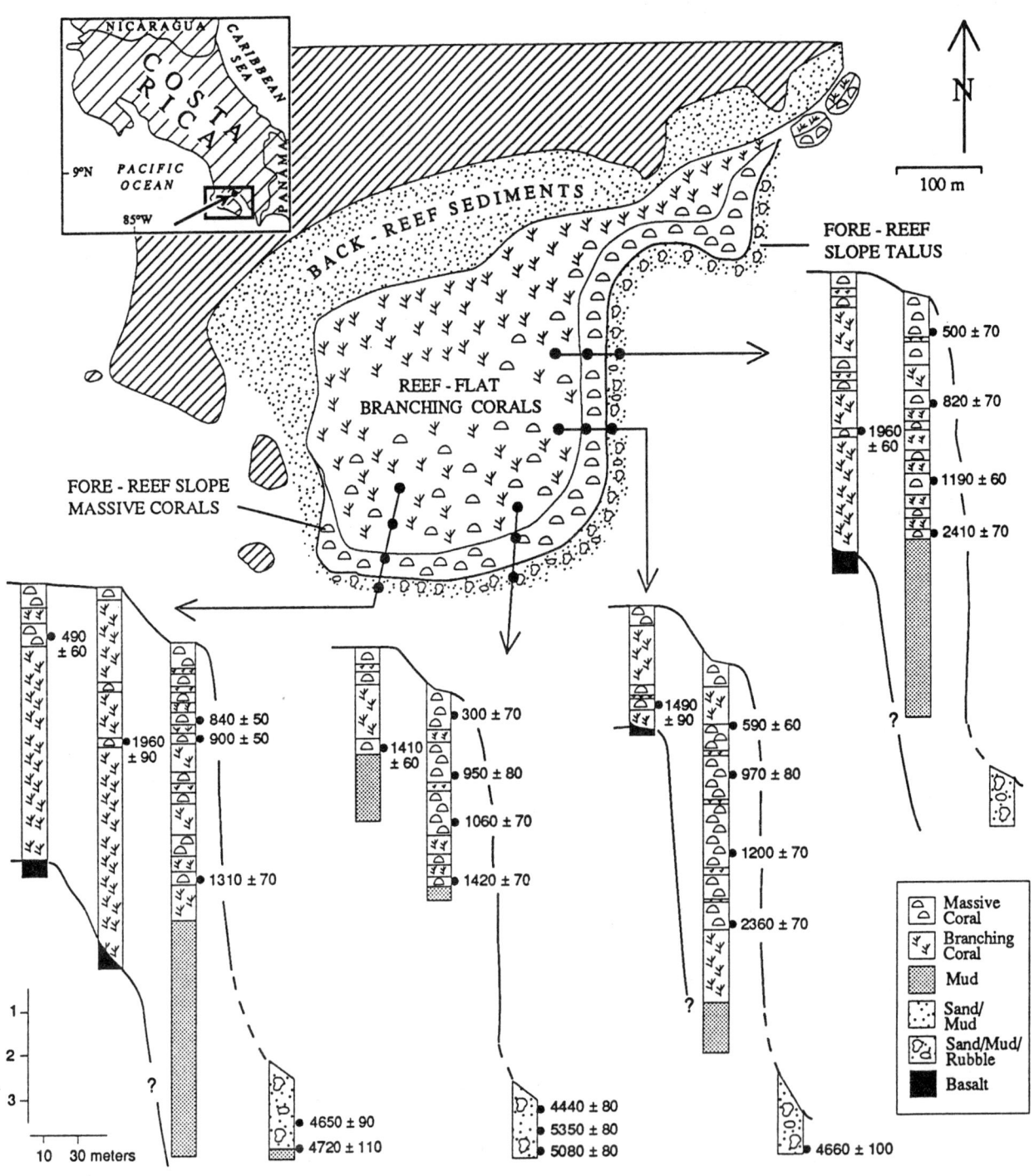

Figure 1. Index map of fringing reef at Punta Islotes in Golfo Dulce (see inset) showing reef-surface zonation and location of four rotary-drill core and vibrocore transects. Cross sections along these transects indicate the sedimentologic units recovered from the cores and the location of 26 radiocarbon-dated samples (after Cortés 1990a; Cortés et al. in prep.).

Figure 2. Underwater views of Punta Islotes reef zones: A. Contact between dead interlocking Pocillopora damicornis framework of the reef flat (left) and large colonies of Porites lobata on fore-reef slope. Depth 1m. B. Fore-reef slope massive corals -- mostly dead overlapping colonies of Porites lobata covered with sediment-rich algal mats. Depth 4m. C. Contact between fore-reef slope massive corals and talus zones. Note coral debris on talus slope. Depth 11m.

recorded on this reef -- 8.4%, but seaward, on the steep outer slope, the live cover decreases sharply to levels of less than 1%.

"Fore-reef slope talus" - On the outer slope below the fore-reef slope zone of massive corals, the abundance of corals decreases sharply giving way to a sediment bottom (Fig. 2c). This transition is marked by a distinct decrease in slope, which eventually levels off at a depth of 15m. This muddy-sand contains varying amounts of coral and molluscan rubble, and contains up to 40% non-carbonate material. Here and there, large coral blocks have slumped off onto the sediment-covered slope.

Subsurface Data

Four short transects consisting of rotary drill core holes collected across the outer edge of this reef and vibracores in the fore-reef sediments indicate that this reef is established on a basaltic terrace, similar to the Cretaceous Nicoya Complex basalts exposed along the adjacent coastline. The surface of this terrace is very uneven, as indicated by the thickness of the overlying reef accumulation, which varies from 3.1 to 9m.

The distribution of reef facies in these cores is similar to that found in present-day reef zones (Fig. 1). In other words, the central and dominant branching-coral facies, consisting of Pocillopora damicornis with minor amounts of Psammocora stellata and Porites lobata, is situated below the reef-flat branching coral zone, which has an identical coral assemblage. Likewise the cores in the fore-reef massive corals and the fore-reef slope talus zones contain coral/sedimentologic units similar in composition to these found on the surface.

The only significant changes in subsurface sedimentological facies patterns are the presence of a distinctive gray clastic mud in the lower sections of all four fore-reef slope core holes, at the base of one vibrocore, and in the one reef-flat core hole that did not reach the basalt base. In addition, relatively thick layers of branching coral debris, including both Pocillopora damicornis and Psammocora stellata were found in fore-reef vibrocores 40cm below the surface. This is in marked contrast to the coral debris on the present-day talus slope, which is limited to fragments of the massive coral Porites lobata.

Extensively bored intervals were periodically found in massive Porites lobata sections. This bioerosion was caused mainly by boring molluscs (Lithophaga spp.) and is identical to the present-day dense patterns of bivalve borings in both live and dead Porites lobata.

The clay mineral assemblage associated with this fringing reef is dominated by smectite with lesser amounts of chlorite and kaolinite and traces of illite (Cortés 1990b). The composition of the clay minerals pumped up from drill holes, is similar to that of clay minerals trapped in coral skeletons collected from these holes, in sediments from vibrocores, and in surface sediments.

Cortés (1990b) noted a present-day shoreward increase in chlorite and suggested that this trend indicated a local source of terrigenous sedimentation from erosion of the chlorite-rich soils of the adjacent coast. The smectite-dominant clay assemblage, however, suggests that most of the clays at this reef site originated in the nearby Esquinas River, where outflowing waters contained mostly smectite with minor amounts of illite, kaolinite, and chlorite (Cortés 1990b).

Twenty six radiocarbon dates of unaltered coral samples (Fig. 1) occur in two distinct groups: 1) Branching coral Pocillopora damicornis recovered in vibrocores from fore-reef talus that yielded dates of 4,440 $\pm$ 80 to 5,350 $\pm$ 80 yrs B.P. 2) Massive coral Porites lobata cored in the main framework of this reef that yielded much younger dates, which ranged from 300 $\pm$ 70 to 2,410 $\pm$ 70 yrs B.P.

DISCUSSION

The earliest evidence of reef growth in this area is limited to branching-coral debris that was transported to the fore-reef slope. The close association of this coral debris with smectite-rich muds indicates that these early pioneer Pocillopora damicornis corals struggled to survive in waters heavily laden with sediments from nearby rivers. Indeed, the lag of about 1,000 years (as indicated by a sea-level curve for the west coast of Mexico [Curray et al. 1969]) between the flooding of the basaltic terrace that underlies this reef and the initial growth indicated by the branching corals, suggest that local reworking of the soil and sediment cover eliminated all early coral recruitment (Cortés, 1990b; Cortés et al. in press; Macintyre et al. in press).

This first stage of reef growth (Fig. 3) probably started about 5,500 yrs B.P. as patches of Pocillopora damicornis established on areas of high relief on the basaltic terrace. Periodically these early small patch reefs were damaged by storms and the coral debris was transported seaward, where it accumulated in the fore-reef talus (Cortés, 1990b; Cortés et al. in press; Macintyre et al. in press).

These initial coral patches apparently only survived for about 1,000 years to about 4,500 yrs B.P. (Fig. 3). Then there was a period of 2,000 years of high turbid conditions that prevented any significant coral growth in this area. The earliest massive coral date of 2,410 $\pm$ 70 yrs B.P. is the first evidence of in situ reef growth, with the appearance of massive colonies of Porites lobata, commonly on Pocillopora debris (Cortés, 1990b; Cortés et al. in press). This initiated the second stage of growth of this reef (Fig. 3) when it truly flourished, achieving growth rates of up to 8.3m/1000 years. The majority of the framework of this reef was formed during this 2,000 year period, at which time massive colonies of Porites lobata dominated the outer slopes (Macintyre et al. in press).

Conditions have deteriorated over the last 500 years, apparently related to the introduction of sediment-laden waters from nearby inner gulf rivers (Cortés 1990b). In this final degradation stage of growth (Fig. 3), there is a marked decrease in the rate of framework accumulation (<3m/1000 years). In addition, the strongly depleted $\delta^{18}O$ values obtained from massive corals in this section, values ranging from -4.8 ‰ to -7.19 ‰, are indicative of the influence of freshwater (Cortés, 1990b; Cortés et al. in press). Gardner et al. (1987) reported that the age of breached beach ridges, along with barbed tributaries and superimposed streams, all indicated that the outflows of the two largest rivers in this area, the Esquinas and Rincón, were diverted into the inner gulf about 500 to 1,000 years ago.

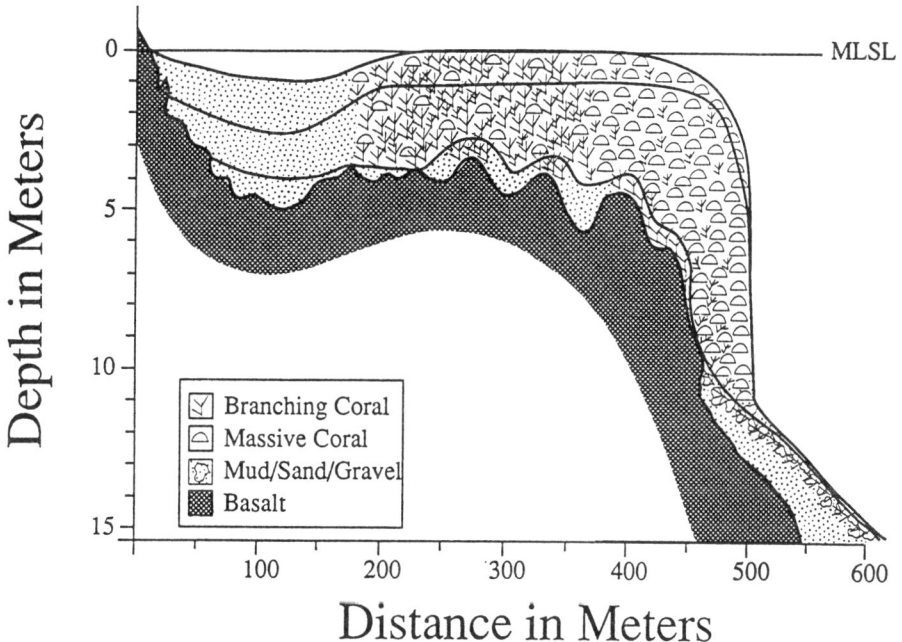

Figure 3. Schematic cross section of Punta Islotes reef showing three postulated stages of reef growth: Initial patch reefs of branching corals, 5,500 - 4,500 years B.P.; main period of flourishing growth, 2,500 - 500 years B.P.; final stage of deterioration, 500 years B.P. - present (after Macintyre et al. in press).

It should be noted, that even during the final stage of degradation, Punta Islotes reef managed to maintain a zonation pattern identical to that of the previous stage of vigorous growth. Indeed, there is some evidence that the present-day degradation of this reef is a relatively recent phenomenon. Although the massive Porites lobata corals are extensively bioeroded, most corals on the reef surface are well preserved and are still in growth position -- even many of the reef-flat branching corals. In 1978, Punta Islotes reef had a much greater live coral cover than it has today (Glynn et al. 1983) -- indicating that this reef is still in a stage of decline.

This final "coup de grace" of the Punta Islotes reef community has been attributed to the recent increase of human activities on the adjacent coasts, including deforestation, mining, and road construction (Cortés 1990b; Cortés et al. in press). Such activities have significantly increased the stress of freshwater runoff and siltation to this reef site.

CONCLUSIONS

Punta Islotes, once one of the best developed reefs in Golfo Dulce, is now almost dead with less than 2% live coral cover. Most of the corals are still in growth position but overgrown with sediment-trapping filamentous algal mats.

This reef had a difficult period of initial growth. Under conditions of heavy sedimentation and freshwater runoff, small coral communities of Pocillopora damicornis survived for about 1,000 years between 5,500 and 4,500 years ago.

These severe stress conditions continued over a long period and it was not until 2,500 years ago that this reef flourished to form most of its framework.

The last 500 years have been marked by a decline in the reef community with a reintroduction of sediment-laden freshwater runoff caused by the diversion of river outflow patterns.

The recent destruction of many adjacent forested areas has given rise to a significant increase in freshwater and siltation stress conditions, so that we are now witnessing the final collapse of this reef community.

Coral reefs in Golfo Dulce are well protected from the oceanic thermal anomalies that restrict coral-reef development in the eastern Pacific. Although some of these reefs have flourished to form impressive reef structures, almost all of the reefs of this area are in a state of deterioration related to terrestrial runoff -- recently aggravated by the destruction of forests surrounding this gulf.

ACKNOWLEDGEMENTS

We thank Axioni Romero, Alvaro Segura, and Captain David West and the crew of R/V Benjamin for their valuable assistance in the field. Technical and logistical support in Costa Rica were provided by CIMAR, Universidad de Costa Rica, and by the Smithsonian Tropical Research Institute in Panama. Mary A. Parrish's drafting and Diane R. Cloyd's typing are acknowledged gratefully. This project was supported by a Scholarly Studies Grant from the Smithsonian Institution to I.G.M. Additional support was provided by a Fulbright Fellowship and by Reitmeister and Rowland Fellowships awarded at the University of Miami to J.C. and by NSF grant OCE 8716726 to P.W.G.

LITERATURE CITED

Cortés, J. 1990a. The coral reefs of Golfo Dulce, Costa Rica: Distribution and community structure. Atoll Research Bulletin 344: 1-37.

Cortés, J. 1990b. Coral reef decline in Golfo Dulce, Costa Rica, eastern Pacific: Anthropogenic and natural disturbances. Ph.D. dissertation, University of Miami. 147 pp.

Cortés, J., I. G. Macintyre and P. W. Glynn. In Press. Holocene growth history of an eastern Pacific fringing reef, Punta Islotes, Costa Rica. Coral Reefs.

Curray, J. R., F. J. Emmel, and P. J. S. Crampton. 1969. Holocene history of a strand plain, lagoonal coast, Nayarit, Mexico. Pages 63-100 in A. Ayala Castañares and F. B. Phleger. eds. Coastal lagoons: A Symposium. UNAM-UNESCO, México D. F.

Macintyre, I. G., P. W. Glynn and J. Cortés. In Press. Holocene reef history in the eastern Pacific: Mainland Costa Rica, Caño Island, Cocos Island, and Galápagos Islands. Proceedings, 7th International Coral Reef Symposium, Guam.

Gardner, T. W., W. Beck, T. F. Bullard, P. W. Hare, R. H. Kesel, D. R. Lowe, C. M. Menges, S. C. Mora, F. J. Pazzagalia, I. D. Sasowskiy, J. W. Troester, and S. G. Wells. 1987. Central America and the Caribbean. Pages 323-402 in W. L. Graf. ed. Geomorphic Systems of North America. Geological Society of America, Centennial Special Vol. 2.

Glynn, P. W., E. M. Druffel, and R. B. Dunbar. 1983. A dead Central American coral reef tract: Possible link with the Little Ice Age. Journal of Marine Research. 41: 605-637.

THE CORAL REEFS OF THE SAN BLAS ISLANDS: REVISITED AFTER 20 YEARS

John C. Ogden[1] and Nancy B. Ogden[1]

[1]Florida Institute of Oceanography, 830 First Street South,
St. Petersburg, Florida, 33701 USA

ABSTRACT

Coral reef sites studied and photographed in the Gulf of San Blas on the Caribbean coast of Panama in 1970-71 were re-visited in 1991. There was a dramatic decline in the most common foliose and branching corals and an increase in algal cover. Agaricia spp. which formed most of the patch reefs and lined the slopes of channels and deep bays were mostly dead or being outcompeted by the brown alga Lobophora. Extensive, shallow Porites porites mounds had been harvested for fill by the Kuna. Deeper mounds were overgrown 50-100% by algae. Only debris fields and scattered small colonies remained of once extensive thickets of Acropora cervicornis and, in higher wave energy areas, A. palmata was mostly dead. In contrast, massive corals appeared generally healthy. These changes, abrupt and startling when viewed in a 20-year interval, have taken place in a context of on-going natural and human impact including the Diadema mass mortality, coral bleaching and diseases, fishing, coral mining, deforestation, and increased nutrients. These results emphasize the sensitivity of coral reefs to global change and the need for long-term comparative research.

INTRODUCTION

Coral reefs have attracted recent attention as potential indicators of global climate change in the oceans (D'Elia et al.,1991; Smith and Buddemeier, 1992; Brown and Ogden, 1993) and as concentrations of marine biological diversity (Jackson, 1991; Ray and Grassle, 1991). It is apparent that coral reefs are declining rapidly nearly everywhere they are in close contact with large human populations and coastal development (Rogers, 1985; Wells, 1988). The few, long-term, quantitative and qualitative studies have indicated that reef communities are dynamic, sensitive to both natural and human impact (Connell, 1976; Davis, 1982; Dustan and Halas, 1987; Hughes, 1989; Porter and Meier, 1992). As interest develops in long-term monitoring of reefs, an important perspective is gained by re-visiting historical field sites. Such an opportunity was afforded us by the Smithsonian Tropical Research Institute (STRI) in 1991 when we returned to coral reef sites in the Gulf of San Blas established during a STRI Post-Doctoral Fellowship in 1970-71 (Ogden and Buckman, 1973; Buckman and Ogden, 1973).

METHODS

The coral reefs of the Gulf of San Blas on the Caribbean coast of Panama were first described by Porter (1972), Glynn (1973), and Robertson and Glynn (1977). The observations reported here were made from July 16-23, 1991 in the vicinity of San Blas Point, where STRI operates a small field station, the Smithsoniantupo. We re-visited our 1970-71 field sites using original notes and photographs as a guide and made general observations on reef status, re-photographing specific areas. Our observations were concentrated at Ulagsukin, Pico Feo, the patch reefs northeast of Pico Feo, Aguadargana, and the Lemon Cays (not shown) across the channel to the east (Figure 1).

RESULTS

In 1970-71 Agaricia spp. formed most of the patch reefs and covered the slopes of bays such as Ulagsukin with a 0.5-1m thick convoluted layer which extended from 0.5m to nearly 30m deep. In 1991, while the complex structure remained, most of the Agaricia spp. were dead and overgrown by the brown alga, Lobophora variegata, remarkably similar to the coral in growth form (Figure 2). Scattered colony tips of Agaricia spp. and Madracis mirabilis pushed up through the thick algae which, when pulled away, revealed the white skeletons of recently killed coral. Other algae abundant on shallow dead Agaricia sp. were Sargassum, three species of Dictyota, and two red algae, Laurencia papillosa and Coelothrix irregularis. The

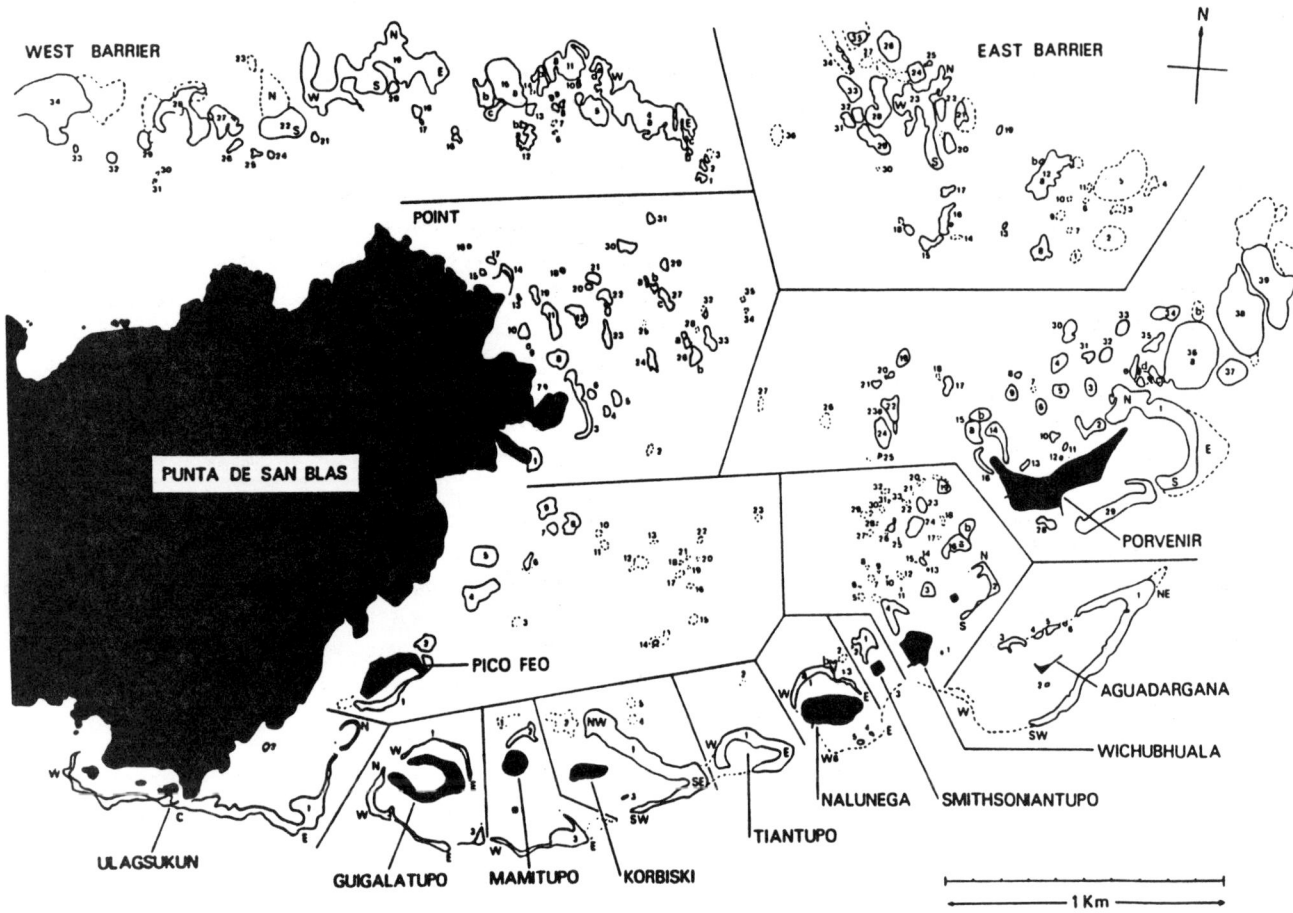

Figure 1: Map of coral reefs in the vicinity of San Blas Point; note Ulagsukin, Pico Feo, Smithsoniantupo, and Aguadargana (from D.R. Robertson, unpubl.)

green alga Halimeda opuntia was abundant as in 1970. Sandy patches had a striking increase in the green alga Penicillus.

The shallow, inner reefs of the Gulf once had extensive mounds of Porites porites (called "chee-wee" by the Kuna after the snack food "Cheetos;" E. Garcia, D.R. Robertson, pers. comm.) which have since been collected for fill. Deeper mounds (>1.5m), spared from collection, were 50-100% overgrown by various species of algae including Dictyota and Galaxaura (Figure 3).

Most reefs had Acropora cervicornis zones, often in extensive thickets, between 1m and 10 m deep. In 1991, we found debris fields of this coral but only a few small, living colonies (Figure 4). As the new colonies attain a suitable size they are apparently taken over and killed by damselfish (mostly Stegastes planifrons; Knowlton et al., 1990). N. Knowlton (pers. comm.) suggests that decline in this species occurred in a series of stages, one in 1987 and the most recent in 1990. The reefs exposed to greater wave action and water movement, particularly at Aguadargana and the Lemon Cays, were once characterized by luxuriant, large colonies of Acropora palmata. In 1991 most A. palmata was dead. Some of the colonies had reduced coverage of living tissue (Figure 5). We found few small colonies.

DISCUSSION AND CONCLUSIONS

Viewed in an interval of 20 years, the declines and overgrowth by algae of the foliose and branching corals on the reefs of the San Blas Islands seem abrupt and startling. It must be remembered, however, that change has taken place in a context of natural and human impacts some of which we can identify, if not assign as causes. Not all corals showed evidence of decline. Massive corals such as Montastrea and Siderastrea at Pico Feo had increased in size and in other locations generally appeared healthy.

In 1982-83, coincident with the strong El Nino event in the eastern Pacific, corals bleached in the San Blas Islands. In some areas most of the Agaricia spp. died (Lasker et al. 1984). The widespread mass mortality of the long-spined black sea urchin Diadema antillarum in 1983-84 released benthic algae from grazing pressure and caused major changes in coral reef communities in the Caribbean (Lessios et al. 1984; Carpenter, 1988). Recovery of Diadema has been very slow in the San Blas Islands (Lessios, pers. comm.) and certainly some of the high algal biomass is attributable to reduced Diadema grazing as well as overfishing. Over the past several decades Acropora cervicornis and A. palmata have declined in much of the Caribbean, in part from suspected diseases (Gladfelter, 1982; Smith and Ogden, in press). These species are dynamic and their slow recruitment may be overwhelmed by predators (Knowlton et al., 1990). Davis (1982) found the two Acropora species to be the major manifestation of change in an interval of 95 years in the Dry Tortugas.

Superimposed on these suspected natural disturbances are direct human impacts, such as coral mining, runoff from deforestation, fishing, and nutrients from sewage, which have certainly increased along with human populations over the 20 year interval. It is difficult to avoid the conclusion that increased human impact, in synergy with a series of natural disturbances, is largely responsible for the dramatic changes that we observed. Similar declines in coral cover have been observed over recent years on reefs between San Blas (eastern Hollandes Cays) and the Panama Canal (J. Jackson and H. Guzman, pers. comm.) and at 14 reef sites around the Caribbean (Ogden, 1987; Smith and Ogden, in press).

Coral reefs are sensitive to human and natural impacts and when viewed at appropriate time and geographic scales may provide threshold indications of change in time for effective management. Discrimination between human impact and natural variation requires long-term comparative research where impacts and influences on the dynamics of reefs may be isolated, studied, and understood (Ogden et al., in press).

ACKNOWLEDGEMENTS

We thank Smithsonian Tropical Research Institute (STRI), particularly I. Rubinoff (Director), E. Bermingham, H. Lessios, J. Jackson, N. Knowlton, and R. Robertson for support and encouragement. In 20 years, reefs and people change, but we were gratified to find all of the Kuna, notably Luis Burgos of Nalunega and Eladio Garcia of Wichubhuala, who helped us in 1970-71 still cheerfully helpful. We are grateful to the Kuna General Congress for their continuing support of the work of STRI in the region.

LITERATURE CITED

Brown, B.E. and J.C. Ogden. 1993. Coral bleaching. Sci. Am. 268(1): 64-70.

Buckman, N.S. and J.C. Ogden. 1973. Territorial behavior of the striped parrotfish Scarus croicensis Bloch (Scaridae). Ecology 54: 1377-1382.

Carpenter, R.C. 1988. Mass mortality of a Caribbean sea urchin: Immediate effects on community metabolism and other herbivores. Proc. Nat. Acad. Sci. USA 85: 511-514.

Connell, J.H. 1976. Competitive interactions and the species diversity of corals. p51-59, In: G.O. Mackie (ed.) Coelenterate Ecology and Behavior. Plenum, New York.

Davis, G.E. 1982. A century of natural change in coral distribution at the Dry Tortugas: A comparison of reef maps from 1881 and 1976. Bull. Mar. Sci. 32: 608-625.

Dustan, P. and J.C. Halas. 1987. Changes in the reef-coral community of Carysfort Reef, Key Largo, Florida: 1974 to 1982. Coral Reefs 6: 91-106.

D'Elia, C.F., R.W. Buddemeier, and S.V. Smith. 1991. Workshop on coral bleaching, coral reef ecosystems, and global change: Report of proceedings. Maryland Sea Grant College, UM-SG-TS-91-03, 49p.

Gladfelter, W.B. 1982. White band disease in Acropora palmata: Implications for the structure and growth of shallow reefs. Bull. Mar. Sci. 32: 639-643.

Glynn, P.W. 1973. Aspects of the ecology of coral reefs in the Western Atlantic region. p271-324. In: O.A. Jones and R. Endean (eds.) Biology and Geology of Coral Reefs, Vol. 2, Biol. 1, Acad. Press, N.Y.

Hughes, T.P. 1989. Community structure and diversity of coral reefs: the role of history. Ecology 70: 275-279.

Jackson, J.B.C. 1991. Adaptation and diversity of reef corals. Bioscience 41: 475-482.

Knowlton, N. J.C. Lang, and B.D. Keller. 1990. Case study of natural population collapse: post-hurricane predation on Jamaican staghorn corals. Smithsonian Contrib. Mar. Sci. 31: 25p.

Lasker, H.R., E.C. Peters, and M.A. Coffroth. 1984. Bleaching of reef coelenterates in the San Blas Islands, Panama. Coral Reefs 3: 183-190.

Lessios, H.A., D.R. Robertson, and J.D. Cubit. 1984. Spread of Diadema mass mortality through the Caribbean. Science 226: 335-337.

Ogden, J.C. 1987. Cooperative coastal ecology at Caribbean marine laboratories. Oceanus 30: 9-15

Ogden, J.C. and N.S. Buckman. 1973. Movements, foraging groups, and diurnal migrations of the striped parrotfish Scarus croicensis Bloch (Scaridae). Ecology 54: 589-596.

Ogden, J.C., J.W. Porter, N.P. Smith, A.M. Szmant, W.C. Jaap, and D. Forcucci. in press. SEAKEYS: A long-term interdisciplinary study of the Florida Keys seascape. Bull. Mar. Sci.

Porter, J.W. 1972. Patterns of species diversity in Caribbean reef corals Ecology 53: 745-748.

Porter, J.W. and O.W. Meier. 1992. Quantification of loss and change in Floridian reef coral populations. Amer. Zool. 32: 625-640.

Robertson, D.R. and P.W. Glynn. 1977. Field guidebook to the reefs of San Blas, Panama. Proc. Third Int. Symp. on Coral Reefs I: 397-403.

Ray, G.C. and J.F. Grassle. 1991. Marine biological diversity. Bioscience 41: 453-457.

Rogers, C.S. 1985. Degradation of Caribbean and Western Atlantic coral reefs and decline of associated reef fisheries. Proc. 5th Int. Coral Reef Symp., Papeete, Tahiti 6: 491-496.

Smith, S.R. and J.C. Ogden (eds.) in press. Status and recent history of coral reefs at the CARICOMP network of Caribbean marine laboratories. Case History: Global Aspects of Coral Reefs: Health, Hazards and History, RSMAS Colloquium, June 1993.

Smith, S.V. and R.W. Buddemeier. 1992. Global change and coral reef ecosystems. Annu. Rev. Ecol. Syst, 23: 89-118.

Wells, S.M. 1988. Coral Reefs of the World. Vol. 1: Atlantic and Eastern Pacific. UNEP/IUCN. 373p.

Figure 2: <u>Agaricia</u> spp. at Ulagsukin, 1970 (left), 1991 (right); note school of <u>Scarus iserti</u> and <u>Acanthurus</u> sp. (left) and massive overgrowth by the brown alga <u>Lobophora variegata</u> (right).

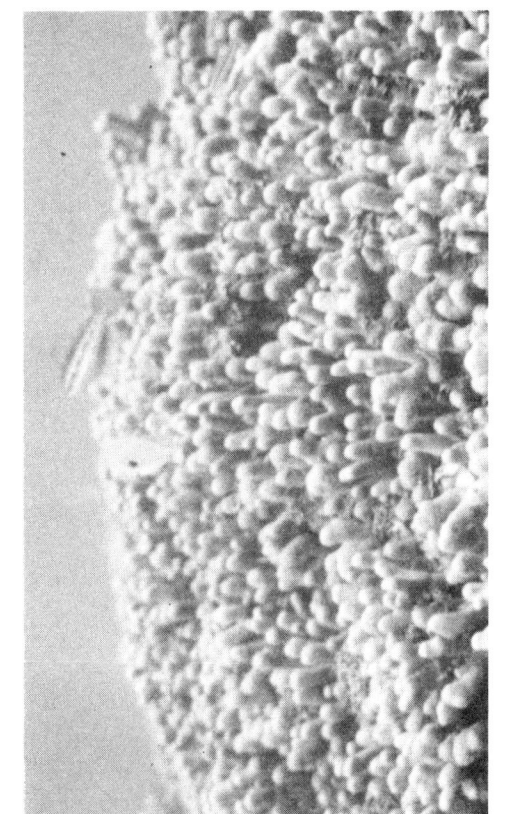

Figure 3: <u>Porites porites</u> mounds at Pico Feo, 1970 (left), 1991 (right); note the green alga <u>Halimeda</u> imbedded in the mound (left) and overgrowth by the brown alga <u>Dictyota</u> (right).

Figure 4: <u>Acropora cervicornis</u> at Ulagsukin, 1970 (left), 1991 (right).

Figure 5: <u>Acropora palmata</u> at Lemon Cays, 1970 (left), 1991 (right); note dead branches in foreground and scattered living colonies in background.

HISTORY OF A FRINGING REEF ON THE WEST COAST OF BARBADOS 1974 - 1992

Terence P. Scoffin

Department of Geology and Geophysics, University of Edinburgh, West Mains Road, Edinburgh,
EH9 3JW, U.K.

ABSTRACT

The northern Bellairs Reef which fringes the west coast of Barbados was surveyed during a $CaCO_3$ budget study in 1974 (Stearn et al, 1977, Scoffin et al, 1980). The region was struck by Hurricane Allen in 1980 and the percentages of substrate types were resurveyed in 1981 by Mah and Stearn (1986) using the same transect lines. After the hurricane the percentage coral cover dropped from 37% to 15% whereas dead coral surfaces increased from 22% to 43% and there was a slight increase in crustose coralline algae from 41% to 42%. The fringing reef corals most damaged were Porites porites and Madracis mirabilis. In 1983 the large population of the urchin Diadema antillarum suffered 94% mortality by an unknown pathogen (Lessios et al, 1984, Hunte et al, 1986). The marked reduction in the grazing fauna had major effects on the fringing reef substrates. A resurvey along the same transect lines in 1992 showed that the cover of crustose coralline algae had dropped from 42% to 25% and dead coral surfaces (with algal turf) had increased from 43% to 60%. The live coral cover had changed little since the 1981 survey; there was no recovery of the Porites porites and Madracis mirabilis populations but the Porites astreoides, Agaricia agaricites and Millepora spp populations showed slight increases. The reported increase in eutrophication may contribute (with the demise of Diadema) to the success of algal cover. The recent seaward extension of sea defences causes seiche waves which further increase inshore turbidity.

INTRODUCTION

During the summer of 1974 a study was undertaken of the calcium carbonate budget of a discrete fringing reef on the west coast of Barbados (Stearn and Scoffin 1978). The object of the study was to compare quantitatively the rate of production of calcium carbonate by the dominant reef-builders (Stearn et al 1977) with the rate of destruction by the major bioeroders (Scoffin et al 1980). The reef chosen was the Northern Bellairs reef (Figure 1) which is about 150m x 150m and isolated from neighbouring reefs on the sides and on the seaward margin by an apron of sand.

The Bellairs fringing reefs have been described and zoned by Lewis (1960) and Stearn et al (1977). The distribution of the reef-builders follows a zonation which roughly parallels the reef front. Consequently for quantitative analysis the reef was subdivided into equal areas by semi-elliptical boundaries each approximately paralleling the reef front. Counts of reef cover were made along six roped transects, taking readings every 10cm for 50cm of each metre of rope. The attributes recorded were: dead coral, crustose coralline algae, living coral, sand and rubble. The living corals present in greater than 1% areal cover of rock surface were: Porites porites, Porites astreoides, Agaricia agaricites, Montastrea annularis, Siderastrea siderea, Millepora spp. Madracis mirabilis and Favia fragum. The counts (total 2175) of substrate type were totalled for each elliptical increment. To take account of the variation in biota with depth and distance from shore the normalised density for each substrate type was calculated for each ellipse and then the trapezoidal integration (Morton 1964) of the ellipses gave the percentage areal cover on the whole reef for each substrate type. The actual areal cover of the various corals and encrusting algae was determined taking into account the planimetric area of the reef and its relief. The rates of growth of the reef builders were determined using stain experiments, planted substrates and skeletal density banding as revealed by x-radiography. The rate of destruction of the reef by bioeroders during fairweather conditions was determined by a variety of techniques (Scoffin et al 1980).

The accessibility of this reef has allowed subsequent surveys to be carried out. Shortly after Hurricane Allen in 1980 Mah and Stearn (1981) made a survey of the percentage cover of the various substrate types along the transect lines used earlier. The damage from the impact of the hurricane was assessed by comparison of the two percentage coral cover surveys coupled with a quantitative analysis of the rubble associated with the reef (Mah & Stearn 1981).

Bellairs reef was one of the sites used in the comparative study of reefs suffering different levels of eutrophication (Tomascik and Sander, 1985, 1987a,b). In their study, the effects of eutrophication on growth rate of Montastrea annularis, structure of scleractinian coral communities and reproduction of Porites porites were investigated. The authors also recorded (Tomascik and Sander, 1985) the physicochemical and biological conditions of the sea water from this area during the period 1981 to 1982. Wittenberg and Hunte (1992) reported the effects of eutrophication and sedimentation on the abundance, mortality and community structure of juvenile corals on fringing reefs in this area of the west coast of Barbados.

During a visit in 1992 while studying the movement of sand-sized sediment around and within the framework of the reef (Scoffin & Tudhope in press) it was again possible to survey the coral cover on the Northern Bellairs fringing reef using the original line transects.

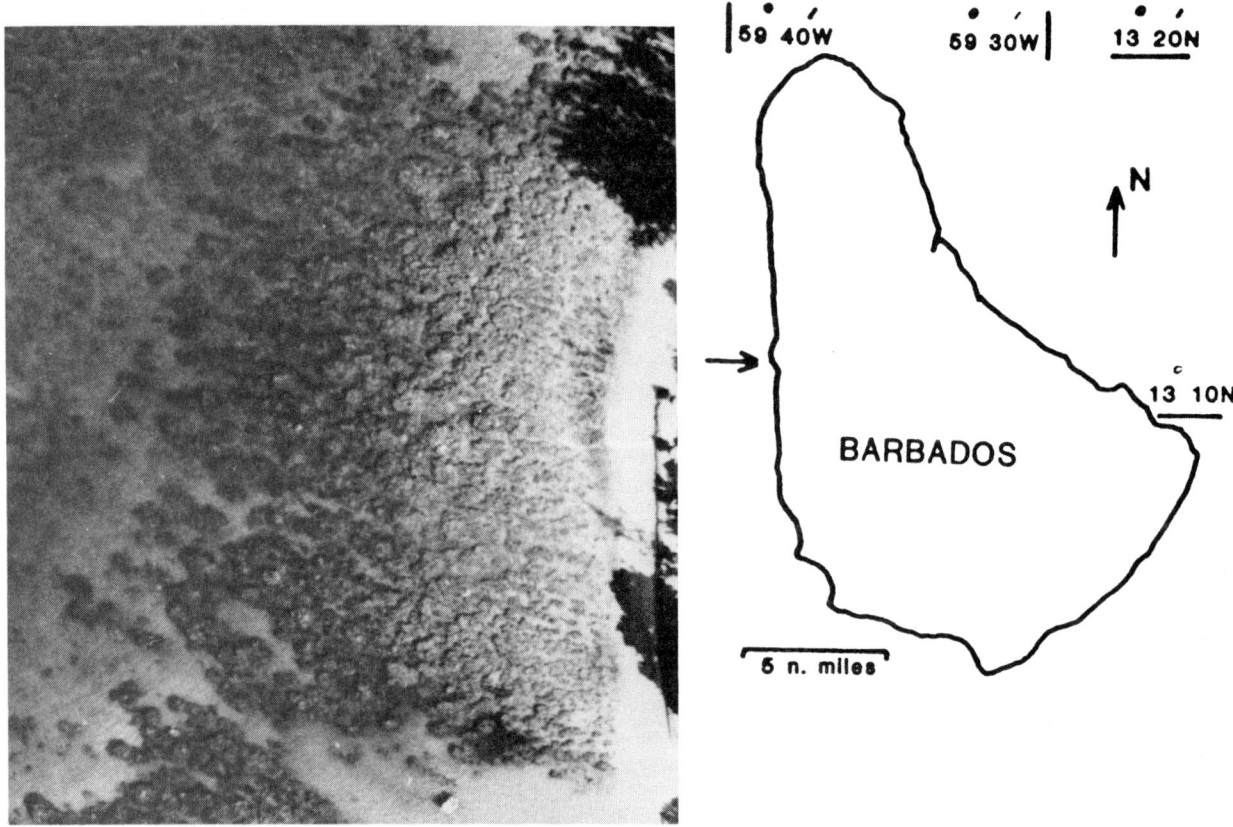

Figure 1 Northern Bellairs reef on the west coast of Barbados

RESULTS

The percentage cover of corals and crustose coralline algae on the rock substrates of the Northern Bellairs Reef during the three periods 1974, 1981 and 1992 is given in Table 1.

Table 1. Percentage cover of different substrate types on reef ellipses (1 inshore, 6 offshore) and whole reef, in 1974, 1981 and 1992 surveys.

	ELLIPSE 1			ELLIPSE 2			ELLIPSE 3			ELLIPSE 4			ELLIPSE 5			ELLIPSE 6			TOTAL REEF		
	'74	'81	'92	'74	'81	'92	'74	'81	'92	'74	'81	'92	'74	'81	'92	'74	'81	'92	'74	'81	'92
Dead coral	47	41	70	18	36	77	16	35	69	18	45	50	14	54	55	16	47	41	22	43	60
Crustose coralline algae	50	54	30	60	49	17	50	50	21	32	47	31	28	28	20	26	26	28	41	42	25
Porites porites	-	-	-	5	1	-	9	tr	tr	17	-	1	21	1	1	17	1	2	12	1	1
Porites astreoides	3	5	-	8	4	4	8	2	5	11	2	6	10	4	6	9	5	7	8	4	4
Agaricia agaricites	-	-	-	2	6	1	6	7	3	9	5	8	8	7	8	10	8	14	6	5	6
Montastrea annularis	-	-	-	1	1	-	5	5	tr	6	-	1	5	4	3	12	6	2	5	3	1
Siderastrea siderea	-	-	-	tr	tr	-	2	tr	-	2	-	1	5	2	6	7	3	2	3	1	1
Millepora spp	-	-	-	2	3	1	3	1	1	2	1	3	4	3	3	2	3	4	2	2	2
Madracis mirabilis	-	-	-	tr	-	-	1	-	-	2	-	-	3	1	tr	1	-	-	1	-	-
Favia fragum	-	-	-	1	tr	tr	tr	-	tr	tr	-	-	1	-	tr	-	-	-	tr	-	-

The relative coral cover expressed as a percentage is given in Table 2.

Table 2. Relative coral cover percentage

CORAL	1974	1981	1992
Porites porites	32	6	7
Porites astreoides	22	25	27
Agaricia agaricites	16	31	40
Montastrea annularis	14	19	6
Siderastrea siderea	8	6	7
Millepora spp	5	13	13
Madracis mirabilis	3	-	-

DISCUSSION

Since the original survey in 1974 there have been both short-lived and prolonged perturbations to this reef at north Bellairs. The dramatic disturbances were the physical damage caused by Hurricane Allen in August 1980 and the mass mortality of Diadema antillarum in summer 1983. The chronic stresses have been the increase in eutrophication as a consequence of nutrient enrichment, sedimentation and toxicity associated with the dumping of domestic and industrial wastes over the last 20 years and an increase in fresh water run off due to man-made modifications of natural drainage streams into major storm drains which empty directly onto most of the fringing reefs. An increase in inshore turbidity at the Bellairs reef has resulted from the reflection of waves from recently extended sea defences which creates nearshore seiche waves during high tide.

Hurricane Allen

Hurricane Allen, though not passing directly over Barbados produced large waves that affected west coast reefs in 1980. Winds were estimated to be 100 knots. The coral population was dramatically reduced from 37% to 15%. Those branching corals that grew on the tops of spurs in shallow water were the most severely affected, Porites porites coverage was reduced by 96%. This breakage lowered the level of the spur tops creating a substrate of freshly truncated branching coral skeletons and added large quantities of coral stick rubble to the reef grooves. Mah and Stearn (1981) noted that the composition of the groove rubble was 40 wt% Porites porites, 32 wt% Acropora cervicornis and 13 wt% Madracis mirabilis. The bulk of the rubble made of A. cervicornis and M. mirabilis were swept up on to the fringing reef from their former positions of growth in the reef-front zone of 7 to 20m depth. The percentage loss of the other important corals was as follows Porites astreoides 71%, Agaricia agaricites 25%, Montastrea annularis 54%, Siderastrea siderea 75% (Mah and Stearn, 1981). The coral diversity (recorded as Shannon-Weaver and Simpson indexes) showed the sharpest decline in the zone of the fringing reef where the storm waves broke (Mah & Stearn 1981). Prior to Hurricane Allen the Bellairs reef was of relatively high diversity between the pioneer stage and the stage of dominance by a late successional species (Porites porites). The hurricane damage reset the successional process back to a pioneer stage of low coral diversity. Agaricia agaricites became the dominant coral species on the reef changing from formerly making up 16% of living coral cover to occupying 31% of the living coral cover. Whereas Porites porites formerly the dominant coral dropped from 32% of the coral cover to 6% of the coral cover.

Mass Mortality Of Diadema Antillarum

As part of the reef $CaCO_3$ budget survey of 1974 - 1975 the number of bioeroding organisms were determined. The spiny black sea urchin Diadema antillarum was especially abundant on the west coast reefs and the population on north Bellairs reef had an average density of 23 individuals per square metre of rocky reef substrate (Scoffin et al, 1980). It has been suggested (Sammarco, 1980, 1982) that corals settle more readily when grazing by urchins is rapid enough to prevent filamentous non-coralline algae from monopolizing available substrate space. A massive mortality of Diadema antillarum occurred in the Caribbean starting in Panama in January 1983 and spreading throughout the Caribbean by January 1984 (Lessios et al 1984). The major impact in Barbados was in September 1983 after which the Diadema population was reduced by 94% (Hunte et al, 1986). The survey of Bellairs in 1992 showed a marked increase in the area of dead coral substrate at the expense of mainly the crustose coralline algae (Table 1). This dead coral surface had dense algal turf which may well be responsible for the slow recruitment of corals on the fresh substrates exposed during the hurricane two years earlier, as well as this displacement of the calcareous red algae.

When we compare the substrate cover figures for 1981 and 1992 (Table 1) all the coral abundances are relatively unchanged except for Montastrea annularis which shows a considerable reduction. The reduction in this coral is initially surprising as it is the massive Montastrea colonies that are so commonly seen to be infested by Diadema urchins which hollow out the dish-shaped profiles to the large colonies by their collective grazing activities. And so it might have been anticipated that a reduction in Diadema would result in recovery of these grazed surfaces and an increase in Montastrea cover on the reef. This is not the case. 1992 is nine years after the mass mortality event and the Diadema population is now increasing and many still actively graze Montastrea heads, for these colonies commonly have lobate surfaces in which discrete 'islands' of living polyps develop separated by channels of dead skeleton which are suitable sites for initial grazing attack. Siderastrea siderea colonies on the other hand, rarely suffer surface grazing by Diadema on account of their extensive cover of living polyps. The remaining coral species whose cover is relatively unchanged (i.e. P. porites, P. astreoides, A. agaricites, Millepora spp) are essentially new recruits after the hurricane, as is confirmed by their colony size and their substrate (commonly truncated P. porites branches). The reduction in Diadema may have affected the mortality rate of the juvenile corals of these species (Wittenberg and Hunte 1992) and contributed to the cause for no marked increase in abundance over the twelve years after the hurricane. Hughes (1985) found that the mortality of juvenile corals rose sharply following an algal bloom caused by this same event of dramatic reduction of Diadema in Jamaica.

Eutrophication

The effects of the increase in eutrophication along the west coast of Barbados has been described by Tomascik and Sander (1985, 1987a,b) and Wittenberg and Hunte (1992). The main consequence of this eutrophication are reported by the above authors to be:

1) Increase in production at other trophic levels affects the coral community directly through competition for space or indirectly through increased bioturbation or sediment trapping.

2) An increase in eutrophication results in a decrease in the population of Diadema which may contribute to the elevated benthic algae biomass.

3) Increase in phytoplankton biomass affects the coral community indirectly through the reduction of light intensity and/or alteration of spectral quality thus affecting zooxanthellae photosynthesis essential for normal coral function.

4) High turbidity and sedimentation rates have been implicated in severely affecting coral diversity cover, abundance and health. Elevated suspended particulate matter concentrations may be responsible for reduced growth rates of some corals.

5) There is a lower recruitment of juveniles and a higher juvenile mortality with increase in eutrophication and this results in community structure changes from one dominated by low recruitment, low natural mortality corals (such as Montastrea annularis, Siderastrea siderea) to one dominated by high recruitment, high natural mortality corals (such as P. astreoides, A. agaricites).

All these trends are supported by the figures of coral cover presented here.

Suspended Sediment

The inshore back-reef zone of Bellairs reef in 1974 was very rich in crustose coralline algae whose skeletogenesis contributed significant $CaCO_3$ to the reef. The strengthening of the sea defences in front of the sea-front property next to the reef has resulted in a seaward extension of the gabion (large limestone boulders) by approximately 2m over the last 15 years. The beach sand has migrated from this shore and now during high tide waves are reflected from the gabion back to sea to form standing waves (seiche wave) where they meet the next advancing wave 10 to 30m offshore. The reinforcement of the wave increases wave height and this causes an increase in the amount and size of suspended sediment particules in this nearshore zone. The crustose coralline algae may have suffered from this sediment loading as well as the other effects that resulted in their greater competition from filamentous algal turf.

CONCLUSIONS

Three surveys of substrate cover on the Bellairs fringing reef of West Barbados were made in 1974, 1981 and 1992 along the same transect lines. The cover of the substrates changed most dramatically after Hurricane Allen struck the reef in 1980. Coral cover dropped from 37% to 15%, with the branching corals living on spur tops (Porites porites and Madracis mirabilis) most severely affected. Dead coral surfaces increased from 22% to 43% during this physical erosion. The dramatic reduction (94%) in the population of the urchin Diadema antillarum in summer 1983 was followed by an increase in filamentous algae and a reduction in crustose coralline algae cover. The increase in non-calcareous benthic algae biomass has also been due to eutrophication and enhanced suspended sediment loading. The relatively unchanged coral population between 1981 and 1992 is thought to be due essentially to the reduction in both recruitment of juvenile corals and reduction in coral growth rate under conditions of increasing eutrophication.

ACKNOWLEDGEMENTS

I am grateful to the director and staff of Bellairs Research Institute for their support and facilities. Part of this work was financed by NERC grant no GR9/325.

LITERATURE CITED

Hughes, T.P. 1985. Life histories and population dymanics of early successional corals. Proc. 5th Int. Coral Reef Symp. Tahiti. 4: 101 - 106.
Hunte, W., I Côté and T. Tomascik. 1986. On the dynamics of the mass mortality of Diadema antillarum in Barbados. Coral Reefs 4 (3): 135 - 139.
Lessios, H.A., D.R. Robertson and J.D. Cubit. 1984. Spread of Diadema mass mortality through the Caribbean. Science. 226: 335 - 337.
Lewis, J.B. 1960. The coral reefs and coral communities of Barbados, West Indies. Can. J. Zool. 38: 1133 - 1145.
Mah, A.J. and C.W. Stearn. 1986. The effect of Hurricane Allen on the Bellairs fringing reef, Barbados. Coral Reefs 4 (3): 169 - 176.
Morton, B.R. 1964. Numerical approximation. Routledge and Kegan Paul Ltd. London. 101pp.
Sammarco, P.W. 1980. Diadema and its relationship to coral spat mortality: grazing, competition and biological disturbance. J. Exp. Mar. Biol. Ecol. 45: 245 - 272.
Sammarco, P.W. 1982. Effects of grazing by Diadema antillarum Phillipi on algal diversity and community structure. J. Exp. Mar. Biol. Ecol. 65: 83 - 105.
Scoffin, T.P., C.W. Stearn, D. Boucher, P. Frydl, C.M. Hawkins, I.G. Hunter and J.K. MacGeachy. 1980. Calcium carbonate budget of a fringing reef on the west coast of Barbados. Part II, Erosion, sediments and internal structure. Bull. Mar. Sci. 30 (2): 475-508.

Scoffin, T.P. and A.W. Tudhope. In Press. The nature of the sedimentary record within Quaternary reefs of Barbados, St Vincent and the Grenadines. Proc. 7th Int. Coral Reef Symp Guam.

Stearn, C.W. and T.P. Scoffin. 1978. Carbonate budget of a fringing reef, Barbados. Proc 3rd Int. Coral Reef Symp. Miami 2: 471 - 476.

Stearn, C.W., T.P. Scoffin and W. Martindale. 1977. Calcium carbonate budget of a fringing reef on the west coast of Barbados. Part I, Zonation and productivity. Bull. Mar. Sci. 27 (3) 479 - 510.

Tomascik, T. and F. Sander. 1985. Effects of eutrophication on reef-building corals. I Growth rate of the reef-building coral Montastrea annularis. Mar. Biol. 87: 143 - 155.

Tomascik, T. and F. Sander. 1987. Effects of eutrophication on reef-building corals. II Structure of scleractinian coral communities on fringing reefs, Barbados, West Indies. Mar. Biol. 94: 53 - 75.

Tomascik, T. and F. Sander. 1987. Effects of eutrophication on reef-building corals. III Reproduction of the reef-building coral Porites porites. Mar. Biol. 94: 77-94.

Wittenberg, M. and W. Hunte. 1992. Effects of eutrhopication and sedimentation on juvenile corals. I. Abundance, mortality and community structure. Mar. Biol. 112: 131 - 138.

REEFS OF JAVA AND SOUTH CHINA SEAS

	PAGES
Natural and Anthropogenic Disturbances on Intertidal Reefs of S.E. Phuket, Thailand 1979-1992 *Barbara E. Brown, Martin D. Le Tissier, Richard P. Dunne, and Terence P. Scoffin*	279 - 285
Health of Fringing Reefs of Asia Through a Decade of Change A Case History from Phuket Island, Thailand *Hansa Chansang and Niphon Phongsuwan*	286 - 292
On the Severe Changes in the Ecology and Sedimentation of Luweitou Fringing Coral Reefs Hainan Island, China *Wang Guozhong, Lu Bingquan, and Quan Songqing*	293 - 297
Sedimentation Damage to Reef Corals *Gregor Hodgson*	298 - 303
Case Histories: A Historical Perspective of the Natural and Anthropogenic Impacts in the Indonesian Archipelago with a focus on the Kepulauan Seribu, Java Sea *Tomas Tomascik, Suharsono, and Anmarie J. Mah*	304 - 310
Status of Coral Reefs in Southeast Asia: Threats and Responses *C.R. Wilkinson, L.M. Chou, E. Gomez, A.R. Ridzwan, S. Soekarno, and S. Sudara*	311 - 317

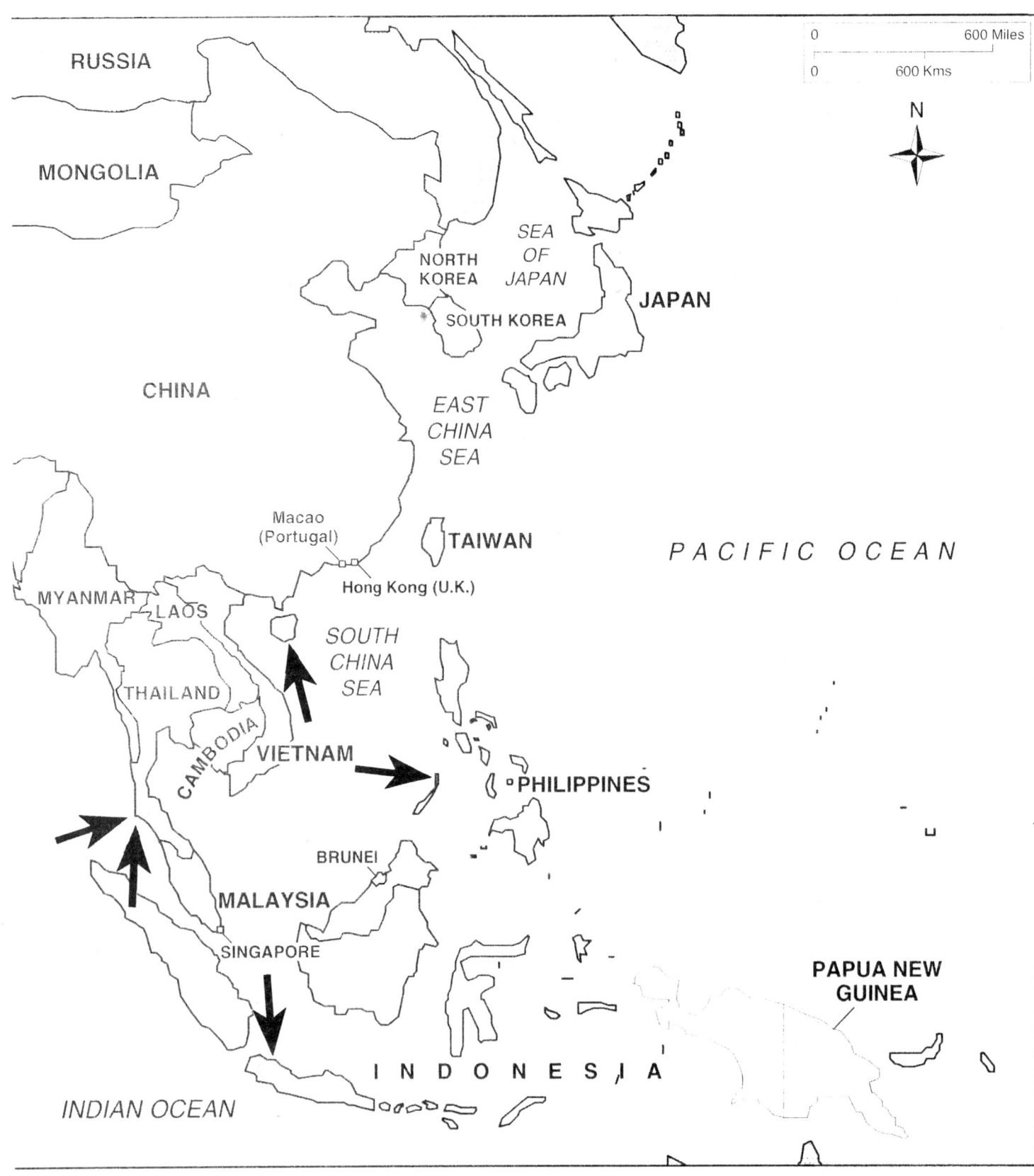

NATURAL AND ANTHROPOGENIC DISTURBANCES ON INTERTIDAL REEFS OF S.E PHUKET, THAILAND 1979-1992.

Barbara E. Brown[1], Martin D. Le Tissier[1], Richard P. Dunne[1] and Terence P Scoffin[2].

[1] Department of Marine Sciences and Coastal Management, University of Newcastle upon Tyne, Newcastle upon Tyne NE1 7RU, U.K. [2] Department of Geology and Geophysics, University of Edinburgh, Edinburgh EH9 3JW, U.K.

ABSTRACT

A series of natural and man-made disturbances have affected the intertidal coral reefs of S.E. Phuket over the period 1979-1992. Man-made influences include the discharge of tin-ore washing liquors on to the reef and the effects of dredging for a deepwater port facility. Natural factors include widespread coral bleaching (possibly as a result of increased seawater temperatures) and the effects of sub-aerial exposure and localised solar bleaching.

Responses of the reefs to dredging in 1987 involved localised reductions in coral cover and species diversity at one site with subsequent rapid recovery 12 months later. Responses to natural factors, apparent since 1990, were more extensive, resulting in reduced cover but generally little alteration in species diversity at all sites monitored. A gradual increase in mean sea level ($\approx$ 10cm) over the years 1979 to 1991 has likely had an impact on both man-made and recent natural influences, possibly accelerating recovery from man-made disturbances but also subsequently rendering the corals more susceptible to solar and sub-aerial influences as they grow up to a higher sea level.

INTRODUCTION

The intertidal reef flats of Ko Phuket were first described by Ditlev (1978). Since that time they have been subject to considerable natural and anthropogenic disturbance. Man-made influences on the reef include reef gleaning, localised effluent discharge from a tin-ore dressing plant (Brown and Holley 1982), and dredging for a deep-water port (Brown et al 1990). Natural disturbances at the site have included increased seawater temperatures (1-2°C above ambient) during the period December-July 1991 which resulted in extensive bleaching of both intertidal and sub-tidal corals and the effects of solar irradiance which have produced localised bleaching in coral colonies on an annual basis since 1990.

While there have been a large number of case-histories documented in recent years which describe the effects of either man-made or natural disturbance on coral reefs (see Grigg and Dollar 1990 for review) few have described both natural and man-made influences at the same location and the relative effects of these factors on the overall reef community structure. In this case-history we review the impacts of acute pulses of disturbance (both natural and man-made) and compare and contrast these with the effects of chronic man-made and natural influences.

METHODS

Site Description

Intertidal reef flats are well developed around the south-east peninsula of Phuket Island, Thailand and have been described in detail in previous studies (Brown et al 1990). The reef flats are wide (being up to 200m in lateral extent) terminating at their seaward edge in a shallow reef slope down to approximately 4-5m.

Results presented in this case-history relate to two locations; a reef below a tin smelting operation adjacent to a deep-water port (site A), and a reef approximately 1km away which has been used as a control area (site B) - Figure 1.

Physical and chemical parameters.-

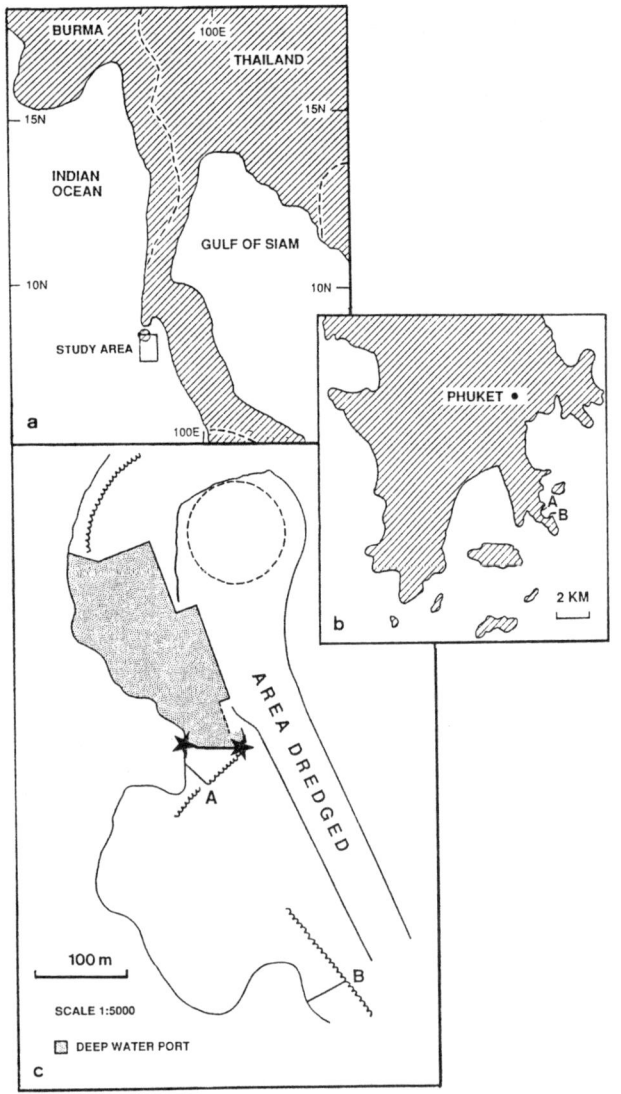

Figure 1. Location of study sites at Ko Phuket, Thailand. (a) Position of the study area on the west coast of Thailand, (b) location of Sites A and B on Phuket Island, and (c) location of the sites with respect to the dredged channel deep-water port and position of the bund (☆——☆)

a) Tidal regime: The tidal form experienced at Phuket is semi-diurnal having a range of 0.6m (neap tides) to 3.1m (spring tides), and with little variation in height between successive high and low waters. Because of this pattern, the typical 14 day cyclical increase and decrease in range, coupled with the tidal period, results in the low water of the spring tides consistently falling either early in the morning or late in the afternoon. It is only on these spring tides that the intertidal coral reefs at Phuket are aerially exposed.

There is considerable seasonal variation in mean sea level as a result of the monsoon influence, data being available from 1940 from a Global Ocean Sea Surface tide gauge 1.5km from site A. The mean sea level is significantly depressed during the north east monsoon months of December - April, with a maximum reduction of up to 20cm during January - March. In addition there is considerable inter-annual variation in mean sea level with maximum differences of 30cm being recorded between some years.

b) Seawater temperature:

Sea surface temperature has been measured at Phuket Marine Biological Centre since 1981 but calibrated temperature measurements have only been recorded since 1991. Data collected in 1992 shows that the seawater temperature ranged from 27-30.5°C, the maximum temperature being reached at the end of the hot north east monsoon in May. In 1991 seawater temperatures ranged from 28°C to almost 32°C over the period January to May when values were 1-2°C above those recorded in 1992. Surface seawater temperature anomalies (from data produced for the Global Ocean Surface Temperature Atlas) showed anomalies of +0.8°C in offshore waters over the period January-May 1991.

c) Heavy metal levels:
Higher levels of heavy metals are found at site A than at other locations in the area as a result of ore washing discharges associated with the tin smelter; elevated levels of copper, zinc and iron have been recorded in sediments, coral and mollusc tissues (Howard and Brown 1987; Brown and Kumar 1990).

Biological parameters.- The intertidal reef flats at locations A and B have a moderately high coral cover, ranging, on average, from between 10-20% live cover on inner reef flats to between 40-65% on outer reef flats. The reefs have a high diversity of corals, being dominated by faviids and massive *Porites* assemblages. Massive *Porites* species dominate the reef flats at all locations, particularly on inner and mid-reef flat positions where *Porites* cover may acount for 60-80% total coral cover.

Summary of environmental history of reefs.- A tin-smelter commenced production at site A in 1964; since 1988 its production capacity was reduced following a fall in the world price of tin. The main effect of the tin smelter has been the discharge of effluent from an ore washing plant on to the reef. At low tides inner reef flat corals find themselves submerged in pools of effluent which is enriched in heavy metals, particularly iron, zinc, copper and lead.

In 1986-87 a deep-water channel was dredged adjacent to site A during construction of a port. Over a ten month period from October 1986 to July 1987 1.3 million m^3 of muddy terrigenous sediment was removed from the channel and deposited as infill behind a bund separating site A from the port area.

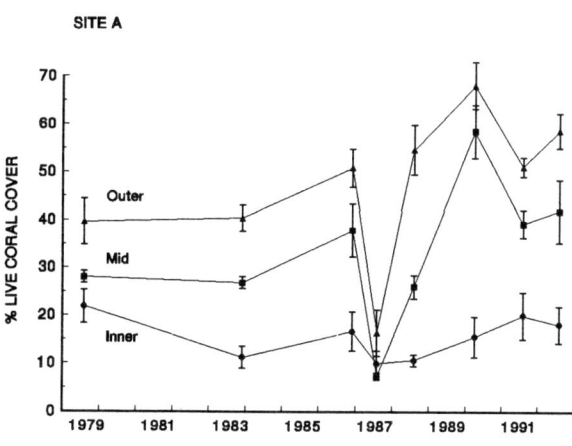

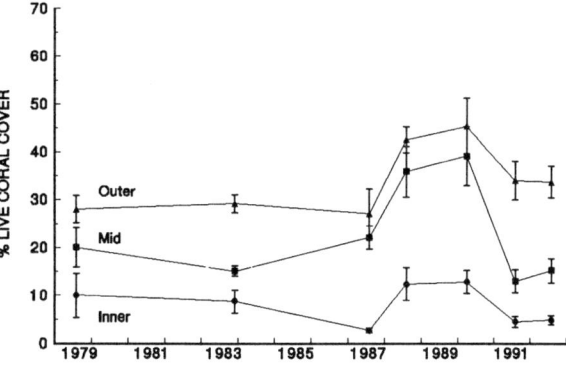

Figure 2. Fluctuations in average percentage live coral cover over time for inner, mid and outer reef transects at sites A and B (standard error of mean shown for each point).

In March 1990 pronounced bleaching was recorded on all intertidal reef flats around the peninsula, the effects being particularly prominent in faviid corals occupying an elevated position on the reef flat. The bleaching was extremely localised and restricted to specific areas of colonies, being correlated with sun altitude and azimuth. Incidence of the bleaching was extremely seasonal occuring maximally in March-May when intertidal corals are subject to long periods of sub aerial exposure and high levels of solar irradiance.

In July 1991 extensive bleaching was recorded on both intertidal and subtidal reefs in the Andaman Sea, an effect which is believed to be principally due to seawater warming over the period January - May.

Ecological Monitoring

Plotless line transects.- Full details of transecting methods are given in Brown et al (1990). Since 1988 fourteen 10m long plotless line transects have been monitored at site A and twelve 10m long transects at site B; transects at sites A and B have been surveyed in 1979, 1983, 1986 (site A only), 1987, 1988, 1990, 1991 and 1992. Parameters measured along transect lines included percentage coral cover of each species and total number of colonies of each species which in turn yielded data on species diversity.

Photography of permanently marked belt transects.- In addition to surveyed transects eight permanent belt transects (each measuring 10x1m) have been period; three since 1983 and the remainder since 1986. To confirm trends observed from the plotless line transects, three ten metre long lines were selected to cover exactly the same position on each photograph set, and coral cover of *Porites* spp. under each line was measured and adjusted for variation in the scale of the photographs.

Using these photographic transects from July 1991 and March 1992 coral colonies which appeared either totally bleached or partially bleached in 1991 were subsequently monitored for their status (recovery or mortality) in 1992. Only corals which were white, partially white or showed conspicuous paling were scored as bleached, with histological tissue samples confirming loss of zooxanthellae.

RESULTS

Plotless line transects

Fluctuations in live coral cover at inner, mid and outer reef transects at sites A and B are shown in Figure 2. The dredging event had a pronounced effect upon coral cover at site A during 1987. Statistical comparison of overall coral cover between years, using the Wilcoxon Matched Pair-Sign Ranked Test, revealed significant differences ($p<0.01$) in live coral cover at site A between 1987 and all other years. Significant differences ($p<0.05$) in coral cover were also evident between 1990 and all other years apart from 1986 and 1992. At site B in 1990 coral cover values differed significantly ($p<0.01$) from coverage results recorded in all other years.

A marked decline in coral cover during the dredging event in 1987 only occurred at site A, with a rapid recovery, in terms of coral cover, taking place in 1988. Fluctuations in coral cover in subsequent years were particularly apparent on mid- and outer reef transects with mid-reef flat transects showing a pronounced decline in coral cover since 1990 when coral cover was relatively high at both sites A and B.

No significant differences ($p>0.05$) in coral species diversity (expressed as H^1c) were noted between years at Site B while significant differences ($p<0.02$) in species diversity were apparent between 1987 and all other years, apart from 1990, at site A.

Photographic Analyses

Confirmation of changes in coral cover at site A were obtained from measurement of *Porites* cover on permanent phototransects. All phototransects showed similar trends with declines in cover during the dredging period 1986-87, a rapid recovery in 1988, followed by a decline in *Porites* cover in 1990-1991 and then some recovery in 1992 (Figure 3).

Analysis of colonies which bleached in 1991 (Table 1) shows that more colonies per transect were affected on outer reef transects (6-8) than on the mid-reef flat transects (1-5). Six months after the bleaching event in February 1992, 9% of bleached colonies had shown 100% mortality, 74% had shown partial mortality and 17% had fully recovered their pigmentation.

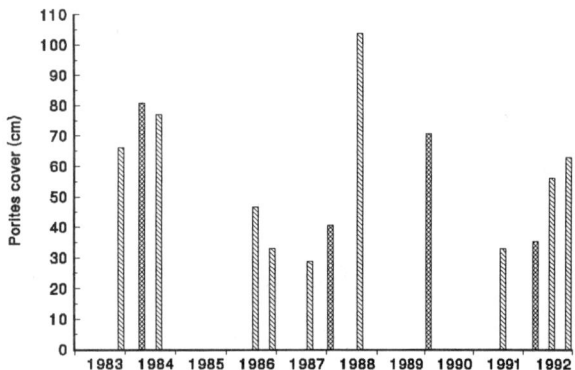

Figure 3. Fluctuations in live *Porites* cover (cm) on chosen line transects on a permanently marked belt transect from the mid reef flat of site A which was photographed regularly over the period 1983-1992.

	Transect N°	Coral Species	1991		1992		
			N° of bleached colonies	Type of bleaching	N° of colonies showing		
					100% mortality	Partial mortality	Recovery
INCREASING WATER DEPTH ⇓	1.	*G. aspera*	5 (56)	P	1	3	1
	2.	*G. aspera*	5 (63)	P	0	3	2
		P. daedalea	5 (71)	P	0	5	0
	3.	*G. aspera*	7 (78)	P	1	2	4
	4.	*G. aspera*	1 (50)	P	0	0	1
		P. daedalea	3 (100)	O	1	1	1
		Porites spp	2 (67)	O	0	2	1
	5.	*G. aspera*	7 (78)	P	1	4	2
		G. retiformis	3 (50)	P	0	3	0
		P. daedalea	1 (20)	P	0	1	0
		F. abdita	2 (50)	O	0	0	1
	6.	*G. aspera*	2 (67)	P	0	1	1
		G. retiformis	3 (60)	P	0	3	0
		P. daedalea	28 (82)	O	1	23	4
		F. abdita	5 (50)	O	2	3	0
	7.	*P. daedalea*	36 (97)	O	0	31	5
		Porites spp	4 (67)	O	1	3	0
		F. abdita	1 (25)	O	0	0	1
	8.	*P. daedalea*	32 (100)	O	2	27	3
		Po. damicornis	3 (75)	O	1	1	1
		F. abdita	8 (50)	O	2	6	0
		Fungia sp	2 (100)	O	2	0	0
	Overall number of colonies (% in brackets)				15 (9)	122 (74)	28 (17)

Table 1. Showing coral species affected by bleaching in 1991 (G = *Goniastrea* P = *Platygyra* F = *Favites* Po = *Pocillopora*) on eight photo-belt transects; number of bleached colonies of each species (numbers in brackets indicate % of total number of colonies of that species) per transect; the type of bleaching shown either P = partial or O = overall and the number of these colonies which showed 100% mortality, partial mortality or recovery in 1992.

DISCUSSION

It has already been shown that the localised effect of metalliferrous discharges had little apparent effect at site A on community parameters such as coral cover and coral diversity (Brown and Holley 1982) although metal discharges compounded with other stresses (sedimentation from dredging) may cause significant increases in metal availability (Brown and Kumar 1990) and subsequent incorporation into into coral tissues (Howard and Brown 1987) and skeleton (Brown et al 1991), where the ultimate effects on physiology are unknown.

The dredging event in 1987 caused significant reductions in coral cover and species diversity at site A which was ascribed to partial mortality of massive *Porites* spp. and faviids (Brown et al 1990). Rapid regeneration of all species followed in 1988 but in particular, *Porites* spp. showed a spectacular recovery, resulting in a reduced species diversity at site A in 1990 when cover by this genus averaged 74% of the total coral cover of all transects, compared with 40-55% in previous years.

We suspect that the decline in coral cover at both sites, after 1990 is most likely associated with the effects of solar bleaching which was conspicuous in that year (Brown et al - in prep) and which caused considerable partial mortality in all massive coral species. Preliminary analysis of plots of mean sea level at this site over the last 50y indicate cyclical changes in mean sea level, possibly mirroring the 18.6 nodal tidal cycle. For the duration of available coral cover records, mean sea level has risen by approximately 10cm, rising most markedly up to 1986, with little further increase beyond that time.

We believe that the extensive solar bleaching witnessed in 1990 was the result of active growth of intertidal reef corals over preceding years to a critical height which rendered them vulnerable to sub aerial exposure and consequently solar irradiance effects. The pronounced decline of coral cover on the mid reef flat transects at both sites A and B where reef basement is approximately 10-20cm above inner and outer reef transects suggests that the mortality is related to sea level effects. Indeed it is possible that rapid recovery of corals following the dredging event may have been linked to the temporary improved conditions for growth effected by higher mean sea levels. Sea water warming in 1991 contributed further to coral mortality together with continued solar bleaching in 1991 and 1992; the latter occuring with lower incidence in recent years.

CONCLUSIONS

1. The effects of heavy metal rich effluent discharges appear to have had little impact on community structure of intertidal reef flats at Ko Phuket, Thailand.

2. Effects of dredging caused localised declines in coral cover and diversity but coral cover and species diversity rapidly regained pre-dredging values one year later.

3. After a period of high coral cover on the reefs in 1988-1990 live cover declined. This decline is attributed to the combined effects of sub-aerial exposure and bleaching due to seawater warming in 1991.

4. This case-history indicates the potential synergistic effects of both man-made (dredging interacting with heavy metals) and natural (solar bleaching interacting with seawater warming bleaching) disturbances on intertidal reef flats. It may be speculated that some natural environmental factors, such as increase in mean sea level, may act positively for intertidal and shallow water coral communities, particularly if the timing of events allows rapid growth and recovery from a man-made disturbance.

ACKNOWLEDGEMENTS

We thank the Director and Staff at the Phuket Marine Biological Centre, in particular Dr. Hansa Chansang and Mr. Niphon Phongsuang, for their long term support. This work is currently supported by a grant from the Overseas Development Administration's Natural Resources and Environment Department.

LITERATURE CITED

Brown, B.E., M.C.Holley. 1982. Metal levels associated with tin dredging and smelting and their effect upon intertidal reef flats at Ko Phuket, Thailand. Coral Reefs 1: 131-137.

Brown, B.E., A.J. Kumar. 1990. Temporal and spatial variations in iron concentrations of tropical bivalves during a dredging event. Mar. Pollut. Bull. 21: 118-123.

Brown, B.E., M.D.A. Le Tissier, T.P. Scoffin, and A.W. Tudhope. 1990. Evaluation of the environmental impact of dredging on intertidal corals reefs at Ko Phuket,Thailand, using ecological and physiological parameters. Mar. Ecol. Prog. Ser. 65: 273-281.

Brown, B.E., A.W. Tudhope, M.D.A. Le Tissier, and T.P. Scoffin. 1991. A novel mechanism for iron incorporation into coral skeletons. Coral Reefs 10: 211-215.

Ditlev, H. 1978. Zonation of corals (Scleractinia: Coelenterata) on intertidal reef flats at Ko Phuket, Eastern Indian Ocean. Mar. Biol. 47: 29-39.

Grigg, R.W., S.J. Dollar. 1990. Natural and anthropogenic disturbance on coral reefs. In Z. Dubinsky, ed. Ecosystems of the World 25: 439-452.

Howard, L.S., B.E. Brown. 1987. Metals in *Pocillopora damicornis* exposed to a tin smelter effluent. Mar. Pollut. Bull. 18: 451-454.

HEALTH OF FRINGING REEFS OF ASIA THROUGH A DECADE OF CHANGE A CASE HISTORY FROM PHUKET ISLAND, THAILAND

Hansa Chansang and Niphon Phongsuwan

Phuket Marine Biological Center
P.O.Box 60, Phuket 83000, Thailand

ABSTRACT

This paper presents the data on changes of live coral covers on 7 transects of reefs of Phuket Island, The Andaman Sea from 1980 to 1992. Description of reefs of the islands was briefly described. Transect studies were conducted by 2 methods, i.e. photographic quadrat transect method during 1980- 1986 and line transect method during 1988 to 1992. Changes in live coral cover was used as the indicator of reef health. The results show trend in decreasing of live coral cover of 5 transects, whereas the coral cover increased at one site and remained more or less the same at the other. The transect which increased in coral cover was the site that was orginally damaged by sedimentation from tin dredging in early 1980s. The recovery occured during southwest monsoon season when sediment was naturally removed. The other site which was also affected by tin dredging but the natural removal of sediment was more limited and subsequently was predated by *Acanthaster planci*. The low coral cover remained the same. Of the 5 sites which showed the decline in coral cover, the causes of decline ranging from natural causes i.e. *Acanthaster* predation, strom damage, coral bleaching and man made effects, especially boat anchoring, damage from tourists, coral collection, fishing in reef areas and possibly eutrophication.

It is concluded that with the information available it is not possible to isolate damage by natural causes from man made damage except effect of sedimentation and damages from natural causes seem to be major factors in causing decline in coral cover on Phuket Island.

INTRODUCTION

Fringing reefs of Phuket Island have been studied since 1980 due to the conflict of coastal tin drerdging and environmental conservation for tourism (Chansang, 1988). Data base on fringing reefs along the west and south coasts were established and reefs were monitored at various interval (Chansang, et al. 1985; Phongsuwan and Chansang, 1992). Since 1980, pattern of coastal land uses have been dramatically changed from tin dredging, mining, and agriculture into expansion of communities for tourism development and increasing uses of coastal waters for recreation. The changes in coastal waters and land uses have coincided with changes in coral reefs conditions along the coast. In trying to understand reef health and stress imposing upon reefs, attempts have been made to correlate various consative events to changes on reefs of Phuket.

Figure 1 shows the location of Phuket Island and the reefs distribution. Phuket Island is located at 8°N 98° 20E. The island is seperated from the mainland South Peninsula by a channel of 200 m width. It has a monsoonal climate. The Northeast Monsoon (Nov. - Apr.) coincides with the dry season, while the Southwest Monsoon (May - Oct.) brings about heavy rainfall from the Indian Ocean. The prevailing wind system on Phuket Island is offshore (NE, E and SE) during the Northeast Monsoon and on-shore (NW, W and SW) during the Southwest Monsoon. The salinity and temperature of nearshore waters around Phuket Island are relatively constant, 32-33%. and 26-28°C respectively. The tide is semi-diurnal. The mean annual tidal range is about 1.8 m although the range may vary up to 3.7 m during certain time of the year.

Reef are located mainly on the south and west coast and nearshore islands as shown in Figure 1. The reefs on Phuket Islnd are different in term of physiomorphology, dominant species and coral coverage. Reefs in protected bays of the south and east coasts are the reefs of shallow turbid waters of 4-5 m depth with extensive intestidal reefs flat. Reefs in the bays along the northwest coast are the reefs with extensive reef slope extending to 15 m depth in clear waters. Besides there are also reefs that are in semi protected areas from southwest monsoon influence along the southwest coast and satellite islands and coral communities on rocky coast in relatively exposed area of the west coast. (Chansang et al., 1985).

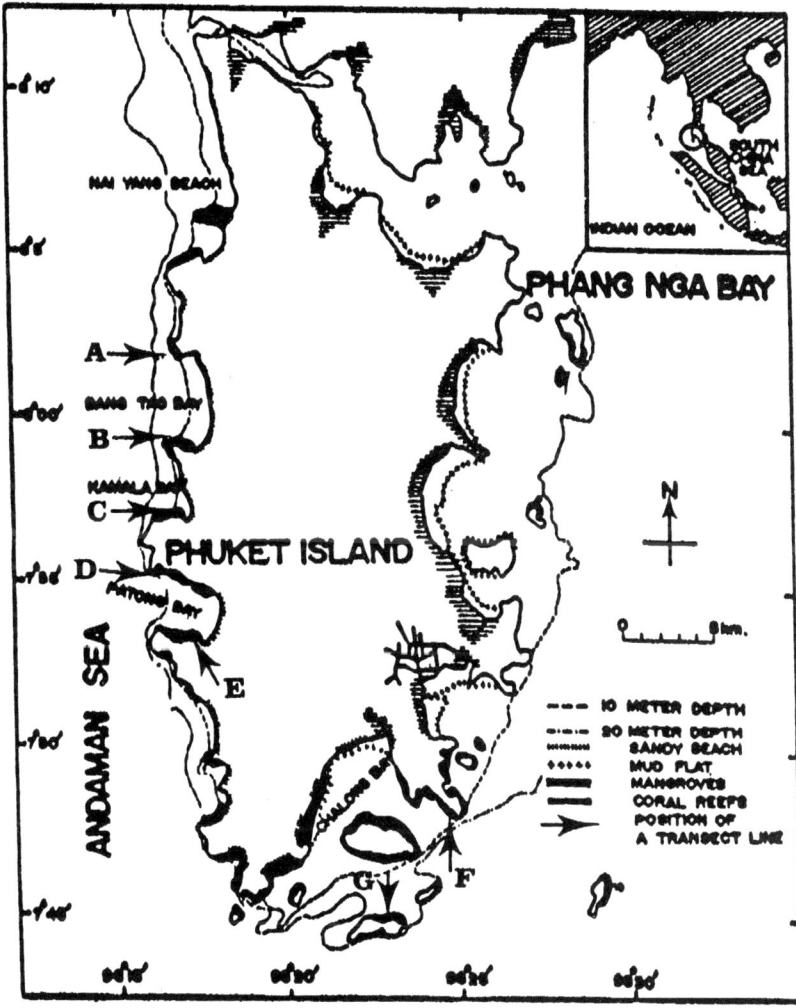

Figure 1. Map show reef distribution on Phuket Island, Thailand with the indicators of transects (A-G)

METHODS

Transect studies were carried out by photographic quadrat transect method during 1980-1986 and line transect method during 1988-1992. The photographic quadrat transect method was designed for inventory of Phuket reefs (Chansang et al., 1985). Estimate of coral coverages was made by photographing 15 m transect lines which were placed parallel to shore line at the interval of about 20 m down to reef slope perpendicular to the profile. On each line, 15 m^2 strip of reef area were photographed by using 1x1 m^2 quadrat as the frame of referernce. Images of live corals (if possible identified to species), dead corals, soft corals, algal cover and substratum were cut from photo and weighed. The coral cover were then recalculate from percentage of total coral cover from each transect

The transect sites on the northwest coast (site A to site E) were subsequently marked with cement blocks for monitoring programme during 1982-1986. The monitoring was conducted every 6 months i.e. in April and November of each year to observe the change due to effect of tin dredging and monsoonal influence. Example of monitoring data was prersented (Chansang, 1988).

In 1988, the ASEAN-Australia Living Resources in Coastal Area Program was established with the assistance of Australia to ASEAN countries. Under this programme, the line transect method was recommended for survey and generation of base line data on coral reef ecosystems through out ASEAN countries. The methodology was as recorded in a manual (Dartnall and Jones, 1989). With some modification as stated (Phongsuwan and Chansang, 1992), the line transect method has been used to replace the photographic quadrat transect method for further monitoring programe since 1988. Line transects were placed on the same photographic transect in reef slope or reef edge areas depend upon sites. Iron rods were placed at various intervals through out the entire 100 m length. Measures of intersection of coral colonies are carried out.

RESULTS

The results shown in Figure 2 present as live and dead coral covers. Seven transects were selected as examples presenting case history of Phuket reefs. The northern most sites presented are reefs in Bang Tao Bay which were damaged by sedimentation from tin dredging activity (Chansang et al 1981). The north Bang Tao (site A) showed increasing coral cover during 1982-1986. Live coral cover in 1988 and 1989 were less than those of 1986 but subsequently increased to 60%. Increase in coral cover depended upon the increasing distance of tin dredging moving away from the coral reef during each dredging season in subsequent year and removing of the sediment from reef during the southwest monsoon season (Chansang et al., 1988). Tin dredging activity in Bang Tao Bay stopped since 1990.

On the south side of Bang Tao Bay (site B), which was also affected by sedimentation, the coral cover remained about 30% during 1980-1984 and declined during 1985 to 1986 which was about the period of *Acanthaster planci* were commonly found in the area. The lowest coral cover was 16% in 1986. Following up in 1988-1992 showed relatively constant coral cover of 30-33%. Eventhough the dredging activity stopped since 1990, the sediment were not easily removed from the reef site. The turbidity remained quite high.

At site C in Kamala Bay, the coral reef suffered from sedimentation from dredging activity for 3 month period during the dry season of 1983. The live coral cover was low in 1984 (26%) by compasion to 77% in 1980. The coral reef showed significant recovery in 1985 and 1986 as dredging stopped and sediment were removed. However reef was also affected by *A. planci* during 1986-1988. whereas the *A. planci* population was highest in 1988 (Chansang, 1988). The coral cover seemed to remain more of less the same ranging from 62.7-67.6%.

At site D, north Patong, the live coral cover declined from 77.5% to 52.9% during 1981-1982 and remained relatively the same through out the monitoring process till 1986. Data since 1988 showed fluctuation in coral cover with the lowest in 1989 (31.1%) and steadily increase to 58.7% in 1992. *A. planci* was also found on this reef with increasing number during 1985-1989. They caused more destruction on the upper reef zone whereas the dominant corals were *Acropora formosa*. (Phongsuwan, unpublished data)

At South Patong (site E), the reef is close to Patong Beach, the center of toursim development than any reefs under this studied. After inventory in 1980, monitoring at this site began in 1988. It was found that the live coral cover steadily declined during 1988-1992. The causes of decline are attributed to various activities i.e. increasing turbidity due to dredging of reef flat, *A. planci* predation during 1988-1989, tourist activities, boat anchoring and recently the possibility of eutrophication. Monitoring nutrient levels and reef responses to increasing nutrients is being conducted at this site.

The reefs on the south coast of Phuket are of shallow reefs. The reef depths range from 5 m in turbid waters of site F to 10 m for reefs of satellite islands such as site G. The reef at Ko Hae (site G) showed the decline in live coral cover from 91% in 1981 to 74% in 1990 and subsequantly to 66.7% in 1992. The decline in 1992 was also due to coral bleaching during May-June 1991 when the water temperature was at 32°C for several weeks. General survey in the area showed severe bleaching of *Acropora* spp which did not recover whereas the massive forms such as *Porites* subsequently recover. The reef site at G was a patch reef infront of a small south beach of the Phuket Marine Biological Center. The reef was destroyed by monsoon strom in May 1986 whereas all the coral debris were washed ashore. Monitoring in 1987 showed no live coral on upper zone and 17% coral cover in lower zone (Phongsuwan, 1992). Data from lower zone is presented in this report. Line transect at this site is only 15 m in length due to the size of communities. The live coral cover increased significantly in 1991 to 43.6% and declined to 33.0% due to bleaching event.

DISCUSSION

In considering the continuity of these data sets, it is necessary to be aware of changing monitoring method from photographic quadrat - transect method prior to 1987 to line transect method. Although in 1988 at each transect both methods were carried out, the data has yet to be analysed. Data sets at site A - D may be interpreted seperately from the period of 1981 to 1986 and 1988 to 1992. Under the current monitoring programme it is intended to conduct repeated monitoring at the same sites within the same period to determine degree of accuracy of this method.

In presenting result of each reef with only one transect line, it may be misleading. The early result from our work using data of parallel photographic transect quadrat method showed that reef condition vary

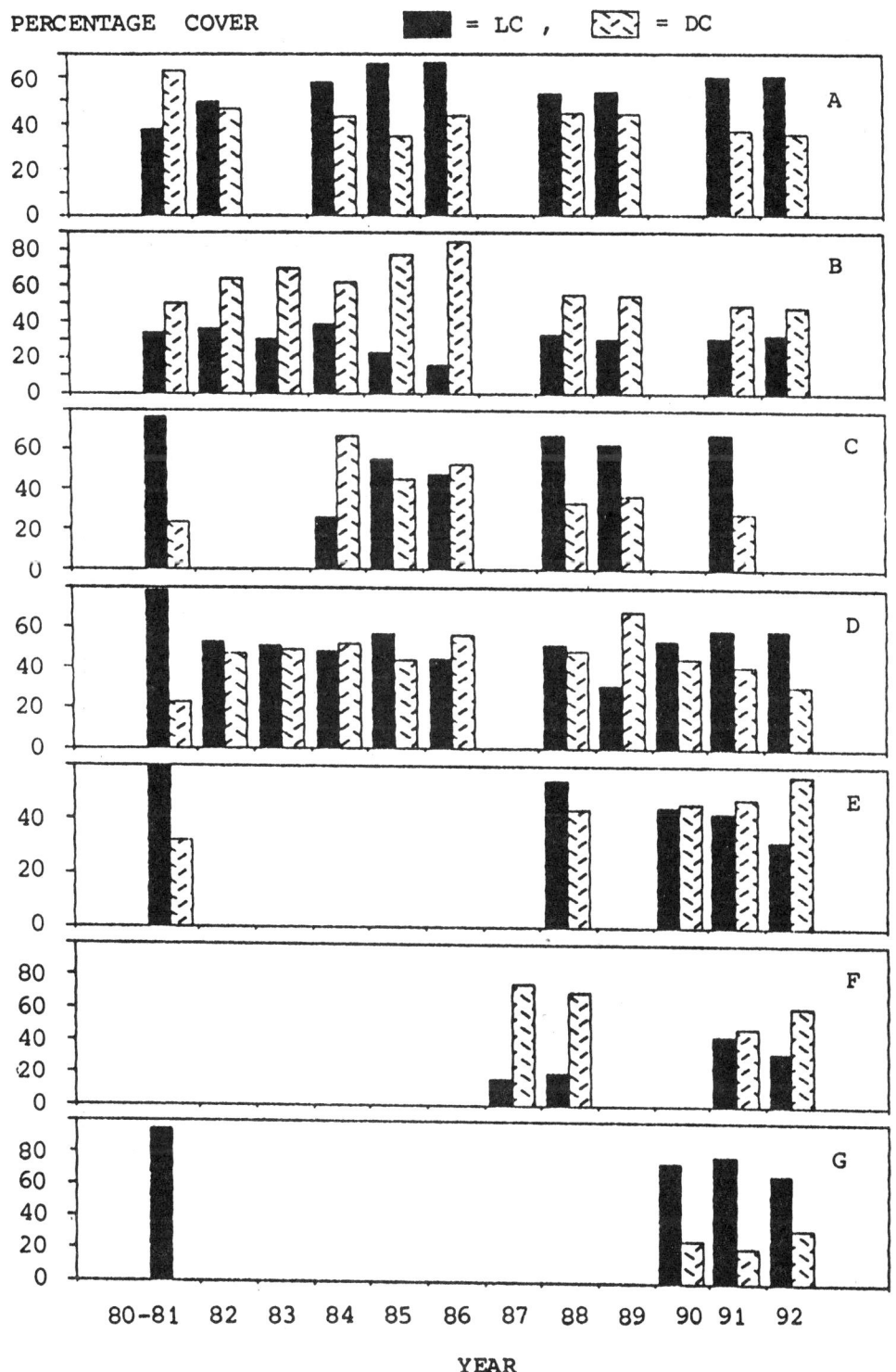

Figure 2 Data from 7 transects on Phuket reefs showing live and dead coral cover during 1980-1992. Alphabets represent site of transect: A, north Bang Tao; B south Bang Tao; C, Kamala Bay; D, north Patong; E, south Patong; F, Laem Panwa and G; Ko Hae. LC and DC are % live coral and dead coral cover.

at each zone of reefs. Even with the effect of sedimentation on same reef at North Bang Tao (Site A) the upper slope areas were more affected that the lower slope i.e. less live coral cover. (Chansang et al., 1981). The present result using line transect method at North Patong also shows the effect of *A. planci* preditation more drastic and hence less coral cover on upper slope whereas *Acropora* were dominant species than lower slope (data presented in this paper) which were dominated by massive forms (Phongsuwan, unpublished data). Although we prefered data which would reflect coverage of corals at different zonation as previously done (Chansang et al., 1981; Chansang, 1988), due to limited in time man power and number reefs to be monitored we adopt the present method for ongoing long term monitoring programme. Thus it is necessary to be aware of intepreting data of quantitative transect method at certain zone to represent the whole reef. The location of transect site on reef should be stated. In addition the zonal condition of reefs even at the same island may vary. For example, the intertidal reef flats of reefs on relatively exposed area on west coast of Phuket Island are cemented dead coral platform with low coral coverage (Chansang et al., 1981,1985) in comparison with luxurious growth of intertidal reef flat in protected bays in southern part of island (Brown and Holley, 1984; Ditlev, 1978).

In considering the result presented from 7 selected reefs for Phuket Island it can be said that live coral cover in 1992 on each reef is less than those in 1980 with the exception of condition at site A which showed the sign of recovery and site B whereas the live coral cover remained more or less the same. As presented in the results, the causes of changes at each reef include both manmade activities and natural events. Sedimentation from dredging at site A, B and C was an obvious major manmade cause which incurred devastating effect on coral reefs. It is also shown that in certain areas whereas sediment were removed from the reefs, recovery of coral growth was possible as shown at site A and site C. The effect of sedimentation on corals may vary according to species and to environmental conditions. Dodge and Visney (1977) reported effect of dredging on growth of corals in Bermuda. On Phuket Island, growth of *Porites* along west coast at site disturbed by sediment and undisturbed site were not significantly different, whereas the seasonal difference seems to be more pronounce (Chansang and Phongsuwan 1992). However there are other manmade causes which are more diffcult to quantitatively presented when they happen in concurrent with other activities, for examples the effects from tourism such as boat anchorage, damage corals from tourist visiting areas. Since early 1980S site B and site C have been increasingly visited by tourists as Patong Beach became a major resort town. During that period the degradation of coral reefs was observed. There was other cause which caused more damage to corals within the area i.e. the outbreak of *Acanthaster planci*, however. *A. planci* was considered a serious detrimental cause during 1986-1989 at site B,C,D and E. The most abundance were around 1988-1989 whereas campaigns for collecting starfish were organized by diving tour operators. By 1990 the number became much less. At present *A. planci* was still observed at each site but in very low number. In the Andaman Sea, it was a major cause in reef degradation within the last decade. Of 25 sites of 'unhealthy' reefs, *A. planci* outbrerak was identified as major cause for 12 sites in comparison with 7 sites being affected by tourism (Phongsuwan and Chansang, 1992).

The other major natural causes are strom damage and bleaching. Only one site was selected to show the result of strom damage and the recovery. The tropical strom in May 1986 caused large scale damage to many islands in the Andaman Sea especially on reefs which were exposed on the south side. Date from site F reports the recovery from such damage despite the water turbidity. However on other reefs, the recovery was not in such order. Reef on Maithon Island, 8 km south of site F still does not recover eventhough the water clarity was much better. This may due to various combination factors. One of possible explanating was the availability of coral larvae to reach the site. Coral bleaching was noticed in May - July 1991 after prolong warming of surface seawater. Surface temperature data shows increasing temperature of $2°C$ above ambient during that period. Brief survey was conducted along the south coast of Phuket Island and in Phang-nga Bay. Bleaching event was observed from surface to 20 m depth. Subsequent monitoring shows significant recovery of massive forms and the death of *Acropora* spp. Thus data in 1992 shows the decline in coral cover aspecially along the south coast was attributed to bleaching event. Unfortunately no spot check was done on the west coast. Thus it could not be definit whether corals at site D were affected.

In the area included in this report, damage from destructive fishing methods are not reported. Dynamite fishing which is the common practice reported in Southeast Asia was not considered as a major threat. It was more prevalent on isolated islands offshore than on major island such as Phuket. However, from our manta tow survey of Andaman Sea, it was not possible to separate sign of reef damage by dynamite from other activities. The clue of such dynamite blasting was patches of coral damages among good whereas strom damage destroyed entire areas. In certain reef with massive form it was possible to indicate the damage by blasting but it was not easily done in *Acropora* dominating areas. Muro ami fishing was carried out among reefs in Phuket and surrounding areas until recently. But, again, to evaluate the extent of damage causes by such activity was not possible due to other activities which occured in the same area.

Thus in Phuket area superimposing of several causes of decline of coral covers seem to be common. This makes it difficult to single out any cause, expecially manmade one, as causing the decline of reef health. On contrary, from data and field observation it seems to be that the natural causes i.e. strom, *A. planci* outbreak and, possibly, bleaching are more of important factor in causing decrease in live coral cover, not only for the sites reported in this paper but also the over all Andaman Sea observation. Increasing concern, however, is on the chronic problem of increasing turbidity, nutrients and sedimentation along the coastline. Eventhough the situation may not affect the coral directly as acute effect from dredging, the result may weaken or decrease the chance of coral from recovering from natural disturbances.

How to define reef health is a subject worth considering. In general there are tendency to relate coral cover with reef health. In Philippines, range of percent of living coral cover are used as indicator of reef condition i.e. 75-100% as excellent, 50-74.9% as good, etc (Gomez, 1990). This criteria is also recommended to be used in ASEAN-Australia project (Wilkinson, personal communication). However, this criteria may not be appropriate to describe natural condition of a many reefs in the region and elsewhere. As in the Andaman Sea some of the naturally undisturbed reefs do not have more than 50-75% of live coral cover due to the nature of reef environment. In the Andaman Sea, the ratio of live to dead coral cover was used instead to define reef condition in order to avoid the problem of substratum cover. (Phongsuwan and Chansang, 1992).

We feel that the definition of reef health and criteria for identification of reef health deserve some critical attention especially if we want better understanding of reef condition on global scale. Use of coral cover which is quantitative information of express the condition in qualitative term such as good or bad should be carefully considered as it can be subjective matter to certain degree. In addition succession of communities generally occur with some natural desturbances such as strom and prerdation as catalysts. Thus change in coral cover and species diversity is also natural process. In relating to 'health' issue some critical questions to be address should be on extent of increasing man made disturbances causing dissuption of natural processes of reef ecosystems.

CONCLUSIONS

This study compiles information from last 10 years, of which is the period of economic expasion of Phuket Island. In most cases, reef health seemed to decline. It is not possible to clearly separate the changes on reefs as causing by natural events or by manmade, however. In most causes, it was combination of both factors. At this point we would conclude that major causes of decreasing in coral cover in Phuket Island as presented in this paper and in the Andaman Sea (as our data available) are causing by natural events. Sedimentation is a major man made disturbance which played significant role in some location. Other man made disturbances are more difficult to quentity. The problem how this man made disturbance disrupt the natural process is a subject to be considered.

ACKNOWLEDGEMENTS

We would like to thank Mr. Ukrit Sattapoomin and Mr. Jumroen Khoekao for preparing this manuscript. This paper is the Miscellaneous Contribution No.   from the Phuket Marine Biological Center.

LITERATURE CITED

Brown, B.E. and M.C. Holley. 1984. Coral assemblages of intertidal reef flat at Ko Phuket, Thailand. Phuket Mar. Biol. Center Bull. 30:1-10.

Chansang, H. 1988. Coastal tin mining and marine pollution in Thailand. AMBIO 17(3):223-228.

Chansang, H., P. Boonyanate and M. Charuchinda. 1981. Effect of sedimentation from coastal mining on coral reefs on the northwestern coast of Phuket Island, Thailand. Proc. 4th Int. Coral Reef Symp. 1:129-136.

Chansang, H., P. Boonyanate and M. Charuchinda. 1985. Features of fringing reefs in shallow water environments of Phuket Island, the Andaman Sea. Proc. 5th Int. Coral Reef Congress. Tahiti. 6:439-444.

Chansang, H., P. Boonyanage, N. Phongsuwan and S. Panrong. 1988. Effect of sediment from tin dredging to coral and growth of some coral species. Technical report submitted to the Department of Mineral Resources. Bangkok, Thailand. 82 p. (in Thai)

Chansang, H., N. Phongsuwan and P. Boonyanate. 1992. Growth of corals under effect of sedimentation along the north west coast of Phuket Island, Thailand. Proc. 7th Int. Coral Reef Symp. (in press)

Dartnall, A. J. and M. Jones. (eds) 1986. A manual of survey methods for living resources in coastal areas: ASEAN-Australia Cooperative Programme on Marine Science. The Australian Institute of Marine Science. Townsville.

Ditlev, H. 1978. Zonation of corals (Scleractinia: Coelenterata) on intertidal reef flats at Ko Phuket, Eastern Indian Ocean. Mar. Biol. 47:29-39.

Dodge, R.E. and J.R. Vaisnys. 1977. Coral populations and growth patterns: responses to sedimentation and turbidity associated with dredging. J. Mar. Res. 35:715-730.

Gomez, E.D. 1990. Coral reef ecosystems and resources of the Philippines Canopy 16(5). Manila.

Phongsuwan, N. 1991. Recolonization of coral reef damaged by a strom on Phuket Island, Thailand. Phuket Mar. Biol. Center Res. Bull. 56:75-83.

Phongsuwan, N. and H. Chansang. 1992. Assessment of coral communities in The Andaman Sea (Thailand). Proc. 7th Int. Coral Reef Symp. (in press)

ON THE SEVERE CHANGES IN THE ECOLOGY AND SEDIMENTATION OF LUWEITOU FRINGING CORAL REEFS, HAINAN ISLAND, CHINA

Wang Guozhong, Lu Bingquan and Quan Songqing

Tongji University, Department of Marine Geology,
Shanghai 200092, China

ABSTRACT

In the famous Luweitou Coral Reef Area, three repeated field investigations were completed and followed by laboratory analyses in 1978 and 1990. These studies revealed severe changes in the ecology of corals, geomorphology, depositional environments and sedimentation. In the reef framework zone, the flourishing, prosperous scene of hermatypic corals had become a miserable one. The coral cover on the reef face had decreased between 1978 and 1990 from 50-90% to 40-60% on the East Reefs, and from 60% to 30-40% on the West Reef. The density of the coral communities had become lower, massive corals (more than 1m in diameter) were rare in 1990, while they had been common in 1978. In the West Reef, the framework was destroyed and the marginal gravel facies zone had disappeared. The submarine relief was planed down and loose sediments in the related zone became coarser, while mud increased. The absence of breakers on the reef crest indicated that the wave action had decreased. Coral reefs have been susceptible to many hazards, particularly in the last years. The causes of these hazards to reefs are either natural or anthropogenic effects. Among these effects, the main destructive activities are the excavation of reef rock for building materials, the collection of coral skeletons for sale as handicrafts, and fishing with the help of explosives. Some significant measures have been taken to protect the reef environment, but it may already be too late.

INTRODUCTION

The Luweitou Fringing Coral Reef Area is located in the south part of Hainan Island, approximately 109° 30' E, 18° 20' N (Figure 1). It was said to be the most developed recent coral reefs in the Northern Continental Shelf of the South China Sea. The reef falls within the tropical biogeographic zone, and the average water temperature is approximately 26.7 ° C. Salinities of the sea water range from 33.5 to 34.0 parts per thousand. The reefs are dominated by the northeasterly-southwesterly monsoons, and in the summer typhoons and hurricanes strike from the southwest. The ocean-facing setting provides a continuous supply of normal sea water. Under these favorable conditions the scleractinian corals and reef organisms flourished and formed fringing coral reefs. It is the most-studied and best-described modern coral reef area in China and a significant educational and research area for carbonate sedimentology. There are many reports on this coral reef area. Biologists and geologists have delineated some zones of coral communities, ecological habitats, and sedimentary facies (Zhou Renlin et al. 1966, Huang Jinsen et al. 1975, Wang Guozhong et al. 1979). However, in the past few years, these coral reefs have undergone serious destruction, caused by a combination of unfavorable natural conditions and especially the impact of human activity.

Through comparison of data collected in repeated field investigations from 1978 and 1990, this case history reveals the serious results of the human impact and how it leads to severe changes in the ecological environments, hydrodynamic conditions, and sedimentation.

METHODS

In May of 1978 and July of 1990, we carried out repeated field investigations of the same Luweitou Coral Reef Area. I measured the submarine relief, observed the reef landscapes and hydrodynamic conditions, documented bottom characteristics in detail, and accounted for biotic cover, coral genera and species in particular, by means of their percentages and growth characteristics along the study transects. Sediment samples and bottom photographs were taken by SCUBA diving. Sedimentary facies zones were divided and examined in the field. The analysis of the size distribution of the loose sediments was based on standard sieve and settling techniques. Weight percentages of the main constituents were estimated for coarser fractions greater than 0.5 mm with the aid of a stereoscope and balance.

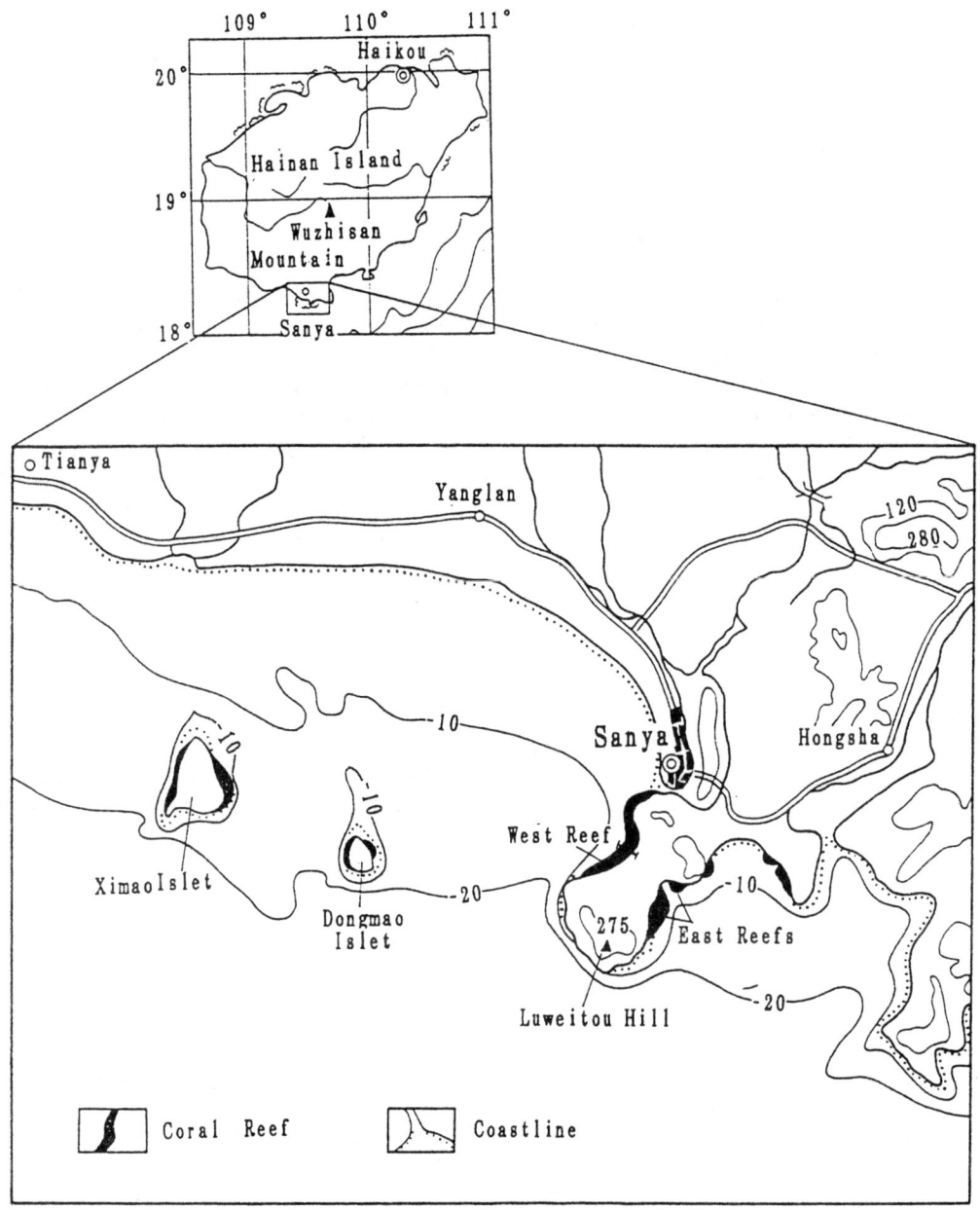

Figure 1. Map of the Luweitou Fringing Coral Reef Area. Bar indicates location of West Reef transect reported in Figure 2.

RESULTS

Tables 1 and 2 and Figure 2 show the results of field observations and laboratory analyses of the samples, collected on of the same reef area in 1978 and 1990. For an additional description of the depositional environments and sedimentary facies, the reader is referred to Wang Guozhong et al. (1979) and Zhou Renlin et al.(1966).

The changes in the intervening 12 years period in the Luweitou Coral Reef Area were phenomenal. In the autochthonous reef facies, or reef framework facies zone of the East Reefs of the Reef Area, the biotic cover, mainly hermatypic coral cover on the reef face decreased from 50-90% in 1978 to 40-60% in 1990. In the same zone of the West Reef the hermatypic coral cover decreased from 60% in 1978 to 30-40% in 1990.

Table 1. Reef habitat and ecology of hermatypic corals in the framework zone of Luweitou Coral Reef Area, 1978 vs. 1990.

Location	East Reef		West Reef	
Date	1978	1990	1978	1990
Living Coral Cover (%)	50-90	40-60	60	30-40
Diameter of massive corals (m)	1-2	1	0.5-1	0.3
Height of massive corals (m)	0.5-1	0.5	0.2-0.4	0.1-0.3
Height of branching corals (m)	0.1-0.3	0.1-0.2	0.1-0.2	0.1-0.2
Hydrodynamic condition	strong	strong	medium	weak
Turbidity of water	clear	clear	clear	muddy

In 1978, the reef framework had a flourishing coral community. The hermatypic corals can be grouped into two broad coral communities: 1) an upper subzone community is dominated by branching and encrusting corals, such as *Acropora* and *Pocillopora*; and 2) a lower subzone community containing mainly plate-like corals such as *Acropora corymbosa* and *surcolosa*.

The hemispherical and massive corals species such as *Porites* and *Favia* are minor components of both subzones. Massive corals, more than 1-2 meters in diameter, were common in 1978. There were 114 species, belonging to 37 genera, of hermatypic corals in the Luweitou Coral Reef Area. There are 128 species in the entire Hainan Coral Reef Region. In 1978 and before, the East Reefs of the Area contained many areas of alcyonarians and sponges, and especially areas of Millepora and coralline algae. The West Reef was home to many *Fungia*. Twelve years later, many species of coral and reef-building organisms were absent in the reef area. Before 1980, this reef had abundant fish, arthropod, and mollusk resources, indeed it was a famous fishing area, but today, those biotic resources are so reduced that no one comes there to fish anymore. In 1978, the reef margin of East Reef had a well-developed boundstone facies zone which consisted of crustose coralline algae and other branching red algae, but in 1990, this boundstone facies zone had deteriorated and was eroded.

A comparison of the same reef transect of West Reef of Luweitou Reef Area between 1978 and 1990 can be seen in Figure 2. The marginal reef-gravel-facies zone, situated at 20 cm above low tide level and consisting of fresh reef rock, gravels and shingles(Figure 2A), was completely absent in 1990. Instead, this same zone was now 1 m below the low tide level and covered by eroded, bored gravel(Figure 2C). Living *Fungia* was also very rare.

The severe changes in the past 12 years are also reflected in the sediments. Results of the analyses of the size distribution of samples collected from the same transect in repeated field investigations are shown in Figure 2B. The median grain size of sediments of the related facies zone had become coarser, the mud content had increased in the reef flat and coastal zone, and the standard deviation had increased.

As a result of the destruction of the coral reef framework zone and the disappearance of the marginal gravel facies zone, there are no breakers in the fore reef area of West Reef. The waves now lash straight across the reef to the coast and destroy coastal roads.

Table 2. Comparative gram size distributions of samples collected in the West Reef of Luweitou Reef Area in 1978 and 1990.

Sedimentary Facies	Year/Sample	Fractions			Size parameter				Nomenclature
		Gravel	Sand	Silt	Mz	σ1	Sk	Kg	
Reef frame-work zone	1978 W1-2	3.02	93.72	3.26	1.96	0.83	-0.19	1.54	Medium-Fine sand
	1990 W901	0.86	99.92	0.22	1.87	0.79	-0.15	1.04	Medium-Fine sand
	W902	1.32	99.64	0.04	1.55	0.77	-0.25	1.18	Fine-Medium sand
Marginal gravel zone	1978 W2-1	1.90	98.10	-----	1.25	0.64	-0.25	1.29	Coarse-Medium sand
	1990 W903	1.02	98.96	0.02	0.74	0.65	0.01	1.08	Medium-Coarse sand
Inner Reef Flat	1978 W4	2.94	97.06	-----	1.24	1.32	0.10	0.87	Medium-Coarse sand
	1990 W906	6.60	93.10	0.20	1.14	1.46	0.16	1.06	Medium sand
Beach zone	1978 W13	0.02	99.98	-----	2.34	0.77	-0.06	0.95	Medium-Fine sand
	W14	0.92	99.08	-----	1.27	0.40	0.10	1.23	Coarse-Medium sand
	1990 W907	22.14	77.86	-----	-0.46	0.85	-0.14	1.20	Gravel-Coarse sand
	W908	14.34	85.62	0.04	-0.02	1.07	-0.06	2.01	Gravel-Coarse sand
Dune	1978 W15	0.52	99.74	-----	1.51	0.64	-0.04	1.09	Medium sand
	1990 W909	1.74	98.26	-----	1.37	1.89	0.05	0.85	Coarse-Medium sand

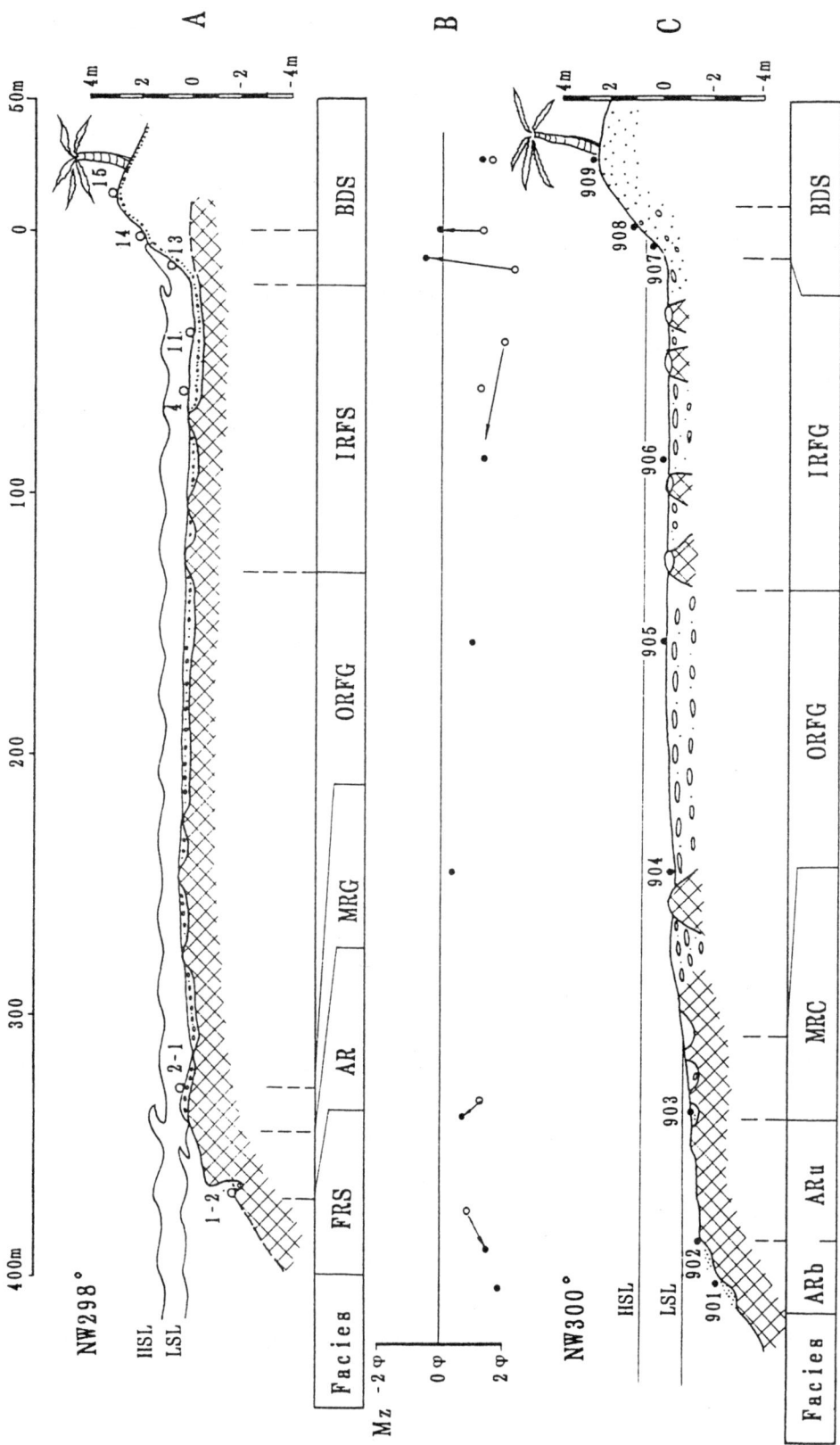

Figure 2. The same transect of West Reef taken in 1978(2A) and 1990 (2C). 2B shows the value of median grain size of loose samples and their changing tendency. Facies: FRS = the off-reef sand facies; ARL = the lower autochtonous reef facies; ARU = the upper autochtonous reef facies; MRG the marginal reef gravel facies; ORFG = the outer-reef flat gravel facies; IRFS = the inner reef flat sand facies; BDS = the beach-dune sand facies.

DISCUSSION

The Luweitou Coral Reefs are relatively immature, which were formed during the Holocene, beginning about 8000 a B.P. (Zhao Xitao et al. 1983). In the last decade, the once-beautiful and flourishing Luweitou Coral Reefs have been exposed to a combination of natural or anthropogenic hazards.

Typhoons and hurricanes are the primary natural hazards of coral reefs. For example, in the summer of 1983, when a typhoon struck the Coral Reef Area, the huge waves swept reef rocks and coral heads onto the reef flat, including a block of *Porites* 2 m in diameter and 1.5 m high. It was a great destruction, but it didn't have a fatal effect on the coral reefs because such storms do not fundamentally destroy the environment of the reef-building biota. Hurricanes will strike coral reef areas and destroy reefs, but they do not stop the development of reef. Cold currents are another natural effect which can be detrimental to reefs. In the winter, they flow southward periodically decreasing the sea water temperature and thereby causing the death of coral communities, as well as an overgrowth of brown algae.

The main destructive forces, however, are anthropogenic. For example, the excavating of reef rocks as building materials, the collection of coral skeletons for sale as handicrafts, and the use of explosives to aid in fishing, all lead to the destruction of the entire reef ecology and sedimentary system. Unfortunately, these effects are intense and widespread.

At present, government agencies and people in general are beginning to recognize the harm of reef destruction, and some major measures are being taken to protect the reef environments against pollution and destruction. The Luweitou Coral Reef Area was designated as a natural coral reef protectorate. Another effective measure that has been passed is the prohibition of the sale of coral skeletons on the open market.

To aid the recovery of this valuable reef area, there is a need to develop methods for transplanting hermatypic corals and monitoring their continual growth. Further study must be done on the methods and techniques of recovery and development of hermatypic corals in the reef area.

CONCLUSIONS

1. The Luweitou Fringing Coral Reefs are one of the most developed modern coral reefs in the Northern Continental Shelf of the South China Sea. It is a famous tourist attraction and field investigation base for modern carbonate sedimentology in China.

2. In the last decade, these reefs have undergone severe destruction, caused mainly by various human activity, including reef rock excavation, coral skeleton collection, and fishing through use of explosives.

3. Results of these destructive human activities are reflected in the reef ecology, landscape, depositional environment, and sedimentation.

4. Some important measures are now taking place to protect the reef environment against pollution, including the designation of a coral reef protectorate and prohibition of the sale of coral skeletons on the open market.

5. Methods of transplanting should be developed to renew deteriorated reefs.

ACKNOWLEDGMENTS

We wish to thank Zhou Fugen and Sun Zhiguo for participating in the field investigations of 1978 and 1990, and Wang Xiuya for drawing the pictures. This project was supported by the National Natural Science Foundation of China.

LITERATURE CITED

Guozhong, Wang, et al. 1979. The Sedimentary facies zones of the Luweitou Fringing Reefs, Hainan Island. J. Tongji University No. 2, 70-89.

Jinsen, Huang, et al. 1982. On the geomorphology and depositional characteristics of islands and reefs in the middle and northern parts of the South China Sea. *in* "The reports of comprehensive investigation and survey in the South China Sea I ", Science Press, 39-67.

Renlin, Zhou, et al. 1966. An original research of vertical distribution of coral reefs, Hainan Island. Oceanologia et Limnologia Sinica, Vol. 8, No. 2, 153-161.

Xitao, et al. 1983. Development of the Holocene coral reefs along the southern coast of Hainan Island. Scientia Geologica Sinica, No. 2, 150-159.

SEDIMENTATION DAMAGE TO REEF CORALS

Gregor Hodgson

Binnie Consultants Ltd.
11/F New Town Tower, Pak Hok Ting St., Shatin, Hong Kong

ABSTRACT

A 12-month study was made of the effects of coastal logging in a Philippine drainage basin, on soil erosion, sediment transport, and the subsequent effects of marine sedimentation on coral reefs located in an adjacent bay. Logging significantly increased soil erosion and sediment transport to the bay. Over 80% of surface erosion came from logging roads. Sediment deposition increased only at the coral reefs closest to the river mouth on most days. During peak river discharge, however, sediment plumes spread over the bay and high rates of sedimentation occurred at all reefs except the control station. Coral cover and number of species declined significantly during the study period. Experimental tests of sedimentation tolerance among 50 species of coral revealed a tolerance hierarchy based on growth form, corallite diameter and polyp extensional ability. The abundance of corals shown by experiment to be highly susceptible to injury from sedimentation declined significantly over the 12-month period. The study demonstrated that coastal logging can damage coral reefs by increasing sediment deposition rates above the tolerance thresholds of some coral species.

INTRODUCTION

Sedimentation in the sea is a natural process that results from erosion of the land and transport of soil to the sea, or from resuspension of sediment previously deposited along coastal margins or on the seabed. Many human activities, particularly land clearing associated with farming, logging and road construction, are believed to accelerate erosion and subsequent marine sedimentation. This anthropogenic sedimentation is a form of pollution. Scleractinian corals are known to be injured by exposure to sedimentation (Rogers, 1990), and sedimentation pollution appears to be widespread and increasing in severity. Sedimentation pollution may pose the single most serious threat to the health of coastal coral reefs in the world.

Few studies have attempted to link the cause of anthropogenic sedimentation, in the terrestrial ecosystem, with the effects on organisms in the marine ecosystem. This paper summarizes the results of a 12-month study of the effects of coastal logging in the Philippines on soil erosion, and the follow-on effects of marine sedimentation on coral reefs located within a nearby bay (Hodgson, 1989; 1990a; 1990b). A detailed analysis of this case from the perspective of ecological economics has been reported separately (Hodgson and Dixon, 1988).

METHODS

Terrestrial

The study was carried out in a forested watershed and adjoining bay in El Nido, Palawan (Figure 1). A six-month site investigation commenced in mid-1985 followed by a 12-month period of quantitative data collection that ended on 31 December 1986. Land use, particularly the extent of logging, was measured from aerial photographs and confirmed by ground truthing. From January to December 1985, the pristine dipterocarp forest was selectively logged, with most activity occurring during the dry season (August-December). Logging was temporarily halted between January and December, 1986.

Rain gages and adjacent erosion plots were built on 30% slopes and used to measure erosion rates in pristine forest, cut forest and on a logging road (Figure 2). An automated gaging station was constructed to measure the flow of the major river (Manlag) draining the logging area. Sediment load in the Manlag River and a nearby river draining pristine forest land were measured using standard USGS procedures (Guy and Norman, 1970).

Marine

Eight permanent stations were monitored on coral reefs in Bacuit Bay (Figure 2). Station 8, near the bay entrance served as a control station. Water current patterns were studied using drogues during both monsoons. Weather conditions and water quality parameters were measured twice monthly. At each station, sediment deposition was measured once per month using replicate traps located at a depth of 3 m and placed 1.5 m above the seabed. Both terrestrial and marine sediments were analyzed for particle-size distribution, calcium carbonate and organic content.

At each station, five 10 m transects were established on the reefs at a depth of 3 m. The transects were surveyed in January and December 1986 using the chord-intercept technique (Loya, 1972). Coral colony-size was also measured and the size of any injured patches was recorded (partial mortality).

The effects of sedimentation on 50 species of corals from 14 Families were studied in the laboratory and the field. In Bacuit

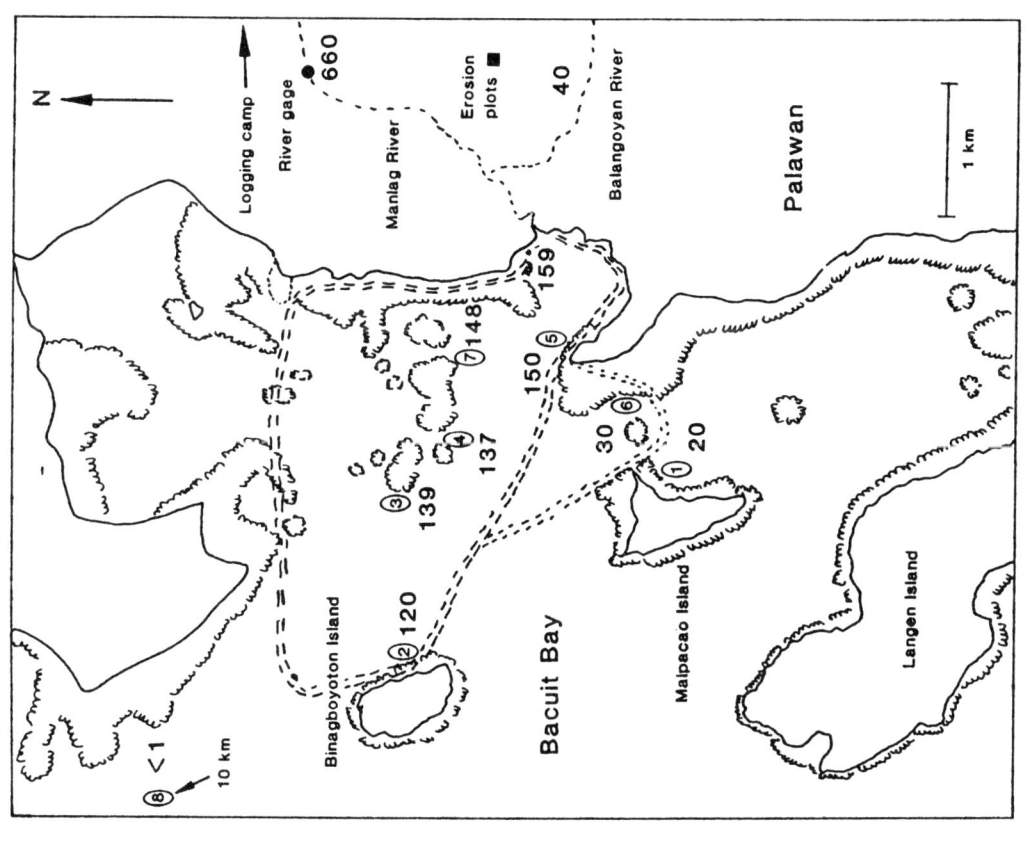

Figure 1. The study area in El Nido, northern Palawan showing coral reefs in Bacuit Bay, the drainage basin, and logging concession.

Figure 2. The study area showing the location of terrestrial and marine monitoring stations (1-8). The control station (8) was located near the bay entrance and is not on the map. The border of a typical sediment plume is marked by a broken double line and sediment concentrations in the river and sediment plume are given (mg/l).

299

Bay, reciprocal transplants were made between corals at a pristine reef (Station 8) and the reef nearest to the mouth of the Manlag River (Station 5), the source of anthropogenic sedimentation. Mortality and the percentage of injured tissue were monitored regularly. Experiments conducted in aquaria were used to assess the tolerance of 22 species of coral to sedimentation. A variety of additional studies were carried out to investigate the process of sedimentation damage to corals and the effects of sediment on the settlement of coral planulae (Hodgson, 1989; Hodgson, 1990a,b).

RESULTS

Terrestrial

At the beginning of the study, when logging had temporarily ceased, 87% of the watershed was still forested and about 6% had been logged (Table 1).

Table 1. Land use in the Bacuit Bay Drainage Basin in January 1986

Land Use	Area (km^2)	% of Drainage Basin
All Forest	**72.8**	**93.0**
Primary	37.0	47.3
Scrub/Secondary	27.1	34.6
Logged	4.8	6.1
Mangrove	3.9	5.0
All Agriculture	**5.5**	**7.0**
Swidden/cashew	3.6	4.6
Rice paddy	1.1	1.4
Coconut planation	0.8	1.0
Total	**78.3**	**100.0**

Drainage basin soils are acidic; the average particle-size distribution is 23% sand, 41% silt and 36% clay. Rainfall in 1986 was 3400 mm, of which about 85% fell from June through November. The annual erosion rate from the road (3.215 kg/m^2) was 50 times the rate in the cut forest and 120 times that from the pristine forest. Mean Manlag River discharge was 112,402 m^3/day (5,742 m3/day/km^2). Mean suspended sediment concentration in the Manlag River was 327 mg/l and annual sediment discharge was 39,154 tonnes (2,000 tonnes/km^2). During five one-week monitoring periods (February, May, June, August and December), the Manlag River sediment concentration (730 mg/l) was significantly higher ($p < 0.005$) than that in the river (Balangoyan) draining adjacent pristine forest (45 mg/l).

Marine

Physical Parameters.——

During 1986, mean wind speed was 2.7 m/s and the wind direction closely followed monsoon directions (southwest from May through October; northeast from November to April). Annual means of other marine parameters are given in Table 2.

Table 2. Marine parameters during 1986: mean (standard error)

Parameter	Stn 1	Stn 2	Stn 3	Stn 4	Stn 5	Stn 6	Stn 7	Stn 8
Temp °C	29 (1)	28 (2)	28 (2)	29 (2)	29 (1)	29 (2)	29 (1)	28 (1)
Salinity (ppt)	34 (1)	33 (2)	33 (3)	33 (3)	33 (2)	33 (2)	33 (3)	34 (1)
Waveheight (m)	0.1 (0.3)	0.1 (0.1)	0.5 (0.4)	0.3 (0.3)	0.4 (0.3)	0.2 (0.3)	0.2 (0.2)	0.4 (0.3)
Sediment deposition (mg/cm^2/d)	1.4 (0.8)	0.5 (0.4)	1.8 (1.1)	1.7 (0.9)	31.6[1] (19.0)	6.8 (5.9)	2.1 (1.3)	0.6 (0.4)
Secchi depth (m)	7.5 (3.8)	9.5 (4.9)	8.0 (3.7)	6.4 (2.3)	3.4 (1.8)	5.4 (1.8)	4.5 (2.5)	13.1 (5.4)

[1] $p < 0.05$ Tukey test

There were some significant differences in wave height among stations (see Hodgson, 1989), however, there was no difference between Station 5 (closest to the terrestrial sediment source) and 8 (control). Sediment deposition was significantly higher ($p < 0.05$) at Station 5 than at all other stations. In the trapped sediment, percent calcium carbonate was significantly lower at Stations 5,6 and 7 than at Stations 1,2,3 and 8. Turbidity was significantly higher ($p < 0.05$) at Station 5 than at Stations 1,2,3 and 8.

The results of routine monitoring indicate that mean temperature and salinity were similar at all stations, however, during periods of high discharge from the Manlag River, low salinity and temperature sediment plumes spread out across the bay for periods lasting up to several days (Figure 2). Depending on the state of the tide, wind direction and speed, and rate of Manlag River discharge, these plumes would occasionally reduce salinity and temperature to a depth of 1 m at Stations 1-7. The concentration of suspended sediment in surface waters during such an event is indicated in Figure 2.

It was not possible to monitor all sediment plumes (peak discharge often occurred at night), however, daily sediment concentrations and discharge rates measured at the Manlag River gaging station allowed estimates to be made of suspended sediment and sediment deposition at all marine stations except the control (Station 8) during peak discharge days. During 1986, there were seven high-discharge days during which sediment deposition at Stations 1-7 probably ranged between 16 and 51 mg/cm^2/day.

Biological Parameters. ——

The results of the aquarium and field experiments with 50 species of corals showed that there was a hierarchy of tolerance to sedimentation that was related to each species' growth form, corallite size and ability to extend polyps above the colony surface. Sediment deposition of 20 mg/cm^2/day was sufficient to injure many species of Bacuit Bay corals. Coral species having a large corallite diameter and extensible polyps were found to be the most resistant to sedimentation damage while those with small corallite diameter, low polyp extensibility and ramose growth form were the most susceptible.

Between January and December 1986, coral cover was reduced at all stations except the control (Figure 3); this reduction was significant ($p < 0.0005$; anova). Recently killed coral increased significantly at Station 5 from near zero to almost 40% of the substrate ($p < 0.01$; Tukey test). There was a significant positive relationship between loss of coral cover at each site and mean sediment deposition (natural log transformed; $p < 0.02$; $r^2 = 0.62$; $y = 6.28x + 1.3$).

In addition to a reduction in coral cover, there was a significant decrease in number of species ($p < 0.0001$; anova) and genera ($p < 0.05$; anova), however, changes in the Shannon diversity index (H'), Fager evenness (F) and mean colony size were not significant. Partial mortality significantly increased ($p < 0.0007$; anova). There was a significant reduction in cover of coral species with the three phenotypes shown by experimentation to be susceptible to sedimentation injury ($p < 0.0001$; anova).

DISCUSSION

Terrestrial

Although intuitively obvious, only a few studies have demonstrated that logging increases soil erosion (Hamilton and King, 1983). The present study was possibly the first to quantify the links between erosion and sediment transport from a logging area, and sedimentation in a tropical marine ecosystem. The erosion and sediment transport results presented here are conservative because prior to the start of monitoring, logging had stopped and only a small portion of the total available concession had been harvested.

To estimate the contribution of roads to erosion, it is necessary to take into account the cut and fill slopes that are generated during road construction on steep slopes. Using this method, logging roads in El Nido comprised 6% of all forest land, but were estimated to contribute 84% of all surface erosion.

Marine

Marine organisms have a wide variety of adaptations that protect them from deleterious effects of sedimentation. Contrary to conventional wisdom, corals commonly grow in turbid water environments and have a variety of mechanisms that protect them from sedimentation damage (Hubbard, 1973; Hubbard and Pocock, 1972; Hodgson, 1989; Rogers, 1990; Stafford-Smith, 1990; Stafford-Smith and Ormond, 1992). In general, sediment deposition is more harmful to corals than high turbidity (Edmondson, 1928). When the rate of sediment deposition exceeds the clearance rate, tissue necrosis follows a well-defined series of microbe-mediated stages until the skeleton is exposed (Hodgson, 1990b). A number of studies have investigated the tolerance of scleractinian corals to sedimentation (see Rogers, 1990; Stafford-Smith, in press). Building on previous work, the present study demonstrated that corals span a wide hierarchy of sedimentation tolerance. Corals with large diameter corallites and high extension ability polyps are most resistant to sediment damage because they can clear their surfaces of sediment accumulation, even when the sediment is composed of large heavy particles. The linkage of certain phenotypic characters such as small polyps and ramose growth form in the speciose Acroporidae makes it difficult to resolve the importance of some individual characters.

There is little evidence to support hypotheses other than sedimentation as the cause of the changes recorded at Bacuit Bay reefs in 1986. In particular, the losses of coral cover consisting of species predicted by experiments to be most susceptible to sedimentation injury is considered strong supporting evidence that sedimentation was a primary causitive agent.

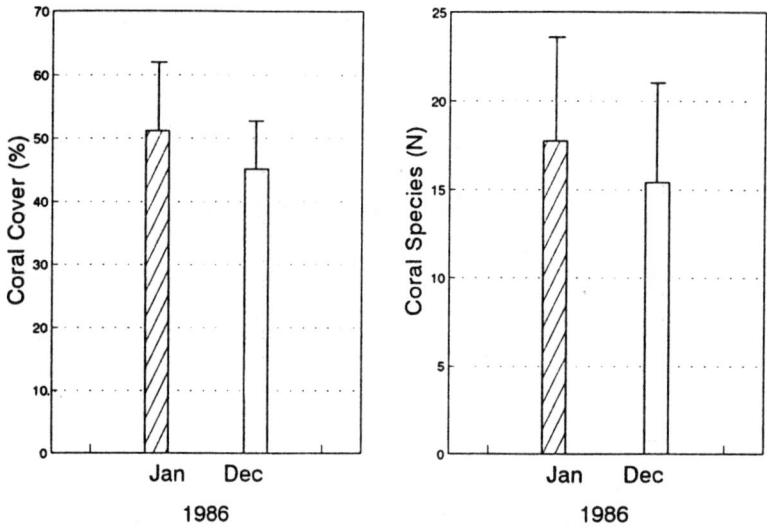

Figure 3. There was a significant decline in mean coral cover and number of species at Stations 1-8 between January and December 1986. Error bar shows S.D., n=5, 10m transects.

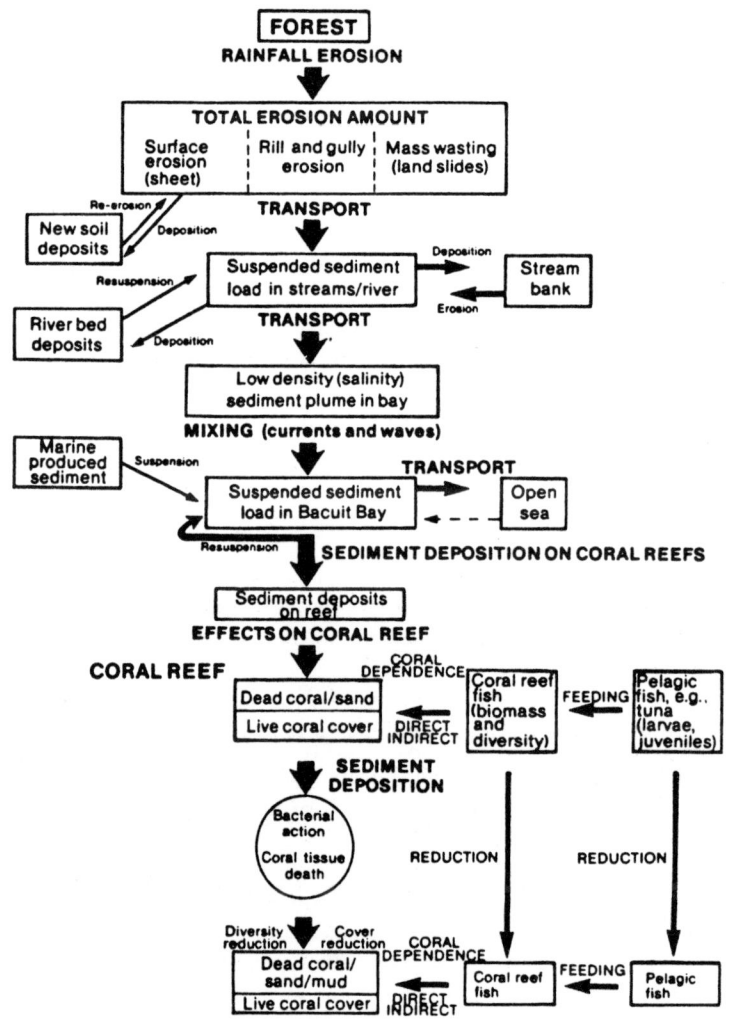

Figure 4. This flow chart indicates the possible pathways of sediment eroded from the El Nido forest, and some potential effects on coral reef communities.

CONCLUSIONS

Logging in the El Nido forest was shown to significantly increase surface erosion of which more than 80% was attributable to roads. Cost-effective erosion control within logging concessions would best be achieved by focusing on the reduction of erosion from roads. Logging significantly increased sediment transport from the drainage basin to Bacuit Bay. Although sediment deposition on most days was significantly increased only at reefs close to the river mouth, on peak discharge days sediment plumes spread out over the bay and deposition was increased to potentially damaging levels (>20 mg/cm^2/day) at all except the control station. Coral cover and number of species declined significantly during the study and the most likely cause was sediment deposition. Coral species shown by experiment to be susceptible to sedimentation injury showed significant mortality. The most susceptible coral species are probably among the least tolerant marine organisms to sedimentation. The study demonstrated the link between the terrestrial and marine ecosystems, and that coastal logging can damage coral reefs by increasing erosion, sediment transport and deposition (Figure 4). The results from El Nido are conservative because only a small fraction of the available forest was logged, logging was not active during the study, and the water volume in Bacuit Bay is relatively large when compared with the discharge volume from the drainage basin. The study confirmed the hypothesis that coastal logging can damage coral reefs and suggests that other forms of land clearing would pose a similar threat. There is potential for large economic losses due to sedimentation damage to coral reefs (Hodgson and Dixon, 1988).

ACKNOWLEDGEMENTS

I am indebted to the many people who assisted in this study. Work was supported primarily by NSF grant INT-8421225 and by the East-West Center.

LITERATURE CITED

Edmondson, C.H. 1928. The ecology of an Hawaiian coral reef. B.P. Bishop Museum Bull. 45.

Guy, H.P. and V.W. Norman. 1970. Field methods for measurement of fluvial sediment. U. S. Geol. Survey Techniques Water-Resources Investig., book 3, chap. c2.

Hamilton, L. and P.N. King. 1983. Tropical forested watersheds. Westview, Boulder, Colorado.

Hodgson, G. 1989. The effects of sedimentation on Indo-Pacific Reef Corals. Dissertation. University of Hawaii, Honolulu. 338 pp.

Hodgson, G. 1990a. The effects of sediment on the settlement of larvae of the reef coral *Pocillopora damicornis*. Coral Reefs. 9:41-43.

Hodgson, G. 1990b. Tetracycline reduces sedimentation damage to corals. Marine Biology. 104:493-496.

Hodgson, G. and J.A. Dixon. 1988. Logging versus fisheries and tourism: environmental and economic dimensions. Occasional Paper No. 7. Environment and Policy Institute, East West Center, Honoluulu, Hawaii, USA 96848. 95 pp.

Hubbard, J.A.E.B. 1973. Sediment shifting experiments: a guide to functional behavior in colonial corals. p. 31-42. In: R.S. Boardman, A.H. Cheetham, W.A. Oliver (eds.) Animal colonies. Dowden, Hutchinson & Ross, Stroudsburg, Pa.

Hubbard, J.A.E.B. and Y.P. Pocock. 1972. Sediment rejection by recent scleractinian corals: a key to paleo-environmental reconstruction. Geolog. Rundsch. 61:598-626.

Loya, Y. 1972. Community structure and species diversity of hermatypic corals at Eilat, Red Sea. Mar. Biol. 13:100-123.

Rogers, C.S. 1990. Responses of coral reefs and reef organisms to sedimentation. Mar. Ecol. Prog. Ser. 62:185-202.

Stafford-Smith, M.G. 1990. The effects of sediments on Australian scleractinian corals. DPhil thesis, University of York, York, UK, 383pp.

Stafford-Smith, M.G. in press. Mortality of the hard coral *Leptoria phrygia* under persistant sediment influx. Proc. 7th Intnl. Coral Reef Symposium, Guam, 1992.

Stafford-Smith, M.G. and R.F.G. Ormond. 1992. Sediment rejection mechanisms of 42 species of Australian scleractinian corals. Australian J. Mar. Freshw. Res. 43:683-705.

Case Histories: A historical perspective of the natural and anthropogenic impacts in the Indonesian Archipelago with a focus on the Kepulauan Seribu, Java Sea.

Tomas Tomascik[1], Suharsono[2], and Anmarie J. Mah[1]

[1] Environmental Management Development in Indonesia (EMDI) Project, Arthaloka building - lantai 12, Jl. Jendral Sudirman 2, Jakarta 10220, Indonesia. [2] Pusat Penelitian dan Pengembangan Oseanologi, Jl. Pasir Putih No. 1, Jakarta Utara, Indonesia.

ABSTRACT

The Indonesian Archipelago with a coastline in excess of 81,000 km consists of some 17,000 islands of various sizes and geologic history. The coral reef ecosystems of the Indonesian Archipelago are considered to be among the most diverse in terms of biodiversity and geomorphology. Environmental degradation is discussed in general terms with a focus on Jakarta Bay and Kepulauan Seribu, a chain of coral cays in the Java Sea approximately 40 km from Jakarta, a metropolis of 9.5 million inhabitants. It is demonstrated that a strong inverse relationship exists between water transparency, a measure of water quality, and a number of coral reef community characteristics as well as coral growth rates. Recent studies suggest that natural disturbances (e.g., El Niño) are greatly exacerbated by anthropogenic impacts. This case history supports the hypothesis that anthropogenic eutrophication is a major forcing function responsible for the demise of scleractinian coral communities in Jakarta Bay. The analysis of historical and current data indicates that acute levels of eutrophication in coral reef ecosystems culminate in an ultimate replacement, a major ecosystem shift, of the animal-algal symbionts by heterotrophic (i.e., filter and deposit feeding) macroinvertebrates.

INTRODUCTION

The Indonesian coral reef ecosystems are highly diverse, rich and indispensable sources of renewable natural resources and amenities, often located in areas of intense economic development. The subsistence and commercial reef fisheries contribute significantly to the national economy. In some parts of Indonesia coral reefs have traditionally served as the fall-back life support systems in times of agricultural crisis (Gordon Claridge 1991, person. comm.). Coral reefs are also valuable tourist attractions generating foreign exchange earnings and local income quite apart from fisheries activities. In many areas, coral reefs protect valuable beach front properties and industrial estates from natural elements of the sea. In addition, there are many social benefits associated with coral reef resources such as support for traditional lifestyles in remote communities throughout the Indonesian Archipelago.

As a result of large scale atmospheric and oceanic processes coral reefs in Indonesia occur throughout the archipelago, however, their greatest development occurs in the eastern part of the archipelago, characterized by clear water free from suspended sediments and excessive freshwater runoff. The Indonesian Archipelago located along the equator is not climatically homogeneous, but rather varies from areas of frequent and intense rainfall (i.e., Irian Jaya), to areas with distinct seasonal shifts between dry and wet (e.g., Nusa Tengara, Java, etc.). The fact that the archipelago lies outside the Indo-Pacific cyclone belt may have had a pronounced influence on the evolution of, and therefore, the function and structure of the coral reef ecosystems in this area. Compared to the Great Barrier Reef province, where cyclones play an important role in the maintenance of high diversity and overall stability of the system, the coral reefs of Indonesia are to a greater degree biologically constrained through biological interactions such as predation, competition, and parasitism. However, in areas of high rainfall and/or volcanic activity, periodic freshwater runoff events, strong pulses of nutrients, lava flows, earthquakes, and tsunamis are important forcing functions.

The focus of this case history is on the coral reefs of Jakarta Bay and Kepulauan Seribu (Fig. 1), an area heavily dependent on coral reef resources in terms of fisheries, sand mining, coral mining and tourism. The synthesis of available data suggests that coral reef communities which have evolved in sedimentary depositional environments (e.g., in close proximity to major rivers), while being relatively resilient with respect to natural environmental impacts, are highly sensitive to environmental impacts associated with a wide spectrum of anthropogenic activities. The case study constitutes a synthesis of previous work done in the Indonesian Archipelago since late 1920s. The quantitative data base used in this case study is derived from a data set produced in 1985 during a UNESCO (COMAR) sponsored regional workshop on the effects of anthropogenic stresses on coral reefs (UNESCO, 1986). Standard techniques were used to measure physical and ecological characteristics of the study reefs (see Harger, 1986, 1992 for further detail). In March 1993, a short field trip was organized to revisit the coral reefs described by Verwey (1931a,b) and Umbgrove (1939) in Jakarta Bay.

RESULTS

"The unrivaled splendor and wealth of forms and the delicate tints of the coral structures, the brilliant colours of fishes, clams, sea anemones, worms, crabs, star fishes and the whole rest of the reef animals are so attractive and interesting that it seems impossible to give an adequate description of such a profusion of serene and fascinating beauty." (Umbgrove, 1939). The author was describing a "thriving reef" surrounding Nyamuk Besar (Leiden) in Jakarta Bay in 1928.

Water Quality. - The strong modifying influence of mainland Java on the 'water quality' of Jakarta Bay and K. Seribu is demonstrated by a strong ($r^2 = 0.76$) inverse relationship between water transparency, as measured by an extinction coefficient k ($k = 1.7/D$; where D is the *secchi disk* depth), and the distance from mainland Java (Fig. 2). In describing thriving coral reefs in Jakarta Bay, Verwey

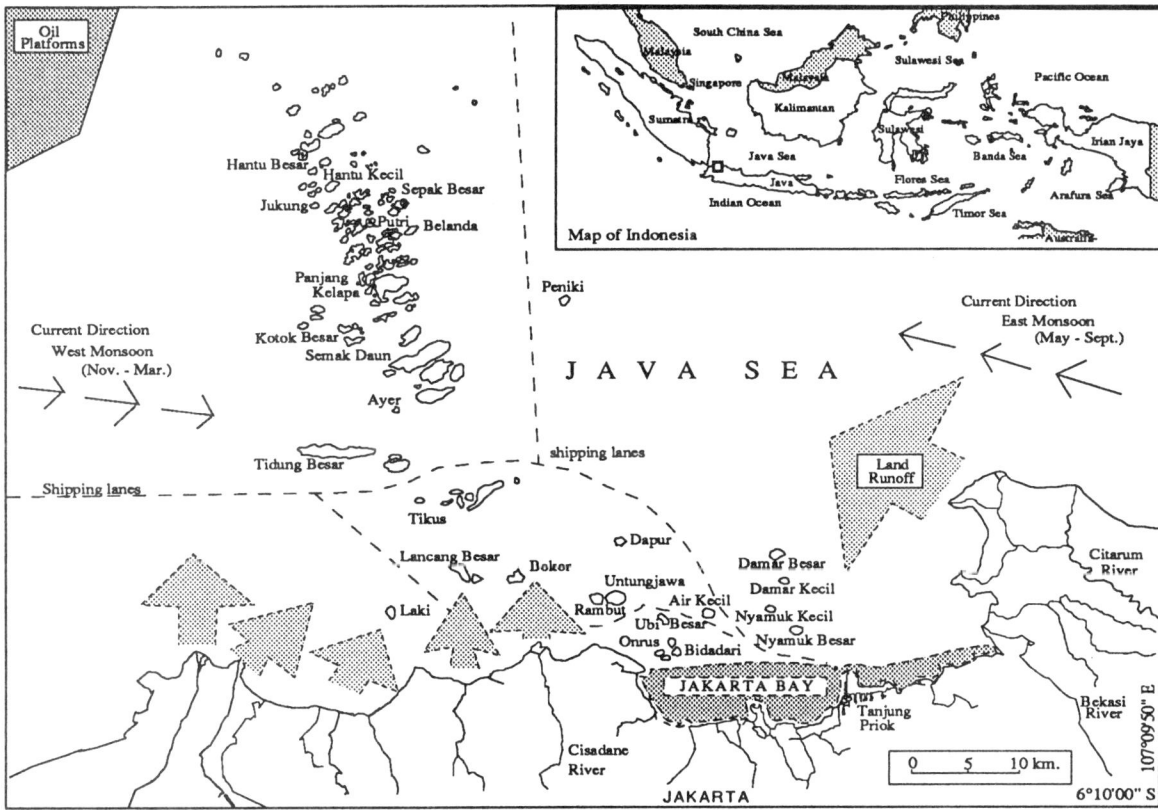

Figure 1. Map of Jakarta Bay, Indonesia. Shading in Jakarta Bay indicates pollution zone.

(1931a) provided some of the earliest information on water transparency in Jakarta Bay through *secchi disk* measurements. Figure 3 provides a temporal and spatial comparison of *secchi disk* depths in Jakarta Bay. The results demonstrate that coral reefs found closer to Java (i.e., Onrus and Kelor) show no difference among the 1929, 1985 and 1993 values, whereas reefs further away from the mainland show a dramatic reduction in water transparency from 1928 to 1993. The historical data suggest that annual land-runoff events during the west monsoon (November-March) are the main forcing function in the development and survival of coral reefs in Jakarta Bay and K. Seribu.

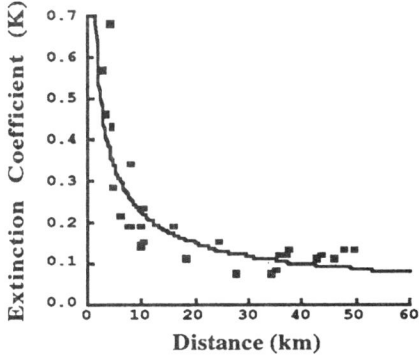

Figure 2. The relationship between extinction coefficient k (k = 1.7/D, where D is the *secchi disk* depth) and the distance from Java. The regression equation is $y = 0.86x^{-0.58}$; $R^2 = 0.76$; $P < 0.000$; $N = 27$. Data from UNESCO, 1986.

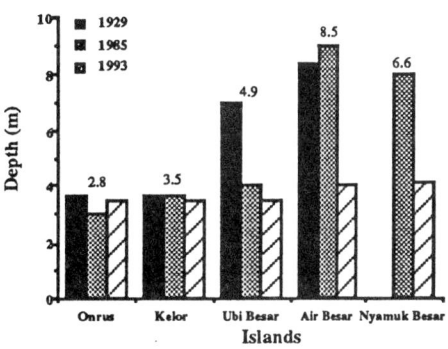

Figure 3. Temporal and spatial comparison of *secchi disk* depths among five coral reefs in Jakarta Bay. The numbers above each column indicate the distance, in km, from Java. Data from Verwey (1931a) and UNESCO (1986).

Review of historical data indicates that Jakarta Bay has become progressively more eutrophic. Table 1 presents a comparison of nutrient concentrations in Jakarta Bay and K. Seribu since 1969. Compared to other parts of the world where eutrophication is a major concern (Bell and Tomascik, this Colloquium), the nutrient concentrations may be considered as extreme.

Table 1. Temporal comparison of average nutrient concentrations (±SD) in the general area of Jakarta Bay from 1964 to 1992. The data are for trend illustration only.

Nutrients	1964 - 1973[1]	1975 - 1978[2]	1985[3]	1992[4]
$PO_4 - P$ (µg-at/l)	0.67 ± 0.32	0.36 ± 0.15	1.09 ± 0.93	1.36 ± 1.35
$NO_3 - N$ (µg-at/l)	0.48 ± 0.22	0.62 ± 0.63	1.41 ± 1.00	2.71 ± 2.70

Data modified from: [1] Institute of Marine Research, 1971, 1973a,b; [2] Ilahude and Liasaputra, 1980; [3] Tjutju, 1988; [4] Siswanto, 1992.

High nutrient concentrations in Jakarta Bay and K. Seribu have been identified as the main cause of increased primary productivity of the surface waters. Chlorophyll *a* concentrations measured in Jakarta Bay in 1977 (Setiapermana *et al.*, 1980) ranged from 1.02 to 3.39 mg/m^3, while Nontji (1978) recorded chlorophyll a concentrations between 5.41 to 12.3 mg/m^3, and suspended particulate matter concentrations in the range of 10 to 79.6 mg/l between 1975 and 1976. Praseno and Andan (1978) documented massive diatom blooms (e.g. mean of 102.24x10^3 cells/l in January 1977).

Harger (1992) has recently demonstrated that phytoplankton biomass distributions in Jakarta Bay, measured from 1986 to 1990, have undergone significant shifts (i.e., phytoplankton blooms are now spreading further offshore). In 1986 massive algal blooms were detected only within 2 km from Tanjuk Priok (Jakarta's port). However, in 1988 the blooms spread out to 5 km offshore, and in 1990 massive algal concentrations were measured 12 km from the port (Harger, 1992).

Jakarta Bay - Community and Environmental Interactions

Anthropogenic influences - Since k is a function of suspended particulate matter concentrations (SPM) in the water column, it is expected that there should be a strong relationship between k and a number of coral community characteristics. Indeed, Fig. 4 and 5 demonstrate a strong inverse relationship between k and two coral community characteristics, namely the % coral cover ($r^2 = 0.58$) and the Shannon-Weaver's index of diversity H ($r^2 = 0.48$).

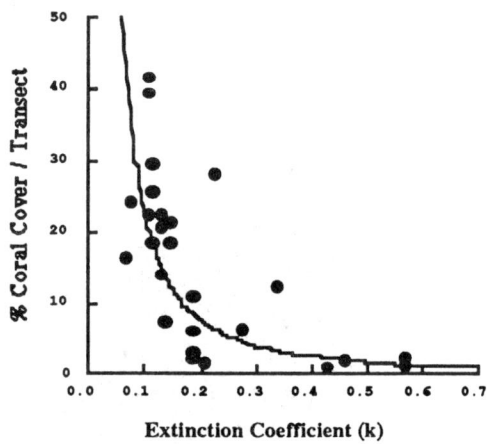

Figure 4. The relationship between the percentage coral cover and water transparency (k= 1.7/D; D is the *secchi disk* depth) in K. Seribu. The regression equation for the relationship is: y=0.55x$^{-1.62}$; R^2=0.58,; P<0.000; N=27. Data from UNESCO, 1986.

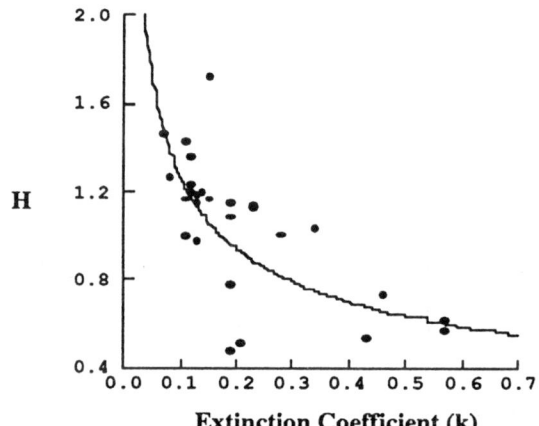

Figure 5. The relationship between the Shannon-Weaver's index of diversity (H), based on abundance, and water transparency (k). The regression equation is: y=0.48x$^{-0.43}$; R^2=0.48; P<0.000; N=27. Data from UNESCO, 1986.

The re-analysis of historical data also revealed a strong negative relationship between k and coral growth rates in K. Seribu and Jakarta Bay. Figure 6 demonstrates a significant ($r^2 = 0.27$; P<0.02) inverse relationship between water transparency (k) and the growth rates of *Porites lutea*. To demonstrate that water transparency is a key environmental factor affecting the vertical distribution of corals as well as the maximum depth of a "functional" coral community, a regression analysis (power function) was performed on the measured maximum depth of functional reef and k. The results demonstrate (Fig. 7) that the maximum depth of a 'functional' coral reef is a strong function ($r^2 = 0.78$) of water transparency, and therefore, water quality. The significant reduction in water transparency (Fig. 3) is paralleled by a dramatic reduction of the maximum depth of a coral community from 1929 to 1993 (Fig. 8).

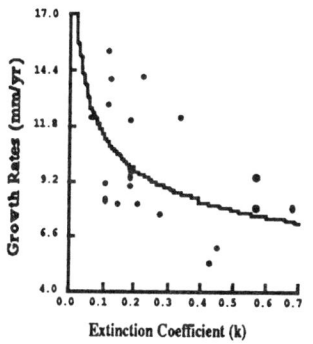

Figure 6. *Porites lutea*. Average yearly growth rates of *P. lutea* versus water transparency (k = 1.7/D; D is *secchi disk* depth) in K. Seribu. The regression equation is: $y = 6.64x^{-0.23}$; $R^2=0.27$, P < 0.02; N = 27. Data from Scoffin, 1986.

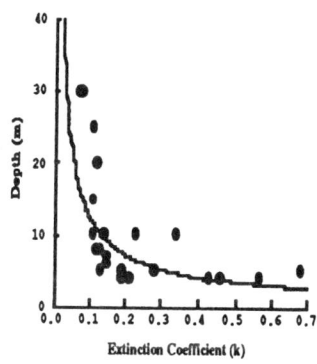

Figure 7. The relationship between the maximum depth of a functional coral reef and water transparency as measured by a *secchi disk* depth. The regression equation is $y = 2.08x^{-0.78}$; $R^2 = 0.49$; P < 0.00004; N=27. Data from UNESCO, 1986.

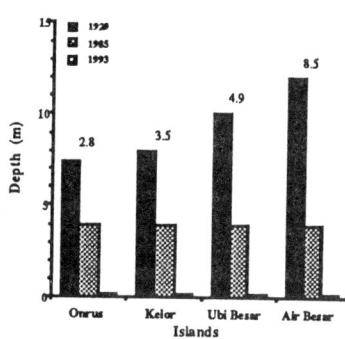

Figure 8. Temporal and spatial comparison of maximum depth of living coral reef among four islands in Jakarta Bay. Numbers above columns are the distance, in km, from Java. Data from Verwey (1931a) and UNESCO (1986).

Natural perturbations. - Since the Indonesian Archipelago lies outside the Indo-Pacific cyclone belt, coral reefs in Jakarta Bay and K. Seribu are relatively free of major physical perturbations associated with cyclones or major storms. However, in 1983 a major ENSO-event took place with some major impacts on reefs worldwide. In March 1983, sea surface temperatures in Jakarta Bay and K. Seribu increased 2 to 4°C above ambient levels for a period of six months. The ENSO-event was responsible for wide scale bleaching, which was however restricted to the reef flat zone (Suharsono, 1990). No bleaching was observed below the depth of 3 m. However, 70 to 90% of coral bleached on the reef flat suffered mortality (Suharsono, 1990). Figure 9 serves to demonstrate that there was a measurable decrease in both coral abundance and species diversity in 1983 - the ENSO year. The data indicate that there has been no 'significant' recovery in coral diversity, while coral abundance (i.e., number of colonies) has reached the pre ENSO-event. Figure 10 demonstrates that while both percentage coral cover and coral diversity based on coral coverage (i.e., H'c) declined during the 1983 ENSO-event, only the percentage coral cover has returned to the pre ENSO-event levels.

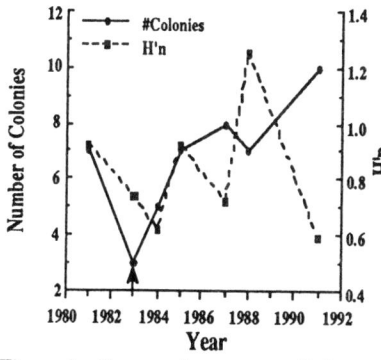

Figure 9. Temporal sequence of changes in coral abundance and H'n (Shannon-Weaver's index of diversity based on colony counts) since the 1983 ENSO (dark arrow) event in K. Seribu. Both abundance (i.e., number of colonies) and H'n are average values based on three (3) permanent 30 m line transects located on a reef flat in Pulau Pari (Suharsono, 1990).

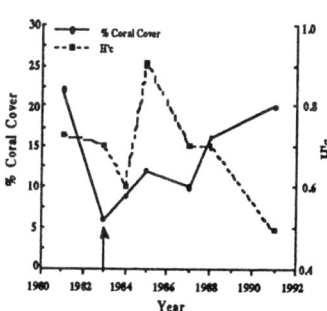

Figure 10. Temporal sequence of changes in the percent coral cover and H'c (Shannon-Weaver's index of diversity based on coral cover) since the 1983 ENSO (dark arrow) event in K. Seribu.. Both percent coral cover and H'c are average values based on three (3) permanent 30 m line transects located on a reef flat in Pulau Pari. Data from Suharsono 1990.

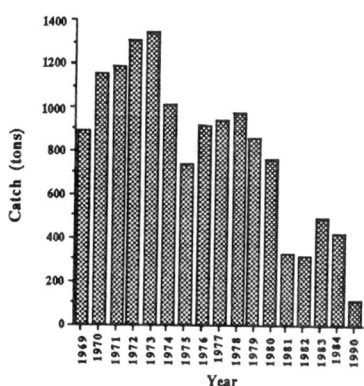

Figure 11. The recent history of declining fish landings (i.e., total catch in tons) from the *muro-ami* reef fishery in K. Seribu. Fish landings from 1985 to 1989 were not available. Data from Subani and Wahyono (1987); and Dinas Perikanan (1990).

DISCUSSION

The coral reef communities in Jakarta Bay are examples "par excellence" of the terminal stage of coral reef eutrophication. The coral reefs of Jakarta Bay and K. Seribu evolved and developed in marine depositional environments, and as such, one would expect them to be well adapted to the seasonal fluxes of land derived sediments and the associated influx of nutrients. Verwey (1931a) was the first to provide concrete data to demonstrate that there was a strong negative relationship between water transparency and the maximum depth of the living reef. Applying regression analysis to Verwey's (1931a) data (*secchi disk* readings converted to k), we obtain the following multiplicative regression model for the 1929 data: $y = 3.74x^{-0.76}$; $r^2 = 0.92$; $P < 0.04$; where y is the maximum depth of the living reef and x is *k* (i.e., water transparency). The striking feature of this relationship is that while the slope of the regression equation is not statistically discernible from the slope in the regression equation in Fig. 7, the y intercept of the former is statistically ($P<0.01$) higher than the y intercept of the latter. This further supports our contention that the maximum depth of a functional coral reef community has been dramatically reduced since 1929.

The data support the hypothesis that sedimentation has been a major forcing function in coral reef development in Jakarta Bay and K. Seribu. Verwey (1932b) suggested that the reef development in Jakarta Bay is made possible by the combination of sedimentation and hydrologic conditions of the area. Verwey (1931a) also recorded clear seasonal patterns and large variations in water transparency in the western part of Jakarta Bay. The high seasonal variability in water transparency was also reported by Verstappen (1953), who, in his 1951 study, showed that water transparency near Nyamuk Besar ranged from 6 to 12 m during the east monsoon (May-September), and between 4 to 6 m during the west monsoon (November-March). Data in Fig. 3 suggest that land-runoff has played a significant, not necessarily detrimental, role in structuring of coral communities in Jakarta Bay.

Verstappen (1953) postulated that most of the silt in Jakarta Bay originates from the Citerum river, since fine-grained sediments are restricted to the eastern part of the bay, with a sharp boundary just west of Nyamuk Besar, Damar Besar, Damar Kecil, and Nyamuk Kecil (Fig. 1). Fine-grained sediments observed west of Ubi Besar are thought to originate from the Cisadane river (Fig. 1). The watersheds of these rivers have undergone major changes in land use and drainage patterns. Umbgrove (1947) points out the fact that the coast line along the western part of Jakarta Bay grew between 200 to 600 m seaward within a period of 30 years.

In 1929 the reefs in the western part of Jakarta Bay were live, "thriving reefs" (Umbgrove, 1939). Umbgrove (1939) recorded 96 coral species from Nyamuk Besar (Fig. 1). Today, only two reefs have 'some' coral colonies. Out of the 96 coral species described by Umbgrove (1939), only 16 species remain and these have very low abundance. Umbgrove (1939) made a qualitative description of Nyamuk Besar, and at the time, the reef was characterized by a prominent *Montipora digitata* ("*ramosa* ") and *M. foliosa* facies. Umbgrove (1939) referred to *M. digitata* (*ramosa*) as "the moat coral par excellence". Today, none of these remain! The large moat of *Acropora aspera* present in 1928 has disappeared as well. Based on historical and current evidence, it is clear that the once "thriving reefs" of Batavia Bay (Umbgrove, 1939) are 'functionally' dead at the present. Clearly, something other than, or in addition to, the natural siltation must have played a significant role in their demise. Data in Fig. 3 suggest that land runoff has increased to such an extent that the river runoff, with its assortment of industrial, agricultural and urban wastes, now reaches further out to sea.

However, pollution and increased land runoff are not the only anthropogenic stresses affecting the reefs in K. Seribu. Verwey (1931b) observed that rapid abrasion of coral cays in Jakarta Bay was a result of coral extraction for road works and construction in Jakarta. It was estimated that approximately 8500 m^3 of coral was being extracted from the reefs. It should be pointed out that the coral mining, then and now, occurs on the shallow reef flats. Ongkosongko and Sukarno (1986) reported that in 1982 approximately 840,000 m^3 (re-analyzed data) of coral was extracted from the reefs.

This massive assault on the reefs is reflected in reduced abundance and diversity of coral reef fishes throughout the island chain (see Sukarno, 1989 for review). Coral reef fish in Jakarta Bay are in very low abundance, and are totally absent from Bidadari, Onrus and Kelor (Fig. 1). However, these reefs have an unusual abundance of benthic crabs (e.g., *Eriphia smithi*, *Ategratis integerrimus*, *Carpilius maculatus* and *Lophozozymus pictor*), indicating an ecosystem shift. Whether the low abundance of coral reef fish is a direct result of over-fishing or the demise of coral communities, or a combination of the two, is an important management question in need of an answer.

The demise of the coral reef communities in Jakarta Bay, and the continuous degradation of reefs in the K. Seribu, is having a dramatic impact on reef fisheries in K. Seribu. Figure 11 illustrates the dramatic reduction in fisheries landings since 1969. In 1990, the total value of the reef fishery (i.e., *muro-ami*) in K. Seribu was estimated at US$ 90,000 (Dinas Perikanan, 1992). This translates to approximately US$ 450 per fisherman per year. Approximately 80% of the catch consists of *Caesio cuning* and *C. lunaris*, both reef associated fish species. It should also be pointed out that *muro-ami* is a very destructive fishing technique. Considering the multi-million dollar tourism industry in K. Seribu, which depends heavily on the continued existence of live coral reefs, the destructive muro-ami fishery clearly needs to be re-evaluated by the managing agencies of the K. Seribu Marine National Park. To what degree have destructive fishing techniques, such as *muro-ami* and reef blasting, contributed to the demise of coral reefs in K. Seribu is speculative, but it is clear that these practices cannot continue for long.

This case history documents a major ecosystem-wide change that has been taking place in Jakarta Bay since 1929. In 1929 the living reefs extended down to 15 m, today none of the coral reefs in Jakarta Bay can be considered as functional coral reef communities. Figure 12 illustrates the current structure of the water column in Jakarta Bay and the general reef profile.

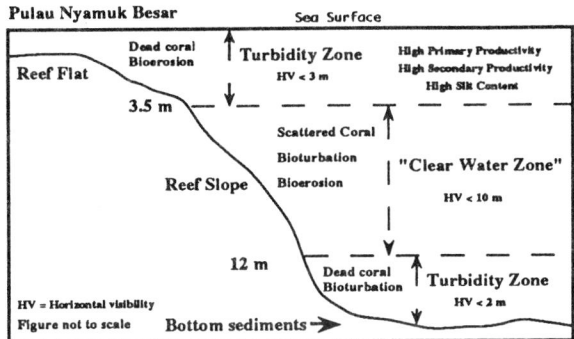

Figure 12. An example of a general reef profile and water column structure, in terms of water clarity, in Jakarta Bay and the summary of major ecological processes that have a direct and/or indirect impact on water transparency. The reef profile and the water column structure illustrated are 6.6 km from Java.

Figure 12 illustrates the existence of two major turbidity zones. The surface turbidity zone (STZ) is associated with high phytoplankton biomass, which, during the west monsoon, is mixed with silt from land runoff. High nutrient concentrations are currently supporting high biomass of 'nuisance' dinoflagellates, mainly *Noctiluca*. The bottom turbidity zone (BTZ) is a result of increased bioturbation. The continual rain of autochthonous and allochthonous detritus has considerably enhanced the benthic macroinvertebrate productivity in the area. The BTZ moves further up the reef slope during periods of heavy seas, when wave energies cause resuspension of bottom sediments. Sandwiched between the STZ and the BTZ is a narrow 'clear water zone' (CWZ). The widest CWZ was measured at Nyamuk Besar, 6.6 km from the mainland. As one moves progressively inshore, the CWZ shrinks, until finally, as in the case of Onrus and Bidadari, the STZ merges with BTZ.

The coral reefs of Jakarta Bay are now functionally dead. The animal-algal symbiont associations, characteristic of coral reef ecosystems, have been replaced by a benthic heterotrophic community dominated by filter feeding and deposit feeding benthos, characteristic of muddy environments. The reef matrix is now perforated by a great profusion of boring organisms dominated by the bivalve *Lithophaga* spp. However, boring sponges are very rare. It is hypothesized that the absence of sponges is a result of high suspended particulate matter concentrations in the water column, which may "suffocate" filter feeders, such as sponges, with a fine mesh filtering apparatus (i.e., small incurrrent pores). Bioerosion, on a massive scale, is currently the main bio-physical process that is contributing to a rapid destruction of the reef matrix. In addition to the boring organisms there is an abundance of benthic mollusks (e.g., *Cypraea tigris* and *Chicoreus ramosus*) and stingrays (*Taeniura lymma*) characteristic of the deeper, muddier parts of the reef slope.

Scoffin (1986) reported an abundance of turf algae as well as *Diadema* on most of the reefs in Jakarta Bay. Data from UNESCO (1986) show that benthic turf algae covered between 37% to 78% of the available substrate. Currently all *Diadema* and the turf algae are missing from Bidadari, Onrus and Kelor, reefs closest to Java. Nyamuk Besar and Air Besar were the only reefs with a few *Diadema setosum* and *Echinotrix diadema*, with only a sparse cover of turf algae. The coralline algae, a fundamental component of a functional reef (Bell, 1992), have been virtually eliminated from these systems.

CONCLUSIONS

Jakarta Bay is not an isolated case of reef degradation, now a worldwide phenomenon. A similar process of reef degradation associated with eutrophication is currently occurring in Barbados, West Indies (Bell and Tomascik, this Colloquium). However, in comparison to the Barbados reefs, the reefs in Jakarta Bay have been effectively destroyed. Based on the data presented in this case history, it can be argued that since most coral reef communities in the archipelago have evolved in regions of relative environmental stability (i.e., small fluctuations in environmental conditions - e.g., temperature or salinity, and intermediate disturbances such as storms and land runoff), they lack the plasticity to tolerate (either at a molecular, organism, population or community level), or to adapt to, the wide spectrum of bio-physico-chemical stresses associated with eutrophication processes and anthropogenic activities. It is therefore essential that sound management guidelines are developed and implemented for all coastal development projects in coral reef areas. Furthermore, it is imperative that all current reef monitoring programs incorporate a comprehensive environmental component into the design matrix. However, monitoring for reef deterioration, and the development of new statistics to deal with high variability, will not prevent the demise of coastal reef ecosystems, but ecologically sound management practices and coastal development based on sustainable principles just might.

ACKNOWLEDGMENTS

The authors wish to acknowledge the support of the Environmental Management Development in Indonesia (EMDI) project through its *Ecology of Indonesian Seas* book component. The EMDI project is a joint project of the Indonesian Ministry of State for Population and Environment, and the School for Resource and Environmental Studies, Dalhousie University, Canada. Funding for the EMDI project is from the Canadian International Development Agency (CIDA). We express our great appreciation to Dr. J. R. E. Harger, UNESCO, Jakarta, for the UNESCO data base. Errol Billing kindly provided the templates for the maps and invaluable assistance with computers.

REFERENCES

Bell, P.R.F. 1992. Eutrophication and coral reefs - some examples in the Great Barrier Reef lagoon. Water Research 26(5): 553-568.

Dinas Perikanan. 1990. Analisis usaha penangkapan ikan muro ami. Laporan Akhir, Dinas Perikanan DKI Jakarta, Fakultas Perikanan IBP Bogor. 142 pp.

Harger, J.R.E. 1992. Environment trends and reef monitoring strategies. Proc. 7th Int. Coral Reef Symp. Guam, 22-26 June 1992 (in press)

Harger, J.R.E. 1986. Community structure as a response to natural and man-made environmental variables in the Pulau Seribu island chain. pp 34-85 *in* S. Soemodihardjo ed. Proceedings of MAB~COMAR Regional Workshop on Coral Reef Ecosystems: Their Management Practices and Research/Training Needs. UNESCO: MAB~COMAR and LIPI, Jakarta.

Ilahude, A.G. and S. Liasaputra. 1980. Sebaran "normal" parameter hidrologi di Teluk Jakarta. pp 1-47 *In* A. Nontji and A. Djamali, eds. Teluk Jakarta: Pengkajian Fisika, Kimia, Biologi dan Geologi, Tahun 1975-1979. LIPI, Jakarta.

Institute of Marine Research. 1971. Oceanographical cruise report (1963 - 1966). Special Issue. National Institute of Oceanology, Indonesian Institute of Sciences, Jakarta.

Institute of Marine Research. 1973a. Hydrological, plankton and pigment observations in the South China Sea and around Seribu Islands by R.V. Samudra, July 22-Aug 2, 1972. Institute of Marine Research Oceanographical Cruise Report 9. National Institute of Oceanology, Jakarta.

Institute of Marine Research. 1973b. Hydrological, plankton and pigment observations in the Jakarta Bay and the South China Sea by R.V. Samudra June 29-July17, 1973. Institute of Marine Research Oceanographical Cruise Report 12. National Institute of Oceanology, Jakarta.

Moll, H, and Suharsono. 1986. Distribution, diversity and abundance of reef corals in Jakarta Bay and Kepulauan Seribu. pp 112-125 *in* B.E. Brown ed. Human induced damage to coral reefs: Results of a regional UNESCO (COMAR) workshop with advanced training. UNESCO Reports in Marine Science 40.

Nontji, A. 1978. Variasi musiman beberapa factor ekologi di perairan Teluk Jakarta. Oseanologi di Indonesia 11: 27-36.

Ongkosongo, O.S.R. 1986. Some harmful stresses to the Seribu coral reefs, Indonesia. pp 133-142 *in* S. Soemodihardjo ed. Proceedings of MAB~COMAR Regional Workshop on Coral Reef Ecosystems: Their Management Practices and Research/Training Needs. UNESCO: MAB~COMAR and LIPI, Jakarta

Ongkosongo, O.S.R. and Sukarno. 1986. Background to the study sites in the Bay of Jakarta and Kepulauan Seribu. pp 56-79 *in* B.E. Brown ed. Human induced damage to coral reefs: Results of a regional UNESCO (COMAR) workshop with advanced training. UNESCO Reports in Marine Science 40.

Praseno, D.P. and Q. Amdan. 1978. *Noctiluca miliaris* SURIRAY perairan Teluk Jakarta. Oseanologi di Indonesia 11: 1-25.

Scoffin, T.P. 1986. Banding in coral skeletons from Pulau Seribu as revealed by x-rays and U/V light analyses. pp 126-134 *in* B. E. Brown, ed. Human induced damage to coral reefs: Results of a regional UNESCO (COMAR) workshop with advanced training. UNESCO Reports in Marine Science 40.

Setiapermana, D., A. Nontji and B.S. Sudibyo. 1980. Klorofil fitoplankton di Teluk Jakarta. pp 99-106 *In* A. Nontji and A. Djamali, eds. Teluk Jakarta: Pengkajian Fisika, Kimia, Biologi dan Geologi, Tahun 1975-1979. LIPI, Jakarta.

Siswanto, E. 1992. Kadar nitrat, fosfat, oksigen terlaryt dan struktur komunitas fitoplankton di perairan teluk Jakarta bagian barat. Fakultas Perikanan, Institute Pertanian Bogor. 72 pp.

Subani, W. and M. M. Wahyono. 1987. Kerusakan ekosistem perairan pantai dan dampaknya terhadap sumberdaya perikanan di pantai selatan Bali, barat dan timur Lombok dan Teluk Jakarta. Jurnal Pen. Perikanan Laut 42: 53-70.

Suharsono. 1990. Ecological and physiological implication of coral bleaching at Pari Island, Thousand Islands, Indonesia. Ph.D. Thesis. University of Newcastle upon Tyne. 279 pp.

Soekarno, R. 1989. Comparative studies on the status of Indonesian coral reefs. Netherlands Journal of Sea Research 23(2): 215-222.

Sukarno, N. Naamin and M. Hutomo. 1986. The status of coral reef in Indonesia. pp 24-33 *in* S. Soemodihardjo ed. Proceedings of MAB~COMAR Regional Workshop on Coral Reef Ecosystems: Their Management Practices and Research/Training Needs. UNESCO: MAB~COMAR, LIPI, Jakarta.

Tjutju, S. 1988. Pengaruh PLTU Muara Karang terhadap kadar fosfat dan nitrat di perairan Muara Karang. Pages 112-118 *In* M.K. Moosa, D.P. Praseno and Sukarno, eds. Teluk Jakarta. Biologi, Budidaya, Oseanografi, Geologi dan Kondisi Perairan. LIPI, Jakarta.

Umbgrove, J.H.F. 1928. De Koraalriffen in de haai van Batavia (with summary in English). Wetenschappelijke Mededeelingen Nr. 7.

Umbgrove, J.H.F. 1939. Madreporaria from the Bay of Batavia. Zoölogische Mededeelingen XXII: 1-64.

Umbgrove, J.H.F. 1947. Coral reef in the East Indies. Bull. Geol. Soc. Amer. 58: 729-778.

UNESCO. 1986. Human induced damage to coral reefs: Results of a regional UNESCO (COMAR) workshop with advanced training, Diponegoro University, Jepara and National Institute of Oceanology, Jakarta, Indonesia, May 1985. Brown, B.E (ed.). UNESCO Reports in Marine Science 40, France. 180 pp.

Verstappen, H.T. 1953. Djakarta Bay, a geomorphological study on shoreline development. Ph.D. Thesis. Utrecht, 101 pp.

Verwey, J. 1931a. Coral reef studies. II. The depth of coral reefs in relation to their oxygen consumption and the penetration of light in the water. Treubia 13(2): 169-198.

Verwey, J. 1931b. Coral reef studies. III. Geomorphological notes on the coral reefs of Batavia Bay. Treubia 13(2): 199-215.

STATUS OF CORAL REEFS IN SOUTHEAST ASIA: THREATS AND RESPONSES

C.R. Wilkinson[1], L.M. Chou[2], E. Gomez[3], A.R. Ridzwan[4], S. Soekarno[5], S. Sudara[6]

[1]Australian Institute of Marine Science, P.M.B. No. 3, Townsville M.C. Q 4810, Australia. [2]Department of Zoology, National University of Singapore, Singapore 0511. [3]Marine Science Institute, University of the Philippines, Diliman, Quezon City 1101 Philippines. [4]Fac Fisheries and Marine Science, Universiti Pertanian Malaysia, Malaysia. [5]Indonesian Institute of Science LIPI, Jl. Gatot Subroto 10, Jakarta 12710 Indonesia. [6]Department of Marine Science, Chulalongkorn University, Bangkok, Thailand.

ABSTRACT

Coral reefs of southeast Asia are **both** at the center of reef biodiversity, especially the archipelagos of Indonesia and the Philippines, and the focus of rapid economic and population growth. This latter growth places increasing pressures on reef resources, such that the ecosystems are close to collapse, with some reefs already destroyed and many species likely to become extinct. The major stresses are anthropogenic: organic and inorganic pollution, sedimentation and over-exploitation. Over-exploitation is exacerbated because dynamite and muro-ami fishing is used frequently to capture the few remaining fishes. Many of countries have enacted strong legislation to protect coral reefs and gazetted some marine protected areas, however, the resources are neither available nor of sufficient priority to ensure adequate protection of their coral reefs. There is evidence that many reefs have already collapsed. Because human populations are expanding and economies are growing, it is predicted that most of the coral reefs in the region will be exterminated within the next 40 years. This situation will only be prevented if governments provide: resources for education for sustainable exploitation practices; management of large areas; and the authority at the local government level for the protection and management of the coral reefs by the people who directly use them.

INTRODUCTION

Southeast Asian contains approximately 30% of the world's coral reef area of 617,000 km^2. These reefs are of particular significance because the region is at the centre of coral biodiversity with the two island archipelagos of Indonesia and the Philippines having the richest diversity of coral species (Veron, 1986) and probably of all other coral reef biota as well e.g. fish (Thresher, 1991).

Southeast Asia is a major center of global economic growth, featuring the new 'economic tigers'; Thailand, Malaysia and Singapore, and Indonesia, the fifth most populous country in the world (Table 1). The Indochina countries will undoubtedly expand their economies rapidly when political stability is assured. Populations are generally stabilising at or below 1.5 to 2.0% increase, except for the Philippines (at 2.5%), where religious pressures inhibit population control programs, and Malaysia (2.6%), which is seeking to increase its population to enhance economic power. The combination of large populations and rapid economic growth is putting great pressures onto coral reef resources. As economies expand and personal incomes improve, demand increases for protein rich foods, which result in greater extraction of fish and other food from the reefs. Already approximately 60% of the regions' animal protein comes from the adjacent seas (Yong, 1989). Fisheries are expanding beyond the nearshore resources to far flung reefs. The Gulf of Thailand fishery is close to collapse and only through increasing the effort by building larger boats that venture further is a marketable catch maintained (p. 49 in World Resources Institute, 1992). Likewise, many Indonesian fishermen from Sulawesi are regularly apprehended fishing illegally on the coral reefs off northwest Australia and a recent report states that the remote Scarborough Reef, 220 km west of the Philippine island of Luzon has been effectively denuded of fish and much of the live coral cover through dynamite and muro ami fishing within the last 2 years (Collard and Collard, 1992).

Large human populations are behind the major stresses that are causing destruction of southeast Asian coral reefs: organic and inorganic pollution from sewage, agricultural and industrial wastes; sediment damage from excessive deforestation, agriculture and land clearing for commercial crops such as rubber and oil palm; over-exploitation, particularly through destructive fishing methods; and pollution by oil, hydrocarbons, complex organic molecules and heavy metals.

Table 1. Population and economic parameters for Southeast Asian countries derived principally from World Resources Institute (1992). For comparison Gross National Product growth for Australia and the USA is 3.0% and 2.6% respectively with fish consumption 18.2 and 21.3 kg per annum. -, data not available.

Country	Population millions	Population change %		GNP per capita $US'000	GNP growth %	Coastline 1000 km	Seafood per capita
		1990	2000				
Burma/Myanmar	44.29	2.09	2.00	-	2.3	3.06	15.3
Cambodia	8.87	2.48	1.75	-	-	0.44	9.1
Indonesia	194.95	1.93	1.60	0.49	6.5	54.72	14.0
Malaysia	19.31	2.64	1.85	2.13	5.7	4.68	30.1
Philippines	67.07	2.49	2.05	0.70	1.8	22.54	33.8
Singapore	2.82	1.25	0.84	10.45	7.2	0.19	29.6
Thailand	58.26	1.53	1.32	1.17	7.3	3.22	20.8
Vietnam	70.99	2.15	2.03	0.22	5.3	3.44	13.0

METHODS

Data for 5 ASEAN countries are drawn from literature published by the ASEAN-Australia Marine Science Project: Living Coastal Resources and reports presented to the Project Management Committee (Gomez *et al.*, 1982; Sudara *et al.*, 1988; ASEAN-Australia Marine Science Project, 1992). The project, funded since 1984 by the Australian International Development Assistance Bureau, has accumulated the largest (spatial) database on reef status in the world (Wilkinson *et al.*, 1993). The reef classification in Fig. 1 is that used in Wilkinson (1993). Categories are based on the percent cover of live coral, the fish populations and the amount of anthropogenic stress. Additional data for these classifications are drawn from the assessments of global reef resources by UNEP/IUCN (1988), other published material, as well as anecdotal evidence and personal observations.

RESULTS

Brunei Darussalam, Burma, Cambodia, Vietnam

There are few reefs associated with these countries because of the high turbidity of the coastal waters. There are some reefs on offshore islands remote from land influence, but they are poorly studied (UNEP/IUCN, 1988). In Brunei, Chou *et al.* (1992) report that coral cover on nearshore reefs is about 30-40% and relatively rich in both coral and fish species, with relatively low fishing pressure. The best reefs in Burma occur towards the border with Thailand where river influence is much reduced. Reefs of the Mergui Archipelago are reported to be in relatively good condition (Sudara, pers. comm.) although many of the larger reef associated animals, such as turtles are unsustainably exploited (UNEP/IUCN, 1988). Vietnamese coral reefs have suffered extensive sediment damage (UNEP/IUCN, 1988), but on some of the offshore reefs, coral growth does extend down to 20 m with reasonably high coral diversity (Titlyanov and Latypov, 1991).

Indonesia

Coral reefs in Indonesia occur over an extensive area (45 degrees of longitude and 18 degrees of latitude) and constitute the most significant reef resource in southeast Asia. The condition of these reefs varies quite widely: reefs near the large population areas of Java and Sumatra show severe damaged from over-exploitation and sediment and organic pollution and many have been mined out of existence (Brown, 1986); whereas reefs in far eastern and northeastern Indonesia are reportedly in excellent condition. Reefs in central Indonesia have been heavily exploited with damaging practices common. The reefs in western Indonesia are under greater influence of anthropogenic stresses and coastal water circulation, such that they have been classified as **critical** category with more degradation the probable outcome as populations continue to grow along with more extensive clearing of forests.

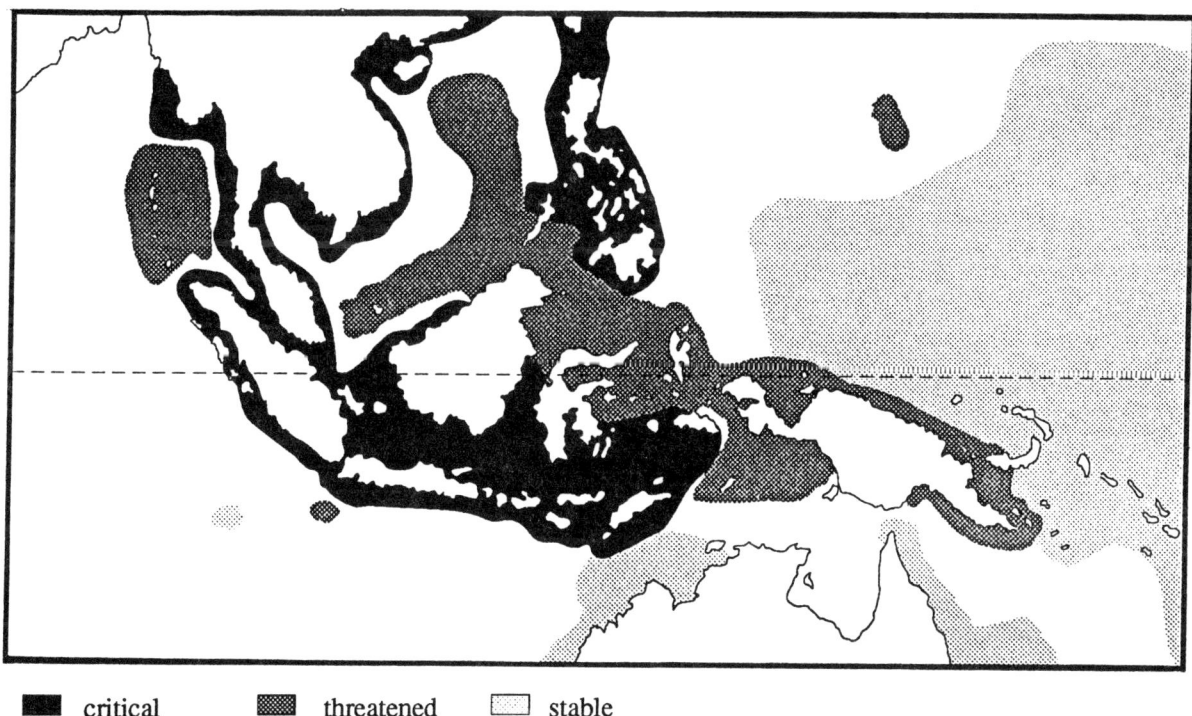

■ critical ▓ threatened ☐ stable

Figure 1. Distribution of coral reefs in southeast Asia categorised into three classes: **critical**: reefs that are obviously damaged and are likely to collapse as coral reef ecosystems within 10-20 years unless the current levels of anthropogenic stress are removed or diverted; **threatened**: reefs that are currently under increasing levels of stress, such that they will collapse within 20-40 years, if populations and associated stresses continue to increase at current rates; **stable**: reefs under low anthropogenic stress with no imminent threats of ecosystem collapse, which should remain healthy in the immediate future (100s-1,000s of years) except for unpredictable events like massive global climate change or large meteor strike.

The reefs of Pulau Seribu are a particularly valuable resource for Java as they provide fishery products for Jakarta, and constitute a considerable focus for Indonesian and international tourists. These reefs are, however, being heavily degraded by pollution from the mainland as well as excessive exploitation of fishery stocks, with dynamite fishing still evident. Coral cover (Table 2) and fish stocks are low. In central Indonesia, the reefs are also classified as **critical**, principally because of over-fishing. Many of the reefs in this area occur in clean oceanic waters away from centers of population, but are visited regularly by fishermen. A recent survey of the remote Taka Bone Rate atoll group (between Sulawesi and Lombok) by the Canadian EMDI group showed that blast damage was extensive, along with over collecting of invertebrates (J. Alder, pers. comm.). Coral cover and fish populations were low. In eastern Indonesia, however, the reefs have been categorised as **threatened**, as population pressures are lower and the predominant influence is the flow of clean oceanic water from the Pacific Ocean. The implementation of effective management will ensure that these reefs will continue and flourish, however, if the migratory boats are allowed to continue the practices of large scale dynamite and muro-ami fishing, then recovery is unlikely. Currently the Government of Indonesia is increasing efforts to manage significant tracts of reefs, but frequently the national and local governments involved do not have the resources to police the protected areas and considerable destructive exploitation continues.

Table 2. Extend of cover of live coral (as %) on reefs of five ASEAN countries collected during the ASEAN-Australia Living Coastal Resources project and during other surveys*. The first column lists the number of transect sites whereas the others list the % of sites with cover >75%; <75% and >50%; <50% and >25%; <25% to 0%. Most data were collected from 1987 to present, with country data being a combination of internal divisions.

Country	Transect Sites	Excellent >75%	Good >50%	Fair >25%	Poor >0%
Indonesia	357	5.3	26.6	30.8	37.3
Western	240	4.6	24.6	30.8	40.0
Central	38	10.5	34.2	42.1	13.2
Eastern	79	5.1	29.1	25.3	40.5
Malaysia	81	4.9	27.2	35.8	32.1
West Peninsular	29	3.4	17.2	48.3	31.0
East Peninsular	52	5.8	32.7	28.8	32.7
Philippines	735	5.3	25.2	39.2	30.3
North	332	3.6	25.3	43.4	27.7
Central	360	6.7	26.2	36.4	30.6
South	43	7.0	14.0	30.2	48.8
Singapore	129	0.8	22.4	39.5	37.2
Outer Reefs	82	1.2	28.0	47.6	23.2
Inner Reefs	47	0.0	12.8	25.5	61.7
Thailand	172	34.9	34.9	25.0	5.2
East Gulf	57	24.6	36.8	38.6	0.0
West Gulf	42	50.0	33.3	11.9	4.8
Andaman Sea	73	34.2	34.2	21.9	9.6

*Live coral determined on triplicate 100 m transects, placed usually at depths of 3 and 10 m on fore-reef slopes.

Malaysia

Coral reefs in Malaysia are situated principally on the east coast and some of the islands off the north west coast of Peninsula Malaysia. There are extensive reefs off Sabah. All reefs are suffering similar problems of organic and sediment pollution and over-exploitation, but the levels are not as severe as in other countries (e.g. the Philippines). Dynamite and other destructive practices appear to be rare near the land and probably only occur on outer islands. Data on the percent cover of corals is not comparable to the other ASEAN countries, however it is evident that cover is decreasing on reefs near land influence (Table 2). Fish stocks on coral reefs are also reported to by low (unpublished data). The first Malaysian marine protected area was established at Pulau Redang as a model for similar protection activities. Unfortunately, development of a tourist facility and golf course has resulted in considerable damage to the adjacent coral reefs with sediment loads increasing by 600% and smothering corals (Mohamed et al., 1992). All reefs in the Peninsula Malaysia region are considered to be **critical** category with further decline being the probable prognosis in the next 20 years (Fig. 1). All these reefs are under the immediate influence of coastal waters with high sediment and pollution loads. The reefs off Sabah are, however, under predominantly oceanic influence and have been regarded as **threatened** with over-exploitation as the major factor threatening the community structure. Many of Malaysian coral reef areas have become the focus for tourism and unless more stringent controls are placed on these developments, the magnet of the reefs will lose its attraction.

Philippines

The reefs in the archipelago are predominantly all in decline. The reasons are principally over-exploitation with dynamite fishing a regular and widespread occurrence as well as sediment and nutrient pollution. Surveys conducted by the Marine Science Institute of the University of the Philippines show that coral cover is predominantly 'fair' to 'poor' (more than 65% of 735 sites studied) in the three major zones of the Philippines (Table 2; ASEAN-Australia Marine Science Project, 1992). At the same sites, fish populations are reported to be low, showing evidence of extensive fishing pressure (NEDA, Region 1, 1992). The degradation of Filipino coral reefs follows a similar pattern to that for tropical rain forests, where more than 60% of the original forest area has been cleared (Hinrichsen, 1990), and at least 80% and possibly 90% of the original mangrove forest area in 1920 has been lost (ASEAN-Australia Marine Science Project, 1992). This clearing has resulted in extensive sediment deposition onto nearshore coral reefs, which predominate in the Philippines, resulting in loss of fisheries (Hodgson and Dixon, 1988). The government currently has insufficient resources to manage effectively the reefs and protect them from over-exploitation. With a stagnant economy and population increasing, there are few prospects that significant national resources will be diverted towards reef management. There is, however, another strategy that is proving effective for coastal resource management. Local governments (barangays) in several parts of the country are adopting local area management plans. These were successfully introduced by Angel Alcala (Alcala and Russ, 1990) and have spread to other regions. Provided central governments assist the decentralisation of power, these local management activities may prove to be most effective at retaining coral reef resources against increasing anthropogenic stress.

Singapore

Singaporean reefs, whilst small in area, constitute a considerable resource for the development of environmental tourism. These reefs, however, are being severely degraded by the destructive engineering practices used to develop the existing maritime areas, (port and oil processing facilities) and expand the land area of Singapore (Chua and Chou, 1992). Percent coral cover is relatively high on some of the outer reefs, particularly those under military control, whereas cover is reduced (>50% cover) on reefs close to land (Table 2). There has been a marked reduction in the cover of coral below 5 m depth, with virtually no coral growth at 10 m. This is principally due to the heavy sediment load in the water (from land reclamation) impeding light penetration (Chou, 1991). The reefs are also being used as a source of live coral for export to aquarium shops; whilst it is illegal, operators collecting in Sumatra often complete their shipment with Singaporean corals. Some reef areas will be destroyed when more land is 'reclaimed' for development using garbage on Pulau Semakau. There is, however, a plan to gazette some of the offshore reefs as marine protected areas by the National Parks Board of the Ministry of National Development. Fish populations are under moderate pressure, compared to the rest of Asia, but there is rather intensive collection of aquarium specimens (Chua and Chou, 1992).

Thailand

The reefs of Thailand are experiencing similar pressures to all others in Asia. Those nearshore are suffering considerable damage from land based activities, whereas offshore reefs still have relatively high coral cover (UNEP/IUCN, 1988). Of the three major regions in Thailand, the eastern Gulf of Thailand reefs are experiencing greatest pressures. Domestic and industrial pollution from Bangkok and nearby Pattaya have resulted in almost total destruction of reefs in the northern part of the Gulf. For example, reefs adjacent to Pattaya have a low average coral cover (Sudara and Nateekarnchanalap, 1988). Away from these pollution 'hot spots' the greatest stresses are over-exploitation, including dynamite fishing, and pollution from the excessive development of prawn (shrimp) ponds resulting in the clearance of approximately 87% of the original mangrove forest area (World Resources Institute, 1992). The prawn ponds operate on an intensive basis with large releases of nutrient and pesticide pollutants, but the ponds have a short production life (5 to 7 years) due to rising acidity from the mangrove peat soils and disease. Reefs on the western side of the Gulf of Thailand are generally in better condition, with coral cover frequently exceeding 50%. Recent reports have shown that reef cover is declining by 20% annually due to pressures from tourism development (Sudara and Nateekarnchanalap, 1988; ASEAN-Australia Marine Science Project, 1992). This development has been uncontrolled with excessive clearing of coastal lands and no treatment of sewage wastes. The major area of concern is around the tourist site of Ko Samui, where the reefs are being simultaneously impacted by rapid development and pollution from intensive prawn farming around to Ban Don Bay. Best reef resources for

Thailand are in the Andaman Sea, particularly those of the Similan and Surin Islands, to the north of Phuket. Coral cover on many of the transects exceeded 75%. Reefs closer to Phuket are experiencing the direct effects of over-fishing and tourist activities. Most serious destructive stresses are the release of sewage and sediment into shallow Phangnga Bay where many reefs occur (e.g. Ko Phi Phi). Protection and management of coastal resources is now more important in Thailand. The conservation ethic is driven by three significant factors: the Thai Royal Family is becoming increasingly involved in conservation projects, often acting with local people to protect their resources; there are a number of marine resources management projects that have been driven by local residents to sustain their resources (Nateekanjanalarp and Sudara, 1992); and the Government has placed a moratorium on the further development of prawn ponds and mangrove clearing with approximately US$32 million allocated for urgent mangrove and coral reef management over 5 years (ASEAN-Australia Marine Science Project, 1992).

DISCUSSION

The prognosis for coral reefs in southeast Asia is not encouraging, as reef degradation is accelerating at approximately the same rate as population increase. Currently approximately 260 million people live near the coast (World Resources Institute, 1992) resulting in two distinct pressures on the adjacent reefs. Virtually all sewage is discharged directly into the nearshore coastal waters, and people extract large quantities of food protein from the sea (Yong, 1989). The region is experiencing 5% or more economic growth which results in trickle down increases in per capita income in virtually all countries - this is putting pressure on the marine environment (including coral reefs) to yield more fisheries products that are a favoured form of animal protein (Table 1). Thus, reefs far from centers of population are being exploited for both the southeast Asian markets as well as those of more prosperous countries such as Japan, South Korea, Taiwan and Hong Kong. All these factors are additive in the rate of collapse of coral reefs. With the human populations in the southeast Asian region set to double within the next 25 to 35 years, problems for coral reefs will exacerbate.

It is concluded that 11% of the reefs in southeast Asia have already collapsed and a further 48% of the reefs are in the **critical** category, with collapse likely within the next 20 years, if urgent management procedures are not adopted (Fig. 1). This leaves approximately 36% of reef area as **threatened** such that reef collapse could occur in 20 to 40 years from now, again dependent on whether effective reef management is adopted. The only remaining reefs that are not considered under serious threat (approximately 5%) are parts of the Spratley Islands under military or tourist development protection, and some remote parts of eastern Indonesia. Reefs around the southeast Asian center of coral biodiversity are similarly threatened. The reefs of Japan are in a serious state as are the reefs in other highly populated parts of Asia (China, Sri Lanka and India; UNEP/IUCN, 1988; Wilkinson, 1993). Reefs to the south (in Australia) and east, however, are virtually all considered as **stable** (Wilkinson, 1993). Global climate change and sea level rise, based on current predictions, are not considered as major threats to reefs. The beneficial and deleterious effects on coral reefs are in approximate balance (Smith and Buddemeier, 1992). The unambiguous effects of direct anthropogenic stress are, however, currently damaging the reefs and will result in disastrous effects if continued. These effects will overwhelm any potential changes from climate change. Where climate change may effect the long term future for coral reefs is on those in the **stable** category (Wilkinson, 1993), however there are virtually none of these in southeast Asia.

Virtually all countries in southeast Asia have enacted strong legislation to protect coastal ecosystems, however, there are insufficient resources to enforce the legislation. There are many marine protected areas, but few have management plans and enforcement officers. These countries will probably require external assistance to plan and manage significant areas of coral reefs, e.g. Bunaken in Sulawesi and reefs in the Sulu Sea. In order to implement sustainable development of coral reefs, there is an urgent need to provide environmental education at the village level and encourage the development of local area management plans incorporating all activities on and around the coral reefs. National governments must be prepared to surrender authority for control of coastal areas to local government as control by the user is the only immediate mechanism for controlling destruction of southeast Asian coral reefs.

REFERENCES

Alcala, A.K. and G.R. Russ. 1990. A direct test of the effects of protective management on abundance and yield of tropical marine resources. J. Cons. Cons. Int. Explor. Mer. 46: 40-47.

ASEAN-Australia Marine Science Project 1992. The status of living coastal resources in ASEAN Countries. Pages 6-17 in S. English, ed. ASEAN Marine Science, No. 19, ASEAN-Australia Marine Science Project: Living Coastal Resources, Australian Institute of Marine Science, Townsville.

Brown, B.E. 1986. Human induced damage to coral reefs. UNESCO Reports in Marine Science No. 40, pp. 179.

Chou, L.M. 1991. Community structure of sediment stressed reefs in Singapore. Galaxea 7: 101-111.

Chua, C.Y.Y. and L.M. Chou. 1992. Coral reef conservation in Singapore - a case for integrated coastal area management. Pages 437-445 in L.M. Chou and C. R. Wilkinson, eds. Third ASEAN Science and Technology Week Conference Proceedings, Vol. 6, Department of Zoology, National University of Singapore and National Science and Technology Board, Singapore.

Chou, L.M., G.S.Y. Lim and C.B. Leng. 1992. Fish communities in natural reef and artificial habitats in the coastal waters of Brunei Darussalam. Pages 75-90 in G. Silvestre et al., eds. The Coastal Resources of Brunei Darussalam: Status, Utilization and Management. ICLARM Conference Proceedings 34, Department of Fisheries, Ministry of Industry and Primary Resources, Brunei Darussalam and International Center for Living Aquatic Resources Management, Manila.

Collard, M. and T. Collard. 1992. Threats to Scarborough Reef in the South China Sea. Reef Encounter No. 12, December 1992, pp 9.

Gomez, E.D., A.C. Alcala and A.C. San Diego. 1982. Status of Philippine coral reefs - 1981. Proceedings 4th International Coral Reef Symposium 2: 275-282.

Hinrichsen, D. 1990. Our common seas:coasts in crisis. Earthscan Publications, London 184 pp.

Hodgson, G. and J.A. Dixon. 1988. Logging versus fisheries and tourism in Palawan: an environmental and economic analysis. Occasional Paper No. 7, East-West Environmental and Policy Institute, Honolulu, Hawaii.

Mohamed, M.I.H., H.A. Aziz and S.B. Ahmad. 1992. The impact of resort development on the coral reefs of Pulau Redang Marine Park. Pages 463-470 in L.M. Chou and C.R. Wilkinson, eds. Third ASEAN Science and Technology Week Conference Proceedings, Vol. 6, Department of Zoology, National University of Singapore and National Science and Technology Board, Singapore.

Nateekanjanalarp, S. and S. Sudara. 1992a. Economic aspects and successful conservation from ASEAN-Australia Living Coastal Resources project. Third ASEAN Science & Technology Week Proceedings, Vol. 6: 447-451.

NEDA, Region 1. 1992. The Lingayen Gulf coastal area management plan. National Economic Development Authority, Region 1, Philippines. ICLARM Tech. Rep. 30, pp. 161.

Smith, S.V. and R.W. Buddemeier. 1992. Global change and coral reef ecosystems. Annual Review of Ecology and Systematics 23: 89-118.

Sudara, S., V. Manthachittra, T. Thamrongnawasawat and S. Nateekanjanalarp. 1988. Change in the coral community structure along the west coast of the Gulf of Thailand. Galaxea 7: 233-239.

Sudara, S. and S. Nateekarnchanalap. 1988. Impact of tourism development on the reef in Thailand. Proceedings 6th International Coral Reef Symposium 2: 273-278.

Thresher, R.E. 1991. Geographic variability in the ecology of coral reef fishes: evidence, evolution, and possible implications. Pages 401-436 in P.F. Sale, ed. The Ecology of Fishes on Coral Reefs. Academic Press, San Diego, pp. 754.

Titlyanov, E.A. and Y.Y. Latypov. 1991. Light-dependence in scleractinian distribution in the sublittoral zone of South China Sea Islands. Coral Reefs 10: 13-138.

UNEP/IUCN. 1988. Coral Reefs of the World, Volumes 1-3. S.M. Wells, D. Sheppard and M.D. Jenkins, eds. UNEP Regional Seas Directories and Bibliographies. IUCN Publication Services, Gland. UNEP Nairobi.

Veron, J.E.N. 1986. Corals of Australia and the Indo-Pacific. Angus and Robertson, North Ryde, pp. 644

Wilkinson, C.R. 1993. Coral reefs of the world are facing widespread devastation: can we prevent this through sustainable management practices? Proceedings 7th International Coral Reef Symposium, in press.

Wilkinson, C.R., L.M. Chou, E. Gomez, I. Mohammed, S. Soekarno and S. Sudara. 1993. A regional approach to monitoring coral reefs: studies in southeast Asia by the ASEAN-Australia Living Coastal Resources project. Proceedings 7th International Coral Reef Symposium, in press.

World Resources Institute. 1992. World Resources 1992-93. The World Resources Institute, the United Nations Environment Programme and the United Nations Development Programme, Oxford University Press, New York, pp. 385.

Yong, S.K.T. 1989. Coastal resource management in the ASEAN region: problems and directions. In T.-E. Chua and D. Pauly, eds. Coastal area management in southeast Asia: policies, management strategies and case studies. ICLARM Contribution No. 543 xi.

REEFS OF THE PACIFIC OCEAN

	PAGES
The Demise of the Fringing Coral Reefs of Barbados and of Regions in the Great Barrier Reef (GBR) Lagoon-Impacts of Eutrophication *Peter R.F. Bell and Tom Tomascik*	319 -325
Impacts of Cyclone-Induced Floods on Fringing Reefs: Case Study of Keppel Bay, Queensland, Australia *Grahame Byron*	326 - 332
Doomsday Ecology Misapplied: Alleged Versus Documented Impacts of a Deep Ocean Sewage Outfall in Hawaii *Richard W. Grigg and Steven J. Dollar*	333 - 338
Reefs In Kaneohe Bay, Hawaii: Two Centuries of Western Influence and Two Decades of Data *Cynthia L. Hunter and Christopher W. Evans*	339 - 345
Can the Great Barrier Reef Model of Marine Protected Ocean Save Reefs World Wide? *Grahame Kelleher*	346 - 352
Biological Limits To Caribbean Reef Recovery A Comparison with Western South Pacific Reefs *Barbara L. Kojis and Norman J. Quinn*	353 - 359
Effects of Coastal Runoff on Coral Reproduction *Robert H. Richmond*	360 - 364
Biodiversity of Reef Corals: Is There a Problem in the Indo-Pacific Centre of Diversity? *J.E. N. Veron*	365 - 370

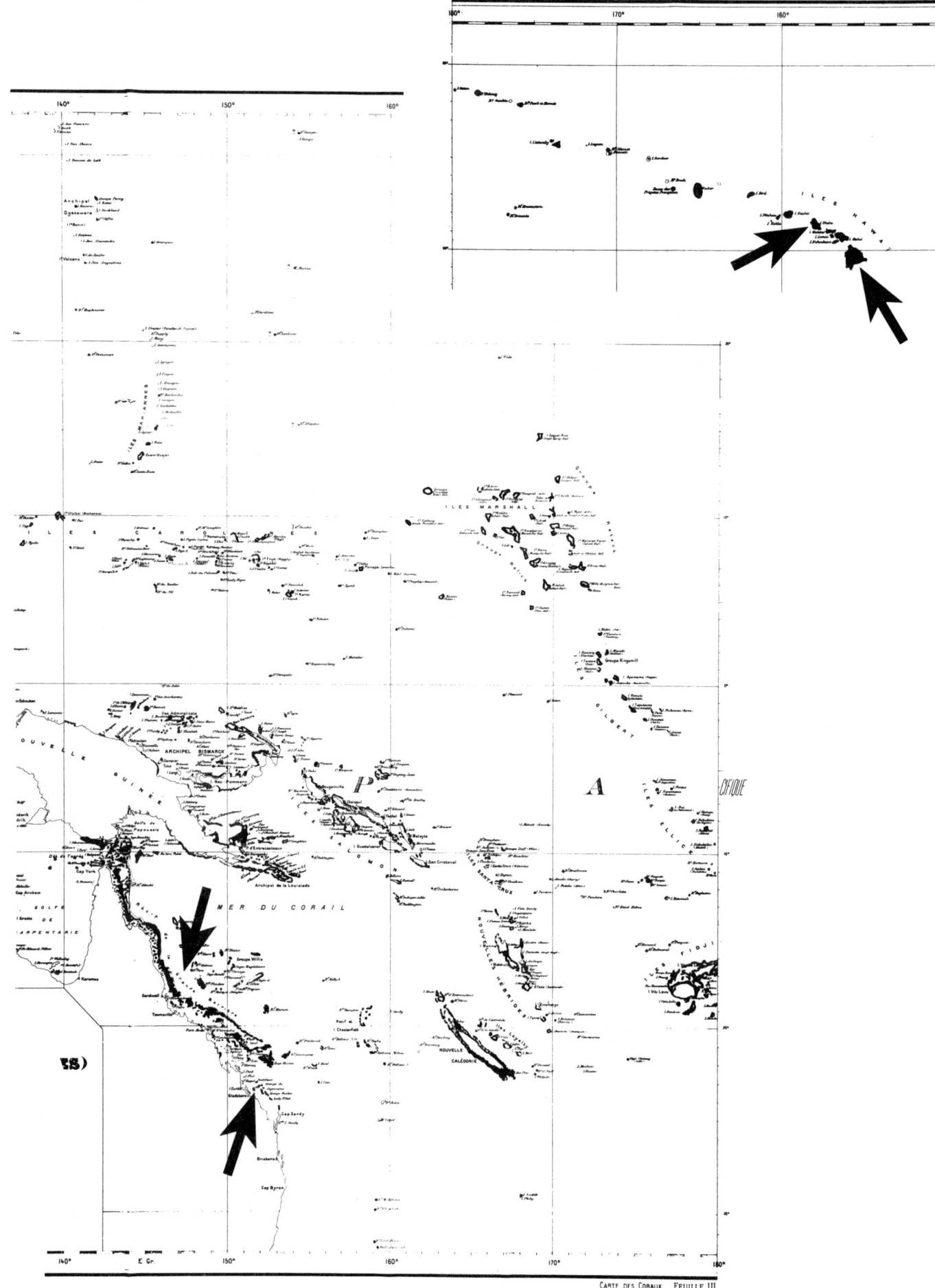

THE DEMISE OF THE FRINGING CORAL REEFS OF BARBADOS AND OF REGIONS IN THE GREAT BARRIER REEF (GBR) LAGOON - IMPACTS OF EUTROPHICATION

Peter R.F. Bell[1] and Tom Tomascik[2]

[1] Department of Chemical/Environmental Engineering University of Queensland St Lucia Brisbane Australia 4072
[2] EMDI Project Kantor Menteri Negara Kependudukan dan Lingkungan Hidup Jl. Medan Merdeka Barat 15 Jakarta Indonesia

ABSTRACT

The fringing reefs of Barbados are in a very poor state of development when compared with earlier descriptions. The historical data demonstrate a close correspondence between the demise of the coral reefs with increased tourist and industrial development and the resulting degradation in water quality and associated eutrophication. The studies indicate that chronic low levels of eutrophication can restrict coral growth and reproduction and in doing so inhibit the recovery of damaged reefs. The virtual extinction of *A. palmata* in recent times indicates that it could be particularly sensitive to eutrophication. The data suggest a eutrophication threshold of 0.3 mg chlorophyll *a* m^{-3} if the demise of *A. palmata* is relevant which is low in comparison with the 0.5 mg chlorophyll a m^{-3} previously suggested for the Great Barrier Reef (GBR) lagoon. Data for the GBR lagoon off Townsville show that the status of eutrophication or fertility of the waters (as determined by chlorophyll *a*) is equivalent to or greater than that which was associated with the demise of reefs in Barbados and Hawaii. Recent data show that the fertility (as measured by total diatom counts) of the lagoon water near to Low Isles is far higher than that measured in 1928-29. The increased fertility in both GBR regions is attributed mainly to agricultural run-off. It is hypothesised that this large scale eutrophication is a significant factor in the demise of corals in the GBR lagoon and in the promotion of outbreaks of *A. planci*.

INTRODUCTION

Various descriptions and scientific studies provide a relatively good history of the demise of the once flourishing fringing reefs on the south and west coasts of Barbados. The data indicate that an underlying cause for the demise is eutrophication and associated suspended particulate matter (SPM) and sedimentation (Tomascik and Sander 1985, 1987a and b; Tomascik 1991; Wittenberg and Hunte 1992; Hunte and Wittenberg 1992). The main cause of the eutrophication in Barbados is the increased loads of nutrients that have occurred with the increased development of tourism (see Figure 3) and industry along the coastal fringe (Tomascik and Sander 1985). The effects of the many point sources along the coast are magnified by the impacts of run-off and the seepage of groundwater. The groundwaters are contaminated by industry, agriculture and sewage (much of the sewage from domestic households and tourist resorts is disposed of through cess pits). Run-off, although it only occurs periodically, is usually highly contaminated with sediment, sewage and agricultural wastes. These waters often discharge near to the fringing reefs thus exposing the corals to an immediate high sedimentation load and the toxic effects of the freshwater and its constituents. Examination of the historical data provides useful relationships between water quality and reef health indicators. This data can be used to establish water quality guidelines or eutrophication threshold levels that can be used for the management of coral reef regions. Based mainly on historical data from Barbados (Tomascik and Sander 1985) and Kaneohe Bay (Smith et al 1981; Laws and Redalje 1979 cited by Bell 1991, 1992) Bell (1991, 1992) suggested a eutrophication threshold level for the Great Barrier Reef (GBR) lagoon corals corresponding to an annual mean concentration of chlorophyll $a \leq 0.5$ mg m^{-3} with corresponding concentrations of nutrients P-PO$_4$ 0.1 - 0.2 µM; DIN (NH$_4$+NO$_3$+NO$_2$) 1 µM. These threshold concentrations were used to define the status of eutrophication or fertility of the waters in the GBR lagoon (Bell 1991, 1992). The nutrient threshold concentrations are of the same order as the half-saturation constants of many marine phytoplankton (and probably attached algae) and hence variations around these concentrations will significantly affect the rate of growth of the algae and hence affect the ability of the algae to compete with the corals. A closer examination of the historical data for Barbados is presented below and this indicates that an even lower threshold level is appropriate for that region and possibly the Caribbean as a whole. The low threshold concentrations for the nutrients means that large nutrient discharges (eg. rivers) can lead to large scale eutrophication and thus affect far distant reefs and even very small discharges can affect nearby reefs. Indeed the impacts of local or small scale inputs of nutrients in Barbados could be magnified by the large scale effects which result from the discharges of the rivers of South America, particularly the Amazon but space does not permit further discussion of this aspect.

Moss et al. (1992, cited by Gabric and Bell 1993) estimate that the annual loads of sediment and nutrients discharged to the GBR lagoon are 3-5 times that prior to European settlement. Their data show that only 11% of the total coastal catchment area is pristine with over 85% under agricultural development. Given the limited flushing of the GBR lagoon and the low eutrophication threshold level for coral reef regions it is quite likely that little if any of the GBR lagoon could be classed as pristine. Indeed historical data for the GBR lagoon indicate that some regions exhibit signs of large scale eutrophication (Bell 1991,1992). In particular it is noted that areas once renowned for their coral growth are now dominated by other benthos eg algae, soft corals and seagrasses (eg Magnetic Island and Low Isles). There is evidence that small scale discharges of run-off, groundwater and sewage have also impacted upon GBR coral reef ecosystems (eg Green Island, Hamilton Island). In the results section below historical data from studies done in Barbados and from studies done at Magnetic Island and Low Isles in the GBR lagoon are summarised. The reader should refer to the original work for the methods used. The 1993 algal cover transect study for Barbados followed the method of Tomascik and Sander (1987a).

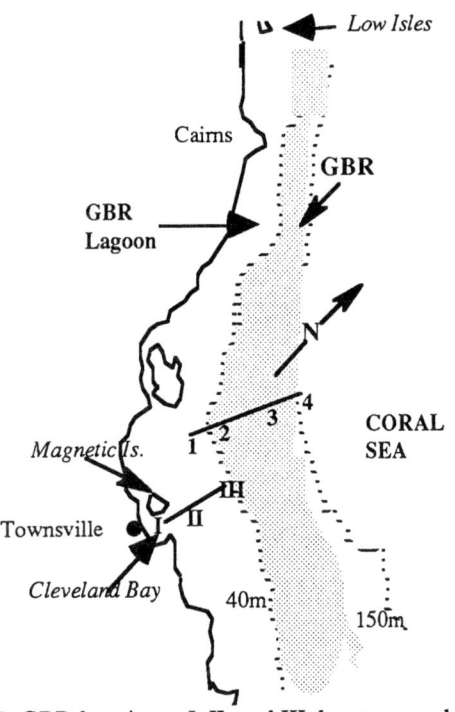

Figure 1. GBR locations. I, II, and III denote cross-lagoon sampling stations and 1-4 show outer shelf sampling stations.

Figure 2. Location of fringing reef sampling stations SR, SG, BRI, SL, FV, SG, BR, in Barbados.

RESULTS

Observations of Demise of Barbados's Fringing Reefs and Water Quality. -- The abundant "good thriving reefs" as described by Nutting (1919) which existed "for miles in the immediate neighbourhood" of Pelican Island (ie. close to Bridgetown) and those off Hastings where there were "acres of bottom crowded with immense fronds of *Isopora (Acropora) palmata* " exist no more. The demise of the south coast fringing reefs coincided with the rapid development of tourism (see Figure 3) and degradation of water quality that has occurred along the south coast since 1950 (Light 1974 cited by Lewsey 1978; Vezina 1974 cited by Tomascik and Sander 1985; Turnbull 1979). Lewsey (1978) demonstrates the extent of the degradation of the reefs, coralline algal and sea-grass beds since 1950 using aerial photographs. The demise is attributed to a combination of anthropogenic activities (eg reef mining, coral collecting, dynamite fishing), natural occurrences (eg hurricanes) and the effects of water pollution and in particular eutrophication.

The extensive *A.palmata* beds were gone by the time of the work of Lewis (1960). By the time of Macintyre (1967) even some of the west coast reefs appeared to be in decline. He notes that the prolific coral growth (>75% cover; also see Lewis 1960) was restricted to the reefs lying between Speightstown and Lower Carlton and between Alleynes Bay and Sandy Lane. The other west coast fringing reefs consisted of reef-rock and coral debris covered with pink coralline algae with only sparse growths of corals. He notes *A.palmata* was still relatively common on the surface of the spurs of some reefs in the mid 1960's. Ott (1971) recorded 28 colonies in a 100 metre square area on the Bellairs Research Institute (BRI) reef. The work of Stearn et al.(1977, as cited by Tomascik and Sander 1985) shows prolific coral growth on the northern section of the BRI reef, the mean cover for the outer half of the reef, which included the spur and groove region and part of the coalesced spur zone, was over 50% live coral and some *A.palmata* was still present. Hurricane Allen in 1980 caused severe damage to the northern BRI reef (Mah 1984 as cited by Tomascik and Sander 1987a) and probably to other west coast reefs.

Table 1. Correlations between coral health indicators (reef mean) (H: Brillouin's diversity index; %CC: % coral cover; GR: growth rate of *M. annularis* cm yr^{-1}) and annual mean water quality parameters (SPM mg l^{-1}; Chl *a* mg m^{-3}; P-PO$_4$ µM; DIN µM)

Correlation	r^2
H = 1.361 - 1.350 Log(SPM)	0.86
H = 0.792 - 1.950 Log(Chl *a* +1)	0.83
H = 0.545 - 5.088 Log(P-PO$_4$ +1)	0.70
H = 0.533 - 0.459 Log(DIN+1)	0.66
Sin^{-1}(%CC)$^{0.5}$ = 30.25 - 64.82 Log(Chl *a* +1)	0.65
Sin^{-1}(%CC)$^{0.5}$ = 47.95 - 43.29 Log(SPM)	0.63
Sin^{-1}(%CC)$^{0.5}$ = 21.25 - 150.15 Log(PO$_4$+ 1)	0.43
Log(1+GR) = 0.866 - 0.729 Log(SPM+1)	0.99
Log(1+GR) = 0.467 - 0.877 Log(Chl *a* +1)	0.92
Log(1+GR) = 0.321 - 1.957 Log(PO$_4$+1)	0.57

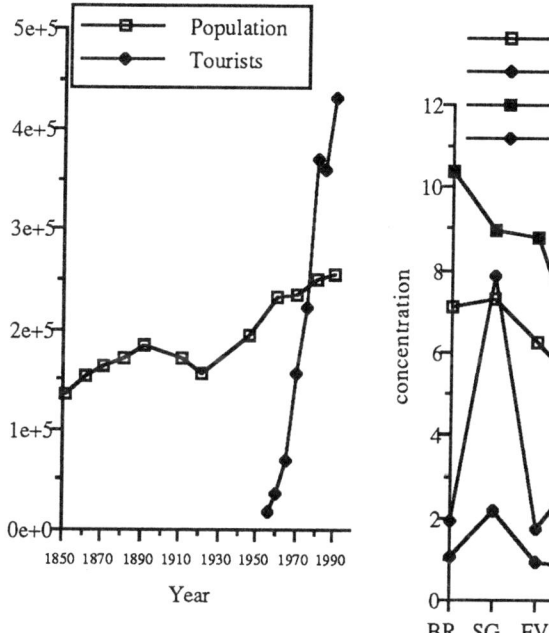
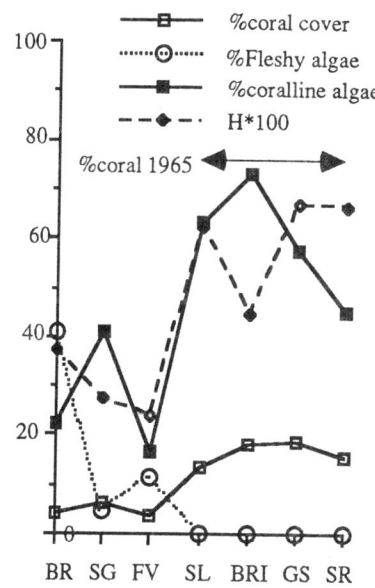

Figure 3. Total general population and and tourist arrivals - Barbados.

Figure 4. Variation in water quality (annual mean values) along the west coast of Barbados.

Figure 5. Variation in mean coral health indicators along the west coast.

In 1982 Tomascik and Sander (1987a) found the southern portion of the BRI reef in a relatively poor state of development with live coral cover of only 18% in the spur and groove zone. They found live coral cover ranging from 3%-19% in the spur and groove zones of the seven reefs surveyed which illustrates a general decline in the west coast fringing reefs when compared with the earlier descriptions. Their data show *A. Palmata* was quite rare. Tomascik and Sander (1985, 1987a) showed that the water quality of the west coast waters had declined over the preceding decade and hypothesised that the increased eutrophication resulted from the tourist and industrial developments along the coast. They concluded that eutrophication is a principal cause of the demise of the west coast reefs. In a more recent study Wittenberg and Hunte (1992) found that the reefs on the west coast are still in a poor state of development with higher fleshy algae cover than measured by Tomascik and Sander (1987a) and coral cover in the spur and groove zone ranging from 2.0-24.9%. A recent survey (by PRFB) in 1993 showed a fleshy algal cover for BRI of >70% (mean of six 20m transects).

Water Quality, Coral Health and Reproduction-Barbados. -- Tomascik and Sander (1985, 1987a) measured various coral reef health indicators and water quality parameters along the west coast of Barbados and analysed for correlations between the health indicators and the water quality parameters. Detailed statistical analysis to test for the significance of the results was performed. Figures 4 and 5 summarise the spatial variation of some water quality (annual mean) and the coral health indicators (reef mean) along the west coast. Some of correlations between the health indicators and the water quality parameters are given in Table 1. Additional studies by Tomascik and Sander (1987b) showed that the reproduction output of *Porites porites* was reduced in the more eutrophic regions. Also Tomascik (1991), Wittenberg and Hunte (1992) and Hunte and Wittenberg (1992) found that coral recruitment was significantly reduced in the more eutrophic regions. In particular these studies showed that in the more eutrophic regions juvenile settlement rates were lower, juvenile mortality was higher and juvenile abundance was lower than in the less eutrophic regions.

Observations of the Demise of Corals on the Reefs of Magnetic Island. -- The demise of the reefs at Nelly Bay and the nearby Geoffrey, Arthur and Florence Bays on Magnetic Island have been attributed to increased sedimentation which results from the dumping of spoil from harbour dredging and also to effects of cyclone "Althea" (Collins, 1978; Endean, 1976 cited by Bell, 1992). Nelly Bay, Magnetic Island, was once renowned for its coral reef platform of *Acropora, Turbinaria* and *Montipora*, much of which emerged at low tide and was known to many as the "coral gardens" (eg see Johannes, 1972 ; Collins, 1978; Endean, 1976, cited by Bell, 1992). "As recently as the latter half of the 1960s the island still possessed coral gardens that were equal, and in fact often superior, to anything on the Great Barrier Reef...the diversity and form and delicate colouring of the corals painted an exquisite picture of unequalled beauty" (T. Brown cited by Bell, 1992). T. Brown noted that seaweed growth invaded the silt-saturated environment which effectively eliminated many of the remaining corals (cited by Bell, 1992). Endean reports (1976, cited by Bell 1992) that algae invaded many areas after destruction of part of the coral cover and this precipitated further destruction by trapping sediment.

Water Quality Data for Townsville Magnetic Island Region. -- The most comprehensive study on nutrients and water column productivity for the GBR lagoon is that of Revelante and Gilmartin (1982) for the region off Townsville (see Figure 1). Figures 6 and

7 compare the results obtained by Revelante and Gilmartin (1982) for chlorophyll *a* and P-PO4 (in surface waters) with the suggested eutrophication threshold concentrations. Figure 8 compares the P-PO4 data for the mid-lagoon Station II with those collected by Marshall at Low Isles in 1928-29 (Bell 1991). Some data for the outer regions of the GBR lagoon are also available (see Figures 6 and 7). These results are probably biased towards the high side because these data were mostly collected during the upwelling periods.

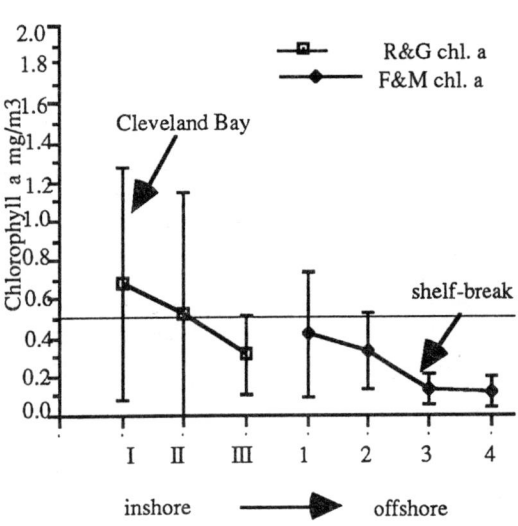

Figure 6. Cross-shelf variation of chlorophyll *a* as recorded by Revelante and Gilmartin (1982), Ikeda et al, (1980) (R&G); Furnas & Mitchell (1984) (F&M) cited by Bell (1992) (see Fig. 1 for sampling station locations)

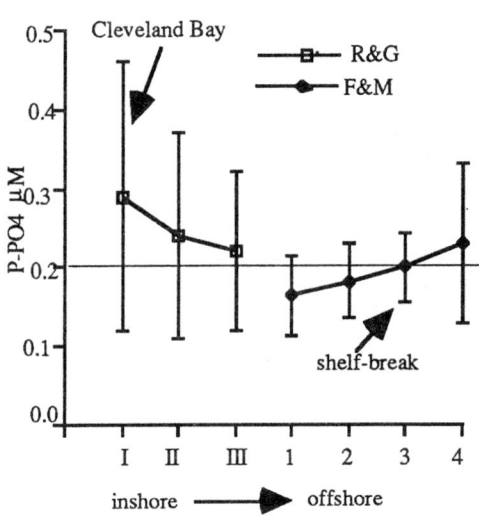

Figure 7. Cross-shelf variation of chlorophyll *a* as recorded by Revelante and Gilmartin (1982), Ikeda et al. (1980) (R&G); Furnas and Mitchell (1984) (F&M) cited by Bell (1992) (see Fig. 1 for sampling station locations)

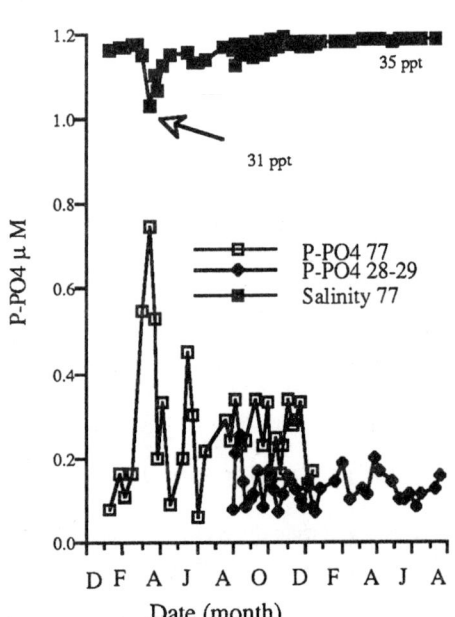

Figure 8. Comparison of seasonal variation of P-PO4 at Station II (see Fig. 1) in 1977 with that measured in 1928-29 at Low Isles. Salinity is for Station II 1977.

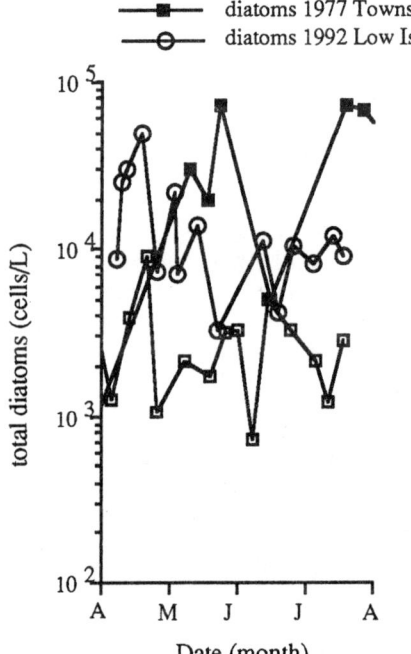

Figure 9. Comparison of variation of total diatom concentrations at mid- GBR lagoon stations 3ME Low Isles in 1929, 3ME Low Isles in 1992 and Station II (see Fig. 1) off Townsville 1977.

Observations of Demise of Coral Cover and Water Quality at Low Isles. -- Our personal observations and a comparison of photographic and descriptive records (eg see GBR 1933) demonstrates that a large portion of the reported flourishing hard coral cover in the shallower waters at Low Isles has been replaced since 1928-29 by soft corals, algae and sea grasses. Since the 1928-29 British Expedition to Low Isles, the corals have been subjected to the destructive forces of cyclones and to attacks by the crown of thorns starfish (*A. planci*). Results for $P-PO_4$ and diatom (>20μm) concentrations of samples collected at a station located 3 miles east (3ME) of Low Isles during the 1928-29 study are summarised in Figures 8 and 9. Figure 9 compares the total diatoms concentrations measured in 1992 at 3ME (Elmetri 1993) with those measured in 1929 at 3ME and those measured at Station II (Fig. 1) off Townsville in 1977.

DISCUSSION

Barbados. -- The early work demonstrates a significant demise of the coral reefs on both the south and west coasts of Barbados since 1950 which coincides with the increase in pollution of the coastal waters by sewage outfalls, storm drainage outlets, contaminated groundwaters and industrial discharges. Macintyre (1967) noted the more southern reefs on the west coast ie. those located closer to Bridgetown, had less coral cover than most of the reefs to the north, however all the substrate not covered by coral was covered by pink coralline algae. The results in Figure 5 indicate that the coralline algal cover of these reefs had been replaced to some extent by fleshy algae (eg turf and filamentous) by 1982. The impact of the rum factory and power plant discharges between BR and SG on DIN concentration is clearly discernible in Figure 4. The results in Figure 5 show a trend towards healthier reefs as one moves from south to north down the eutrophication gradient, with increases in the following reef characteristics: coral diversity, coral cover and coralline algal cover (at the expense of fleshy algal cover). Coralline and fleshy algal cover are included as health indicators because (i) live coralline algae are the preferred substrate for settlement of many corals, some species will not settle on fleshy algae (ii) fleshy algae have been identified as a competitor for space for both adult corals and juvenile corals and (iii) fleshy algae may promote disease (eg see review by Van Moorsel, 1989; Bell, 1992). Also the coral and coralline algal fragments are the main source of sediment to replenish beaches and to maintain and build the coral reefs themselves (Lewsey 1978; Scoffin et al. 1980 cited by Tomascik and Sander 1985). Eutrophication, by promoting fleshy algae and preventing the growth of corals and coralline algae, could therefore be a significant factor in the reef and beach erosion that is occurring on the west and south coasts of Barbados.

Figure 5 shows no fleshy algal cover in the spur and groove zone for the less eutrophic reefs in 1982. Today the coral rock areas of all of these reefs have significant cover of fleshy algae. A recent survey (6 transects 1993) of BRI showed over 70% of the spur and groove is covered with fleshy algae. Also Wittenberg and Hunte (1992) recorded significant increases in fleshy algal cover over that shown in Figure 5 for the spur and grove zones for SG (60.7%) and FV (50.2%). The increased fleshy algal growth is attributed to both eutrophication and reduction of grazing pressure brought about by the die-off of *Diadema antillarum* in 1983 (Wittenberg and Hunte 1992). However it is important to note Tomascik and Sander's (1987a) results pre-date the 1983 die-off and these results did show far higher fleshy algae, lower coral diversity and lower coral cover in the more eutrophic region than in the less eutrophic region. A confounding factor is that Tomascik and Sander (1987a) found lower numbers of *D. antillarum* on the more eutrophic reefs. However there is evidence that eutrophication may decrease the recruitment of *D. antillarum* (see Wittenberg and Hunte 1992) which supports Tomascik and Sander's (1987a) conclusion that the primary cause for increased fleshy algal growth on the more southern reefs was eutrophication and not a reduction in grazing pressure. Wittenberg and Hunte (1992) also found fewer *D. antillarum* on the more eutrophic reefs. This finding following the severe die-off of *D. antillarum* supports the hypothesis that recruitment of *D. antillarum* is inhibited by eutrophication. It is concluded that the impact of the eutrophication has been magnified on all reefs by the reduction in grazing pressure that resulted from the *D. antillarum* die-off.

The results of correlation analyses between water quality parameters and coral health indicators are summarised in Table 1. These results show that both growth rate (GR) of *Montastrea annularis* and Brillouin's species diversity index (H) are highly correlated with chlorophyll *a* and SPM. This simple analysis supports Tomascik and Sander's (1987a) conclusion that the species diversity is the key community index in delineating the impacts of eutrophication. Of the water quality parameters that are specific measures of eutrophication, namely concentrations of nutrients and chlorophyll *a*, chlorophyll *a* exhibited the highest (negative) correlation with the coral health indicators. This indicates that chlorophyll *a* is the best water quality parameter for measuring the status of eutrophication. Laws and Redalje (1979) (cited by Bell, 1992) came to the same conclusion for their work in Kaneohe Bay. It is noted that because the water column would usually be well mixed in the shallow fringing reef areas the chlorophyll *a* of surface water samples reflects the fertility of not only the water column but also the substrata as well. In particular the sediment could be a source of nutrients and some components contributing to the chlorophyll *a* could originate from the substrata eg. dislodged attached algae and pennate diatoms. Pennate diatoms are a major contributor to the phytoplankton biomass in the coastal waters of Barbados (Partlo, 1975). The observed sensitivity of coral diversity to small changes in chlorophyll *a* (ie. eutrophication) is supported by the results of Maragos et al. (1985) and the analysis of Bell (1991, 1992) which show significant coral recovery of some rarer coral species in the northern (least polluted) region of Kaneohe Bay for a decrease in annual mean chlorophyll *a* concentration from 0.68 to 0.55 mg m^{-3}.

Tomascik and Sander's (1985 and 1987a) statistical analyses show that a significant reduction in the growth rates of *Montastrea annularis* (when compared with the growth rate at SR) occurs at stations with annual mean chlorophyll *a* concentrations ≥ 0.5 mg m^{-3} and that a significant reduction in Brillouin's diversity index occurs at stations with an annual mean chlorophyll *a* concentration ≥ 0.6 mg m^{-3}. Both of these values are in general agreement with the threshold concentration of 0.5 mg m^{-3} suggested by Bell (1991,

1992). However other data suggest that a lower threshold level may be relevant for Barbados. Firstly the more southern reefs were in a poor state of development in the mid 1960s (Macintyre, 1967) and these were characterised by an annual mean chlorophyll a concentration of around 0.4 mg m^{-3} in 1972-73 (source Vezina, 1974 cited by Tomascik and Sander 1985). Secondly in 1970 the outer region of BRI was characterised by a mean chlorophyll a concentration of 0.23 mg m^{-3} (Sander 1971, cited by Tomascik and Sander 1985). At this time $A.$ $palmata$ was relatively plentiful on BRI (Ott, 1971) yet was becoming a rarity in other regions. If it is assumed that the demise of $A.$ $palmata$ was due to eutrophication then these data suggest a threshold concentration of between 0.23 and 0.4 mg chlorophyll a m^{-3}. A value of 0.3 mg chlorophyll a m^{-3} is chosen. This threshold concentration may appear low but is in fact twice the open water background level (Kidd 1978, cited by Tomascik and Sander 1987a). The hypothesis that the recent demise of $A.$ $palmata$ was due to eutrophication seems reasonable when one considers (i) its sensitivity to sedimentation (ii) its susceptibility to physical damage by storms and predators and hence to overgrowth by algae (eg see Pastorok and Bilyard 1985 cited by Tomascik and Sander 1987a). Tomascik and Sander's (1987a) data also show that significant fleshy algal growth only occurred in the spur and groove zone of regions characterised by a mean chlorophyll a concentration >0.8 mg m^{-3}. It is hypothesised that beyond this second threshold level grazers cannot cope with the pressures of increased fleshy algal growth.

The effect of Hurricane Allen on BRI reef suggests that many of the other fringing reefs were probably severely damaged. The poor development of all the reefs along the west coast to-day in comparison with the earlier descriptions is attributed to their recovery being inhibited by eutrophication and in particular through its ability to restrict coral growth and reproduction. Tomascik and Sander (1985; 1987b), Tomascik (1991), Wittenberg and Hunte (1992) and Hunte and Wittenberg (1992) found that coral growth, reproduction potential and recruitment (settlement and survival of spats) were significantly reduced in the more eutrophic regions. Other workers have observed that attached algae inhibits recolonisation of damaged corals (eg Ott 1971, Endean, 1976 cited by Bell 1992). Also Wittenberg and Hunte (1992) found that both fleshy algae and sediment were directly responsible for the mortality of some of the settled spats. These latter observations confirm the work of other workers (eg see Van Moorsel 1989). While a reduction in growth and reproduction ability of the adult corals may be important in the more eutrophic regions of Barbados, the lack of coral recovery in the less eutrophic regions is attributed largely to a reduction in recruitment and recolonisation which would have resulted from the increase in fleshy algal cover. As noted above the increase in fleshy algal growth due to eutrophication and hence its impact on coral recruitment and recolonisation would have been magnified by the reduction in grazing pressure due to the $D.$ $antillarum$ die-off. It is interesting to note that Van Moorsel (1989) found that coralline algae was an important competitor for settled spats and hence it is hypothesised that in the early stages of eutrophication that increased growth rate of coralline algae could reduce the survival of spats. This could explain the lack of coral development on the fringing reefs described by Macintyre (1967).

Townsville and Magnetic Island . -- The demise of the reefs at Nelly Bay and the invasion by macrophytes of nearby Geoffrey, Arthur and Florence Bays on Magnetic Island are consistent with the region being eutrophic. After cyclone "Althea" no recruitment of *Acropora* spats was observed in the following 15 months (Collins 1978 cited by Bell 1992). Collins noted that both increased sedimentation and algal growth make the conditions unsuitable for such settlement and also eludes to the possibility that eutrophication was causing the increased algal growth. The results of Revelante and Gilmartin (1982) (see Figures 6-8) show elevated concentrations of nutrients and phytoplankton for Cleveland Bay and for the mid-lagoon in the late 1970s. If the eutrophication threshold criteria are valid for the GBR lagoon then these results suggest that coral reefs in this region would have been experiencing stress through the effects of eutrophication (Bell 1991;1992). It is important to note that, in the vicinity of the fringing reefs, mean concentrations of nutrients and chlorophyll a would probably be significantly higher than those given in Figures 6 and 7 due to the effects of local discharges and "island mass" effects. Revelante and Gilmartin (1982) concluded that riverine discharge is the principal source of the elevated nutrient concentrations for the near shore region. The results do indeed demonstrate a close correspondence between $P-PO_4$, silicate and lowered salinity which indicates they are river derived (eg see Figure 8). However decaying antecedent algal blooms and wind driven resuspension could be important factors contributing to the DIN flux (see review by Bell 1992). The results in Figure 8 suggest that the concentrations of $P-PO_4$ may have more than doubled in the inner lagoon since 1928 (Bell, 1991), which is consistent with the increased loads of phosphorus suggested Moss et al (1992; cited by Gabric and Bell 1993). The data of Revelante and Gilmartin (1982) also show the concentration of micro-phytoplankton (ie. phytoplankton > 20µm) in the mid-lagoon is some 1-2 orders of magnitude greater than that recorded by Marshall at Low Isles in 1928-29 (Bell 1992 eg see Figure 9). Bell (1992) notes that the mean concentration of nanoplankton (<20µm) is quite high and is in fact greater than the critical level suggested by Lucas(1974; 1982 cited by Bell 1992) for promotion of the growth of *Acanthaster planci*. Thus eutrophication of the inner GBR lagoon could be a significant factor in the outbreaks of *A. planci* (cf. Birkeland's hypothesis see Bell, 1992). The high concentrations of nutrients in the outer regions are attributed to upwellings and in the case of DIN, also to nitrogen fixing algae and bacteria which inhabit the sub-strata of the coral reefs. In addition to the large scale impact of river discharge on Cleveland Bay there are a number of local or small scale impacts. The harbour channel is dredged regularly and the spoil is dumped into Cleveland Bay. Sewage effluent (35,000 m^3 d^{-1}) and sludge from the city of Townsville flows to Cleveland Bay. A recent tourist development at Nelly Bay has not only destroyed much of the existing buffering capacity of the foreshores for the septic seepage from the existing local population but will also increase run-off to the fringing reefs. A most beautiful headland dotted with large granite boulders and majestic pines was literally blasted apart and dumped into Nelly Bay to reclaim land and to construct a marina. The entrance to the marina requires the mining of the fringing coral reef. This development ensures that the "coral gardens" will never reestablish in Nelly Bay.

Low Isles. -- The observed reduction in coral cover at Low Isles, although not conclusive evidence, is consistent with the region being eutrophic. The principal cause of the eutrophication is surmised to be due to river discharges transporting nutrients from agricultural areas. The fact that the Low Isles region is impacted by river run-off has be recognised by various workers. Fairbridge and Teichert (Johannes, 1972 cited by Bell 1992) note that many of the corals in the vicinity of Low Isles had apparently been killed by sedimentation which they attribute to "colossal soil erosion due to unplanned agriculture". Yonge came essentially to the same conclusion on revisiting Low Isles, 50 years after the 1928 British expedition (Brown and Howard 1985 cited by Bell 1992). The CSIRO data summarised by Bell (1992) certainly show significant freshwater influence at Low Isles and the nitrate concentrations are of similar a magnitude to that measured by Revelante and Gilmartin (1982) for the river-affected inner lagoon off Townsville. A repeat of the 1928-29 study is underway. Preliminary results (see Figure 9) indicate that the diatom concentrations were much higher (~x 10) in 1992 than they were in 1928-29 (Elmetri 1993). Preliminary results for the concentrations of *Trichodesmium* indicate that they are also far higher now than they were in 1928-29. These results suggest that the GBR lagoon in the Low Isles region is far more fertile now than in 1928-29 which supports the hypothesis that GBR lagoon in this region is eutrophic. It is recognised that there could be a year to year variation in the phytoplankton concentrations and hence it is important that a monitoring programme be maintained.

CONCLUSIONS

The data demonstrate a close correspondence between the demise of the coral reefs in Barbados with increased development and the resulting degradation in water quality and associated eutrophication. The studies indicate that chronic eutrophication is inhibiting the reproduction of the corals and in doing so is inhibiting the recovery of damaged reefs. The effect of the eutrophication is magnified by the reduction in grazing pressure brought about by the *D. antillarum* die-off. Eutrophication, by promoting fleshy algal growth at the expense of coralline algal growth and reducing coral growth, could be a significant factor in the reef and beach erosion that is occurring on the west and south coasts of Barbados. The virtual extinction of *A. palmata* in recent times indicates that it could be particularly sensitive to eutrophication and if so the data suggest a relatively low eutrophication threshold of 0.3 mg chlorophyll a m^{-3}. Data for the GBR lagoon indicate that some river impacted regions exhibit signs of large scale eutrophication. There is some evidence that discharges of sewage are also impacting upon GBR coral reef ecosystems. The large scale eutrophication, which is attributed to agricultural run-off, could well be a factor in the demise of corals in the GBR lagoon and in the promotion of outbreaks of *A. planci*.

LITERATURE CITED

Bell P.R.F 1992. Eutrophication and coral reefs-some examples in the Great Barrier Reef lagoon. Water Research 26(5): 553-568.
Bell P.R.F. 1991. Status of eutrophication in the Great Barrier Reef lagoon. Mar. Poll. Bull. 23: 89-93.
Elmetri I. 1993. Usefulness of the 1928-29 Phosphate and Micro-Phytoplankton Data for Low Isles as a Baseline for Eutrophication in the Great Barrier Reef Lagoon. MSc thesis Univ. Queensland, Brisbane Australia.
Gabric A.J. and Bell P.R.F. 1993. A Review of the Large Scale Effects of Nutrient Loadings on Coastal Ecosystems - Use of Satellite Remote Sensing for Monitoring. Aust. J. Mar. Freshw. Res. (In Press).
GBR 1933. Sci. Rep. Gt. Barrier Reef Exped., Brit Museum. Nat. Hist. Vol. 1-7
Hunte W and Wittenberg M. 1992. Effects of eutrophication and sedimentation on juvenile corals II. Settlement Mar. Biol. 114, 625-631.
Lewis J.B. 1960. The coral reefs and coral communities of Barbados. W.I.Can J Zool 38: 1133-1145.
Lewsey C.D. 1978. Assessing the environmental effects of tourism development on the carrying capacity of small island systems "The case for Barbados". Ph. D. thesis Cornell University. Uni. Micro. Int. Ann Arbor Michigan.
Macintyre I.G. 1967. Recent Sediments off the west coast of Barbados, W.I. PhD thesis McGill University, Montreal, Quebec.
Maragos J.E., Evans C. and Holthus P. 1985. Reef corals in Kaneohe Bay. Six years before and after termination of sewage discharges (Oahu, Hawaiian Archipelago). In Proc. 5th Int Coral Reef Congress Tahiti Vol. 4 pp 189-194.
Nutting C.C. 1919 Barbados-Antigua expedition. Univ. Iowa Stud. Nat. Hist. 8:1-274
Ott B.S. 1971. Hermatypic coral predation at Barbados, West Indies, by *Coralliophila abbreviata* (Gastropoda, Prosobranchia) and *Hermodice carunculata* (Polychaeta, Errantia). MSc Thesis McGill University, Montreal Quebec.
Partlo J.K. 1975. Ecological aspects of a semi-enclosed, eutrophic, tropical marine environment. MSc thesis McGill Uni. Montreal
Revelante N. and Gilmartin M. 1982. Dynamics of phytoplankton in the Great Barrier Reef lagoon. J. Plankton Res. 4(1), 47-76.
Tomascik T 1991. Settlement patterns of Caribbean juvenile scleractinian corals on artificial substrata along a eutrophication gradient, Barbados, West Indies. Mar Ecol Prog. Ser. 77:261-269.
Tomascik T and Sander F 1985. Effects of eutrophication on reef-building corals I. Growth rate of the reef building coral *Montastrea annularis* Mar Biol 87:143-155
Tomascik T and Sander F 1987a. Effects of eutrophication on reef-building corals II. Structure of scleractinian coral communities on fringing reefs, Barbados, West Indies. Mar Biol 94: 3-75
Tomascik T. and Sander F 1987b. Effects of eutrophication on reef building corals Part III. Reproduction of the reef building coral *Porites porites*. Mar Biol 94: 77-94.
Turnbull A.A. 1979. The water quality characteristics and distribution of benthic invertebrates in a polluted harbour, Barbados, West Indies. MSc thesis Marine Sciences Centre McGill University Montreal.
Van Moorsel G.W.N.M. 1989. Juvenile ecology and reproductive strategies of reef corals. Profschrift ter verkrijging het doctoraat (PhD thesis), door G.W.N.M. Van Moorsel. Printed by Artigrafica, Den Helder
Wittenberg M and Hunte W 1992. Effects of eutrophication and sedimentation on juvenile corals. I Abundance, mortality and community structure. Mar. Biol. 112: 131-138.

IMPACTS OF CYCLONE-INDUCED FLOODS ON FRINGING REEFS: CASE STUDY OF KEPPEL BAY, QUEENSLAND, AUSTRALIA

Grahame Byron
Department of Environment and Heritage
Yeppoon Road Parkhurst, Rockhampton Queensland Australia 4702

ABSTRACT

In January of 1991 Tropical Cyclone Joy crossed the coast near Ayr, northern Queensland. The ensuing rainfall caused extensive flooding throughout the Fitzroy catchment in central Queensland. In excess of 18.5 million megalitres of flood runoff escaped down the Fitzroy River into Keppel Bay. Large-scale clearing of this catchment in the last twenty five years has led to increased silt loads in flood waters.

This runoff and the associated sediment had a major impact on the fringing reefs surrounding the continental islands within Keppel Bay. The shallow fringing reefs on the southern and western shores of Great Keppel, North Keppel, Middle and Miall Islands were devastated with mortality of 90% common.

The path of travel of the flood plume was monitored. The predominant winds and tidal conditions were found to strongly influence the shape and direction of movement of the plume.

The comparative analysis of the physical characteristics of the flood plume and the extent of coral mortality clearly showed that the variable extent and persistence of floodwaters throughout the Bay created disparate patterns of overall effect.

INTRODUCTION

The Fitzroy River basin covers an area of 140,000 square kilometres on the North East coast of Australia. The climate throughout the basin is distinctly seasonal, with heavy summer rainfall and protracted dry winter spells.

Most of the large volume flood flows in this basin are due to extremely high, short-term rainfall, resulting from monsoonal or cyclonic activity. Widespread flooding is common throughout the broad floodplains of the catchment, with the subsequent runoff taking a considerable time to discharge into Keppel Bay through the Fitzroy River (Fig.1).

The Islands in Keppel Bay are continental in origin, and many support well developed fringing reefs up to 200 metres wide. These generally occur as isolated reef patches adjacent to headlands or on the protected south and western sides of the island. These reefs are generally dominated by Acropora spp.

Keppel Bay supports an important commercial fishery with trawling for scallops and prawns, trolling for pelagic species, commercial aquarium fish and coral collection, oyster gathering and inshore gillnet enterprises.

The Bay also receives extensive tourist, commercial and recreational use. There is an underwater observatory on Middle Island and tourist resorts on Great Keppel and Pumpkin Islands. These developments have been located to take advantage of the adjacent coral reef communities, with water based activities such as snorkelling, scuba diving and fishing being important recreational activities.

On 26 December 1990, Tropical Cyclone Joy crossed the north Queensland coast, and produced heavy rainfall and flood runoff. It resulted in the third largest flood in the Fitzroy since records began in 1860. In excess of 18.5 million megalitres were discharged from the Fitzroy River in the 25 days from 28 December 1990 to 21 January 1991 (Keane, 1992).

The magnitude of this event was such that severe impacts were experienced throughout the fringing reefs of Keppel Bay. Such impacts directly influence the use of the area, creating significant economic difficulty for industries based on the natural resources. Consequently, this study was initiated to determine overall patterns of impact, so that future management and, in particular, zoning decisions for this part of the Great Barrier Reef Marine Park may be made with an understanding of major natural perturbations.

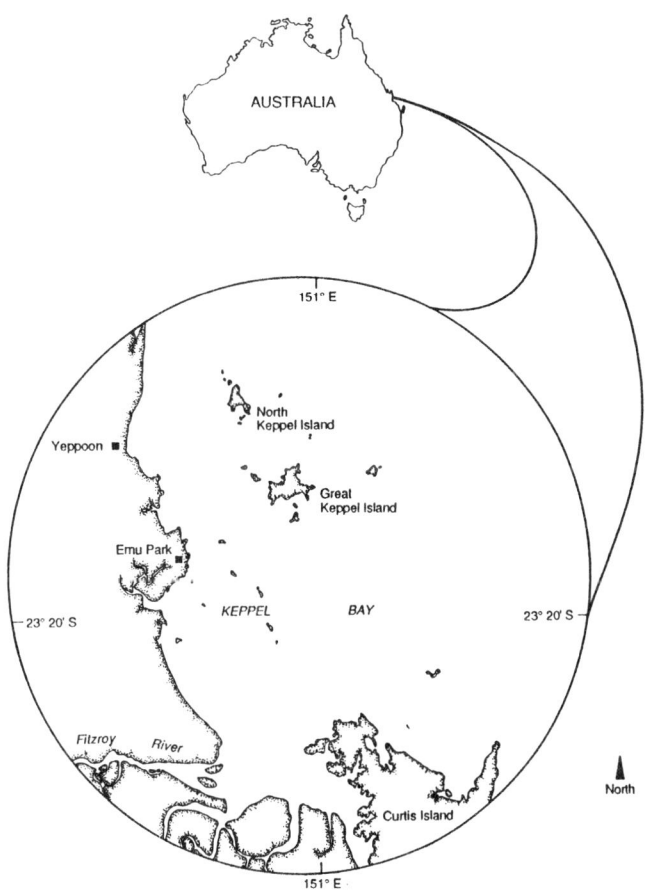

Figure 1 Location Map Scale 1:2 000 000

METHODS

Low level aerial flights over Keppel Bay on January 12, 19 and 23 were undertaken to map and photograph the extent, distance and direction of travel of the flood plume.

Measurements of salinity, turbidity and temperature were taken at 14 stations along five transects across Keppel Bay between January 17 and January 23, 1991.

Each station was sampled initially over a two day period (January 17 and 18), and then relocated using a Global Positioning System (GPS) and resampled on January 23, 1991.

A total of 22 fringing reefs were chosen for analysis of impacts on the basis of, known previous coral condition, level of human use and accessibility.

The selected sites, were surveyed by two observers using manta tow techniques (Moran, et. al. 1989). The observers were towed at 2 knots, approximately 20 m behind a vessel and separated by less than 3 m. Tow transects were run parallel to the reef edge, with each tow lasting two minutes. Sites 1 - 6 were observed on 30 April, Sites 9 - 13 on 2 May and Sites 14 - 22 on 7 May. At the commencement of each tow, a position fix, using a JRC JLU-121 Global Positioning System, and depth to bottom, using a JRC, JFV-86 colour echo sounder, were recorded. At the conclusion of the tow another position fix and depth to bottom measurement were recorded.

RESULTS

The January 1991 flood was the third largest recorded this century for the Fitzroy River, both in terms of peak river height and total discharge volume (Keane, 1992). After a protracted period of drought minimal flow had been recorded for the Fitzroy River for most of December 1990. However, on 28 December, the flow increased by over 42, 000 megalitres and within nine days it had risen to over one million megalitres per day, remaining above this level for nine days. By 21 January the height had dropped sufficiently for the river to again be contained within its banks, although the flow rate was still high, relative to the pre-flood values.

Extremely low salinities (< 10 ppt) were recorded at the surface over most of the inshore section of Keppel Bay on 17 and 18 January. Salinity levels on these dates increased with northward and eastward travel, and with increasing depth (refer Figure 2).

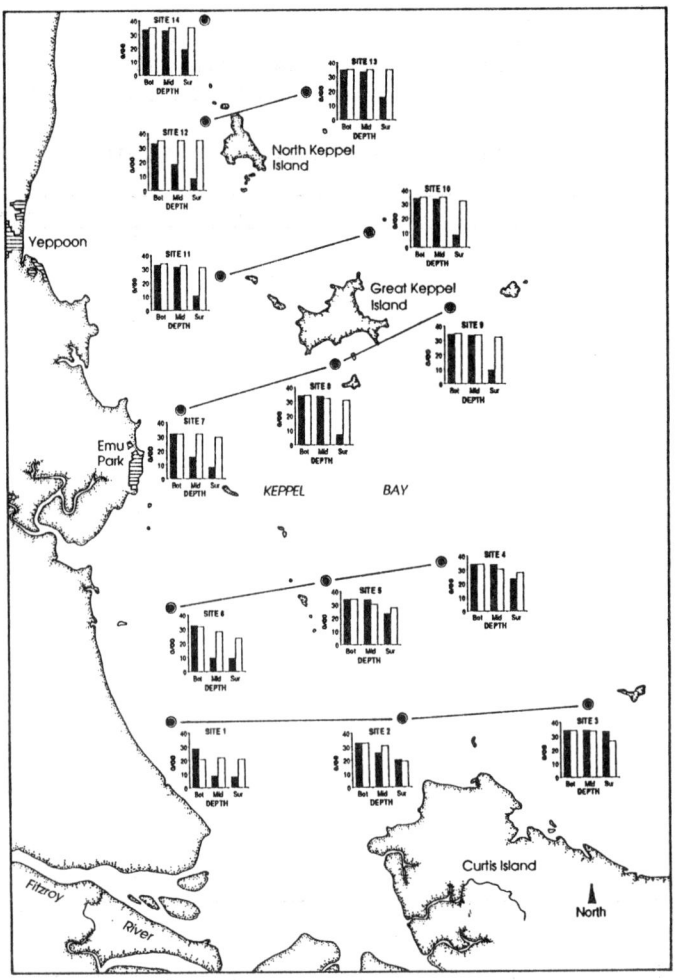

Figure 2. Salinity Values in Keppel Bay, January 1991 Scale 1:500 000
Notes: Solid Fill Columns = Data collected on 17 &18. 1.91
Clear Fill Columns = Data collected on 23.1.91
Bot = Within 1 metre of bottom, Mid = mid stratum, Sur = Surface

Recordings from the southern inshore stations (Stations 1, 6, & 7) indicated that the freshwater had penetrated to a greater depth than at the northern inshore stations. At the northern sites the mid-stratum salinity levels were closer to that of seawater (~ 35 ppt).

Stations 9, 10 and 13 also recorded relatively low surface salinity values on 18 January. These stations were not contained within the main body of the plume moving northwards, but rather within a southward moving back-eddy created by the interference presented by the Keppel Islands.

By 23 January the shape, position and concentration of the plume had changed markedly. At this time the discharge from the river had also dropped to its lowest level since 27 December, 1990, and the wind had now been blowing lightly from the north-west for a number of days. Diurnal tidal range was also at a minimum. Only the stations at the southern end of Keppel Bay now had salinity values of less than 30ppt and the fresh water effect was very much restricted to the near-surface samples. Salinity values at all points in the stratum had returned to above 30ppt at all stations from Great Keppel Island north.

There was significant mortality of corals on fringing reefs in Keppel Bay following this flooding event, with up to 90% mortality common on the shallower sections (<3m) of fringing reefs on the southern and western sides of North Keppel, Miall, Middle and Great Keppel Islands (Sites 3,4,9,10,13-19),(refer Table 1 and Figure 3). These areas suffered extensive mortality across the reef flat and down the crest with only the deeper fringes of these reefs surviving.

Sites on the exposed or eastern sides of the same islands (11,21), sites in deeper water (>4 m.), such as Passage Rocks (12), the edges of Miall and Middle Islands, and the coral communities further offshore at Outer Rock (7) and Barren Island (8) exhibited comparatively little recent mortality, (<30%).

Table 1. Coral cover estimates and level of mortality of fringing reefs in Keppel Bay.

Site No.	Estimated coral cover	Estimated coral mortality (%)	Depth of Impact
1	3	65	-
2	1	60	-
3	4	61	2.16m.-1.66m.
4	4	93	1.91m.-1.86m.
5	5	81.5	-
6	5	92.7	-
7	4	0	-
8	5	10	-
9	3	55	1.71m.
10	5	95	2.31m.-1.16m.
11	5	20	-
12	3	5	-
13	5	70	-
14	5	90	-
15	2	80	-
16	4	70	-
17	4	90	-
18	4	90	2.21m.
19	4	70	2.11m.
20	5	50	-
21	4	60	-
22	5	50	-
23	4	30	-

Note: Coral cover was divided into categories from 0(min) to 5(max) following Moran, P.J. et al (1989);

Mortality at various sites was limited by depth (*Acropora spp.* only),with an obvious boundary between live and dead coral at 6 sites (Refer Table 1). This boundary varied between and within these sites.

Percentage mortality varied between genera with *Acropora spp.* experiencing greater than 80% mortality in at least 9 sites. However, *Favia*, *Fungia*, and *Porites spp.*, remained healthy in many areas where *Acropora spp.* had succumbed (Sites 13-18).

Generally soft corals appeared not to suffer as badly as the hard corals. At Miall Island (Site 9), however, soft corals had also died.

Approximately 5% of the corals at Sites 14,20,22 also exhibited a loss of colour (ie. bleaching). This bleaching reportedly occurred at the time of flooding (B Morris, pers.comm.). Whilst there was no specific monitoring of the affected colonies during the surveys, it was noted during follow up surveys that this bleaching did not last greater than 5 months. By this time all bleached corals had either died or recovered.

At Monkey Point, which is a boulder reef dominated by small massive corals, (Site 14), many of the massive coral colonies were bleached. These colonies were conspicuous by their numbers and represent an uncommon community within Keppel Bay. Observations of this community over a 5 month period indicated that most coral colonies recovered.

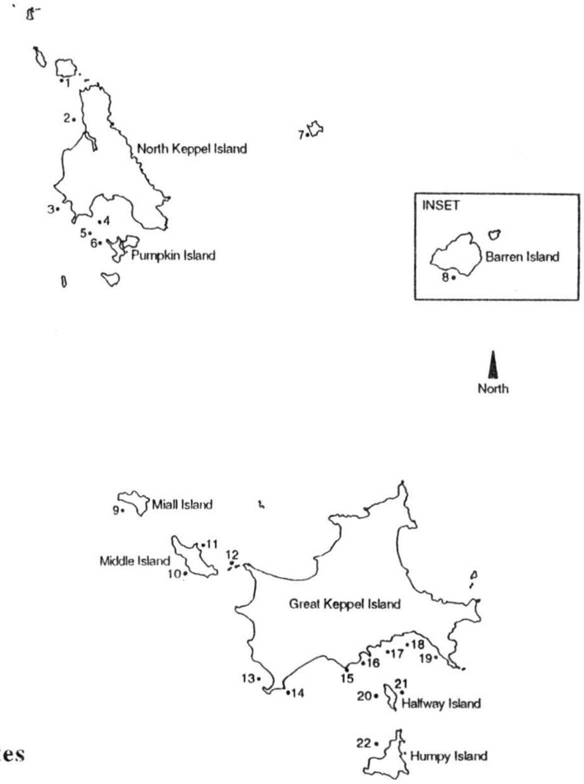

Figure 3. Survey Sites   Scale 1:200 000

DISCUSSION

Plume movement appeared to be largely controlled by localised weather influences. Aerial surveillance flights undertaken during the flood indicated that the shape and location of the plume was not static. At all times the eastern edge of the plume was very clearly defined, the coffee coloured flood waters presenting a stark contrast to the adjacent seawater. Changes in location of the eastern edge of the plume were at times observable within a period of hours, however the general direction of travel and shape of the plume remained stable in the period before about January 19. During this period the plume travelled generally northwards and on January 12 was plotted some 70 kilometres north of the Fitzroy River mouth.

The tidal range in the area is relatively large (up to 5m.), and this resulted in large quantities of water being moved toward and away from the coast on a daily basis. A consistent pattern of northward flood flow and southward ebb flow has been observed along most of the coast between the Keppel Islands and the mainland (Beach Protection Authority, 1979). However, the interference of coastal islands, reefs and channels is known to cause abrupt changes both in tidal velocities and flow direction. These tidal currents are difficult to separate from the wind induced drift currents often present in this area.

There was a consistent pattern of south east winds from late December 1990 until about 18 January, 1991. These winds contained the plume inshore and maintained a northward flow of floodwaters. On 19 January, the south easterly winds were replaced by north-westerlies, and the plume began to move easterly. By 23 January the plume had reached the Capricorn Bunker Group of islands, some 48 nautical miles to the east.

The significant overall increase in water clarity recorded in Keppel Bay on 23 January reflected a change in direction of plume movement rather than a general lessening of plume turbidity levels. Turbidity levels at the three southern sites changed little during this period of time, and actually increased at site 3 on the later date, due to the main body of freshwater then moving through this area.

The thickness of the freshwater surface layer (<20ppt) around the Keppel Islands during this time was variable, but tended to remain between 3 and 5 metres. This layer moved up and down with tidal movement, affecting marine life in deeper waters on the low tides. The duration of freshwater innundation at particular depths is difficult to determine retrospectively. However, with a tidal range during this period up to 4.18 metres, it is likely that on the high tides even organisms in the lower intertidal zone were innundated by water with salinity less than 30ppt.

The freshwater flood effects from the Fitzroy River were evident in the majority of reefs throughout Keppel Bay. Of those reefs affected, the inshore expansive fringing reef communities on the southern and western sides of islands were most devastated. These reefs are dominated by large banks of fast growing *Acropora formosa, A.millepora* and *A.micropthalma*, (Van Woesik, 1990).

It was evident that various species of corals were affected in different ways to exposure to the flood plume. Mortality was highest in shallow coral communities dominated by *Acropora spp*. The coral communities further offshore which are both taxonomically and bathymetrically more diverse showed little if any damage that could be attributed to the flood, due to the shorter time of exposure to the plume. Additionally, at these sites the plume was more saline and thinner in profile than at the sites closer inshore.

The relatively high mortality and dominance of *Acropora spp*. on most affected reefal areas suggests high turnover and growth rates of these species, particularly on the reef flats. The staghorn *Acropora* do not cope well with such stress, but have a shorter regeneration time (Oliver, 1985). Species of *Favites* and *Porites* on the other hand appear to cope with these stressors in this situation. If the critical limits of the *Favites* and *Porites* species were reached, however, because of their long recovery times local extinction could occur. This would create a situation where *Acropora spp*. could overgrow the area.

The relationship between depth and mortality was highly variable. Previous reports of freshwater impacts on corals in the Great Barrier Reef have referred to a critical depth (Hedley, 1925), (Van Woesik, 1991). In contrast this study indicates that coral mortality as a result of flooding varies with depth, location and species.

As would be expected, there was no consistent correlation between these variables as the floodwater was unevenly and irregularly distributed throughout the bay with varying degrees of persistence. Clearly, managers need to consider these dramatic environmental changes when planning for the future use of areas. Anecdotal evidence from previous major flooding events (1954,-83,-88) record a similar pattern of effect on the corals in Keppel Bay.

Flooding is undoubtedly a primary regulator of the pattern of development and succession of fringing reefs within Keppel Bay. These common but irregular pulses of mass mortality probably determine the spatial and temporal extent of these reefs.

Natural perturbations such as this must have always affected coral reef development. It is suspected, however, that actions such as land clearing would indirectly exacerbate the impacts.

The development of the lands of the brigalow belt, (*Acacia harpophylla*), for agriculture in the mid 1960's to the early 1970's resulted in the clearing of several million hectares of central Queensland, primarily in the Fitzroy catchment (Webb, 1984). The two major problems of soil erosion and soil salinity that were associated with this extensive clearing have not dissipated (Johnson, 1985). Whilst mud fractions are continually removed from Keppel Bay by the strong northerly currents (Beach Protection Authority, 1979), large volumes of sediment from the brigalow lands are continuing to be deposited in Keppel Bay.

Differential recruitment to the affected areas may also result if the sediment loads exceed a level which will support developing recruits. Whilst no overall measurement of the silt load was available for this event, initial estimates made by the Water Resource Commission suggest that 10-20 million tonnes of silt passed down the Fitzroy River during the flood period, (Keane, pers. comm.). Soil loss estimates of 1300 tonnes per hectare were recorded in the cultivated areas of the floodplain, and in one instance 430,000 tonnes of alluvial soil was removed when a new channel was created (Chapman, 1992).

Historic evidence suggests that this recent flood was simply another event in a long series of natural environmental perturbations. However, due to changes in land use practices throughout the Fitzroy catchment, (Johnson, 1985), which have significantly elevated sediment loads in the river, the severity of impact of such natural events is very likely increasing. The cumulative effects of increasing silt deposition combined with irregular massive freshwater immersion, may be reducing the viability and potential for reestablishment of the coral communities in certain locations throughout Keppel Bay.

CONCLUSIONS

Even though the floods have abated, there will be long term ongoing stress of fringing reefs as the waters of the bay are continually muddied by the resuspension of bottom sediment stirred up by winds, tides and currents. These irregular events might prevent long term survival of some species in areas where their tolerance to stressors is exceeded, particularly if recruitment is unreliable. Whilst many fringing reefs do grow in highly turbid situations the severity of the effect of these natural events is likely to change with time as a result of changes in land use and management practices in the catchment area. This topic is currently being investigated in a number of studies underway in the Great Barrier Reef Region.

Cyclones and their consequent impacts are a major force shaping the development and use of the Great Barrier Reef Marine Park. Considerable effort is expended on a regular basis, monitoring and managing anthropomorphic impacts throughout the Great Barrier Reef Marine Park. Comparatively less management-oriented research effort is directed to understanding the natural changes occuring in our resources. Quite often, as managers we have limited understanding of the extent of natural changes in our resources and we are unable to manage or plan for major environmental events such as floods or cyclones. When such events do occur we take a reactive role in measuring the impacts and managing the consequences.

REFERENCES

Beach Protection Authority, (1979) Capricorn Coast Beaches. A detailed Study of Coastline Behaviour along the Capricorn Coast of Queensland, Australia. BPA, Dec., 1979.

Chapman,D.G. (1992) Erosion Observation and Land Management Recommendations for the Floodplains Following Cyclone Joy Floods in January 1991, in: Workshop on the Impacts of Flooding, ed: G.T.Byron, GBRMPA Townsville pp. 94-96

Hedley C. (1925), The natural destruction of a coral reef, transactions of the Royal Geographical Society in Report of Great Barrier Reef Committee 1:3540.Canberra.

Johnson, R.W. (1985) The impact of agricultural development on the vegetation of the Brigalow lands of Queensland, in. Gasteen,J., Henry,D. and Page, S. (eds.) Agriculture and conservation in Inland Queensland. Wild. Pres. Soc.Qld., Brisbane pp 10-12.

Keane, M. (1992) Assessment of the 1991 Fitzroy River Flood. How Much Water? in: Workshop on the Impacts of Flooding, ed:G.T.Byron,GBRMPA Townsville. pp 16-35

Moran P.J. et al (1989), A Guide to the AIMS Manta Tow Technique, Australian Institute of Marine Science, Townsville.

Oliver J. (1985), Recurrent seasonal bleaching and mortality of corals on the Great Barrier Reef. Proc 5th Int Coral Reef Cong Vol. 4.

Van Woesik, R. (1990) An assessment of the coral reef communities of the Keppel Isles, report to the Great Barrier Reef Marine Park Authority, Townsville.

Van Woesik, R. (1991) Impact of the 1991 floods on coral communities of the Keppel Islands, report to Great Barrier Reef Marine Park Authority, Townsville.

Webb, A.A. (1984) Consequences of agricultural land use in the Brigalow belt. in.The Brigalow Belt of Australia, ed. Bailey, A. The Royal Soc of Qld Symp. Oct 82 (Bris) pp.131-147

DOOMSDAY ECOLOGY MISAPPLIED: ALLEGED VERSUS DOCUMENTED IMPACTS OF A DEEP OCEAN SEWAGE OUTFALL IN HAWAII

by

Richard W. Grigg and Steven J. Dollar

School of Ocean, Earth, Science & Technology
University of Hawaii, Honolulu, Hawaii 96822

ABSTRACT

In 1991 and again in 1993, the City and County of Honolulu, State of Hawaii, was sued by the Sierra Club Legal Defense Fund for alleged violations of the U.S. Clean Water Act, mainly for discharging primary treated sewage wastewater into the ocean through deep outfalls off Oahu. However, a multitude of scientific studies have failed to document any public health hazard, or any environmental impact caused by the discharges. This case history documents the results of one of these lawsuits including a review of the scientific evidence presented at trial.

INTRODUCTION

"Doomsday ecology" is becoming increasingly popular in the public media. And for good reason. With world human population growth exploding at an out of control annual rate of about 1.9%, the specter of global warming and ozone depletion hanging over the next century, rampant destruction of tropical rain forests and other natural resources, and increasing tensions over human food supply worldwide, there are plenty of valid reasons for legitimate concern. In fact, it may well be that the solutions to these and other disaster scenarios will arise out of this increasing environmental awareness. It is therefore of utmost importance that concern over these impending problems is founded on a strong factual basis. Sewage pollution of the world's ocean is a case in point.

In the United States, federal law (the Clean Water Act of 1972) required that all sewage discharged into navigable waters be treated at the secondary level. Recognition by the U.S. Environmental Protection Agency (EPA) that secondary treatment may not be required to protect human health and the marine environment resulted in an amendment (the 301(h) waiver program) to the Clean Water Act in 1977. Under the waiver program, discharge of advanced primary treatment is allowed in cases where it can be demonstrated that such a practice is environmentally sound.

Such was the case in Honolulu, Hawaii when the City and County applied to the EPA for a 301(h) waiver permit to discharge effluent treated at the advanced primary level for the Honouliuli Waste Water Treatment Plant (HWWTP) located in Ewa, on the Island of Oahu. EPA approved and granted the permit to the City and County, but immediately thereafter the Sierra Club Legal Defense Fund (SCLDF) filed a lawsuit against the City and County. By virtue of this lawsuit, the waiver permit was stayed, and the City and County was in technical violation of discharging less than secondary effluent during the period when the waiver permit was in preparation. Because the waiver was not in effect during the period stipulated in the lawsuit, a federal judge ruled that the City and County was in violation of the Clean Water Act. A separate trial was held to determine the penalties for the cited violations based on the impacts to public health and the marine environment caused by the Honouliuli discharge. In effect, by filing these lawsuits, the SCLDF challenged the judgement of the EPA to issue a 301(h) waiver.

DISCUSSION

The basis of the SCLDF suit was that the discharge "...resulted in serious threats to public health and marine life" (SCLDF, 1993). However, the scientific record presented at trial demonstrated that no negative environmental impacts or public health hazards could be attributed to the discharge of primary treated effluent at Honouliuli over the 10-year period that the outfall has been in operation. The evidence that supports this conclusion is summarized as follows:

• The HWWTP has been discharging primary treated effluent off Ewa Beach on the southern coastline of Oahu since 1982. The ocean outfall system extends 2,670 m from shore and terminates at a water depth of 61 m (see Figure 1). Sewage is dispersed through 148 ports (5-9 cm in diameter) along a 533 m long diffuser at the end of the outfall pipe. At present, the discharge is approximately 90×10^6 liters day^{-1} (≈ 25 million gallons per day (mgd)). Peak wet weather flow capacity is approximately 400×10^6 liters day^{-1} (≈ 112 mgd). Industrial flow to the Honouliuli system is negligible and storm water is not routed to the outfall. None of the priority pollutants specified by EPA exceeded water quality criteria following initial dilution. Effluent consists of domestic sewage composed primarily of dissolved and particulate C, N, and P.

• Along the entire Ewa coastline between Pearl Harbor and Barbers Point coral communities are sparse and patchily distributed between the depths of 5 to 20 m. Inshore of 5 m, and deeper than 20 m, corals are essentially absent. Coral reef ecosystems inshore of the outfall and along the adjacent shoreline have been shown to be controlled primarily by storm wave stress, sediment scour, and inappropriate substratum resulting from the predominance of sand cover across the entire area (R.M. Towill, 1976;

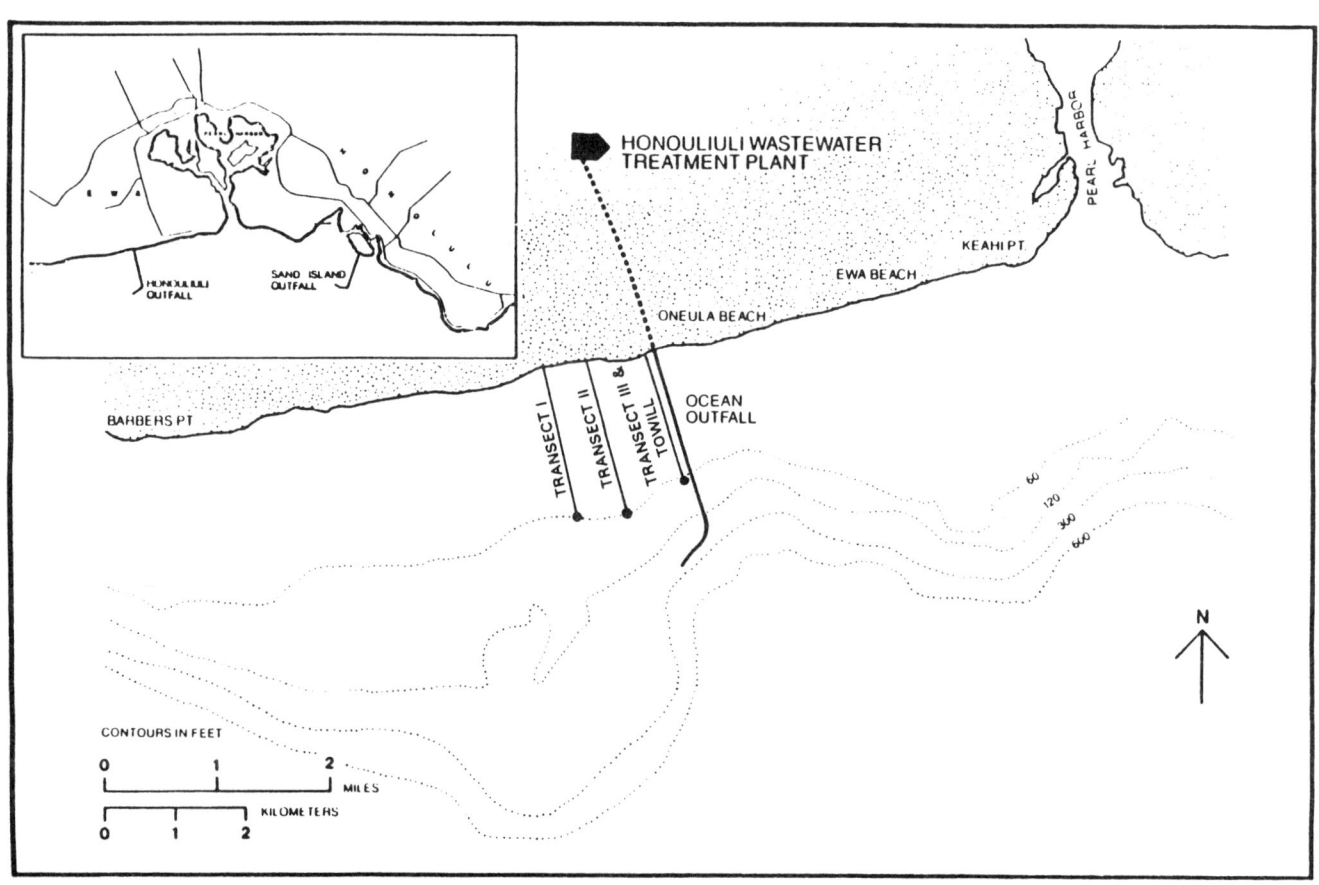

FIGURE 1. Location of the Honouliuli ocean outfall off Ewa Beach, Oahu, Hawaii. Also shown are the locations of three transects where coral community structure was surveyed at depts of 4.5, 9.1 and 18.3 m. See Table 1 for survey results.

Marine Research Consultants 1991; Brock, 1992). Percent coral cover is typically less than 10% (Table 1, Figure 1), although small localized areas of coral have been recorded up to about 40% as a result of higher relief of the bottom which reduces the lethal effects of scour and smothering from shifting sand. No gradient in the abundance of coral or other benthos is associated with the outfall. Nor is there any indication of any significant temporal change in coral abundance since the outfall was constructed. Data collected in 1974 (Towill, 1976) do not differ significantly ($p > 0.05$) from data collected in 1990 (Marine Research Consultants, 1991)(see Table 1).

- The EPA model "UMERGE" was used to estimate dispersion of the Honouliuli effluent plume (EPA, 1985). UMERGE models a positively buoyant discharge by tracing a plume particle through the course of its trajectory and dilution, based on current speeds, water depth, and orientation and spacing of the diffuser ports. Model results predict that the worst case instantaneous initial dilution of the submerged plume is about 1,000, with a chronic dilution on the order of 20,000. Initial dilution is defined as the dilution that takes place while the effluent plume is rising until it reaches neutral density and stabilizes, or until it reaches the surface. During the winter months when vertical stratification of the water column is deeper than the discharge, effluent can reach the surface, and southerly winds can carry the plume toward the shoreline. At the 20 m depth contour (the maximum depth where corals are common), the worst case instantaneous dilution is predicted to be 1,700 (occurring about 6 hours per year) with a chronic dilution of 50,000-100,000. At shallower depths, dilution is substantially greater.

- At the worst case instantaneous dilution of 1,700, the subsidy of dissolved NH_4^+, NO_3^- and PO_4^{3-} from the effluent at the 20 m contour would be about 0.7 μM, 0.005 μM and 0.003 μM, respectively. These subsidies account for less than a 10% increase for NO_3^- and PO_4^{3-} over mean ambient concentration, while the increase of NH_4^+ equals about a 2-fold increase over the ambient water column concentrations. However, these increases in dissolved nutrients appear to be well within the range that corals can tolerate with no alteration of community structure or function. In fact, these worst case concentrations are at least ten times less than values of nutrients known to affect normal coral metabolism (Kinsey and Domm, 1974; Kinsey and Davis, 1979). In another study, Stamber et al. (1991) used concentrations of 2 μM NH_4^+ and 0.1 μM PO_4^{3-} as <u>controls</u> in experiments to determine the effects of nutrient enrichment on *Pocillopora damicornis* in Hawaii. These control concentrations are at least twice the concentrations off Honouliuli. At the level of chronic dilution, nutrient enrichment in the areas where corals occur is undetectable.

- At the worst case instantaneous dilution of 1,700, suspended solids from the discharge would contribute 30 μg l^{-1} to the water column, representing an increase of less than 10% over mean ambient conditions. Such an increase in suspended sediments is not likely to result in any alteration to coral settlement, growth or survival. Experiments to determine the effect of

TABLE 1. Percent cover at selected transect stations off Ewa Beach (From Marine Research Consultants, 1991, and R. M. Towill, 1976). The Towill Transect and Transect III are parallel to the Honouliuli outfall pipe; Transects II and I are about 200 m and 300 m to the west, respectively (see Figure 1).

Depth (m)	Transect I	Transect II	Transect III	Towill Transect
4.5	0.3	0.0	4.6	1.1
9.1	12.2	8.4	3.2	7.8 (12.2 m)
18.3	2.6	41.0	2.6	9.9

sediment on the settlement of *Pocillopora damicornis* planulae in Hawaii showed no significant effects at sediment treatments up to 1,000 mg l^{-1} (Te, 1992), four orders of magnitude greater than the worst case increase from effluent discharge. Similarly, Randall and Birkeland (1978) and Pastorok and Bilyard (1985) demonstrated that sedimentation rates of 2-13 g m^{-2} hr^{-1} are not detrimental to corals in the vicinity of a river outflow in Guam. The average deposition rate for the Honouliuli effluent within the Zone of Initial Dilution (ZID) was estimated at 0.003 g m^{-2} hr^{-1} (Tetra Tech, 1987), 3 to 4 orders of magnitude less than that noted to have no apparent effect on a healthy reef. Similar assessments for the changes in dissolved oxygen, BOD, salinity and pH indicate that even at the worst case dilutions, negative impacts to coral communities do not appear possible. At the chronic dilutions, virtually no changes in the concentrations of these factors can be detected in the water column.

• Experiments conducted at the sediment-water interface within a sampling grid near the Honouliuli Outfall (Smith and Dollar, 1986), as well as calculations based on effluent particle size and current velocities (Tetratech, 1987), indicate that less than 1% of the particulate material released from the diffuser settles to the bottom. Particulate material that reaches the benthos is rapidly metabolized at the interface, with virtually no incorporation into the sediment column (Smith and Dollar, 1986). Repetitive benthic infaunal sampling at seven stations within and beyond the ZID revealed no significant differences between stations with respect to mean abundance of infaunal organisms or numbers of species (Nelson et al. 1991; 1992). Fish community structure was enhanced along, and over, the outfall diffuser structure compared to neighboring soft bottom areas (Russo, 1986; 1989).

• The effluent plume also does not appear to affect phytoplankton or zooplankton community structure (AECOS, 1983; M&E Pacific, 1983; Tetratech, 1987). Mean measurements (n=200) of Chl $\underline{a}$ and secchi depth from 3 depths at ten stations within and outside the Zone of Mixing collected over a 6-year period reveal there was no effect on phytoplankton from the effluent (E. Laws, personal communication). There are, however, statistically significant relationships between the distance from the mouth of Pearl Harbor and Chl $\underline{a}$ (negative correlation) and secchi depth (positive correlation). At the Honouliuli outfall, dilution and dispersal of dissolved nutrients is apparently too rapid to result in uptake by phytoplankton at levels different than ambient conditions.

• No evidence of any human health problems associated with the effluent discharge was produced during the trial. In addition, officials from the State of Hawaii Department of Health report that there are no records of public health problems (Bruce Anderson, personal communication). It was estimated that a person at the shoreline would have to drink 57 gallons of sea water to inject one plaque forming unit (PFU) originating from the discharge (M&E Pacific, 1989). Expressed in terms of dilution from the outfall, the probability of infection was calculated to be 4.7×10^{-5}. An acceptable risk based on Federal standards and epidemiological criteria is 19 per 1000 swimmers (population) or 1.9×10^{-2}. In other words, the risk of bacterial or enterovirus infection caused by outfall pathogens is insignificant.

Given the overwhelming weight of evidence produced by the defense (and lack of evidence produced by the plaintiffs), concerning the detrimental effects of discharge of less than secondarily treated effluent, the question must be asked: Why did the SCLDF file suit in the first place? The history of a similar lawsuit filed by the SCLDF against the City and County of Honolulu over another sewage treatment plant at Sand Island may provide the answer. In that lawsuit, filed in 1991, the issue was nearly the same. The discharge at Sand Island was at the primary level, and the SCLDF argued that secondary treatment was legally required and necessary to prevent environmental degradation, even though they had no data to support this charge. However, because the City and County was technically in violation of the Clean Water Act because of bypasses during power outages, they settled the case out of court for $14 million. The settlement paid all of the SCLFD legal expenses incurred in filing the suit. It also provided funds for future studies to further quantify effects of the discharge. It was a profitable victory for the SCLDF and came without so much as even a test of their allegations in court.

An editorial written by the Editor of the journal Science recently described such tactics as "Get rich quick science" (Koshland, 1993).

For the SCLDF, the Honouliuli case may have appeared to be another easy settlement. This time however, the City and County decided to fight the lawsuit in court. Two more sewage treatment plants on Oahu had been named by the SCLDF as the subjects of future lawsuits over violations of the Clean Water Act. At Honouliuli, the City and County of Honolulu drew a line in the sand and said "not without first proving it in court". If the City and County prevails, it is likely that the other impending lawsuits will be dropped and millions of dollars required for unnecessary upgades of facilities will be saved.

CONCLUSIONS

Depending on the outcome of the Honouliuli case, the SCLDF could lose there court cost fees and operating expenses. Perhaps more importantly, they could also lose a considerable amount of credibility and power. In the future, we hope the SCLDF will redirect their energies to fight the real doomsday world problems for which there seems to be no shortage. There can be no question that their environmental awareness and concern is needed to wage these battles. We hope that other environmental groups will also get the message and focus more on the really serious environmental issues facing the world. As a society we must use the best scientific information available, and we must apply it where it is needed most. At the world conference on the environment in Rio de Janeiro in 1992 (UNCED), the global population explosion was treated as a local problem needing more "appropriate demographic policies". Such diversions will only delay our collective ability to solve world problems. If doomsday ecology is to *save* the environment it must be applied to both the symptoms and the cause of resource depletion, and environmental degradation, and that means reining in the human population explosion.

REFERENCES

AECOS, 1983. Zooplankton and larval fish near the Honouliuli deep ocean outfall. Unpublished report. 28 pp.

Brock, R. E. 1992. Community structure of fish and macrobenthos at selected shallow water sites in relation to the Barbers Point Deep Ocean Outfall, 1991. Water Resources Research Center Special Report. 10.07.92. 33 pp.

EPA. 1985. Initial Mixing Characteristics of Municipal Ocean Discharges: Vol. 1. Procedures and Applications. USEPA 600/3-85 073a. Environmental Research Lab. Narraganset, R.I. 132 pp.

Kinsey, D. W. and P. J. Davies. 1979. Effects of elevated nitrogen and phosphorus on coral reef growth. Limnol. and Oceanogr. 24:95-109.

Kinsey, D. W. and A. Domm. 1974. Effects of fertilization on a coral reef environment - primary production studies. Proc. 2nd Int. Coral Reef Symp., Brisbane, Australia. 1:49-66.

Koshland, D. E. 1993. Get rich quick science. Science, 259:1103.

Marine Research Consultants. 1991. Ewa Marina, Ocean/marina monitoring program. Reef community structure. Report No. 1. 11 pp.

M & E Pacific. 1983. Reapplication for secondary treatment modification, Honouliuli Treatment Facility. Unpublished Report, M & E Pacific, Inc. Engineers and Architects, Honolulu, Hawaii.

M & E Pacific. 1989. Assessment of the public health risks of the discharges from the Sand Island, Barbers Point, and Waianae outfall systems. Vol 1. Unpublished Report, M & E Pacific, Inc. Engineers and Architects, Honolulu, Hawaii.

Nelson, W. G., J. H. Bailey-Brock, W. J. Cooke, and E. A. Kay. 1991. Benthic faunal sampling adjacent to Barbers Point ocean outfall, Oahu, Hawaii, February 1990. Water Resources Research Center Special Report 04.01.91, University of Hawaii.

Nelson, W. G., J. H. Bailey-Brock, W. J. Cooke, and E. A. Kay. 1992. Benthic faunal sampling adjacent to Barbers Point ocean outfall, Oahu, Hawaii, July 1991. Water Resources Research Center Special Report 06.30.921, University of Hawaii.

Pastorok, R. A. and G. R. Bilyard. 1985. Effects of sewage pollution on coral reef communities. Mar. Ecol. Prog. Ser. 21:175-189.

Randall, R. H. and C. Birkeland. 1978. Guam's reefs and beaches. Part II: Sedimentation studies at fouha Bay and Ylig Bay, University of Guam, Marine Laboratory Report No. 47. 75 pp.

Russo, A. R. 1986. Fish community structure on a deep ocean outfall, Barbers Point, Oahu, Hawaii, 1981-86. Water Resources Research Center Special Report 11:86. 9 pp.

Russo, A. R. 1989. Fish community structure on a deep ocean outfall, Barbers Point Oahu, Hawaii. Int. Revue ges. Hydrobiol. 74(5):499-506.

Sierra Club Legal Defense Fund. 1993. In brief, A quarterly newsletter on environmental law. 11 pp.

Smith, S. V. and S. J. Dollar. 1986. Responses of the benthic ecosystem to deep ocean sewage outfalls in Hawaii: a nutrient cycling approach to biological impact assessment and monitoring. EPA Report, 172 pp.

Stambler, N., N. Popper, Z. Dubinsky and J. Stimson. 1991. Effects of nutrient enrichment and water motion on the coral *Pocillopora damicornis*. Pac. Sci. 45:299-307.

Te, F. T. 1992. Response to higher sediment loads by *Pocillopora damicornis* planulae. Coral Reefs 11:131-134.

Tetra Tech, Inc. 1987. Technical review of the Honouliuli wastewater treatment plant section 301(h) application for modification of secondary treatment requirements for discharge into marine waters. EPA Report, 206 pp.

Towill, R. M. 1976. Oceanographic data collection and analysis, Barbers Point ocean outfall system. Unpublished Report. 173 pp.

REEFS IN KANEOHE BAY, HAWAII:
TWO CENTURIES OF WESTERN INFLUENCE AND TWO DECADES OF DATA

Cynthia L. Hunter[1] and Christopher W. Evans[2]

[1]University of Hawaii, Hawaii Institute of Marine Biology, P.O. Box 1346, Kaneohe, HI 96744.
[2] University of Hawaii, Department of Geography, Honolulu, HI 96822.

ABSTRACT

Kaneohe Bay, an estuarine and coral reef ecosystem on the windward coast of Oahu, Hawaii, is often cited as an exemplary illustration of the resiliency of an ecosystem to environmental insult. Impacts to Kaneohe Bay coral reefs have resulted from various effects of natural processes such as freshwater flooding and erosional runoff. Additional impacts to the reef communities have resulted from activities concomitant with urbanization, including extensive dredging, increased sedimentation, stream channelization, and municipal sewage discharges.

After twenty-five years of discharge, two large sewage outfalls were diverted from the Bay in 1977-78, followed by a rapid and dramatic decrease in nutrient levels, turbidity, and phytoplankton abundance in the previously affected areas. There was a corresponding change in community structure from one dominated by the green bubble algae, Dictyosphaeria cavernosa, and filter or deposit feeders, to one more closely approaching the "coral gardens" described by Kaneohe Bay visitors prior to W.W.II. By 1983, D. cavernosa had decreased to 1/4 of its previous abundance while coral cover (mainly Porites compressa and Montipora verrucosa) had doubled. The last point-source sewage discharge into the bay was diverted in 1986. Although recovery of coral reef community in Kaneohe Bay was expected to continue, a 1990 survey indicated that algae cover had increased and coral recovery had slowed relative to 1983 levels. This paper discusses the recent history of Kaneohe Bay in light of anthropogenic alterations, describes changes on reefs in the bay over the past two decades, and discusses potential factors involved in these changes.

INTRODUCTION

Kaneohe Bay has been one of the most intensively studied coral reef systems in the world. As one of the premier locations for tropical marine research and the site of Hawaii Institute of Marine Biology, the oldest research institute of the University of Hawaii, researchers have produced over 1000 publications, reports, theses, and dissertations that address various aspects of the diverse flora and fauna in the estuarine and reef habitats of this semi-tropical embayment.

Environmental Setting

The physical setting of Kaneohe Bay has been described in numerous publications (e.g. Banner, 1974; Smith, et al. 1973, 1981; Devaney, et al., 1982; Holthus, 1986; Jokiel, et al., 1991; Hawaii Office of State Planning, 1992). The 31.5 km^2 bay on the windward (northeast) coast of Oahu, Hawaii, is approximately 12.7 km long, 4.3 km across at its widest points, and bordered by 28 km of shoreline. The seaward boundary of the bay is marked by the only barrier reef in the Hawaiian archipelago (and the northern-most barrier reef in the Pacific), cut by two natural channels. A dredged ship channel runs the length of the bay, connecting the north and south passages and allowing deep-draft access. Watersheds adjacent to the bay have a combined area of 97 km^2. These watersheds consist of gently rolling hills and valleys that abut nearly vertical cliffs at their landward boundaries.

Much of the shoreline of Kaneohe Bay is bordered by shallow fringing reefs punctuated by the entry of twelve streams and their associated estuarine components. Scattered throughout the bay, but concentrated near the channels, are 79 patch reefs ranging in size from 0.6 to 358 x 10^3 m^2. Mean depth of the bay is 8.4 m, with a maximum depth of about 17 m (Smith, et al. 1981). About half (47%) of the bay area is lagoonal (>10 m depth) with mud bottom, a third is shallow reef flat (<1.5 m), and the remaining area (20%) is steep reef slope where coral abundance is high.est Water circulation in the bay involves net transport of ocean seawater across the barrier reef toward shore, with most of the water exiting the bay through the two channels (Bathen, 1968). Mean monthly seawater temperature varies from 19.5-28.9° C, about 0.7° C above mean ocean temperatures.

Annual rainfall in the Kaneohe region averages 140-240 cm/year and total stream discharge rate is approximately 214,000 m^3/day, although episodic storms may result in flow rates almost an order of magnitude higher (2,120,000 m^3/day; Jokiel, et al., in press). Severe rainfalll events (e.g. 1965 and 1987) have led to significant mortality of benthic organisms on shallow (<120 cm) reef flats and slopes (Banner, 1968; Jokiel, et al., in press). Depth-averaged bay salinity approximates oceanic conditions (35 ppt), with occasional decreases in salinity (to 20 ppt, Jokiel, et al., in press) occurring in near-shore, shallow waters due to storm runoff. The impacts of two major freshwater flooding events on the biota of the bay have been documented over the past 25 years (Banner, 1968; Jokiel, et al., in press). Both of these events resulted in heavy mortality to nearshore, shallow water, benthic reef communities. Coral mortality due to the most recent (1987) freshwater "kill" extended to a depth of 120 cm below reef crests, and particularly near stream mouths. As coral species show differential sensitivities to reduced salinities, episodic freshwater kills on Kaneohe Bay reefs play an important role in structuring these reef communities.

Kaneohe Bay can be characterized by distinct north-south gradients in rural to urbanized watersheds and oceanic to land-influenced waters. Most of the population in the surrounding watersheds is concentrated in the southern sections. The bay waters adjacent to these watersheds have the most restricted water circulation and have also been the most affected by dredging and the impacts of urbanization.

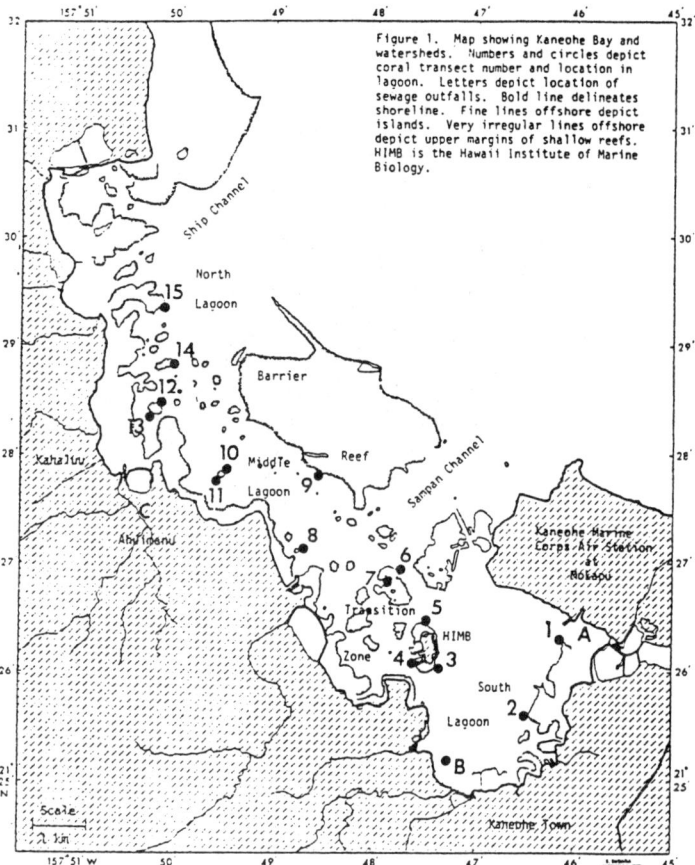

Figure 1. Map of Kaneohe Bay, Oahu and reef survey sites.

Historical Overview of Kaneohe Bay

The recent history of Kaneohe Bay (post-western contact in 1778) involves a series of changes in utilizations of the bay and its surrounding watersheds. From the 1800's through the early part of this century, land use changed from primarily taro culture to cultivation of pineapple, sugarcane, rice, and pasturage for cattle, horses, and goats. Approximately 40% of stream flow into Kaneohe Bay was diverted between 1916 and the 1930's to irrigate central and leeward Oahu through a massive system of ditch tunnels.

Just prior to and during World War II, the U.S. Navy constructed a military base on Mokapu Peninsula at the southern end of the bay (now Kaneohe Marine Corps Air Station), and dredged over 15 million cubic yards of reef from the bay to use as fill for approximately 280 acres of the new facility. The ship channel and numerous fringing and patch reefs were dredged for seaplane runway areas during this time period. Between bathymetric surveys conducted in 1927 and 1969, measured water depths decreased throughout the bay due to infilling and shoaling (Roy, 1970). Estimates of the composition of aragonitic (reef-derived) material in shoaled sediments vary from 25-75% (Roy, 1970; Smith, et al., 1973; Hollett, 1976) and a large proportion may have been derived from military dredge spoils (Devaney, et al., 1982). Deposition of land-derived sediments in the bay also increased over the past 60 years due to soil erosion runoff from agriculture and urbanization (Smith et al., 1973l; Devaney, et al., 1982; Jokiel, et al. 1991).

After W.W.II, Kaneohe experienced a "boom" as it began to develop into a bedroom community of Honolulu. The population increased 450% between 1940-1960, from 5,387 to 29,622. In 1990, population of the area was estimated at 66,760 (State of Hawaii, 1992). Housing developments, road construction, and other impacts of urbanization have accompanied these population increases. Nine of the original 30 fishponds built by early Hawaiians were filled to create more land for housing developments between 1946-1948. Beginning in the 1960's, most of the streams in the southern sector of the Kaneohe area were channel-lized for at least part of their lengths to facilitate flood control. Two major highways constructed in the 1960's connected Kaneohe to Honolulu, further augmenting urbanization.

Sewage was discharged into the bay (up to 7.5 mgd) from three primary treatment plants (later upgraded to secondary treatment) between the early 1950's and the late 1970's. Sewage discharge from two of the plants was diverted from south Kaneohe Bay to a deep ocean outfall in 1977-78; discharge into the north-central bay from a third plant was diverted in 1986. Approximately 85% of the current population is now served by municipal sewerage, with the remaining 10,000 individuals utilizing 2900 cesspools (Office of State Planning, 1992). Currently, the four watersheds around the southern and central sectors of the bay are urbanized (residential, commercial, and light industry), while most of the northern half of the bay remains rural/agricultural.

STATUS OF REEFS IN KANEOHE BAY: 1971-1990

Prior to the late 1960's, descriptions of reefs in Kaneohe Bay were anecdotal. It seems clear that, through geological time to the present, reef communities in the bay have developed and evolved under significant terrestrial influences. In the latter part of the last century, Agassiz (1889) recorded that, although corals flourished on slopes of fringing reefs, they had succumbed to sedimentation in nearshore reef areas. However, in the early 1900's, reefs in the south bay were described as "coral gardens" (Mackaye, 1915) consisting of a variety of species and forms.

There have been no formal long-term monitoring studies of the status or health of reefs in Kaneohe Bay. Concerns about the impacts of sewage discharge in the early 1970's prompted bay-wide surveys of coral and algal abundance (Banner and Bailey, 1970; Maragos, 1972; Smith, et al., 1973). High nutrient levels at this time supported a luxuriant growth of the "green bubble alga", Dictyosphaeria cavernosa. The alga overgrew and smothered the living coral colonies, particularly in the central sectors of the bay where standing crop of D. cavernosa reached 1000 g dry weight/ m^2 (Soegiarto, 1972). There was little to no coral in the south bay, apparently due to a combination of high turbidity, sedimentation, and, possibly, toxicity from anoxic conditions fostered by high nutrient levels. Smith, et al. (1981), anticipating the natural experiment presented by diversion of sewage discharge from the bay in 1977-78, initiated a comprehensive study of the response of nutrients and biota between 1976 and 1979. Their

340

study demonstrated a marked and rapid decline in nitrogen and phosphorus concentrations over a period of several months after sewage diversion. Although phytoplankton and Dictyosphaeria abundance began to decrease during this time period, and filter-feeders showed a dramatic decline, benthic biomass and community composition in the south and central sectors of the bay had not returned to "pre-sewage conditions" during the period of this study. Smith et al, (1981) proposed that: 1) the post-diversion monitoring time interval was insufficient to track complete recovery, 2) there had been irreversible shifts in community structure, or 3) observed shifts were due to factors other than sewage enrichment

A series of surveys conducted over the past two decades provides insight into the long-term trends of "recovery" of Kaneohe Bay after sewage diversion. Coral and algal abundances were quantitatively censused at fifteen reef sites in 1970-71 by Maragos (1972) and Jokiel (unpublished). These sites (Figure 1) were re-surveyed using similar methods in 1983, six years after sewage diversion (Maragos, et al., 1985; Evans, et al., 1986) and again in 1990 (Evans and Hunter, in press). Similarity of sites, methodology, and comparisons of the resulting data sets was facilitated by the overlap of investigators conducting the censuses. Methods of data collection and statistical analyses of the three data sets prsented here are as described by Evans and Hunter (in press).

Changes in coral and algal cover.-

Although there was a remarkable recovery of coral communities between 1971 and 1983, the trend established by those two data sets was not observed in the 1990 survey. On a baywide basis, percent cover of coral remained essentially unchanged between 1983-1990, while the abundance of Dictyosphaeria doubled (Figure 2a,b).

Variations in coral and Dictyosphaeria abundance by depth are presented for eight of the survey sites in Figure 3 (space limitations preclude presentation of data from all 15 sites, but those shown are representative). What is apparent from these graphs is that there have been different patterns of change in the relative abundance of coral and alga cover at different sites and depths.

Coral and algal cover remained very low and essentially unchanged on the southernmost reefs in the bay (Site1, and Site 2, [not shown]). The southern part of the bay was heavily dredged in the late 1930's and early 1940's, and Site 1 still had considerable amounts of fine sediments (75% of total cover) vs. hard substratum (22%) in 1990. However, Site 2 had approximately 61% bare hard substratum that had not been recolonized by corals or algaein 1990 The reasons for this lack of recruitment are unknown.

In contrast, Site 3, on the south side of Coconut Island, showed a dramatic and continuous increase in coral abundance between 1971-1983 and again between 1983 -1990, while Dictyosphaeria remained uniformly low (<1% at all depths). A few hundred meters north, at Site 5, the increase in coral abundance seen between 1971-1983 reversed between 1983-1990, particularly at depths <5m, where Dictyosphaeria abundance rose. A similar pattern can be seen for Site 7, on the leeward side of a patchreef just north of Coconut Island. While Dictyosphaeria abundance at this site declined sharply between 1971-1983, algal cover approached pre-sewage diversion levels in 1990, particularly at depths >3m.

a)

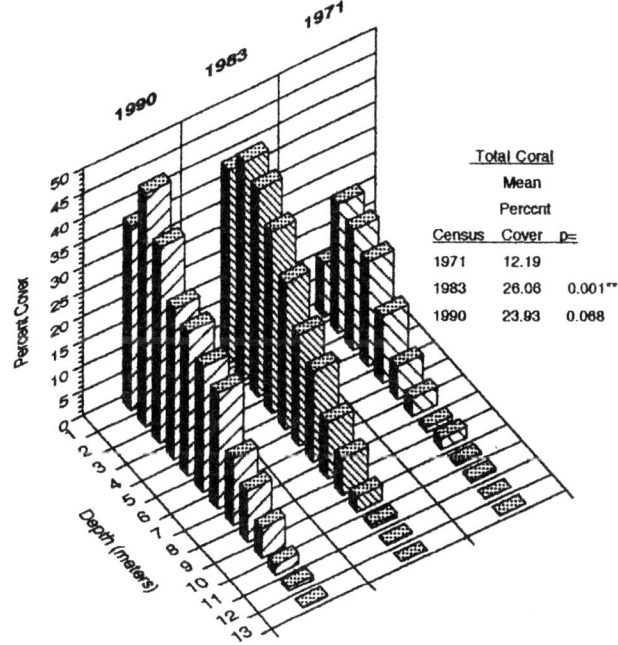

b)

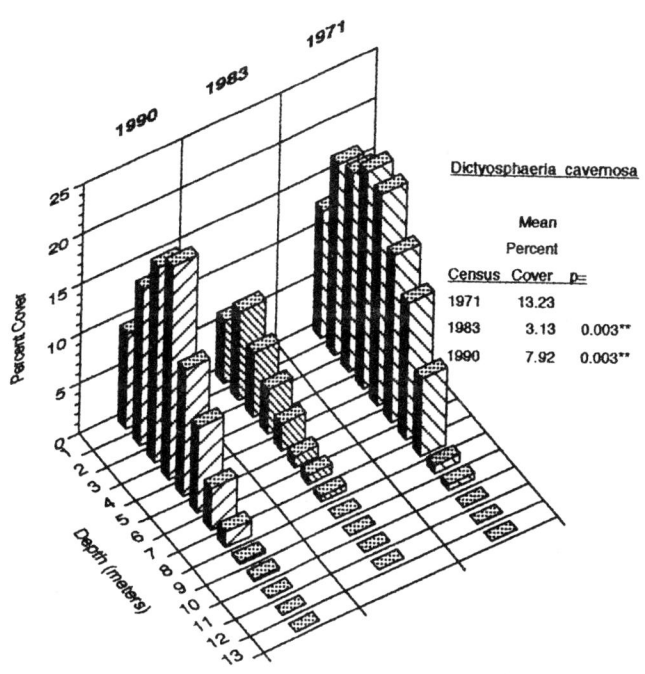

Figure 2. Depth profiles of mean percent cover of a) total coral and b) Dictyosphaeria cavernosa averaged over 15 survey sites in Kaneohe Bay censused in 1971, 1983, and 1990.

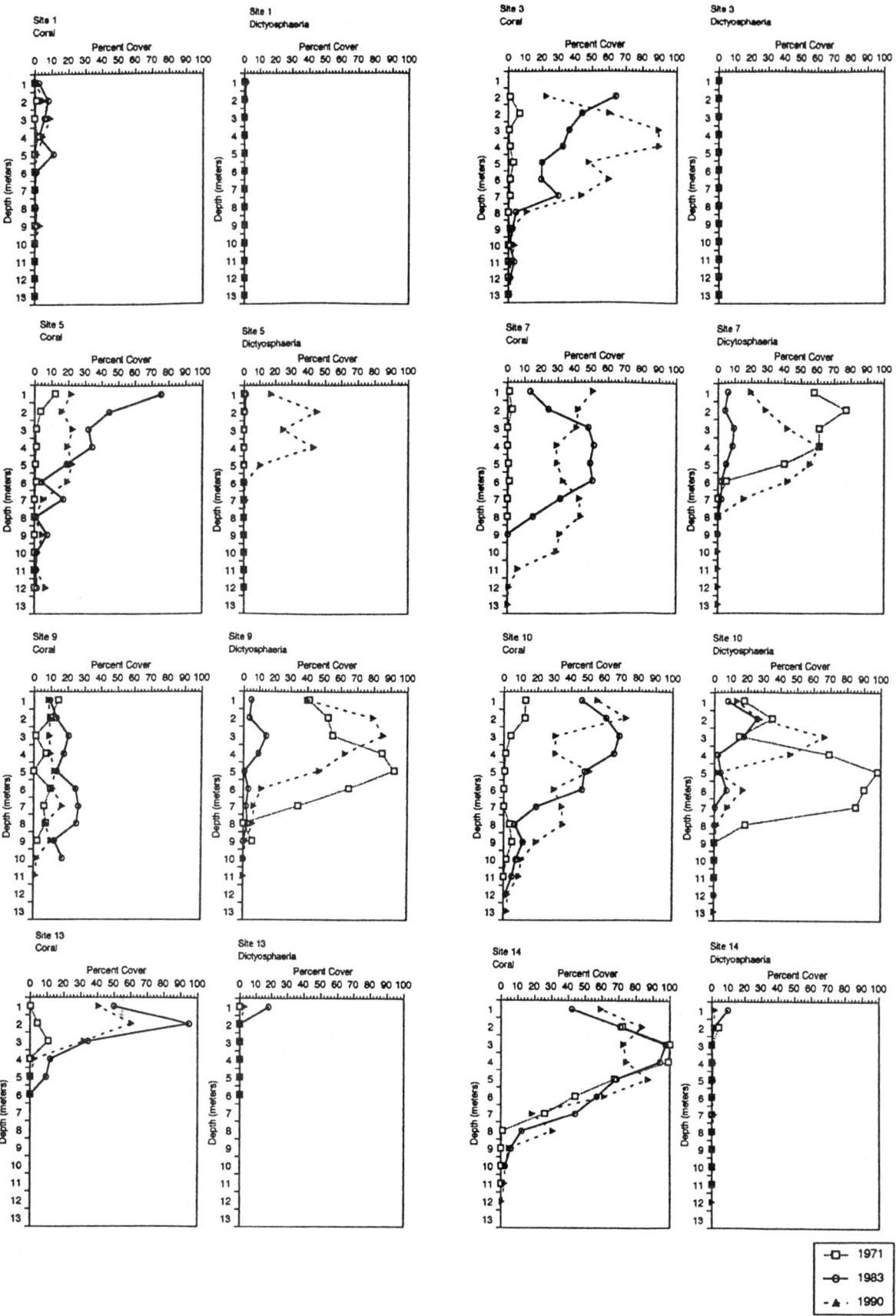

Figure 3. Depth profiles of percent cover of total coral and Dictyosphaeria cavernosa at eight reef sites in Kaneohe Bay censused in 1970-71 (open squares), 1983 (open circles), and 1990 (closed triangles).

Total coral abundance declined and Dictyosphaeria cover increased on 3 out of 4 reefs (Sites 8, 9 and 10) in the central bay between 1983-1990. These sites had shown an opposite trend of increased coral cover between 1971-1983. Dictyosphaeria occupied a shallow depth range on the reef slopes of Sites 9 and 10 in 1990 compared to its 1971 range at these sites. At the fourth central bay reef site (#11), coral abundance increased and algal cover declined at both the 1983 and 1990 censuses relative to 1971 levels.

North bay sites showed the least amount of change in coral and algal cover over the 20 year period. Only Site 13 (nearer a reef mouth than any of the other sites) showed significant changes in coral cover, with an increase between 1971-1983 and a (smaller) decline between 1983-1990. Site 15, the northern-most survey site, was the only reef on which coral declined and Dictyosphaeria cover increased between 1971-1983; between 1983-1990, both coral and algae increased slightly at this site.

Site 14 (Figure 3, bottom right) is notable in exhibiting the least amount of change in coral or algal abundance over the past two decades. In general, coral abundance increased from about 50% cover on the reef flat to nearly 100% at 3-4 m depth, and gradually declined down the reef slope to the mud bottom of the lagoon. (The decline in percent cover of coral at 3-4 m depth in 1990 appeared to be due to abrasion from a boat grounding. Dictyosphaeria cover has remained low at this site (<1% overall) from 1971 to present.

Changes in species diversity.-

The relative abundance of the two most common corals in Kaneohe Bay, Porites compressa and Montipora verrucosa, increased substantially between 1971 and 1983 (41-72% and 6-10% of total cover, respectively) and remained high and essentially unchanged between the 1983 and 1990 surveys (73% and 12%, respectively). Other common coral species in the bay, Pocillopora damicornis, Cyphastrea ocellina, and Fungia scutaria showed different patterns of occurrence and abundance (Figure 4). Pocillopora and Cyphastrea abundance increased dramatically after sewage diversion, but showed a significant decline between 1983 and 1990. Most of the change in these two species, which typically occur mainly on reef flats, was seen at 1 m depth or less suggesting that the 1987 freshwater kill may have been responsible, at least in part, for the observed declines. Declines at deeper depths suggest that mortality of the large numbers of colonies on reef flats may have resulted in a depression of reproductive /recruitment success over the time interval between the freshwater kill and 1990 census (2 1/2 years). In contrast, the abundance of Fungia. increased at depths less than 1 m, while decreasing on the reef slopes. Although Fungia is sensitive to decreased salinity (many "dead" coralla were observed after the 1987 flood), these coralla sprouted hydrocauli (asexual buds) from apparently residual tissues over the next several years (Jokiel, et al., in press), resulting in a rapid recovery of this species on reef flats. Of interest is the lack of recovery, and actual decline, of Fungia at depths > 1 m in 1983 and again in 1990. A possible explanation for the decline in Fungia may be an increase in souvenir collection of this "portable" species.

Overall declines in total coral abundance at <1 m depth in 1990 were positively correlated (r^2=0.508, p<0.01) with mortality due to the 1987 flood for the 11 sites for which 1988 and 1990 surveys overlapped. At Sites 3, 4 and 5 (all on Coconut Island) this mortality explained most of the measured negative change in coral cover. However, for the other 12 sites surveyed in 1990, significance values for declines in coral cover did not change when the upper 1 m was omitted from paired comparisons.

DISCUSSION

Kaneohe Bay was described in 1973 as "a reef ecosystem under stress" (Smith et al, 1973). The authors identified the basis of this stress as due to the large population increases in the surrounding watersheds during the previous 30 year period, and the concomitant impacts of urbanization (increased sedimentation from runoff, dredging, and reef erosion; freshwater kills due to stream channelization, and nutrient stress from sewage outfalls in the south bay). As a result of such scientific attention and public outcry, local government responded and sewage outfalls were diverted from the bay. A rapid and dramatic change was documented in nutrient concentrations, phytoplankton abundance, and water clarity in the south and central bay. Surveys within the first six years after diversion indicated that coral communities had begun to recover (Smith et al, 1981; Maragos, et al, 1985; Evans, et al, 1986). However, as indicated by the 1990 reef survey, these initial trends of recovery appear to have slowed or even reversed at some sites. We submit that limitations in the scope and methodology of the surveys, along with the potential for natural variability of ecosystems, emphasize the need for further data over longer time periods to confirm these trends.

Overall coral abundance in Kaneohe Bay has not continued to increase from 1983 levels, while the green bubble alga, Dictyosphaeria cavernosa, previously believed to be an indicator of eutrophic conditions, has doubled in percent cover. It has been suggested that recent increases of this macroalga may reflect a response to nutrient subsidies from sediment release, fixation and export from reefs, land runoff, cesspools, municipal sewage bypasses, and human wastes from commercial and recreational boaters. However, limited data have failed to detect a degradation in water quality in Kaneohe Bay as measures of nutrient levels, turbidity, and chlorophyll a have remained essentially the same or declined slightly over the past decade.

At present, factors contributing to the health or decline of reefs in Kaneohe Bay are more subtle and complex than the point-source sewage outfalls of the past. Although grading ordinances have been enacted over the past several decades, compliance is not always achieved. A large highway construction project begun in 1988 increased sediment loads in a Kaneohe stream six-fold compared to pre-construction levels (Hill and DeCarlo, 1991). Channelization of most streams in the southern and central sectors of the watershed has no doubt accelerated freshwater delivery to the bay during heavy rainfall events, resulting in potentially higher suspended sediment loads and more extreme fluctuations in salinity. A major storm in 1987 resulted in substantial mortality of shallow water benthos followed by a protracted period of

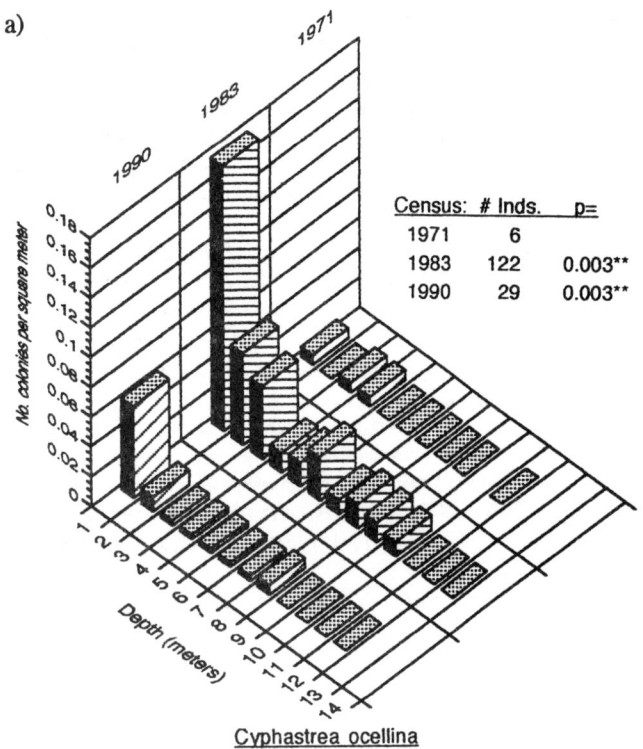

Figure 4. Depth profiles for number of colonies/m^2 of: a) <u>Cyphastrea ocellina</u>, b) <u>Pocillopora damicornis</u>, and c) <u>Fungia scutaria</u> from 1971, 1983, and 1990 reef surveys of Kaneohe Bay.

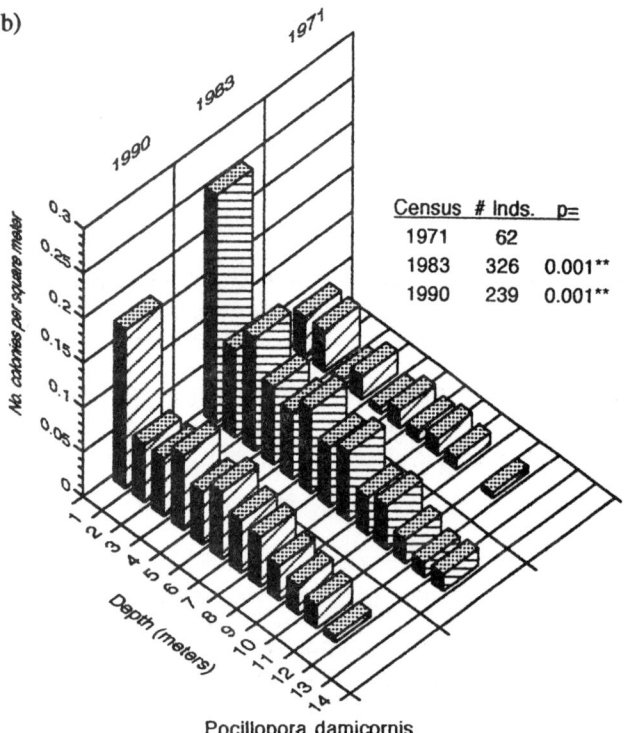

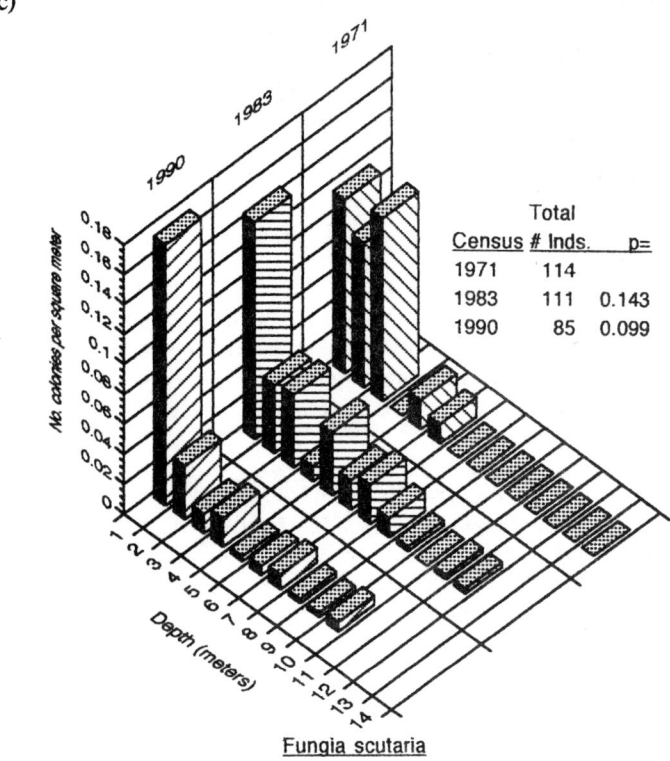

phytoplankton growth (Jokiel, et al, in press). Nutrients released during and after the freshwater kill may have augmented cycling of nutrients between the plankton and benthos, ultimately favoring the growth of macroalgae. Although spills and bypasses of raw sewage still occasionally occur (particularly during large rainfall events and maintenance operations), cesspool drainages and an antiquated sewage collection system may also provide a relatively small but chronic source of nutrients to bay waters. Planned and accidental bypasses of sewage into the bay are estimated at up to 32 million gallons per event; cesspools and faulty septic systems contribute approximately 800,000 gallons of sewage per day to groundwater, particularly in the central and northern bay watersheds (City and County of Honolulu, Department of Public Works).

Alternatively to an increased nutrient scenario, 1990 reef surveys may reflect inter-annual variations in algal abundance that have not been previously quantified. What "should" a healthy reef look like in Kaneohe Bay in terms of total coral and macroalgal abundance? We propose that the "inverted J" pattern of coral coverage (observed at Site 14 in the north bay) may represent the "normal" Kaneohe Bay reef type, based on our observations of other reefs in more "pristine" areas of the bay. Proximity to shore (and land influences) and algal overgrowth appear to be prominent factors responsible for deviations from this "norm" on other reefs. Whether this pattern represents a historical "norm" (beyond the short period of time for which we have quantitative data) is open to conjecture, but is supported by the morphology of existent reef structures and proposed patterns of reef development in the bay (Roy, 1970).

After diversion of point-source sewage discharges into Kaneohe Bay, the rapid initial indications of recovery abecame a textbook exemplification of the resiliency of ecosystems to anthropogenic stress. However, numerous other environmental stresses have not been remediated: long-term impacts of dredging, sedimentation, stream channelization, additional nutrient subsidy, and the introduction of potential toxicants. Although the data presented in this summary are limited and preliminary, they provide the beginnings of a database by which long-term changes on Kaneohe Bay reefs may be measured and evaluated. Further research will be necessary to determine if changes in coral and algal abundance represent equilibrium shifts and/or long-term trends.

Kaneohe Bay ecosystem dynamics are the subject of current research emphases, including nutrient input sources and rates, uptake parameters of primary producers, and investigations of the potential influence of algal grazers on Dictyosphaeria abundance. Of much interest also are recent findings that the phytoplankton community in the bay has shifted from N-limited to P-limited (E. Laws, pers. comm); in addition, there appears to be a substantial subsidy (approximately 40 uM) of dissolved organic nitrogen to the bay water column (E. Laws, M. Atkinson, pers. comm.). Levels and potential bioaccumulation of toxic contaminants in bay fauna have also been the subject of recent attention. Samples of oyster tissues collected near a stream mouth in the southern sector of the bay showed high levels of some metals and persistent pesticides (e.g. dieldrin and chlordane, which have been banned from use in Hawaii for more than five years). Recent work has begun to focus on the effects of various toxicants on corals and their larvae.

The impacts of nutrient enrichment from urban sewage (Smith, et al, 1981) and periodic freshwater kills (Banner, 1968; Jokiel, et al., in press) on structuring the ecological distributions of shallow-water reef corals in Kaneohe Bay have been well documented. Data on recovery of near-shore areas after the 1987 flood have supportednd expanded what has been learned over the past decade about the modes and relative contributions of sexual and asexual reproduction and recruitment of corals in the bay. In addition, studies on the effects of UV light, temperature, and water motion regimes conducted in Kaneohe Bay have contributed greatly to our understanding of coral distributions and environmental tolerances. Although a large body of work has been accumulated on Kaneohe Bay coral reef communities, much remains to be learned about the long-term dynamics of what is perhaps one of the best-developed (and best-studied) reef systems in the world adjacent to an urbanized and growing population center.

LITERATURE CITED

Agassiz, A. 1889. The coral reefs of the Hawaiian Islands. Bull. Mar. Comp. Zool., Harvard, 17(3):121-170.

Banner, A.H. 1968. A freshwater "kill" on Hawaiian coral reefs. Hawaii Inst. Mar. Biol. Tech. Rep. #15. 29 pp.

Banner, A.H. 1974. Kaneohe Bay, Hawaii: Urban pollution and a coral reef ecosystem. Proc. 2nd Intl. Coral Reef Symp., Brisbane, 2:685.

Banner, A.H. and J.H. Bailey. 1970. The effects of urban pollution upon a coral reef system. Hawaii Inst. Mar. Biol. Tech. Rep. # 25. 66 pp.

Bathen, K.H. 1968. A descriptive study of the physical oceanography of Kaneohe Bay, Oahu, Hawaii. Hawaii Inst. Mar. Biol. Tech. Rep. #14. 353 pp.

Devaney, D. M., M.Kelly, P.J. Lee, and L.S. Motteler. 1982. Kaneohe: A History of Change (1778-1950). B.P. Bishop Museum, Honolulu. 271 pp..

Evans, C.W., J.E. Maragos, and P. Holthus. 1986. Reef corals in Kaneohe Bay. Six years before and after termination of sewage. In P.L . Jokiel, R.H. Richmond, and R. A. Rogers, eds. Coral Reef Population Biology. Hawaii Inst. Mar. Biol. Tech. Rep. #37. pp 91-100.

Evans, C.W. and C.L .Hunter. 1992. Kaneohe Bay: an update on recovery and trends to the contrary. Presented at 7th Intl. Coral Reef Cong., Guam, in press.

Hill, B.R. and E.H. DeCarlo. 1991 Effects of highway construction on suspended sediment concentrations in two small drainage basins on Oahu, Hawaii. Proc. Tech. Sess. Reg. Conf. Nonpoint Source Pollution. Tacoma, WA pp 303-313.

Hollett, K.J. 1977. Shoaling of Kaneohe Bay, Oahu, Hawaii, in the period 1927-1976, based upon bathymetric, sedimentological, and geographical studies. M.S. thesis, Univ. Hawaii, 145 pp.

Jokiel, P.J., C.L. Hunter, S. Taguchi, and L. Watarai. in press. Ecological impact of a fresh water "kill" on the reefs of Kaneohe Bay, Oahu, Hawaii.. Coral Reefs.

MacKaye, A.L. 1915. Coral of Kaneohe Bay. *Hawaiian Almanac and Ann. for 1916.*. pp 135-139.

Maragos, J.E. 1972. A study of the ecology of Hawaiian corals. Ph.D. Disserrtation, University of Hawaii., 290 pp.

Maragos, J.E, C.W. Evans, and P. Holthus. 1985. Reef corals in Kaneohe Bay six years before and after termination of sewage (Oahu, Hawaiian Archipelago). Proc. 5th Intl. Coral Reef Congress, Tahiti, 4:189-194.

Office of State Planning. 1992. Kaneohe Bay Master Plan. Kaneohe Bay Master Plan Task Force. State of Hawaii, 115 pp.

Roy, K.J. 1970. Changes in bathymetric configuration, Kaneohe Bay, Oahu, 1882-1969. Hawaii Inst. Geophy. Rep. 70-15. 226 pp.

Smith, S.V., K.E. Chave, and D.T.O. Kam. 1973. Atlas of Kaneohe Bay: a reef ecosystem under stress. Univ. Hawaii Sea Grant Pub. TR-72-01. 128 pp.

Smith, S.V., W.J. Kimmerer, E.A. Lawa, R.E Brock, and T.W. Walsh. 1981. Kaneohe Bay sewage diversion experiment: perspectives on ecosystem responses to nutritional perturbation. Pacific Sci. 35(4): 279-395.

Sogiarto, A. 1972. The role of benthic algae in the carbonate budget of the modern reef complex, Kaneohe Bay. Ph. D. Dissertation, University of Hawaii.

Acknowledgements.- The individuals who have contributed to the research efforts summarized in this case history are innumerable. We gratefully acknowledge their contrib-utions, and particularly wish to thank J.E. Maragos, P.J. Jokiel, M.D. Stephenson, J. Oetting, G.J. Smith, and S. V. Smith for their assistance and/or editorial comments. We also thank E.A. Laws and M. Atkinson for providing unpublished data.

Can the Great Barrier Reef Model of Protected Areas Save Reefs Worldwide?

Graeme Kelleher AM FTS, FIE Aust

Chairman, Great Barrier Reef Marine Park Authority, Professor of Systems Engineering, James Cook University, Townsville
GPO Box 791, Canberra, ACT, 2601, Australia

ABSTRACT

This paper suggests that the conservation of the world's coral reefs requires integrated planning and management of coastal seas. Australia's Great Barrier Reef Marine Park, the world's largest marine protected area, provides a management model for such integration. Through initiatives such as IUCN's global representative system of marine protected areas, this model could be applied in other countries to achieve ecologically sustainable use of coastal resources and conservation of the world's coral reefs.

INTRODUCTION

As a general statement, one can summarize the state of the world's marine environment as suffering from a number of stresses caused by human activity that has caused observable and in many cases gross reductions in environmental quality. They can be summarized as pollution, over fishing, physical alteration of the seabed or coastline, introduction of exotic species and climate change.

There are two major deficiencies in our scientific and administrative systems, which place in jeopardy the attainment of ecologically sustainable use of coastal waters and coral reefs. The first is the absence of comprehensive, long term monitoring programs covering each of the large marine ecosystems which impinge on the coastline. This deficiency prevents us from defining the level of stresses that exist now and the trends in those levels. The second is the lack of integration of planning, management and research in the coastal zone. Without integrated programs, there is little chance that nations will be able to take the actions, on both land and sea, that will be necessary to prevent insidious degradation of the marine environment.

In the last century, there have been three principle approaches to marine management. The first and oldest consisted of regulation and management of individual marine activities, such as commercial fishing, by specialist agencies, with varying degrees of co-ordination of regulation between different agencies. Usually there was little or no co-ordination with management of adjacent coastal lands.

The second approach involved the creation of small marine protected areas which provided special protection for particularly valuable areas within the broad areas which were subject to regulation of the first type or, in some cases, to no regulation. This is the most common application of the concept of marine protected areas. It is usually the first stage in marine conservation initiatives which go beyond fisheries restrictions which limit gear, catches and effort.

The third approach is a recent development. It consists of the establishment of a large, multiple use protected area with an integrated management system providing levels of protection varying throughout the area. Ideally this integration should extend to co-ordinated management of marine and terrestrial areas in the coastal zone and beyond. However, in many circumstances, the complexity of boundaries and competition between governments and government agencies regarding jurisdictional responsibility effectively preclude this.

It is conceptually possible for the same management results to be achieved with either of the last two approaches. However, the integrated multiple use protected area approach has the advantage that co-ordination of regulation of different human activities can be automatically achieved when the overriding responsibility for management rests with one agency. Co-ordination of management in the marine environment is in many ways even more important than it is in the terrestrial sphere. This is because the high degree of connectivity in the seas facilitates the transmission of substances and effects throughout the water column. The tradition of common property rights in the sea has led to actual or potential conflict between users and between forms of use. Under these circumstances there is a positive incentive for individual users to maximize their exploitation of the resource, even if destruction of the resource is an inevitable result -- the tragedy of the commons.

We are entering a new and more difficult phase. Direct use of coastal waters and of coral reefs is increasing; there are proportionately fewer resources for management and management agencies are being forced to recover costs from users who are reluctant to pay.

The need for and the difficulties of managing uses so that they are ecologically sustainable forever are common to all coastal waters. Coral reefs in particular are frequently an important source of resources for a coastal nation. The system of management which has been developed on the Great Barrier Reef has been shown to be effective in achieving ecologically sustainable use of these resources. Its principles have been incorporated in the policies of IUCN, the World Conservation Union and have been unanimously endorsed in a major workshop recently by representatives of fisheries and environmental management agencies of the ASEAN countries. They could be applied widely in Australia. Let us look at these principles and assess their effects on commercial and sport fishing, exploration and tourism.

The Goal and Aims of Large Multiple Use Marine Protected Areas (MPAS)

Primary Goal

The IUCN -- the World Conservation Union -- has derived a primary goal for marine management (Kelleher and Kenchington, 1991):

"To provide for the protection, restoration, wise use, understanding and enjoyment of the marine heritage of the world on perpetuity through the creation of a global, representative system of marine protected areas and through the management in accordance with the principles of the World Conservation Strategy of human activities that use or affect the marine environment."

Policy Statement

It is the policy of IUCN to foster marine conservation by encouraging governments, the non-governmental community and international agencies to cooperate in (IUCN, 1988):
A) Implementing integrated management strategies to achieve the objectives of the World Conservation Strategy in the coastal and marine environment and in so doing to consider local resource needs as well as national and international conservation and development responsibilities in the protection of the marine environment.
B) Involving local people, non-government organizations, related industries and other interested parties in the development of these strategies and in the implementation of various marine conservation programs.

It is also the policy of IUCN to recommend that, as an integral component of marine conservation and management, each national government should seek cooperative action between the public and all levels of government for development of a national system of marine protected areas.

Such a system should have the following objectives:
- to protect and manage substantial examples of marine and estuarine systems to ensure their long-term viability and to maintain genetic diversity;
- to protect depleted, threatened, rare or endangered species and populations and, in particular to preserve habitats considered critical for the survival of such species;
- to protect and manage areas of significance to the life cycles of economically important species;
- to prevent outside activities from detrimentally affecting the marine protected areas;
- to provide for the continued welfare of people affected by the creation of marine protected areas;
- to preserve, protect, and manage historical and cultural sites and natural aesthetic values of marine and estuarine areas, for present and future generations;
- to facilitate the interpretation of marine and estuarine systems for the purposes of conservation, education, and tourism;
- to accommodate within appropriate management regimes a broad spectrum of human activities compatible with the primary goal in marine and estuarine settings;
- to provide for research and training, and for monitoring the environmental effects of human activities, including the direct and indirect effects of development and adjacent land-use practices.

The Authority has derived a similar primary goal and a set of aims from the provisions of the Act and recognition of the political, legal, economic, sociological and ecological environment in which it operates.

Not only the physical aspects of marine management need to survive. If the ecology is to be protected, administrative arrangements also must be durable.

In Australia the major determinant of administrative survivability of organizations is public support. In the long run, government support flows from it. It follows that marine management agencies must act in ways which sustain or increase that support. What are those ways?

In general the public is likely to continue to support a MPA and the management Authority if the primary goal is seen to be being achieved efficiently. For this to occur, the public will have to be aware of what the Authority is doing and the way it is doing it, the effectiveness and costs of its programs and the reasons for them, and to the extent practicable, to be involved in the establishment and management of the protected area. A set of aims has been derived from this and related observations. They are subordinate to the primary goal and must be read in conjunction with it and with each other.

1. The Authority's principle aim is to protect the ecology of the Great Barrier Reef, while allowing reasonable use. Reasonable use must provide for the special values and interests of Aboriginals and Torres Strait Islanders and must protect the cultural values of all Australians.
2. The Authority will achieve its goal only if it employs people of high caliber, provides them with rewarding and useful work and ensures their continued personal and professional development.
3. The Authority must achieve its goal, and be seen to do so, efficiently. This will depend on:
    - providing sound and timely policy advice to the government
    - involving the community meaningfully in all aspects of the Marine Park
    - minimizing the costs of management
    - minimizing regulation
    - making decisions on the basis of the best available information
    - adapting the operations of the Authority to changing circumstances
    - The Authority being, and being seen as, a world leader in natural resource management.

Taken together, this goal and these aims provide a policy framework for evaluation of proposed programs and actions. We believe that much of the success of the Great Barrier Reef Marine Park is the result of applying these policies. We believe further that they can (and should) be applied in natural resource management anywhere. Much to the thrust of policy is communication with and involvement of the public in the development and care of the Marine Park. Education and information programs are therefore critically important elements of the Authority's work.

The Marine Park and Its Zoning System

The Great Barrier Reef Marine Park is not a National Park. It is a multiple-use protected area, fitting the definition of Category VIII of the classification system used by IUCN (McNeely & Miller, 1984), the World Conservation Union. It also meets the criteria for selection and management as a Biosphere Reserve (Category IX), although it has not been formally proposed or established as one. The Reef was inscribed on the World Heritage List in 1981 as a natural site (Category X).

Through the use of zoning, conflicting activities are separated, areas are provided which are suitable for particular activities and some areas are protected from use. Levels of protection within the Park vary from almost complete absence of restriction on activity in some zones to zones within which almost no human activities are permitted. The only activities which are prohibited throughout the Park are Oil exploration, mining (other than for approved research purposes), littering, spearfishing with SCUBA and the taking of large specimens of certain species of fish.

In the zoning plans which have been developed so far, there are three major categories of zones:
1. Preservation zones: Equivalent to IUCN Category I - or Scientific Research/Strict Nature zones Reserve. The only human activity permitted is strictly controlled scientific research.
2. Marine National Park: Equivalent to IUCN Category II zones National Park. The major uses permitted are scientific, educational and recreational.
3. General Use zones: Equivalent to IUCN Category IV - Managed Nature Reserve and VI - Resources Reserves. Uses are held at levels with do not jeopardize the ecosystem or its major elements. Commercial and recreational fishing are generally permitted, although bottom trawling is prohibited in one of these two zones.

The zones are fixed during the life of a zoning plan (generally five to seven years). They are complemented by generally smaller areas which give special protection from time to time to animal breeding or nesting sites, to sites in general use and other zones which are required to be protected to allow appreciation of nature free from fishing or collecting and to sites suitable for scientific research.

Because there has been a dramatic increase in the use of the Marine Park by tourists, the original zoning system, which focused on fishing proved inadequate. There is increasing competition for tourism use of particular sites. Usually these sites are near major areas of coastal development (e.g. Cairns or Townsville) or have particular attributes which make them suitable for tourism - the Whitsunday Islands, for example.

At a special conference arrange by the Authority in late 1988, participants agreed that there was a need to incorporate into the zoning system a tourist strategy. This strategy would identify those areas which are particularly suited to tourism development and those that should be retained in their natural state, undisturbed by such development.

The strategy is being implemented through the zoning system, initially in the rezoning of the Cairns Section of the Marine Park. It will be extended to the other three Sections as they are rezoned during the next five years. Initial zoning of the entire Marine Park was completed on schedule in 1988.

A major constraint in zoning for tourism has been that many tourists like to observe the natural qualities of the Great Barrier Reef undisturbed by fishing. Modern technology allows them to do this from semi-submersible vessels and from underwater observatories. If carried out with care these activities can have very little if any effect on the Reef's ecosystem. They are, in other words, compatible with the Authority's goal. The need to provide for such activities in zones which are protected from fishing has led the Authority to divide each of the zones other than the Preservation Zone into two categories:

    Category 1 - no structures (for example, floating hotels, pontoons or mariculture) will be permitted. Mooring buoys may be permitted.

    Category 2 - such structures are permitted provided they meet environmental guidelines. A permit is required.

The adoption of this new zoning scheme will allow the Authority, in association with interested members of the public and with other agencies, to develop and apply a tourism strategy for the whole of the Great Barrier Reef. The aim will be to ensure that the whole Reef will not become dotted with tourist and other structures while at the same time providing for careful development on reefs which are suitable for that purpose. The strategy should allow the Authority to continue to provide for protection of the Great Barrier Reef while allowing careful development - in other words, to provide for ecologically sustainable development.

The graphical representation of a zoning map is supported by a document (the formal Zoning Plan) which defines in legal terms the purposes for which a zone may be used or entered.

The Global Representative System of Marine Protected Areas

IUCN and its Commission on National Parks and Protected Areas (CNPPA) are promoting the establishment of a global representative system of marine protected areas as a key means of conserving important parts of the marine environment, such as coral reefs. As Vice-Chairman (Marine) of IUCN's Commission on National Parks and Protected Areas it has been my job to contribute to the development of this system through the CNPPA, GBRMPA has been fortunate enough to have received financial and other support from the World Bank.

We started by writing "Guidelines for Establishing Marine Protected Areas" and then established a network of 18 working groups covering all the marine geopolitical subdivisions of the world. Since 1990 these working groups have directed their efforts towards the following aims:

    1. divide each region's marine environment into its major constituent biogeographic zones;

    2. identify gaps in the representation in MPA's of those zones; and,

    3. identify areas suitable for the establishment of MPA's.

Each working group is coordinated by a working group leader. The group's role is to collect information on individual MPAs and on national and regional MPA systems, to determine the biogeographic framework in which a representative MPA system will be developed, to determine regional and national priorities for the establishment and management of MPAs, and to maintain a network of regional contacts to contribute to this work.

A principle objective in developing a global representative system of marine protected areas is to adequately represent biogeographic, ecosystem, habitat and species diversity. Coral reefs are of particular importance.

The Great Barrier Reef Marine Park Authority (GBRMPA) was asked by the World Bank Environmental Department to begin a project to undertake a preliminary assessment of the world's marine protected areas and identify priority areas for the conservation of global marine biodiversity. The Bank recognized the need to build on existing activities and in particular the CNPPA program.

Through this project GBRMPA has produced a draft report (Kelleher & Bleakley, 1993) that includes:

- a biogeographic framework for each marine region
- the location of all the world's existing MPA's
- priority areas and actions for the conservation of marine biodiversity, particularly as relates to marine protected areas.

Following the revision of the draft report in the coming months, the CNPPA Marine Protected Areas Program will begin to address individual regions and countries in greater detail. It will be at that stage, hopefully within the next year, that projects suitable for funding under the GEF should be developed.

In promoting the global representative system of marine protected areas for IUCN and with the support of the World Bank, we hope that other countries will be able to benefit from the knowledge and experience developed in managing the Great Barrier Reef Marine Park. It is our belief that the development of this global system is a vital contribution to the maintenance of marine biodiversity and to the achievement of ecologically sustainable development of the coastal marine environment, including coral reefs.

CONCLUSIONS

The Great Barrier Reef Marine Park is an example of the practical application of the principles defined in the World Conservation Strategy. It can be seen as a model for development of the kind described in the report of the World Commission on Environment and Development - "Our Common Future."

Attaining ecologically sustainable development of coral reefs will depend on the management of coastal waters in an integrated way. One option is the establishment of Marine Management Authorities, with representatives of national and state governments as well as a small number of representatives of local government and community interests, with the specific function of achieving integrated planning, research and management of the marine coastal zone in accordance with the principles of ecologically sustainable development.

Because of the proven difficulty that organizations and individuals have in simultaneously attempting to achieve two goals - in this case, economic development and ecological protection - these Authorities should not be responsible for detailed management of individual sectoral activities, such as tourism or fisheries. Such activities should continue to be managed by specialist agencies. However, the Authorities could have the following responsibilities and functions:

- development, in association with interest groups and the community generally of a strategic plan for the marine coastal zone;
- oversight of coastal development to ensure that it is ecologically sustainable;
- design and management of comprehensive monitoring programs which will define the state of the marine coastal environments and the trends in environmental parameters;
- design and management or contracted, multi-disciplinary, ecological research programs aimed at solving environmental problems;
- design and implementation of comprehensive community involvement and education programs designed to achieve voluntary acceptance by the community of policies, programs and actions which will lead to ecologically sustainable development. Particular emphasis should be placed on educating the young.

To the maximum extent practicable, specific management programs and actions should be carried out by existing agencies, with the Authorities concentrating on policy, strategy, planning, design and supervision of research programs and coordination. The enabling legislation should override conflicting provisions of existing legislation.

and supervision of research programs and coordination. The enabling legislation should override conflicting provisions of existing legislation.

In the absence of an organizational framework that provides for integrated management of our coral reefs, the energies of people and governments will continue to be dissipated in intersectoral conflicts, incompatible activities, inefficient developments, and research that is not relevant to achieving ecologically sustainable development.

LITERATURE CITED

IUCN. 1988. Resolution 17.38 of the IUCN (World Conservation Union) General Assembly. San Jose, Costa Rica, February 1988.

Kelleher, G.K., C.J. Bleakley (eds.). 1993. A Global Representation System of Marine Protected Areas. Draft report to the World Bank Environmental Department prepared by the Great Barrier Reef Marine Park Authority in association with IUCN's Commission on National Parks and Protected Areas.

Kelleher, G.K., R.A. Kenchington. 1991. Guidelines for Establishing Marine Protected Areas. A Marine Conservation and Development Report. IUCN, Gland, Switzerland.

McNeely, J.A., K.R. Miller (eds.). 1984. National Parks, Conservation, and Development. The Role of Protected Areas in Sustaining Society. Proceedings of the World Congress on National Parks, Bali, Indonesia, October 1982, Smithsonian Institution Press, Washington, D.C.

BIOLOGICAL LIMITS TO CARIBBEAN REEF RECOVERY A COMPARISON WITH WESTERN SOUTH PACIFIC REEFS

BARBARA L. KOJIS[1] AND NORMAN J. QUINN[2]

[1]COASTAL ZONE MANAGEMENT, GOVERNMENT OF THE VIRGIN ISLANDS OF THE UNITED STATES, ST. THOMAS, UNITED STATES VIRGIN ISLANDS 00802. [2]ENVIRONMENTAL RESEARCH UNIT, EASTERN CARIBBEAN CENTER, UNIVERSITY OF THE VIRGIN ISLANDS, #2 BREWERS BAY, ST. THOMAS, UNITED STATES VIRGIN ISLANDS 00802.

ABSTRACT

Both Caribbean and western South Pacific reef communities have experienced serious damage in the last two decades resulting in major declines in coral cover in many areas. However, Caribbean reef communities differ substantially from western South Pacific communities and appear to be less resilient. Caribbean reefs have fewer than one sixth the number of hard coral species found on the Great Barrier Reef. Furthermore, Caribbean reef communities are dominated by only three scleractinian species. Populations of two of these, *Acropora palmata* and *A. cervicornis*, were decimated more than a decade ago. These species populations have shown little signs of recovery and no other corals have replaced them. Quick growing, moderately sized, opportunistic species, such as *Pocillopora damicornis*, are absent and recruitment rates of corals in general are an order of magnitude lower in the Caribbean. Recovery of Caribbean reefs in the short term (past decade) has not occurred. Medium and long term recovery is predicted to be highly variable within and between reefs. Studies of coral recruitment and community recovery in the Atlantic and Pacific have used various techniques, in different habitats, for less than one half of the species described. Long term, Caribbean-wide, standardized studies of recruitment and post-settlement mortality are needed.

INTRODUCTION

During the past two decades, there has severe damage inflicted on reef building corals and important reef associated organisms by apparently natural events. In the Pacific, the Crown-of-thorns starfish, *Acanthaster planci* (Done, 1992), has devastated coral communities. In the Caribbean, white band disease has severely reduced *Acropora* populations (Gladfelter, 1982) and disease has decimated populations of the long-spined sea urchin, *Diadema antillarum*, an important reef herbivore (Lessios et al., 1984). Coral bleaching has been reported in both ocean systems (Jaap, 1979; Harriott, 1985; Roberts, 1987) and cyclonic storms have devastated specific reefs (Rogers et al., 1991). In contrast to studies on the Great Barrier Reef (GBR), which indicate rapid recovery of reefs in shallow water and slow recovery of deeper reefs (Done, 1992), there has been little sign of recovery on Caribbean reefs during the last ten years (Jackson, 1992). In fact, reefs are apparently continuing to decline (Porter and Meier, 1992).

The aim of this paper is to the compare coral community structure and life history strategies of coral species in the Caribbean with the western South Pacific. We will concentrate on the dominate Caribbean species and compare their life history strategies with that of taxonomic groups in the western South Pacific that are either related or exhibit similar life history strategies to determine some factors that may be contributing to the lack of recovery on Caribbean coral reefs.

REGIONAL SPECIES DIVERSITY

Species diversity of Scleractinia in the Caribbean is much lower than on the Great Barrier Reef. There are over 60 species in the Caribbean (Glynn, 1973) compared to more than 350 species on the Great Barrier Reef (Veron, 1986). Of the 60+ species in the Caribbean, only three, according to Jackson (1992), dominate present day coral reef community structure and the Pleistocene geological record: *A. palmata*, *A. cervicornis* and the *Montastrea annularis* "complex" (Knowlton, et al., 1992).

LIFE HISTORY TRAITS OF *ACROPORA*

In the Caribbean, the family Acroporidae has one genus and three species, the two listed above and *A. prolifera*, a less common species. *A. palmata* and *A. cervicornis* dominate the shallow and mid-water reef community structure (Jackson, 1992). In Indo-Pacific seas "*Acropora* is by far the most important genus of extant Scleractinia, having the greatest number of species and also greatest abundance on most reefs..." (Veron and Wallace, 1984). On the GBR there are over 70 species of *Acropora* found in a wide range of reef habitats. Regional dominance of a reef habitat by any species of coral is uncommon on the GBR.

Growth and Morphology

Acroporan species are the fastest growing scleractinian corals in both the Indo-Pacific and Caribbean. Compared to many massive species, such as *Porites* that grow outward at a rate of 0.5 - 2.5 cm yr^{-1} (Endean et al., 1988), *Acropora* spp. grow rapidly. The branch extension rate of *A. palmata* is up to 10 cm yr^{-1} (Gladfelter et al., 1978; Shinn, 1989) and *A. cervicornis* grows at 12 cm yr⁻¹ (Tunnicliffe, 1983). Studies of *Acropora* species in the South Pacific indicate growth rates are also high (Oliver, 1984).

A. palmata forms tall (2-3 m), robust colonies with a thick trunk and plate-like branches. No GBR *Acropora* has a similar morphology. *A. cervicornis*, the staghorn coral, forms thinner branched, more fragile colonies very similar to a number of arborescent species found on the GBR. In contrast, *Acropora* on the GBR exhibits not only the arborescent growth form of *A. cervicornis* (with a wider range of branch thicknesses), but a myriad of other morphological forms, e.g. hispidose, corymbose, caespitose, digitate, plate-like, wedge shaped and encrusting (Veron and Wallace, 1984). Local recruitment through growth, fragmentation and regeneration is also common among the arborescent species of the GBR. However, it is uncommon among the digitate, plate-like, corymbose and caespitose forms. These species maintain their abundance by recruiting sexually and are probably the dominant *Acropora* species recruiting to settlement plates.

Reproduction

Species of *Acropora* belong to one of two subgenera: *A. (Isopora)* or *A. (Acropora)*. Species of both genera are simultaneous hermaphrodites. *A. (Isopora)* is found only in the Pacific, eggs are fertilized internally and colonies brood large (>1mm) larvae. *A. (Acropora)* is found in both the Pacific and Atlantic and all species of this subgenus release eggs and sperm, fertilization is external and larvae develop in the plankton (Harrison and Wallace, 1990).

On the GBR, many *A. (Acropora)* species spawn synchronously during the spring mass spawning event. While there is no evidence that any individual colony of an *A. (Acropora)* species on the GBR spawns more than once per annum, colonies within a population may spawn at different times of the year (Kojis and Quinn, 1990). The eggs and subsequent larvae of this subgenus on the GBR are large, >0.6mm mean diameter (Wallace, 1985a). In the Caribbean, *A. palmata* and *A. cervicornis* produce eggs about half the size of GBR species (0.3mm diameter) (Szmant, 1986). A study in Puerto Rico indicated that both Caribbean species spawn in August and, at least in the case of *A. palmata*, only once per annum (Szmant, 1986).

Recruitment

Coral recruitment studies can be divided into two groups: those concerned with "invisible" recruitment (<1 cm diameter) and "visible" recruitment (>1 cm diameter) (Wallace, 1983). The former can only be accurately detected using a removable substrate, while the latter can be detected in the field. Recruits in the "invisible" category can seldom be confidently identified to species. In the South Pacific, owing to the large number of genera and species, "invisible" recruits are usually only readily identified to family. However, in the case of the subgenus *Isopora*, recruits were distinguished from other Acroporidae based on size (Harriott, 1992). Recruits of non-isoporan Acroporidae primarily belong to the genera *Montipora* and *Acropora* (Wallace, 1985b) and frequently make up 64 - >80% of the recruits to settlement plates (Wallace, 1985b; Fisk and Harriott, 1990). Isoporan *Acropora* recruitment was low on the Great Barrier Reef (Fisk and Harriott, 1990) and only recruited in substantial numbers at Lord Howe Island, an isolated island which is well south of the GBR (31°S). Studies of recruitment of juvenile *Acropora (Acropora)* on the GBR have shown high sexual recruitment of non-arborescent species and low sexual recruitment of arborescent species (Wallace, 1985a). The difference was correlated with rates of colony multiplication by fragmentation. Year-round fragmenters had few larval recruits, non fragmenting species had many, and rough-water fragmenters had an intermediate number of larval recruits (Wallace, 1985a).

In contrast, Caribbean studies indicate that *Acropora* rarely, if ever, recruit sexually to settlement plates (Rogers *et al.*, 1984; Tunnicliffe, 1983) and sexual recruitment is often non-existent in permanent quadrats (Porter and Meier, 1992). Egg size of both species is much smaller than GBR species and this may increase mortality of both eggs and larvae. Both Caribbean species maintain and garner space primarily by rapid growth, fragmentation and regeneration. Large stands of either species may be derived from few sexual recruits.

Fertilization Success

Differences in the fertilization rates of species may be an important factor in the success of sexual reproduction. Acroporids are simultaneous hermaphrodites and self fertilization is known to occur in some species. However, self fertilization rates may be low. Heyward and Babcock (1986) found *Acropora tenuis* had a very low level (2 to 3%) of self fertilization. Similarly, Richmond (1992) in Guam found that self-fertilization was usually low in the species studied, but increased with time. He also found that hybridization could occur between related species. Willis *et al.* (1992) did hybridization experiments on the GBR and found that closely-related and distantly related *Acropora* species were able to hybridize.

Several studies indicate that fertilization success is dependent on the close proximity of genetically dissimilar colonies. Studies of dioecious, brooding, soft corals have shown that sperm densities drop to levels at which fertilization is unlikely within meters of a colony (Brazeau and Lasker, 1992). When colonies form large clones, most branches of a clone may be far from other genetically distinct clones and cross fertilization may occur only when currents bring gametes together. Hybridization may be an important factor in fertilization success in the Pacific where synchronized mass spawning of many acroporid species occurs. It is unclear if coral species spawn synchronously in the Caribbean and, therefore, it is unclear if hybridization can play a role in fertilization success in the Caribbean. If, as is suggested by the above studies, self-fertilization is low, gamete wastage in the Caribbean may be high and larval recruitment low because few planulae are produced.

Habitat Dominance

Prior to the destructive events of the last two decades, pure stands of *Acropora palmata* dominated reef crests in the Caribbean wherever there was some protection from the full force of oceanic storm activity. It formed such dense, largely mono-specific, stands that scientists assumed it shaded out other coral species (Porter *et al.*, 1981). This was also, to some extent, an assumption made for *A. cervicornis* which formed huge "haystacks" (Tunnicliffe, 1983) and predominated at intermediate depths. This dominance through vegetative reproduction may have resulted in low genetic variation and, along with very high abundance, greatly increased these species susceptibility to epidemic disease (UNESCO, 1982). It is obvious today, that despite the absence or low abundance of *A. palmata* and *A. cervicornis* and, therefore, the lack of competition in habitats where it previously predominated, no other Caribbean coral species has substantially replaced these species within the last ten years.

While *Acropora* dominates in many habitats on the GBR seldom does a single species predominate. Exposed and semi-exposed shallow and intermediate depth habitats such has outer reef slopes, reef flats, and lagoons are colonized by multi-species assemblages of *Acropora* (Table 1) along with species of other families. Stubby branching digitate and wedge shaped species predominate on shallow reef habitats directly exposed to ocean waves. More diverse morphologies, e.g. plate-like and corymbose, are found in shallow habitats where some protection from oceanic swells are provided. On wave exposed forereef slopes, thick branching isoporan *Acropora* are common. Irrespective of morphology, these wave exposed species must recruit primarily by means of a sexually produced larvae. At intermediate depths, where wave action is not so severe, the multi-species assemblages include bottle brush, arborescent (staghorn) and sub-arborescent species. However, it is usually only in protected lagoonal waters that branching *Acropora*, similar to *A. cervicornis*, form large stands, often covering large areas of sandy bottoms.

Table 1: Representative distribution in different biotopes of 19 common *Acropora* species on the Great Barrier Reef.

Outer Reef Slope Exposed Reefs	Back Reef	Reef Flat	Lagoon	Turbid Waters	Depth >12 m
1,2,3,4,5,6,7,9, 13,14,15,16,17, 18,19	1,3,5,7,9, 11,15,19	1,2,4,5,9, 12,13,15,17, 18,19	1,3,5,7, 9,12,14, 15,19	1,3,7, 8,10,11, 15,19	8,15

Code for numbers: 1) *A. aspera*, 2) *A. bruggemanni*, 3) *A. cuneata*, 4) *A. danai*, 5) *A. formosa*, 6) *A. gemmifera*, 7) *A. grandis*, 8) *A. horrida*, 9) *A. humilus*, 10) *A. kirstyae*, 11) *A. microphtalma*, 12) *A. millepora*, 13) *A. monticulosa*, 14) *A. nobilis*, 15) *A. palifera*, 16) *A. polystoma*, 17) *A. robusta*, 18) *A. samoroensis*, 19) *A. selago*.

Habitat preferences derived from Veron and Wallace (1984).

LIFE HISTORY TRAITS OF *MONTASTREA ANNULARIS* AND THE COMPARABLE GBR TAXONOMIC GROUPS

Montastrea annularis belongs to the family Faviidae, the largest Caribbean scleractinian family in terms of genera (Veron, 1986) and species. *M. annularis* ranks *Acropora palmata* and *A. cervicornis* in its contribution to Caribbean reef structure (Jackson, 1992). We will compare *M. annularis* with species of the family Faviidae and the genus *Porites* on the GBR where the genus *Porites* (subgenus *Porites*) has 3 large, common, massive species with similar life histories to *M. annularis*.

Growth and Morphology

The *M. annularis* "complex" exhibits different variations of a massive growth form (Knowlton *et al.*, 1992). Colony growth rates are slow (<1cm yr^{-1}) (Gladfelter, 1978), but colonies can grow large (many meters across in some cases) and live for hundreds of years. GBR faviids have similar slow colony growth rates, although many species do not grow so large or live so long. However, several *Porites* species on the GBR achieve similar colony sizes, are long lived, and exhibit similar growth rates (Potts *et al.*, 1985; Done and Potts, 1992).

Reproduction

All GBR faviids are hermaphroditic, release eggs and sperm and fertilization occurs externally. *M. annularis* also releases sperm and eggs and has external fertilization, but colonies are dioecious (Szmant, 1991). *Porites* of the GBR are dioecious (Kojis and Quinn, 1982). Egg sizes of both *M. annularis* and GBR faviids are moderate in size (diameters of 0.35mm to about 0.5mm; Szmant, 1986), while egg sizes of *Porites* are small to moderate (Kojis and Quinn, 1982). Self-fertilization success was found to be significant, but low, in one faviid (Heyward and Babcock, 1986), and high in another (Kojis and Quinn, 1981a; Heyward and Babcock, 1986). In general, faviids are long lived, slow growing and have low to moderate rates of sexual recruitment and fragmentation. While settlement plate studies show fairly low rates of larval recruitment for *Porites* (Wallace, 1985a), high rates of juvenile colonies were reported following mass coral mortality caused by *Acanthaster planci* (Done and Potts, 1992). It is unclear if Done and Potts (1992) were able to distinguish *Porites* recruits originating from brooding and broadcasting species. The low rate of sexual recruitment by *M. annularis* may be exacerbated because it is dioecious and this may inhibit fertilization success as indicated above.

Habitat Dominance

Montastrea annularis is the most abundant and wide-ranging Caribbean coral (Knowlton *et al.*, 1992), sometimes forming monospecific reef crest communities in wave protected habitats (Geister, 1977) and at 5-10 meter depths in leeward habitats on St. John, U.S. Virgin Islands. At depths below 15 m it often makes up about 40% of the coral cover (Jackson, 1992). The geological record shows dominance of *M. annularis* below 15 m as well and indicates that *M. annularis* was co-dominant with *A. cervicornis* 120,000 years ago at depths of 5-10 m (Jackson, 1992). It apparently dominates habitats because of its longevity and the ability of dislodged colonies or parts of colonies to survive.

No single species of faviid predominates on the GBR, although some species can be abundant in unfavorable environments, e.g. turbid, shallow water habitats. However, the three most common, large *Porites* species can dominate communities on leeward margins of nearshore platform and fringing reefs. The *Porites* in these communities have a propensity to fragment, a propensity for fragments and entire colonies to survive transportation, and are comprised of very few genotypes (Done and Potts, 1992). *M. annularis* forms similar communities in a similar manner.

GENERAL CORAL RECRUITMENT

Recruitment of coral larvae in general is considerably higher on the Great Barrier Reef than in the Caribbean (Figure 1). At a depth of 6 m Wallace (1985b) on the GBR (18°C) observed 523 recruits per m^2 yr^{-1} at 17°S while Rogers *et al.* (1984) in the Caribbean at St. Croix at approximately the same depth recorded only 30 recruits m^{-2} yr^{-1}. Recruitment was higher in Jamaica (Rylaarsdam, 1983) with 94 to 165 recruits m^{-2} yr^{-1} at depths of 15 and 11 m respectively, but still less than that observed on the GBR.

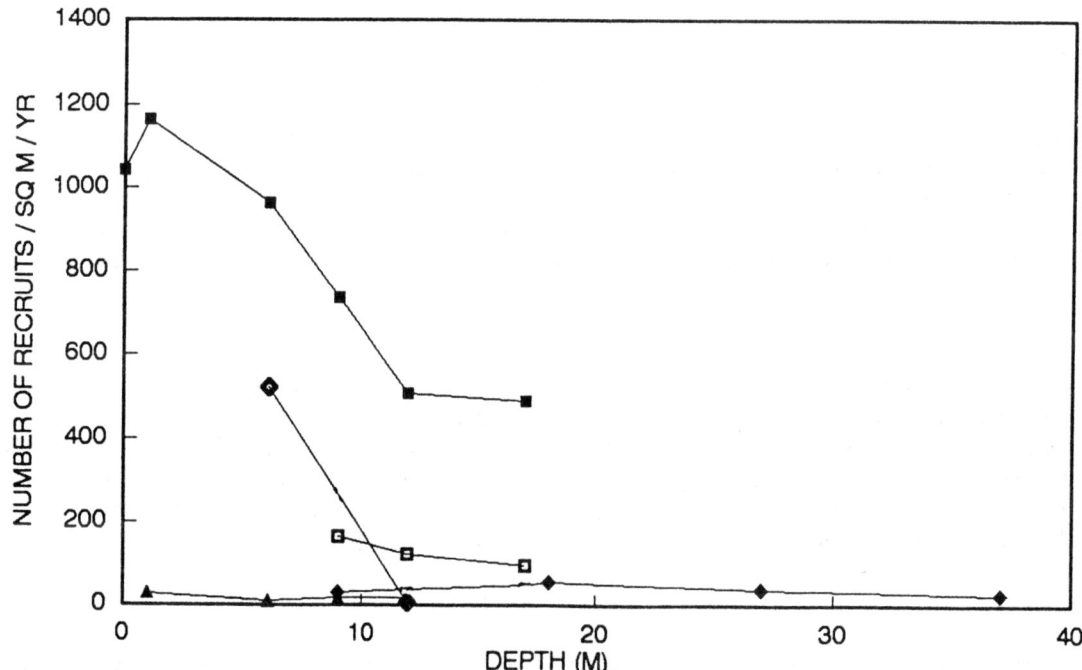

Figure 1: A comparison of rates of recruitment of Scleractinia on artificial substrates on Caribbean versus Australian east coast reefs. Great Barrier Reef 18°S (-■-) (Wallace, 1985b); Lord Howe Island 31°S (-♦-) (Harriott, 1992); Jamaica 17°N (-□-) (Rylaarsdam, 1983); St. Croix 17°N (-▲-) (Rogers *et al.*, 1984); Dry Tortugas 24°N (-●-) (Kojis *et al.*, 1992).

Even the high latitude (31°S) isolated reef system at Lord Howe Island in the western South Pacific had about 500 recruits $m^{-2} yr^{-1}$ at 8-12 m. The two dominant groups found recruiting on settlement plates in the GBR are the broadcast spawning acroporids and the brooding pocilloporids. Species of the latter family have a branching habit; recruit rapidly, often year-round; and grow quickly to a moderate size. Both families are represented in the Caribbean, but are rarely found on studies using settlement plates. Most recruits to settlement plates in the Caribbean are brooding *Agaricia* spp. and *Porites* spp. Low recruitment rates lead to low recolonization rates after severe perturbations. Recovery of many Caribbean reefs may be limited by lack of larval recruits in general and of the important reef building species in particular.

ROLE OF LIFE HISTORY IN CORAL RECOVERY

The life histories of Caribbean *Acropora* and *Montastrea annularis* retard recovery after massive local and/or regional mortality. When local extinction occurs, larval recruitment is the only natural means of recolonization. If larval recruitment is a rare, chance event, recovery will be delayed and may not occur for many decades.

The chance and patchy recruitment of the Caribbean *Acropora* spp. and *M. annularis* complex despite suitable habitat is apparent in anomalous coral distributions. For example, the *A. cervicornis* zone is absent at the southwest corner of Aruba. Here the *A. palmata* zone is bordered by a dense stand of *M. annularis* at its seaward edge (UNESCO, 1982). No *M. annularis* community inhabits the normal head coral zone on the eastern tip of the island. Instead only scattered gorgonians and small corals occur (UNESCO, 1982). At Curacao and Bonaire the *A. cervicornis* zone alternates with long stretches of sandy bottom inhabited by a few gorgonians and scattered corals (UNESCO, 1982).

Barbados may also exemplify the problem. *A. palmata* flourished in Barbados into the present century and was the major shallow water reef builder (Lewis, 1974). It is now uncommon on the reefs of Barbados and has been so for at least four decades (Lewis, 1974). It has never recovered its former abundance. Barbados is the eastern-most island in the Caribbean and up-current of other Caribbean reefs. *A. palmata* in Barbados may have to rely on self-seeding for new recruits. When a species becomes rare, such as in this case, successful cross-fertilization may be infrequent and sexual reproduction impaired. Low production of sexual recruits may severely hamper recovery. Populations of two of the three major Caribbean species have severely declined in the last two decades. *M. annularis* has also declined but not so severely. It is somewhat immune to storm damage because of its depth distribution and massive growth form. It has not been affected by white band disease. However, its slow growth and low recruitment rate means that recovery after damage to populations will be slow. This species is vulnerable if perturbations are moderately frequent and do not allow enough time for recovery.

SOFT CORAL RECRUITMENT

Large numbers of soft corals are more characteristic of healthy Caribbean reefs than of western Pacific reefs. Are damaged scleractinian sites in the Caribbean likely to be recolonized by soft corals? Smith (1985) monitored natural recolonization of hard and soft corals over a 5 year period at a ship grounding site on a Bermuda reef. He found that, although there was active recruitment of hard corals into the damaged area, an average of 25 $cm^{-2} m^{-2} yr^{-1}$ of coral cover has been generated there by natural means. Surprisingly, no new octocorals appeared despite the fact that they are normally abundant on Bermudan reefs.

Another ship grounding in 1985 on Molasses Reef in the Florida Keys yielded a different set of results. Hudson and Diaz (1988) reported that there were only a few successful scleractinian recruits, while soft corals, primarily *Pseudopterogorgia americana*, colonized large areas of the impact site.

There is presently no consistency in the evidence whether soft corals are capable of rapidly colonizing Caribbean reefs previously dominated by scleractinian corals and function as a successional species in rebuilding the reef community structure.

RELICT SPUR AND GROOVE FORMATIONS

Spur and groove formations form in shallow water on wave exposed reefs. They are active structures on exposed reefs along the Great Barrier Reef. The are generally relict Pleistocene features on Caribbean reefs lying at depths of about 12 meters. Caribbean spur and groove formations in shallow water are currently inhabited by colonies of *Millepora* and zoanthids on Looe Key Reef, Florida (Wheaton and Jaap, 1988). This is the zone described by Geister (1977) as the second most wave exposed community in shallow water. These spur and groove formations whether shallow or deep do not appear to be actively accreting structures. To these two biologists it appears that shallow water reefs are currently not actively accreting in the Caribbean.

CAN TECHNOLOGY SAVE THE REEFS?

Transplantation of hard corals as a means of accelerating the regeneration of damaged coral reefs has been tested in Hawaii (Maragos, 1974), Guam (Birkland *et al.*, 1979), Australia (Harriott and Fisk, 1988), Philippines (Yap and Gomez, 1985) and in the Red Sea (Bouchon, 1981). Kojis and Quinn (1981b) discussed the selection of Pacific corals for transplantation. In these experimental studies transplantation was generally successful with survival rates ranging in most cases from 50% to 100% when corals were transplanted into similar habitats to those from which they were collected. The process appears to have a potential role in the repair of reefs, but the method is very expensive and would only probably be used in specific localities where the expense could be justified.

Experiments in transplanting coral in the Caribbean are uncommon. Hudson and Diaz (1988) transplanted 11 large individuals from eight species in the Florida Keys in an effort to repair a swath of destruction created from a ship grounding. At the time of publication of their report in 1988, all hard corals were in excellent health. Recently, Wheaton et al. (1992) began another transplantation experiment at a ship damaged site in the Florida Keys.

At the time of writing, Walter Jaap and his team are again surveying damaged coral reefs associated with the freak storm of March 12-13, 1993, which produced winds in excess of 100 miles an hour in the Keys. We suppose the scientific community should thank the shipping industry for the opportunity to engage in experiments that otherwise would not be permitted.

Although the technique appears to have limited practical potential, further experiments are necessary to assess the ability of Caribbean corals to survive transplantation. The technique may have the most applicability and greatest success with *A. palmata* and *A. cervicornis* which are essential components of Caribbean coral reefs, and have high fragment survival rates and low sexual recruitment.

CONCLUSION

Coral communities are recovering on the GBR, but not in the Caribbean. This is at least in part, Caribbean corals generally have low larval recruitment rates. It is also due to difference in the life history strategies of dominant taxonomic groups. *Acropora*, the most abundant group of corals on the GBR, has a large number of species exhibiting a wide range of life history strategies. Many GBR *Acropora* combine fast growth rates with high sexual recruitment rates enabling them to successfully recolonize reefs after perturbations. Recovery of *Acropora* populations in the Caribbean is hindered by high growth rates, frequent fragmentation and low larval recruitment rates. High growth and fragmentation is a successful strategy to increase recruitment locally, but may inhibit sexual recruitment by reducing allocation of resources to sexual reproduction and decreasing fertilization success. Colonies of *Montastrea annularis* are slow growing, large and long lived with low larval recruitment rates. It too is vulnerable to major perturbations.

LITERATURE CITED

Birkeland, C., R. H. Randall and G. Grimm. 1979. Three methods of coral transplantation for the purpose of re-establishing coral community in the thermal effluent area of the Tanguisson Power Plant. Univ. of Guam Marine La. Tech. Rep. 60: 1-24.

Bouchon, C., J. Jaubert and Y. Bouchon-Navaro. 1981. Evolution of a semi-artificial reef built by transplanting coral heads. Tethys 10(2): 173-176.

Brazeau, D. A. and H. R. Lasker. 1992. Reproductive success in a marine benthic invertebrate, the Caribbean octocoral *Briareum asbestinum*. Mar. Biol. 114: 157-163.

Done, T. 1992. Constancy and change in some Great Barrier Reef coral communities: 1980-1990. American Zoologist 32: 655-662.

Done, T. and D. C. Potts. 1992. Influences of habitat and natural disturbances on contributions of massive *Porites* corals to reef communities. Mar. Biol. 114: 479-493.

Endean, R., A. M. Cameron and L. M. DeVantier. 1988. *Acanthaster planci* predation on massive corals: the myth of rapid recovery of devastated reefs. Proc. 6th Int. Coral Reef Symp., Australia. 2: 143-148.

Fisk, D. A. and V. J. Harriott. 1990. Spatial and temporal variation in coral recruitment on the Great Barrier Reef: implications for dispersal hypotheses. Mar. Biol. 107: 485-490.

Gleister, J. 1977. The influence of wave exposure on the ecological zonation of Caribbean coral reefs. Proc. 3rd Int. Coral Reef Symposium. 1: 23-29.

Gladfelter, E. H., R.K. Monahan and W. B. Gladfelter. 1978. Growth rates of five reef-building corals in the northeastern Caribbean. Bull. Mar. Sci. 23(4): 728-734.

Gladfelter, W. B. 1982. White band disease in *Acropora palmata*: implications for the structure and growth of shallow reefs. Bull. Mar. Sci. 32(2): 639-643.

Glynn, P. W. 1973. Aspects of the Ecology of Coral Reefs in the Western Atlantic Region. Pages 271-324 *in* O. A. Jones and R. Endean, ed. Biology and Geology of Coral Reefs, Vol. 2. Academic Press.

Harriott, V. J. 1985. Mortality rates of scleractinian corals before and during a mass bleaching event. Mar. Ecol. Prog. Ser. 21: 81-88.

Harriott, V. J. 1992. Recruitment patterns of scleractinian corals in an isolated sub-tropical reef system. Coral Reefs 11: 215-219.

Harriott, V. J. and D. A. Fisk. 1988. The natural recruitment and recovery process of corals at Green Island. G.B.R.M.P.A. Technical Memorandum 15.

Harrison, P. L. and C. C. Wallace, 1990. Reproduction, dispersal and recruitment of scleractinian corals. Pages 133 - 207. *in* Dubinsky, Z. (ed) Coral Reef ecosystems. Elsevier, Amsterdam.

Heyward, A. J. and R. C. Babcock. 1986. Self- and cross-fertilization in scleractinian corals. Mar. Biol. 90: 191-195.

Hudson, J. H. and R. Diaz. 1988. Damage survey and restoration of M/V Wellwood grounding site, Molasses Reef, Key Largo National Marine Sanctuary, Florida. Proc. 6th Int. Coral Reef Symp., Australia. 2: 231-236.

Jaap, W. C. 1979. Observations on zooxanthellae expulsion at Middle Sambo Reef, Florida Keys. Bull. Mar. Sci. 29: 414-422.

Jackson, J. B .C. 1992. Pleistocene perspectives on coral reef community structure. American Zoologist 32: 719-731.

Knowlton, N., E. Weil, L. A. Weight and H. M. Guzman. 1992. Sibling species in *Montastrea annularis*, coral bleaching, and the coral climate record. Science. 255: 330-333.

Kojis, B. L. and N. J. Quinn. 1981a. Aspects of sexual reproduction and larval development in the shallow water hermatypic coral *Goniastrea australensis* (Edwards and Haime, 1857). Bull. Mar. Sci. 31: 558-573.

Kojis, B. L. and N. J. Quinn. 1981b. Factors to consider when transplanting hermatypic corals to accelerate regeneration of damaged coral reefs. Conf. on Environ. Engin. Townsville, 8-10 July 1981, pp.183-187.

Kojis, B. L., and N. J. Quinn. 1990. Reproduction in Scleractinian corals at Lizard Island, Great Barrier Reef, with an emphasis on species spawning outside the mass spawning event. American Zoologist 30: 521.

Kojis, B. L., K. Boomer Donnelly, W. C. Jaap and W. C. Wheaton. 1992. Coral recruitment patterns at Dry Tortugas and Western Sambo reefs, Florida, a Seakeys Cooperative research project. 29th Annual Marine Benthic Ecology Meeting (abstract).

Lessios, H. A., D. R. Robertson and J. D. Cubit. 1984. Spread of *Diadema* mass mortality throughout the Caribbean. Science 226: 335-337.

Lewis, J. B. 1984. The *Acropora* inheritance: A reinterpretation of the development of fringing reefs in Barbados, West Indies. Coral Reefs 3: 117-122.

Maragos, J. E. 1974. Coral transplantation: a method to create, preserve and manage coral reefs. Sea Grant Advisory Report UNIHI-Sea Grant-AR-74-03, CORMAR-14. 30 pp.

Oliver, J. K. 1984. Variation in the growth of *Acropora* formosa: Extension rates and skeletal structure of white (Zooxanthellae-free) and brown-tipped branches. Coral Reefs 3: 139-147.

Porter, J. W., J. D. Woodley, G. J. Smith, J. E. Neigel, J. F. Battey and D. G. Dallmeyer. 1981. Population trends among Jamaican reef corals. Nature 294: 249-250.

Porter, J. W. and O. W. Meier. 1992. Quantification of Loss and Change in Floridian Reef Coral Populations. American Zoologist 32: 625-640.

Potts, D. C., T. J. Done, P. J. Isdale and D. A. Fisk. 1985. Dominance of a coral community by the genus *Porites* (Scleractinia). Mar. Ecol. Prog. Ser. 23:79-84.

Richmond, R. H. 1992. Fertilization in corals: Problems and puzzles. Page 89 *in* R. Richmond, ed. 7th International Coral Reef Symposium: Abstracts. Guam.

Roberts, L. 1987. Coral bleaching threatens Atlantic reefs. Science 238: 1228-1229.

Rogers, C. S., H. C. Fitz III, M. Gilnack, J. Beets and J. Hardin. 1984. Scleractinian Coral Recruitment Patterns at Salt River Submarine Canyon, St. Croix, U.S. Virgin Islands. Coral Reefs 3: 69-76.

Rylaarsdam, K. W. 1983. Life histories and abundance patterns of colonial corals on Jamaican reefs. Mar. Ecol. Prog. Ser. 13: 249-260.

Shinn, E. A., 1989. What is really killing the corals. Sea Frontiers 35(2): 72-81.

Szmant, A. M. 1986. Reproductive ecology of Caribbean reef corals. Coral Reefs 5: 43-55.

Szmant. A. M. 1991. Sexual reproduction by the Caribbean reef corals *Montastrea annularis* and *M. cavernosa*. Mar. Ecol. Prog. Ser. 74: 13-25.

Tunnicliffe, V. 1983. Caribbean staghorn coral populations: Pre-Hurricane Allen conditions in Discovery Bay, Jamaica. Bull. Mar. Sci. 33: 132-151.

UNESCO. 1983. Coral reefs, seagrass beds and mangroves: Their interaction in the coastal zones of the Caribbean. Report of a Workshop held at West Indies Laboratory, St. Croix, U.S. Virgin Islands, May 1982. UNESCO Reports in Marine Science. 133 pp.

Veron, J. E. N. and C. C. Wallace. 1984. Scleractinia of Eastern Australia. Part V. Family Acroporidae. Australian Institute of Marine Science Monograph Series. Vol. 6. 485 pp.

Veron, J. E. N. 1986. Corals of Australia and the Indo-Pacific. Angus & Robertson Publishers, North Ryde, NSW, Australia. 644 pp.

Wallace, C. C. 1983. Visible and invisible coral recruitment. Pages 295-261 *in* Proceedings of the Inaugural Great Barrier Reef Conference, Townsville, 1983.

Wallace, C. C. 1985a. Reproduction, recruitment and fragmentation in nine sympatric species of the coral genus *Acropora*. Marine Biology 88: 217-233.

Wallace, C. C. 1985b. Seasonal peaks and recruitment in juvenile scleractinian corals. Mar. Ecol. Prog. Ser. 21: 289-298.

Wheaton, J. L. and W. C. Jaap. 1988. Corals and other prominent benthic Cnidaria of Looe Key National Marine Sanctuary, Florida. Florida Marine Research Publications, No. 43. 25 pp.

Wheaton, J. L., W. C. Jaap, B. L. Kojis, G. P. Schmahl, D. L. Ballantine and J. E. McKenna, Jr. 1992. Transplanting organisms on a damaged reef at Pulaski Shoal, Ft. Jefferson National Monument, Dry Tortugas, Florida, U.S.A.: An experiment to enhance recruitment. Page 108 *in* R. Richmond, ed. 7th Int. Coral Reef Symp.: Abstracts. Guam.

Willis, B. L., R. C. Babcock, P. L. Harrison and C. C. Wallace. 1992. Experimental evidence of hybridization in reef corals involved in mass spawning events. Page 109 *in* R. Richmond, ed. 7th Int. Coral Reef Symp.: Abstracts. Guam.

Yap, H. T. and E. D. Gomez. 1985. Growth of *Acropora pulchra* III. Preliminary observations on the effects of transplantation and sediment on the growth and survival of transplants. Mar. Biol. 87: 203-209.

EFFECTS OF COASTAL RUNOFF ON CORAL REPRODUCTION

Robert H. Richmond

Marine Laboratory, University of Guam, UOG Station, Mangilao, Guam 96923 USA

ABSTRACT

Erosion, sedimentation and runoff are problems many tropical islands are experiencing as they come under development pressure from the construction of hotels, resorts, condominiums, golf courses, roads and increased housing. Previous studies have shown the detrimental effects of sediment on living corals, which can destroy reefs through shading, burial and interference with the ability of corals to feed heterotrophically. Experiments with coral gametes demonstrate that runoff also effects the reproductive success of corals, with an observed 86% drop in fertilization rate accompanying a 20% decrease in salinity from 35 o/oo to 28 o/oo. Success of larval development following fertilization was also reduced by runoff, in some cases by as much as 50%. This is of particular concern as many corals on Indo-west Pacific reefs (e.g. Guam and Okinawa) reproduce during mass-spawning events which occur during the rainy season, when seawater temperatures reach their seasonal peak, and coastal water quality is most likely to be affected by runoff. As most tropical marine invertebrates and fishes also reproduce by spawning gametes into the water column, the evidence of reproductive failure in corals has far-reaching implications for the management and preservation of tropical marine communities.

INTRODUCTION

Scleractinian reef-building corals can either brood larvae after internal fertilization or spawn gametes into the water column, with subsequent external fertilization. Of the over 200 species which have been studied, the vast majority are simultaneous hermaphrodites which broadcast spawn (Richmond and Hunter, 1990). More than 150 species of corals have been observed to spawn gametes either on the same night, or over the course of a week on the reefs of Australia, Okinawa, and the Pacific Islands (Harrison and Wallace, 1990). Some species spawn only one night per year. The timing of these mass spawning events are temperature related seasonally, and further synchronized by nocturnal illumination, occurring during or soon after the summer full moon. This peak reproductive period coincides with the rainy season for the islands sampled in this study.

While the decline in health of numerous reefs throughout the world has been reported, the actual causes have not always been identified. Nearshore reefs are often impacted directly by sedimentation, leaving little doubt as to the cause of problems. Offshore reefs have also been reported to show signs of reduced coral cover, with no evidence of sediment-related problems. There are a number of natural causes of coral mortality including predation from echinoderms and gastropods, storm-related damage, and competition with other benthic encrusting organisms. After several reports and observations of declining coral cover and low coral recruitment levels on reefs off southern Guam, a study was initiated to determine if reproductive failure on upcurrent "source" reefs combined with natural (and anthropogenic) coral mortality could be the problem.

METHODS

Gamete Collection

During June, 1990, colonies of Acropora digitifera were collected from the reefs surrounding Sesoko Island, Okinawa, Japan. Colonies were placed in flowing seawater tables at the Sesoko Marine Sciences Center, University of the Ryukyus, and observed starting one hour after sundown beginning the night prior to the full moon. By 8:00 PM on June 9, expanded polyps took on an orange color, as gamete clusters were pushed up from the polyps' mesenteries towards their mouths. At this point, individual colonies were placed into separate 20 liter aquaria containing seawater. Over the next two hours, gamete clusters composed of from 9 - 16 eggs surrounding a sperm packet moved to the area just below the polyp tentacles, with release occurring from 10:00 - 10:30 PM.

The egg/sperm clusters floated to the surface and remained intact for 10 to 20 minutes before bursting apart, allowing eggs and sperm to mix. Immediately upon release, gamete clusters were collected, placed on a 80um screen, and washed with filtered seawater to separate the sperm from the egg. The sperm were collected in a beaker, while the eggs were placed into filtered seawater.

Fertilization Bioassays

Okinawa 1990.-- To determine if coastal runoff had an effect on reproductive success in spawning corals, water samples were collected from the surface 10 cm above a fringing reef near the mouth of the Okobori River, Motobu-Cho, Okinawa. This water had a salinity of 28.5 o/oo and lateritic suspended solids of 1.28 g/l. This site was selected for its accessibility, and the fact that coral gametes were being released into these waters during the spawning period. The control seawater from the nearby Sesoko Marine Science Center seawater system had a salinity of 34.42 o/oo, and was filtered through a Millepore 0.45 um filter prior to use.

One hundred to 150 eggs were placed into the following treatments: fertilization control (eggs alone, filtered seawater); experimental control (eggs treated with sperm from a different colony of the same species at ca. 10^5 sperm/ml); experimental, performing the fertilization experiment in the coastal water sample. The fertilization control was performed to eliminate the possibility of parthenogenesis or selfing from confounding the results. It was necessary to use sperm and eggs from different colonies of the same species as self-fertilization rates were found to be low in this species.

Guam 1990.-- Experiments performed during the summers of 1988 and 1989 found that the major period of coral spawning took place one month later on Guam, Marianas Islands, than on Okinawa. In July, 1990, experiments were performed on Guam which included comparisons of fertilization success of Acropora digitifera in seawater at 34 o/oo versus seawater diluted with distilled water to a salinity of 28 o/oo.

Okinawa 1991.-- During the June, 1991, spawning at Sesoko Island, Okinawa, experiments were performed using Acropora digitifera, with 100 - 150 eggs placed into 15 ml plastic scintillation vials under the following replicated treatments: a fertilization control (eggs only, filtered seawater); an experimental control using filtered seawater with a salinity of 35 o/oo; a 10% dilution with distilled freshwater (31.5 o/oo); a 20% dilution (28 o/oo); a 30% dilution (24.5 o/oo); a 40% dilution (21 o/oo); and a 50%

dilution (17.5 o/oo). As in the initial experiment, sperm cells from a different colony of the same species were added to each treatment except the fertilization control at a concentration of ca. 10^5 sperm/ml. The results are summarized in Table 1.

RESULTS

Okinawa 1990.-- After 10 hours, none of the eggs from the fertilization control were fertilized, 72% of the experimental control eggs were fertilized, and 34% of the experimental treatment's eggs (lower salinity, higher suspended solids) were fertilized. The fertilized eggs from this experiment were observed over the following 3 days for development to the planula larva stage. All of the fertilized eggs from the 34.4 o/oo control developed into actively swimming planulae, while only 51% of the fertilized eggs from the coastal water treatment developed successfully. The observed 53% drop in fertilization rate and subsequent 49% decrease in embryo viability between the two groups of gametes in the control and runoff affected seawater provided the basis for further experimentation.

Guam 1990.-- In the 1990 Guam experiment comparing success at the salinities of 34 o/oo versus 28 o/oo, fertilization was 88% at the higher (ambient) salinity, compared to 25% for the lower salinity treatment.

Okinawa 1991.-- A drop in percent fertilization from 58% to 34% was observed in response to a 10% decrease in salinity from 35 o/oo to 31.5 o/oo. The data from the range experiment are summarized in Table 1.

Table 1. Fertilization success of Acropora digitifera eggs under conditions of altered salinity (n = 2 replicates, 100-150 eggs each).

Salinity (o/oo)	Mean Fertilization (%)
Guam, 1990	
34	88
28	25
Okinawa, 1991	
35	58
31.5	34
28	8
24.5	1
21	0
17.5	0

DISCUSSION

The experiments at different sites and on different years were consistent in showing a marked decrease in fertilization rate of coral eggs in conditions of reduced salinity. During the rainy season, large quantities of fresh water impinge on coastal reefs throughout the tropics. The experiment performed in 1990 is relevant to the real world, as water into which gametes were released was tested for its effects on fertilization success, demonstrating a decrease in reproductive success from egg to planula larvae from 72% to 17%. The experiments performed in 1991 dealt with the effects of freshwater dilution alone, demonstrating that a 10% dilution of seawater with freshwater caused a 41% decrease in fertilization rate, and that a 20% dilution caused an 86% reduction. These experiments did not take any other substances into consideration which would likely be included in runoff water such as petroleum products washing off roads, and herbicides and pesticides from agriculture and golf courses. Considering coral eggs are lipid-rich, floating at the surface for hours until fertilized, and the subsequent embryos remain positively buoyant for days, reproductive products of corals will be subjected to the waters of lowest salinity and highest levels of contamination during the limited periods during which fertilization and development can occur.

It is important to note that most of the marine tropical shallow-water organisms of economic importance, including both fishes and invertebrates, are broadcast spawners. Their reproductive products and hence reproductive success are also affected by water quality. The data presented here indicate that terrestrial runoff may be sublethal to adult marine organisms at certain levels, but can interfere with reproduction, development and subsequent recruitment. Coral reefs may be killed rapidly, via sedimentation, or slowly through attrition and reproductive failure.

Artisinal fishermen, who are excellent marine biologists by necessity and experience, have brought the problem of coral reef decline to the attention of scientists before. Death of reefs via sedimentation and burial has been relatively easy to observe. Decline of coral reefs through attrition has been harder to document. As corals have natural predators, including mollusks, fish, and echinoderms, and may suffer mortality from anchor and wave damage, reefs removed from sedimentation may still be adversely affected by coastal runoff through loss of recruits from affected coastal sources. This appears to be the situation on Anae Island off the southern coast of Guam, where large corals are abundant, but few recruits in the smaller size classes can be found. The data presented here clearly demonstrate that reproductive failure is a very real problem for spawning corals, intensified by the pattern of mass-spawnings during the rainy season. As development, erosion and freshwater runoff continue to increase on tropical islands, the fate of corals and other reef-associated spawning organisms is of concern. These data make a compelling argument for better erosion control practices needed on tropical islands, least the reefs and coastal marine resources which support the islands and their developing tourist industries be lost. The accepted engineering scheme for allowing storm runoff to pour into the coastal zone needs to be rethought in the tropics, where economically valuable coral reefs depend on water clarity and quality to exist and reproduce. Limiting clearing and grading activities to the dry season through the permitting process is one suggestion Islands may adopt. Appropriate ponding basins in addition to stricter erosion control measures are also partial solutions. More detailed toxicological data are needed to determine synergisms which are likely to exist.

CONCLUSIONS

The time period prior to disruption of the gamete clusters is believed to be an adaptation to increase the probability of out-crossing during the mass-spawning events. This observed time delay also increases the time gametes are subjected to any contaminants that may be in surface waters. Reduced coastal water quality can cause reproductive failure in corals and other spawning marine organisms. This is believed to be responsible for reduced coral cover on reefs affected by both natural and anthropogenic disturbance. Reproductive failure, and subsequent reductions in recruitment are serious problems affecting coral reefs, and often escape detection as the results occur over longer time period than acute disturbances.

ACKNOWLEDGEMENTS

I thank Dr. Kiyoshi Yamazato for his support and use of the facilities at the Sesoko Marine Science Center, Okinawa, Japan, and H. Sakai, F. Te and D. Hopper for field and laboratory assistance. Research was supported in part by grant # 53-LA-61158-511 from the National Institutes of Health, # BSR 8813350 from the National Science Foundation, and a cooperative research grant from the Monbusho (Japan). M.G. Hadfield provided helpful comments on the manuscript.

LITERATURE CITED

Harrison, P.L., R.C. Babcock, G.D. Bull, J.K. Oliver, C.C. Wallace, and B.L. Willis. 1984. Mass spawning in tropical reef corals. Science 223:1186-1189.

Harrison, P.L., and C.C. Wallace. 1990. Coral reproduction. In Z. Dubinsky (ed.), Ecosystems of the World: Coral Reefs, pp. 133-208. Elsevier Science Publishers B.V., Amsterdam.

Richmond, R.H. 1990. Relationships among reproductive mode, biogeographic distribution patterns and evolution in scleractinian corals. Pages 317 - 322 in M. Hoshi and O. Yamashita, eds. Advances in invertebrate reproduction 5, Elsevier Press.

Richmond, R.H., and C.L. Hunter. 1990. Reproduction and recruitment of corals: comparisons among the Caribbean, the Tropical Pacific, and the Red Sea. Mar. Ecol. Prog. Ser. 60:185-203.

Rogers, C.S. 1990. Responses of coral reef organisms to sedimentation. Mar. Ecol. Prog. Ser. 62:185-202.

BIODIVERSITY OF REEF CORALS:

IS THERE A PROBLEM IN THE INDO-PACIFIC CENTRE OF DIVERSITY?

J.E.N. Veron

Australian Institute of Marine Science, Townsville, Australia

ABSTRACT

Continuous taxonomic and biogeographic studies of hermatypic corals over the past 20 years has yielded a clear picture of the global distribution of genera, together with details of distribution patterns of species within the Indo-Pacific Centre of Diversity. In global terms, most of the world's coral reefs are in developing countries where conservation is either not practiced, or cannot be enforced. In the Central Indo-Pacific, the highest diversity occurs in the Indonesian and Philippine archipelagoes, a region with a very high population density, where eutrophication and over-fishing are ubiquitous and explosive fishing and commercial collecting is effectively unregulated. The Ryukyu Is. of Japan, and the Great Barrier Reef of Australia, are at the northern and southern extremities of the Centre of Diversity (respectively). Conservation of coral reefs of Japan is currently at a critical phase where bad land management, coastal construction, and lack of a conservation ethic are creating a scenario for widespread extinction through environmental deterioration. Australia's low population density and strictly enforced conservation laws are effectively protecting reef biota. In the foreseeable future, the diversity of reef corals and other reef biota is likely to decline to the point where Australian reefs become the global refuge for a significant proportion of the world's reef biodiversity.

INTRODUCTION

This study was initiated twenty years ago by a small group of coral taxonomists who produced a five-volume monograph *Scleractinia of Eastern Australia*. This work was progressively extended to the reefs of Western Australia and thence to many countries of SE Asia. The last part of the study was undertaken in Japan. Biogeographic data from these studies has recently been condensed into to a database which provides the basis for detailed observations about species distributions and diversity (Veron, 1992a).

Japan has become the focus of concern, partly because reef degradation is both recent and rapid and partly because Japan and Australia are the two developed countries in the Indo-Pacific Centre of Diversity which have the capacity to control environment degradation to the point where long-term conservation is achievable.

RESULTS

The global generic distribution of coral is illustrated in Fig. 1. There is a well-defined Indo-Pacific Centre of Diversity and that occurs in the Central Indo-Pacific. West from this Centre, diversity remains approximately uniform across the coral regions of the Indian Ocean and into the Red Sea. East from the Centre, diversity attenuates across the central and south Pacific, with depauperate outlying regions occurring in Hawaii in the north, Eastern Island in the south-east, and in the Far Eastern Pacific.

Figure 1

Global generic contours of hermatypic coral diversity.

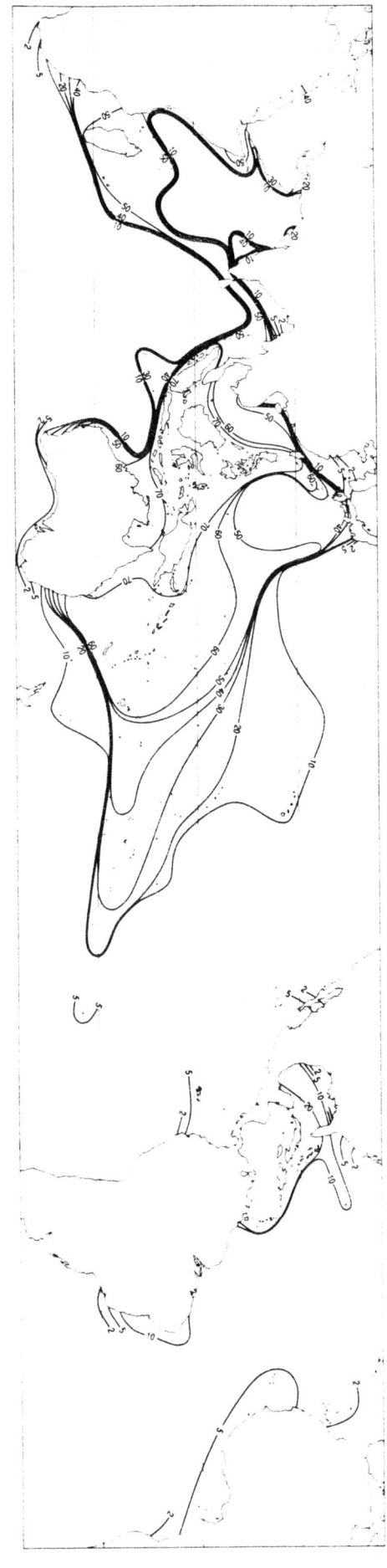

Within the Central Indo-Pacific, latitudinal attenuation occurs north from the Philippines to mainland Japan (Fig. 2) and south along the western and eastern Australian coasts (Fig. 3 and 4, respectively).

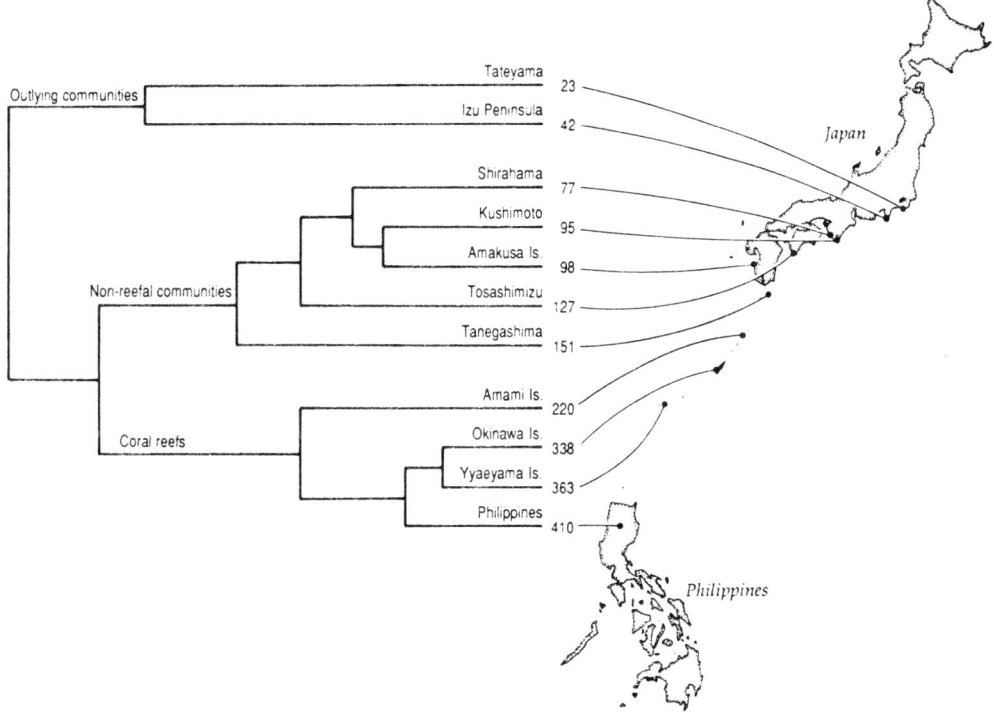

Figure 2 Agglomerative hierarchical classification of the hermatypic corals of Japan using the Bray-Curtis dissimilarity coefficient and flexible unweighted pair mean averages.

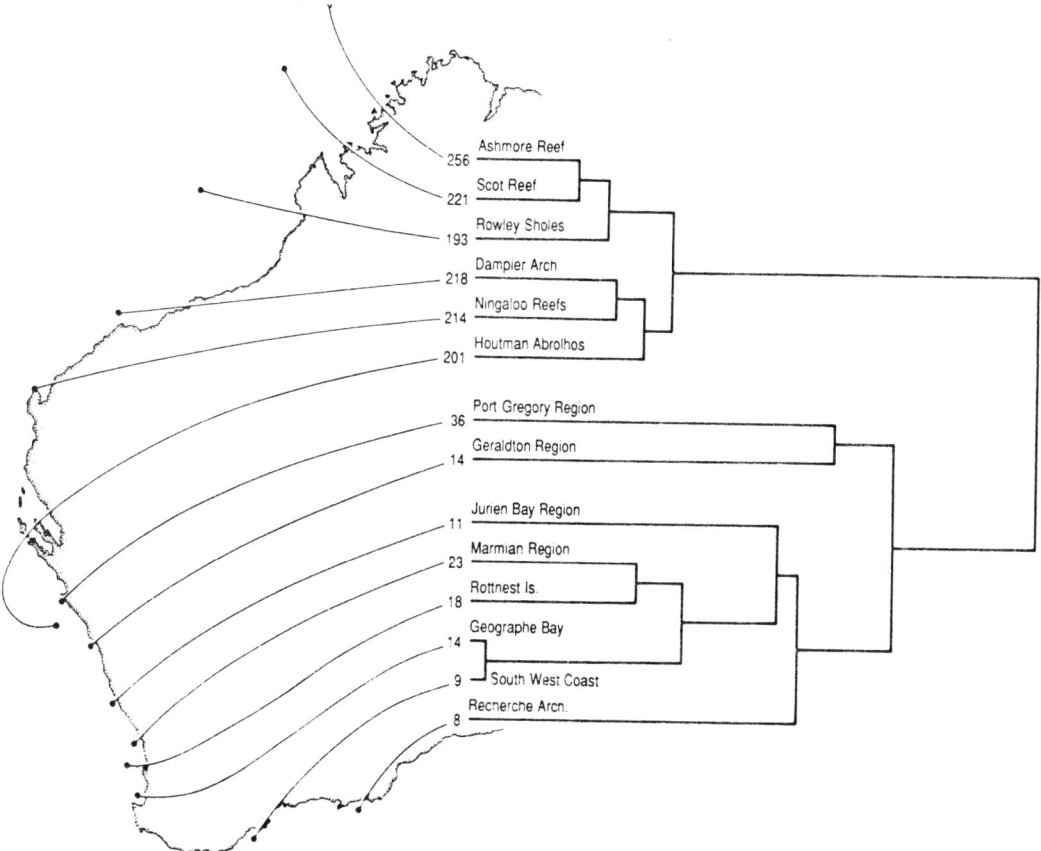

Figure 3 Agglomerative hierarchical classification of the hermatypic corals of Western Australia (procedures as described for Fig. 2).

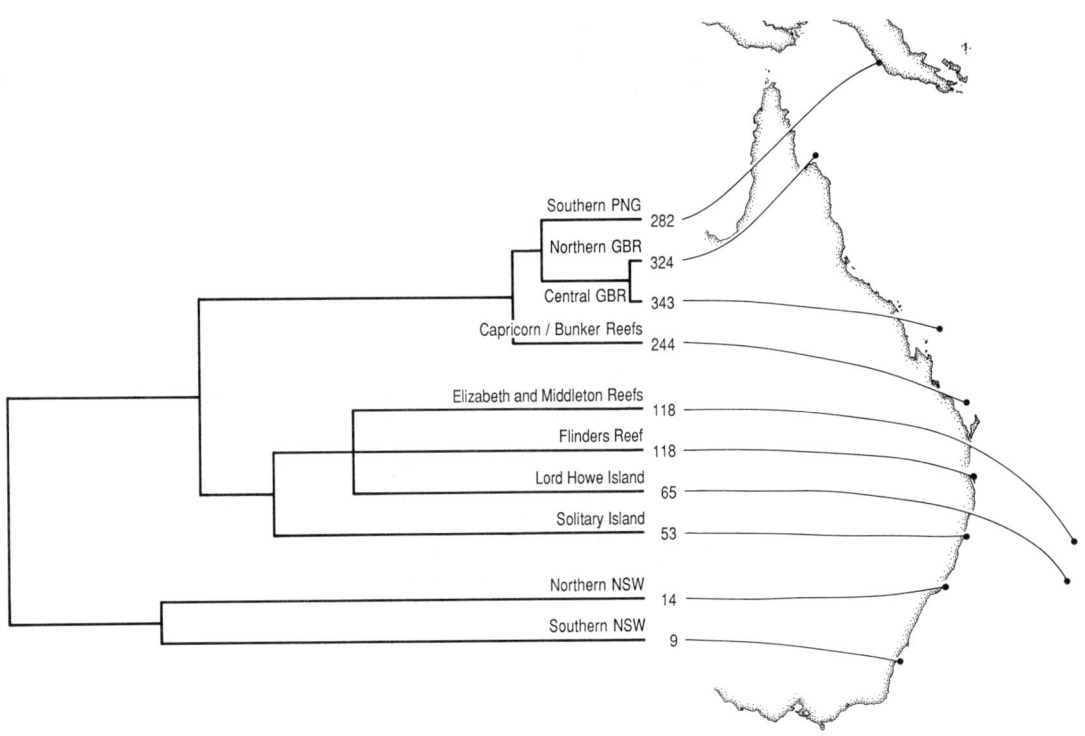

Figure 4 Agglomerative hierarchical classification of the hermatypic corals of Eastern Australia (procedures as described for Fig. 2).

The first of these regions is the focus of the present report (Veron 1992b). Ninety-eight sites in Japan were studied, allowing detailed comparison between the three main groups of the Ryukyu Is. (Yaeyama, Okinawa and Amami Groups) and seven principal coral regions of mainland Japan (Tanegashima, Amakusa Is., the Tosashimizu and Kushimoto regions, and the Shirahama, Izu and Tateyama Peninsulas) (see Fig. 2).

Within this area, 400 species have been recorded and 9 additional species are recorded from the literature, from additional localities, or with doubt, from the Ryukyu Is. In non-mutually exclusive distribution and abundance categories for the Ryukyu Is. and mainland Japan, 129 species are common in at least some Japanese localities, 24 are widely dispersed within the Indo-Pacific, but occur in small, perhaps disjunct populations in Japan, 149 are uncommon throughout their Indo-west Pacific distribution ranges including Japan; 38 are restricted to the Yaeyama Group where all but three are uncommon or rare; 69 purely reefal (Ryukyu Is.) species are rare; 17 are rare in the Ryukyu Is. but are relatively common in mainland locations and 8 species appear to be endemic to mainland Japan and adjacent Asian countries. Some 37% of all Japanese hermatypic corals are uncommon throughout their range in Japan and are at some risk of regional extinction, 29% of others are rare and at substantial risk as they occur only in very limited areas of high diversity or in species-specific refuges. These sites are identified. Five endemic species are primarily restricted to species-specific refuges.

A relatively small proportion of the species of the Central Indo-Pacific as a whole are endemic (Fig. 5)

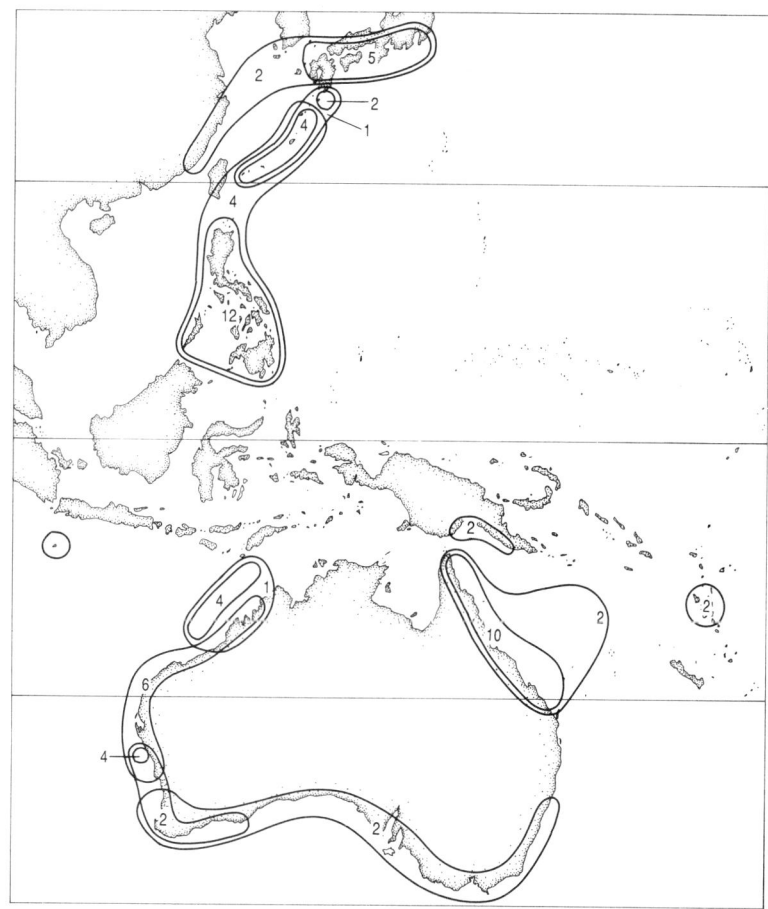

Figure 5 Patterns of endeminism in the Central Indo-Pacific. Numbers are numbers of species.

DISCUSSION

At least one third of all hermatypic corals of Japan appear to exist in an unstable state and are at serious risk of extinction within Japan if the present apparent rate of environmental deterioration continues. The risk of total extinction for most of the currently endangered species (number unknown number, but not less that 50) is not confined to Japan, as most also occur in the Philippine and Indonesian archipelagos. These, however, are developing countries where effective conservation measures are not implemented as completely or effectively as they have been in Australia, or could be in Japan.

In the absence of effective recruitment from the Philippines, a major part of the regional diversity of Japanese corals is dependent on the conservation within Japan of adequate areas of high biodiversity together with other areas of high environmental diversity, including species-specific refuges. In both cases it is the environment, not just the fauna, that must be managed. The two most essential regions for long-term conservation, containing major areas of healthy reef as well as wide environment heterogeneity, are Iriomote I. and Sekisei lagoon (part of the Yaeyama Groups of islands) and the Kerama Is. of the Okinawa Group. The case for general conservation of other regions (except for species-specific refuges) is less a biological one than a question of value judgement. Optimism can be found only if widespread, effective, coastal zone management practices, combined with multiple user management procedures for the reefs are urgently adopted.

LITERATURE CITED

Veron, J.E.N. 1992a A biogeographic database of hermatypic corals; species of the Central Indo-Pacific, genera of the world. AIMS Monograph Ser. 10: 442pp.

Veron, J.E.N. 1992b Conservation of biodiversity: a critical time for the hermatypic corals of Japan. Coral Reefs 11: 13-21.

REEFS OF THE INDIAN OCEAN

	PAGES
Damage to Shallow Reef Corals in the Gulf is Caused by Periodic Exposures to Air During Extreme Low Tides and Low Water Temperatures (Tarut Bay, Eastern Saudi Arabia) *Y.H. Fadlallah, K.W. Allen and R.A. Estudillo*	371 - 377
The Houtman Abrolhos Reefs of Western Australia: Environmental and Anthropogenic Change in the Structure and Function of Reef Communities at High Latitude *Bruce G. Hatcher and Lindsay B. Collins*	378 - 384
The Growth of Coastal Tourism in the Red Sea: Present and Possible Future Effects on Coral Reefs *Julie P. Hawkins and Callum M. Roberts*	385 - 391
Status of Kenyan Coral Reefs *T.R. McClanahan and D. Obura*	392 - 396
Effect of Nutrient Excess on a Modern Fringing Reef (Reunion Island, Western Indian Ocean): Geological Implications *Lucien F. Montaggioni, Pascale Cuet and Odile Naim*	397 - 403
Three Adjacent Coral Reefs in North-Western Sri Lanka; Biology and Human Disturbances *Marcus Ohman, Arjan Rajasuriya and Olof Linden*	404 - 409
Present Status of Coral Reefs in Sri Lanka *Arjan Rajasuriya*	410 - 416

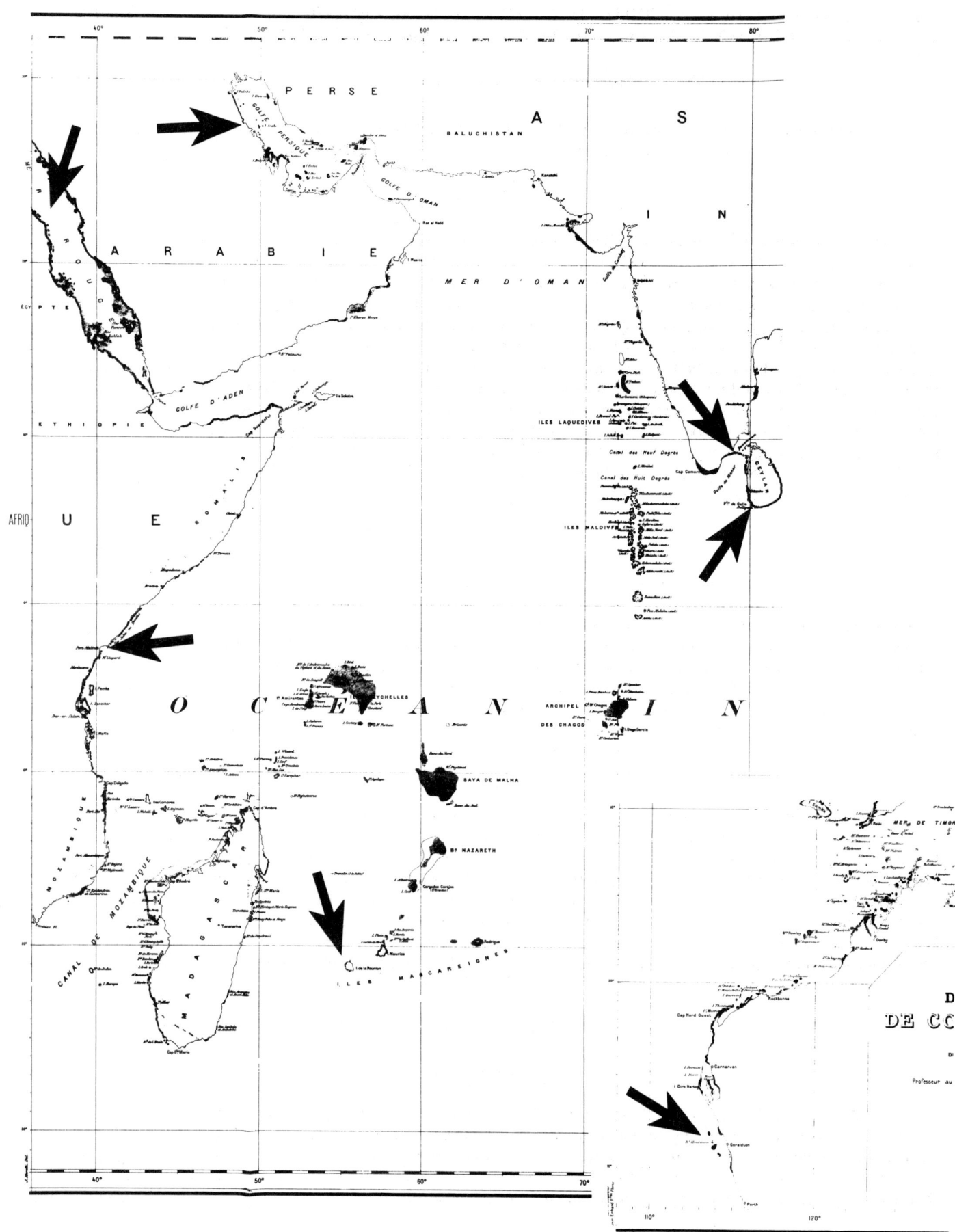

DAMAGE TO SHALLOW REEF CORALS IN THE GULF IS CAUSED BY PERIODIC EXPOSURES TO AIR DURING EXTREME LOW TIDES AND LOW WATER TEMPERATURES (TARUT BAY, EASTERN SAUDI ARABIA)

Y.H. Fadlallah[1], K.W. Allen[2], and R.A. Estudillo[1]

[1]Research Institute, King Fahd University of Petroleum and Minerals, Dhahran 31261, Saudi Arabia. [2]Environmental Engineering Division, Saudi Aramco, Dhahran 31311, Saudi Arabia.

ABSTRACT

Corals were exposed to air repeatedly during a cluster of extreme low spring tides (below Lowest Astronomical Tide-LAT), from December 1991 through April 1992 on patch reefs in Tarut Bay adjacent to the Ras Tanura Peninsula, Saudi Arabia. Most affected were colonies occurring at the highest levels on the tops of patch reef platforms. Corals (Genus *Acropora* and *Stylophora*) fully exposed to air apparently suffered total mortality, while those not fully exposed suffered tissue damage to their upper parts.. Evaporative cooling and heat radiation may have caused coral tissue temperatures to drop below their normal range of thermal tolerance. Exposure to air occurred during winter months when air and water temperatures are at their lowest in the Gulf. Evaporative cooling and heat radiation may have caused coral tissue temperatures to have dropped below their normal range of thermal tolerance. The coupling of extremely low spring winter tides with wind-induced setdowns below LAT are not regular events but are not infrequent. Comprehensive records of observed tides assisted in determining the events that preceded the coral mortalities in Tarut Bay, and provided the tool with which we were able to relate coral death to tidal exposure This phenomenon is probably responsible for previously observed coral die-off events western Gulf coast of Saudi Arabia and other Gulf countries, coincidental with low water temperature. It is highly unlikely that the Gulf War oil spill and oil well fires of 1991 played any role in the observed damage to corals in western Gulf reefs in 1992.

INTRODUCTION

In 1992, independent observations of damage to corals on nearshore and offshore reefs in the western Arabian/Persian Gulf (herein referred to as the Gulf) lead to questions about possible impacts from the oil spilled during the 1991 Gulf War, or other war-related effects. In the winter of 1991, oil slicks moved over reefs in northern Saudi Arabia and Kuwait, but as tides were unseasonably high direct contact of oil with reef corals was not observed (KFUPM/RI, 1991). Neither was there any immediate deterioration in conditions of reefs in nearshore areas, where oil damage to coastal habitats was most apparent. Similarly, there was no apparent impact on reefs from reduced solar radiation in 1991, due to the massive smoke plumes from the oil-well fires. During that period there was a significant drop in near-surface sea water temperature (McCain et al, 1993). Thus it was remarkable that reefs would begin to show signs of impact more than a year after the oil was spilled. It was also remarkable that shallow water reefs farther south of the oil-affected areas were involved in these bleaching and die-off events. It is those reefs that finally provided the clues for the most likely cause to most of the coral bleaching and partial die-off observed in 1992.

Between December 1991 and April 1992, extreme low astronomical spring tides and meteorological effects combined to lower water level below Lowest Astronomical Tide (LAT), thus exposing upper sections of patch reefs in Tarut Bay, eastern Saudi Arabia (Figure 1) to air. In this paper we describe the observed impacts of these events on reef corals in Tarut Bay and compare historical meteorological and tide data in support of exposure-related coral mortality. Although not documented, this phenomenon may have occurred during the same period on a wider scale along the west coast of the Arabian/Persian Gulf. Tidal records also suggest that past exposures may have been responsible for previously recorded coral mortality in the inshore waters of the western Arabian Gulf. We suggest that extreme meteorological conditions, which result in rapid and severe drops in air and water temperatures, and coincident coral emergence during minimum tides, contribute to small scale localized mortality of corals in high latitude reefs.

MATERIALS AND METHODS

Sites Description

The Tarut Bay Reef (Figure 1) near the entrance to Tarut Bay (26° 37' N, 50°08' E) is an unusual patch reef (8 hectares) divided into a windward north facing *Stylophora*-dominated platform zone, and a leeward *Acropora*-dominated patch reef zone. The demarcation line between the two zones is quite distinct. *Stylophora pistillata* colonies form an almost continuous cover on a heavily eroded platform. *Pocillopora damicornis* and *Acropora* spp. are found in small numbers in this zone. *Acropora clathrata*, covers up to 95% of the southern leeward side, along with the less common *Acropora arabensis* colonies, and occasional microatoll-

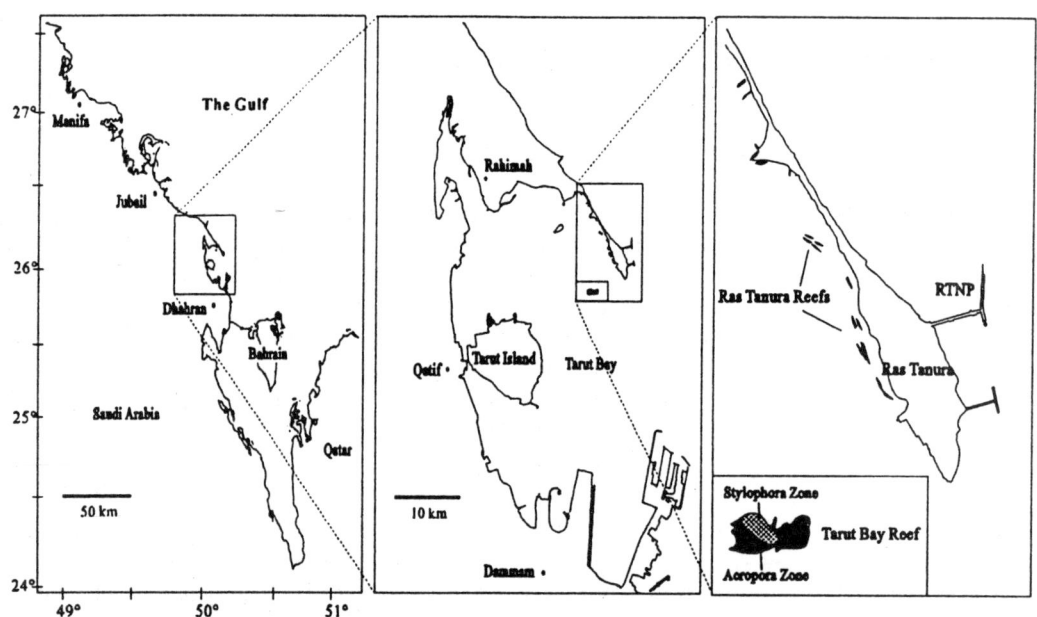

Figure 1. Gulf coast of Saudi Arabia, Tarut Bay, and the reefs near Ras Tanura Peninsula

like colonies of *Platygyra daedalea* and *Cyphastrea micropthalma*. Most of the patch reef sits in water no deeper than 3-4 meters at high tide, while the *Stylophora* zone is distinctly shallower than the *Acropora* zone. Low sea levels have been observed on occasions, where the water level is less than 1 m. above the shallow *Stylopohora* assemblage. The reef is heavily exploited for line and trap fishing by local fishermen, and thus subject to substantial damage from traps and small-anchors. Tarut Bay Reef has been monitored since 1985.. Semidiurnal tides produce strong currents which cause considerable disruption to diving activity, thus increasing the number of visits to this reef. Despite strong currents, anchor damage, fishing pressure, and proximity to an oil refinery, large scale mortalities or bleaching have not been observed during tens of visits to this reef

Coral communities near Ras Tanura shoreline include 5 tracts of *Acropora*-dominated patch reefs (Figure 1). *Acropora* thickets occur on soft bottom sandy sediment between 1 and 4 meters deep. The structural framework of the reefs at Ras Tanura consist of almost 100% *Acropora clathrata* cover. The distance from shore for these thickets varies from 20 m to 400 meters; and depths varies between 1-1.5m at the flat and 3-3.5m at the base. Strong tidal currents and heavy sediment transport have been observed around the reefs.

Coral cover was monitored in Tarut Bay Reef and Ras Tanura reefs after the Gulf war oil spill. Permanent transects and photoquadrats were established on all reefs. Tarut and Ras Tanura Reefs are among a group of inshore and nearshore reefs on the Saudi coast, which were monitored quarterly or more frequently (KFUPM/RI, 1992). The reefs, both located inside Tarut Bay are about 100 km south of the spill's southern extension. During a pre-scheduled visit to Tarut Reef on 24 December 1991, colonies of *Stylophora* were observed exposed to air although predicted low tide for the day was LAT+2. The reefs at the two locations had been visited during 1991 and prior to this first observed low tide event. During those visits line transects and photoquadrat surveys were carried out. Subsequent visits in 1992 also included Photoquadrat surveys and visual searches for bleached or killed corals (Table 1). Photoquadrats were established by November 1991, thus data for coral cover were compared for changes after the observed low tide events.

Table 1. Schedule of visits to Ras Tanura (RT) Reefs and Tarut Bay Reef during 1991 and 1992.

Month-Year	May 91	Oct-91	Nov-91	Dec-91	Feb-92	Apr-92	May-92	Aug-92	Sep-92
Tarut Bay Reef	21st	•	4th	24th	15th, 17th	28th	5th, 20th, 26th	11th	1st
Ras Tanura Reefs	•	23rd	5th	•	10th	27th	3rd, 20th, 26th	11th	1st, 14th

Tide Data

Observed Tide height data are recorded by at the Ras Tanura North Pier (RTNP) located on the gulf side of Ras Tanura peninsula (Figure 1) by Saudi Aramco's Hydrographic Survey Unit (Williams and Allen, 1991/92). Observed tide records are referenced against the Lowest Astronomical Tide (LAT) datum, the lowest level that can be predicted to occur under average meteorological conditions and any combination of astronomical conditions at a specific location. In the absence of any meteorological influences, a value of zero (0) is the lowest possible tide level. LAT at RTNP is 122 cm below Mean Sea Level (MSL). When observed tides occur which are above or below predicted tides, meteorological factors, especially north winds have been shown to be the cause of the residual tidal oscillations (CEA, 1986)

Tidal data were compiled (Table 2) for dates from 1980 through 1992 in which the lowest recorded tides were measured at RTNP, the measured tide level relative to LAT, the estimated exposure interval for exposed corals, and the time of day. It is important to note here that the hourly records stored in the tide archives do not necessarily record the absolute lowest tide which occurred. The listed values are hourly values, and the lowest tides will almost always occur sometime between the hourly records. The difference may be negligible but its an important consideration in some cases since the low tides may have been several (or even more) centimeters below the values recorded. Corresponding meteorological data, which also appear in Table 2, include wind speed and direction, air temperature and water temperature, 24-hr means and monthly ranges of temperature where available.

Coral Kill Zone and Tide Level

Table 2 available separately.

The relationship between the coral kill zone and tide level was established with a simple survey on a calm day at Reef 6 in Ras Tanura. On 14 September, 1992, low tide at Ras Tanura North Pier was predicted to be 55 cm above LAT at 12:05 PM. Just before expected low tide, a pole was stuck in the sediment and a rubber band was set at the water height. This "tide staff" was used to reference changes in tidal height and to determine the actual time of low tide (since the Ras Tanura Reefs are around the bend from RTNP). Low tide occurred about 12:34 PM, when the tide staff recorded a minimum of 0.5 cm. below the rubber band. Following that point, the tide began to rise. The staff was visited periodically to ascertain the state of the tide. Aided by recent aerial photographs we were able to locate areas of substantial coral kills. A PVC pipe with several rubber bands and markings was used as a measuring device. Knowing that the predicted low tide for this tidal cycle was 55 cm above LAT on this day, we assumed that during low tide, any coral at 55 cm below the water surface would be at the level of LAT (with respect to RTNP datum). A rubber band that would have been 19 cm below LAT was also placed on the pipe, as that marked the lowest sub-LAT tide experienced in 1992. Measurements were taken at the top of the dead corals and then at points which appeared to be the average depth at which live corals appeared.

Meteorological Data

Meteorological data are recorded at Rahimah (Figure 1) by Saudi Aramco's Air Quality Monitoring/Meteorological Network (AMMNET). We used records from the Rahimah AMMNET station to obtain recent and historical data on wind speed and direction, air temperature, and solar radiation. Time-series water temperature data for Tarut Bay Reef are obtained by a thermograph deployed by at the base of a pipeline marker adjacent to the reef (KFUPM/RI, 1992). Other temperature data come from single readings by hand-held thermometers during visits to the study sites, and, for 1980-84, from single daily automatic temperature records from the Ras Tanura Refinery water intake..

RESULTS

Observations in Tarut Bay Reef

As indicated in the previous section, visits to Tarut Bay Reef were ongoing for a number of years (Table 1). We had established transects for observation in the year (1991) preceding the low-tide event. Quantitative records of the transect quadrats are available from November 4, 1991, only a month before the first low tide event at Ras Tanura Reef. At that time there was no indication of stress or die-off of corals in the reef. The next scheduled (24 December 1991) visit to the reef coincided with low tides (at 12:40 PM), and large sections of the *Stylophora* zone were exposed in the northern part of the reef. The southern *Acropora* zone was not exposed. The water temperature was 17.6°C, not unusually low for that time of year (Table 2). There were no signs of coral bleaching or recent coral mortality. The reef was exposed again on the 15th (11:00 AM; T = 15.3°C), and partial exposure of the windward (*Stylophora*-dominated) side was observed. Tide records indicate that the observed tide at RTNP on the 16th of February 1992 was 14 cm below LAT. One the 17th of February 1992 (12:50 PM; T = 15.6°C) coral transects were surveyed, quadrats photographed, and observations were made on the condition of corals on the reef. In the shallowest portions of the reef, the majority of *Stylopohora* colonies appeared dead, and the few *Acropora* and *Pocillopora* colonies found in this zone were all dead. A large number of *Stylophora pistillata* colonies suffered sub lethal to lethal injuries, to the extent that the percentage of live coral (i.e. Stylophora) recorded in our photoquadrats had dropped to zero by February and March (Figure 2) Other coral species appeared moderately or severely bleached. With only two days of relatively high tide, the corals were again subjected to two more days (19 and 20 February) of low tide (Table 2). The observed low tide on 20 February was 19 cm below LAT, the lowest recorded for 1992. It is expected that more colonies of *Stylophora* and parts of *Acropora* colonies in the shallower sections of the Acropora-dominated areas would have been exposed on that day. The next survey was carried out on 28 April 1992. (T=23.5°C). More colonies of *Stylophora* appeared dead. On 5 May 1992. (25.5°C), recently dead colonies of *Acropora* were found on the deeper leeward (southern) *Acropora* zone of the reef transect.

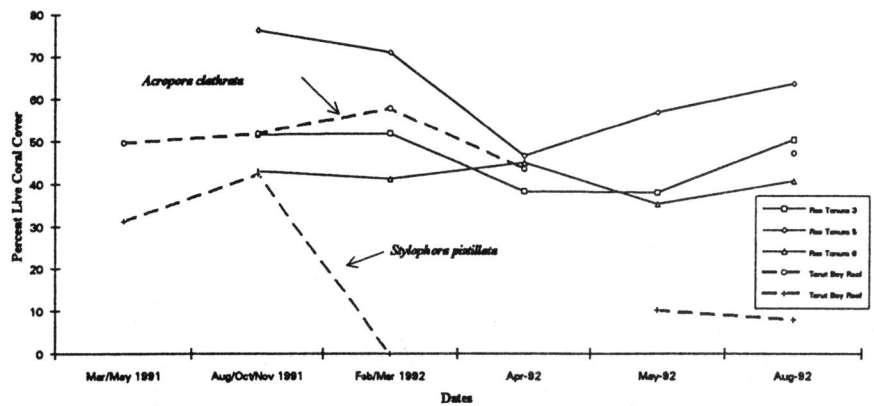

Figure 2. Percent live cover of *Stylophora pistillata* (only one plot), and *Acropora clathrata* in Tarut Bay Reef and Ras Tanura Reefs. Note that the data for the A. clathrata cover was obtained from transects which were mostly deeper than the reach of extreme low tides.

On 20 May 1992 we observed that a substantial number of colonies of *Stylophora* had lost tissue from all but the base of the skeleton, while many other colonies were completely dead. The skeletons were covered with brownish detritus. It became obvious that colonies closest to the surface were those most affected. We again noted that the few *Acropora* colonies within this zone were all dead. However, at the demarcation zone between the windward *Stylophora* zone and the leeward *Acropora* zone, many healthy and fecund *Acropora* colonies were found next to shallower dead *Stylophora* colonies. Observations on 20 May 1992 were carried out during storm conditions; and only portion of the *Stylophora* zone and the demarcation zone were visually surveyed. The reef was carefully inspected on 26 May, *Stylophora* still showed signs of stress. Three months later (11 August, 1992; T = 34.0°C), all live *Acropora* colonies in the transect quadrats appeared healthy. The remaining live colonies of *Stylophora* appeared less stressed. On 1 September 1992 (T = 32.4° C), all *Acropora*, *Stylophora*, and *Pocillopora* colonies not exposed during the low tide event appeared healthy, and surviving portions of the impacted *Stylophora* colonies were recovering. Dead colonies of *Stylophora* were beginning to erode, and the latest photoquadrat records from |March 1993, indicate that the skeletons have eroded some more, and have been utilized as substrate by seasonal macroalgae. The common sea urchin, *Echinometra mathai* was now observed foraging on these eroded skeletons.

Observations in Ras Tanura Reefs

The transects we established in the Ras Tanura patch reefs were positioned in deeper water to enable use of a 1.2 m tall Photoquadrat camera stand. As such the quantitative photoquadrat data (Figure 2) fail to demonstrate the extensive coral mortality we would discover in the shallower portions of the reefs. As such, we observed no ill effects on *Acropora* colonies during five visits made to the Ras Tanura reefs between 23 October 1991 and 27 April 1992. On 10 February and 27 April (16.3°C and 23.6°C) the tissues of *Acropora* were a healthy dark brown, and no bleaching or mortality was observed around the transect areas.

In the course of separate survey on 3 May 1992, of the shallower parts of the Ras Tanura reefs, the upper parts of considerable numbers of *Acropora* colonies were dead, and a light growth of brown filamentous algae covered the impacted portions of the corals, suggesting that some time had passed since bleaching and death had occurred. The impact zone appeared from the tops of the shallowest colonies to a level approximately 30 cm below the top of the reef. Partial or total mortality was dependent on proximity to the surface. The impacts had been relatively recent. A very obvious dead coral zone was observed. Preliminary measurements indicated the dead coral bands began at approximately Ras Tanura North Pier (RTNP) LAT datum and continued down to approximately 20-30 cm. below LAT. On 11 August 1992 we were able to establish that coral mortality had occurred in large patches of *Acropora clathrata*. There was a distinct dead coral zone throughout these patch reefs, with dead whole or upper portions of colonies in a horizontal band that varied in height from 10-30 cm. An assemblage of organisms, including algae, was growing on much of the dead *Acropora* skeletons. Below the dead coral zone, colonies of *Acropora* and other coral species appeared healthy.

Tide and Meteorology

Historical Tide Levels (1980-1992).--

The most extreme spring tides in the study area occur in the winter season, with the lowest of the two daily semidiurnal lows occurring during the early afternoon hours during that season (Williams and Allen, 1991/1992). We plotted the observed hourly (on the hour) minimum tide records from the Ras Tanuura North Pier for the months of December through May from 1980 through 1992 (Figure 3). These are not necessarily the absolute lowest tides which occurred during that period. Since these are hourly records, the actual low tide levels may have been several to many centimeters below the values recorded within the hour, which is an important consideration in some cases (e.g. December 1991 observed tide of 2 cm above LAT at RTNP, when we observed exposed corals at the Tarut Bay Reef).

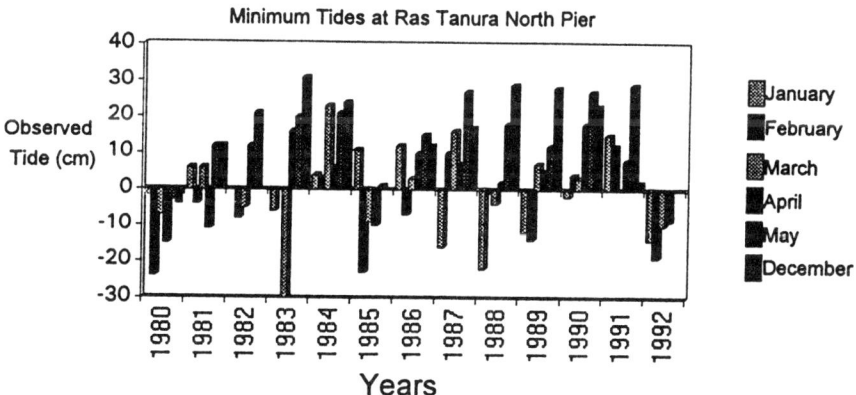

Figure 3. Observed single hourly minimum tide records from Ras Tanura North Pier, Ras Tanura Peninsula (Saudi Arabia), for the months of January, February, March, April, May, and December 1980-1992. Lowest Astronomical tide is at 0 cm.

Between 1980 and 1992, tides below LAT occurred in 10 of 13 years. Clusters of three or more consecutive months with tides below LAT, with one or more significant (> -10cm) low, occurred in 1980, 1985, 1989 and 1992 (Table 2). Other years with significant single lows are 1981, 1983, 1987, and 1988. The absence of extreme low tides in 1991 is remarkable, and perhaps fortunate for reef corals, as the months which normally produce significant low tides, witnessed the massive Gulf war oil spill.

Tide Levels and Dead Coral Bands.--

In the Tarut Bay Reef, The *Stylophora* zone is closer to the surface than the *Acropora* zone. At only LAT+2 cm (RTNP observed tide) on 24 December 1991, the *Stylophora* zone was observed partially exposed. Subsequent and much lower tides (see Figure 3) would have exposed wider areas of the reef, including portions of the *Acropora* zone. This conclusion is based on evidence from photoquadrats, which show mortalities in *Stylophora* and *Acropora* zones, which were not exposed during the low tide of 24 December. Although we have not established the position of the dead coral bands areas in the *Stylophora* zone relative to tide level, there is strong indication that portions of the *Stylophora* platform occur at levels higher than LAT.

Exposure at low tide was not observed at Ras Tanura Reefs. The position of dead corals with respect to tide datum was measured in detail under controlled conditions. The predicted low tide for Ras Tanura North Pier on 14 September 1992 was LAT+55 cm at 12:34 PM. The residual tide (difference between predicted and observed tide) between 11:00 AM and 13:00 ranged from -2 to -1 cm; thus the observed tide was off only by 1 to 2 cm from the predicted tide. The almost perfect congruence of predicted and observed tide levels indicate that the tides during this period were minimally affected by meteorological forcing, thus providing confidence in our estimation of LAT level relative to tide level for that period. Measurements were made at Ras Tanura reefs on the same day between 12:27 and 13:31. The average tide-corrected distance measured from the top of dead *Acropora* to the water surface was 52 cm (n=37; range 47 to 59 cm). Therefore we conclude that the highest occurring *Acropora* tables in Ras Tanura reefs are at about level with LAT (or LAT + 0). The average height (depth) of the dead-coral band is 15 cm (n=37; range 10 to 25 cm), coinciding with an average tidal height of 15 cm below LAT (Figure 4). Based on observed tide measurements (Figure 3), we conclude that partial exposure of *Acropora* thickets in Ras Tanura reefs occurred during any/all of the low tide events between December 1991 and April 1992. Various levels (depths) of exposure occurred every month and was capped by the lowest observed tide (LAT -19) in March 1992. The proximity (about 2.5 km) of the Tarut Bay Reef would suggest that the same events would have occurred on this reef.

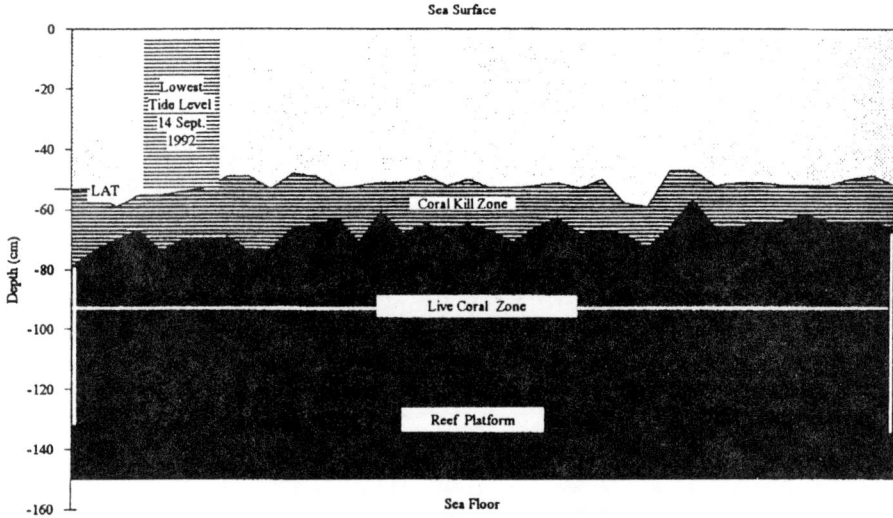

Figure 4. Width of coral kill zone at Ras Tanura Reef 6. The coral kill zone schematic is generated by joining point plots of 37 separate measurements of distances from the surface to the upper level and surface to lower level of dead corals. The position of upper level of the coral kill zone is around LAT. Depths of live coral zone and sea floor are approximate.

DISCUSSION

This episode of coral die off was limited to those corals closest to the water surface. Subsequent analysis of observed and predicted tide data, and field surveys and observations, suggest that the observed dead-coral zones in both areas were exposed to air when water levels were below LAT. Therefore we conclude that resultant coral mortality is associated with repeated exposure to air during the coldest months of the year.

Until now, exposure of Saudi Gulf corals at low tide was considered a rare if unlikely event, despite anecdotal reports from Kuwait (Downing, 1985, 1988) of exposure and associated impacts. The common wisdom was that high air temperatures and solar irradiance were so extreme that corals stood little chance of surviving very short periods of exposure (Basson et al, 1977). It was not anticipated that shallow reef corals in Saudi Gulf waters, like their counterparts to the north, were rather under control of the opposite weather extremes, low tides combined with extreme low air and water temperatures. We suggest that repeated exposure to air during extreme low winter tides in Tarut Bay, and possibly other shallow coastal reefs the western Gulf coast, caused significant mortality to coral colonies in elevated areas of platform and patch reefs. Tide records and meteorological data (as in Table 2) may enable retrospective analysis of previously recorded coral die-offs in the western Gulf (e.g. Coles and Fadlallah, 1991). The actual cause of mortality of corals as reported by Coles and Fadlallah (1991) may have been low water temperatures, but we now think that emergence of reef tops during extreme low water and air temperatures were responsible for mortality of corals on platform reefs in the northern area of the Saudi Gulf coast during 1983, 1985 and 1989. Invariably, extreme low tides in the winter are brought about by cold northwesterly winds (Shamal) which rapidly cool the shallow waters of the western Arabian Gulf and cause subtidal very long period oscillations of the sea level. The result is emergence of reef tops in the nearshore and exposure of corals to evaporative and radiative cooling.

Inshore reef corals in the western Gulf are particularly subject to the most extreme water temperature fluctuations (Coles and Fadlallah, 1991). During cold fronts corals invariably turn 'pale' (see Brown and LeTissier, 1992) but often recover their normal light or dark brown color. Extreme cold fronts (air temperature below 10°C) produce water temperatures below 15°C (Downing, 1985, 1988; Coles and Fadlallah, 1991). Long term temperature records indicate that even more extreme lowering of water temperature has been experienced by reef corals in the Gulf (Shinn, 1972, 1976; Coles and Fadlallah, 1991). These events apparently lead to various levels of coral mortalities, especially to corals occurring in shallow reef flats. Downing (1985) reported that reef flats in Kuwait dry out regularly at low spring tides, and suggested that they may be exposed to air temperatures approaching 55°C in the summer and 0°C in the winter. The same report indicated that on one occasion (13 January 1982) the reef flat at Kubbar Island was exposed in the early morning for a period of two hours. Downing (1988) also monitored exposure of Kuwaiti reef flat corals to air during low spring tides in the late winter/early spring of 1985, and reported mortality of apparently large areas of the reef flat corals from "chilling", followed by significant recovery of branching corals (*Acropora*) within three years. Downing (1988) again reasserted that the reef flat, which comprises by far the most extensive area, dries out periodically at very low spring tides. When this coincides with low air temperatures the exposed corals will die from chilling. Tidal ranges are widest (up to 3 meters) in the northern waters of Kuwait, far exceeding those experienced several hundred kilometers to the south. This may explain the apparent infrequency of reef exposure in southern areas such as Tarut Bay.

While Downing (1985, 1988) drew attention to the impact of low tides in Kuwait, the attention of our group was focused on extreme low water temperature as the major cause of coral die-off in the western Gulf, and a major obstacle for species expansion to the northern parts of the Gulf. We do not dismiss this important factor, and in fact, until demonstrated otherwise, extreme lowering of sea water temperature will remain a major consideration as a cause of coral die-offs in the Gulf. However, after examining the tidal and temperature records for the past 12 years, and correlating those with reported or known coral kills, it is becoming evident that the co-occurrence of low water temperature and exposure to air or "chilling" (Downing, 1985, 1988), is the preeminent mode of impact on western Gulf corals. Repeated exposures (dose-duration) over a period of days and in consecutive months appear to play a major role in determining whether impacts will be effected. When we examined all the documented coral kills since 1980, we found that they occurred during the winters of 1983 (Burchard, 1984; McCain et al, 1984), 1985 (Downing, 1988), 1989 (Coles and Fadlallah, 1991); and 1992 (this study). The most salient feature of this grouping is the occurrence of low tide events in the winter months. Additionally, these are multi-day and multi-month events. Shallow reef corals were exposed to air for durations of 1-4 hours a day, often for two or more consecutive days, and in the cluster years, for 2-4 consecutive months. These exposures usually occur under conditions of low air and sea water temperatures.

In 1964, chilling, followed by extensive mortality of corals was well documented off the coast of Qatar (Shinn, 1972, 1976). In this instance water temperatures dipped far below 10°C (4-5°C in inshore waters) apparently causing immediate coral kills. This event apparently affected only the branching coral *Acropora*, but was followed by complete recovery in less than five years. Similar "chilling" events may have occurred in the last few decades, as daily temperature records from 1945 through 1975 suggest (Coles and Fadlallah, 1991). However, in the 1980's, temperatures were not lowered to levels experienced in the preceding decades. In the winter of 1988/1989, the shallow waters of the western Gulf experienced prolonged drops in temperature and a coral kill was recorded in one reef about 150 km to the north of the present study (Coles and Fadlallah, 1991). What was not done at the time was examine the possibility of tides as a primary or secondary cause of the kill. In 1983, the same reef experienced massive mortality of the reef flat *Acropora*. At the time, that was attributed to oil pollution (McCain et al, 1984). Low tides and cold temperatures were not suspected, but might have likely been the cause of the kill.

How much do low tide events influence the distribution and structure of shallow reef coral communities in the Gulf is not known. Stoddart (1972) suggested that low tides prevent the establishment of reef flat corals in southwestern Indo-Pacific reefs. Shinn (1972), based on evidence from Florida, implied that lower temperature limits control the distribution of less temperature-tolerant (i.e. *Acropora*) species in the Gulf. However, the occurrence of *Acropora* on inshore and offshore Kuwaiti reefs (Downing, 1985), and in Kharg Island (Iran) (Shinn, 1972) demonstrate that in the absence of other limiting factors, normal low winter temperatures in the northern Gulf are not sufficient to cause repeated coral kills. But cyclic exposures to extreme low tides, combined with extreme low temperature excursions, are in fact sufficient to cause mortalities in *Acropora* as well as other species. We offer evidence that the coral kill of 1992 in Tarut Bay was tide-related; that although temperatures were relatively low, *Acropora* spp. and *Stylophora pistillata* which were not exposed did not die. In fact, *Acropora* spp. from Tarut Bay successfully completed their reproductive season by spawning in May (Fadlallah, Unpublished data). *Acropora* spp. and *Stylophora pistillata* have successfully invaded nearshore reefs in the northwestern Gulf (where *Porites compressa* is the main frame builder), perhaps only to the extent that the populations would recover from episodic localized disturbances or extinctions by recruitment from the large offshore coral islands or from the southern populations in Bahrain, Qatar, and the United Arab Emirates, followed by rapid growth. Recruitment to the reefs of Kuwait may come via reefs along the Iranian coast for which little or no information is available.

CONCLUSIONS

Nearshore reef corals in the Gulf occur in a unique high latitude marine system. Severe fluctuations in water temperatures are routine daily and annual phenomena in the shallow water coastal habitats. Extreme low tides however occur periodically during winter months, and are more pronounced in the northern part of the Gulf. Extreme low tides and cold water combine to cause sporadic die-offs of shallow water species of *Acropora* and *Stylophora*.

ACKNOWLEDGMENTS

We wish to thank R. Gonzaga and R. Lindo for field support. The trip to the Gulf by the senior author in May 1992 was made possible by NOAA in connection with the R/V Mt. Mitchell Gulf Cruise. We owe much to our respective institutions for providing the time and material support to investigate this event. We thank JS Pearse for reading an earlier version of our manuscript.

THE HOUTMAN ABROLHOS REEFS OF WESTERN AUSTRALIA: ENVIRONMENTAL AND ANTHROPOGENIC CHANGE IN THE STRUCTURE AND FUNCTION OF REEF COMMUNITIES AT HIGH LATITUDE

Bruce G. Hatcher[1] and Lindsay B. Collins[2]

[1] Dalhousie University, Oceanography Dept., Halifax, N.S., Canada, B3H 4J1.
[2] Curtin University, School of Applied Geology, GPO Box U1987, Perth, Western Australia, 6001.

INTRODUCTION

Benthic communities of coral reefs in marginal environments are characterized by transitions between small algae (zooxanthaellae, endolithic, epipelic and epilithic turf algae) and large plants (macroalgae and seagrasses with epiphytic and understory flora) as the dominant primary producers. The contrasting structures appear to be alternate stable states for reef benthos (Hatcher, 1984; Littler & Littler, 1984). They support fundamentally different food webs and patterns of materials' flux, with profound implications for productivity, accretion, biodiversity, and susceptibility to resource exploitation and alteration by man. In the reef context, transitions from microalgal ($\approx$ coral) to macrophyte dominance is undesirable because it results in reduced abundance of live corals and the associated structural and biotic diversity they support.

High latitude reefs are good places to study community transitions because the magnitude and temporal variability of environmental factors stress coral reef communities in parallel with anthropogenic impacts, and because alternate community types are juxtaposed such that the process of transition may be observed over logistically manageable topologies. As study of the moribund and the athletic contributes to knowledge of human physiology, the study of coral reefs at the limits of existence can teach us about processes fundamental to all reef ecosystems.

Here we examine a well-studied high latitude reef system (the Houtman Abrolhos: southernmost coral reefs of the Indian Ocean) in the context of this Colloquium's goals. The pertinent questions are:
1) Are the Abrolhos reefs "Healthy" despite environmental stresses?
2) How significant are anthropogenic "Hazards" to their health?
3) What does the "History" of the reefs and their usage tell us about natural and anthropogenic change?

RESULTS

Coral Reef Structure and Function at 29°S Indian Ocean

The Abrolhos comprise three ca. 100 km^2 carbonate platforms supporting over 100 low islands on the edge of the 80 km wide continental shelf off central Western Australia (Fig.1). Each platform has a central core of (often emergent) Pleistocene substratum surrounded by windward (western) and leeward (eastern) reef margins enclosing shallow and deep lagoons respectively. Wind and swell forcing is predominantly from the exposed, southwest quadrant. The adjacent coast is arid. A poleward-flowing eastern boundary current (The Leeuwin Current, Cresswell, 1991) dominates the regional oceanography. Advective transport and thermal anomalies associated with this unusual current have been invoked as causative factors in the development and maintenance of the Abrolhos reefs Hatcher, 1991). The reefs are located in a zone of overlap between major tropical and temperate biogeographical provinces (Morgan & Wells, 1991).

The most striking ecological feature of the Abrolhos is the juxtaposition of extensive macrophyte communities (including dense kelp

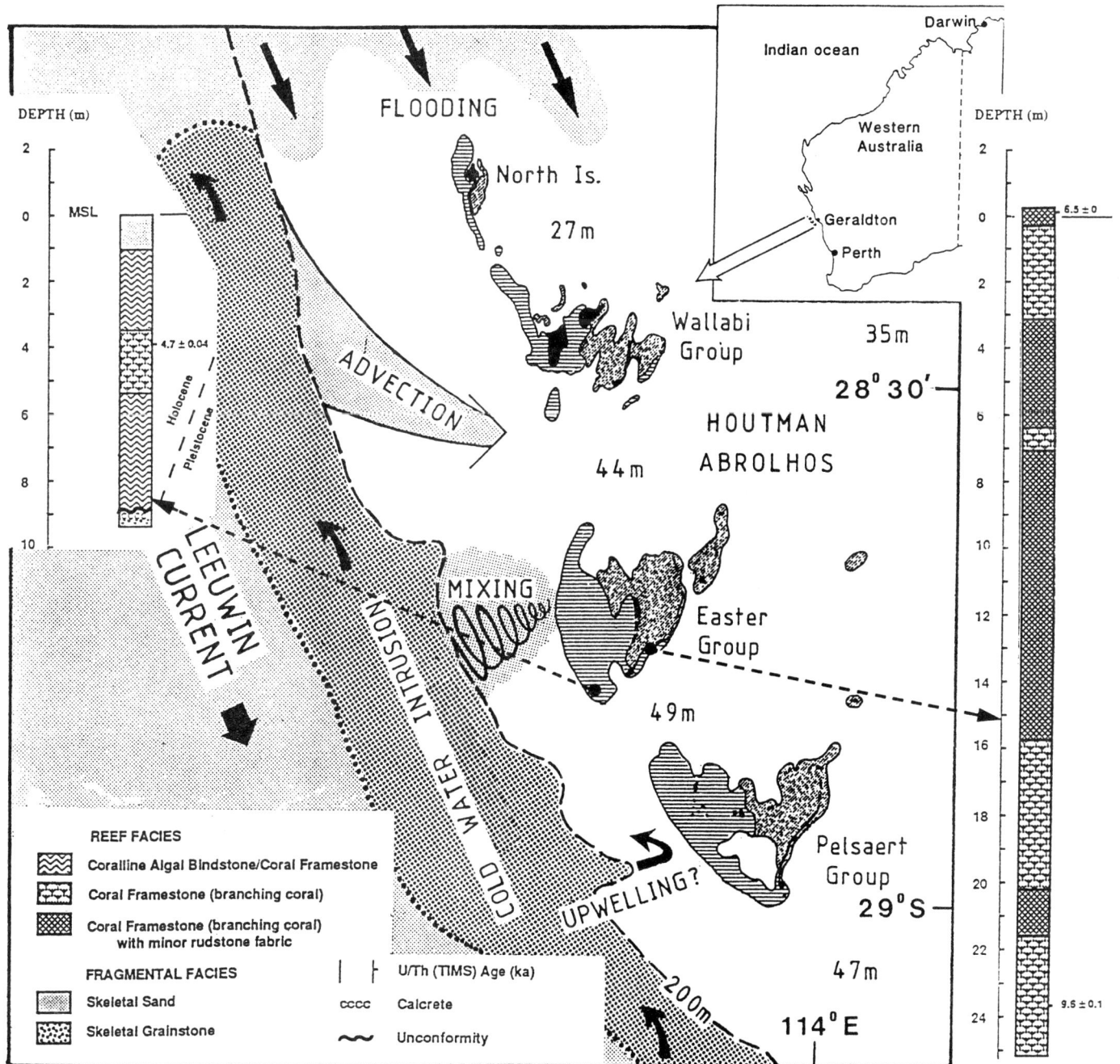

Figure 1. Location, geomorphology, stratigraphy and oceanography of the Houtman Abrolhos reefs. Three platforms (island groups) are located on the continental shelf (representative depths shown), within 20 km of the 200 m contour. Benthic communities (mapped after Hatcher et al, 1990) dominated by macroalgae (horizontal shading) and by corals (diagonal shading) surround the islands (black). Representative core samples (after Collins et al, 1993) are shown for western and eastern platforms (see key). Generalized circulation features (based on analysis of NOAA-AVHRR imagery, Pearce et al, 1991) depict three mechanisms by which Leeuwin Current water (light stipple) and sporadic colder intrusions (dark stipple) influence the reefs.

canopies) on the western portions of the reef platforms, and diverse coral communities (often reaching 100% cover) on the eastern portions (Fig. 1, Table 1). The dominant kelp species occurs at its upper temperature limits, suffering higher mortality and growing at lower rates and densities than its southern conspecifics (Hatcher et al, 1987). Massive production of macrophyte detritus on the upstream margins of the western platforms inundates the lagoons with an organic nutrient subsidy, maintaining high dissolved nutrient concentrations within the water column (Crossland et al, 1984) and supporting a large and diverse detrital food web. Extravagant secondary production of benthic invertebrates on these reefs supports a large and stable monospecific fishery. Fully 15% of Australia's most valuable catch (the western rock lobster) is taken from the Abrolhos, which comprise only 3% of the area fished (Hatcher, 1985).

Table 1. Characteristic attributes of reef structure and function at the Houtman Abrolhos. Most measurements are from sites on the west (windward) and east (leeward) portions of reefs and lagoons in the Easter Group.

ATTRIBUTE		MAGNITUDE & UNITS	SOURCE
Holocene reef thickness	-west:	> 9 m	Collins et al,
	-east:	< 26 m	1993
Vertical accretion rate	-west:	$0.6 - 0.7$ mm yr^{-1}	"
	-east:	$6.0 - 7.4$ mm yr^{-1}	"
Scleractinian coral diversity		184 spp. 42 genera	Veron & Marsh, 1988
Live coral cover	-west:	$0 - 60$ %	Hatcher et al,
on hard substrata	-east:	$35 - 100$ %	1990
Coral growth rate (P. damicornis)		$10 - 15$ mm yr^{-1}	Crossland, 1981;
-mean elongation. (A. formosa)		$35 - 50$ mm yr^{-1}	Crossland, 1984
(Pavona minuta)		$6 - 22$ mm yr^{-1}	Hatcher, unpubl.
Macroalgal biomass	-west:	$100 - 1350$ g m^{-2}	Hatcher & Rimmer
-dry weight.	-east:	$50 - 450$ g m^{-2}	1985
Kelp growth rate	-west:	$0.9 - 1.3$ mm d^{-1}	Hatcher et al,
-annual mean elongation.			1987
Algal detritus input to	-west:	$0.1 - 0.2$ g m^{-2} d^{-1}	Crossland et al,
lagoon -dry wt.			1984; Hatcher, unpul.
Herbivore grazing rates	-west:	$0.3 - 0.6$ g m^{-2} d^{-1}	Hatcher & Rimmer
-summer means)	-east:	0.08 g m^{-2} d^{-1}	1985
Calcification rate	-east:	$13 - 50$ g CaCO$_3$ m^{-2} d^{-1}	Smith, 1981
Gross productivity rate	-east:	$12 - 21$ g C m^{-2} d^{-1}	"
Community P/R ratio	-east:	$0.84 - 1.07$	"

The coral communities of the Abrolhos are of exceptional diversity for the latitude (Table 1), but lack many species which characterize high energy environments in the tropics (Veron and Marsh, 1988). Luxuriant stands of branching and tabulate corals dominate the leeward outer and lagoonal slopes, but the annual elongation rates of two common branching species are only 20 and 70% of their tropical conspecifics (Table 1). Calcification by an abundant coral is highly seasonal due to low winter temperature and irradiance, resulting in a poorly infilled skeletal matrix and unusual fragility for the species (Crossland, 1984). Growth analysis of a massive coral colony (Table 1) also shows strong seasonality, but annual increments approximate those of tropical species of the genera.

Benthic community production and calcification rates measured on reef flats at the Abrolhos fall within the range recorded for tropical reef flats (Table 1). These integrated measures do not demonstrate reduced metabolic performance at high latitude, emphasizing the large contribution of primary producers and calcifiers other than corals (e.g. coralline algae and gastropods) to the shallow reef communities (Smith, 1981).

Competition occurs in transition zones where corals and macroalgae meet on platform margins and in the lagoons. Experimental evidence demonstrates that macroalgae can overgrow and kill even fast-growing corals at the Abrolhos (Crossland, 1981: Hatcher, 1985). Physical damage to 6 m² coral plots has resulted in overgrowth and competitive exclusion of corals by macroalgae for periods of up to eight years (Hatcher, unpub. data). Recovery of coral communities over these time scales has occurred in plots which are grazed by large herbivorous fish, despite the fact that the intensity of grazing by herbivores on Abrolhos reef substrata is only 5 to 25% of that measured on tropical reefs (Table 1). The tropical fish fauna at the Abrolhos is depauperate, with many taxa of important functional groups (e.g. surgeon fish) poorly represented, and others restricted to the coral-dominated communities (Morgan & Wells, 1991).

Differences between the two benthic community types are reflected in the hard substratum. Coralline algal bindstones underlie macrophyte beds on the western reef platforms, while flourishing coral communities create characteristic reef topographies to the east (Fig.1, Table 1). Dead corals of Holocene age underlie hectare-scale areas now covered by a macroalgal veneer in transition zones. Data are insufficient to determine whether apparent shifts from coral to macroalgal domination are directional or stable at decadal time scales. Anecdotal evidence spanning 50 years suggests that coral-dominated communities were more extensive in the recent past, leading to concern that transitions are anthropogenic Hatcher et al. 1990).

Human Activities at the Abrolhos

The Abrolhos are not pristine reefs. The site of European man's first residence in Australia following an infamous shipwreck, they have a long history of human presence and exploitation (Table 2). Mining of guano for phosphate and munitions over a century denuded the larger islands and decimated populations of many of the 20 bird species which breed there.

Table 2. Chronology, characteristics and effects of human activities at the Houtman Abrolhos. Information sourced in UNEP/IUCN (1988) Anon (1989).

DATES	ACTIVITY	MAGNITUDE & UNITS	EFFECTS
1629 -1908	Shipwrecks	16 ships (20 - 2,000 tons)	discovery & notoriety physical damage to reefs
1840 -1940	Fishing & sealing	???total catch??? few, small boats	recognition of resources minimal harvests of fish
1847 -1946	Guano mining	≈ 50 k tonnes from 13 islands	removal of soil horizon disrupt bird populations extinctions & introductions
1885 -1993	Scientific research	> 150 publications ≈ 40 expeditions	recognition of values improved management
1927 -1993	Line & spear fishing	?? total catch ?? > 200 tonnes yr⁻¹ (since 1980)	deplete demersal fish stock plastics pollution anchor damage to reefs
1927 -1993	Lobster fishing	≈ 65 k tonnes from ≈ 50 M trap sets (20 islands used)	economic prosperity physical damage to reefs development & pollution
1929 -1993	Management	access restrictions protected species	limit disruption & pollution maintain populations
1947 -1993	Tourism (present)	≈ 14 k man-days yr⁻¹ by boat & 'plane	disruption of fauna anchor damage to reefs
1967 -1993	Scallop fishing	≈ 1.1 M tonnes meat from 4 beds	disruption of benthos shell waste pollution

The trap fishery for lobster at the Abrolhos presently yields an annual catch of ca. 1.5 kt (value ≈ $20 M), taken by ca. 200 boats over 5 months (Table 1). Over 80% of ca. 1.2 million trap sets per year occur on the western reef platforms, where effort intensity ranges from 10 to over 250 (mean = 39) sets ha^{-1} yr^{-1} (Hatcher et al, 1990). The high potential for physical damage to benthic communities as a result of trap impact and jet-boat grounding is ameliorated by the low sensitivity of the robust limestone and macrophyte-dominated substrata, which is the primary lobster habitat. Significant areas of sensitive, coral-dominated communities do experience effort intensities as high as 110 sets ha^{-1} yr^{-1}, and show evidence of structural damage and loss of live coral cover. Access to the fishery and trap numbers have been strictly limited since the 1960's, but fishing effort, gear efficiency and catches continue to increase.

A commercial line fishery for large demersal finfish currently involves about 30 vessels at the Abrolhos (Table 2). The yield is greatly augmented by an unmeasured recreational catch. Highly variable catches of scallops (10 - 200 tonnes yr^{-1}) are dragged from the channels between the reef platforms. In total, the fisheries of the Abrolhos exhibit remarkably high yields for a coral reef system (Hatcher, 1985) and are a major source of wealth to the small population of central Western Australia.

Tourism at the Abrolhos has been sporadic due to their isolation and lack of facilities. Recreational use and ecotourism has increased rapidly since the America's cup bonanza of 1987. About 600 lobster fishermen and their families live in unserviced shanty-towns on the islands during fishing season. Conflicts between user groups have escalated recently (Wright et al, 1988), forcing development of a management strategy under the jurisdiction of the state Fisheries Department (Anon, 1989).

Reef Development During the Holocene

Modern coral reef growth at the Abrolhos was initiated at least 9.6 ka ago as rising seas flooded the calcretized limestone platforms of the Last Interglacial (Collins et al, 1993). Fast-growing corals framed large vertical accretions on the perimeter of the eastern reefs, which kept pace with rising sea level to reach ca. 0.5 m above present sea level during the high stand ca. 4.7 ka B.P.(Fig.1, Table 1). The vertical rates are comparable to tropical reefs, and lateral accretion of these rich reef communities into the eastern channels and lagoons is apparent. Growth on the western platforms originated more recently, as the antecedent surface lies only a few metres below present sea level there. The Holocene vertical accretions are an alternating sequence of slow-growing corals and coralline algal associations, which did not reach present sea level until well after the high stand (Fig.1), and show little evidence of lateral accretion into the shallow, sediment-covered western lagoons.

Asymmetrical development and contrasting lithographies of reef platforms reflect the present distribution of benthic communities at the Abrolhos. While palaeoenvironmental conditions have clearly varied over Holocene time scales, they have consistently supported coral dominance to the east, while usually favouring macroalgal communities to the west.

DISCUSSION AND CONCLUSIONS

The pattern of Holocene reef development at the Abrolhos is apparently at variance with both the Pleistocene development and the contemporary oceanography. Coral reefs flourished in the region during the Last Interglacial, as evidenced by the antecedcent topography and fossil outcrops on (Collins et al, 1991; 1993). The Leeuwin Current inhibits upwelling and maintains a westward gradient of increasing sea surface temperature and decreasing nutrient concentrations across the shelf during winter (Cresswell, 1991). This, plus the wave climate, should favour coral growth on the western reefs: yet it has been poor throughout much of the Holocene. We suggest that variations in the strength and pattern of the Leeuwin Current permit sporadic upwelling on the western reef margins that inhibit coral and enhance macrophyte community development. Analyses of satellite imagery and sub-surface temperature data reveal occasional intrusions of cold water to the west (Fig.1), which may favour kelp growth in otherwise unfavourable conditions as it does seasonally elsewhere in the tropics (hatcher et al, 1988). The competitive superiority of macrophytes in the high nutrient concentrations maintained by re-cycling through detritus in the eastern lagoons could allow their persistence even when environmental conditions are also suitable for coral growth (Johannes et al, 1983; Crossland et al, 1984; Hatcher, 1985; 1991).

While explanation of the pattern of reef growth at the Abrolhos awaits further research, it is clear that extensive coral communities there are healthy in terms of their diversity, productivity and persistence in environmental extremes. Coincidentally, equally healthy macrophyte communities have come to dominate extensive areas of reef substratum during the Holocene transgression. A balance between the two community types appears to have persisted since the stabilization of sea level, although anecdotal and experimental data indicate dynamic boundary conditions. The pattern is not unique. High latitude reefs at Bermuda, French Polynesia and Japan, and tropical reefs at Barbados, Galapagos and Oman are characterized by extensive macroalgal communities (Crossland, 1988). The fact that there are at least as many contrary examples from tropical and sub-tropical coral reefs demonstrates that latitude per se is an inappropriate predictor of transitions between community type. Exposure to high dis-solved nutrient concentrations, which permit the accumulation of macro-algal biomass, is the best guess we have to explain why a coral reef stops being one (Johannes et al, 1983; Hatcher & Larkum, 1983; Littler & Littler, 1984; Hallock & Schlager, 1986; Birkeland, 1988).

At the reefal scale, elevated nutrient levels resulting from anthropogenic inputs are unlikely to duplicate the effects of oceanographic delivery because of the hydrology and evolutionary time scales of the latter. Reefs which have developed under nutrient and temperature stresses support comparatively low diversity of consumers and high sustainable export yields to terrestrial harvesters such as birds and humans. The Abrolhos have done so throughout the Holocene, first to seabirds, and then to the men that displaced them. The anthropogenic hazard to these reefs is not nutrient pollution (indeed, a localized source of nutrients was removed as guano), but physical damage to corals which may allow competitive exclusion by macro-algae. To date, however, there is no substantive evidence that this has occurred at ecologically significant scales. The geologic history of the Abrolhos shows that the balance has shifted on the western reefs, probably in response to regional oceanographic forcing. The lack of a monitoring program in the proposed management plan for the Abrolhos ensures that the required evidence will not become available.

The Abrolhos case history is a fortunate one. It seems that these coral reefs can survive both the natural stresses of existence at environmental limits, and the anthropogenic impacts of intensive fisheries. Perhaps, like athletes, reefs which "train" under severe conditions will prove to be the most robust in competition. The onus to maintain the health of these unusual reefs in the face of local and global anthropogenic change in their environment is a rewarding challenge to Western Australians.

LITERATURE CITED

Anonymous. 1989. Abrolhos Islands planning strategy: Final report. Abrolhos Islands Consultative Committee, Geraldton, W.A. 29 pp.

Birkeland, C. 1988. Geographic comparisons of coral reef community processes. Proc. Sixth Int. Coral Reef Symp. Townsville, 1: 117-220.

Collins, L.B., K-H. Wyrwoll and R.E. France. 1991. The Abrolhos carbonate platforms" geological evolution and Leeuwin Current activity. J. Roy. Soc. West. Aust. 74: 47-58.

Collins, L.B., Z.R. Zhu, K-H. Wyrwoll, B.G. Hatcher, P.E. Playford, J.H. Chen, A. Eisenhauer and G.J. Wasserburg. 1993. Late Quaternary evolution of coral reefs on a cool-water carbonate margin: the Abrolhos carbonate platforms, SW Australia. Mar. Geol. In Press.

Cresswell, G.R. 1991 The Leeuwin Current - observations and recent models. J. Roy. Soc. West. Aust. 74: 1-14.

Crossland, C.J. 1981. Seasonal growth of Acropora cf. formosa and Pocillopora damicornis on a high latitude reef (Houtman Abrolhos, Western Australia). Proc. Fourth Int. Coral Reef Symp., Manila, 1: 663-667.

Crossland, C.J. 1984. Seasonal variation in the rates of calcification and productivity in the coral A. formosa on a high-latitude coral reef. Mar. Ecol. Prog. Ser. 15: 135-140.

Crossland, C.J. 1988. Latitudinal comparisons of coral reef structure and function. Proc. 6th Int. Coral Reef Symp. Townsville, 1: 221-226.

Crossland, C.J., B.G. Hatcher, M.J. Atkinson and S.V. Smith. 1984. Dissolved nutrients of a high latitude coral reef, Houtman Abrolhos Islands, Western Australia. Mar. Ecol. Prog. Ser. 14: 159-163.

Hallock, P. and W. Schlager. 1986. Nutrient excess and the demise of coral reefs and carbonate platforms. Palaios 1: 389-398.

Hatcher, A.I., G.D. Wright and B.G. Hatcher. 1990. Resolving the conflict between conservation values and extractive use of the Abrolhos coral reefs. Proc. Ecol. Soc. Aust. 16: 55-70.

Hatcher, B.G. 1984. A maritime accident provides evidence for alternative stable states in benthic communities on coral reefs. Coral Reefs, 3: 199-204.

Hatcher, B.G. 1985. Ecological Research at the Houtman Abrolhos: High latitude reefs of Western Australia. Proc. Fifth Int. Coral Reef Cong., Tahiti, 6: 291-297.

Hatcher, B.G. 1991. Coral Reefs in the Leeuwin Current: an Ecological Perspective. J Roy. Soc. West. Aust. 74: 115-127.

Hatcher, B.G. and A.W.D. Larkum. 1983. An experimental analysis of factors controlling the standing crop of the epilithic algal community on a coral reef. J. Exp. Mar. Biol. Ecol. 69: 61-84.

Hatcher, B.G. and D.W. Rimmer. 1985. The role of grazing in controlling community structure on a high latitude coral reef: measurements of grazing intensity. Proc. Fifth Int. Coral Reef Cong., Tahiti, 6: 229-236.

Hatcher, B.G., H. Kirkman and W.F. Wood. 1987. The growth of the kelp Ecklonia radiata near the northern limit of its range in Western Australia. Mar. Biol. 95: 63-73.

Johannes, R.E., W.J. Wiebe, C.J. Crossland, D.W. Rimmer and S.V. Smith. 1983. Latuitudinal limits of coral reef growth. Mar. Ecol. Prog. Ser. 11: 105-111.

Littler, M.M. and D.S. Littler. 1984. Models of tropical reef biogenisis: contribution of algae. Pages 323-364 in E.E. Round and D.J. Chapman, eds. Progress in pycological research. Biopress.

Morgan, G.J. and F.E. Wells. 1991. Zoogeographic provinces of the Humbolt, Benguela and Leeuwin Current systems. J. Roy. Soc. West. Aust. 74: 59-70.

Pearce, A.F., B.G. Hatcher and K-H. Wyrwoll. 1991. Using satellite imagery to interpret the growth history and palaeoceanography of the Houtman Abrolhos reefs: patterns of the Leeuwin Current around the Abrolhos. CSIRO/UWA Final Report, CSIRO, Perth, 20pp.

Smith, S.V. 1981. The Houtman Abrolhos Islands: carbon metabolism of coral reefs at high latitude. Limnol. Oceanogr. 26: 612-621.

UNEP/IUCN. 1988. Coral reefs of world. Vol. 2. UNEP, Nairobi, pp. 13-18.

Veron, J.E.N. and L.M. Marsh. 1988. Hermatypic corals of Western Australia. Recs. West. Aust. Mus. Suppl. No. 29, 136 pp.

THE GROWTH OF COASTAL TOURISM IN THE RED SEA: PRESENT AND POSSIBLE FUTURE EFFECTS ON CORAL REEFS

Julie P. Hawkins and Callum M. Roberts

Eastern Caribbean Center, University of the Virgin Islands, St Thomas, US Virgin Islands, 00802, USA.

ABSTRACT

Coral reefs provide a major impetus for tourist development throughout the tropics. Their increased popularity has led to extremely rapid growth of many resorts. Using the Red Sea as a case history we examine the impacts that expanding coastal tourism has had on coral reefs. Present development is restricted almost entirely to Egypt, Israel and Jordan. The short coastlines of the latter two countries mean that most of their reefs are already or soon will be influenced by tourism. Approximately 19% of Egypt's reefs are currently affected but this is expected to rise to over 26% by the year 2000. However, the intensity of effects on reefs is likely to increase much more during this period. Israel plans a further 50% increase in coastal tourism, Jordan 100% and Egypt a massive 13 fold expansion. 83% of the planned expansion in Egypt will occur around the established resorts of Hurghada and Sharm-el-Sheikh. Tourist development has already caused substantial damage to inshore reefs near Hurghada from infilling, sedimentation and over-fishing for marine curios. Elsewhere new constructions are also beginning to modify reef habitats. Until now damage to Sharm-el-Sheikh's reefs has been mainly caused by the direct effects of diving and snorkelling. Whilst current levels of recreational use appear to be sustainable the massive expansion planned throughout the region will place the long-term future of reefs in doubt. Unless the pace of tourist development in the northern Red Sea is soon significantly reduced the carrying capacity of coral reefs seems sure to be exceeded with widespread reef degradation the likely result.

INTRODUCTION

Nestled between the desert sands of Africa and Arabia, the Red Sea has lured adventurous explorers for hundreds of years. Now it attracts thousands of tourists! Once exotic and remote it is now provisioned with airports, hotels and diving package deals. The story is familiar wherever coral reefs occur. An unprecedented growth in global tourism now threatens reefs throughout the world. Using tourist development in the Red Sea as a case study we focus on a problem that has worldwide dimensions.

Almost all tourism to the Red Sea occurs in the north within Egypt, Israel and Jordan. Rapid development over the past twenty years has dotted the coastline with numerous resorts, and ambitious expansion plans will potentially quadruple the number of tourists visiting the area by the year 2000. In order to assess how coastal tourism has already, and may yet affect Red Sea coral reefs this paper will draw on examples from these three countries, in particular the Egyptian resorts of Sharm-el-Sheikh and Hurghada. We will describe current levels of development and examine the implications of future expansion plans.

ENVIRONMENTAL PROFILE OF THE RED SEA

Extending betweeen 13°N and 30°N the Red Sea contains unusually warm water for its more northerly latitudes. Fringing reefs occur throughout almost the entire length but are best developed in the deep clear waters of the northern and central regions. In the south the narrow continental shelf broadens and inshore reef growth tends to peter out in the shallow turbid conditions. However, there are extensive reef systems around the southern island groups of Farasan and Dhalak. Reefs in the Gulf of Aqaba have typical northern Red Sea characteristics with a narrow reef-flat and a reef-slope which plunges almost vertically from the reef-edge into very deep water. By contrast, reefs in the shallow Gulf of Suez are poorly developed and resemble those of the Southern Red Sea, becoming sparse moving north as low temperature and high turbidity restrict coral growth. Minimum temperatures in the far northern Red Sea approach the lower limit for reef development (Sheppard et al. 1992).

Apart from the occurrence of extreme low tides, which predominantly affect reef-flat communities in the far north (Loya 1976), reefs in the Red Sea are subject to few natural disturbances. The Red Sea is narrow and enclosed, thus having a short fetch for winds from most directions and so waves are generally small. Storms are rare and cyclonic storms do not occur (Reiss and Hottinger 1984). Consequently reefs are not subject to high levels of turbulence and there is rich coral growth right up to the surface. Futhermore, low wave action allows the development of coral communities composed of relatively easily-broken corals, particularly in more sheltered areas.

Rainfall in the Red Sea region is extremely low and no permanent rivers flow into it. Occasional heavy downpours may cause dry river beds to flood, resulting in freshwater runoff and large amounts of sediment input. However, the majority of reefs in the central and northern region lie adjacent to very deep water and sediments quickly drop out of the range of reef growth and are not usually resuspended. This, together with low plankton productivity and a lack of freshwater runoff, results in very clear water.

The combination of calm seas, clear water and rich marine life form the basis for the Red Sea's rising popularity as a tourist destination.

PRESENT AND PLANNED TOURIST DEVELOPMENT

Egypt

The first tourist resorts on the Red Sea coast were at Hurghada in Egypt and Eilat in Israel (Figure 1). Hurghada was founded by the British in 1909 to support the oil industry in the Gulf of Suez, but did not attract tourists in any numbers until the late 1970s, following the return of stability to the region after the 1967 war with Israel. Tourist villages now sprawl for 20km south of the old town (Figure 2). There are currently 4000 hotel beds in and around Hurghada plus 300 beds in hotels south to Safaga (Figure 1). A further 30,000 are in the development stage along this stretch of coast (ARICON 1990).

At present Hurghada is the only large tourist destination on the mainland Egyptian Red Sea coast. About 50% of the tourists are foreign and diving plays an important role in the town's economy (Jobbins 1989). In the early 1980s diving pressure was very low with only 2 or 3 dive boats, each carrying about 10 people in operation (Ormond 1982). By the middle of the decade this had increased to 20 boats (Ormond 1987). Although we have no data on present diving activity we assume that this has increased along with additional hotel developments.

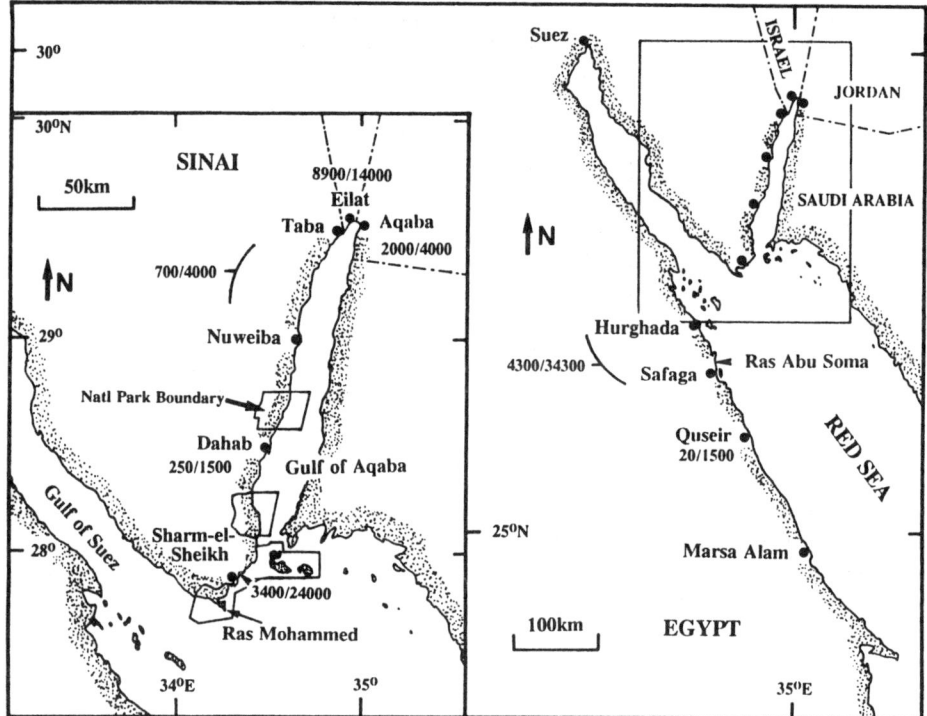

Figure 1: Map of the northern Red Sea showing the locations of coastal tourist resorts. Levels of present and planned development are indicated by the figures; the left hand figure of each pair refers to the present number of hotel beds available in that area, whilst the right hand figure shows the numbers expected by the year 2000.

South of Hurghada the towns of Safaga and Quseir currently attract only a handful of visitors. This is all set to change as a tourist "riviera" spreading south from Hurghada to Safaga, a distance of 61km, is envisaged for the future (Figure 1) (Jobbins 1989). Development is already underway in Quseir with three hotels nearing completion, totalling around 1500 beds (Wager and Roberts 1991).

During their occupation of Sinai (1967-82), the Israelis established small-scale tourism in the newly built towns of Nuweiba and Dahab on the Gulf of Aqaba coast, and Sharm-el-Sheikh situated on the tip of the peninsula (Figure 1). Since Sinai was returned to Egypt in 1982, the Egyptian government have vigorously promoted tourism development and Sharm-el-Sheikh has expanded into a major international resort. Initially development was centred in Na'ama Bay, about 10km north of Sharm-el-Sheikh town (Figure 2). However since this bay is only 1km long, it was filled very rapidly.

Recent hotel constructions have started to spread outwards from Na'ama Bay, particularly in and around Sharm-el-Sheikh itself (Figure 2). Over the past ten years the number of beds has risen from 460 to 3,400, and the area now attracts upwards of 50,000 divers out of some 200,000 visitors per year (Hawkins and Roberts in press). Future plans for expansion aim to increase the number of beds over sevenfold to 24,000 to accommodate over 300,000 divers and a total of 1.2 million visitors (Hawkins and Roberts in press). As a result all the available building land along a 24km strip of coast spreading north from Sharm-el-Sheikh town has been sold to developers. In order to foster rapid growth, the government has stipulated that developers must begin construction within three years of land purchase (O. Melika pers. comm.). Unfortunately, this has led to poorly conceived plans and uncoordinated development.

Development elsewhere in Sinai has proceeded much less rapidly. Nevertheless there are similarly ambitious plans for expansion. At present there are just over 700 beds in the 63km between Nuweiba and Taba (Figure 1). From plans approved up to 1988, this figure is set to increase to over 4000 (Anon. 1989)

An increase of a similar scale is planned for Dahab, which at present primarily caters for budget travellers. In 1992 Dahab had around 250 beds, of which under half were in the one international-style hotel. The remainder were in low cost Bedouin campsites. Plans for three large international hotels totalling some 1500 beds, will provide the up-market accommodation that now dominates in Sharm-el-Sheikh (Wager et al. 1990).

Israel

As in Egypt tourism in Israel was initially retarded by wartime conflicts in the late 1960s and early 1970s, although less so domestically than internationally. With only 11km of coast, every bit is precious. Demands for recreation, port facilities and housing mean all have had to be crammed into this tiny stretch of land (Feitelson and Elgar 1991). Unsurprisingly much of the available coastline has been rapidly built up.

Initially tourism in Eilat was centred along the northern coast with a residential area to the south separating it from the port (Feitelson and Elgar 1991). More recently development has progressed on the southern shore, where most of Israel's reefs lie, and is now encroaching on the Eilat Coral Reserve (Ullian 1992). In 1988 there were an estimated 8,900 hotel beds in Eilat but projections suggested that this would increase to 14,000 by 1995 (ARICON 1990). If realised this would amount to over 50% growth in only seven years. Around 32% of all visitors to Eilat are engaged in water sports (ARICON 1990).

Jordan

Tourist development in Jordan has progressed more slowly than in Egypt or Israel. Aqaba is the only town of any size on the short 27km coastline, and like Eilat it shares the combined role of port and resort, as well as being an industrial centre. By the late 1980s there were just over 2000 hotel beds on the Jordanian Red Sea coast, but a further 2000 were planned by the year 2000 (DAHC 1986) Most of this development is envisaged to take place along the south coast where the majority of the reefs lie. In addition the government hopes to encourage Jordanian residents to build holiday homes in this area (DAHC 1986). The development of holiday homes has already begun in Egypt around Sharm-el-Sheikh and Hurghada.

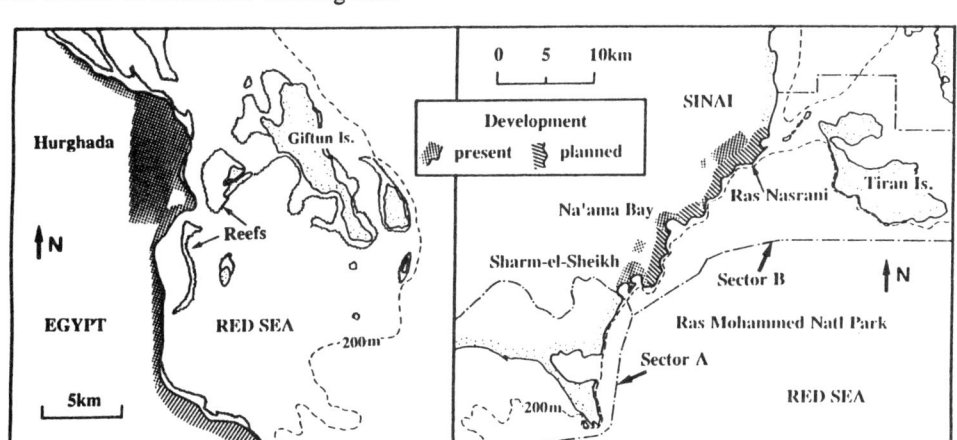

Figure 2: Present and planned tourist development in the two major Egyptian resort areas of Hurghada and Sharm-el-Sheikh. Most of the inshore fringing reefs around Hurghada have now been infilled to create new building land.

EFFECTS OF PRESENT DEVELOPMENTS ON REEFS

In the following, we examine the effects that tourist development has had on coral reefs in the northern Red Sea, focusing on Hurghada and Sharm-el-Sheikh as case studies. These two resorts fall under the jurisdiction of different local governorates and show contrasting styles of development. The expansion of Hurghada has caused substantial damage to reefs whilst Sharm-el-Sheikh has so far had little impact. There are a number of reasons for this difference. The later emergence of Sharm-el-Sheikh as a tourist destination probably enabled some of the early mistakes made during development in Hurghada to be avoided. Furthermore the presence of the Ras Mohammed National Park has perhaps been a restraining influence on environmentally damaging developments there (Figure 2). Differences in coastal topography between the two resorts have also modified the extent of impacts on the marine environment. Inshore reefs around Hurghada lie in shallow water and the shoreline is generally flat (Figure 2). By contrast the coastal waters around Sharm-el-Sheikh are deep and the shore lined with cliffs over much of its length. The significance of these differences is explained below.

Effects of construction and infrastructure

The coastal strip around Hurghada has for years more closely resembled a building site than a tourist resort. This development has caused serious damage to inshore reefs around Hurghada, such that what remains is "of little interest to divers or snorkellers" (Edwards et al. 1982). Offshore reefs 4-16 kilometers from the coast now support the diving industry (Figure 2). In Sharm-el-Sheikh, both fringing reefs and those further offshore remain healthy and are still greatly acclaimed by divers.

Infilling

Coastal infilling has been widespread throughout Hurghada despite a setback requirement prohibiting development within 30m of the high-tide line. This law has been flouted by town officials and developers alike causing major damage to fringing reefs, both directly by construction and indirectly through the effects of sedimentation. Landfill has proceeded unchecked probably because it creates prime but inexpensive land, improves access to the sea and helps line the pockets of corrupt government officials.

Aside from one example in a sandy bay, there has been no coastal infill around Sharm-el-Sheikh. This may be partly because the damage done by infilling in Hurghada has been widely noted, but is probably because most construction to date has occurred in sandy bays without any reefs, or on the tops of cliffs. As new developments extend to areas where infilling could occur, it is hoped that pressure from the increasingly influential Ras Mohammed Marine Park will prevent such a practice.

Sediment from construction

Because there is so little rain along the Red Sea coast very little of the sediment released during construction is washed into the sea. Nevertheless huge amounts of building dust blows offshore. Corals are very sensitive to sediment which can kill them directly by smothering, reduce their growth rates and ability to settle (Rogers 1990). Around Sharm-el-Sheikh dust from construction has so far caused little damage to reefs. Most of it is blown out to sea from high cliff-tops where it drops into deep water and does not become resuspended. By contrast, the low lying coast at Hurghada allows dust to settle directly onto reefs and shallow water means that sediment is continually resuspended by wave action from the strong northerly winds. Dust from construction has probably added to other stresses imposed on inshore reefs near Hurghada.

Beach enhancement may also cause local damage to reefs. Along large parts of the Gulf of Aqaba and Red Sea coasts, uplifted fossil reefs rise close behind the living, submerged reef resulting in narrow or non-existent beaches. Consequently attempts have been made to enhance them. At Quseir, on the southern Egyptian coast, developers are excavating at the edges of both the fossil and the living reef to make a broader beach and deeper swimming area (Wager and Roberts 1991). Although no comparable beach enhancement has so far taken place around Sharm-el-Sheikh, there may be future pressure to do so as development extends to more rocky shorelines. In other places such as Dahab, in the Gulf of Aqaba, the natural shoreline consists of coarse alluvial gravel. The three large hotels currently under construction plan to import fine sand to improve their beaches, much of which will eventually end up in the sea where it may damage reef organisms.

Sewage disposal, desalination, irrigation and rubbish

An increasing threat to coral reefs throughout the world is eutrophication (Wittenburg and Hunte 1992). Nutrient enrichment of coastal waters enables algae to thrive, overgrow and kill corals (Walker and Ormond 1982). Sewage disposal causes much of this nutrient input. At the moment Sharm-el-Sheikh directs all its sewage inland to fertilize a citrus farm. Although the President of the Hurghada City Council stresses that none of the town's sewage goes directly into the sea (Arkell 1991), there is plenty of evidence to suggest that treatment prior to discharge is inadequate (pers. obs.). Riegl and Velimirov (1991) found that algal overgrowth of corals was significantly higher on inshore fringing reefs of Hurghada than on offshore patch reefs, and suggested this was an effect of waste discharge.

A more localised source of nutrient input to reefs, but one which could have damaging effects over the long term, comes from seepage of nutrient-rich irrigation water derived from hotel gardens. Many hotels water their gardens with treated waste water which will gradually percolate through porous coastal rock and enter the sea.

As new developments spring up in more remote areas they will have to take responsibility for their own sewage treatment on site and generate their own electricity and supply of fresh water. The hot brine effluent produced by desalination plants and generator cooling water can cause local damage to reefs (Doty and Marsh 1977). Hotels under construction at Quseir and Dahab plan to discharge these effluents via pipelines across the fringing reef (Wager et al. 1990, Wager and Roberts 1991). Many more hotels now in the planning stage are expected to do this in the future.

Rubbish litters the whole of the Red Sea coast but is particularly abundant around centres of population. Some of it eventually ends up underwater where as well as being unsightly it can cause damage. For example plastic bags can smother corals and rubbish litters the sea bed in the Eilat Coral Reserve (D. Shapiro, pers. comm.). In the past few years the litter problem around Sharm-el-Sheikh has been much reduced owing to an initiative by the local dive centres. They now organise rubbish to be collected from the bins which were installed several years earlier by a Cairo diving club. Nevertheless large quantities of rubbish still blow onto beaches and into the sea from local landfill sites.

Effects of tourism on local fisheries

Large-scale tourist development brings with it a great demand for fresh seafood. A huge appetite for lobster has led to over-fishing and severely depleted stocks around Sinai. Immature individuals are regularly served in restaurants and even those too small to eat are used for garnishes. Recognising there was a problem the Governorate of South Sinai recently imposed a size restriction on lobsters but this has not been enforced and is apparently being flouted due to pressure from the hotel lobby (O. Melika pers. comm.).

Large individual reef-fish used as a centre-piece on the buffet dinner table are also heavily in demand, particularly groupers, snappers and emperors. A recent survey along the Gulf of Aqaba coastline showed that stocks of these fishes are not yet over-exploited (Roberts and Polunin, in press). Nevertheless fishing pressure is increasing and there is a trend towards Egyptian fishermen from the north taking over from local Bedouins, shifting the emphasis from sustainable to extractive harvesting.

Reefs around Hurghada have been heavily fished for a number of years. Ormond (1982) suggests that serious over-fishing occurred between 1967 and 1979 when military security prohibited local fishermen from using the Gulf of Suez. Finding virtually no reasonably sized edible fish on inshore reefs he also concluded that spear-fishing was partly to blame. Although all diving centres in Egypt ban spear-fishing this is still a problem around Hurghada where there is poor enforcement of a new law prohibiting it. Spear-fishing has not been a problem around Sharm-el-Sheikh although some evidently does take place there.

The marine curio trade is a cause for much concern around Hurghada. At least ten shops sell a wide variety of curios from shells, corals, sea urchins and starfish, to turtles, shark jaws and stuffed or dried out fish (Ormond 1982). As well as posing a threat to the numbers of individual target species this trade can also affect wider reef ecology. Ormond (1982) suggested that sea urchin population explosions around Hurghada in the early 1980s were partly due to removal of their pufferfish and triggerfish predators for sale as souvenirs. Population explosions of sea urchins after removal of these fishes have been demonstrated on Kenyan reefs (McClanahan and Muthiga 1988). The large number of sea urchins at Hurghada have caused extensive reef erosion whilst feeding on filamentous algae which they scrape from the reef. Ormond (1982) reported that densities of urchin predators near Hurghada were down to one twentieth of those on little-fished reefs elsewhere in the Red Sea.

So far there has been virtually no trade in marine curios at Sharm-el-Shiekh. A few stuffed fish decorate bars and restaurants and some shops exhibit jewellery around shells and corals. Several of the dive centres feature posters against the marine curio trade and all prohibit collection of souvenirs by their guests. By contrast the last word from Hurghada is a roadside farewell sign showing a happy tourist caricature setting off home with pufferfish lampshade tucked under his arm.

Direct impacts of diving and snorkelling

Many visitors to the Red Sea go either diving, snorkelling or do both. The impact on corals can be striking in very popular areas. Large amounts of broken coral litter the reef and many of the broken colonies appear bleached or overgrown with algae (Hawkins and Roberts 1992). Direct damage is caused by tourists kicking, trampling or holding onto corals which, once damaged, could become more susceptible to disease and algal competitors. Additional, often very serious damage occurs when misplaced boat anchors scour the reef (Tilmant 1987).

The most detailed studies of diver impact have been made around Sharm-el-Sheikh (Hawkins and Roberts 1992, 1993, in press) where the Egyptian Tourist Authority estimates that about a quarter of the visitors are divers (Anon. 1989). A study made in 1990 by Hawkins and Roberts (1992) showed there was significantly more broken coral, fragments of coral reattached to the substratum, partially dead and abraded corals in areas heavily used by divers than in control areas. They concluded that although damage rapidly accumulated within new dive sites, once a certain level of use had been reached the impact appeared to stabilise.

Despite very high levels of diving around Sharm-el-Sheikh, Hawkins and Roberts (in press) found only 37 sites were used in a 48.5km stretch of coast (Figure 2). Assuming each site covers 500m, this means that 38% of the local coastline is subject to the direct effects of diving. Six dive sites were used very intensively with between 35,000 and 50,000 dives per year and it was feared that the carrying capacity of these reefs was being exceeded. Since then in one of several positive management steps, the Ras Mohammed Marine Park has limited each diving centre to only one boat a day visiting the popular Ras Mohammed peninsula.

However problems lie ahead. Hawkins and Roberts (in press) concluded that if future plans to increase the number of divers visiting Sharm-el-Sheikh by over sixfold were realised then the carrying capacity of the area for diving would be completely outstripped, even if the number of dive sites were increased and restrictions placed on use of the most popular sites.

Similar problems from diving and snorkelling face reefs around Hurghada (Riegl and Velimirov 1991). Although divers form a smaller proportion of visitors than in Sharm-el-Sheikh, the actual diving pressure is comparable, particularly since the bad state of inshore reefs magnifies pressures put on offshore dive sites. Unfortunately there is as yet no National Park or management plan for Hurghada which might regulate against the damaging effects of divers and snorkellers.

In Eilat where management does exist in the form of the Nature Reserves Authority the pressures are so great on such tiny areas of reef (reefs cover only 6.2km) that most appear badly knocked about (L. Montgomery pers comm.) and management might not seem very successful. Nevertheless Riegl and Velimirov (1991) showed that only 11% of the coral colonies they sampled around Eilat were actually broken. This compares closely with breakage levels of 10% found by Hawkins and Roberts (1993) on popular reefs around Sharm-el-Sheikh. Interestingly the subjective impression amongst divers and reef scientists was that the Sharm-el-Sheikh reefs were in much better condition than those of Eilat (D. Shapiro pers. comm.). This may be because other stresses, such as pollution from the nearby port (Loya 1975), exacerbate impacts from tourism.

PLANNING AND FUTURE DEVELOPMENT

Many of the current problems from coastal development have arisen due to a lack of planning or at least a lack of adherence to development restrictions aleady on the statute books. In Egypt, government incentives to developers have created the massive scale coastal construction presently underway before any coordinated development plans were drafted. Although it now appears to recognise the need for better coastal planning (Government of Egypt 1992) government initiatives to expand tourist development over 13 times by the year 2000 (Figure 1) pose a significant threat to reefs.

At present approximately 19% of Egypt's reefs are under the influence of tourism. This will increase to over 26% if the above mentioned plans materialize. In terms of reef area affected by tourism such expansion does not seem excessive. However the huge increase in intensity of use can be expected to exceed the carrying capacity of reefs and widespread degradation will ensue. Reefs cannot for example, support the same density of visitors that a sandy coast can. In Israel, 100% of reefs are currently affected by tourism but future development will intensify their use. Similarly, Jordan's planned tourism expansion will extend tourist effects to all of the country's reefs.

There is little prospect of feedback control discouraging further growth from tourists opting not to visit the region after environmental damage becomes evident. Whilst degraded reefs won't exactly lure people into repeat diving holidays, dive centres will remain in business because many divers want to dive in warm clear water regardless of what there is to see. It is also likely that if reefs become heavily degraded there will be a change in the type of tourist visiting the Red Sea; sun-worshippers replacing divers for example. Facilities can thus continue to expand well beyond the point at which coral reefs have been severely damaged. For this reason, it is necessary to regulate development in areas with reefs to prevent such deterioration.

Increased coastal tourism can also be expected to lead to increased coastal urbanisation. As well as hotels, facilities must be developed to support their staff and local infrastructure improved to provide necessary services. In Egypt, facilities for workers in resort towns are currently sparse and most workers leave their families elsewhere. However with Egypt's population set to double by 2020 expanding tourist resorts are likely to become a focus for new settlement.

Some efforts towards integrated reef management and tourist development are now being belatedly introduced. In 1988 a project was initiated to develop a management plan for the Ras Mohammed Marine Park (Pearson 1989). Although the Israelis had first proclaimed the area a reserve and later legislation in 1983 made it an Egyptian Marine Park, it existed in name only for the next five years. Following initial success of this new management initiative, the park's boundaries have recently been extended to include the whole of the Sharm-el-Sheikh resort area plus two additional pockets of coast further north in the Gulf of Aqaba (Figures 1 and 2) (Commission of the European Community 1991).

In the near future Egypt is expected to receive a multi-hundred million dollar loan from the World Bank for coastal development. The Bank plans to incorporate environmental conditions into the loan, such as a setback zone on all coastal building (Jan Post pers. comm.). Meanwhile USAID recently funded a study which first identified and then suggested how to rectify the most pressing environmental problems facing the Gulf of Aqaba (RDA Int., pers. comm.). A similar study was also commissioned by the Egyptian Environmental Affairs Agency in 1990 to examine the effects of tourism development (TMRU pers. comm.).

Whilst the stated intention of the Red Sea Governorate is to transform the coast between Hurghada and Safaga into a tourist riviera, at least part of that area will hopefully avoid mistakes made in earlier construction. Developers planning a resort covering 3200 hectares around the beautiful headland of Ras Abu Soma (Figure 1) have brought in consultants from the Ras Mohammed Marine Park to help them draft their plans.

CONCLUSIONS

Overall the present effects of coastal tourism on Red Sea coral reefs are worrying rather than alarming. Despite various examples where tourist development has caused damage, the impacts arising from industry and ports have usually been worse (Loya 1975, Ormond 1987, Sheppard et al. 1992). One positive influence of tourism is that it tends to hold back industrial development. It should also provide a powerful economic reason to preserve reefs (Spurgeon in press). With careful planning and development tourism should bring prosperity to the region and need not threaten reefs. In reality the environmental implications of tourist development are frequently overlooked and future plans for tourism expansion are a cause for great concern.

The region now stands at a crossroads where there is still a choice between sustainable tourist development or widespread decline of the Red Sea's outstanding coral reefs. It is a choice which also faces many other nations. Recent initiatives in Egypt to control development have been encouraging but will need powerful backing to overcome the temptation for short-term financial gain offered by a booming tourist industry. Unless restrictions are swiftly imposed to slow down the accelerating pace of tourist development in the northern Red Sea and to cap its ultimate growth, the future of the region's reefs will remain in doubt.

ACKNOWLEDGEMENTS

We would like to thank the Eastern Caribbean Centre of the University of the Virgin Islands for providing office facilities during this work, and also the many people who gave us access to unpublished information.

LITERATURE CITED

Anonymous. 1989. Unpublished report on tourism development in Sinai for Movenpick Hotels. Cairo, Egypt.
Arkell, C. 1991. Blue water, Red Sea. Green Magazine January 1991: 60-63.
ARICON 1990. Priority Action Plan. Unpublished report. Arab International Consultants, Cairo, Egypt.
Commission of the European Community. 1991. Financing proposal EC/Egypt cooperation agreement. VIII/692/91-EN.
DAHC. 1986. Hashemite Kingdom of Jordan. The south coast tourist area. Aqaba. Interim Report. Vol. 2, Tourism and Recreation. Aqaba Region Authority. Dar Al-Handasah Consultants (Shair & Partners).
Doty, J.E. and J.A. Marsh. 1977. Marine survey of Tanapag, Saipan: the power barge "Impedance". Technical Report No. 33 March 1977, The Marine Laboratory, University of Guam, Guam.
Edwards, A.J., S. Hind and D. Rosenthal. 1982. General report of the Cambridge University Underwater Exploration Group. Red Sea Reefs Study 1981. Cambridge University, UK. 44pp.
Feitelson, E. and A. Elgar. 1991. Eilat: Multiple conflicts in an inherently uncertain environment. Coastal Manage. 19: 357-369.
Government of Egypt, 1992. Arab Republic of Egypt National Environmental Action plan. Aide Memoire. March 1992.
Hawkins, J.P. and C.M. Roberts. 1992. Effects of recreational SCUBA diving on fore-reef slope communities of coral reefs. Biol. Conserv. 62: 171-78.
Hawkins, J.P. and C.M. Roberts. In press. Can Egypt's coral reefs support ambitious plans for diving tourism? 7th Int. Coral Reef Symp., Guam. June 1992.
Hawkins, J.P and C.M. Roberts. 1993. Effects of recreational diving on coral reefs. Trampling of reef-flat communities. J. Appl. Ecol. 30: 25-30.
Jobbins, J. 1989. The Red Sea Coasts of Egypt. Sinai and the Mainland. The American Univ. in Cairo Press, Cairo, Egypt. 115pp.
Loya, Y. 1975. Possible effects of water pollution on the community structure of Red Sea corals. Mar. Biol. 29: 177-185.
Loya, Y. 1976. Recolonization of Red Sea corals affected by natural catastrophes and man-made perturbations. Ecol. 57: 278-289.
McClanahan, T.R. and N.A. Muthiga. 1988. Changes in Kenyan coral reef community structure and function due to exploitation. Hydrobiologia 166: 269-276.
Ormond, R.F.G. 1982. Report on the need for management and marine parks in the Egyptian Red Sea. Institute of Oceanography and Fisheries, Academy of Sciences, Cairo, Egypt.
Ormond, R.F.G. 1987. Conservation and management. In: Edwards, A.J. and S.M. Head (eds), Red Sea Key Environments, Pergamon Press, Oxford. pp 405-423.
Pearson, M.P. 1989. Specification study for the development of a management plan for the Ras Mohammed Marine National Park. The Egyptian Environmental Affairs Agency, Cairo, Egypt.
Riegl, B. and B. Velimirov. 1991. How many damaged corals in the Red Sea reef systems? A quantitative survey. Hydrobiologia 216/217: 249-256.
Reiss, Z. and L. Hottinger. 1984. The Gulf of Aqaba. Springer-Verlag, Berlin. 354 pp.
Roberts, C.M. and N.V.C. Polunin. In press. Effects of marine reserve protection on northern Red Sea fish populations. In: Proc. 7th Int. Coral Reef Symp., Guam, 22-27 June, 1992.
Rogers, C.S. 1990. Responses of coral reefs and reef organisms to sedimentation. Mar. Ecol. Prog. Ser. 62: 185-202.
Sheppard, C.R.C., A.R.G. Price and C.M. Roberts. 1992. Marine Ecology of the Arabian region. Patterns and processes in extreme tropical environments. Academic Press, London. 359pp.
Spurgeon, J. In press. The Economic valuation of coral reefs. Mar. Poll. Bull.
Tilmant, J.T. 1987. Impacts of recreational activities on coral reefs. In: Salvat, B. (ed), Human impacts on coral reefs: facts and recommendations, Antenne Museum EPHE, French Polynesia, pp 195-214.
Ullian, R. 1992. Frommers budget travel guide. Israel 93-94 on $45 a day. Prentice Hall Travel, New York. 408pp.
Wager, J. and C.M. Roberts. 1991. Report on the potential environmental impacts from the development of two hotels at Quseir el Qadim. Cobham Resource Consultants, Manchester, UK.
Wager, J., C.M. Roberts and J.P. Hawkins. 1990. Report on the potential environmental impact from the development of a hotel on El Kura spit, Dahab, Egypt. Cobham Resource Consultants, Manchester, UK.
Walker, D.I. and R.F.G. Ormond. 1982. Coral death from sewage and phosphate pollution at Aqaba, Red Sea. Mar. Poll. Bull. 13: 21-25.
Wells, S. M. 1988. Coral reefs of the world. Vol. 2: Indian Ocean, Red Sea and Gulf. IUCN, Gland, Switzerland and Cambridge, U.K./UNEP, Nairobi, Kenya. 389 pp.
Wittenberg, M. and W. Hunte. 1992. Effects of eutrophication and sedimentation on juvenile corals. 1. Abundance, mortality and community structure. Mar. Biol. 112: 131-138.

STATUS OF KENYAN CORAL REEFS

T.R. McClanahan[1,2] and D. Obura[2]

[1] NYZS - Wildlife Conservation Society - International, Coral Reef Conservation Project, P.O. Box 99470, Mombasa, Kenya.
[2] Rosenstiel School of Marine and Atmospheric Sciences, University of Miami, 4600 Rickenbacker Causeway, Miami, Florida 33149, USA.

ABSTRACT

Kenyan coral reefs have been relatively well-studied from the view of human impacts largely due to the existence of four marine parks and numerous reefs experiencing intense human resource use. Studies indicate that the removal of finfish is having the largest impact on unprotected reefs and has a number of secondary and tertiary effects on other faunal groups and ecological processes. The high abundance of sea urchins in unprotected reefs may results from a reduction in their predators due to overfishing. Sea urchins are associated with reefs of lower coral cover, topographic complexity, and reduced calcium carbonate deposition rates. Some species of gastropod appear to be affected by shell collecting, but the total fauna seem more impacted by removal of their predators. River sediment discharges and eutrophication are of secondary importance but are not severe as yet and cannot be distinguished from natural variations over geologic history.

INTRODUCTION

Kenya's coral reefs experience two extremes of management. Coral reef lagoons in Malindi, Watamu, Kisite, and Mombasa receive total protection from fishing and shell and coral collection. All other reef lagoons are exposed to largely unregulated human resource use which principally includes fishing and shell and coral collection. The impacts of these two management plans result in large differences in the ecology of these lagoons. Additionally, river discharges from the Sabaki and Tana Rives in northern Kenya release large quantities of sediment and nutrients. The impacts of these discharges has been poorly studied until recently. This paper briefly summarizes some of the findings of research undertaken by the Coral Reef Conservation Project on the human impact on coral reefs.

FINFISH

Surveys of the fish fauna were completed using visual transects (usually five replicate 5 meter x 100 meter transects per reef) in 1985, 1992, and 1993. Surveys indicate that fish population densities and sizes are much smaller in unprotected than protected reef lagoons with a few exceptions. Additionally, the numbers of species of finfish is reduced by about 50% in unprotected reefs and many species were never observed outside the marine parks. All families of fish except for pufferfish (*Diodontidae*), wrasses (*Labridae*), and parrotfish have higher population densities (i.e. numbers of fish) in protected reefs. Wrasses and parrotfish are considerably smaller in unprotected reefs than protected reefs, and unprotected areas have somewhat higher population densities of the smallest size class of fish (3-10 cm). The population densities of the edible surgeonfish (*Acanthuridae*) and snappers (*Lutjanidae*) are very low in unprotected reefs as are the edible and ornamental triggerfish (*Balistidae*) and butterflyfish (*Chaetodontidae*). No angelfish (*Pomacanthiidae*) were observed in the 1992 unprotected surveys, in which 7500 m^2 were covered.

Comparisons of fish populations in unprotected reefs between 1988 and 1992 indicate population reductions in surgeonfish, butterflyfish, angelfish, and other families while triggerfish densities have increased somewhat during this time interval. Overall, total fish populations have remained unchanged in unprotected reefs.

With the parks, most fish families, with the exception of damselfish, have remained constant over time. Damselfish populations have been reduced to around 30% of their previous population density and this appears to have occurred in both Malindi and Watamu reefs. The cause of this massive population reduction is unclear at present. The transition reef (Mombasa MNP) has undergone population increases in all fish categories. Therefore, it is clear that fishermen were having a large impact on fish populations in the studied coral areas.

SEA URCHINS

Sea Urchins, in general, and in particular the rock-boring sea urchin (*Echinometra mathaei*), which is one of the reef's major substrate eroders, continue to display very high populations in unprotected reefs and very low populations in protected reefs. Overall, there has been an increase in sea urchin populations since 1987, but this is variable among the studied reefs, with population increases occurring in Diani Beach, reductions in Kanamai, and stability in the other studied reefs. Predation rates on tethered sea urchins indicate that predation is very intense in protected reefs and the population density of sea urchins in studied reefs appears to be well-predicted by predation and the abundance of triggerfish (the Red-lined triggerfish, *Balistapus undulatus*, and the Picasso triggerfish, *Rhinacanthus aculeatus*). Within the Mombasa MNP, the transitional reef, there have been reductions in some species of sea urchin (*Diadema* and *Tripneustes*) and overall, a significant reduction in the abundance and biomass of sea urchins. Yet, the very large-bodied sea urchin *Echinothrix* has not changed since previously surveyed. Experiments on herbivory have shown that *Echinothrix* is the major herbivore on the Mombase MNP reef although the abundance of finfish herbivores (parrot and surgeonfish) have increased since protection.

SUBSTRATE COVER

Studies on the cover of the lagoonal substratum indicate differences between protected and unprotected reefs and over time. Protected reefs have a greater abundance of hard coral, calcareous (*Halimeda*), and coralline algae while unprotected reefs have a greater abundance of large macroalgae, algal turf ("bare substrate"), seagrass, soft coral and sponges. These differences indicate higher overall herbivory from finfish in protected reefs, but localized intense herbivory by sea urchins associated with spots of bare substrate in unprotected reefs. Additionally, unprotected reefs had lower reef topographic complexity. This low topographic complexity has been attributed to the low abundance of corals (the coral reef's major substrate builder) combined with a high abundance of sea urchins (the coral reefs major substrate eroders).

The Mombasa MNP transitional reef sites show increases in hard coral cover (250% in four years), calcareous algae, topographic complexity and benthic diversity while a decrease in bare substrate has been measured. These results are consistent with the transition from dominance by sea urchins to herbivorous fish as the reef's major herbivores and is strong support for the model of the impacts of fishing on coral reefs developed by Dr. McClanahan.

An analysis of the present state of growth (calcium carbonate growth) of Kenyan coral reefs is presented by comparing the abundance of coral (major reef builders) versus sea urchins (major reef eroders). The model indicates that the Diani beach reef is a decaying reef while other Kenyan reefs are either close to the line of zero growth (i.e. Kanamai and Vipingo) or growing reefs (i.e. the protected reefs). Analysis of monitoring data on Diani reef collected from 1985 indicates that the abundance of hard substrate and coral have consistently been going down over this period while seagrass appears to be colonizing coral sand which replaces the coral reef's hard substrate.

SIMULATION MODELS

A computer model (differential equations solved by computer algorithms) of the coral reef has been developed which includes some of the main components (i.e. algae, coral, fish) of the coral reef discussed above. This model has been used to make predictions concerning the ecology of the coral reef under different levels of fishing. One model experiment allows fishermen to fish all of the main finfish groups while the second experiment allows the fishermen to fish piscivorous (i.e. groupers) and herbivorous fishes (i.e. surgeon and parrotfish) but leaving triggerfish ("invertivores") unfished. Model results plot the model's predictions for the abundance and processes of different reef components as a function of the density of fishermen. Simulation model results indicate that fishing all groups will eventually result in a dominance of the reef by sea urchins which will reduce both fisheries and substrate productivity and cause the reef substratum to decay or grow negatively. This simulation suggests that this transition from finfish to sea urchin dominance can occur for a very small increase in fishermen once triggerfish numbers are already low. Leaving triggerfish alone avoids the above losses and results in higher fisheries yields of mostly herbivorous fishes.

SHELL COLLECTING

Collection of shells for sale to tourists is a conservation concern due to the possibility of local or global extinctions and the possible imbalance in reef ecology that may occur due to their overcollection. But, attempts to find impacts on the shell populations indicate that only a few species may be affected by shell collection. Population density comparisons of thirty commercially collected species were compared between protected and unprotected reefs (i.e. no shelling and shelling). Only two commercial wing shells (*Lambis truncata* and *L. chiragra*) and the egg cowrie (*Ovula ovum*) appeared to have reduced populations in unprotected reefs. A comparison of the Mombasa Marine National Park before and after protection found population increases in four commercial species since protection. These species included the above three species and the Tiger cowrie (*Cypraea tigris*). Within six southern Kenyan reef lagoons total gastropod density was negatively correlated with triggerfish and total fish densities which suggests the removal of gastropod predators may be having a greater impact on the shell fauna than shell collection.

RIVER DISCHARGE AND EUTROPHICATION

The geographic distribution of coral reefs in East Africa reflects freshwater and nutrient influences (river discharge and upwelling) over geologic time. The southern coastal strip, which has little freshwater input is bounded by a continuous fringing reef. The northern coastal zone is dominated by the Tana and Sabaki rivers, which drain central and southern Kenya. The coral reefs in the Malindi Marine Park are the northern tip of the southern fringing reef, 15 kilometers south of the Sabaki River mouth. River discharge flows over the Malindi reefs from December to April, controlled by the northerly North-East monsoon winds and the short rains upcountry. Increases in soil erosion and runoff associated with human land use patterns upcountry have resulted in increases in sediment delivery to Malindi by the Sabaki River over the last 30 years.

During high river discharge, visibility in reef waters can be reduced to 1 meter over several weeks. Sedimentation rates are highly variable, however do not greatly exceed "normal" values, which may be due to the high flushing rate of water caused by a tidal fluctuation of 3 meters twice daily. Reef sediments in Malindi have a high terrigenos fraction that remains throughout the year and is resuspended during storms, extending conditions of river sediment resuspension beyond its seasonal occurrence. Substrate cover, coral diversity, and coral genus abundance patterns on reefs less than 2 meters depth at low tide were comparable to non-sedimented reefs. Coral growth rates (measured by colony diameter and buoyant weight) showed some seasonal and between-reef differences but with little consistency and high variation. Field comparisons of three dominant coral genera, *Porites*, *Acropora,* and *Pocillopora* indicate that the last two are more susceptible to sediment stress with higher mortality rates. *Porites lutes* is more susceptible to reductions in growth rates, however it has lower mortality rates. Overall, shallow reefs in Malindi do not show the reduced diversity that is characteristic of sediment stressed reefs. Observed differences in coral genus distributions and abundances cannot simply be attributed to river influence. The affects of eutrophication associated with river discharge may also be hard to determine, as these continental fringing reefs are heavily influenced by freshwater and terrestrial runoff.

The coral reefs in Malindi exhibit resistance to change under the influence of increasing environmental sediment stress. Research will be broadened with the aim of measuring community and ecosystem parameters related to sediment stress in order to perform modelling experiments to explore the possible effects of increases in sediment delivery by the Sabaki River, a likely occurrence in the coming years.

Through reefs in the Malindi Marine Park do not appear to be suffering ecologically from human induced changes in river discharge, the tourism resource value of the park has been eroded -- during low visibility events (which coincide with tourist high season), tourists are diverted to nearby unaffected reefs.

TOURIST DAMAGE

Heavy use of snorkeling sites in the marine parks and in unprotected reefs adjacent to tourism developments results in varying degrees of physical damage. The most heavily visited sites in the Malindi and Watamu Marine Parks have a higher proportion of damaged coral colonies than at adjacent non-visited sites. In patches, coral cover can be less than 1 percent, though with high diversity (10 genera) of small colonies in crevices. Due to the limited extent of these snorkeling sites, tourist damage does not represent a threat to the reef system as yet. The proximity of nearby undamaged reefs and the presence of small corals in refuges suggests that the recovery potential of damaged sites is high.

RECOMMENDATIONS

PROTECTED SITES

Kenya's marine parks continue to be a haven for fish, corals, gastropods, and many other unstudied organisms. The existence of these parks has made this comparative study possible, and as a result our understanding of Kenyan and Indian Ocean coral reefs ecology has greatly increased. Additionally, we are more knowledgeable and therefore better able to manage Kenya's coral reef resources. We therefore suggested that these marine parks should continue to receive the kind of protection they receive, but some additional studies should be undertaken on two issues uncovered by our research. These issues are:

1) fish population studies indicate a 30% reduction in total fish numbers which is entirely attributable to the more than 60% reduction in damselfish numbers both in Malindi and Watamu MNP

2) there has been a measured reduction in the coral reefs topographic complexity. Topographic complexity is essential for providing shelter to reef animals.

Consequently, we recommend that park-related research and consequent management be focused on:

1) a study of damselfish populations; focusing on their habitat requirements, possible migrations, effects of tourism (i.e. coral breakage, feeding of Sargeant majors (*Abudefduf*) and subsequent competitive effects on other species of damselfish), and impacts of water quality changes on damselfish ecology and behavior.

2) a study of the factors that effect coral reef topographic complexity such as tourist breakage, sedimentation, coral predators, and coral community composition be undertaken to develop management plans to increase the reef's topographic complexity.

3) a thorough research and monitoring program of the impacts of sediment discharge from the Sabaki on Malindi's coral reefs be completed.

TRANSITION SITE

The creation of the Mombasa MNP has resulted in the full protection of a previously heavily exploited coral reef. The protection of this reef signals a continued commitment to marine conservation by the Kenyan government and has also initiated an important experiment on the impacts o fishing and human resource use on coral reefs. Results o the survey indicate a very rapid response to the removal of fisherman with increase in fish and coral, and reductions in many sea urchin species. Studies on the coral fauna also indicate that the Mombasa MNP coral fauna is one the most species rich sites measured along the Kenyan coast. The Mombasa MNP may soon become Kenya's premier marine park in terms of species diversity, water quality, and as the largest income generator among protected areas. Consequently, we recommend:

1) that the designated park area continue to receive full protection

2) that research and management focus on the reserve area, in the southern end of the gazetted area, with a focus on developing a) a fisheries management plan which is nondestructive to the coral reef's ecology and maximizes fisheries sustained yields, and b) provide small protected areas for tourists to visit and enjoy a high abundance and diversity of fish and corals.

and

3) a small-scale sea urchin removal experiment be performed within the park to determine the impact that the removal of the large-bodied sea urchin *Echinothrix* will have on the reef's substrate and fish fauna. Because *Echinothrix* appears to be the major herbivore at present (eating > 90% of the experimental seagrass and algae placed in the reef) we have hypothesized that the removal of *Echinothrix* will result in further increases in finfish diversity and abundance as additional food is made available to these fish species.

UNPROTECTED SITES

Unprotected coral reef lagoons continue to show signs of extreme overfishing which occurred before the beginning of this monitoring program in 1987. Unprotected areas have a large abundance of sea urchins, low coral cover, and populations of small fish. Nonetheless, the recovery of the Mombasa MNP suggests that heavily overfished reefs can, in some instances, quickly recover from overuse. Additionally, other studies indicate that fish abundance is high in deep-water reef edges. Therefore, in order to increase the fisheries sustained yields of these coral reefs, we suggest the following:

1) a ban on the removal of triggerfish (the three species to include in this ban are the red-lined triggerfish (*Balistaphus undulatus*), Picasso triggerfish (*Rhinecanthus aculeatus*), and the Wedge-tailed triggerfish (*Rhinecanthus rectangulus*)) by both aquarium and subsistence fishermen.

2) a temporary ban (i.e., 1 to 3 years) be established on the collection of Angelfish (Pomacanthides) by aquarium and commercial fishermen from reef lagoons until Angelfish populations show signs of recovery (to be determined by this monitoring program).

3) the Diani beach reef lagoon and reef edge should be temporarily closed (i.e., 2 to 5 years) or receive regulation of human resource use (i.e., fishing and coral collection) in order that the reef recovers from extreme overuse which is threatening its long-term sustainability.

4) minimum size restrictions be places on food fishes caught in reef lagoons in order to increase the size of fish caught and therefore increasing fish biomass and sustainable yields of the commercial fisheries.

5) fishing in off-shore areas (i.e., water deeper than 3 meters beyond the reef edge) should be encouraged by promoting the use of engines and off-shore fishing equipment to local fishermen.

6) preliminary small-scale sea urchin removal experiments should be undertaken in unprotected reef lagoons to determine the impacts of sea urchins on the fish and coral fauna and as a way to increase fish production on heavily fished reefs.

We suggest that initiation of these management plans will result in the recovery of many overfished reefs and reestablish them as more productive fishing grounds in the near future. In order to temporarily compensate fishermen who might suffer short-term losses due to these management plans, alternative sources of employment, income, and resources are needed. This can be achieved by promoting off-shore fishing, aquaculture, artificial reef programs, sea urchin removal programs, and including fishermen in the tourist-generated income or economy.

ACKNOWLEDGEMENTS

This research, monitoring, education and conservation program were established through financial support from Wildlife Conservation Society International, The Pew Charitable Trust, the Conservation, Food & Health Foundation, and the Rockefeller Foundation. Logistical, field and personnel support were provided by Kenya Marine & Fisheries Research Institute and Kenya Wildlife Services. Field assistance of N.A. Muthiga, J. Mutere, and S. Mwachireya is greatly appreciated. Research clearance was granted by Kenya's office of the President.

EFFECT OF NUTRIENT EXCESS ON A MODERN FRINGING REEF (REUNION ISLAND, WESTERN INDIAN OCEAN). GEOLOGICAL IMPLICATIONS.

Lucien F. Montaggioni[1], Pascale Cuet[2], and Odile Naïm[2]

[1]URA-CNRS 1208, Université de Provence, 13331 Marseille Cedex 3, France·

[2]Université de la Réunion, 97490 Sainte Clotilde, Réunion island, France D.O.M.

ABSTRACT

In Réunion island (Indian Ocean), La Saline fringing reef is subjected to varying biotic disruption due to discharge of nutrient-rich waters. A multidisciplinary study including water chemistry and bionomy allowed us to define the relationships between nutrient availability and reef community structure. Based on the eutrophication levels and the state of health of the initial biotic communities, three main areas have been recognized on the reef studied. The oligotrophic areas are typified by normal salinity, nitrate and phosphate levels lower than $1\mu M$; biota is dominated by living corals both in high and low energy settings. The mesotrophic areas are slightly hyposaline (<34.5‰), with nitrate and phosphate concentrations of about 2 and $1\mu M$; respectively; biota is characterized by the abundance of calcareous or fleshy algae. In the eutrophic areas, reef-overlying waters are hyposaline and contain high concentrations of nitrate and phosphate (5 and $1.2\mu M$ respectively); benthic communities are dominated by algal-cyanobacterial mats and bioeroders (clionid sponges). Since calcification rates (0.66 kg $CaCO_3 m^{-2}.yr^{-1}$) cannot balance carbonate export, the reef is assumed to be in process of drowning. A predictive model of community replacement sequence indicative of increased eutrophication is proposed as a modern analog for the fossil record.

INTRODUCTION

In the fossil record, drowned carbonate sedimentary systems display evidence of the negative influence of nutrients on benthic biota (Hallock and Schlager, 1986). Similarly, eutrophication is regarded as instrumental in the demise of modern coral reefs in a number of areas (Hallock, 1988). Réunion island is situated in the southwestern Indian ocean (Fig.1), and exhibits discontinuous fringing reefs along the western coast (Montaggioni and Faure, 1980). In such high volcanic islands, local nutrient sources (i. e. runoff) can produce mesotrophic to eutrophic conditions on reefs ecosystems within an oligotrophic province (Cuet *et al.*, 1988).

In this paper, we report chemical and biological results from La Saline reef that exhibits varying levels of biotic disruption by nutrients. Subsequently, we discuss the implications for the geological record through a predictive model of community replacement sequence.

METHODS

Subsurface and bottom sampling of reef-overlying waters was conducted hourly during 24 hour-periods in the rainy season (Feb. and Dec. 1985) for nutrient determination. Correlatively, salinity was determined using a Beckman salinometer. Furthermore, in April 1987, salinity and reactive silicate concentrations were mapped from subsurface water samples. Analysis was performed using the standard manual method described by Aminot (1983). Reef calcification was estimated using the alkalinity depression method (Smith, 1983) in Dec. 1985 (austral summer) and May 1986 (austral winter). Detailed mapping of dominant benthic communities was carried out during a series of extremely low tides (July 1986), using aerial colour photographs.

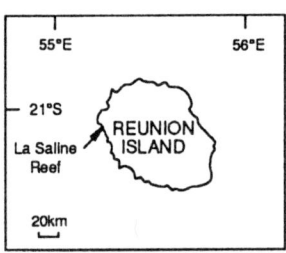

Figure 1. Location of La Saline reef, western coast of Réunion island, Western Indian Ocean

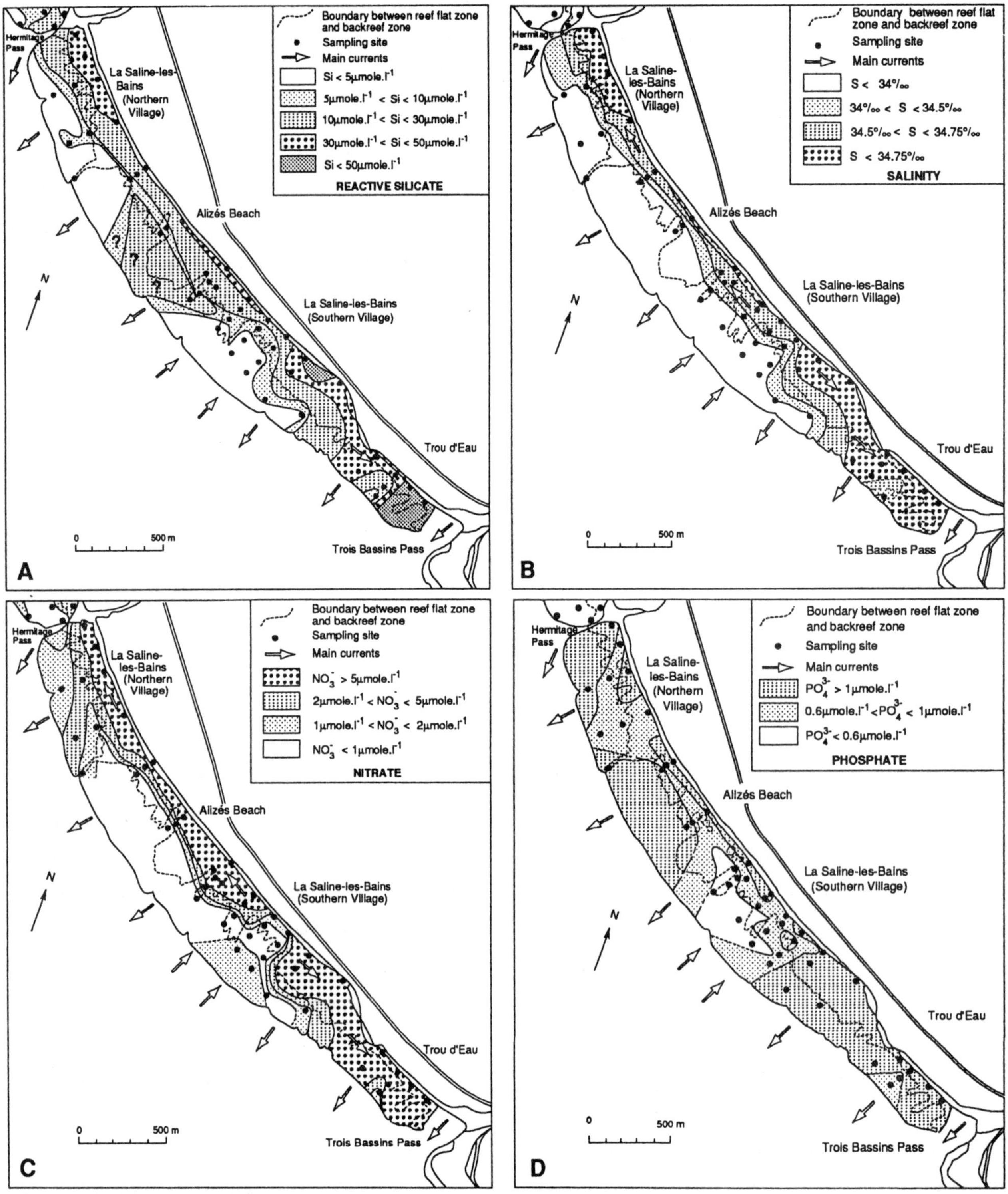

Figure 2. Surface isoplets of reactive silicate (A), salinity (B), nitrate (C) and phosphate (D), La Saline fringing reef, Réunion island.

RESULTS

Distributional patterns of freshwater and nutrient supply.

Reactive silicate concentrations can be used as a marker of submarine groundwater discharge (SGD) which is the major source of freshwater inputs on the reef considered (Cuet et al., 1988).

The good consistency between the distribution of isopleths from surface reactive silicate (Fig.2A), salinity (Fig.2B) and nitrate (Fig.2C) indicates that freshwater aquifer is likely to produce significant input of terrestrial nutrient onto the reef. Correlation between reactive silicate and nitrate is weaker on the reef flat than in the back reef zone, but still significant; mean nitrate content of La Saline coastal groundwaters is 2.47 $\mu mole.l^{-1}$ (μM). Phosphate concentration in reef waters shows no clear relationship with reactive silicate content (compare Fig.2A and 2D), neither along the shoreline nor on the reef flat. However, phosphorus was probably brought in by SGD, since mean values of PO_4^{3-} from La Saline coastal freshwaters may locally reach $3.7\mu M$ ($1.5\mu M$ on average). According to the distributional patterns of reactive silicate, nitrate, phosphate contents and salinity, the reef under study can be divided into three distinct areas related to eutrophication rates : 1) oligotrophic to mildly oligotrophic areas, 2) mesotrophic areas , and 3) eutrophic areas.

The oligotrophic to mildly oligotrophic areas are typified by normal salinity (higher than 34.75‰), reactive silicate content lower than $10\mu M$, nitrate and phosphate concentrations lower than $1\mu M$. They are situated facing the Northern and Southern villages respectively (Fig. 2). The northern area is drained by an active groove system that seems to prevent the residence of SGD-rich flows on the reef flat, while occurring along the inner reef zone. This is evidenced from aerial photography : the southern area corresponds to the dividing line between sea water masses flowing across the reef, and coming back to open sea through the Hermitage and Trois Bassins passes.

The mesotrophic areas basically display salinity values ranging from 34.0 to 34.5‰, reactive silicate content less than $30\mu M$, nitrate and phosphate concentrations averaging 2 and $1\mu M$ respectively. They are restricted in an area opposite Trou d'Eau locality (Fig. 2). Driven by the southward dominant currents, southerly generated SGD waters have a short time of residence on the reef, prior to flow out toward the Trois Bassins Pass.

The eutrophic areas exhibit salinity lower than 34‰, reactive silicate content higher than $30\mu M$, nitrate and phosphate concentrations averaging 5 and 1.2 μM respectively. These areas are mainly close to the northern and southern passes. Due to the strong current induced northward by the adjacent Hermitage pass, the northernmost part of the reef from beachline seaward undergoes SGD that flows away from South to North; in addition, it is influenced by an important seepage operating along the shoreline south of the Hermitage pass (salinity = 31.28‰). Near the Trois Bassins pass, the reef experiences lowest salinities (33.5 to 22.6‰). The southward main current controls southerly generated freshwater discharge, flowing over the reef toward the pass. The third eutrophicated area is located in the middle part of the reef, facing Alizés Beach. The relevant reef flat zone is strongly affected by SGD that gets sucked off through the adjacent groove system, after spreading over the coral-built zone.

Distributional patterns of reef-dwelling communities

As shown in Figures 3A-B, La Saline reef can be subdivided into 3 distinct areas on the basis of preservation rate of the initial coral communities : 1) relatively healthy areas; 2) partly altered areas, and 3) severely altered areas.

The relatively healthy reef flat areas exhibit dense, living coral assemblages. The outer parts are typified by the occurrence of a pavement (i.e. compact reef flat) mainly built up by *Acropora humilis, A. digitifera, Pocillopora damicornis*, associated with *Porites (Synarea) iwayamaensis* and, to a lesser extent, *Montipora circumvallata* (Faure, 1982). The cover rate averages 50% of the total substrate. Coralline algal crusts occupy around 25% of the available surface. The inner parts are dominated by branching forms (*Acropora pharaonis, A. hyacinthus, A. abrotanoïdes*) as trips and patches, whose coverage reaches 60%. Locally, *Porites lobata* micro-atolls and *Pavona divaricata* macrocolonies occur. In most exposed areas of the inner reef flat, *Montipora* and *Porites* develop in the forms of corallites. Calcified and non-calcified algae are scarcely distributed. Corallines colonize rubble deposits; the pheophyte *Vaughaniella* can develop in the form of scattered, thin turfs over rubble during hot season, under moderately oligotrophic areas, while this algal cover is totally missing from typically oligotrophic settings (Cuet *et al.*, 1988). The relatively well-preserved initial reef flat communities are found facing the Northern and Southern villages respectively.

The partly altered reef flats have a lower coral coverage (35%). In higher energy zones (outer reef flat), there is an active competition between coral colonies and coralline algal crusts (*Neogoniolithon, Porolithon*). In most protected zones, the fleshy rhodophyte *Gracilaria crassa* form small, localized patches. The backreef zone is locally colonized by cyanobacteria-bearing *Vaughaniella* mats. Filamentous cyanobacteria (*Nodularia, Lyngbya, Plormidium*) are scattered and short-lived. Whatever the diversity of algal associations is, they never occupy more than 10% of the substrate. As a whole, boring sponges (*Cliona inconstans*) and non boring forms (*Dysidea, Paratettila*) display a low cover rate (less than 1% on average), though higher Clionid abundance can be found in lower salinity settings (less than 32.30‰ along the shore). The partly altered reef zones have been encountered close to Trou d'Eau area.

In the severely altered areas, the living coral communities have a cover rate never exceeding 15% of the substrate. Two scenarios may be considered according to local hydraulic conditions. Under higher energy conditions, the coral assemblages, that tend firstly to diminish in density, are progressively dominated by the opportunistic *Pocillopora damicornis*; later, most of the coral-built areas are overgrown and choked by calcareous algae, that finally occupy 50-60% of the total substrate. Cyanobacteria and sponges are scarce or absent. In lower energy zones, coral over growth by *Gracilaria* turfs is optimal. *Vaughaniella*, highly epiphyted by cyanobacterial populations (*Schizothrix*), occurs as dense, 10-30 cm thick networks, reaching 30% in coverage. Boring clionids increase significantly in abundance; in the backreef zone, thay can occupy 60 to 90% of the substrate. The most poorly preserved areas are situated at the vicinity of the two passes and in the middle part of the reef.

Reef calcification rates

Table 1 summarizes available data of net calcification rate (net precipitation minus dissolution) for the coral built-reef flat of La Saline (Cuet, 1989). The latter appears to calcify during diurnal hours, more actively in summer, while, at night, it mainly undergoes dissolution that is three times higher in summer.

	Austral summer (1985)	Austral winter (1986)
Diurnal net calcification g $CaCO_3 m^{-2}.h^{-1}$	+ 0.35	+ 0.30
Nocturnal net calcification g $CaCO_3 m^{-2}.h^{-1}$	- 0.32	- 0.08
Daily net calcification g $CaCO_3 m^{-2}.d^{-1}$	1.51	2.11
Seasonal net calcification[1] kg $CaCO_3 m^{-2}.yr^{-1}$	0.55	0.77
Annual net calcification[1] kg $CaCO_3 m^{-2}.yr^{-1}$	0.66	

[1]These average values have been obtained assuming that there is no significant intraseasonal variability.

Table 1 - Calcification rates, La Saline reef flat (determined by the total alkalinity method).

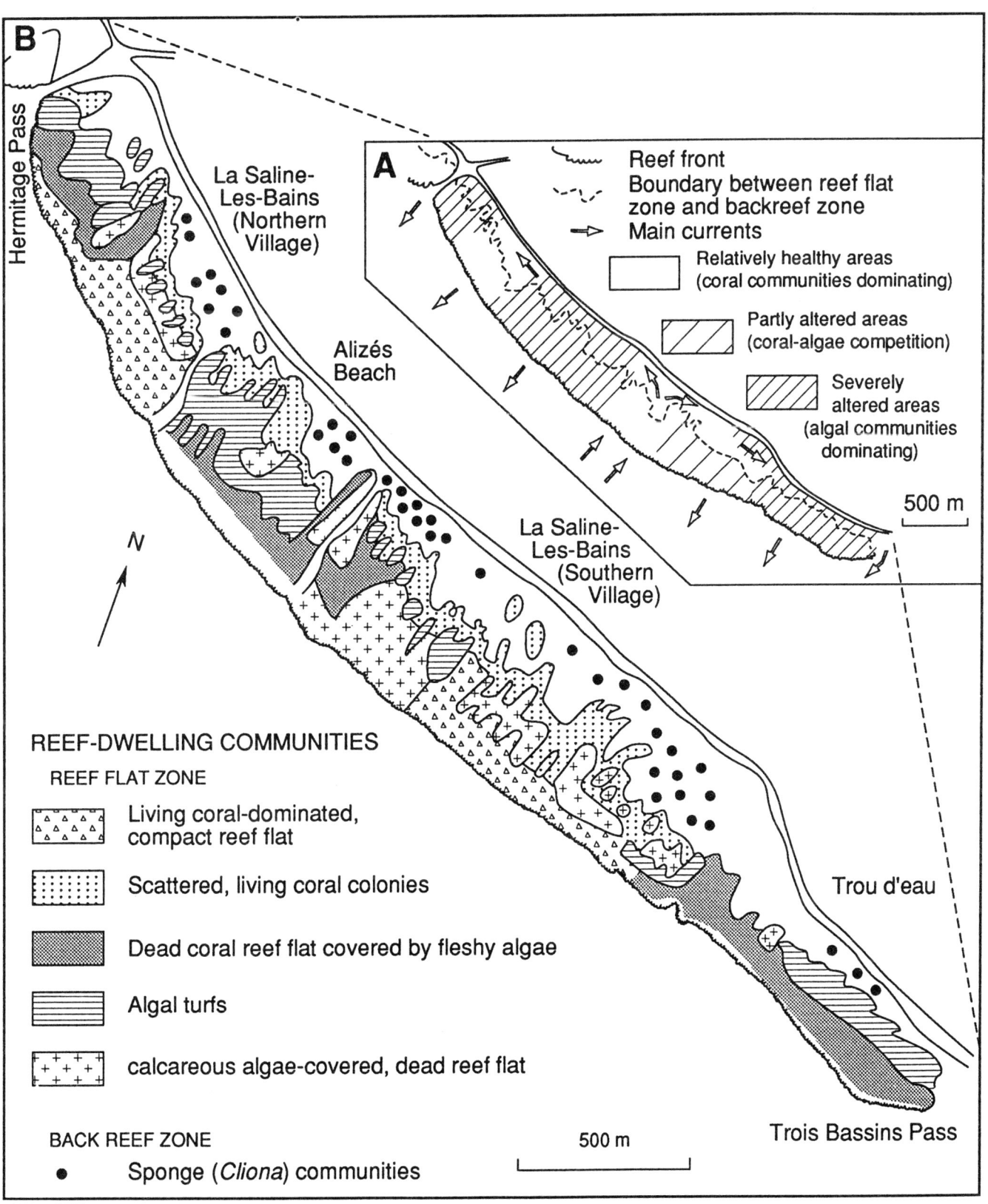

Figure 3. Distributional patterns of dominant benthonic communities on La Saline fringing reef, Réunion island. A : Location of areas of different states of health.
B : Distribution of the main biotic assemblages.

DISCUSSION

Relationships between nutrient avaibility and reef community structure.

As contended by Hallock and Schlager (1986), nutrient avaibility may influence the development of carbonate buildups. On La Saline reef, the distributional scheme of nutrient levels in overlying waters seems to coincide with biozonal patterns, from compared analysis of figures 2 and 3. This further implies that the degree of oligotrophy or eutrophy controls the structure of reefal communities. Under relatively oligotrophic conditions, reef biota is dominated by corals. Under mesotrophic conditions, both calcareous and fleshy algae compete with corals for space. Algal overgrowths, development of algal-bacterial mats, and infestation by boring sponges reflect eutrophic conditions. According to previous studies (cf. references in Hallock and Schlager, 1986), excess of nutrients appears clearly to be deleterious to normal reef biota and to calcification, through overfeeding-enhanced competition, subsequent reduction of coverage by carbonate-secreting organisms, increasing of density of bioeroders, and carbonate crystal poisoning. The described horizontal biotic gradient from oligotrophic to eutrophic reef environments in Réunion island may represent a vertical, low-to high-nutrient ecosequence for the fossil record (Table 2). This model is consistent with that of Hallock (1988), concerning the influence of nutrient availability on the relationships between water energy and carbonate facies; it may provide clues to paleo-nutrient analysis, when bioerosion did not totally erase the record of the eutrophication event.

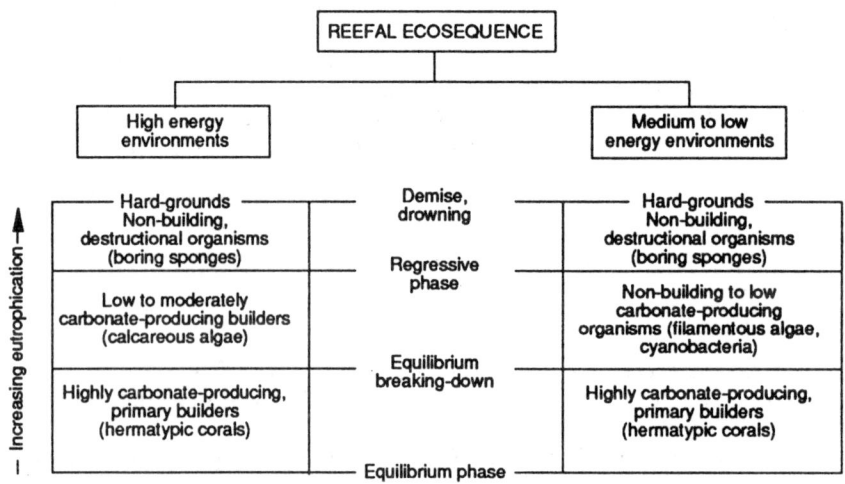

Table 2. Predictive model of community replacement sequence on a nutrient-stressed fringing reef flat

Effects on reef calcification rates

The results presented in Table 1 are in good agreement with previous works, which indicate that healthy reefs dissolve (Sournia *et al.*, 1981; Pichon, 1985) or do not calcify (Atkinson and Grigg, 1984) during night. However, the annual calcification rate recorded on La Saline reef (0.66 kg $CaCO_3 m^{-2} \cdot yr^{-1}$) is markedly lower than the "standard performance" indicated by Smith (1983) for a reef flat (4.0 kg) or even for a whole reef system (1.0 to 1.2 kg). This may partly result from phosphate poisoning of calcium carbonate crystal, acting at concentrations as low as $0.01 \mu M$ (Kinsey and Davies, 1979). Since an average carbonate production less than 1 kg cannot balance export of dissolved or particulate carbonate (Smith, 1983), the reef studied can be regarded as being in process of demise, even if net dissolution does not exceed calcification. The seasonality patterns of calcification clearly sustain this contention. Generally, the summer/winter ratio in calcification for the standard low-latitude reef flats range from 1.3 to 1.4 (Kinsey, 1985), due to higher reef metabolism in summer. In contrast, the summer/winter ratio found in Réunion is 0.71. According to Hutchings (1986), this value may reflect increasing chemical dissolution of the coral substrate at the beginning of the hot season. Clionid sponges, one of the most effective bioeroders (Neumann, 1966), stimulated by excess nutrients, in turn promote carbonate dissolution. Since clionids are widespread in the inner parts of the reef, they contribute to modify chemistry of reefal waters and to induce decreasing calcification rate.

CONCLUSIONS

The enhancement of nutrient supply on La Saline reef results in : 1) replacement of high carbonate producers by slow-growing carbonate organisms in high energy settings; 2) replacement of primary carbonate producers by weakly to non-building organisms, then eroding organisms in medium to low energy areas. Correlatively, the calcification rates recorded are below the threshold of performance required for the reef keeps pace with sea level. From biotic composition and calcification rate, this reef can be considered in process of drowning.

LITERATURE CITED

AMINOT, A. 1983. Eléments nutritifs dissous. Pages 93-150 *in* A. Aminot and M. Chaussepied, eds. Manuel des analyses chimiques en milieu marin, C.N.E.X.O. Press.

ATKINSON, M.J. and GRIGG, R.W. 1984. Model of coral reef ecosystem. II. Gross and net benthic primary production at French Frigate Shoals, Hawaï. *Coral Reefs* 1 : 13-22.

CUET, P. 1989. Influence des résurgences d'eau douce sur les caractéristiques physico-chimiques et métaboliques de l'écosystème récifal à la Réunion. Unpubl. Ph. D. thesis, University of Marseille, 295 pp.

CUET, P., NAÏM, O, FAURE, G. and CONAN, J.Y. 1988. Nutrient-rich ground water impact on benthic communities of La Saline fringing reef (Réunion island, Indian Ocean) : preliminary results. *Proceedings of the 6th International Coral reef Symposium*, Australia 2 : 207-212.

FAURE, G. 1982. Recherche sur les peuplements de Scléractiniaires des récifs coralliens de l'archipel des Mascareignes (Océan Indien occidental). Unpubl.D. Sc. thesis, University of Marseille, 204 pp + 246 pp.

HALLOCK, P. 1988. The role of nutrient availability in bioerosion : consequences to carbonate buildup. *Palaeogeogr., Palaeoclimat., Palaeoecol.* 63 : 275-291.

HALLOCK, P. and SCHLAGER, W. 1986. Nutrient excess and the demise of coral reefs and carbonate platforms. *Palaios* 1 : 389-390.

HUTCHINGS, P.A. 1986. Biological destruction of coral reefs - a review. *Coral reefs* 4 : 239-252.

KINSEY, D.W. and DAVIES, P.J. 1979. Effects of elevated nitrogen and phosphorus on coral reef growth. *Limnol. Oceanogr.* 24 : 935-940.

MONTAGGIONI, L.F. and FAURE, G. 1980. Les récifs coralliens des Mascareignes (Océan Indien). Collections Travaux Centre Univ. La Réunion, 149 p.

NEUMANN, A.C. 1966. Observations in coastal bioerosion in Bermuda and measurements of the boring rate of the sponge *Cliona lampa. Limnol. Oceanogr.* 11 : 92-108.

PICHON, M. 1985. Organic production and calcification in some coral reefs of Polynesia. *Proceedings of the 5th International Coral Reef Congress*, Tahiti, 6 : 173-177.

SMITH, R.V. 1983. Coral reef calcification. Pages 240-247 *in* D.J. Barnes, ed. Perspectives on coral reefs. brian Clouston Publisher, Manuka, Australia.

SOURNIA, A., DELESALLE, B. and RICARD, M. 1981. Premiers bilans de production organique et de calcification d'un récif-barrière de la Polynésie Française. *Oceanol. Acta* 4 : 423-431.

Three Adjacent Coral Reefs in North-Western Sri Lanka; Biology and Human Disturbances.

by

Marcus Öhman[1], Arjan Rajasuriya[2] and Olof Linden[1]

[1] Department of Zoology
University of Stockholm
10691 Stockholm, Sweden

[2] National Aquatic Resources Agency
Crow Island
Mattakkuliya
Colombo 15, Sri Lanka

Introduction

Well over one third of the population of Sri Lanka lives in the coastal areas, and the coastal ecosystems provide a number of important goods and services to these people including food, building material, etc. On average, approximately 65 percent of the animal protein in the national diet comes from marine soures, particularly coastal fisheries. For the population in the coastal areas this figure is close to 100 percent. In addition, the coastal zone is also a key area for tourism, one of the the country's most important sources of income. However, the population pressure in the coastal areas is increasing. In several coastal provinces, considered to be rural areas, there are now well over one thousand inhabitants per km^2, a value more typical of urban zones. Due to this increasing population pressure and expanding economic activity in the last decades, several of the important coastal habitats including the coral reefs are under increasing pressure. The coral reefs in Sri Lanka are threatened by a range of activities including mining for lime production, destruction by tourism, siltation from land etc. In particular, modern fishing techniques such as beach seining and bottom set nets have cased considerable damage in many areas. The damage caused by bottom set nets is related to the heavy anchors and the lead line used to keep the net in place on the reef. Such techniques in combination with dramatically increased fishing effort resulting from the introduction of new fiberglass outboard motorboats, have made it possible not only to extend the range covered by fishermen during their daily operations, but also to fish in areas, such as coral reefs, where traditional techniques would not be used. Also, dynamite fishing is commonly practiced in many coral areas and the collection of coral reef organisms for the aquarium trade (ornamental fish and invertebrate collection) is widely practiced. Ornamental fish collection is a lucrative and rapidly expanding business with exports worth several million dollars per year.

In addition to the human induced degradation of the reefs, some natural phenomena may also be mentioned. Specifically, the "Crown of Thorns

Starfish", *Acanthaster planci*, has been observed in certain areas including the area where the present study was carried out.

The investigation reported here was carried out during some 300 SCUBA dives during a 4 year period (1989-1993) in the area off the Puttalam Lagoon on the north western coast of Sri Lanka. The study was conducted by Sri Lankan and Swedish scientists from the National Aquatic Resources Agency (NARA) in Colombo and the University of Stockholm, Department of Zoology. The work was funded by NARA and the Swedish Agency for Research Cooperation with Developing Countries (SAREC). The full results of the studies are being published separately (Öhman et al. in prep.)

Methods
Three different reefs west and north-west of Kalpitiya Peninsular were studied: Bar Reef, Talaiwila Reef, and Kandakuliya Reef. The results reported here were collected over a depth range between 0 and 8 m.

The investigations were carried out using general survey techniques according to Kenchington (1978) and White (1984), in conjunction with detailed transect survey techniques described for example by De Silva (1984) and Russ and Alcala (1989). The general surveys provided a descriptive picture of the reefs where obvious signs of natural or human damage were noted, while the transect studies provided detailed information on species distribution and abundance of the fauna, live and dead coral cover, reef relief and profile. In total 53 transects were laid out among the different reefs, each one being 50 m long.

For each reef the mean figure for each measured characteristic was calculated. This included coral genera diversity, live coral cover, proportion coral rubble, chaetodontid diversity and fish species richness. Relief was expressed as additional length per 50 m transect. This was derived through graphical representation of the bottom topography and calculating the total length of the graph using a MOP video plan (Kontron Image Analysis Division).

When comparing the reefs the following ecological indices were used:

Live coral cover: The percentage live hard coral cover divided by number of transects on each reef (% live coral cover)

Coral rubble: Total percentage bottom cover of coral rubble divided by number of transects on each reef (% coral rubble)

Coral genera richness: The average number of coral genera per transect on each reef (cor gen/tr)

Fish species richness: The number of fish species per transect on each reef (fish sp/tr)

Chaetodontidae diversity: The average number of Chaetodontidae (Butterfly fish) species per transect on each reef (chaet sp/tr)

Topographic relief: The average additional length in meters per transect on each reef (add m/tr)

Results

Bar Reef is a relatively remote reef with no nearby fishing communities. Both the general and the detailed transect surveys showed a reef in good condition with a pristine character. The level of human disturbances appeared to be insignificant. Only minor impacts were observed, originating from fishing practices and ornamental fish collection. Natural destruction caused by *Acanthaster* had locally affected the reef.

The live coral cover at Bar Reef was found to be 78.5 % per transect (Table 1). The corals were in good condition with *Acropora* being the most dominant genus in the shallow areas followed by *Echinopora* and *Montipora*. Also, 215 species of fish from 39 families were recorded in the initial general survey (Öhman et. al in press). The average number of fish species per transect was found to be 31.5 on Bar Reef (Table 2). The dominant species in the shallow areas were pomacentrids such as *Chromis viridis*, *Dascyllus aruanus*, *Abudefduf vaigiensis* and *Stegastes nigricans* (Öhman et. al in prep.). Common acanthurids recorded included *Acanthurus leucosternon*, *A. xanthopterus* and *Ctenochaetus striatus*. The more abundant labrids observed were *Labrichthys unilinieatus*, *Thallasoma lunare*, *T. hardwicke* and *Halichoeres marginatus*. Also among the siganids, *Siganus canaliculatus*, *S. javus* and *S. lineatus* were common. Other families found which also were highly abundant and diversified were *Caesionidae*, *Haemulidae*, *Lethrinidae*, *Lutjanidae*, *Pomacanthidae*, *Scaridae* and *Serranidae*. The chaetodontid diversity was on average 7.5 species per transect in the transect survey (Table 2). In total 27 species of chaetodontid have been recorded on the reef.

Table 1

	Bar Reef	Talavilla Reef	Kandakuliya Reef
live coral cover (%/transect)	78.5	58.7	21.6
coral rubble (% / transect)	3.8	0.5	21.3
coral genera (no / transect)	2.3	10.9	8.2

In comparision, Talawila Reef is situated approximately 500 m from the Talawila fishing community and the general survey showed a reef with a poor fishstock but a relatively healthy and diversified bottom fauna. There were no reports of fish collectors working in the area and *Acanthaster plancii* was not observed. Further the structure of Talawila Reef was found to be different from the other reefs in the region with massive and encrusting species dominating. Mean coral genera diversity was 10.9 per transect (Table 1), and the most common coral genera were *Favia* and *Porites*. The average proportion of live coral cover and coral rubble were 58.7 and 0.5 % respectively and an average of 4.2 species of butterfly fishes were recorded. The mean number of fish species noted on the transects was 29.3.

Table 2

	Bar Reef	Talavilla Reef	Kandakuliya Reef
fish species richness (sp / transect)	31.5	29.3	27.4
chaetodontid diversity (sp / transect)	7.5	4.3	2.3

The third reef in the present study, Kandakuliya Reef is situated close to the dense fishing communities of Kandakuliya and Kudawa. The beaches of these communities are used for the storage of fiberglass fishing boats and also serve as a dumping site for garbage and other local wastes. Also, considerable beach erosion has taken place during the last decades. The most common fishing methods practiced in the area are bottom set nylon nets and gill nets. SCUBA surveys showed that large areas which previously had been dominated by *Acropora*, are now covered with broken dead coral, algae and sponges. In some areas there were huge underwater piles of coral rubble and the proportion of coral rubble on one transect was more than 80 %. The average percentage of rubble cover per transect was 21.3 % (Table 1) which compares to the mean proportion of live coral cover which was found to be 21.6 % and including an average of 8.2 genera per transect. The most common living corals were *Porites spp.*, *Acropora spp.* and *Favites spp*. The mean number of chaetodontids and all species per transect was 2.7 and 27.4 species respectively.

Discussion
Bar Reef appeared from these investigations to be relatively intact with only minor traces of human impact. Both the general and the detailed transect surveys showed a reef in good condition with a pristine character. The amount live coral cover was very high when compared with the other two reefs and the coral rubble appeared not to have been produced by human activities; it is more likely that it was the result of wave action over the shallower parts of the reef. Also, relatively higher numbers of chaetodontid species indicated an apparently undisturbed reef environment. Due to the almost total dominance of *Acropora* and *Echinopora* in the shallower areas,

the coral diversity was relatively low in these areas. In contrast, there were far more coral genera per unit area in the deeper areas. In addition, the general survey showed a higher abundance of fish than in any of the other reefs studied in this investigation.

By comparision with Bar Reef and Kandakuliya Reef, Talawila Reef showed intermediate values with regard to live coral cover, fish species richness and chaetodontid diversity. In addition, compared with the other reefs, Talawila reef had a low abundance of *Acropora spp.* and other branching or foliaceous species, but a high abundance and diversity of massive and encrusting species. The proportion of coral rubble was also low. An explanation for the particular character of Talawila Reef could be its proximity to the shore which generates a different environment compared with the other reefs in the investigation. Also, different fishing practices, such as the use of beach seine nets on the Talawila Reef may have had an impact.

The general survey showed that the Kandakuliya Reef was in poor condition with very low figures for live coral cover and chaetodontid diversity. Large areas which previously had been dominated by *Acropora* had turned into coral rubble covered by algae and sponge. The modifications to the bottom fauna observed on Kandakuliya Reef was probably the result of the use of destructive fishing methods. In particular, bottom set gill nets made of nylon have been widely used in this area and are known to cause severe damage to coral organisms. Furthermore, boat anchoring has caused very destructive effects on the coral reefs in the area. From interviews with fishermen in the area, it can be established that the destruction of the reef started with the introduction of bottom set nylon nets ten to fifteen years ago. When such nets are used, the anchoring devices (usually relatively large stones) cause the breaking of all erect corals such as *Acropora* and *Echinopora*. This leads to the flattening of the coral reef and gradual increase in the exposure of the adjacent shoreline to wave action producing increased erosion. It cannot be excluded that other factors such as an increasing sea level may have played a role in increasing the problems with coastal erosion. However, the relationship with increasing fishing pressure using destructive methods seems most likely.

About one year ago the Bar Reef was decared a Marine National Park. The area which now is under formal protection include in addition to the coral reefs also parts of the lagoon systems of Dutch and Portugal Bays, and boarders the extensive Wilpatu National Park. Thus the area under protection forms a very valuable unit which includes both terrestrial, coastal and marine ecosystems; systems which are likely to be interlinked in various ways.

References

De Silva, M.W.R.N. 1984.
Coral reef assessment and management methodologies currently used in Malaysia. Unesco Reports in Marine Sciences. 21:47-55.

Öhman, M.C., Rajasuriya, A. and Linden, O. 1993.
Human Disturbances on Coral Reefs in Sri Lanka; a Case Study. *Ambio*, in press.

Russ, G.R. and Alcala, A.C. 1989.
Effects of intense fishing pressure on an assemblage of coral reef fishes. *Mar. Ecol. Prog. Ser.* 56:13-27.

White, A.T. 1984.
Marine Parks and Reserves: Management for Philippine, Indonesian and Malaysian coastal reef environments. University of Hawaii, Honolulu, Hawaii, 275 pp.

Present Status of Coral Reefs in Sri Lanka

by
Arjan Rajasururiya
National Aquatic Resources Agency
Colombia, Sri Lanka

Introduction

The coastline of Sri Lanka, which is about 1,585 kilometres in length support extensive areas of salt marshes, mangroves, estuaries, lagoons, sandy beaches and dunes. Seawards, the continental shelf covers about 26,000 square kilometres, which is approximately half the land area of the island. The coastal waters is characterised by highly productive marine habitats. It supports a number of important eco-systems such as coral reefs and Sea Grass Beds. This narrow coastal belt supports 34 percent of the country's total population in 24 percent of its land area. In the coastal belt, fishing is the most important economic activity. Marine fisheries contribute almost 65 percent of the total animal protein consumed by the population. Coastal fisheries classified as within 40 kilometres of the shore consitute over 90 percent of the marine fish production. All of Sri Lanka's coral reefs and sea grass beds are within 25 to 30 kilometres from the shore. Therefore the major part of the fisheries production depends on the well being of these highly productive but fragile eco-systems.

In the past fishing activities in the coastal region have mainly been confined to non-destructive, traditional methods such as the use of hand lines and beach seines. However, fishing in coastal waters has increased tremendously during the past two to three decades due to a rapid increase of the population, mechanisation of fishing crafts together with more efficient fishing methods to increase production. As a result, once highly productive coastal habitats have been adversely affected within a very short period. Recognising the need of proper management practices for the sustainability of these important eco-systems, the Government of Sri Lanka formed the National Aquatic Resources Agency (NARA) in 1981, with a mandate to carry out research and development on all aquatic eco-systems.

NARA commenced a Coral Reef Research Programme in 1985 with the primary aim of monitoring the status of the coastal reefs, identify causes and issues related to reef degradation and to formulate practical management plans. Since 1985, the Coral Reef Research Project has carried out investigations at 23 locations from the Kalpitiya Peninsular in the north-west to Tangalle in the south. Over 10 seperate sites have been investigated at each location. Several species of stony corals new to Sri Lanka were discovered including one genus which was not previously recorded for the Indian Ocean. In addition two locations were recommended to be made into Marine Sanctuaries based on the research conducted during these surveys. One of these areas is in Hikkaduwa in the south-west and the other is Bar Reef in the north-west. The Hikkaduwa Marine Sanctuary has a size of .5 km^2 and the Bar Reef 306.7 km^2.

Types and Locations of Reefs

Reefs within the coastal waters of Sri Lanka are found mainly as nearshore fringing reefs and deep water reefs, located several kilometres from the shore (Figure 1). They are found mainly on the bathymetric contours formed as a result of fluctuating sealevels in the past, and on consolidated marine substrates such as hard clacareous growths as well as rock substrates. The majority of them are confined to within the 30 metre bathymetric contour. They can be divided into three major groups, based on their different structures. Namely, coral reefs, beachrock or sandstone reefs and rock boulder reefs.

True coral reefs occur as fringing reefs around the Jaffna Peninsular in the north, from Trincomalee to Kalmunai in the east coast, from Tangalle in the south to Akurala in the south-west. Coral reefs in the north-west are found from Mannar Island to west of the Kalpitiya Peninsular. Some are located several kilometres offshore on the shallow continental shelf of the north-west. Coral reefs also found on two underwater ridges off the south-eastern coast called the Great and Little Basses Reefs.

Beachrock reefs occur as discontonous bands on the bathymetric contours around the Island. Rockboulder reefs, are common in the south and eastern shores of Sri Lanka, where corresponding rock outcrops could be seen on land. A superficial coral cover of reef building or stony corals are found on the both substrates.

Nearshore coral reefs are lagoonal reefs which tend to form small lagoons with coral patches on their leeward side. Offshore, they form shallow banks and patch reefs.

Diversity of Reefs

A high diversity of corals and other reef organisms are found in Sri lanka. A total of 171 species of stony corals devided among 65 genera have been recorded for Sri Lanka, one species new to the Indian Ocean (Zoopilus echinatus) was discovered on the sandstone reefs at Kandakuliya. Common reef building corals belong to the families of Acroporidae, Faviidae, Poritidae, Pocilloporidae, Agariciidae, Caryophyllidae, Mussidae, Merulinidae and Oculinidae. Fungid corals are generally found at a depth of greater than 15 metres.

A coral reference collection for Sri Lanka is being built by the coral reef research project of NARA. This collection contains over 300 specimens including 64 species of hermatypic corals which had not been previously recorded for Sri Lanka. A field guide to the corals of Sri Lanka is also under preparation based on this reference collection and the field investigations carried out since 1985.

There are 30 species of butterfly fish that inhabit the coastal waters. Six species are very rare, (Chaetodon unimaculatus, C. bennetti, C. ephippium, C. raffelsi, C. ornatissimus and C. semeion). The Semeion buttrfly fish is the rarest of them, only four specimens have been sighted in the country (in the Bar Reef Marine Sanctuary).

Utilization of Coral Reefs and their Present Status

In Sri Lanka coral reefs are utilized mainly for commercial purposes. Main uses are for fishing, removal of corals for building construction, extraction of live marine organisms for the aquarium industry and for tourism.

Reefs in coastal waters of Sri Lanka are easily accessible. As mentioned initially, fishing pressure has been increasing rapidly due to a rising population and mechanisation of fishing crafts and the introduction of new techniques. Traditionally, coastal waters have been fished using non-destructive methods. Recently reefs have been adversely affected due to coral mining, destructive fishing methods such as the use of 'tangle nets' or 'bottom-set nets', Uncontrolled collection of ornamental reef organisms and destructive collecting methods, blast fishing, negative impacts of tourism and pollution.

Corals within lagoon reefs are damaged due to boat anchoring and the discharge of waste oil into the sea. Glass bottom boats also damage corals at the Hikkaduwa Marine Sanctuary.

The marine environment is the dumping ground for solid wastes and sewage from cities and towns located in the coastal areas. Effluents from industrial establishments eventually end up in the sea. In addition unplanned land clearance practices and deforestation in the central hills contribute to an increasing load of siltation discharged into coastal waters.

In the south a cottage industry that manufacture coconut fibre products utilize calm back waters of fringing reef to season the fibre. Health of corals have been affected in such areas.

Coral are also destroyed by natural causes such as the 'Crown of Thorns starfish' (Acanthaster planci). A population explosion in the 1970's caused large scale damage to reefs in the north-west and eastern coasts. Recent investigations have revealed that their numbers are increasing in the same areas.

Tropical storms and cyclone damage is not common. A cyclone in the late 1970's caused minor damage to the fringing reefs in the east coast around Batticaloa.

Anthropogenic activities, their impacts and the level of natural causes of reef damage are listed in table 1.

TABLE 1.

CAUSES	IMPACT
Coral mining	Very High
Dynamite fishing	High
Tourism	High (Site specific)
Collection of souvenirs	Moderate
Ornamental fish collection	High
Destructive fishing methods	Very High
Anchoring of boats	High (Site specific)
Discharge of waste oil	High (Site specific)
Pollution	Unknown
Seasoning coconut fibre	Unknown
Siltation	High (Site specific)
Crown of Thorns starfish	Very High (Site specific)

Research conducted by NARA has revealed that the nerashore reefs in the west and southern coasts have been seriously affected due to the reasons given above. More than half the reefs in the south-western and southern coasts have disappeared due to coral mining.

Reefs in the north-west (Between Mannar Island and the Kalpitiya Peninsular) and south-east (Great and Little Basses) remain relatively undamaged. These reefs are located in remote areas, further they are several kilometres away from the coast and are not easily accsessible due to difficulties encountered in transport and other infrastructure facilities.

The status of the reefs in the east coast except Trincomalee is not known, as they have not been investigated due to civil unrest in recent times.

Protected Areas (Marine Parks and Sanctuaries)
As mentioned above there are two Marine Sanctuaries in Sri Lanka. They are both established under the Fauna and Flora Protection Ordinance of the Department of Wild Life Conservation. The Hikkaduwa Marine Sanctuary in the south-west and the Bar Reef Marine Sanctuary west of the Kalpitiya Peninsular was established in 1989 and 1992 respectively. They were established based on recommendations forwarded by NARA to the Interministerial Committee on Marine Parks and Sanctuaries.

Legislative Framework and Management Aspects of Coral Reefs
In Sri Lanka, protection of coral reefs is the responsibility of several Departments and Ministries. These are: Department of Coast Conservation, Department of Wild Life Conservation, Ministry of Fisheries and Aquatic Resources, National Aquatic Resources Agency and the Central Environmental Authority.

Coral mining is regarded as a traditional activity in southern parts of the island, therefore implementation of the Coast Conservation Act has been difficult. Recently the Department of Coast Conservation has taken positive steps to control coral mining and the removal of sand in the southern coast. However, in some areas this has not been successful mainly due to lack of alternative employment for displaced miners and others affected due to government action.

Steps are also being taken by the Ministry of Fisheries and Aquatic Resources to control the collection and export of ornamental aquarium fishes and invertebrates.

Although two Marine Sanctuaries have been established, presently they are not managed. This is mainly due to lack of trained personnel, funding and a concerted effort in maintaining the protected areas. As a result destructive fishing practices will undoubtedly affect the Bar Reef Marine Sanctuary in the future. The Hikkaduwa Marine Sanctuary continues to degrade mainly due to tourist related activities.

Acknowledgements
I wish to thank the Chairman and Director General of the National Aquatic Resources Agency (NARA), the Director General of the Natural Resources, Energy and Science Authority (NARESA), the Swedish Agency for Research Co-operation with Developing Countries (SAREC) and the United Nations Development Programme (UNDP) for their support given to the research on coral reefs and to The Coral Reef Research Team of NARA.

References

Baldwin, Malcolm (ed.) Natural Resources of Sri Lanka, Conditions and Trends (1991). Report prepared for the Natural Resources, Energy and Science Authority of Sri Lanka by The United States Agency for International Development (USAID).

De. Silva, M.W.R.N. (1983). Status of South-Asian Coral Reef Resources, Utilization and Problems of Management, Report prepared for ESCAP/UN 1983.

Hale, Lynne Zeitlin and Kumin, Enid (1992). Implementing a Coastal Resources Management Policy, The Case of Prohibiting Coral Mining In Sri Lanka.(Coastal Resources Center, University of Rhode Island, 1992).

Rajasuriya, A. and De Silva, M.W.R.N. (1988). Stony Corals of the Fringing Reefs of the Western, South-Western and Southern coasts of Sri lanka. (Proceeding of the 6th International Coral Reef Symposium, Australia,1988).

Rajasuriya, A. (1991). Location and Condition of Reefs along Sri lanka's Coast. (Seminar on Causes of Coast Erosion in Sri lanka, Colombo, 1991).

Wood, Elizabeth. (1986). Explotation of Coral Reef Fishes for the Aquarium Trade,(Report prepared for the Marine Conservation Society, UK).

Figure 1

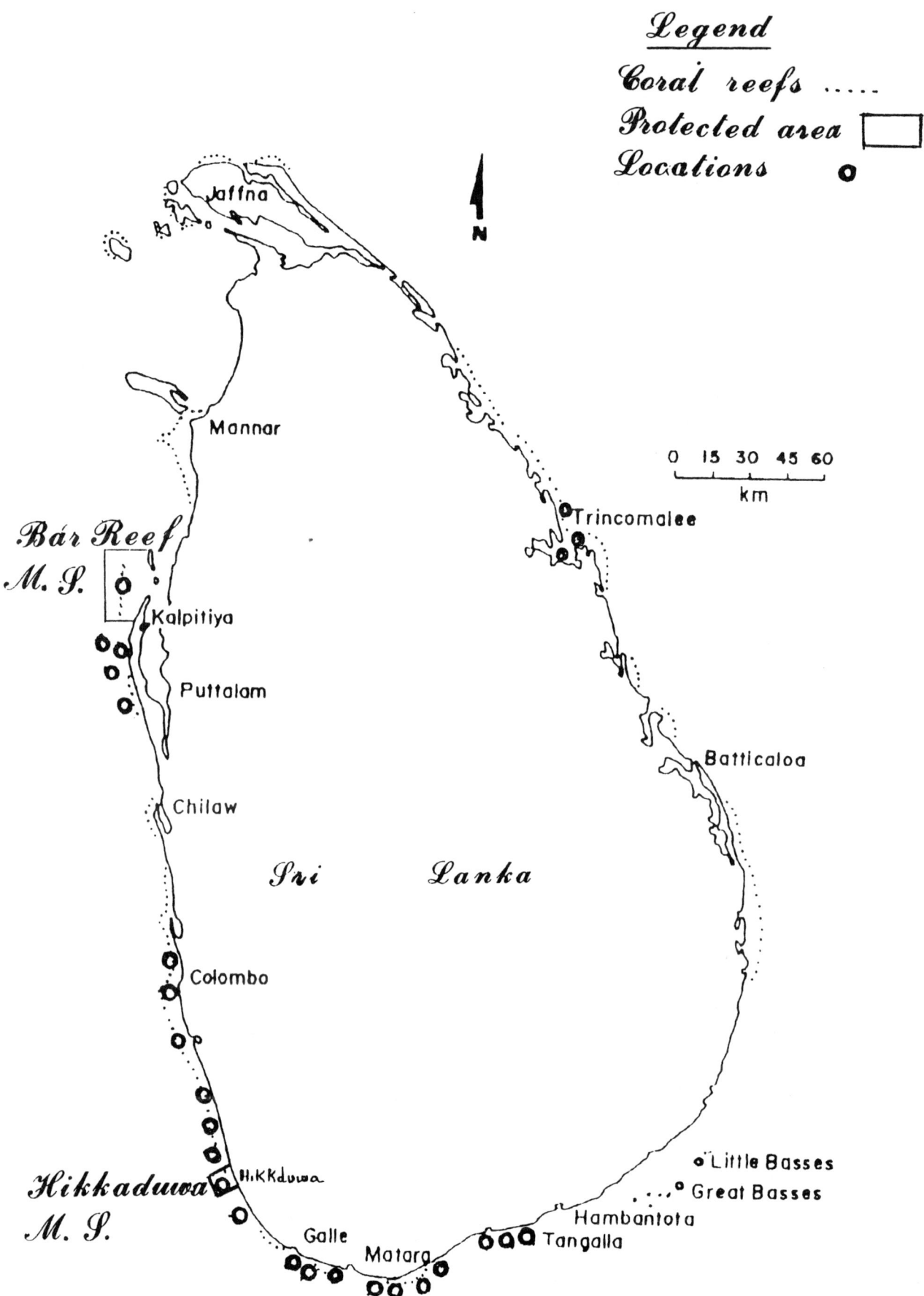

INDEX BY AUTHOR

AUTHOR	PAGES
Acosta M., Alberto	233-239
Alcolado, Pedro M.	27-33; 73-79
Allen, K.W.	371-377
Allison, William R.	66-72
Aronson, Richard B.	189-195
Bak, R. P. M.	154-159
Bell, Peter R. F.	319-325
Bingquan, Lu	293-297
Bloom, Arthur L.	1-6
Bohnsack, James A.	196-200
Bone, David	73-79
Bright, Thomas J.	174-187
Brown, Barbara E.	279-285
Budd, Ann F.	7-13
Bulhoes, Helio A.	254-260
Burke, Randolph B.	14-20
Bush, Phillippe	73-79
Byron, Grahame	326-332
Bythell, John C.	201-213
Chansang, Hansa	286-292
Chiappone, M.	80-86
Chou, L. M.	311-317
Clark, Mark W.	106-112
Collins, Lindsay B.	378-384
Cook, C.B.	160-166
Cortes, Jorge	73-79; 240-246; 261-266
Cruz-Aguero, Gustavo de la	120-125
Cuet, Pascale	397-403
Curran H. Allen	147-153
Dennis, George D.	167-173
Dodge, Richard E.	87-93; 160-166
Dollar, Steven J.	333-348
Downing, Nigel	132-138
Dullo, Wolf-Christian	34-37
Dunn, Jennifer J.	66-72
Dunne, Richard P.	279-285
Dustan, Phillip	38-51
Eakin, C. Mark	139-145
Ebersole, John P.	189-195
Estudillo, R. A.	371-377
Evans, Christopher W.	339-345

417

Fadlallah, Y. H.	371-377
Feingold, Joshua S.	139-145
Garzon-Ferreira, Jaime	73-79; 247-253
Ginsburg, Robert N.	21-26
Gittings, Stephen R.	174-187
Gladfelter, Elizabeth H.	201-207
Glynn, Peter W.	139-145; 261-266
Gomez, E.	311-317
Greer, Mary Lisa	147-153
Grigg, Richard W.	333-338
Guozhong, Wang	293-297
Hagman, Derek K.	174-187
Hallock, Pamela	94-100
Hatcher, Bruce G.	378-384
Hawkins, Julie P.	385-391
Heiss, Georg A.	34-37
Herrera-Moreno, Alejandro	27-33
Hodgson, Gregor	298-303
Horrill, Chris	66-72
Hubbard, Dennis K.	201-207
Hughes, Terence P.	208-213
Hunter, Cynthia L.	339-345
Jaap, Walter C.	101-105
Johnson, Kenneth G.	7-13
Keilman, Margriet	247-253
Kelleher, Grahame	346-352
Kikuchi, Ruy K. P.	254-260
King, Allison J.	45-51
Knap, Anthony H.	87-93
Kojis, Barbara L.	353-359
Lang, Judith C.	45-51
Lapointe, Brian E.	106-112
Latin, Howard	113-119
Laydoo, Richard	73-79
Le Tissier, Martin D.	279-285
Leao, Zelinda M.A. N.	261-266
Linden, Olof	404-409
Macintyre, Ian G.	261-266
Maguire, Jr., Bassett	45-51
Mah, Anmarie J.	304-310
Martinez-Estalella, Nereida	27-33
Martinez-Osegueda, Enrique	120-125
Matzie, William R.	106-112
McClanahan, T. R.	392-396
Meier, Ouida W.	52-58

Meigs, Lucy Chambers	147-153
Montaggioni, Lucien F.	397-403
Munoz-Chagin, Ricardo	120-125
Naim, Odile	397-403
Nieuwland, G.	154-159
O'Connell, Douglas S.	126-131
Obura, D.	392-396
Ogden, John C.	73-79; 267-272
Ogden, Nancy B.	267-272
Ohman, Marcus	404-409
Oxenford, Hazel A.	73-79
Peters, E. C.	80-86
Phongsuwan, Niphon	286-292
Porter, James W.	52-58
Price, Andrew R. G.	132-138
Pufall, Ann E.	147-153
Quinn, Norman J.	353-359
Rajasuriya, Arjan	404-416
Reaka-Kudla, Marjorie L.	126-131
Reese, Ernst S.	59-65
Regan, James D.	126-131
Richmond, Robert H.	360-364
Ridzwan, A. R.	311-317
Risk, Michael J.	66-72
Roberts, Callum M.	132-138; 385-391
Roca, R.	80-86
Rogers, Caroline S.	214-219
Ruiz, Francisco	73-79
Ryan, Joe	73-79
Sargent, Frank J.	101-105
Scoffin, Terence P.	273-278; 279-285
Sebens, Kenneth P.	189-195
Sforza, Roberto	254-260
Shinn, Eugene A.	21-26
Singth, Joth	73-79
Smith, Durelle P.	147-153
Smith, S. R.	160-166
Smith, Struan R.	73-79
Soekarno, S.	311-317
Songquig, Quan	293-297
Stemann, Thomas A.	7-13
Steneck, Robert S.	220-226
Sudara, S.	311-317
Suharsono	304-310
Sullivan, K. M.	80-86

Talge, Helen K.	94-100
Telles, Marcelo D.	254-260
Tomascik, Tom	304-310; 319-325
Tschirky, John	73-79
Veron, J. E. N.	365-370
Vincen, Vance P.	227-232
Vries, Elja de	34-37
White, Susan	73-79
Wickland, Robert I.	126-131; 167-173
Wilkinson, C. R.	311-317
Woodley, Jeremy	73-79

NOTES

NOTES

NOTES

NOTES

NOTES

NOTES

NOTES

NOTES

NOTES

NOTES